EYEWITNESS TO HISTORY

FROM ANCIENT TIMES TO THE MODERN ERA

Stephen G. Hyslop, Bob Somerville
and John Thompson

Foreword by
James Reston, Jr.

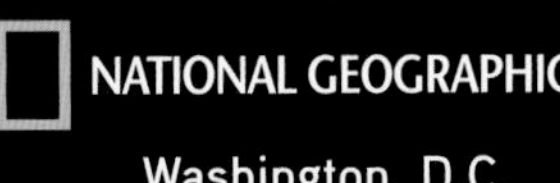

NATIONAL GEOGRAPHIC
Washington, D.C.

CONTENTS

Preceding pages: Onlookers watch the launch of the space shuttle *Atlantis* from Cape Canaveral, Florida.

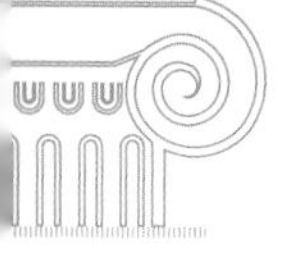

FOREWORD

> “*All history is modern history.*” —WALLACE STEVENS

When someone is said to have a sense of history, what does that mean? And why is such an attribute considered a compliment and a virtue?

For a long time it was said that this country had a short history. It was as if our time began with Columbus. Our roots were in Western civilization. Our politics began with the American Revolution. The Civil War saved our nation, and World War II our civilization. Our youth as a nation gave us energy, made us separate and special, and perhaps even a bit better than the rest of the world.

But the past half-century, partly through setbacks, sometimes through social advances, has imparted a more mature view of our connection to events far beyond our shores and before the arrival of Europeans in North America. This greater appreciation has often been forced upon us by current events. The civil rights movement of the sixties led to a renewed interest in African history. The Vietnam War forced us to concentrate on the shadow of China, with its great dynasties and magnificent culture, over the rest of Asia. For all its horror, 9/11 forced us to grapple with Islamic history and the Arab world. When President George W. Bush proclaimed a crusade, after 9/11, the intense reaction in the Middle East drew our attention to prior instances in history where Christianity and Islam have come into conflict. It could be said that we finally joined world history.

With the arrival of the new Christian millennium in the year 2000, we had an opportunity to view history in multiples of a thousand years. We are still at the dawn of the third millennium, and how good it is to have this book as a memento for the transition we are experiencing. It is still time to take the long view.

Eyewitness to History is more ambitious; it covers more than merely a thousand years. It presents the whole feast of human history, delivered in short takes on the notable figures and the great empires and dynasties, on the driving themes of history in the arts, in religion, in economics and trade, in human migrations and dramatic voyages, in law and fashion and the lot of women. When heard from beginning to end, the whole of history is an exciting story. Simply written and therefore accessible to all ages, beautifully illustrated, its material carefully chosen and cleverly spiced with pithy statements from the wise and witty and appointed with Twitter-like “takeaways” to serve as guideposts to the memory and appetizers for further study, this is a gift to endow the library or coffee table of every educated person and citizen of the world.

—*James Reston, Jr.*
HISTORIAN AND AUTHOR

OPPOSITE: Henry Ford confides in his friend, Thomas Edison.

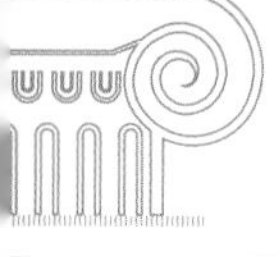

ABOUT THIS BOOK

The history of the world can hardly be summarized in 464 pages. But with informative text, a wealth of illustrations, and firsthand narratives, we can gain a personal and vivid impression of the course of life in ancient Rome, Ming dynasty China, or colonial America. In *Eyewitness to History,* the story of cultures from prehistoric times to the present day—their conflicts, personalities, and arts; the daily lives of great and small—is conveyed through a diverse array of text and pictures. Woven throughout are voices from the past, the words of kings and poets, explorers and scientists, farmers and scribes. And anchoring each chapter is a key document from world history examined more closely, giving us all an intimate look at the masterworks that have defined their times.

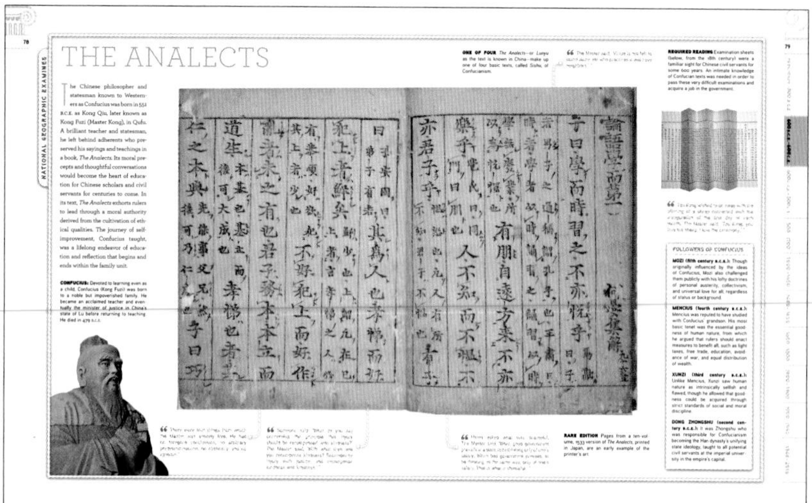

NATIONAL GEOGRAPHIC EXAMINES

Each chapter features a single influential document from its era—the Code of Hammurabi, for instance, or Darwin's *Origin of Species*. The central image displays a portion of the document, either in its original form or in a very early version. Text and additional illustrations put the work into context; quotes pulled from the work (not necessarily from the portion on view) highlight significant passages.

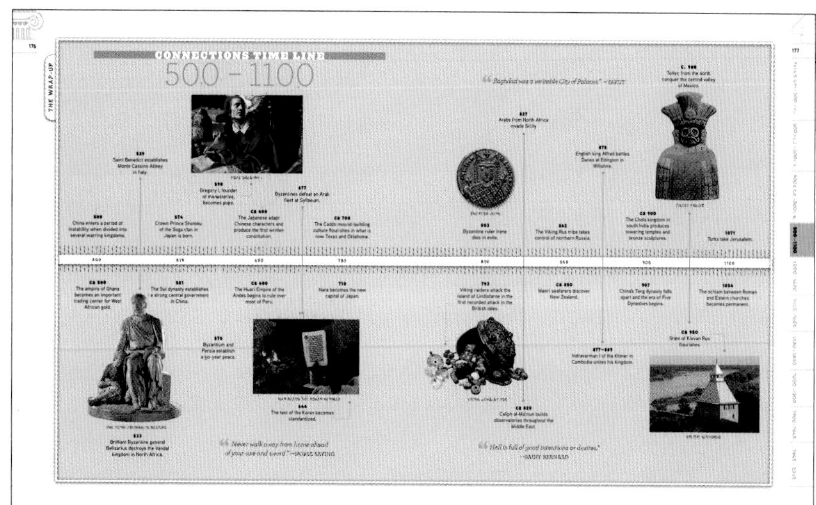

TIME LINE

Time lines underscore the text in each section of each chapter, pointing out significant dates and events for the culture and time period. Every chapter ends with an illustrated Connections Time Line, giving a sense of the simultaneous histories of different regions.

Chapters follow in chronological order, but among the chapters and within them some time periods will be longer, shorter, or overlapping. Chapters 2 and 3, for instance, cover roughly the same time period but two different regions. Chapters and their dates are identified by tabs along the right-hand side of each page.

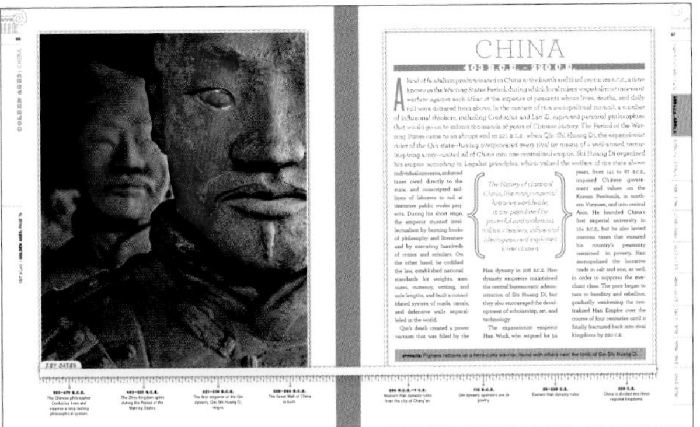

CHAPTER OPENER/ASIDES

Chapters are organized by time period and broken down by cultures or regions: the Americas, for instance, or the Middle East and Africa. Some have special sections on cultural phenomena, such as modern science. Each section begins with an overview, pointing out trends and common themes in the pages to come.

On these pages and interspersed throughout the text are bracketed "asides" that serve either as brief summaries or simply as interesting sidelights—curious facts about the subject at hand.

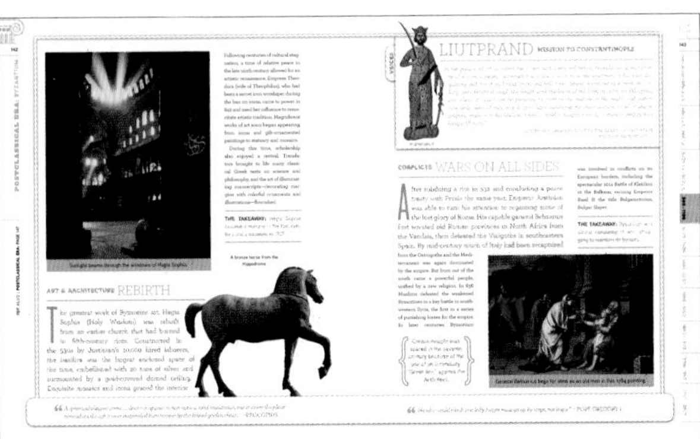

VOICES

Throughout the pages you will find "Voices" features. These contain excerpts from letters, memoirs, speeches, testimony, poetry, novels, and more, from the time and culture. These verbatim, firsthand accounts intimately convey the personalities and happenings, major and minor, of each era—ranging from the graffiti of Pompeii to a description of gas warfare in the trenches of World War I.

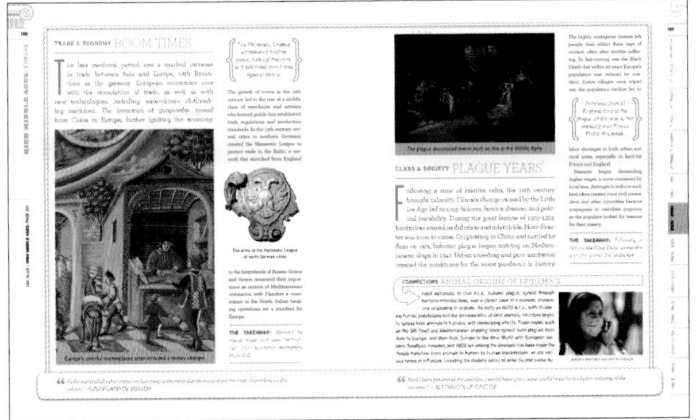

CONNECTIONS

"Connections" features reveal the historic roots of today's issues. Accompanied by modern photographs, they link modern conflicts, products, phrases, and practices to their origins. The beginnings of the Sunni/Shiite divide, the first household pets, the source of modern epidemics, the derivation of popular phrases, and more are traced to their sources.

THUMBS UP/THUMBS DOWN

Biographical profiles of influential historical figures are given a twist in these sidebars. Here we examine people who have made a difference, though not always a good one, in history, and deliver an admittedly opinionated judgment on their positive or negative effects (or sometimes a mixture of both) on the world: thumbs up or thumbs down.

EPIC JOURN

SAGAS OF CREATION

PREHISTORY TO 500 B.C.E.

CHAPTER

1

Phoenician traders once sailed graceful vessels like this one in Tyre, Lebanon.

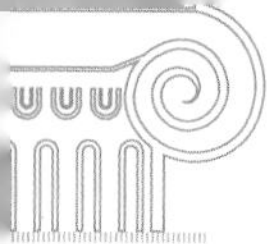

SEE ALSO | EPIC JOURNEYS: PAGE 16

KEY DATES

100,000 B.C.E.
Modern humans begin migrating out of Africa to other parts of the world.

40,000 B.C.E.
Early humans are buried in Australia.

30,000 B.C.E.
Prehistoric painters decorate cave walls in Europe.

10,000 B.C.E.
Humans begin to domesticate plants and animals and settle in villages.

OUT OF AFRICA

100,000–3500 B.C.E.

The story of humanity has hazy beginnings, yet distinct milestones—represented in bone, stone, and other artifacts—mark the progression from our prehistoric roots to the dawn of history, when we began to speak about ourselves, commencing a narrative now some 6,000 years old. Although anthropologists continue to debate the precise origins of the species known as *Homo sapiens,* they generally agree that modern humans evolved in eastern Africa as much as 250,000 years ago. Their ancestors, apelike creatures known as hominids, had diverged from earlier primates some 4 million years earlier in response to climatic and geological changes that increased open grasslands. The major development in hominids was the ability to stand upright and walk on two legs, which allowed them to scan the savanna, travel distances in pursuit of nourishment, and use their hands to gather and carry food.

About 2.5 million years ago, members of the first species of the human family, *Homo habilis,* started using their hands for other purposes, making tools and weapons by chipping sharp fragments from flinty stone. They also built rudimentary shelters by piling up rocks. Their descendants, *Homo erectus,* took advantage of these skills to travel farther afield, leaving Africa for the Middle East, then Europe and Asia.

Back "home" in Africa, modern humans emerged as the eons spun on. What made them different? Most significantly, they had bigger brains, which gave them the edge over competing species. They learned to master naturally occurring fires and to communicate in more complex forms of spoken language. They divvied up tasks, with women taking responsibility for the gathering of food and men using their weapons to hunt.

Environmental changes and an increasingly broad range of skills helped humans move beyond their origins in eastern Africa to the wider world. Societies grew more complex, and civilization emerged.

About 100,000 years ago, modern humans too started venturing beyond Africa. During the Ice Age that peaked about 30,000 years ago, when ice built up and sea levels dropped, they were able to reach formerly inaccessible landmasses—including Britain, the Americas, and perhaps even Australia—by way of land bridges. Migrations continued, but some groups began to settle, having learned not only to gather and hunt for food but also to grow it. By 8,000 years ago, towns were beginning to flourish, and complex societies emerged.

OPPOSITE: Aboriginal rock art, perhaps 3,500 years old, reflects the human need to leave an imprint.

6500 B.C.E.
One of the world's first cities, Catal Huyuk, is built in Anatolia.

5000 B.C.E.
Villagers in Mesopotamia begin practicing irrigation.

4000 B.C.E.
Bronze objects are produced in Thailand.

3500 B.C.E.
Sumerians develop cuneiform writing.

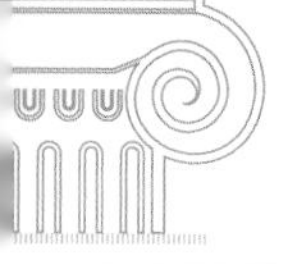

SEE ALSO | EPIC JOURNEYS: PAGE 25

The Poulnabrone dolmen is an Irish tomb dating back 5,000 years.

RELIGION ORIGINS OF BELIEF

Thinking about things beyond the here and now was a hallmark of human development during the Paleolithic period, from 2.5 million to about 10,000 years ago. Did such abstract thought rise to the level of religious belief? Some evidence suggests that it did.

Ceremonial rites may have first emerged in relation to hunting. Buried mammoth skeletons were adorned with jewelry, cave bear skulls had decorative marks carved into them, and reindeer were submerged in bogs and lakes with wooden stakes or stones placed in their chest cavities. These gestures seem to indicate veneration of the beasts of the hunt or perhaps the dedication of some portion of the kill to a hunting deity.

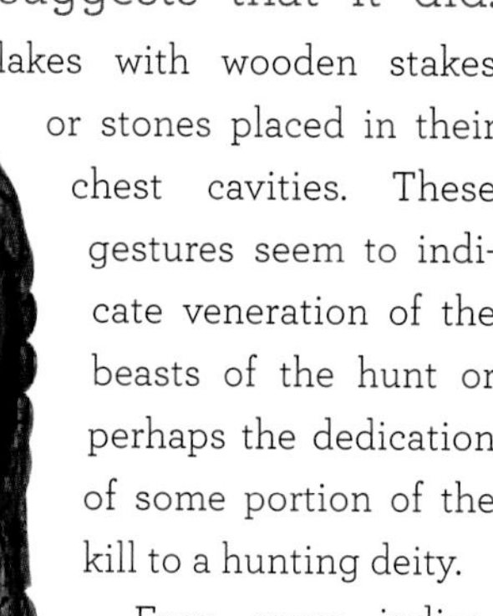

Paleolithic carving Venus of Brassempouy

Even more indicative of a religious sensibility in early humans was the way they treated their own dead. One site in northern Spain from 300,000 years ago shows that even these early hominids performed ritual burials, casting bodies into a limestone fissure. More elaborate treatments date to later Paleolithic times. Graves have been found beneath stone slabs, the carefully arranged remains daubed with red ocher and accompanied by jewelry and stone tools—signs not only that the dead were revered but also that the living had some hopes of an existence beyond death.

THE TAKEAWAY: Their treatment of the dead suggests that early humans had religious beliefs.

PREHISTORIC CULTURES

VIPs

Homo sapiens, 250,000 B.C.E.
Modern humans who first appeared in Africa

Neanderthals, 130,000 B.C.E.
Subspecies of *homo sapiens* or separate species who moved into Europe before 30,000 B.C.E.

Aborigines, 40,000 B.C.E.
The first Australians, who arrived from Southeast Asia via a land bridge

Clovis culture, ca 13,500 B.C.E.
Tool-making culture from the North American southwest

Jomon culture, ca 10,000 B.C.E.
Japanese tool-makers and potters

Anatolians, 6500 B.C.E.
Builders of the early city of Catal Huyuk

“*When of the gods none had been called into being, / And none bore a name, and no destinies were ordained; / Then were created the gods in the midst of heaven.*” —BABYLONIAN CREATION MYTH

VOICES

AFRICA TWIN GODS

"Liza and Mawu were twins. Liza was the Sun god and lived in the East. His sister Mawu was the Moon god and lived in the West. When there is an eclipse, it is because Liza and Mawu are making love. They had a son, Gu, who had the shape of an iron sword. They used him to form the world. Gu taught the people the art of ironworking."

—FON (DAHOMEY) MYTH

SOLAR ECLIPSE BRINGS DARKNESS

ARTS DRAWING ON LIFE

Art was the first form of history, a record of what was most important in life. And the first artists, whose works consecrate caves throughout Europe and elsewhere, painted prey animals, their chief means of survival. Using everything from pigmented minerals to plant juices, egg whites, charcoal, and blood, they created images of astounding detail and realism—and even signed their works with stenciled handprints. Other artists carved images in bone and stone and made small figurines, typically of the female form with exaggerated breasts and hips, which may have been talismans of fertility.

THE TAKEAWAY: Prehistoric art tells us what was most important in the artists' lives.

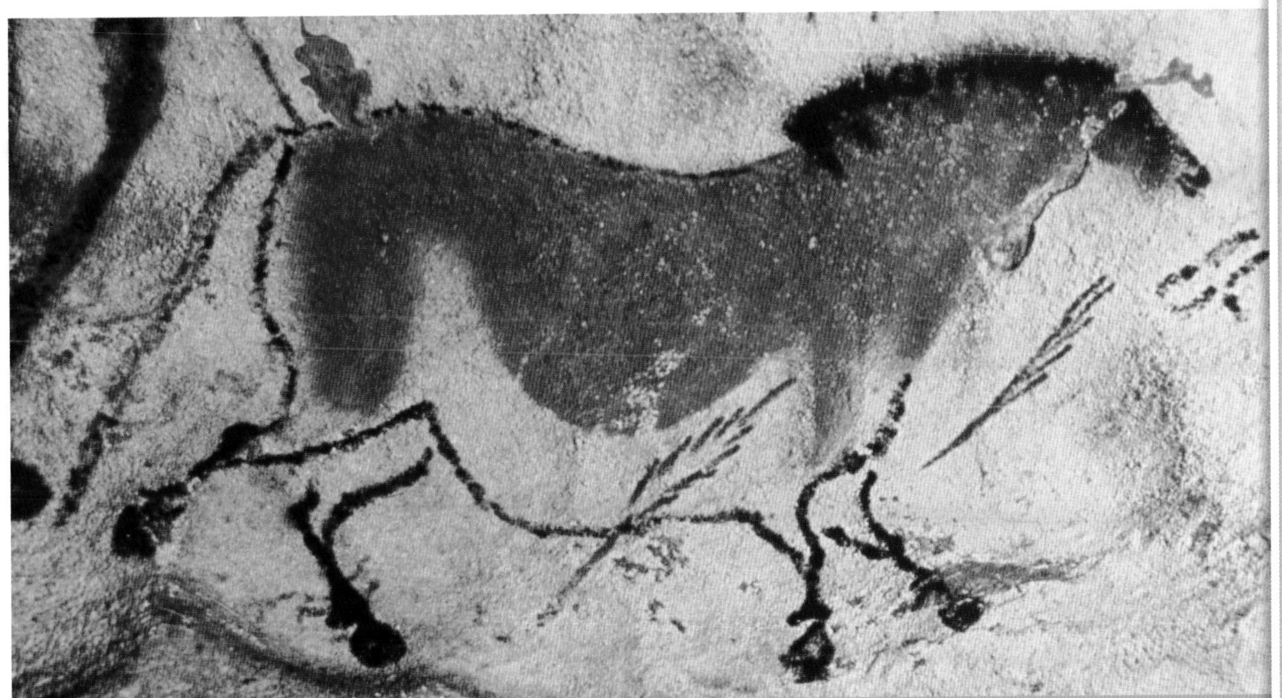

Paintings from France's Lascaux caves depict many prey animals, including this horse.

"For millions and millions of years, the earth may be said to have resembled oil floating, medusa-like, upon the face of the waters." —THE KOJIKI, JAPANESE CREATION MYTH

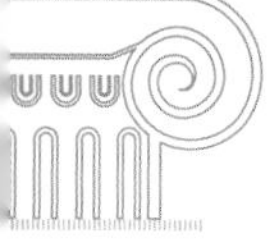

SEE ALSO | EPIC JOURNEYS: PAGE 18

SOCIETY THE HUNT

Searching for food across a given territory was hardly a trait exclusive to prehistoric humans. But they and their ancestors had developed a range of skills and behaviors related to the process of feeding themselves that did set them apart not only from other animals, but also from the apes from which they evolved. Because they could stand and walk, leaving their hands free as they roamed, early humans were able to gather up the nuts, fruits, seeds, grains, and plants they found to eat later. The human species *Homo erectus,* which emerged about 1.8 million years ago, cached food supplies and may have used stone implements to dig up, scrape, and mash edible roots and tubers into a more digestible form. Humans and their forebears also scavenged meat from animal carcasses and crushed the bones with rocks to get at the nutrient-rich marrow inside—a nourishing food that may have accelerated brain development.

Giant rhinoceroses charge Stone Age hunters.

> Early humans became so adept at killing game that they hunted certain species, such as the cave bear, to extinction.

Humans were soon getting fresh meat for themselves. The first type of hunting involved driving herds of animals into ravines or over cliffs, but by 400,000 years ago and perhaps earlier, humans were hunting with weapons. Horse skeletons have been found with wooden lances piercing their sides, and cave paintings show animals being hunted with stone-tipped spears or being driven into nets.

Saddle quern and stone used to grind grain

Pursuing herds and hunting individual large animals required cooperation among the members of the group, and perhaps even involved the dividing up of hunting territories among different groups. Ever more sophisticated forms of food preparation, including roasting meats over fires, also involved a more complex social organization. Scholars speculate that sometime during this period, hunter-gatherer societies came into being, with the women taking charge of gathering vegetable foods and tending fires, and the men focusing on procuring meat.

THE TAKEAWAY: As prehistoric humans learned to gather foods and hunt for meat, they developed new skills.

> “*There was a world before this world, but the people in it did not know how to behave themselves or how to act human. The Creating Power was not pleased with that earlier world.*” —SIOUX CREATION MYTH

VOICES

AUSTRALIA THE COMING OF DEATH

"[The first woman] could not resist the lure of the honey. Letting her sticks fall to the ground, she began to climb the tree. Suddenly there was a rush of air and a dark shape with huge black wings enveloped her. It was Narahdarn the Bat, whom Baiame had put there to guard his yarran tree. . . . The evil she had done could never be remedied. She had released Narahdarn into the world, and from that day onward he became the symbol of the death that afflicts all the descendants of [the first man]."

—ABORIGINAL FABLE

WESTERN MYALL TREE, AUSTRALIA

TECHNOLOGY TOOLMAKING

Researchers believe the very first stone tools were fashioned more than 2.5 million years ago when early humans used one stone to chip fragments off another to make a sharp edge. Over time, toolmakers became increasingly skilled at creating implements of remarkable precision and proportion, designed to fit in the palm of the hand with the cutting edge at a perfect angle. These hand axes allowed humans to butcher carcasses quickly and thoroughly—an important factor with animal predators always nearby—and to chisel wood and carve bone. Scrapers served a multitude of functions, including removing flesh from hides to make clothing that was stitched together with bone or wooden needles and twine made from plant fibers. Stone workers also produced weapons, chipping away tinier and tinier fragments to create extremely sharp and narrow spear points and arrowheads that were lethally effective.

Toward the end of the Paleolithic period, all sorts of other crafts were emerging, including the firing of clay pots in kilns, a technique that began about 9,000 years ago. In the Middle East, kilns were soon being used to smelt copper, which was mostly employed in decorative objects. A major breakthrough came about 6,000 years ago, as metalsmiths found that smelting copper with tin produced an even stronger metal, bronze, which in molten form could be shaped into an almost limitless array of implements.

THE TAKEAWAY: Prehistoric human ingenuity displayed itself in an increasingly sophisticated array of tools and objects.

A willow-leaf point (left). A Stone Age man digs out a canoe (below).

"The gods did leave one pathway from earth to heaven. That is the bridge that appears in the sky as a rainbow, and its perfect arc and brilliant colors are a sign of its origin with the gods." —NORSE MYTH

SEE ALSO | EPIC JOURNEYS: PAGE 44

CULTURES THE FIRST FARMS

A fragment of stonework from Uruk, Mesopotamia, shows cows in wickerwork stables.

As the Ice Age began to wane about 15,000 years ago, wild grasses with edible seeds proliferated, and some hunter-gatherer groups that had formerly been nomadic took up residence near plentiful supplies of these grains. Researchers speculate that periods of drought about 11,000 years ago made wild grain harder to come by, so communities began to cultivate their own crops, tilling the soil with rudimentary implements, growing plants, and then harvesting the kernels. It was the earliest form of farming, allowing groups to stay where they had established settled lives.

Scholars used to think that farming commenced in the rich lands of the Middle East and then spread to other parts of the world. But evidence now suggests that farming arose independently in different places. Regional variations in climate and soil led to specialization in different crops: early forms of barley and wheat in the Middle East, Europe, and India; sorghum in Africa; rice and millet in China and Southeast Asia; and corn in the Americas. Animal domestication followed, leading to full-fledged agricultural communities.

> The potter's wheel enabled people to make better grain containers—and may have planted the idea of wheeled vehicles.

THE TAKEAWAY: Climatic changes encouraged nomadic peoples to settle in communities and grow their own food.

CONNECTIONS COMPANIONS AT THE FIRE

WHEN THE RELATIONSHIP BETWEEN DOGS AND HUMANS that endures to this day first developed is a matter of ongoing conjecture. Genetic studies link most modern dogs to gray wolves from the Middle East. The likeliest scenario is that about 30,000 years ago, or perhaps much earlier, wild dogs began to approach human campsites to scavenge tossed-away bones and scraps of meat. The least-timid ones were soon being trained to help in the hunt or, later, with herding livestock. Their barking also served as an alarm against intruders. By 14,000 years ago the bond had become so special that grave sites have been found with human and canine remains placed side by side.

LABRADOR RETRIEVER

> *"The fireball even set the earth to spinning, as it still does today. Olorun then blew his breath across Ife, and Obatala's figures slowly came to life as the first people of Ife."* —YORUBA CREATION MYTH

CULTURES THE FIRST CITIES

Productivity in the fields led to a reproductive boom, and simple villages soon expanded. Agriculture meant fewer people could grow food for the entire group, so more members of the community were free to develop other skills. Potters and weavers made storage vessels; millers, bakers, and brewers turned grain into bread and beer; builders constructed dwellings and defensive walls; artists and priests satisfied the people's aesthetic and spiritual inclinations; and officials made sure the machinery of society ran smoothly.

One of the first such communities to leave its mark on history was Jericho, in modern-day Palestine. By 10,000 years ago, it had a population of 2,000—ten times larger than a typical hunter-gatherer group—and its people were making houses and other buildings out of mud bricks. Their greatest achievement was a 30-foot-high stone tower and a massive, 12-foot-high defensive wall—celebrated in the Bible—that may have been designed to protect against nomadic raiders. In Anatolia, in today's Turkey, a similar settlement—Catal Huyuk—included clay-brick houses with decorated rooms and signs of a flourishing barter economy.

{ Houses in Catal Huyuk were so tightly clustered that occupants had to enter through openings in the roof. }

THE TAKEAWAY: Agricultural success gave birth to complex communities and urban life.

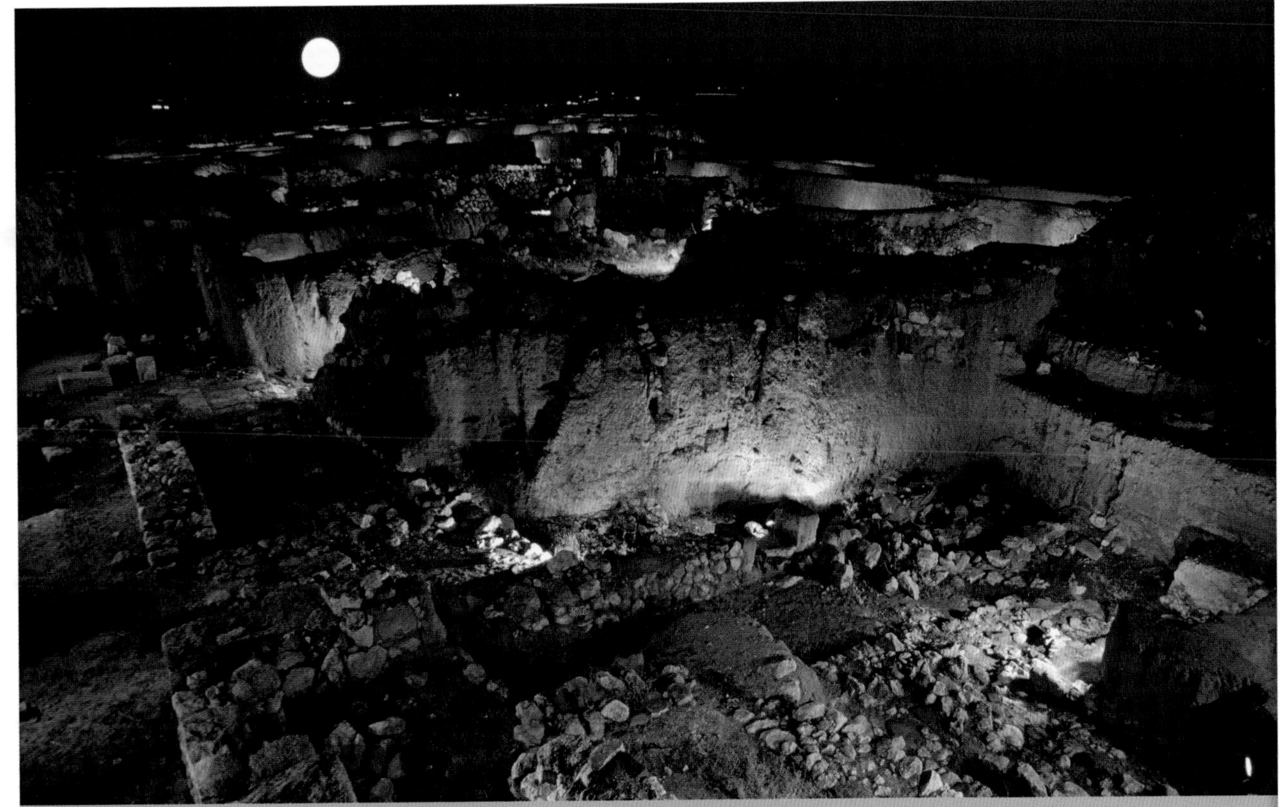

The royal palace of Ebla, in modern-day Syria, dates from the third millennium B.C.E.

"And the Lord God formed man of the dust of the ground, and breathed into his nostrils the breath of life, and man became a living soul." —GENESIS 2:7

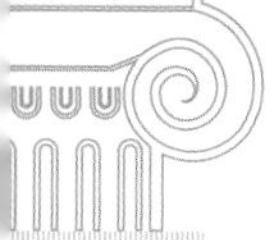

SEE ALSO | GOLDEN AGES: PAGE 88

KEY DATES

3500 B.C.E.
Sumerians develop a complex society with urban areas built around temple centers.

3000 B.C.E.
Camels are domesticated.

2334 B.C.E.
King Sargon of Akkad conquers Sumer and goes on to forge a Mesopotamian empire.

1792 B.C.E.
Hammurabi takes power in Babylon and establishes the first Babylonian Empire.

FIRST STATES

3500–600 B.C.E.

The emergence of urban centers such as Jericho was the initial phase of the next great development in human history: the rise of civilization itself. The word comes from a Latin root meaning "citizen," and includes the concept of the individual being a member of a state. And with statehood, almost inevitably, comes powerful rulers. As they grew more complex, communities that had once seemed to run themselves required more administration, with officials of all sorts managing daily life, from religious observances to economic exchanges to the increasingly frequent practice of trading with other regions. The most successful of these communities were those with strong leaders, who inevitably bred—and sometimes arose from—bands of armed men that evolved into armies. Rulers with armies feel the need to use them, and soon cities were becoming city-states with nearby regions under their control and sometimes even entire empires stretching across hundreds or thousands of miles.

The world's first civilizations were city-states and empires that arose from urban communities with particularly powerful rulers. Trade and cultural development marked the newly civilized world, but so did warfare.

The first civilizations arose in the Fertile Crescent, the broad swath of the Middle East extending from the eastern Mediterranean shore to Mesopotamia, the "land between the rivers"—the Tigris and Euphrates. At the southern end, toward the Persian Gulf, the city-states of Sumer, chief among them Ur and Uruk, came to prominence beginning in 3500 B.C.E. Empire builders followed, from the Akkadian Sargon to Hammurabi of Babylon and, in their turn, the leaders of Assyria to the north and the Hittites from Anatolia.

Wars between empires raged, but so did trade with other societies to the west. Along the eastern Mediterranean coast, the Phoenicians became masters of the waters, establishing a maritime trading empire with colonies as far away as the Iberian Peninsula. The Minoans developed a culture of extraordinary sophistication and refinement on Crete, and the Mycenaeans ruled the lands that would become Greek city-states.

But there were dozens of other "first" civilizations in the surrounding lands of Europe, Africa, and Asia, as well as great, long-lasting empires in Egypt, India, China, the Americas, and other far-flung places. Civilization was in many ways a vast outbreak around the world.

OPPOSITE: An ancient Hittite ruler strikes a kingly pose in this bas-relief.

1595 B.C.E.
Hittites sack Babylon, ending the Babylonian dynasty.

900 B.C.E.
Assyrians in northern Mesopotamia begin imperial expansion.

ca 740 B.C.E.
Babylonians begin detailed recording of celestial phenomena.

612 B.C.E.
Babylonians defeat the Assyrians and regain control of their empire.

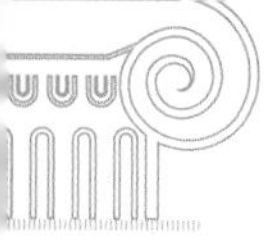

Servants carry dishes for a royal Mesopotamian meal.

CLASS & SOCIETY SUMER'S STRATA

Civilization brought with it the division of people into distinct social classes. In the city-states of Sumer and other Mesopotamian societies, a nobility emerged among the wealthiest citizens, including landowners, top administrative officials, and the family of the king, who was usually a military leader appointed by a council of elders. He stood alone at the pinnacle of society and had many responsibilities, initiating major public projects, such as the building of step-pyramid temples called ziggurats; managing bands of warriors; and serving as the religious leader.

Next in rank were the priests, who conducted religious ceremonies, managed temple complexes, and controlled the storage and distribution of food, making them major players in economic life. Everyone else was a commoner or a slave, but there were many ranks among the masses. Officials not in the nobility were at the top, followed by scribes, merchants, and practitioners of various crafts—from metallurgy to woodworking, weaving, and baking. The peasantry worked the land or tended small shops.

> Priests collected taxes and controlled food storehouses clustered at the base of their ziggurats.

The lowest ranking of all were slaves, who may originally have been captured in battle or seized in slave raids. In fact, the Sumerian word for slave meant "foreigner." The poorest peasants could sell themselves or their children into slavery. Slaves had few if any rights, although in Babylon they could conduct business and even own slaves themselves. In Sumer, the children of a slave and a free person were free.

THE TAKEAWAY: Sumerian society ranged from the king and nobles to commoners and slaves.

FIRST CITIES

VIPs

Gilgamesh,
Third millennium B.C.E.
Semi-legendary ruler of Uruk who became the hero of an early epic poem

Sargon of Akkad,
Reigned 2334–2279 B.C.E.
Emperor famous for his conquests of Sumerian city-states

Hammurabi, 1810–1750 B.C.E.
First king of the Babylonian Empire and creator of one of the first written codes of law

Sennacherib, Reigned 704–681 B.C.E. King of Assyria who established a capital at Nineveh

Nebuchadrezzar II,
634–562 B.C.E.
Ruler of Babylon who conquered Judah and Jerusalem

> *"Urlumma, ruler of Umma drained the boundary canal of Ningirsu, the boundary canal of Nina; those steles he threw into the fire, he broke [them] in pieces."* —SUMERIAN INSCRIPTION

SEE ALSO | EPIC JOURNEYS: PAGE 32

DAILY LIFE BEING CIVIL

As civilizations developed, the needs of everyday life didn't change, but people no longer spent their time collecting, growing, or catching their own food. Instead, they depended on a complex, interwoven economic system, exchanging labor, finished goods, or even administrative or artistic skills for daily sustenance, clothing, and the like. Civilization for most people thus meant going to work to earn a living. Agriculture employed the majority, but archaeological finds indicate the making of pottery was also a major business in Sumer that doubtless relied on a large export market.

MINOAN GOLD PENDANT

Even those who didn't work nurtured new forms of specialized industry. The elite sponsored artists and musicians—paying for lavish jewelry, and encouraging entertainments. Being civilized also meant being civil, following rules of conduct that applied not only to public interchanges but also to family life.

Marriages in Sumer, for example, required the consent of the bride's family, and both husband and wife were bound by a legal contract to stay faithful. In some city-states, a woman could own property and testify in court, but only a woman could be executed for adultery, and her husband could also cast her aside for failing to produce children.

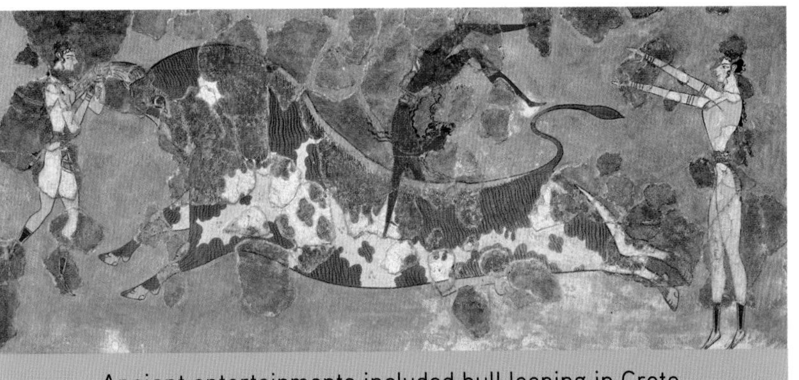

Ancient entertainments included bull leaping in Crete.

> In the Mediterranean, Minoan Crete developed a rich civilization with palaces, villas, and gold artifacts.

THE TAKEAWAY: Rules of conduct for public and private life kept society running smoothly.

VOICES

MESOPOTAMIA FATHERLY ADVICE

AKKADIAN TABLET

"*Do not set out to stand around in the assembly. Do not loiter where there is a dispute, for in the dispute they will have you as an observer. Then you will be made a witness for them, and they will involve you in a lawsuit to affirm something that does not concern you. In case of a dispute, get away from it, disregard it! If a dispute involving you should flare up, calm it down. A dispute is a covered pit, a wall which can cover over its foes.*"

—ADVICE FROM AN AKKADIAN FATHER TO HIS SON, CIRCA 2200 B.C.E.

"*I placed wild bulls and ferocious dragons in the gateways and thus adorned them with luxurious splendor.*"

—NEBUCHADREZZAR'S DEDICATION ON THE ISHTAR GATE

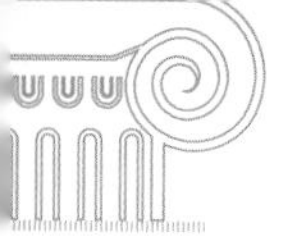

SEE ALSO | EPIC JOURNEYS: PAGE 45

ARTS FIRST WRITING

Writing began in the Middle East as recordkeeping. Merchants had long used clay tokens to represent commodities, and by 3500 B.C.E. they employed hollow clay balls as receptacles for the tokens. Images pressed into the ball's surface represented the number and types of tokens inside, and this label soon made the tokens themselves unnecessary. Scribes then flattened the clay balls into tablets that were easier to write on. Inscribed images, or pictographs, were originally stylized representations of the things they stood for, but the symbols became more and more abstract. Sumer developed a system of writing called cuneiform (from the Latin for "wedge") that used combinations of simple marks made with the wedge-shaped end of a cut piece of reed.

A scribe records distribution of grain (above). Cuneiform script on a letter seal from Ugarit, Syria (below, left).

> Some forms of writing remained pictographic; others became phonetic, with characters representing sounds or syllables.

What scribes were writing was changing, too. Written reports from generals made governing easier; written customs became codified rules; and epic tales became the first forms of literature.

THE TAKEAWAY: Writing led to the recording of history and the beginnings of literature.

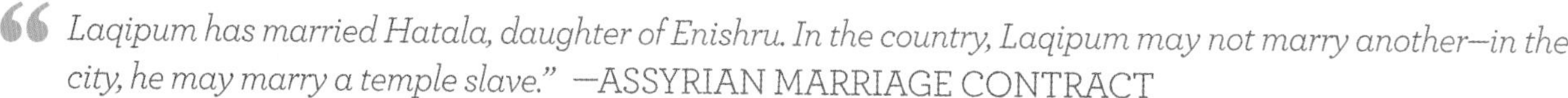

"*Laqipum has married Hatala, daughter of Enishru. In the country, Laqipum may not marry another—in the city, he may marry a temple slave.*" —ASSYRIAN MARRIAGE CONTRACT

VOICES

SUMER GILGAMESH DISCOVERS DEATH

*"Enkidu, my young friend (the panther of the field),
Who surpassed in strength everything so that we ascended the mountain,
Seized the heavenly bull and slew him,
Overthrew Humbaba, who dwelt in the forest of cedars.
What is the sleep that has now seized thee?
Thy appearance is somber; thou dost not hear my voice.'
But he does not lift up his eyes.
Gilgamesh touched his heart; it beat no more.
Then he covered his friend like a bride.
Gilgamesh for Enkidu, his friend,
Weeps bitterly, rushing across the roads.
'I myself will die, and will then be like Enkidu.
Woe has entered my heart,
Fear of death has seized me, therefore I wander across the roads.'"*

—FROM THE *EPIC OF GILGAMESH*, FIRST MILLENNIUM B.C.E.

HERO, POSSIBLY GILGAMESH, TAMING LION

RELIGION MANY GODS

The fact that priests controlled the society's larder demonstrates the centrality of religion in Sumerian life. Everything depended on the success of the crops, so people worshipped gods of the harvest and of the elements. Originally each city-state had its own god, but as relations developed among different communities, these gods became organized into an official pantheon. At the top were three main deities: Anu, the father of all the gods; Enlil, god of earth and air who shaped the world; and Enki, the god of wisdom and of life-giving waters who managed Enlil's creation. There were dozens of other deities with unique responsibilities—a god of the plow, for instance, and a goddess of both love and war known as Ishtar.

Hammurabi praying

When Babylon rose to prominence early in the second millennium B.C.E., the city's local god, Marduk, intruded on the old Sumerian order. The Babylonian king Hammurabi claimed that Anu and Enlil had put Marduk in charge of all the other gods, just as they wanted Hammurabi to rule all of Mesopotamia. It may have been a political ploy, but Marduk survived the gambit, remaining supreme among the gods of Mesopotamia well into the first millennium B.C.E.

THE TAKEAWAY: Sumerians turned to many gods to ensure successful harvests and ventures.

"When Jupiter goes with Venus, the prayer of the land will reach the heart of the gods. Marduk and Sarpanit will hear the prayer of their people, and will have mercy on my people." —NERGAL-ETIR

SEE ALSO | GOLDEN AGES: PAGE 76

The death of Priam during the Trojan War, in a painting by Regnault.

CONFLICTS CLASH OF EMPIRES

The city-states of Mesopotamia entered a new phase during the waning centuries of the third millennium B.C.E. Armed conflict became more common as strong leaders realized they could simply overrun their neighbors to achieve fame and enrich their economies. In the person of Sargon of the central Mesopotamian city of Akkad, the warrior-king took on the new role of empire builder. Sargon overthrew the sitting king of Akkad in 2334 B.C.E. and launched a 56-year expansionist reign that saw the Akkadian Empire stretch from the shores of the Mediterranean to lands just east of the Persian Gulf.

Sargon was the first of many rulers to assert dominance beyond Mesopotamia, and more than a few were foreign invaders attracted to the obvious riches of the land and its cities. Raiders from the east and north, such as Hittites, at times claimed empire status; later, kings from Sumer, Babylon, and Assyria ruled supreme behind thousands of spear-bearing and chariot-mounted warriors; Assyrian armies topped 200,000.

> The Hittites, who sacked Babylon in 1595 B.C.E., were fierce warriors who attacked in swift two-wheeled chariots.

The imperialistic urge cropped up elsewhere. Conflict between the Mycenaeans of Greece and peoples to the east in Anatolia turned into the most famous legendary battle of all time, the siege of Troy. Homer wrote that it was all about love and honor; whatever really happened was undoubtedly more about extending an empire.

THE TAKEAWAY: Empires rose and fell across a 1,500-year period of almost continual warfare.

Mycenae's cyclopean walls and Lion Gate still stand.

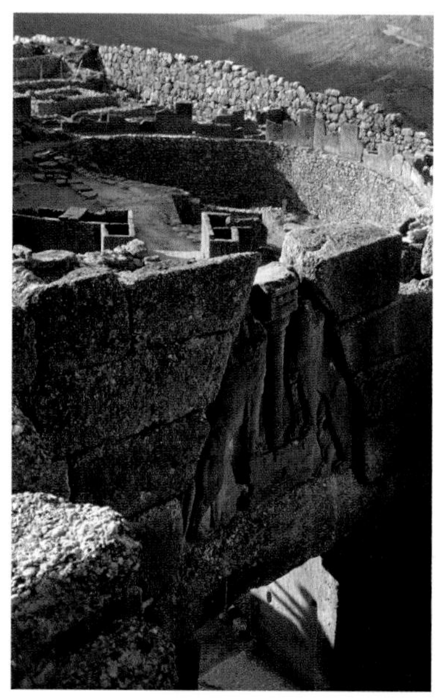

> *"Terillos, the son of Crinippos . . . brought into Sicily at this very time an army of 300,000 men—Phoenicians, Libyans, Iberians, Ligurians, Helisykians, Sardinians, and Corsicans."* —HERODOTUS

VOICES

HOMER GREEKS VS. TROJANS

"So did the serried phalanxes of the Danaans march steadfastly to battle. The chiefs gave orders each to his own people, but the men said never a word; no man would think it, for huge as the host was, it seemed as though there was not a tongue among them, so silent were they in their obedience; and as they marched the armour about their bodies glistened in the sun. But the clamour of the Trojan ranks was as that of many thousand ewes that stand waiting to be milked in the yards of some rich flock-master, and bleat incessantly in answer to the bleating of their lambs."

—FROM *THE ILIAD* OF HOMER, ca 800 B.C.E.

HOMER

TRADE SMART BUSINESS

Trade was one of the key ingredients spurring the rise of civilizations in the Fertile Crescent and the eastern Mediterranean. Agriculture in Mesopotamia would not have thrived without the importation of stone and then metal to make better plows and scythes, and the lands they traded with needed Sumerian grain in return. Over time every trading culture was enriched by an increasingly diverse range of foreign goods. Caravan drivers ran a steady business with pack camels on routes that led north and west from Mesopotamia to the Mediterranean and east to India. In southern Sumer, seafaring traders plied the coastlines of the Persian Gulf and perhaps beyond. They couldn't hold a rudder, though, to the Phoenicians of the eastern Mediterranean coast, whose wooden ships powered by sail and oar reached clear across the Mediterranean. The canny Phoenicians established colonies near lucrative markets while back home, their two great city-states, Tyre and Sidon, kept business going for centuries with smart alliances.

Ancient Phoenician coin with ship (above)

{ The Phoenicians told other cultures that terrifying monsters lay beyond the western end of the Mediterranean. }

THE TAKEAWAY: Early cultures gained from trade routes on land and sea.

THUMBS UP / THUMBS DOWN

SARGON REIGNED 2334–2279 B.C.E.

SARGON

HIS NAME MEANT THE "TRUE KING," and Sargon of Akkad took advantage of that presumed legitimacy to establish a vast empire. Fierce in battle, Sargon claimed in one inscription to have brought a vanquished king "in a dog collar to the gate of Enlil." But he was an effective administrator, standardizing practices and unifying a multicultural empire by making Akkadian the official language of all Mesopotamia. Although he appointed Akkadian governors to rule in captured Sumerian city-states, he left Sumerian religion in place. Later emperors modeled their reigns on his. **CONCLUSION: THUMBS UP**

"Four pounds of copper cost one half-shekel of silver; one tub of lard, one half-shekel of silver; two cheese one half-shekel of silver; a gown twelve half-shekels of silver." —THE CODE OF THE NESILIM

CODE OF HAMMURABI

Greater than any of his conquests was the legacy King Hammurabi of Babylon left in the form of the legal code that bears his name. Consisting of 282 separate laws that were compiled around 1790 B.C.E., the code was based on Sumerian legal precedents. Most of the laws consisted of a single sentence and stipulated punishments for various crimes, established rules for business dealings, and even covered judicial misconduct, stating that a judge in error would have to pay 12 times the amount of any fine he had imposed and would be removed from office.

HAMMURABI Coming to power in 1792 B.C.E., the new king immediately launched military campaigns against neighboring city-states and established the first Babylonian Empire. Of his own code of laws he wrote: "My words are well considered; there is no wisdom like mine."

“If a woman quarrel with her husband, and say: 'You are not congenial to me,' the reasons for her prejudice must be presented. If she is guiltless, and there is no fault on her part, but he leaves and neglects her, then no guilt attaches to this woman, she shall take her dowry and go back to her father's house.”

“If any one steal cattle or sheep, or an ass, or a pig or a goat, if it belong to a god or to the court, the thief shall pay thirtyfold therefore; if they belonged to a freed man of the king he shall pay tenfold; if the thief has nothing with which to pay he shall be put to death.”

STONE TESTAMENT The most complete version of the code was found etched into a stone stele more than seven feet tall displayed in Babylon. Other copies were rendered on baked clay tablets.

“If any one take a male or female slave of the court, or a male or female slave of a freed man, outside the city gates, he shall be put to death.”

KING AND GOD At the top of the stone stele listing the code's 282 laws, Hammurabi solicits advice from Shamash, the god of justice, who sits regally with flames at his shoulders.

“If any one bring an accusation against a man, and the accused go to the river and leap into the river, if he sink in the river his accuser shall take possession of his house. But if the river prove that the accused is not guilty, and he escape unhurt, then he who had brought the accusation shall be put to death, while he who leaped into the river shall take possession of the house that had belonged to his accuser.”

“If any one owe a debt for a loan, and a storm prostrates the grain, or the harvest fail, or the grain does not grow for lack of water; in that year he need not give his creditor any grain, he washes his debt-tablet in water and pays no rent for this year.”

LOCAL LANGUAGE Inscribed in the cuneiform characters of the Akkadian language spoken in the streets, Hammurabi's code was more accessible to the common folk than previous Sumerian laws recorded in esoteric priestly tongues. The section shown above is taken from columns 14 and 15.

AN EYE FOR AN EYE

If a son strike his father, his hands shall be hewn off.

If a man put out the eye of another man, his eye shall be put out.

If he break another man's bone, his bone shall be broken.

If he put out the eye of a freed man, or break the bone of a freed man, he shall pay one gold mina.

If he put out the eye of a man's slave, or break the bone of a man's slave, he shall pay one-half of its value.

If a man knock out the teeth of his equal, his teeth shall be knocked out.

If the slave of a freed man strike the body of a freed man, his ear shall be cut off.

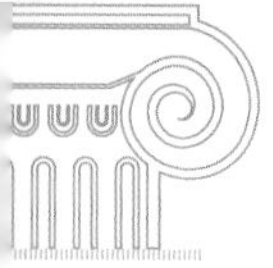

SEE ALSO | THE CLASSICAL AGE: PAGE 103

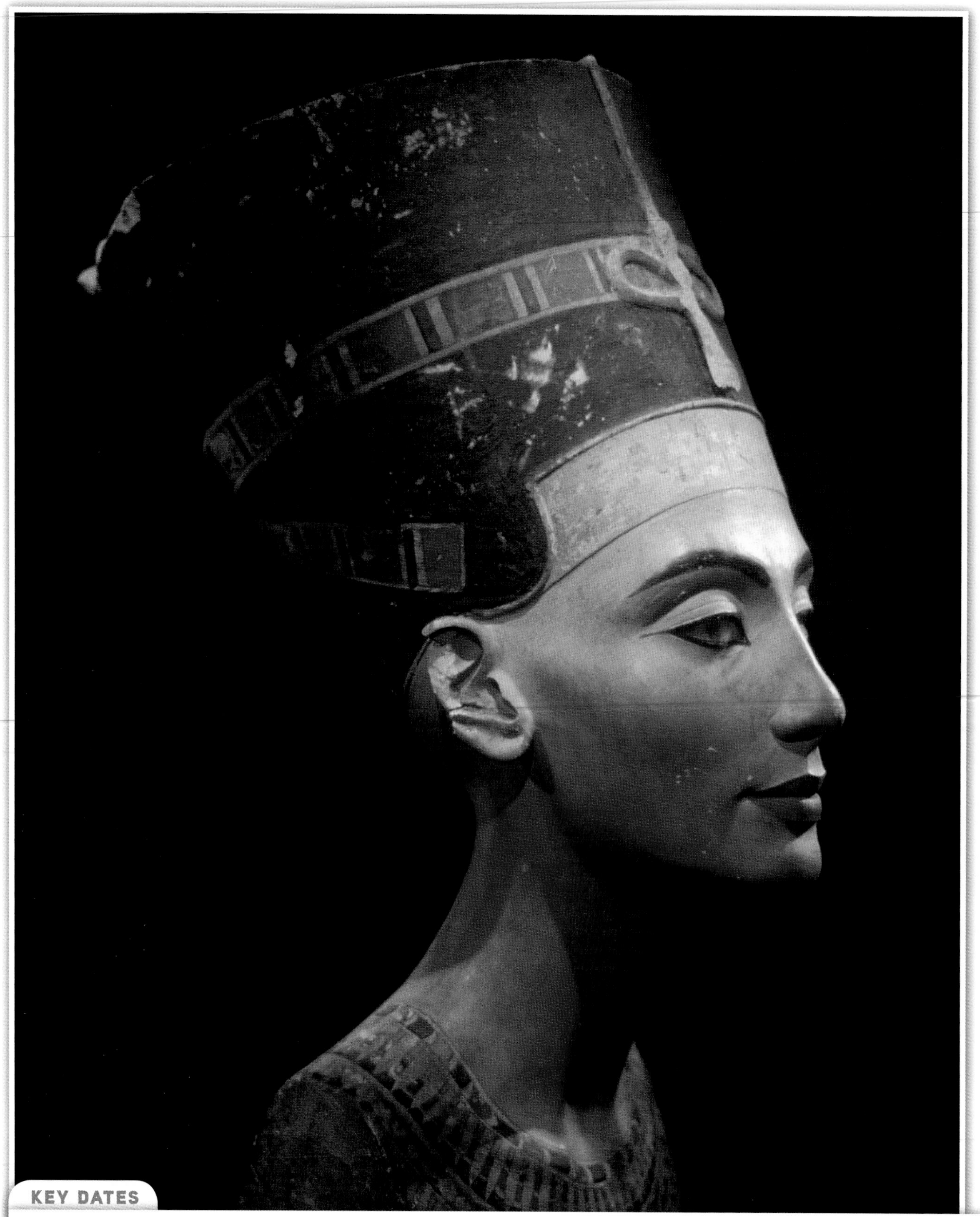

KEY DATES

3100 B.C.E.
King Narmer from Upper Egypt conquers the Nile Delta region, unifying the country.

2650 B.C.E.
The beginning of the Old Kingdom.

2550 B.C.E.
Pharaoh Khufu orders construction of the Great Pyramid at Giza.

2150 B.C.E.
Drought disrupts the seasonal flooding of the Nile, destabilizing the Old Kingdom.

LANDS OF THE NILE

3050–525 B.C.E.

The Nile River gave birth to civilization in Egypt just as the Tigris and Euphrates did in Mesopotamia, but Egypt was an altogether different kind of child. It never developed independent city-states; its cities were religious and political centers, with palaces, temples, and monuments. But the people lived in villages or slightly larger market towns, all clustered near the river's fertile floodplains, and the river kept them all in touch. Early on, the communities in the southern region known as Upper Egypt, where the habitable land is narrower and the river more hemmed in by cliffs and desert, became a united kingdom; Lower Egypt, where the Nile and its tributaries form a vast delta, followed, and powerful leaders emerged to rule each domain. Sometime around 3100 B.C.E., the king of Upper Egypt, known as Menes, or Narmer, conquered Lower Egypt, united the kingdoms, and established his capital on the border between them, at Memphis.

Egyptian civilization flourished for more than 3,000 years under 31 dynasties, fed by the rich deposits of the Nile and bolstered by a homogeneous society that treated their leaders as gods.

Egypt's subsequent history, spinning out for some 3,000 years, is defined by a succession of 31 dynasties, royal families headed by a ruler who only latterly was called pharaoh. Scholars divide the whole stretch into three major stable periods, known as the Old, Middle, and New Kingdoms, punctuated by times of upheaval. During these so-called Intermediate Periods, one of which was brought on by a prolonged drought, the old separation between Lower and Upper Egypt returned, and regional disputes flared. Stable times, though, saw expansion and accomplishment. During the Old Kingdom, the pharaohs Djoser, Sneferu, and Khufu built the first and greatest pyramids, enduring monuments to their power and to the importance they placed on the rituals of death. Pharaohs of the Middle Kingdom looked south to the kingdom of Nubia, annexing its lands—and its gold mines. The New Kingdom's rulers established a new capital, Thebes, and expanded Egyptian hegemony north into Canaan and Syria.

By about 1000 B.C.E., Egypt seemed to have lost its will to rule itself effectively, and for the next half dozen or so centuries fell subject to a variety of foreign invaders. Most of them retained Egyptian customs and ruled as pharaohs. Foreign cultural conquest had to wait for Alexander the Great and then the Romans, who unseated Egypt's last pharaoh, Cleopatra.

OPPOSITE: Powerful queen Nefertiti ruled in the 14th century B.C.E., during Egypt's New Kingdom.

1975 B.C.E.
Egypt is reunified by rulers from Thebes, ushering in the Middle Kingdom.

1353 B.C.E.
Pharaoh Akhenaten takes power and makes Aten, the sun, Egypt's supreme deity.

1070 B.C.E.
New Kingdom ends and Egyptian power declines.

730 B.C.E.
Nubians conquer Egypt and rule for several decades until the Assyrians take control.

SEE ALSO | EPIC JOURNEYS: PAGE 34

CLASS & SOCIETY BORN IN PLACE

A tomb mural shows the goddess Isis (left) and Queen Nefertari (right) of the New Kingdom.

Class defined everyone in Egypt, and the stability of its hierarchical system—its rootedness in birth and its attachment to occupation—helps account for the remarkable staying power of Egyptian society. At the bottom, of course, were slaves, who served in the households of the rich or performed menial tasks, but they were not a massive workforce, as once thought. Peasant workers built the pyramids, dug irrigation channels, and tilled the fields. Above them socially were skilled workers in many crafts, as well as painters and sculptors devoted to decorating royal tombs; scribes serving in a vast government bureaucracy run by a further tier of officials, provincial governors, and viziers handling affairs of state for the pharaoh; a priestly class with abundant privileges; and the pharaoh and his or her family. Pharaohs were considered gods, and maintaining the line was paramount.

THE TAKEAWAY: Egypt's stable society rested on a solid tier of skilled workers.

LANDS OF THE NILE

Narmer, reigned ca 3100 B.C.E. Egyptian pharaoh who unified Upper and Lower Egypt.

Khufu, reigned 2558–2551 B.C.E. Pharaoh of Egypt's Old Kingdom who built the Great Pyramid at Giza

Hatshepsut, reigned 1473–1458 B.C.E.Female pharaoh of Egypt

Akhenaten (Amenhotep IV), reigned 1353–1334 B.C.E. Egyptian pharaoh who introduced the worship of Aten

Ramses II, reigned 1279–1213 B.C.E. Powerful pharaoh who led several expeditions to the Mediterranean

VIPs

"Hail to thee, O Nile! Who manifests thyself over this land, and comes to give life to Egypt! Mysterious is thy issuing forth from the darkness, on this day whereon it is celebrated!" —HYMN TO THE NILE

VOICES

NEBMARE-NAKHT SCRIBE

"Love writing, shun dancing; then you become a worthy official. Do not long for the marsh thicket. Turn your back on throw-stick and chase. By day write with your fingers; recite by night. Befriend the scroll, the palette. It pleases more than wine. Writing for him who knows it is better than all other professions. It pleases more than bread and beer, more than clothing and ointment. It is worth more than an inheritance in Egypt, than a tomb in the west."

—FROM A SCRIBE TO HIS APPRENTICE, LATE NEW KINGDOM

SCRIBE

DAILY LIFE WORK AND PLAY

To help them in the afterlife, pharaohs had their tombs filled with objects both precious and utilitarian and the walls painted with scenes from daily life. These artifacts give a detailed, if idealized, picture of how Egyptians of every status lived. Numerous tasks occupied the workaday folk, from guiding plows and cutting grain to making papyrus, building boats, decorating pottery, and preparing food. The wealthy lounged at elaborate feasts, playing board games while musicians and dancers entertained. They could also have an active life: Murals in King Tutankhamun's tomb show him shooting arrows from a chariot, swimming, fishing, and hunting. Despite the benefits of their land's bounty, life was precarious for high and low. The average Egyptian lived only 20 years, an age Tutankhamun himself never reached, likely dying from a gangrenous leg wound.

Workers stack pot lids in an Egyptian bakery.

THE TAKEAWAY: The masses spent their days working; the elite enjoyed sports and music.

CONNECTIONS LOOKING MARVELOUS

Egyptians of the upper classes took pains to look their best. While their servants wore little more than breechcloths, they dressed in fine white linen robes with bead collars and adorned themselves with jewelry of gold, silver, and precious stones. But elite Egyptians—men, women, and children—weren't fully dressed without their makeup. Red ochre gave cheeks and lips a rosy glow, and henna dyed nails yellow and orange. The finishing touch was black kohl eyeliner painted out to a tapering point. Skin care went with the program: Daily lotioning with perfumed oil kept skin lubricated in the dry climate.

APPLYING MODERN COSMETICS

"And when I expected a child, they told the king, and he was most heartily glad; and he sent me many things, and a present of the best silver and gold and linen." —PRINCESS AHURA

SEE ALSO | THE CLASSICAL AGE: PAGE 113

RELIGION LIFE AND AFTERLIFE

Religion was an intimate part of everyday life for Egyptians. As in other civilizations, each early community originally had a patron deity, typically represented in animal or animal-human form. With the consolidation of Egyptian society, some of these local gods achieved loftier status, and an elaborate mythology developed. The falcon-headed god Horus, once the patron of Nekhen in Upper Egypt, became in pharaonic times the god-king of all Egypt, and pharaohs were said to rule as his incarnation.

When the first pharaohs of the Middle Kingdom came to power, they began a cult that worshipped a newly synthesized god, Amun-Ra, a combination of the old sun god Ra and the ram-headed god Amun, patron of the new capital, Thebes. During the New Kingdom, Akhenaten established Aten, a solar deity represented only by a disk, as the one supreme god, but after Akhenaten's death, self-interested priests quickly reinstated the old order.

Pharaoh Horemheb enters the afterlife.

One of the gods, Horus, was descended from two of Egypt's most important gods. According to the mythology, his father, Osiris, was torn to pieces by his own brother Seth, but their sister Isis, mother of Horus, resurrected him; Horus became god-king by killing Seth in an epic battle. Isis was worshipped as the goddess of love and creation, and Osiris as the god of the dead and of the afterlife.

> People of high status might be buried within three coffins that were nestled within a sarcophagus.

Religion was personal for Egyptians when it came to the afterlife. By the Middle Kingdom, all Egyptians—not just the pharaoh and his

EGYPT THE NEGATIVE CONFESSION

VOICES

"I have not sinned against men. I have not oppressed (or wronged) [my] kinsfolk. I have not committed evil in the place of truth. I have not known worthless men. I have not committed acts of abomination. I have not done daily works of supererogation. I have not caused my name to appear for honours. I have not domineered over slaves. I have not thought scorn of the god. I have not defrauded the poor man of his goods. I have not done the things which the gods abominate. I have not caused harm to be done to the slave by his master. I have caused no man to suffer. I have allowed no man to go hungry. I have made no man weep."

—PART OF THE CONFESSION BEFORE OSIRIS, FROM THE BOOK OF THE DEAD

CASE FOR BOOK OF THE DEAD

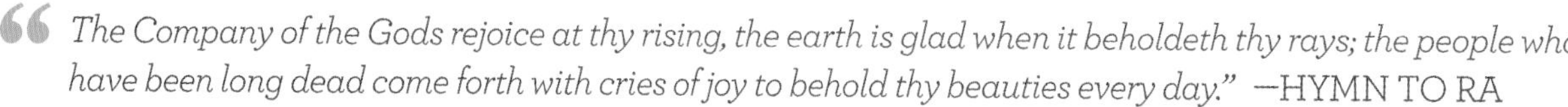

"The Company of the Gods rejoice at thy rising, the earth is glad when it beholdeth thy rays; the people who have been long dead come forth with cries of joy to behold thy beauties every day." —HYMN TO RA

VOICES

EGYPT THOU ENEMY OF RA

"Get thee back, Apep, thou enemy of Ra, thou winding serpent in the form of an intestine, without arms [and] without legs. Thy body cannot stand upright so that thou mayest have therein being, long is thy tail in front of thy den, thou enemy; retreat before Ra. Thy head shall be cut off, and the slaughter of thee shall be carried out. Thou shalt not lift up thy face, for his flame is in thy accursed soul. The odour which is in his chamber of slaughter is in thy members."

—FROM AN EGYPTIAN INCANTATION AGAINST REPTILES

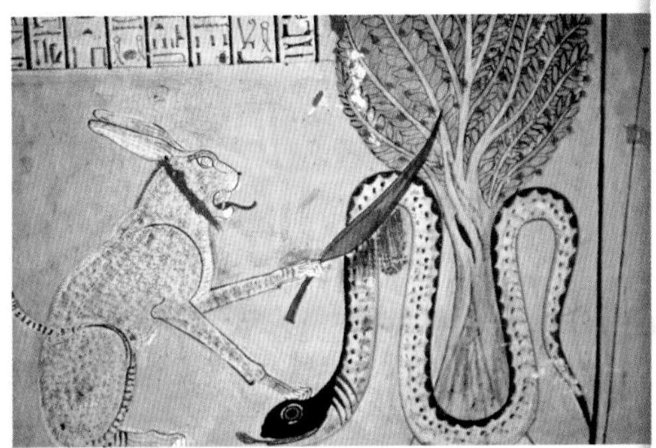

RA IN CAT FORM KILLS SNAKE DEMON APOPHIS

line—were considered eligible for a life of happiness after death if they passed the favorable judgment of Osiris at a tribunal of the dead. The ruling class lavished so much on funerary preparations because they believed it would ease their passage into bliss. Upon arrival in the Netherworld, Egyptians believed, the heart of the deceased would be weighed on a balance against an ostrich plume. If the scales balanced, the deceased would pass on to the fields of the blessed. If not, he or she would be consumed by the Eater of the Dead.

THE TAKEAWAY: Egyptians worshipped many gods but gave primacy to a few, including Osiris.

A scene of mourning with the god Anubis, on papyrus

"Let there be given unto me bread-cakes in the House of Refreshing, and sepulchral offerings of cakes and ale, and propitiatory offerings in Anu, and a permanent homestead in Sekhet-Aaru." —HYMN TO OSIRIS

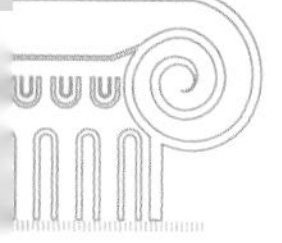

ARCHITECTURE BUILDING THE PYRAMIDS

Concern for status in the afterlife prompted Egypt's pharaohs to have tombs built to house their mummified bodies and everything they would need in the life beyond. The first such graves were simple squared-off mud-brick platforms known as mastabas, the largest of which was only 17 feet high. But in the Third Dynasty, King Djoser commissioned a more impressive memorial at Saqqara, and he put his chief counselor, Imhotep, in charge. Imhotep's architectural genius was to stack a series of mastabas of diminishing size one atop another, creating the world's first step pyramid—and also the first building ever constructed completely of quarried stone.

The Step Pyramid, which tops 200 feet, was soon surpassed by others, the most magnificent of which is the Great Pyramid at Giza, rising some 480 feet and consisting of more than two million limestone blocks weighing as much as 15 tons apiece. Tens of thousands of laborers hauled the stones using rollers or sleds and likely dragged them up earthen ramps into position. The steps were then filled in with rubble and encased in limestone to create smoothly sloping sides said to imitate the rays of the sun.

THE TAKEAWAY: Pharaohs were so powerful that they could command massive workforces to build pyramids and other monuments.

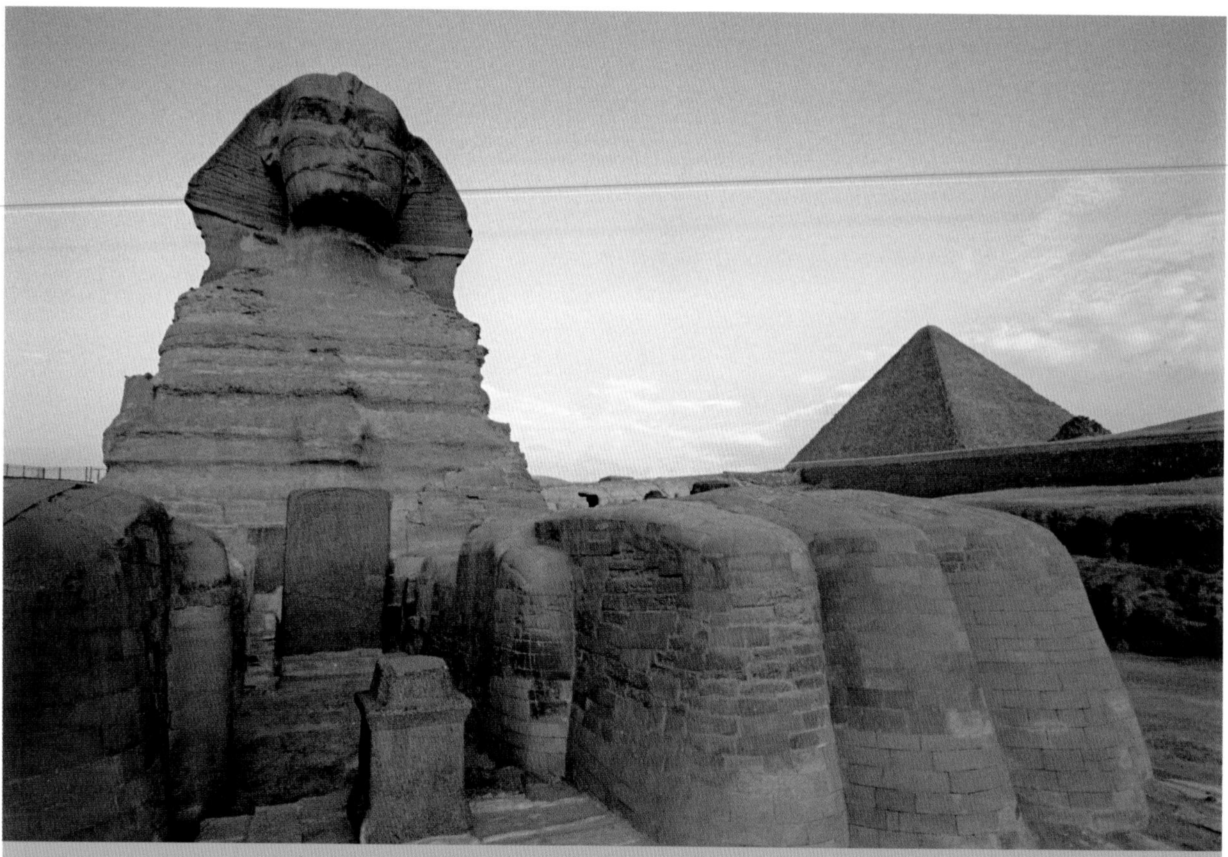

The Great Sphinx was probably built by the Pharaoh Khafre of the Old Kingdom; it may represent his face.

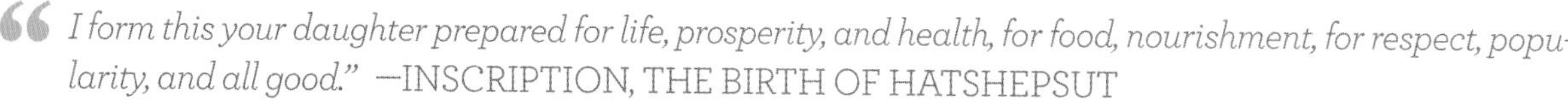

"I form this your daughter prepared for life, prosperity, and health, for food, nourishment, for respect, popularity, and all good." —INSCRIPTION, THE BIRTH OF HATSHEPSUT

SEE ALSO | THE CLASSICAL AGE: PAGE 114

Ramses II uses two-wheeled chariots to battle Nubian rebels.

CONFLICTS EMPIRES IN FLUX

Throughout its history, Egypt was both conquering and conquered. During the Old Kingdom, pharaohs sent armies into the rich lands of Canaan, and Middle Kingdom rulers made empire-expanding military moves into Nubia. They established standing armies for the first time, but thought of few other innovations. In fact, long after the Mesopotamians and others had improved their armaments, Egyptians were still fighting with spears and simple bows, protected only by unwieldy body-sized shields.

Little wonder that Egyptian defenders fell victim in about 1630 B.C.E. to the Hyksos, nomadic warriors from central Asia equipped with scimitars, longer-range bows, and two-wheeled chariots. Only by adopting these innovations were Egyptians able to win back their land.

> Hieroglyphs detail the plunder—including 924 chariots—seized from Canaanites in battle in the 15th century B.C.E.

After battling the Hittites to a standoff in Syria in 1285 B.C.E., Ramses II achieved a temporary peace by marrying a Hittite princess. But Egypt's glory was soon to wane. Libyan, Nubian, Assyrian, and Persian armies all took their turns defeating Egyptian forces before Alexander, and then the Romans, finished the job.

THE TAKEAWAY: Strong pharaohs led conquering armies, but in time Egyptian power waned.

CONNECTIONS COUNTING BY TENS

THE EGYPTIANS WERE OBSESSED WITH NUMBERS, and it paid off in the precision of their measurements; the lengths of the Great Pyramid's sides, for example, vary by less than .1 percent. The Babylonians made more-significant advances in mathematical theory, but the Egyptians contributed two major features to our modern system of enumeration. One was counting by tens: There are hieroglyphs for every tens place up to a million. The other was fractions. Unit fractions ($\frac{1}{3}$ $\frac{1}{4}$, $\frac{1}{100}$ and the like) were represented by a "fraction" hieroglyph set above hieroglyphs for the denominator. Special hieroglyphs stood for the frequently used $\frac{1}{2}$ and the non-unit fractions $\frac{2}{3}$ and $\frac{3}{4}$.

DICE

> *"Then Ramses uprose,/ like his father, Montu in might, / All his weapons took in hand,/ And his armor did he don,/ Just like Baal, fit for fight."* —INSCRIPTION, RAMSES II'S VICTORY OVER THE HITTITES

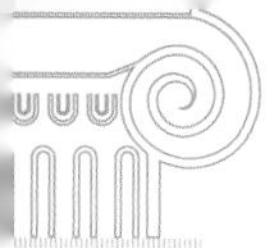

SEE ALSO | GOLDEN AGES: PAGE 57

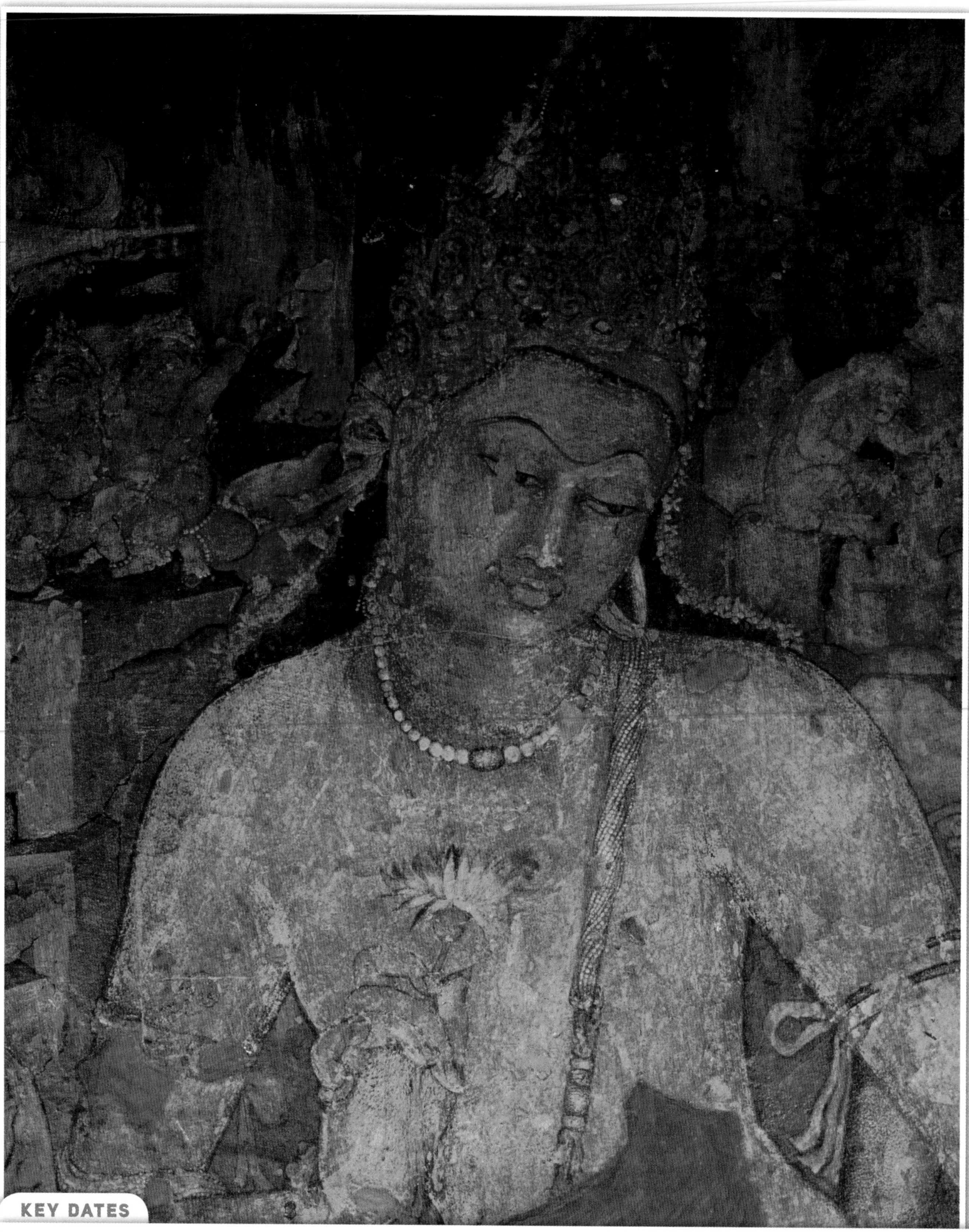

KEY DATES

2500 B.C.E.
Harappan civilization develops in the Indus River Valley as cities emerge.

2000 B.C.E.
Harappan civilization declines and cities are abandoned.

1500 B.C.E.
Aryans invade and take control of the Indus Valley.

1000 B.C.E.
Aryan chieftains expand their domain from the Indus Valley into the Ganges River Valley.

INDIA

2500–500 B.C.E.

Just as it had in the Fertile Crescent and in Egypt, civilization first flowered on the Indian subcontinent along the banks of a river, in this case the Indus, gushing with sediment-rich meltwater from some of the planet's loftiest mountains. The river's vast floodplain offered ample opportunities for managed irrigation, which encouraged strong social organization and led to an abundance of grain that in turn helped the society flourish. Villages came first, but by 2500 B.C.E. the Indus Valley was home to more than a dozen cities on the order of those already established in Mesopotamia. Chief among them were Mohenjo Daro in the south and Harappa in the north, whose name came to represent the entire culture. These two cities exemplified the extraordinary sophistication of the whole society, with streets laid out in a grid and channels carrying wastewater out to sewers. Public hygiene was obviously important and helped Mohenjo Daro's dense population to grow to 40,000.

The Indus and Ganges rivers gave rise to two waves of civilization on the Indian subcontinent, beginning with the Harappans and followed by the invading Aryans. Traditions melded over time to create a richly diverse culture.

The Indian cities carried on an active trade with Mesopotamia. Merchants stamped or inscribed symbols and pictographs onto clay seals and copper tablets, which led to the development of a writing system consisting of some 400 characters.

Floods fed the land but were also destructive; archaeological evidence indicates that Mohenjo Daro was rebuilt nine times. Scholars debate whether this flooding or some other cause brought Harappan civilization down, but during the first two centuries of the second millennium B.C.E., the cities were abandoned, writing disappeared, and the door lay open for invaders from the north.

By 1500 B.C.E. people known as Aryans had swept in from the Eurasian steppes, bringing with them new gods and establishing a whole new class structure. By about 1000 B.C.E. the invaders had laid claim to the lush Ganges Valley to the east, and over the next 300 years, chiefs who had taken the title of raja, or king, ruled 16 distinct Aryan states throughout India.

More changes were afoot. Persians conquered the Indus Valley in about 520 B.C.E., and shortly thereafter the kingdom of Magadha in the Ganges Valley rose to prominence. Its kings formed an empire from which later Indian civilization emerged, its roots still planted in long-standing Aryan and Harappan traditions.

OPPOSITE: A first-century painting from India's Ajanta caves portrays a bodhisattva with a lotus.

ca 900
The Law Code of Manu compiles the rules for moral living.

700 B.C.E.
Indian teachers reinterpret Aryan beliefs in scriptures called Upanishads, which form the basis of Hinduism.

560 B.C.E.
Siddhartha Gautama, known as Buddha or "the enlightened one," is born.

520 B.C.E.
Persians conquer the Indus Valley.

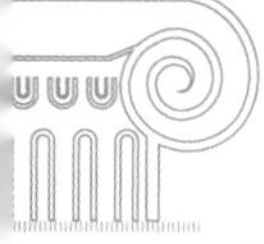

SEE ALSO | GOLDEN AGES: PAGE 82

RELIGION MANY GODS

Arguably the world's oldest religion, Hinduism contains vestiges of both Harappan and Aryan beliefs, the latter formalized in the Vedas, a collection of hymns, prayers, and rituals first compiled in 1400 B.C.E. Later teachers known as gurus challenged some Aryan tenets in their own sacred texts, the Upanishads, which posited that every soul could unite with the universal spirit, known as Brahman. Hinduism itself emerged by the sixth century B.C.E., combining the quest for salvation with veneration of a wide assortment of gods. Then in 528 B.C.E., a man named Siddhartha Gautama began teaching that spiritual enlightenment, or nirvana, could be reached through a Middle Way of moderation and moral conduct. He himself became known as the "enlightened one," or the Buddha, and a new religion was born.

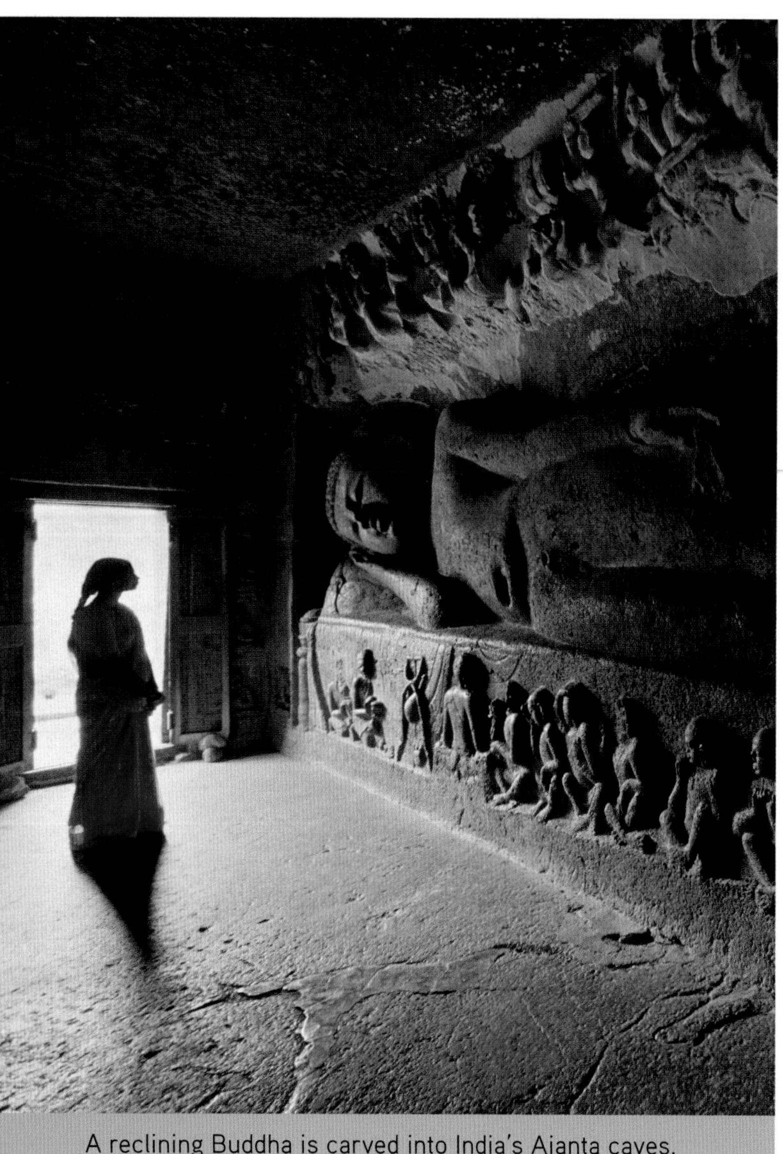

A reclining Buddha is carved into India's Ajanta caves.

{ Some Hindus believe that the Buddha was an incarnation of Vishnu, the god who preserves life and guards the world. }

THE TAKEAWAY: Long-revered sacred texts and adapted forms of ancient gods contributed to the multifaceted tenets of Hinduism.

INDIAN GODS

VIPs

Indra, Chief of the gods in early Hinduism and a great warrior

Varuna, In early Hinduism, a god who rules the heavens and monitors the moral behavior of humans

Vishnu, A principal god of Hinduism who protects and maintains the universe

Shiva, A principal god of Hinduism who is the destroyer of evil

> "*Way must be made for a man in a carriage, for one who is above ninety years old, for one diseased, for the carrier of a burden, for a woman, . . . for the king, and for a bridegroom.*" —LAW CODE OF MANU

VOICES

INDIA INDRA THE FIERCE

"He is the wielder of the thunderbolt, the slayer of robbers, fearful and fierce, knowing many things, much eulogized, and mighty, and like the Soma juice, inspiring the five classes of beings with vigour: may Indra, associated with the Maruts, be our protection."

—FROM THE RIGVEDA, SEVENTH CHAPTER, HYMN VII

THE GOD BRAHMA HOLDS A PAGE OF THE VEDAS

CLASS & SOCIETY CASTES

It is history's first recorded instance of racism. When the Aryans took over in India, they distinguished themselves, a light-skinned people, from the local folk, who belonged to a darker-complexioned ethnic group known as Dravidians. The Aryans had two classes in their own society, Brahmans (priests) and Kshatriyas (warriors), and by 1000 B.C.E. they had divided everyone else—people whom they called *dasas,* or "dark ones"—into occupation-based groups called *varnas,* a word that meant both "class" and "color." Of higher rank were the Vaishyas, who included farmers, merchants, and craftsmen. Shudras, or landless peasants, laborers, and slaves, were a step below. A few centuries later, one more distinction appeared: Those who performed the most unpleasant tasks, such as burying the dead, were outside the class system altogether and deemed "untouchable."

Indus Valley figure with infant

> By 600 B.C.E., class separation had gone further with the identification of subcastes called jatis.

This caste system had rigid rules; you could not, for instance, marry, work with, or even eat with someone from another varna.

THE TAKEAWAY: Aryan dominance brought with it a strict social structure.

CONNECTIONS CASTE TODAY

THE ANCIENT INDIAN CASTE SYSTEM survives to the present day in modified form. The traditional varna distinctions have disappeared, but *jatis,* or subcastes, now numbering nearly 3,000, remain as community-based groups that share an occupation, a dialect, or a set of religious beliefs. Although defining someone as untouchable was outlawed in 1950, discrimination still exists. Calling themselves *dalits,* which means "suppressed" or "crushed," members of this hereditary group still face rejection in some communities. But rights movements that began in the mid-20th century have made major strides. Many dalits have risen to the top of professions in medicine, the law, and government.

TRADITIONAL WOMAN FROM BIHAR, INDIA

"Which, O Bhikkhus, is this Middle Path... which leads to insight, which leads to wisdom, which conduces to calm, to knowledge, to the Sambodhi, to Nirvana?" —SIDDHARTHA GAUTAMA (BUDDHA)

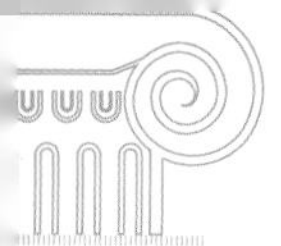

SEE ALSO | GOLDEN AGES: PAGE 75

KEY DATES

2296 B.C.E.
Chinese astronomers make one of the earliest records of a comet sighting.

2200 B.C.E.
Chinese civilization begins to emerge along the Yellow River.

1750 B.C.E.
The Shang dynasty takes control of a kingdom on the Yellow River.

1300 B.C.E.
Shang rulers move their capital to Anyang.

CHINA

2000–500 B.C.E.

In some ways, the conditions were very much the same in ancient China as they were in Mesopotamia and India: two great rivers with fertile floodplains that gave early agriculture a boost, food surpluses that allowed populations to grow, and small village settlements whose social organization became more complex and led to the emergence of cities. But in other ways China was fundamentally different. Isolated by deserts and mountains to the west and north, jungles to the south, and the Pacific Ocean to the east, Chinese civilization developed its own patterns, unaffected by trade or warfare with other peoples. Frequent flooding on China's two major rivers caused strong rulers to direct efforts to dig irrigation ditches and canals to control flooding. One such leader was the legendary Yu the Great, who was credited with taming the floods in 2200 B.C.E. and founding the Xia dynasty, the first of several royal lines that advanced Chinese culture for the next 1,500 years.

By 1750 B.C.E., the Shang dynasty had taken over, and more cities sprang up. The Shang kings took on a semi-divine mantle and were buried in splendor, with captives sacrificed to consecrate the site. But the last Shang ruler, Di Xin, apparently took things too far, torturing opponents and imposing burdensome taxes. Challengers from the west ousted him in 1100 B.C.E. and established the Zhou dynasty, which extended its control south to the Yangtze Valley.

Strong rulers established China's first dynasties and advanced civilization throughout the empire. But increasingly powerful vassals and decentralized authority led to a period of fragmentation.

Zhou emperors wielded authority over the enlarged empire through vassals bound by kinship. Initially, during the Western Zhou period, the king remained strong, but within the rigorous feudal system that had developed were the seeds of dissolution. In 771 B.C.E., marauding nomads forced the Zhou to move their capital east, marking the beginning of the Eastern Zhou period and a weakening of the central ruler's power. The forging of iron weapons, a new technology, had become widespread, and vassals now fully controlled their own territory, looking to the emperor only as a figurehead. Several rival states emerged, and clashes were frequent. The Zhou state responded by building a massive earth-and-stone defensive structure known as the Square Wall. Others followed suit. Remnants of these walls were later incorporated into the Great Wall.

OPPOSITE: Emperor Mu of the Zhou dynasty travels abroad in his chariot.

1100 B.C.E.
Di Xin, the last ruler of the Shang dynasty, is overthrown by the founders of the Zhou dynasty.

1000 B.C.E.
Iron metallurgy becomes widespread in China.

771 B.C.E.
The Zhou move their capital to Luoyang, marking the divide between Eastern and Western Zhou.

CA 600 B.C.E.
Chinese philosopher Lao Zi, founder of Daoism, is born.

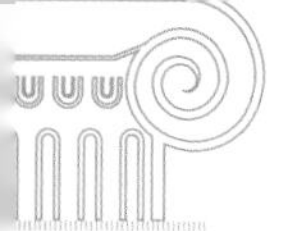

SEE ALSO | EPIC JOURNEYS: PAGE 18

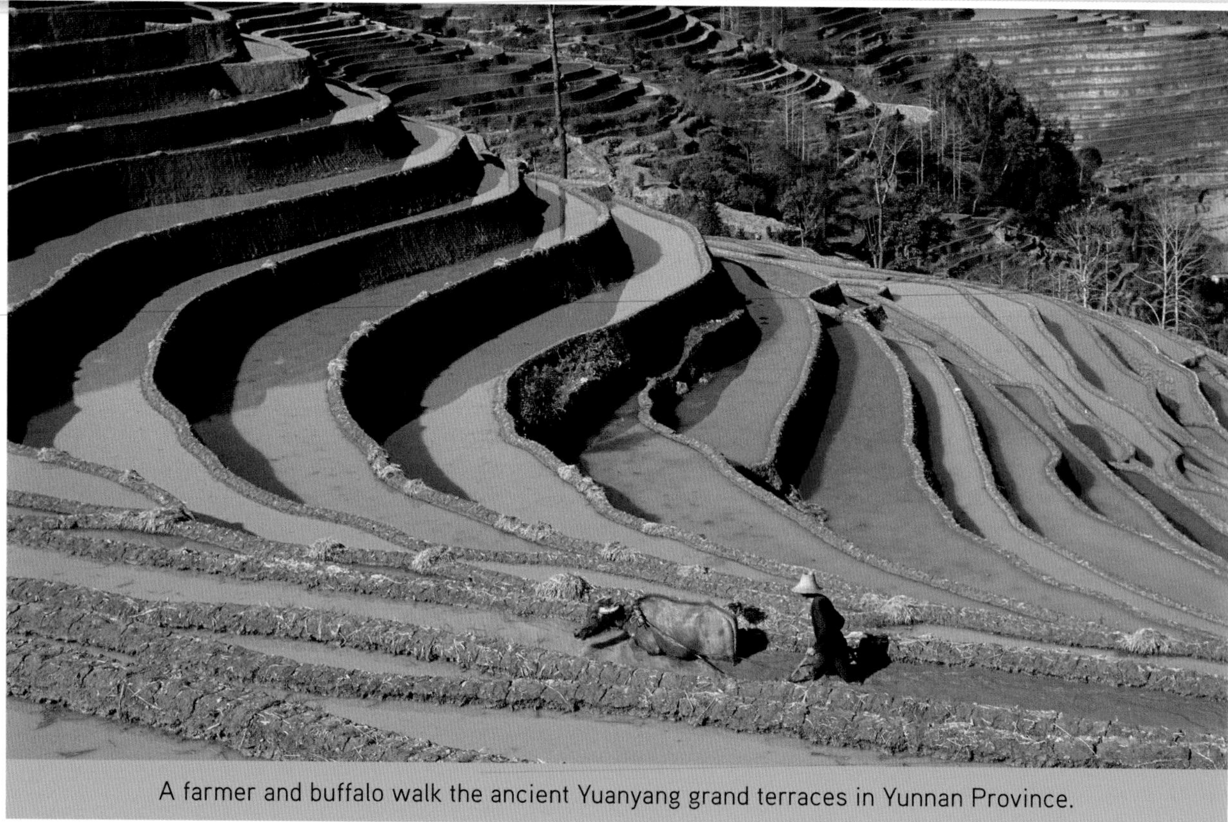

A farmer and buffalo walk the ancient Yuanyang grand terraces in Yunnan Province.

FARMING WET, DRY, AND SILKEN

Climatic and topographic differences caused agriculture to develop differently near China's two main rivers. Wetlands bordering the Yangtze River and a tropical climate led to the cultivation of rice there; the invention of the plow and the domestication of the water buffalo also helped southern farmers prosper. In the north, conditions were harsher and drier, making rice-growing impractical, and the land itself was different. The Yellow River takes its name from a thick blanket of compacted yellow dust called loess that winds and floods had sculpted into an undulating terrain. The resulting soil was easy to till and was extraordinarily rich in minerals that were perfect for growing a once-wild local grain called millet. Farmers increased the amount of tillable land by building terraces into the slopes. With the development of irrigation systems, the Yellow River region became ancient China's breadbasket.

Early on, northern agriculture also produced one of the finest fabrics the world has ever known. Mulberry bushes, perhaps grown for their fruit, also fed a type of caterpillar that secreted a light but strong fiber to make its cocoon. Weavers learned to unravel these strands of silk to spin thread for the lustrous cloth that became one of China's most valuable resources.

> Desert dust blown by northwest winds over eons piled up on the Yellow River plateau as deep as 450 feet.

THE TAKEAWAY: Rice, millet, and silk benefited from different conditions in the south and north.

> *"A wise general makes a point of foraging on the enemy. One cartload of the enemy's provisions is equivalent to twenty of one's own."* —SUN ZI

VOICES

CHINA WRITTEN IN BONE

"In the next ten days, there will be no misfortune. There will be no harm; there will perhaps be the coming of alarming news."

"On day hsin mao, *it is divined on this day* hsin *that it will rain or not rain."*

—TRANSLATIONS OF INSCRIPTIONS ON TWO SHANG DYNASTY ORACLE BONES

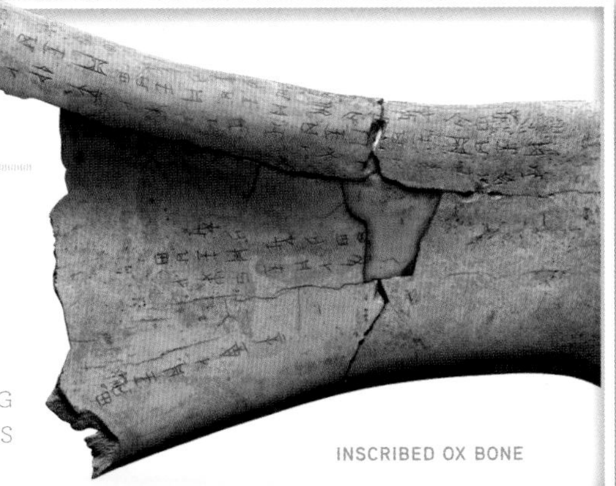

INSCRIBED OX BONE

ARTS

WORDS IN PICTURES

The origins of Chinese writing are lost in the mists of prehistory. The markings may have begun as pictorial symbols representing different clans—in effect, name tags. But true writing, scholars concur, requires an association between symbols and sounds of a spoken language. However Chinese writing emerged, the earliest evidence of it dates to the Shang dynasty. Archaeologists have discovered fragments of bone and tortoiseshell inscribed with pictographic characters and dating to about 1700 B.C.E. Apparently, Shang rulers employed scribes who carved the pictographs into bone or shell to represent questions the ruler wished to ask; the object was then heated until it cracked, and diviners interpreted the cracks as the ancestors' responses. Numerous examples of writing on these oracle bones and on bronze vessels—and later on bamboo and silk scrolls—have led scholars to identify upward of 3,000 characters already in use.

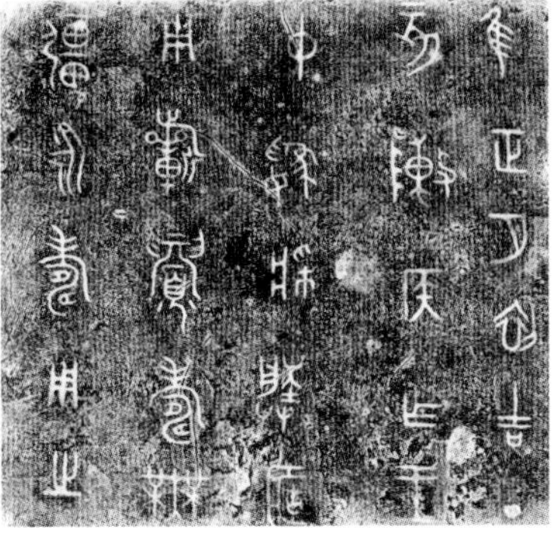

Captured in a rubbing is a Zhou dynasty inscription (above). Pictographs decorate this Zhou bronze food vessel (left).

THE TAKEAWAY: Symbols representing clan names evolved into pictographic writing.

{ The I Ching, one of the first works of Chinese literature, includes thousands of characters combined into symbols called logograms. }

"When armies are mobilized and issues joined, / The man who is sorry over the fact will win." —LAO ZI

SEE ALSO | GOLDEN AGES: PAGE 78

CLASS & SOCIETY INSIDE/OUTSIDE

As in so many other cultures, Chinese society consisted of a privileged elite and masses of commoners who were subdivided into skilled artisans and poorer peasants and laborers. For the vast hordes of farm workers and slaves, life was brutal. They alternated between spending the winter months in simple mud huts and moving in summer to temporary camps where they could manage livestock or tend the fields. They were subject to physical punishment, including mutilation, by their overseers. Even after major urban centers developed, these peasants were typically relegated to villages outside the city walls.

Things were markedly different for the nobility. The king and the aristocracy that supported him spent their time hunting and directing commoners to fight for them in wars. They lived in palace complexes, and increasingly skilled craftsmen made life more pleasant with utilitarian objects of bronze and fired clay, as well as splendid jewelry wrought from jade.

Kinship was vital to the elite. All members of the nobility belonged to clans; during the Zhou dynasty, there were about 100 clans.

The end of the Shang era was said to be a time of drunken excess among the nobility.

THE TAKEAWAY: Commoners supported the elite with backbreaking labor.

CONNECTIONS MEASURED BY THE STARS

CHINESE ASTRONOMY DEVELOPED EVEN BEFORE THE ERA of the first great dynasties. Records note the sighting of a comet as early as 2296 B.C.E., an achievement that depended on an intimate knowledge of the skies. The first astronomers were also adept at predicting solar and lunar eclipses, events that were thought to foretell key events in the life of the emperor; happenings in the heavens also served as mileposts in the reign of kings. Such observations had practical applications, and from them the ancient Chinese were able to develop a precise calendar that proved useful in determining planting times.

COMET HALE-BOPP

> *"The spirits of the hills and rivers alike were all in tranquility; and the birds and beasts, the fishes and tortoises, all enjoyed their existence according to their nature."* —THE SHU JING

VOICES

HARVESTING RICE

LAO ZI THE PEOPLE SUFFER

"The people suffer from famine because of the multitude of taxes consumed by their superiors. It is through this that they suffer famine.

"The people are difficult to govern because of the (excessive) agency of their superiors (in governing them). It is through this that they are difficult to govern.

"The people make light of dying because of the greatness of their labours in seeking for the means of living."

—FROM THE *DAODEJING*, ATTRIBUTED TO LAO ZI

RELIGION YIN AND YANG

THE TAKEAWAY: Chinese religion was a mixture of nature and ancestor worship and philosophy.

Before the advent of civilization, it's likely that the Chinese worshipped deities representing all the aspects of the natural world; when rulers rose to power, one of their responsibilities was propitiating the gods of the mountains and rivers. The primacy of kinship relations added ancestor worship to the mix. Funeral rituals were important. Like the Egyptians, wealthy Chinese were buried in tombs containing vessels and weapons for use in the afterlife. Families made offerings to their dead ancestors to propitiate their spirits.

A more formal religion developed after the writing of the *Book of Changes* (I Ching) in about 800 B.C.E. The book was essentially a manual of divination, but it also reflected a philosophical concern about events that can be controlled and those that cannot.

Sometime in the sixth century B.C.E., according to some histories, two important philosophers were born. Legends tell that Lao Zi was the first to promulgate a philosophy known as Daoism (or Taoism), based on the concept of the Dao, or the Way, an approach to life that navigated between the opposing forces of yin and yang. Shortly afterward Kong Fuzi, known more familiarly as Confucius, was born: His writings would become a keystone of later Chinese culture.

> Yin, according to ancient Chinese lore, is the cosmic female principle, and yang is the cosmic male principle.

Kong Fuzi (Confucius)

"With coarse rice to eat, with water to drink, and my bended arm for a pillow—I have still joy in the midst of these things." —CONFUCIUS

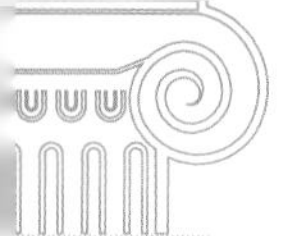

SEE ALSO | THE CLASSICAL AGE: PAGE 121

KEY DATES

2000 B.C.E.
People living between the Pacific Ocean and the Andes Mountains begin laying the foundation for civilization.

2000–1800 B.C.E.
The center of El Paraiso is built in the Peruvian highlands.

1300 B.C.E.
Moses leads the Israelites out of Egypt into the promised land of Canaan.

1200 B.C.E.
An outbreak of plague may be the cause of destruction among the Philistines.

NOMADS AND NEW WORLDS

50,000–500 B.C.E.

Humans have been rovers from the very beginning of the species, but at the same time they have also demonstrated an urge to settle and put down roots. Perhaps the best example of these strains coming together involves the ancient Israelites. Scholars believe that the biblical account of the patriarch Abraham, while perhaps not verifiable as historical fact, has the ring of truth. Abraham and his nomadic clan of herders had been roaming the pastures of southern Mesopotamia in the 22nd century B.C.E., but under a divine dictate they moved into the lands bordering the Mediterranean, known as Palestine, or Canaan. The journey continued when a famine forced Abraham's descendants to migrate to Egypt, where they were enslaved. The Israelites' next wandering began about 1300 B.C.E., when Moses led them out of Egypt and back into the promised land of Canaan.

Although many humans settled in cities and empires, others continued to follow an apparently ingrained urge to wander. Great cultures developed among these peoples nonetheless, from the Israelites to the Celts.

The Israelite's greatest ruler, David, established Jerusalem as the capital, and his equally renowned son, Solomon, began massive building projects, including the first temple. After his death in 925 B.C.E., his sons split the realm in two, with Israel in the north and Judea in the south. In the centuries that followed, Assyrians overran Israel and eventually, under the Babylonian king Nebuchadrezzar, Judea and Jerusalem also fell.

Still other cultures in Europe continued to follow nomadic ways well after the first civilizations emerged. Europe was peopled by such groups, one of which, the Celts, rose to prominence in about 1000 B.C.E. Their earliest settlement was at Hallstatt, in Austria, where the people mined rich deposits of salt and became the first Europeans to master the skill of ironworking. But rather than building a great stable kingdom, they continued to move, spreading their culture into Germany, France, northern Spain, and the British Isles by 500 B.C.E.

Human migration didn't stop at the ocean borders of the Eurasian landmass, and that inherent wanderlust took the species into the regions known much later as the New World.

OPPOSITE: King Solomon of Israel built an extensive empire using a powerful army.

1100 B.C.E.
Indo-European tribes stream into Italy from the north.

1000 B.C.E.
Israel becomes a kingdom.

750 B.C.E.
Celts in Hallstatt, Austria, learn ironworking, which helps them in trade and war.

ca 500 B.C.E.
The great Olmec civilization in Mesoamerica falls into decline.

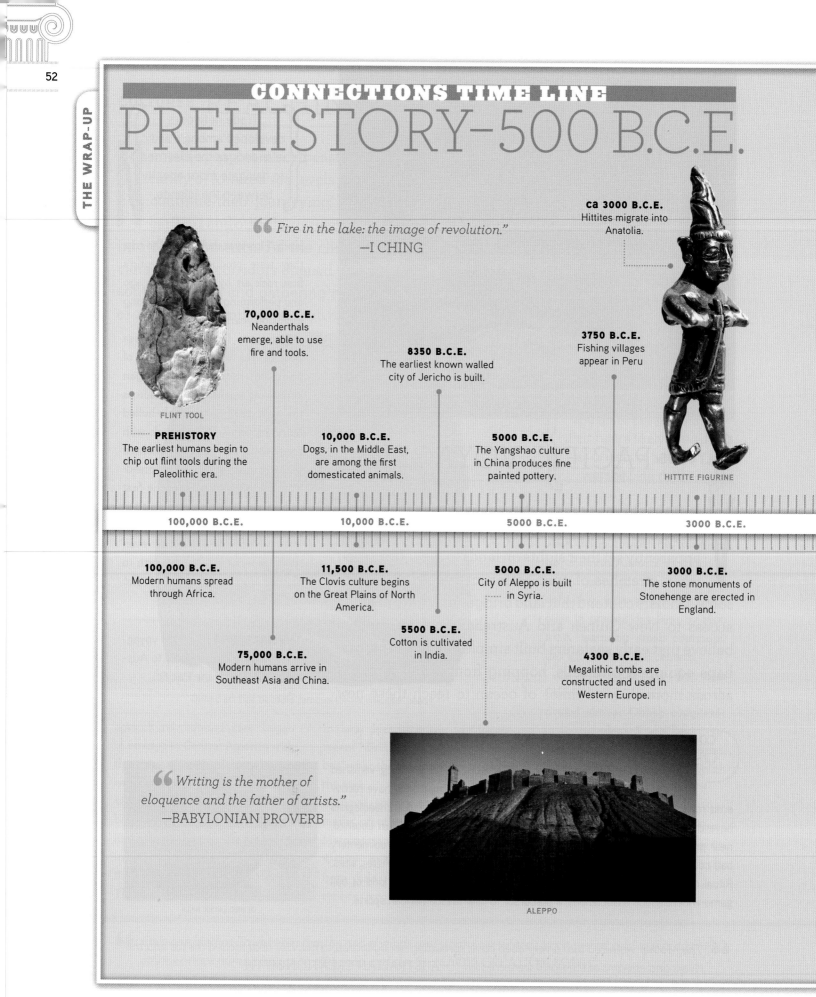

CONNECTIONS TIME LINE

PREHISTORY–500 B.C.E.

"Fire in the lake: the image of revolution."
—I CHING

FLINT TOOL

PREHISTORY
The earliest humans begin to chip out flint tools during the Paleolithic era.

100,000 B.C.E.
Modern humans spread through Africa.

75,000 B.C.E.
Modern humans arrive in Southeast Asia and China.

70,000 B.C.E.
Neanderthals emerge, able to use fire and tools.

11,500 B.C.E.
The Clovis culture begins on the Great Plains of North America.

10,000 B.C.E.
Dogs, in the Middle East, are among the first domesticated animals.

8350 B.C.E.
The earliest known walled city of Jericho is built.

5500 B.C.E.
Cotton is cultivated in India.

5000 B.C.E.
The Yangshao culture in China produces fine painted pottery.

5000 B.C.E.
City of Aleppo is built in Syria.

4300 B.C.E.
Megalithic tombs are constructed and used in Western Europe.

3750 B.C.E.
Fishing villages appear in Peru

ca 3000 B.C.E.
Hittites migrate into Anatolia.

3000 B.C.E.
The stone monuments of Stonehenge are erected in England.

HITTITE FIGURINE

100,000 B.C.E. | 10,000 B.C.E. | 5000 B.C.E. | 3000 B.C.E.

"Writing is the mother of eloquence and the father of artists."
—BABYLONIAN PROVERB

ALEPPO

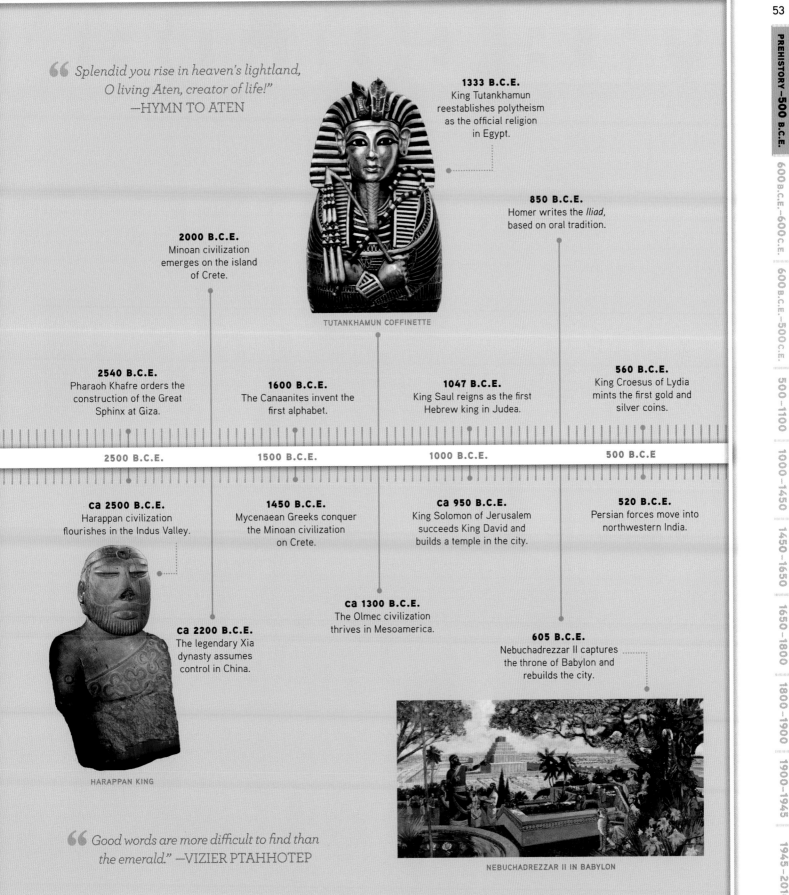

"Splendid you rise in heaven's lightland, O living Aten, creator of life!" —HYMN TO ATEN

TUTANKHAMUN COFFINETTE

1333 B.C.E. King Tutankhamun reestablishes polytheism as the official religion in Egypt.

850 B.C.E. Homer writes the *Iliad,* based on oral tradition.

2000 B.C.E. Minoan civilization emerges on the island of Crete.

2540 B.C.E. Pharaoh Khafre orders the construction of the Great Sphinx at Giza.

1600 B.C.E. The Canaanites invent the first alphabet.

1047 B.C.E. King Saul reigns as the first Hebrew king in Judea.

560 B.C.E. King Croesus of Lydia mints the first gold and silver coins.

2500 B.C.E. | 1500 B.C.E. | 1000 B.C.E. | 500 B.C.E

ca 2500 B.C.E. Harappan civilization flourishes in the Indus Valley.

1450 B.C.E. Mycenaean Greeks conquer the Minoan civilization on Crete.

ca 950 B.C.E. King Solomon of Jerusalem succeeds King David and builds a temple in the city.

520 B.C.E. Persian forces move into northwestern India.

ca 2200 B.C.E. The legendary Xia dynasty assumes control in China.

ca 1300 B.C.E. The Olmec civilization thrives in Mesoamerica.

605 B.C.E. Nebuchadrezzar II captures the throne of Babylon and rebuilds the city.

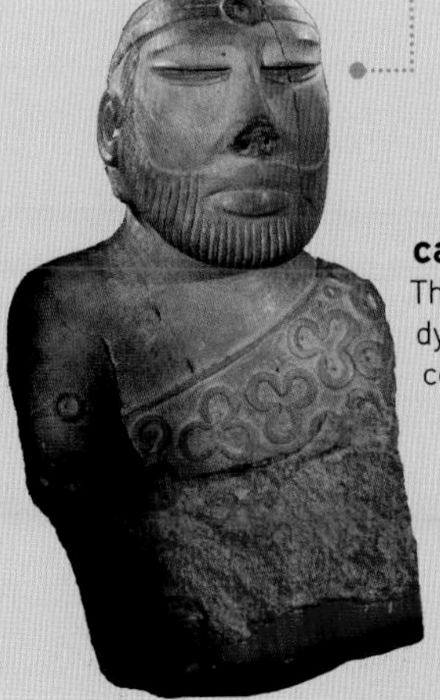

HARAPPAN KING

NEBUCHADREZZAR II IN BABYLON

"Good words are more difficult to find than the emerald." —VIZIER PTAHHOTEP

THE GOLDEN

AGES

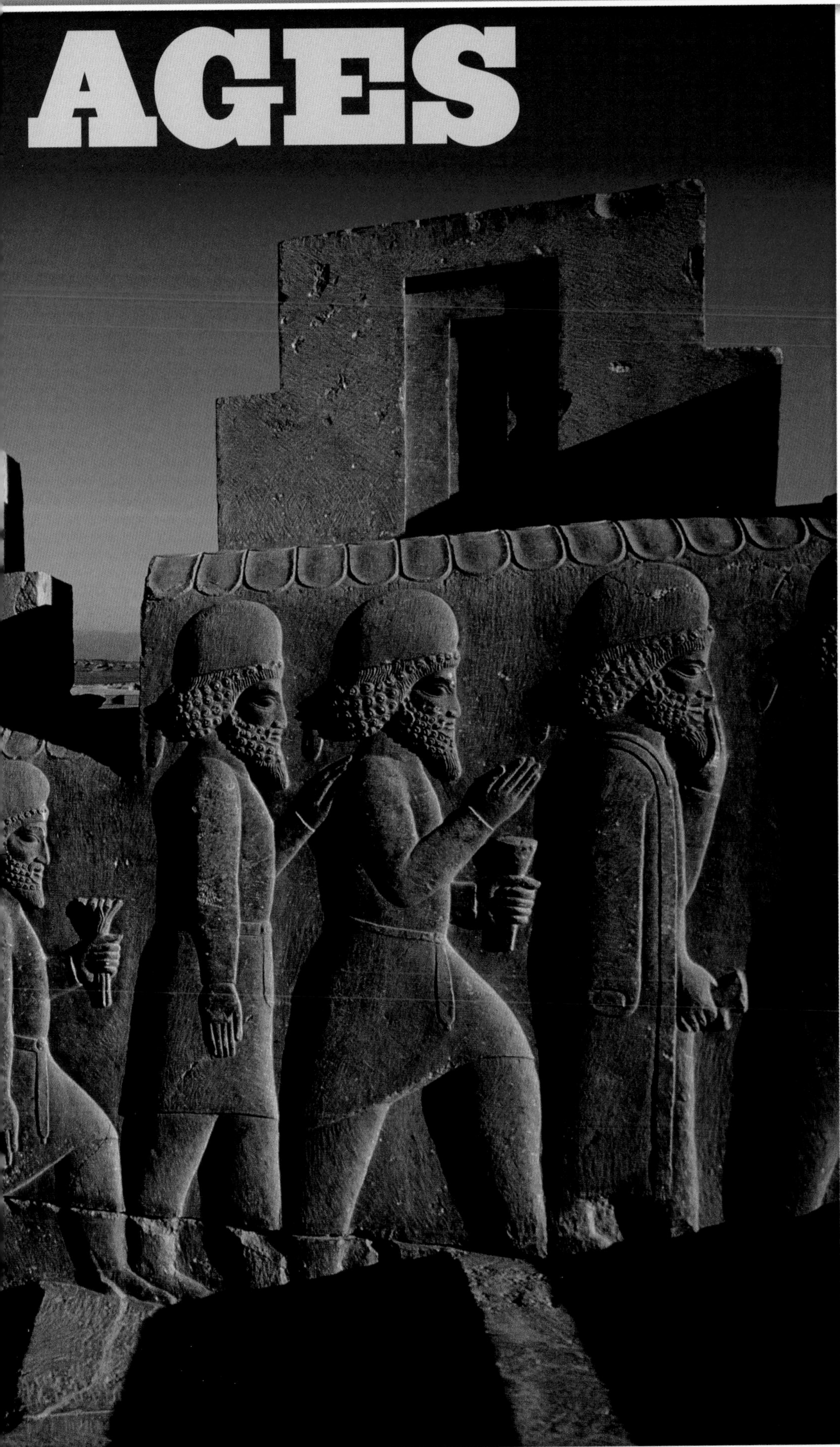

LEGENDS FROM THE EAST

600 B.C.E.–600 C.E.

CHAPTER

2

Carved along the steps of Persepolis, a parade of envoys pays tribute to Persia's king.

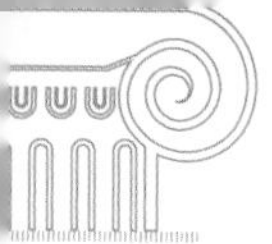

SEE ALSO | THE CLASSICAL AGE: PAGE 102

KEY DATES

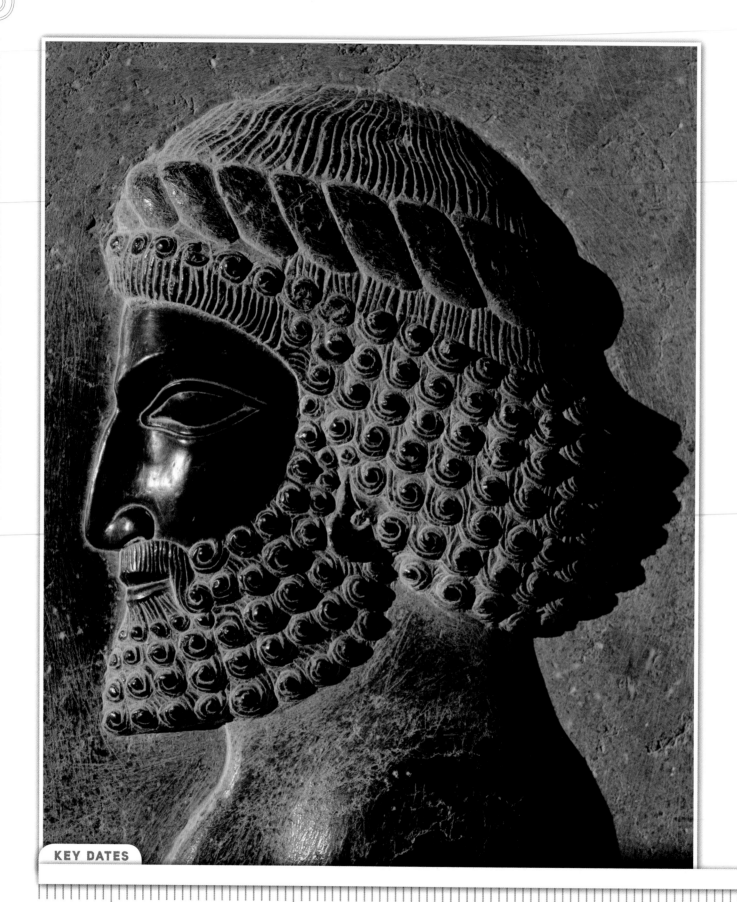

558–529 B.C.E.
Cyrus the Great, first ruler of the Achaemenid dynasty, reigns over Persia.

522–486 B.C.E.
Darius I rules Persia and extends the boundaries of the Persian Empire.

492–449 B.C.E.
Greek city-states and Persia fight a series of wars, eventually won by the Greeks.

330 B.C.E.
Alexander the Great defeats Persian forces and enters and burns Persepolis.

PERSIA

550 B.C.E.–651 C.E.

Starting around 1000 B.C.E., nomadic peoples moved into today's Iran from Central Asia. Then about 550 B.C.E. the strongest and most organized group, the Persians, overcame and absorbed the Medes and other groups. The Persians' leader during this critical period was a brilliant military strategist known as Cyrus the Great, a member of the Achaemenid family that would occupy the throne for centuries to come. An ambitious but fair-minded ruler, Cyrus gained control of Lydia, Babylonia, and current Iran, stretching his empire from Egypt to India. He died in 529 B.C.E., and seven years later another powerful ruler was able to unite the many kingdoms and tribal groups that had been conquered. Darius I coined money, thus stabilizing the economy, and annexed Egypt and northwestern India. Cyrus and Darius were able to maintain their hold over a vast area in part because of their tolerant policy toward local customs and religions. Cyrus adopted the use of coins from the Lydians and administrative practices from the Babylonians. Nor did the Persians try to convert conquered people to their religion, Zoroastrianism. For instance, after Cyrus captured Babylon in 539 B.C.E., the Jews living in captivity there were allowed to return to Jerusalem.

Emerging in the mid-sixth century B.C.E., the Persian Empire expanded to include a vast region from Egypt to India. The Persian Sassanids dominated Iran until being overrun by Islam.

To help control its sprawling territory, the Achaemenid dynasty placed governors known as satraps in charge of the realm's 20 provinces, which were linked by a system of roads, including the 1,600-mile Royal Road from the Aegean coast of western Anatolia (in Turkey) to what is now western Iran. These roads enabled the army to speed to problem areas and eased merchant travel.

The Persian Empire flourished for more than 200 years. Excavations of one of its four capitals, Persepolis, reveal a city of wealth, splendid architecture, and extravagant works of gold and silver.

Darius made inroads into Europe, but he couldn't conquer Greece. The Achaemenid dynasty finally gave way to Alexander the Great of Macedonia in 330 B.C.E. Upon Alexander's death in 323 B.C.E., his generals divided his realm into three portions, which became the Seleucid, Parthian, and Sassanid Empires. Conflicts with Rome doomed the first two, but the Sassanids held on to the region between the Caspian Sea and the Persian Gulf until toppled by Islam in 651 C.E.

OPPOSITE: A detail of a bas-relief, found in Persepolis, portrays the head of a Persian soldier.

312–84 B.C.E.
The Seleucid dynasty takes over Persia.

247 B.C.E.
The Parthians break away from the Seleucids.

224 C.E.
The Sassanids overthrow the Parthians and establish a long-lived empire.

483 C.E.
Nestorian Christians, persecuted by Orthodox emperor Zeno, take refuge in Persia.

SEE ALSO | GOLDEN AGES: PAGE 60

CLASS & SOCIETY PERSIAN PYRAMID

The class structure in early Persia drew from earlier Indo-Iranian societies that had three basic groups—aristocrats and warriors, priests, and farmers and herdsman. Patrilineal clans formed tribes, which were ruled by kings elected by the warriors; particular regions were controlled by men known as kings of kings. Even under the later Achaemenids, a similar pyramidal structure prevailed. A highly evolved legal system intertwined both local and imperial laws; Darius was particularly known for instituting legal reforms.

Kings enjoyed a luxurious lifestyle in stone palaces, while a middle class of merchants, priests, translators, and craftsmen occupied a variety of dwellings, from stone houses to mud huts. At the bottom were the peasants and, just beneath, a class of slaves.

Persian men could have several wives at a time. Long robes, jewelry, and false hair were typical male attire. A formerly nomadic people, the Persians continued to pass down the traditions of horseback riding, bow shooting, and truth telling—lying and incurring debts were considered particularly dishonorable practices.

> Darius ordered that the Old Persian language be given a written form so that his life could be recorded for posterity.

THE TAKEAWAY: Persian society was built upon a pyramidal structure topped by the king, who allowed for regional variations in culture.

VIPs

PERSIA

Zoroaster, ca 628–ca 551 B.C.E. Prophet who inspired the official religion of Persia

Cyrus II (the Great), ca 585–529 B.C.E. Leader who extended the empire from Egypt to India

Darius I, 550–486 B.C.E. King of Persia, brilliant administrator and builder

Xerxes, 519–465 B.C.E. Persian king who invaded Greece

Seleucus, 358–281 B.C.E. Macedonian officer who became the first ruler of the Seleucid dynasty

The legendary feast of Ahasuerus—another name for Xerxes—allowed the Persian king to display his wealth.

> *"Then Cyrus, taking of the several meats, is said to have distributed them to the servants about his grandfather, saying to each, 'I give this to you, because you take pleasure in teaching me to ride.'"* —XENOPHON

VOICES

HERODOTUS EARLY ADOPTERS

"There is no nation which so readily adopts foreign customs as the Persians. Thus, they have taken the dress of the Medes, considering it superior to their own; and in war they wear the Egyptian breastplate. As soon as they hear of any luxury, they instantly make it their own: and hence, among other novelties, they have learnt unnatural lust from the Greeks. Each of them has several wives, and a still larger number of concubines. Next to prowess in arms, it is regarded as the greatest proof of manly excellence to be the father of many sons. Every year the king sends rich gifts to the man who can show the largest number."

—FROM *ON THE CUSTOMS OF THE PERSIANS,* HERODOTUS, ca 430 B.C.E.

HERODOTUS

LEADERS DARIUS I

Son-in-law of Cyrus the Great, Darius I came to power at age 28 and quickly proved himself a great military leader and an even greater administrator. Organizing his empire into 20 provinces, he fixed the annual tribute due from each; he also standardized coinage, weights, and measures. Under his rule, Zoroastrianism became the state religion, providing a cohesive Persian sense of identity to his far-flung empire.

Darius built a grand capital of lavish proportions at Persepolis; created a system of underground canals to increase agriculture; and began construction of the Royal Road, outfitting it with 111 courier stations at equal intervals. Through his use of imperial spies—the "eyes and ears of the king"—he kept sedition to a minimum. These measures along with a liberal policy regarding the cultures of conquered areas helped Darius stimulate trade and productivity. Accordingly, the standard of living in Persia rose, and Persian dominance in the Near East became entrenched. For more than a thousand years, Persia would continue as a political entity, and its traditions endure even today.

THE TAKEAWAY: The foresighted civic and economic policies of Darius I set Persia on a firm path to national unity.

THUMBS UP / THUMBS DOWN

CYRUS THE GREAT 585–529 B.C.E.

CYRUS THE GREAT

FOUNDER AND FIRST GREAT RULER of the Achaemenid dynasty, Cyrus II (the Great) conquered the mighty Lydian kingdom in Anatolia in 546 B.C.E., turning an inherited kingdom into an empire. Seven years later he took Babylon, the greatest city in the ancient world, along with large swaths of Syria and Palestine. A benevolent ruler, Cyrus permitted conquered lands to retain their own religions and cultures, famously freeing the captive Jews. He managed to placate the formerly powerful Medes by involving them in government, and from the proud Elamites he borrowed habits of dress and ornamentation. Cyrus's rule set the tone for more than two centuries of Achaemenid rule and expansion, and his life and exploits became the stuff of legend. **CONCLUSION:** **THUMBS UP**

"The Persians say that Darius was a huckster, Cambyses a master, and Cyrus a father." —HERODOTUS

SEE ALSO | THE CLASSICAL AGE: PAGE 126

Winged figures from Susa, Iran, may represent the god Ahura Mazda.

RELIGION PERSIA

Around the sixth century B.C.E., a new faith arose in Persia, becoming the official religion of the state. Called Zoroastrianism, after its founder Zoroaster (Zarathustra), it viewed the universe as an unending moral battle between good and evil (or chaos). In this universe, humans could contribute to the ultimate triumph of good. Fire played an essential role in the Zoroastrian religion, symbolizing the one deity, known as Ahura Mazda. Rituals were practiced at numerous fire temples, some of which still exist. By the late Sassanid period, rigid rules defined elaborate purification rites, and anything outside these rules was considered an insult to Ahura Mazda.

The prophet Zoroaster was of Indo-European descent, from the same ancestry as the polytheistic Etruscans to the west and the Hindi to the south. Like the medieval prophet Muhammad, he reputedly shone with a radiating light while still in his mother's womb. Like Siddhartha Gautama (the Buddha), who lived not long afterward, he was born into privilege, but then scorned his upbringing to follow his own transcendent vision. And like Jesus a few centuries later, he wandered in the desert to test his faith. As though ushering in a new

> After the Islamic takeover of Persia, a persecuted minority of Zoroastrians hung on in small enclaves.

CONNECTIONS INDIA'S ZOROASTRIANS

STARTING IN THE TENTH CENTURY, Zoroastrians in Iran began migrating to India, where they were cut off from their fellow practitioners in the homeland for about five centuries. Known as Parsis, these followers of Zoroaster became properous by moving into commerce. By limiting or discarding such rituals as animal sacrifice, they were able to fit in with the local Hindus, and after criticism by Christian missionaries for their dualistic beliefs, they emphasized their religion's essential monotheism. Adopting the dress and habits of the West, they grew into a thriving community centered in Mumbai and now number about 100,000.

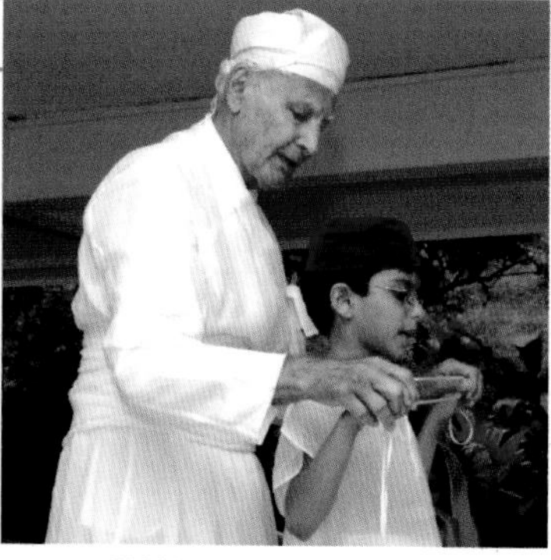
PARSI INITIATION CEREMONY

> *"[The Persians'] wont, however, is to ascend the summits of the loftiest mountains, and there to offer sacrifice to Zeus, which is the name they give to the whole circuit of the firmament."* —HERODOTUS

VOICES

YASNA THE BIRTH OF GOOD AND EVIL

"In the beginning there were two primal spirits,
Twins spontaneously active,
These are the Good and the Evil, in thought, and in word, and in deed.
Between these two, let the wise choose aright.
Be good, not base!

"And when these Twin Spirits came together at first,
They established Life and the Denial of Life."

—FROM THE *YASNA*, ZOROASTRIAN TEXTS, ca THIRD CENTURY C.E.

ZOROASTRIAN PRIEST

religion, the three magi who supposedly visited the newborn Jesus were Zoroastrian priests.

Unlike many prophets, Zoroaster was widely accepted in his own time and considered a great sage. With the rise of Darius I to the Persian throne in 522 B.C.E., Zoroastrianism spread from the Indus River in the east to the Aegean Sea in the west, thus becoming the religion of the largest empire in the world to date. Elements of Zoroaster's moral teachings were to echo through many religions that followed him: the concepts of heaven and hell; judgment day; a holy path; and his credo "good thoughts, good words, good deeds."

Perhaps the key concept of Zoroastrianism was dualism: the fight between good and evil that exists within the human spirit and is mirrored on a cosmic scale by the opposition of the good creator spirit (represented by the purity of fire) and the evil destructive spirit. Life is understood to be an ongoing battle between these forces.

Depiction of Zoroaster with sacred fire

However, the essentially optimistic philosophy of Zoroastrianism teaches that good is stronger and will eventually win out within humanity and in the world at large.

Persian king Artaxerxes II, who reigned from 404–358 B.C.E., began to move Persian religion away from strict Zoroastrianism by restoring some of the old Persian gods. Image worship was not practiced in Persia until Artaxerxes erected statues of Mithra and Anahita, deities from Iranian folk religion. Ancient cults and beliefs crept into Zoroastrianism, so that by the time of the Sassanids, who came into power in the third century C.E., the religion had become a conglomeration of various faiths and rituals.

THE TAKEAWAY: Zoroastrianism took root in Persia from the state's earliest imperial days and continued as the official religion.

"We have accepted this holy religion from Ahura Mazda, and we will not give it up, and we will drink next month the drink of immortality without you." —MEMOIRS OF ZARIR

SEE ALSO | THE CLASSICAL AGE: PAGE 102

ARTS & ARCHITECTURE PALATIAL SPLENDOR

In creating his palace at Susa, in southwestern Iran, Darius erected a work of grandeur unrivaled in the ancient world. The sixth-century B.C.E. palace brought together materials and artisans from far and wide—gold from Sardis in Asia Minor, lapis lazuli from Sogdiana in northeastern Persia, silver and ebony from Egypt, ivory from Nubia. An inscription from the building proudly lists the many nationalities: "The goldsmiths who wrought the gold, those were Medes and Egyptians. The men who wrought the wood, those were Lydians and Egyptians. The men who wrought the baked brick, those were Babylonians. The men who adorned the wall, those were Medes and Egyptians."

The nearby cities of Pasargadae, capital of Cyrus the Great, and Persepolis, founded by Darius, also exhibited many fine works of Persian architecture and embellishment. Metalwork, jewelry, weaponry, and pottery reached highly refined levels during this early era.

Nearly as accomplished, the Sassanid Empire saw an artistic renaissance. Among its achievements are giant rock sculptures, carved in relief, of kings, battles, and the god Ahura Mazda carved into limestone cliffs in the southwestern province of Fars. The palace at Ctesiphon, built by Khosrow I in what is now Iraq, is an outstanding example of period architecture, its brickwork barrel vaulting a Sasanian hallmark. Zoroastrian fire temples in Fars were built as square buildings, a dome surmounting four arches.

Sassanid craftspeople were also famous for their rich, embroidered textiles and colorful carpets, much admired by contemporaries.

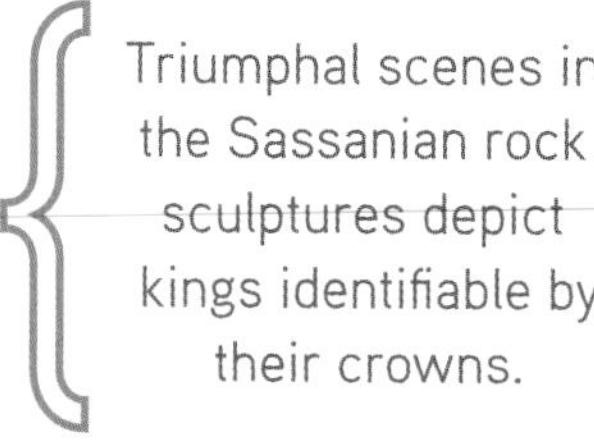

Triumphal scenes in the Sassanian rock sculptures depict kings identifiable by their crowns.

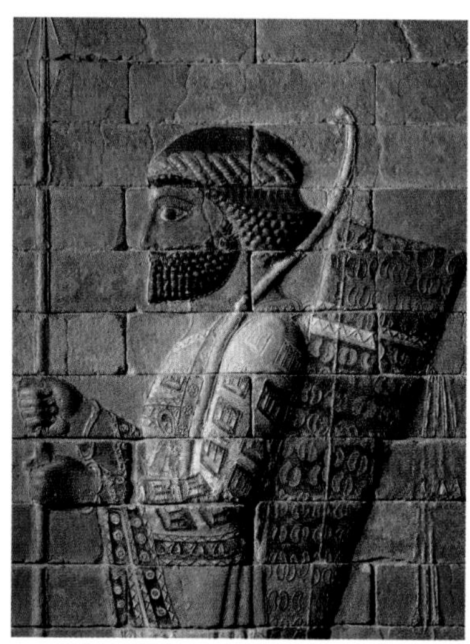

Enameled tiles form an archer in the palace of Darius I at Susa (above); a gold dragon or griffin is an Achaemenid treasure (left).

THE TAKEAWAY: Early Persian palace architecture and decoration were superb artistic achievements.

> *The [king] reclines on a couch supported by feet of gold . . . and throughout the dinner his concubines sing and play the lyre."* —ATHENAEUS

Persian king Xerxes, builder and campaigner, prepares to cross the Hellespont early in his reign.

ARCHITECTURE STATELY HALLS

No city of ancient Persia was more splendid than Persepolis, begun by Darius I in the early sixth century B.C.E. as a palace and capital complex. Built in a remote mountainous area of southwestern Iran, the city escaped Greek notice until Alexander the Great discovered and plundered it in 330 B.C.E. The remaining ruins bespeak the handiwork of a great civilization. Walls surround three sides, while inside are grand staircases, columned halls, harem quarters, fortifications, an *apadana* (audience hall), a treasury, and other massive buildings of cut stone. At the edge of the city are the tombs of Artaxerxes II and III, father and son who ruled a combined 66 years.

THE TAKEAWAY: Home to Darius and succeeding kings, Persepolis was one of the greatest palace-cities of the ancient world.

VOICES

XERXES GATE OF ALL NATIONS

"I am Xerxes, the Great King, King of Kings, King of countries containing many kinds (of men), King in this great earth far and wide, son of King Darius, an Achaemenian.

"Proclaims Xerxes the King: By the favor of Ahura Mazda I built this Gateway of All Nations. I built many other beautiful things in Persia. I built them and my father built them."

—INSCRIPTION ABOVE XERXES' GATE, PERSEPOLIS, ca 490 B.C.E.

GATE OF ALL NATIONS

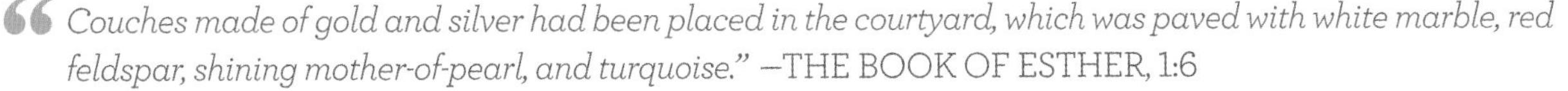

"Couches made of gold and silver had been placed in the courtyard, which was paved with white marble, red feldspar, shining mother-of-pearl, and turquoise." —THE BOOK OF ESTHER, 1:6

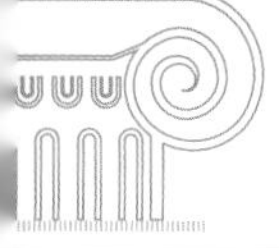

SEE ALSO | THE CLASSICAL AGE: PAGE 94

CONFLICTS EXPANSION & PROTECTION

The Achaemenid dynasty, and thus the history of the Persian Empire, began with the swift rise of Cyrus the Great. In 550 B.C.E., at about age 35, he defeated the Medes; he then diplomatically placated the Babylonians while launching a campaign against the kingdom of Lydia in Asia Minor. Lydia appealed in vain to Babylon for help, and in 546 B.C.E. Cyrus took the kingdom along with its fabulously rich king, Croesus. He then went on to capture the Greek city-states along the western coast of Asia Minor.

Now without an ally, Babylon was ripe for picking, and Cyrus turned his attention thither. Fanning the flames of internal dissent, he was able to quickly move in and conquer in 539 B.C.E.; his policy of letting Babylon remain Babylonian smoothed the transition to the Persian umbrella. By now, the Persian army, which could number 100,000, had a core Persian guard of 10,000, the so-called immortals, 1,000 of whom composed the king's guard.

Cyrus's son, Cambyses, conquered Egypt in 525 B.C.E. His successor, Darius I, invaded Greece in 490 B.C.E. in the first of a 43-year-long series of wars, now known as the Persian Wars, with the Greek city-states. Darius's first invasion

A Sassanid plaque (left) shows a triumphal parade.

DIODORUS PERSEPOLIS BURNS

"One of the women present, Thaïs by name and Attic by origin, said that for Alexander it would be the finest of all his feats in Asia if he joined them in a triumphal procession, set fire to the palaces, and permitted women's hands in a minute to extinguish the famed accomplishments of the Persians. . . . She was the first, after the king, to hurl her blazing torch into the palace."

—AN ACCOUNT OF THE BURNING OF PERSEPOLIS, POSSIBLY APOCRYPHAL, FROM *THE LIBRARY OF HISTORY*, DIODORUS, FIRST CENTURY B.C.E.

ALEXANDER AND THAÏS BURN PERSEPOLIS

VOICES

"This is the command of Cyrus, Emperor of Persia: . . . You are to go to Jerusalem and rebuild the Temple of the Lord, the God of Israel." —THE BOOK OF EZRA, 1:2-3

Alexander and his army fight Darius III's troops in the Battle of Issus, 333 B.C.E.

failed when his troops were overcome by Athenian soldiers on the Marathon plain. (According to legend, a messenger ran 26 miles back to Athens to proclaim victory before dropping dead.) Darius's son Xerxes later renewed the conflict. The Persians had a numerical advantage but encountered difficulty supplying and coordinating their diverse forces, which came from many countries. In 480 B.C.E., Xerxes broke through to Athens and burned the city, but then his forces suffered setbacks—his fleet was destroyed at Salamis (480) and his army at Plataea (479).

During a 480 B.C.E. siege of Athens, the Persian army used arrows wrapped with oil-soaked fibers—the first known projectile torches.

Following the death of Xerxes, Persia waned in power, and in 334 B.C.E. Alexander the Great invaded with a small, well-trained army of Macedonian soldiers. Within three years, the Achaemenid empire was finished, its remnants destroyed at the Battle of Gaugamela (in today's northern Iraq). Alexander's general Seleucus occupied Babylon in 312 B.C.E., ushering in the Seleucid dynasty. In 250 B.C.E., the Parthians, a group of nomadic Persians, regained control of Persia. For the next several hundred years, the Parthians and then the Sassanids would battle Rome for Persian territory. Around 299 C.E., a treaty between Persia and Rome brought peace to the borderlands. The Sassanians then established buffer states and moved their armies north to the Caucasus and central Asia.

THE TAKEAWAY: War gave the Achaemenids vast territory; Greek influences arrived with conqueror Alexander the Great.

“ *[The god Marduk] took the hand of Cyrus, king of the city of Anshan, and called him by his name, proclaiming him aloud for the kingship over all of everything.”* —THE CYRUS CYLINDER

SEE ALSO | GOLDEN AGES: PAGE 74

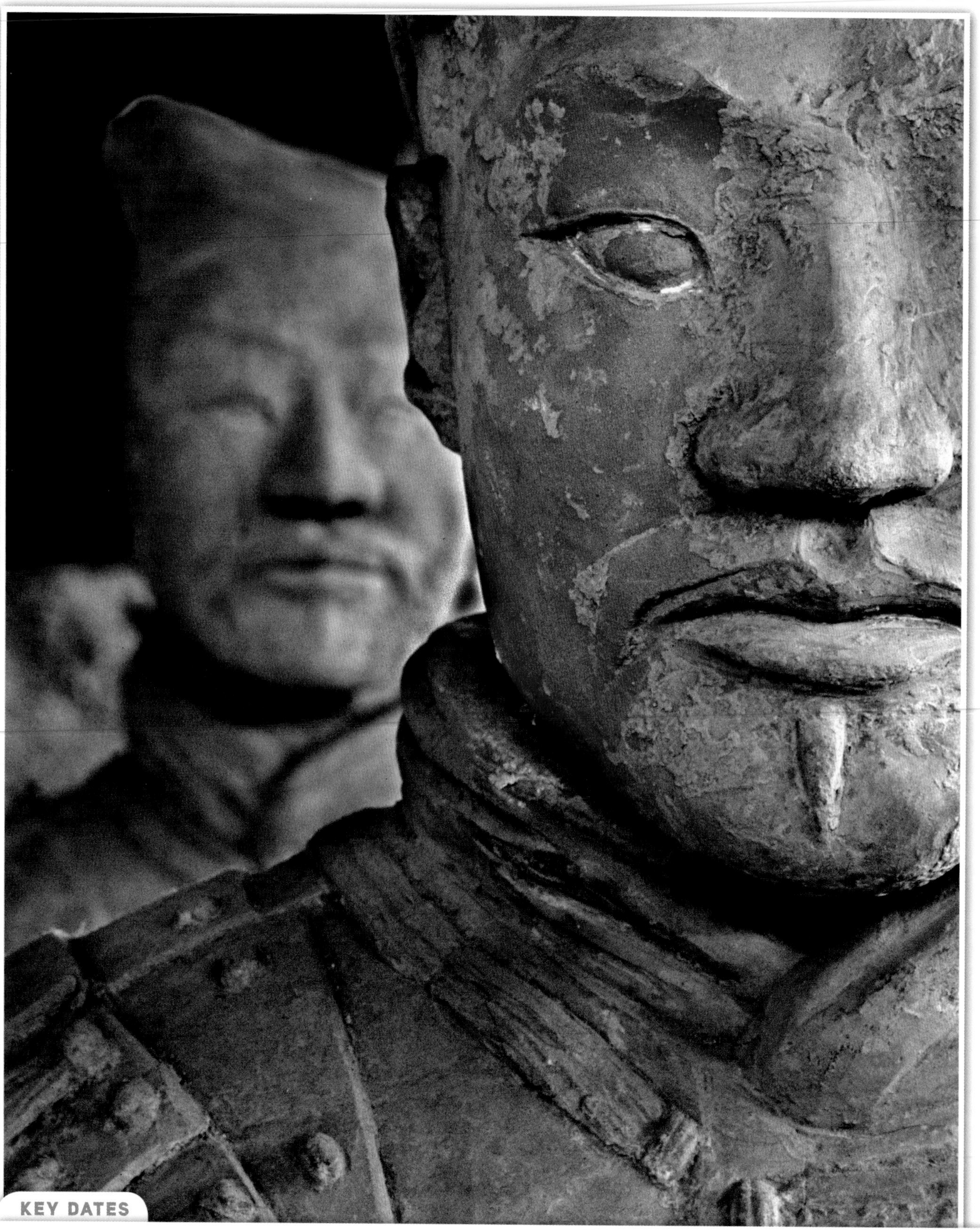

KEY DATES

551–479 B.C.E.
The Chinese philosopher Confucius lives and inspires a long-lasting philosophical system.

403–221 B.C.E.
The Zhou kingdom splits during the Period of the Warring States.

221–210 B.C.E.
The first emperor of the Qin dynasty, Qin Shi Huang Di, reigns.

220–206 B.C.E.
The Great Wall of China is built.

CHINA

403 B.C.E.–220 C.E.

A kind of feudalism predominated in China in the fourth and third centuries B.C.E., a time known as the Warring States Period, during which local rulers waged almost incessant warfare against each other at the expense of peasants whose lives, deaths, and daily toil were dictated from above. In the context of this sociopolitical turmoil, a number of influential thinkers, including Confucius and Lao Zi, espoused personal philosophies that would go on to inform thousands of years of Chinese history. The Period of the Warring States came to an abrupt end in 221 B.C.E., when Qin Shi Huang Di, the expansionist ruler of the Qin state—having overpowered every rival by means of a well-armed, terror-inspiring army—united all of China into one centralized empire. Shi Huang Di organized his empire according to Legalist principles, which valued the welfare of the state above individual concerns, enforced taxes owed directly to the state, and conscripted millions of laborers to toil at immense public works projects. During his short reign, the emperor stunted intellectualism by burning books of philosophy and literature and by executing hundreds of critics and scholars. On the other hand, he codified the law, established national standards for weights, measures, currency, writing, and axle lengths, and built a consolidated system of roads, canals, and defensive walls unparalleled in the world.

The history of classical China, like many imperial histories worldwide, is one populated by powerful and ambitious military leaders, influential ideologues, and exploited lower classes.

Qin's death created a power vacuum that was filled by the Han dynasty in 206 B.C.E. Han dynasty emperors maintained the central bureaucratic administration of Shi Huang Di, but they also encouraged the development of scholarship, art, and technology.

The expansionist emperor Han Wudi, who reigned for 54 years, from 141 to 87 B.C.E., imposed Chinese government and values on the Korean Peninsula, in northern Vietnam, and into central Asia. He founded China's first imperial university in 124 B.C.E., but he also levied onerous taxes that ensured his country's peasantry remained in poverty. Han monopolized the lucrative trade in salt and iron, as well, in order to suppress the merchant class. The poor began to turn to banditry and rebellion, gradually weakening the centralized Han Empire over the course of four centuries until it finally fractured back into rival kingdoms by 220 C.E.

OPPOSITE: Pigment remains on a terra-cotta warrior, found with others near the tomb of Qin Shi Huang Di.

206 B.C.E.–9 C.E.
Western Han dynasty rules from the city of Chang'an.

112 B.C.E.
Qin dynasty sponsors *yue fu* poetry.

25–220 C.E.
Eastern Han dynasty rules

220 C.E.
China is divided into three regional kingdoms.

SEE ALSO | GOLDEN AGES: PAGE 76

CLASS & SOCIETY IRON AND SILK

Scholars show classical texts to the last Han emperor, Xiandi.

As peasants in classical China produced more food with the aid of iron tools and yoked oxen, the wealthy created greater demands for luxury goods in this life and the next. Peasants made do with hemp clothing and sandals, while the rich were frocked in silk and leather and buried in jade suits sewn with gold thread. Between a third and a half of a peasant's harvest was sequestered by the state, while high taxes forced many small landowners to sell their property and sometimes themselves to satisfy their debts. Dependent on the support of the wealthy, the Han rulers did little to aid the poor until the throne was usurped in 9 C.E. by social reformer Wang Mang. His attempts to redistribute wealth failed, setting off widespread revolts throughout the empire. The Han regained power, but were beset by repeated rebellions, such as the Yellow Turban uprising of 184 C.E., led by a Daoist faith healer against the eunuchs who controlled much of the government. The uprising was put down after much bloodshed.

THE TAKEAWAY: The discrepancy between rich and poor in classical China was a source of centuries of conflict.

Han dynasty bronze model of horse carriage and driver

CHINA — VIPs

Confucius, 551–479 B.C.E. Chinese thinker who inspired an influential system of philosophy

Mencius, 372–289 B.C.E. Chinese philosopher regarded as the second most important figure in Confucianism

Qin Shi Huang Di, 259–210 B.C.E. The first emperor of unified China, builder of the original Great Wall

Han Wudi, 156–87 B.C.E. Han dynasty emperor who vastly expanded China's territory

Wang Mang, 45 B.C.E.–23 C.E. Reformer who lead rebellion during the Han dynasty.

> *"The rich, being haughty, acted evilly; the poor, being poverty stricken, acted wickedly."* —WANG MANG

VOICES

BAN ZHAO A WOMAN'S ROLE

"Let a woman modestly yield to others; let her respect others; let her put others first, herself last. Should she do something good, let her not mention it; should she do something bad let her not deny it. Let her bear disgrace; let her even endure when others speak or do evil to her. Always let her seem to tremble and to fear. When a woman follows such maxims as these then she may be said to humble herself before others.

"Let a woman retire late to bed, but rise early to duties; let her not dread tasks by day or by night. Let her not refuse to perform domestic duties whether easy or difficult. That which must be done, let her finish completely, tidily, and systematically, When a woman follows such rules as these, then she may be said to be industrious."

—FROM *RULES FOR A WOMAN*, BAN ZHAO, ca 80 C.E.

BAN ZHAO

DAILY LIFE AN ORDERED SOCIETY

The vast majority of the people in classical China were farmers who raised crops such as rice, wheat, millet, and soybeans. With their livelihood dependent on their productivity, Chinese peasants needed a supply of reliable iron tools, which were provided by local craftsmen. These same craftsmen experimented with the production of utilitarian household goods, such as pots, stoves, and knives, made of iron instead of bronze. Chinese metallurgists also produced iron armor and weapons for use by the military, into which any healthy man of the lower classes could be conscripted for two years of service. A man of little wealth could also—in theory, though not always in practice—enter the imperial university to become a low-ranking clerk in the civil service.

Silk was a commodity coveted throughout much of Eurasia and sericulture, the cultivation of silk, was of great importance to classical China. The Chinese state fervently guarded the processes by which silk textiles were made.

A fragment of a wall painting from Xinjiang province shows men swimming.

> Eunuchs, often born poor, became a powerful force in the Chinese court during the Han era.

At home, the Confucian ideals of filial piety and womanly devotion were the rule of the day. To the Confucianist, the well-ordered patriarchal family unit, characterized by respect for the proper roles of family members, was the very foundation of a well-ordered society.

THE TAKEAWAY: Social mobility was rare but possible in classical China, while Confucian roles ruled the family.

"When people submit to virtue, they are happy from the bottom of their hearts, and they submit sincerely, the way the seventy disciples submitted to Confucius." —MENCIUS

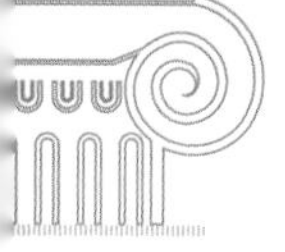

SEE ALSO | GOLDEN AGES: PAGE 78

PHILOSOPHY THREE ROUTES TO HARMONY

Confucius contemplates the course of a river (20th-century engraving).

One of the first Chinese thinkers to reflect on the proper ordering of people and society was Kong Fuzi, better known as Confucius, who lived from 551 to 479 B.C.E. Confucius did not concern himself with abstractions, religiosity, nor even the structural framework of the state; rather, he believed that social harmony would naturally follow from the proper ordering of individuals in relation to one another, with the family unit as the basic building block of society. He therefore stressed the cultivation of personal qualities such as benevolence, reciprocity, and filial piety as essential to the formation of well-educated, conscientious individuals who would benefit society through public service. Though largely ignored in his own day, Confucius's teachings were set down by his adherents in *The Analects*, a book that would go on to inform over 2,000 years of Chinese history.

More immediately applicable to resolving the chaos of the early warring states was a school of thought known as Legalism, which stressed the welfare of the state at the expense of the individual. The Legalists saw obedience to authority as the only route to social harmony—an enforced harmony seen for a short while under the ruthless

LAO ZI WALKING SMOOTHLY IN DAO

VOICES

"He who is enlightened by Dao seems wrapped in darkness. He who is advanced in Dao seems to be going back. He who walks smoothly in Dao seems to be on a rugged path.

The man of highest virtue appears lowly. He who is truly pure behaves as though he were sullied. He who has virtue in abundance behaves as though it were not enough. He who is firm in virtue seems like a skulking pretender. He who is simple and true appears unstable as water."

—FROM THE SAYINGS OF LAO ZI

STONE SCULPTURE OF LAO ZI

"He who exercises government by means of his virtue may be compared to the north polar star, which keeps its place, while all the stars turn toward it." —CONFUCIUS

> An ideal Daoist society was one composed of small, self-governed, self-sufficient communities, so content that they did not seek to conquer, trade with, or even visit their neighbors.

reign of China's first emperor, Qin Shi Huang Di.

Daoism was a third school of thought prevalent in classical China—a philosophy that encouraged disengagement from society and from self-righteous actions that engender conflict. As set down by the semi-historical sage Lao Zi in his *Daodejing,* Daoism was concerned with understanding the principles that promote harmony in nature as a model for promoting harmony among people. During centuries of conflict in China, Daoism offered the means to a tranquil, introspective way of life.

A bronze mirror depicts Confucius meeting a hermit.

THE TAKEAWAY: The Period of the Warring States was a time of upheaval, but it was also an era of intellectual reflection on society.

Early Daoists worshipped constellations, personified here on silk.

> *There is nothing in the world more soft and weak than water, yet for attacking things that are hard and strong, there is nothing that surpasses it, nothing that can take its place.*" –LAO ZI

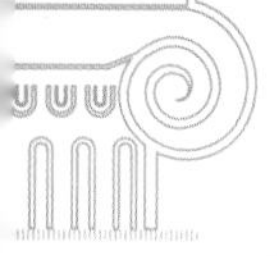

SEE ALSO | GOLDEN AGES: PAGE 75

The Han dynasty's Wudi emperor departs from his palace.

ARTS HAN RENAISSANCE

The art of the Warring States eras had one purpose: to support the ostentatious displays of wealth among competing feudal lords. Bronze pieces inlaid with gold and silver were popular among the wealthy, as were polished bronze mirrors that were thought to provide protection from evil spirits. Works of carved jade achieved a high level of technical perfection, even lauded by the sage Confucius himself.

Art and culture was all but snuffed out during the 11 years of the Qin regime, with the exception of those works commissioned by Emperor Qin Shi Huang Di. Chief among these commissioned works was the emperor's immense palace, which was said to contain a hall of state 1,500 feet square that could accommodate up to 10,000 guests. Qin also commissioned a mausoleum that may have rivaled his palace in lavishness and grandiosity.

The Han era was more favorable to the arts. Chinese mastery of bronze work continued in the form of ornate vessels and sculptural representations of humans, animals, and mythical creatures. The horse, revered for its power and beauty, was particularly prominent in Han art, akin to representations of the lion or bull in the West. Jade body suits, sewn together with gold thread, were increasingly common in wealthy burials. According to ancient belief, one aspect of the human soul remained in the body after death, while the other fled to the afterlife. Hence it was important that the earthbound soul be made comfortable and feel no inclination

A ceramic model of a guard tower, Han dynasty

"If the ruler is greedy, insatiable, attracted to profit, and fond of gain, then ruin is possible." —HAN FEI TZU

VOICES

FU XUAN WHEN A GIRL IS BORN

"No one is glad when a girl is born:
By her the family sets no store.
Then she grows up, she hides in her room
Afraid to look a man in the face.
No one cries when she leaves her home—
Sudden as clouds when the rain stops.
She bows her head and composes her face,
Her teeth are pressed on her red lips."

—FROM "WOMAN," BY FU XUAN, THIRD CENTURY C.E.

SEATED WOMAN, EARTHENWARE

to return from the grave. Jade body suits were thought to be so powerful that the body would be protected from decay and its spirit remain comfortable for eternity.

Many other examples of Han art have been unearthed from the tombs of the wealthy, including miniature terra-cotta servants and soldiers, as well as tiny ceramic homes, granaries, and even pigsties. Some examples of painting survive from royal tombs, as well as stone reliefs of stylized figures and mythological scenes. Upper-crust homes held silk weavings dyed in geometric patterns and lacquered pottery more expensive than bronze.

> After the fall of the Qin, the ensuing Han dynasty ushered in a new era of Chinese art by actively encouraging cultural accomplishments from its civil servants.

Music was well documented by civil servants in the Music Bureau, who compiled detailed descriptions of instruments, songs, and playing styles. These record keepers even created a kind of dance notation to record the movements of large, synchronized groups of performers who participated in temple rituals. Other performers of the time practiced a form of theater that dramatized the fabled exploits of celebrated warrior-heroes. Poetry also flourished during the Han period in the form of a new genre known as *yue fu,* a kind of creative writing that employed prosaic rhyming within long expository compositions.

THE TAKEAWAY: The artistic flowering of the Han became a model for Chinese culture.

CONNECTIONS MANY LANGUAGES, ONE SCRIPT

ONE OF EMPEROR QIN SHI HUANG DI'S most important contributions to Chinese culture was his simplification and standardization of the written Chinese language. Even while he burned books of philosophy and literature, Shi Huang Di aimed to ensure a universal application of his laws and policies by mandating the use of a common script throughout his empire. At that time as now, there were many spoken varieties of Chinese, and the new script was even pronounced differently, according to regional dialects. Nevertheless, use of the standardized script opened up distant lines of communication and promoted a cultural cohesion evident throughout China today.

CHINESE CALLIGRAPHY

"After rain, the forest is sleek, / Between the pines, the moon startles my heart." —YUE FU SONG

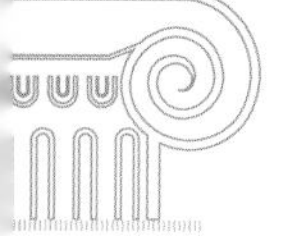

SEE ALSO | KINGS AND NOMADS: PAGE 203

China's Great Wall has been rebuilt extensively over the centuries.

ARCHITECTURE QIN'S WALL

Plagued by raids from the Xiongnu, a nomadic group of horsemen from the central Asian steppes, China's first emperor, Qin Shi Huang Di, set out in 214 B.C.E. to consolidate and enlarge already existing walls in northern China into one immense defensive barrier. He accomplished this through the efforts of an estimated 300,000 conscripted laborers toiling under the gaze of military officials. After ten years, the wall is said to have stretched some 3,000 miles, through mountainous terrain. It was garrisoned with beacon towers from which watchmen could in a single day—by means of smoke and fire—relay messages along the entire length of the structure.

THE TAKEAWAY: China's first contiguous defensive wall was built with millions of hours of conscripted human labor.

BUILDING THE WALL

SIMA QIAN THE GREAT WALL

VOICES

"*I have traveled to the northern border and returned by the direct road. As I went along I saw the outposts of the Great Wall which Meng Tian constructed for the Qin. He cut through the mountains and filled up the valleys, opening up a direct road. Truly he made free with the strength of the common people!*"

—FROM *RECORDS OF THE GRAND HISTORIAN*, SIMA QIAN, ca 230 B.C.E.; MENG TIAN WAS A QIN DYNASTY GENERAL WHO TOOK PART IN THE CONSTRUCTION OF THE GREAT WALL

"*Men delight in his rule, / All understanding the law and discipline. / The universe entire / Is our Emperor's realm.*" —INSCRIPTION PRAISING QIN

VOICES

SUN ZI CRUSH THE ENEMY

SUN ZI

"All warfare is based on deception.

"Hence, when able to attack, we must seem unable; when using our forces, we must seem inactive; when we are near, we must make the enemy believe we are far away; when far away, we must make him believe we are near.

"Hold out baits to entice the enemy. Feign disorder, and crush him."

—FROM *THE ART OF WAR*, ca FIFTH CENTURY C.E., ATTRIBUTED TO SUN ZI

ARCHITECTURE TOMB OF THE FIRST EMPEROR

Soldiers from Qin's terra-cotta army stand excavated near his tomb.

Obsessed with immortality, China's first emperor, Qin Shi Huang Di, began construction on his mausoleum complex at the age of 13. Built over the course of 36 years by a workforce of some 700,000 conscripted laborers, the mausoleum covers an area of over 20 square miles and is flanked by a battle-ready vanguard of around 8,000 life-size terra-cotta warriors, each vividly painted and with individualized facial features. Half-size bronze horses and chariots have also been unearthed, along with rare and valuable artifacts made of silk, linen, jade, and bone. Craftsmen, concubines, and sacrificed slaves were buried in the compound as well, along with a stable of horses, an assemblage of exotic animals, and the remains of seven people who may have been Qin's children. Though still unexcavated, the tomb itself is said to contain a scale model of the entire empire, replete with birds of gold and silver, flowing rivers of mercury, and a map of the sky with constellations of pearls.

{ Modern remote sensing shows that Qin's tomb has an inner chamber with stairlike walls. }

THE TAKEAWAY: Qin's huge mausoleum was guarded by an army of terra-cotta soldiers.

"*To win one hundred victories in one hundred battles is not the acme of skill. To subdue the enemy without fighting is the supreme excellence.*" —SUN ZI

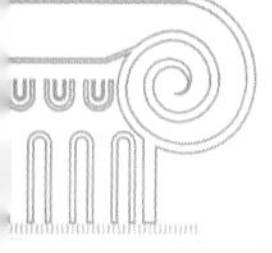

TRADE SILK ROADS

Rough-hewn and often dangerous, the Silk Road—trade routes linking East and West—wound through tracts of rugged mountains, expanses of barren deserts, and vast stretches of open water in an extensive network of footpaths, caravan trails, and sea lanes. When Chinese emperor Han Wudi sent his immense armies into central Asia, he brought under Chinese control a long corridor of land extending almost to the borders of Bactria, an important crossroads of Eurasian trade. With trade in mind, Wudi established a string of Chinese colonies at oases straddling the Taklamakan Desert. From these outposts, he imported central Asian horses and high-quality jade in exchange for manufactured silk, ginger, and cinnamon.

Chinese products reached Roman roads in Italy, where, by the first century C.E., silk garments had become high fashion. Asian products traveled by sea as well from China's port city of Guangzhou through the straits of southeast Asia to markets in India, Arabia, and Africa. Trade goods were not the only cargo on these caravans though, as ideas, religions, and contagions reached new populations in the centuries to come.

> Few traders traveled the entire length of the Silk Road, but instead sold their goods through a chain of middlemen along the way.

THE TAKEAWAY: The Silk Road of the classical era wove continents into an integrated web of commerce.

A half-ounce coin (above) dates to the Qin dynasty.

A junk, based on designs from the Han dynasty, sails the South China Sea.

> *"Boats, carts, and merchants are spread throughout the four quarters. Their stocks of goods held back for speculation fill up the principal cities."* —THIRD-CENTURY C.E. OBSERVER

SEE ALSO | KINGS AND NOMADS: PAGE 201

SCIENCE EARLY INNOVATORS

From the earliest days of Chinese history, technological innovation has been a thing of necessity. China's main food crop, rice, is dependent on human control of the nutrient-rich, but often destructive, flooding of the country's major rivers. Hence canals and irrigation systems, accessed by a network of roads, were a priority of the Qin dynasty. Iron tools also greatly increased the agricultural productivity of China's peasants, so technological advances in the production of high-quality cast iron were relatively quick to arise. There is evidence the Chinese may even have produced heat-treated steel by the second century C.E., 1,500 years before it appeared in Europe. To process the surplus grains produced, Chinese agriculturalists were employing the world's first waterwheels and wheelbarrows under the Han dynasty, technologies that may have traveled centuries later to Europe via the silk roads.

Han dynasty oil lamp (above), and seismoscope (below left).

The Han also oversaw the world's first use of coal as a fuel, and they established gear-and-pulley operations for mining salt from wells as deep as 1,900 feet below ground. On open water, Chinese mariners produced ships outfitted with an easily controlled rudder and some of the world's most advanced sails, still in wide use today.

THE TAKEAWAY: From the clothes iron to the seismoscope, classical Chinese inventions were some of the most advanced in the world.

CONNECTIONS THE INVENTION OF PAPER

An important innovation of classical China, one with effects felt to the present day, was the development of modern papermaking. Imperial court official Cai Lun described the method of creating matted sheets of paper from hemp fibers, fishnets, and old rags about 105 C.E., though the oldest known fragments date as far back as the second century B.C.E. Much less expensive than silk and easier to inscribe than bamboo or bone, paper soon became the primary medium for written communication in China. The technology was slow to travel though, reaching central Asia and the Arab world by the eighth century and Europe by the fourteenth.

MODERN PAPER

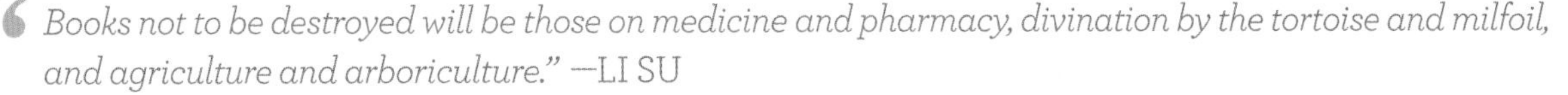

"Books not to be destroyed will be those on medicine and pharmacy, divination by the tortoise and milfoil, and agriculture and arboriculture." —LI SU

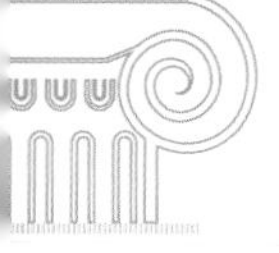

THE ANALECTS

The Chinese philosopher and statesman known to Westerners as Confucius was born in 551 B.C.E. as Kong Qiu, later known as Kong Fuzi (Master Kong), in Qufu. A brilliant teacher and statesman, he left behind adherents who preserved his sayings and teachings in a book, *The Analects*. Its moral precepts and thoughtful conversations would become the heart of education for Chinese scholars and civil servants for centuries to come. In its text, *The Analects* exhorts rulers to lead through a moral authority derived from the cultivation of ethical qualities. The journey of self-improvement, Confucius taught, was a lifelong endeavor of education and reflection that begins and ends within the family unit.

CONFUCIUS: Devoted to learning even as a child, Confucius (Kong Fuzi) was born to a noble but impoverished family. He became an acclaimed teacher and eventually the minister of justice in China's state of Lu before returning to teaching. He died in 479 B.C.E.

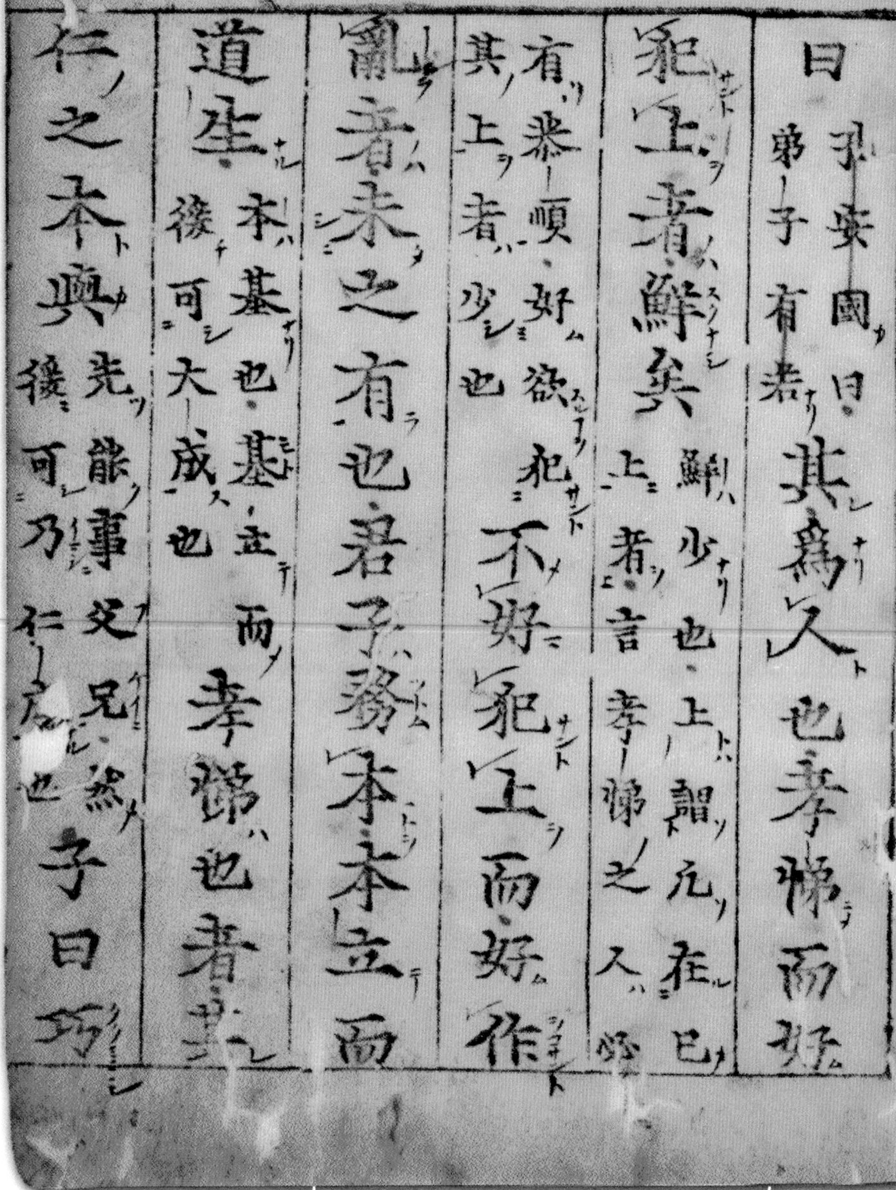

曰孔安國曰弟子有若其為人也孝悌而好
犯上者鮮矣鮮少也上謂凡在己上者言孝悌之人必
有恭順好欲犯其上者少也不好犯上而好作
亂者未之有也君子務本本立而
道生本基也基立而後可大成也孝悌也者其
仁之本與先能事父兄然後仁道可大成也子曰巧

> “There were four things from which the Master was entirely free. He had no foregone conclusions, no arbitrary predeterminations, no obstinacy, and no egotism.”

> “Someone said, 'What do you say concerning the principle that injury should be recompensed with kindness?' The Master said, 'With what then will you recompense kindness? Recompense injury with justice, and recompense kindness with kindness.' ”

ONE OF FOUR *The Analects*—or *Lunyu* as the text is known in China—make up one of four basic texts, called *Sishu*, of Confucianism.

“ The Master said, ‘Virtue is not left to stand alone. He who practices it will have neighbors.’ ”

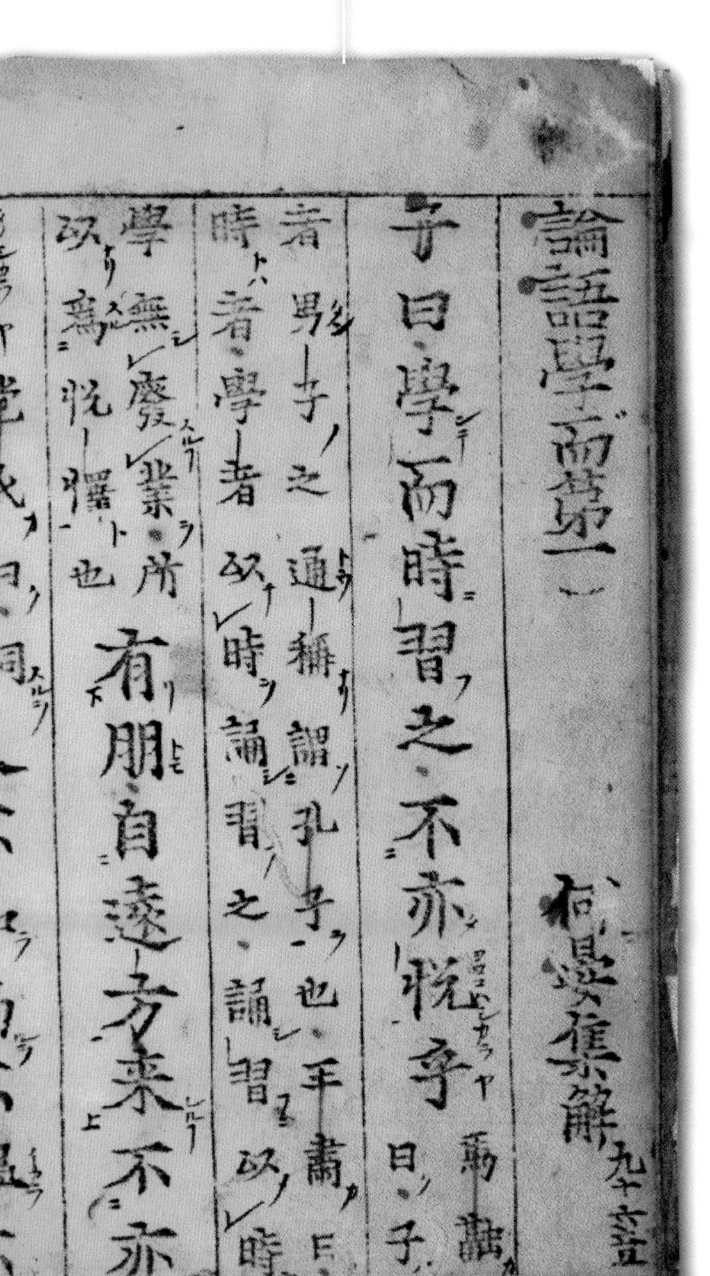

論語學而第一 何晏集解

子曰學而時習之不亦說乎 馬融曰子者男子之通稱謂孔子也王肅曰時者學者以時誦習之誦習以時學無廢業所以為說懌也

有朋自遠方來不亦樂乎 包氏曰同門曰朋也

人不知而不慍不亦君子乎 慍怒也凡人有所不知君子不慍也

有

“ Hsien asked what was shameful. The Master said, ‘When good government prevails in a state, to be thinking only of one’s salary. When bad government prevails, to be thinking, in the same way, only of one’s salary. That is what is shameful.’ ”

RARE EDITION Pages from a ten-volume, 1533 version of *The Analects*, printed in Japan, are an early example of the printer’s art.

REQUIRED READING Examination sheets (below, from the 18th century) were a familiar sight for Chinese civil servants for some 600 years. An intimate knowledge of Confucian texts was needed in order to pass these very difficult examinations and acquire a job in the government.

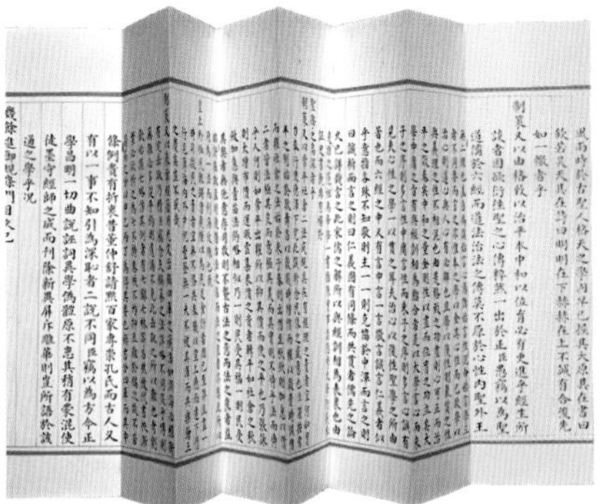

“ Tzu Kung wished to do away with the offering of a sheep connected with the inauguration of the first day of each month. The Master said, ‘Tzu Kung, you love the sheep; I love the ceremony.’ ”

FOLLOWERS OF CONFUCIUS

MOZI (fifth century B.C.E.): Though originally influenced by the ideas of Confucius, Mozi also challenged them publicly with his lofty doctrines of personal austerity, collectivism, and universal love for all, regardless of status or background.

MENCIUS (fourth century B.C.E.): Mencius was reputed to have studied with Confucius’ grandson. His most basic tenet was the essential goodness of human nature, from which he argued that rulers should enact measures to benefit all, such as light taxes, free trade, education, avoidance of war, and equal distribution of wealth.

XUNZI (third century B.C.E.): Unlike Mencius, Xunzi saw human nature as intrinsically selfish and flawed, though he allowed that goodness could be acquired through strict standards of social and moral discipline.

DONG ZHONGSHU (second century B.C.E.): It was Zhongshu who was responsible for Confucianism becoming the Han dynasty’s unifying state ideology, taught to all potential civil servants at the imperial university in the empire’s capital.

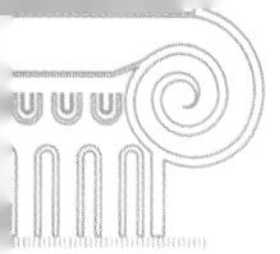

SEE ALSO | **GOLDEN AGES:** PAGE 82

KEY DATES

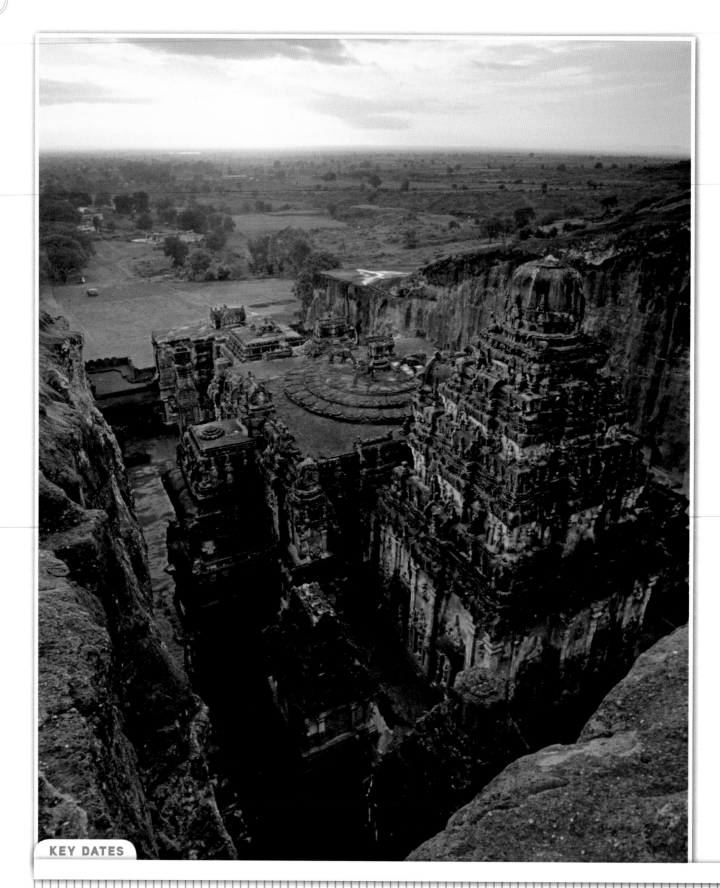

327–325 B.C.E.
Alexander the Great and his armies enter India.

321–185 B.C.E.
The Maurya dynasty rules in India.

268–232 B.C.E.
The emperor Ashoka rules the Maurya dynasty.

ca 250 B.C.E.
Sponsored by Emperor Ashoka, Buddhisms begins to spread through India.

INDIA

327 B.C.E.–550 C.E.

India's classical era was marked by the rise of two great dynasties, the Maurya and the Gupta. Though they did not rule throughout the Indian subcontinent, they brought order and peace to large sections of India, especially the north. Persian overlords had occupied northern India for some two centuries when Alexander the Great stormed through in 327 B.C.E. and toppled the government. His departure two years later resulted in a struggle for power. Into the fray stepped Chandragupta Maurya, former slave and mercenary soldier. The powerful leader took over the Punjab region in 322 B.C.E., and by the following year he had united his holdings into a kingdom. He reigned until 297 B.C.E., reputedly fasting to death in grief for victims of a famine. It was not long before his descendants had firm control of northern India between the Ganges and Indus rivers.

The most renowned of the Mauryans was the emperor Ashoka, who expanded the empire by acquiring the kingdom of Kalinga in east-central India around 260 B.C.E. He then set up an efficient, centralized government, improved agriculture, and built roads to support the empire's trade.

Following the departure of Alexander the Great, the Maurya and Gupta dynasties unified northern India, bringing stability and a golden age of achievement in the arts and sciences.

But Ashoka is perhaps best known for his spiritual contributions to India. The suffering he saw while on military campaigns so affected him that he renounced violence and turned to the peaceful doctrines of Buddhism, a religion which had been growing more popular since its introduction in the sixth century B.C.E. Ashoka gave up hunting, banned animal sacrifice, and took up a vegetarian diet. To foster Buddhism in India, he built monasteries and sent missionaries throughout Asia.

With Ashoka's death in 232 B.C.E., the Maurya Empire began crumbling. A collection of sparring kingdoms was once again united by the Gupta dynasty, founded by Chandra Gupta I in 320 C.E. Sculpture, philosophy, Sanskrit literature, and Ayurvedic medicine blossomed during the Gupta era, a golden age for India.

During this time, Buddhism and the older Hinduism coexisted peacefully, and trade and agriculture boosted the empire's economy. The prosperity, stability, and creativity of Gupta Indian civilization had a great influence on surrounding regions of southern Asia. The Gupta era came to an end around 550 C.E.

OPPOSITE: The Hindu Kailash Temple at Ellora, in western India, was cut into a scarp from the top down.

ca 160–135 B.C.E.
Indo-Greek king Menander rules over the Punjab.

320–550 C.E.
Gupta dynasty, founded by Chandra Gupta I, rules for over two centuries.

450 C.E.
The White Huns invade India across the Hindu Kush.

550 C.E.
The reign of Visnugupta Chandraditya, last of the Gupta kings, ends.

SEE ALSO | EPIC JOURNEYS: PAGE 40

RELIGION BUDDHISM

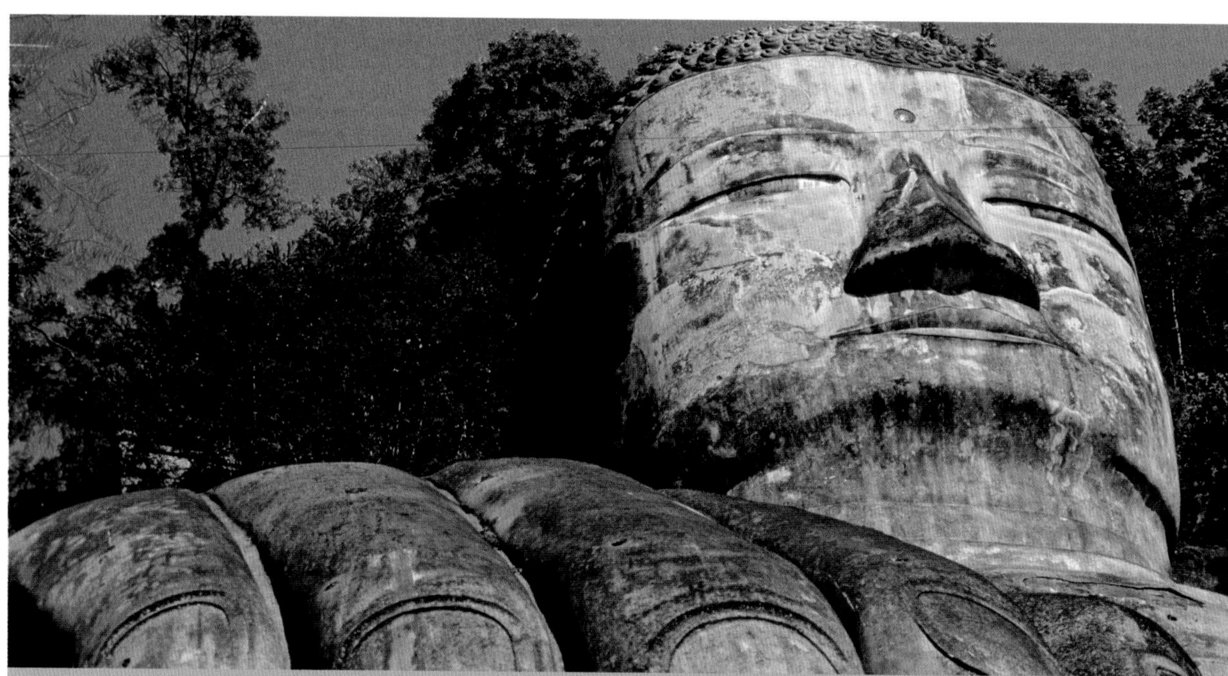

As Buddhism spread, statues of the Buddha, such as this Great Buddha of Leshan, appeared across Asia.

Founded by Siddhartha Gautama, the Buddha, in about the sixth century B.C.E., Buddhism soon spread across India and much of Asia. Hailing from Nepal (northeastern India), Siddhartha introduced the concept of peace through inner discipline. His meditations taught him that suffering came from desire—the craving for sensory pleasures. Therefore he laid out an Eightfold Path to inner holiness: right views, right aspirations, right speech, right conduct, right livelihood, right effort, right-mindedness, and right concentration. Through meditation, discussion, humility, and denial, he taught, a person can achieve a perfect, peaceful state known as nirvana.

Buddhism had great appeal to those who, like Emperor Ashoka, needed an answer to the sufferings and frustrations of life. It offered a way to peace unavailable in the older Brahmin religion, in which salvation through knowledge was promised to only a chosen few.

The religion eventually split into three main movements. Theravadans emphasized the brotherhood of Buddhist monks, though laymen could also achieve nirvana

VIPs

INDIA

Chandragupta Maurya, ca 321–297 B.C.E. Emperor, founder of the Maurya dynasty and unifier of India

Ashoka, reigned 268–232 B.C.E. Powerful emperor in the Mauryan dynasty who renounced violence and turned to Buddhism

Menander, reigned ca 160–135 B.C.E. Indo-Greek ruler in northern India and patron of Buddhism

Bhasa, third century C.E. Sanskrit dramatist who wrote *The Dream of Vasavadatta*

Chandra Gupta I, reigned 320–333 C.E. Indian king, founder of Gupta dynasty, who expanded his territory through marriage

> *"Be not anxious, great king!" said the Brahmans, "A child has planted itself in the womb of your queen . . . he will become a Buddha, and roll back the clouds of sin and folly of this world."* —THE JAKATA

VOICES

BUDDHA NOBLE TRUTHS

"This, O Bhikkhus [Buddhist monks], is the noble truth of the cause of suffering: Thirst, which leads to rebirth, accompanied by pleasure and lust, finding its delight here and there. This thirst is threefold, namely, thirst for pleasure, thirst for existence, thirst for prosperity.

"This, O Bhikkhus, is the noble truth of the cessation of suffering: it ceases with the complete cessation of thirst—a cessation which consists in the absence of every passion with the abandoning of this thirst, with doing away with it, with the deliverance from it, with the destruction of desire."

—FROM THE BUDDHA'S FIRST SERMON, ca SIXTH CENTURY B.C.E., WRITTEN DOWN AFTER HIS DEATH

RELIEF DEPICTING THE BUDDHA'S FOOTPRINTS

by supporting monks. Around the first century C.E., the Mahayana stream of Buddhism surfaced. It focused on the existence of souls known as bodhisattvas, who had attained enlightenment but opted to refrain from entering nirvana so that they could help others on their spiritual path; they were worshiped as deities. Tantric Buddhism developed around the sixth century, adding supernatural deities and even demons who could be summoned for help during rituals.

> According to the concept of karma, actions in this life directly influence a person's future lives.

As the years went on, Buddhist monks in increasing numbers began fanning out across central and western Asia, China, and Southeast Asia, acting as missionaries to promote the faith.

Hindu deity Krishna plays the flute for his beloved, Radha.

In addition to Buddhism, Hinduism and Jainism thrived during the period. Though not as numerous as Buddhists, Jains were prevalent in western India, Kalinga, and the Mysore and Tamil regions of southern India. Founded in the sixth century B.C.E., Jainism was similar to Buddhism in preaching liberation of the soul through right conduct, right knowledge, and right faith. The Jains also had a mendicant order and believed that all living things were sacred. Meanwhile, the ancient Hindu beliefs of karma and rebirth became part of Buddhist doctrine, influencing the growth of both religions.

THE TAKEAWAY: Monks spread the faith of Buddhism in India and throughout Asia.

"Gentle winds clear the ground before him; the clouds let fall drops of water to lay the dust in his pathway, and then become a canopy over him." —THE SUMANGALA-VILASINI

SEE ALSO | GOLDEN AGES: PAGE 82

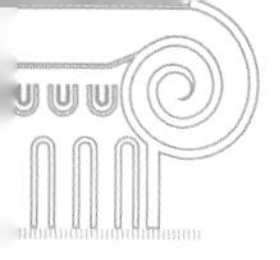

A watercolor portrays a marriage scene from the *Mahabharata.*

ARTS GODS AND HEROES

Literature and visual arts, particularly religious sculpture, made great strides during India's classical era. The first known Sanskrit dramatist, Bhasa, wrote during the second or third century C.E. His greatest play, *Svapnavāsavadattā (The Dream of Vasavadatta),* recounting a king's tribulations, drew themes from the two great Indian epics: the heroic quest *Ramayana* and the *Mahabharata,* a chronicle of Hindu life and legend.

Detailed depictions of the life of Buddha appeared throughout India. Fifth-century murals and sculptures from the Ajanta caves in south-central India are notable examples, as are the intricate carvings on the fifth-century Great Stupa at Sanchi in north-central India.

THE TAKEAWAY: Sanskrit literature became popular as writers drew on ancient Indian epics.

Lion pillar of Ashoka

INDIA PRINCE ARJUNA ON THE EVE OF BATTLE

VOICES

"Krishna! as I see these kinsmen, come here to shed their common blood, my limbs fail, my tongue dries in my mouth, a shudder thrills my body, and my hair bristles with horror; from my weak hand slips Gandiv, the goodly bow; a fever burns my skin to parching. I can hardly stand; the life within me seems to swim and faint. Nothing do I foresee save woe and wailing! It is not good, O Keshav! nothing good can spring from mutual slaughter! I hate triumph and domination, wealth and ease, won in this way!"

—FROM THE *BHAGAVADGITA,* A SECTION OF THE HINDU EPIC, THE *MAHABHARATA,* ca SECOND CENTURY C.E.

"There are monks who remain devoted to the mindfulness of in-and-out breathing. Mindfulness of in-and-out breath, when developed and pursued, is of great fruit, of great benefit." —THE PALI CANON

ARCHITECTURE CARVED IN STONE

Many Hindu temples from the Gupta period were rudimentary, with a shrine room holding an image of a deity and leading to a porch. Much more elaborate and durable were the Buddhist centers, consisting of monasteries, halls of worship, and stupas, dome-shaped mounds or towers that served as shrines. A stupendous feat of art and engineering over several generations during the Gupta dynasty resulted in the architectural monuments carved from a basalt cliff at Ellora, in west-central India. Brahmanical, Buddhist, and Jain craftsmen created the cliffside's 34 buildings of sculpted stone and their statuary.

From about the first century B.C.E. to the sixth century C.E., Buddhist monks turned layers of granite, gneiss, and basalt into the labyrinthine temples at the Ajanta caves. Vaulted ceilings, pillared assembly halls, meditation cells, and devotional shrines were hewn using techniques that historians can only speculate on. Hundreds of sculptural figures animate the walls.

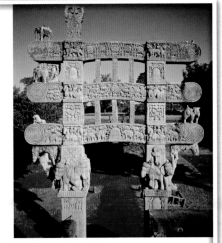

A gate from the Great Stupa of Sanchi, built by Ashoka.

{ The Ajanta caves contain not only sculptures, but also vivid, fresco-style paintings on Buddhist themes. }

A Buddhist stupa's domed shape derives from ancient times.

THE TAKEAWAY: Buddhist sites from the Gupta period include spectacular edifices carved into hillsides and caves.

> *"Be lamps unto yourselves. Be a refuge unto yourselves. Do not turn to any external refuge. Hold fast to the teaching as a lamp."* — THE PALI CANON

THE CLASSI

LIVES ON PARCHMENT

600 B.C.E.–500 C.E.

CHAPTER

3

A Greek temple has weathered the ages in Agrigento, Sicily.

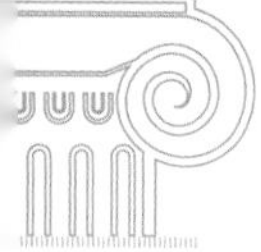

SEE ALSO | THE CLASSICAL AGE: PAGE 107

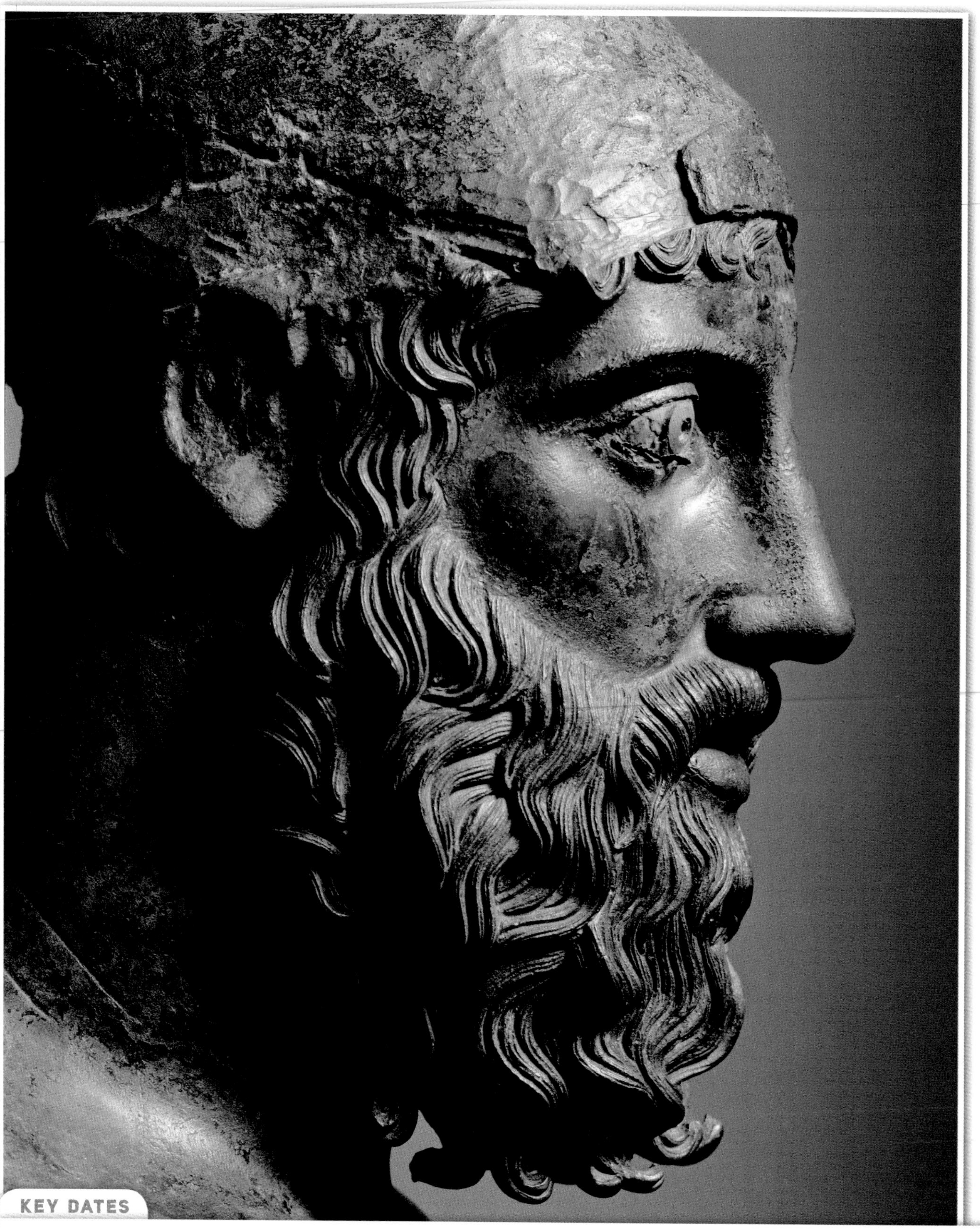

KEY DATES

SIXTH CENTURY B.C.E.
Political reforms in Athens and elsewhere lead to the rise of democracy.

594 B.C.E.
Solon becomes chief magistrate of Athens.

525–456 B.C.E.
Dramatist Aeschylus writes the Oresteia.

ca 500 B.C.E.
Golden Age of intellectual and artistic achievement begins

THE GREEK WORLD

800 B.C.E.–30 C.E.

The Greeks left us riches of every order. We see their magnificent architectural styles all around us, and their works in bronze, marble, paint, and clay still stand as models of artistic perfection. But there can be no doubt that what speaks to us most powerfully down through the centuries are the myriad achievements of the Greek mind—in politics and science and mathematics and philosophy and theater and even in the study of history itself. Though the Greeks themselves were citizens of various city-states, their legacy has passed to us in the Greek language as a single powerful influence, visible in everything from mathematics textbooks to the very way we think about ourselves and the world. Greece's cultural and intellectual blossoming came in the fifth and early fourth centuries B.C.E., a period known as the classical age or, sometimes, Greece's Golden Age. But Greek society traces further back, roughly to 800 B.C.E., when family-based tribes on the mountainous peninsula began organizing themselves based on the concept of the *polis,* or city-state, a trade and defensive center for an urban community and the surrounding lands.

Throughout its history, Greece had moments of glory on the battlefield, but its achievements in the arts and in all manner of intellectual pursuits, from politics to mathematics, stand as its enduring legacy.

Over time, different city-states were ruled as monarchies, with single leaders known as tyrants; as oligarchies, with a few wealthy landowners in charge; and, ultimately, as democracies of a sort, with free male citizens—but not women or immigrants or slaves—having a voice in civic matters. City-states would also sometimes form leagues with or against each other.

The two most prominent city-states, Athens and Sparta, came together in the early fifth century B.C.E. to defeat the mightier Persian Empire. But their coalition was short-lived. As societies they were polar opposites, Sparta glorifying all things military and Athens encouraging the arts. Their differences festered into open conflict, with Athens suffering military defeat in 404 B.C.E., an event that effectively marked the end of its primacy in political affairs.

Greece would go on to other glories, chiefly behind the mounted charges of the young Macedonian warrior-king Alexander the Great. By that time the city-states and their fledgling democracies had fallen, and the world stage would soon belong to others. But Greek influence was already widespread, and what the Greek mind had achieved in those golden days would live on.

OPPOSITE: The head of a bronze statue, possibly by Phidias, displays the Greek ideal of proportion.

492–479 B.C.E.
The Persian Wars are fought, ending in Greek victory.

ca 431–404 B.C.E.
The Peloponnesian War pits Athens against rival Sparta.

334 B.C.E.
Alexander crosses into Asia Minor and begins conquests.

30 B.C.E.
Rome takes control of Egypt, ending Hellenistic rule.

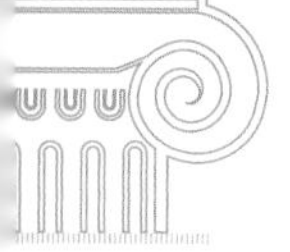

SEE ALSO | THE CLASSICAL AGE: PAGE 105

Poet Sappho rejected the typical Greek woman's role.

CLASS & SOCIETY THE ELITE

The birthplace of democracy was far from a classless society. Greek aristocracy consisted of both old landowning families and those who had accumulated wealth in other ways. Rich merchants and traders might share the privileges of the upper class, but because they had to work for a living, they were considered a step beneath the landed gentry, who saw leisure as a virtual prerequisite for status. Chief among the privileges of Greek men was citizenship itself, which included the power to elect leaders, make decisions in council, and seek redress of grievances. In some city-states, democracy eventually extended citizenship to all free men, but the elite maintained their elevated status. They were cultivators of the arts and theater attendees; leaders in politics, military affairs, and sports; purveyors of education through the hiring of private tutors and sponsorship of academies; and ultimately the supporters of the full catalog of Greek intellectual pursuits. It wasn't all about wine-soaked banquets . . . although there was that, too.

THE TAKEAWAY: Money and hereditary status spelled power in the Greek city-states.

THE GREEK WORLD

VIPs

Homer, Ninth Century B.C.E.
Poet who composed *The Iliad* and *The Odyssey*

Solon, 638–558 B.C.E.
Leader who reformed politics, "fathers" democracy

Pythagoras, 581–497 B.C.E.
Philosopher who developed mathematical principles

Aeschylus, ca 525–455 B.C.E.
Dramatist who wrote tragedies, transformed theater

Pericles, ca 495–429 B.C.E.
Statesman who led Athens to greatness

Aristotle, 384–322 B.C.E.
Philosopher who systematized the sciences

APHRODITE

“*Sweet mother, I cannot ply the loom, vanquished by desire for a youth through the work of soft Aphrodite.*” —SAPPHO

DAILY LIFE GREEK WOMEN

For women as for men, social status determined quality of life, but high-born women lived in a domestic world that set them quite literally apart from men. A five-year-old girl could expect to be betrothed to her future husband in a public ceremony, her father or other guardian intoning to the groom, who was typically ten or more years older, "I give you this woman for the plowing [procreation] of legitimate children." The marriage ceremony, years later, was the procession to her husband's house, where the bride would spend most of her time in rooms set aside for her, including her bedroom and an enclosed courtyard.

The elite woman was expected to manage the household and its slaves, spin wool for clothing, and raise children. She might visit friends, but to be seen even at a banquet was shameful. A few upper-class women found respectable lives outside the home as priestesses, but most women seen on the streets were entertainers or vendors.

> An Athenian woman could only do business if the transaction was worth less than a bushel of grain.

Women weave a woolen cloth on a sixth-century B.C.E. vase.

THE TAKEAWAY: Elite women had fewer cares than the working classes, but their lives were dominated by household management.

VOICES

ARISTOTLE ON A GOOD WIFE

ARISTOTLE

"It is fitting that a woman of a well-ordered life should consider that her husband's wishes are as laws appointed for her by divine will, along with the marriage state and the fortune she shares. If she endures them with patience and gentleness, she will rule her home with ease; otherwise, not so easily. Therefore not only when her husband is in prosperity and good report must she be in agreement with him, and to render him the service he wills, but also in times of adversity. If, through sickness or fault of judgement, his good fortune fails, then must she show her quality, encouraging him ever with words of cheer and yielding him obedience in all fitting ways—only let her do nothing base or unworthy. Let her refrain from all complaint, nor charge him with the wrong, but rather attribute everything of this kind to sickness or ignorance or accidental errors. Therefore, she will serve him more assiduously than if she had been a slave bought and taken home."

—FROM *OIKONOMIKOS*, ca 330 B.C.E.

"When love is in excess it brings a man nor honor nor any worthiness." —EURIPIDES

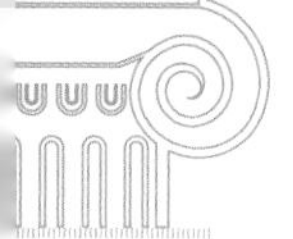

SEE ALSO | GOLDEN AGES: PAGE 64

Leonidas's doomed last stand at Thermopylae became a military legend.

CONFLICTS ON GREEK GROUND

There was an acknowledged superpower in the Mediterranean during the middle of the first millennium B.C.E., and its name was Persia. Its conquests stretched from the Indus Valley in the east to the Nile, the Black Sea, and the very edges of Greece itself. The Persian navy was enormous, with perhaps more than 1,000 vessels, and its equally overwhelming army numbered upwards of 100,000 troops organized as cavalry, charioteers, and skilled archers who were said to be able to darken the skies with their flying arrows.

Against this might, Greece's city-states could muster far fewer numbers, but they still had advantages. The Greek trireme, centerpiece of the Athenian navy, had three decks of oars and could reach destructive ramming speeds the Persians couldn't match. Greek soldiers wore more armor, carried a spear and a large shield, and attacked in tightly packed units known as phalanxes, which were virtually impregnable. And in all the battles known collectively as the Persian Wars, the Greeks were defending home turf and home waters, territory they knew well and used to their benefit.

The first of these David-and-Goliath confrontations occurred in 490 B.C.E., when a Persian force under Darius I attacked by sea just north

Early Greek helmet

> "Turning the lyre and handling the harp are no accomplishments of mine, but rather taking in hand a city that was small and inglorious and making it glorious and great." —THEMISTOCLES

VOICES

XENOPHON

THE APPEARANCE OF THE SPARTAN SOLDIER

"The following inventions are attributed to Lycurgos: the soldier has a crimson-colored uniform and a heavy shield of bronze; his theory being that such equipment has no sort of feminine association, and is altogether most warrior-like. It is most quickly burnished; it is least readily soiled. He further permitted those who were about the age of early manhood to wear their hair long. For so, he conceived, they would appear of larger stature, more free and indomitable, and of a more terrible aspect."

—XENOPHON, ca 375 B.C.E.

MEDIEVAL VIEW OF XENOPHON AND GREEK ARMY

of Athens. The plains of Marathon were actually rough and broken ground, too narrow for the Persians to deploy their cavalry and charioteers effectively. Phalanxes of the Athenian army charged first and seized the victory; later, the Athenian navy defeated a Persian fleet near Athens, and the invaders retreated.

> Herodotus says some 6,400 "barbarians" fell at Marathon; he numbers the Athenian dead at 192.

Sparta had done little to help Athens despite joining it in a defensive league, but such was not the case ten years later when Darius's son Xerxes launched an overland assault, advancing down the Greek coast supported by his navy. Under their king, Leonidas, Spartans bottlenecked the Persians at the pass of Thermopylae, ultimately falling but crucially delaying the Persian advance. Although Xerxes managed to reach Athens and torch it, his much larger navy lost the Battle of Salamis, in part because of what the Greeks knew about the hazards of local waters and weather. A mop-up action at Plataea ended in a crushing defeat of the Persians in 479 B.C.E.

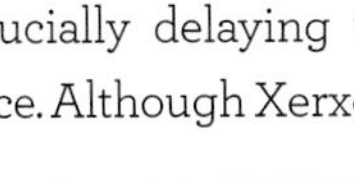

Sparta and Athens later faced off in the Peloponnesian War, battling between 431 and 421 and again in 415. Besieged and starving, the Athenians capitulated in 404.

THE TAKEAWAY: Skilled Greek forces defeated Persia before they turned on each other.

THUMBS UP / THUMBS DOWN

ALCIBIADES ca 450–404 B.C.E.

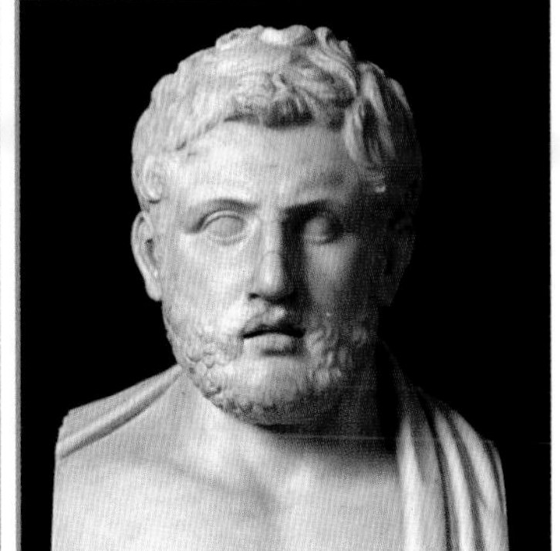

ALCIBIADES

ALLIES AGAINST PERSIA, Athens and Sparta were foes during the 27 years of the Peloponnesian War. A key figure of the time was Alcibiades, who knew how to play both sides—and then some. A prominent member of Athenian society, he advocated aggression, professing that, as Thucydides reported, "If we cease to rule others, we are in danger of being ruled ourselves." A growing cadre of enemies ousted him, and Alcibiades promptly turned to Sparta, organizing and launching several campaigns against Athens. Rivalries again led to his ouster, and he eventually returned to serve Athens as a general and sometime peacemaker before being exiled a second time. Ancient historians weren't sure how to judge him. Plutarch said his strongest passion was "his ambition and desire of superiority," but his brilliance and charm won him supporters wherever he went. The debate continues among historians to this day. **CONCLUSION: THUMBS UP AND DOWN.**

"Anarchy, anarchy! Show me a greater evil! / This is why the cities tumble and the great houses rain down / This is what scatters armies." —SOPHOCLES

SEE ALSO | THE CLASSICAL AGE: PAGE 115

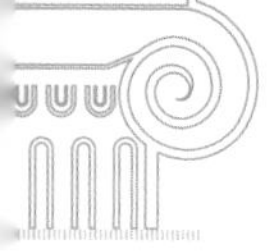

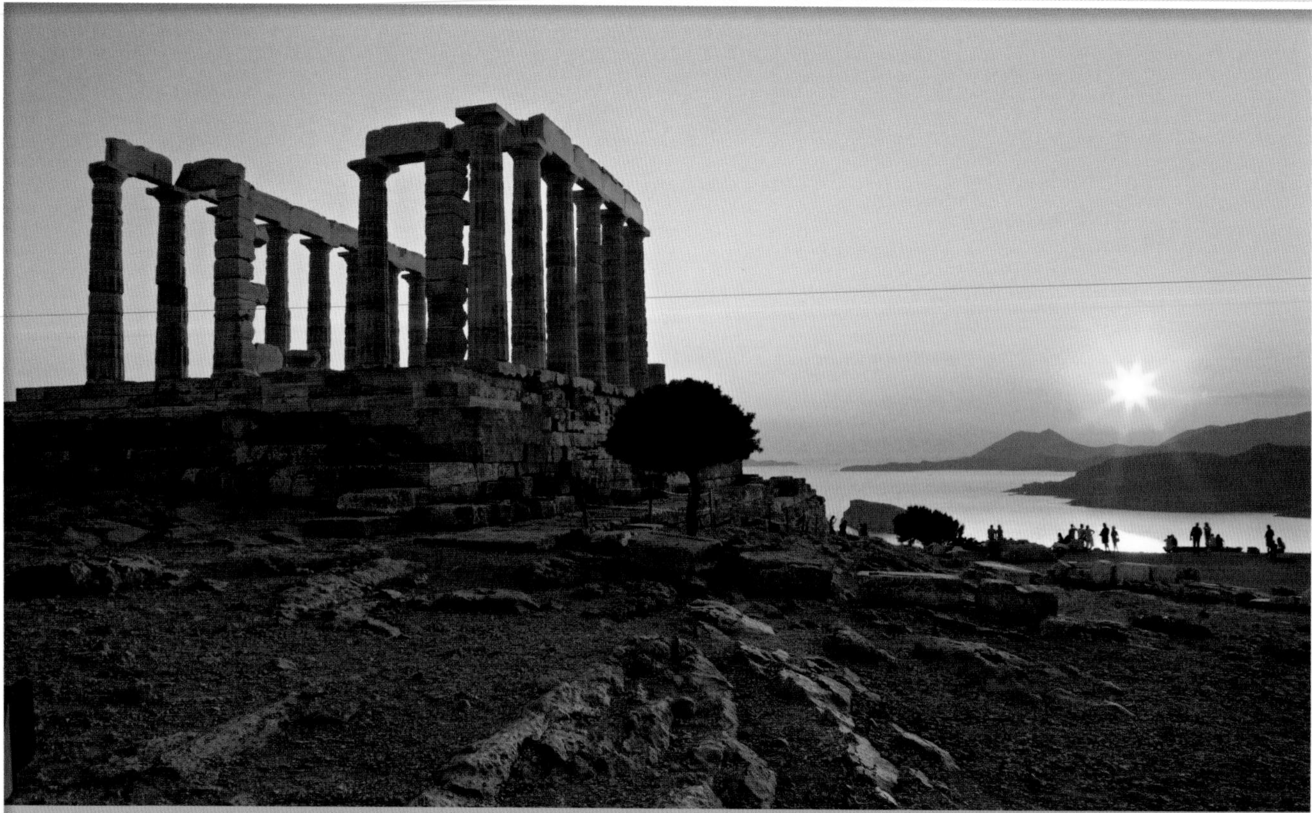

Sunset illuminates the temple of Poseidon on the coast of Cape Sounion.

RELIGION ON OLYMPUS

The precise origins of the Greek pantheon of gods and goddesses are lost, but as early as 776 B.C.E., Zeus and others were being honored at the first Olympic Games. Humans learned of the gods through the stories told about them, which were first written down in the ninth century B.C.E. Mount Olympus, Greece's highest peak, became the place where the 12 important gods held their banquets, but other religious centers developed, such as at Delphi, where a priestess who served as Apollo's oracle read the future under the god's protection.

Greeks were like other peoples in many religious practices. They asked the gods for help and saw misfortune as punishment from on high; they also sacrificed animals to thank the gods for blessings or appease them for sins committed. But the Greek gods were unique in one regard: their faults. They could represent ideal human qualities like wisdom and sobriety, but they also fell prey to such foibles as drunkenness and lust. For the Greeks, the gods were very much a part of a human world.

Plaque of religious offering

THE TAKEAWAY: The Greeks told stories about their gods, revealing themselves in the process.

> *Homer and Hesiod attributed to the gods everything that is a shame and a reproach among men.*"
> —XENOPHANES

ARTS TOWARD THE IDEAL

Greece's literary tradition began with Homer's *Iliad* and *Odyssey*, epic poems first written down in the ninth century B.C.E. but arising from a much older oral tradition. Greek literature took new forms in the hands of the poet Hesiod, who told of farm life in *Work and Days*, and the tragedians Aeschylus, Sophocles, and Euripides, who transformed poetry into theater and helped make Athens the cultural center of the Greek world.

Homer sings the *Iliad* at the gates of Athens.

{ Almost all Greek sculpture was public art, displayed for all to see by rich patrons. }

The visual arts had borrowed roots. Early Greek pottery, murals, and sculpture show Eastern and Egyptian influences, but as artists developed more naturalized depictions, distinctly Greek styles emerged in an extraordinary blending of naturalism and idealization.

Much has remained to influence our own times, but much has also been lost. Homer supposedly composed eight other epic poems, and while the noble columns and plinths of the Parthenon still stand, the gold and ivory statue of Athena it once housed is gone.

THE TAKEAWAY: The Greek arts fashioned enduring masterpieces from older models.

VOICES

SOPHOCLES CHORUS FROM *ANTIGONE*

“*Strophe: Love, unconquered in the fight, Love, who makest havoc of wealth, who keepest thy vigil on the soft cheek of a maiden; thou roamest over the sea, and among the homes of dwellers in the wilds; no immortal can escape thee, nor any among men whose life is for a day; and he to whom thou hast come is mad.*

Antistrophe: The just themselves have their minds warped by thee to wrong, for their ruin: 'tis thou that hast stirred up this present strife of kinsmen; victorious is the love-kindling light from the eyes of the fair bride; it is a power enthroned in sway beside the eternal laws; for there the goddess Aphrodite is working her unconquerable will.”

—FROM *ANTIGONE* BY SOPHOCLES, 441 B.C.E.

APHRODITE, GODDESS OF LOVE

“*One race there is of men, one of gods, but from one mother we both draw our breath.*” —PINDAR

SEE ALSO | BREAKING BONDS: PAGE 220

PHILOSOPHY LOVE OF WISDOM

Some ascribe the Greek love of wisdom—the literal meaning of "philosophy"—to the society's widespread literacy, which itself traces back to the easy phonetics of the Greek alphabet. But Greeks were also inherently curious, believing that the world made rational sense and that an inquiring mind could fathom its many intricacies. However it came to be, the Greek passion for contemplation reached a pinnacle during Athens's Golden Age, when you were as likely to meet a philosopher as you were a politician in the city streets—and as likely to get into a serious argument with him. The Sophists, who charged fees to verse young men in such subjects as "excellence" and "virtue," touted the power of rhetoric to uncover truth and explain human behavior, but others vilified them and their methods; Xenophon called them "prostitutors of wisdom," and Plato defined the Sophist as "an athlete in contests of words."

> Philosophers could face punishment for their thoughts. Anaxagoras was banished from Athens for theorizing that the sun is a molten ball of iron.

Socrates, who would suffer fortune's slings and arrows himself (see sidebar, opposite), brought a new spirit to philosophy, focusing on the moral responsibility of the individual and the importance of knowing oneself. His student Plato described an ethics-based order in the universe and posited an ideal realm of which this world was only a poor reflection. His version of the ideal state had a ruler he called the philosopher-king. The Academy, which he founded in the 380s B.C.E., was Greece's earliest example of a university-like institution.

This legacy of critical thinking continued with Aristotle, who attended the Academy but took Plato's philosophy in a profoundly different direction. While Plato felt that human senses actually interfered with knowledge, Aristotle embraced observation and evidence gathered through the

PLATO

PLATO THE ALLEGORY OF THE CAVE

VOICES

"Imagine men in an underground cave with an entrance open toward the light which extends through the whole cave. Within the cave are people who from childhood have had chains on their legs and their necks so they could only look forward but not turn their heads. There is burning a fire, above and behind them, and between the fire and the chains is a road above, along which one may see a little wall built along. . . . Imagine then by the side of this little wall men carrying all sorts of machines rising above the wall, and statues of men and other animals wrought in stone, wood, and other materials, some of the bearers probably speaking, others proceeding in silence. . . . [Do you think] that such as these [chained men] would have seen anything else of themselves or one another except the shadows that fall from the fire on the opposite side of the cave? [S]uch persons would believe that truth was nothing else but the shadows of the exhibitions."

—FROM *THE REPUBLIC*, PLATO, FOURTH CENTURY B.C.E.

"It is in the character of very few men to honor without envy a friend who has prospered." —AESCHYLUS

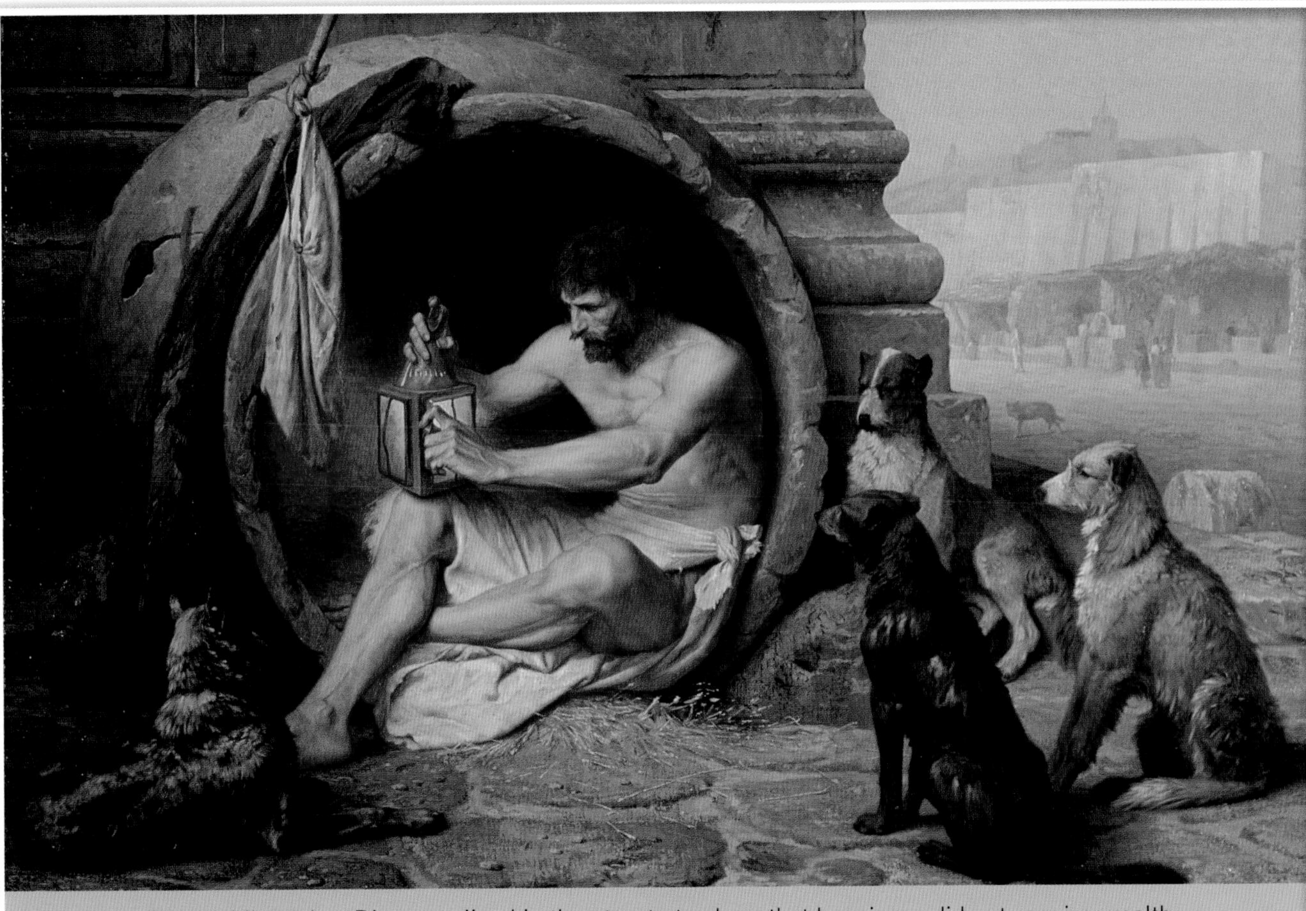

Greek philosopher Diogenes lived in the streets to show that happiness did not require wealth.

senses. In the process, he launched studies into everything from physics and astronomy to biology, psychology, and politics. He got some things right (describing the earth as a sphere, for example) and other things wrong (placing it at the center of the universe), but he deserves credit for establishing rigorous methods of intellectual investigation that have guided the human pursuit of knowledge up to the present.

THE TAKEAWAY: Greek philosophers were insatiably curious about humanity's role.

THUMBS UP / THUMBS DOWN

SOCRATES ca 470–399 B.C.E.

DEATH OF SOCRATES

One of western civilization's most vivid figures, Socrates began his adult life as a soldier and later served as an Athenian magistrate. But his true love was the pursuit of knowledge, particularly of oneself, and the question of what it means to lead a life of integrity. His approach was simple—a series of questions that invariably led his students to deeper levels of understanding—but the effects were profound on the philosophy of the day. Indeed, Socrates' concepts of individualism and virtue were considered so revolutionary that they led Athenian magistrates to charge him with impiety and the corruption of the city's youth. Rather than renounce his beliefs, Socrates agreed to commit suicide, drinking a mixture of hemlock sap and declaring to his attending followers that "no evil can happen to a good man, either in life, or after death." **CONCLUSION:** THUMBS UP

"All men's souls are immortal, but the souls of the righteous are immortal and divine." —SOCRATES

SEE ALSO | NEW WORLD ORDER: PAGE 280

MATHEMATICS SEEING NUMBERS

Pythagoras demonstrates mathematical harmonies to astrologers.

Early on, mathematics became a distinct branch of the intellectual pursuits known broadly as philosophy, and the Greeks excelled at it. To this day, students learn basic mathematical principles named for some of the giants of these early investigations into how numbers make the world work. Perhaps coincidentally, two of the most renowned Greek achievements in mathematics occurred away from the homeland.

Euclid's Elements begins with 23 definitions and 10 geometric axioms that serve as the basis of hundreds of theorems, all reached through deductive logic.

The first came from Pythagoras, a native of the Aegean island of Samos who migrated to a Greek colony in Sicily around 525 B.C.E. There he founded an academy dedicated to describing physical phenomena in numerical terms. His adherents helped establish the study of geometry and the closely related discipline of astronomy.

More than 200 years later, in the intellectual hub of Alexandria in Egypt, Euclid made an eternal name for himself with his 13-volume treatise on all things mathematic, the *Elements,* which codified the principles of geometry. The work served as the only textbook in its field for centuries.

THE TAKEAWAY: Greek mathematicians saw the world in geometric terms.

CONNECTIONS THE ORIGINS OF GEOMETRY

It may not have originated with Pythagoras himself, but out of his academy in the sixth century B.C.E. came the mathematical theorem that bears his name: In a right triangle, the square of the hypotenuse is equal to the sum of the squares of the other two sides. Most children of a certain age can recite it in their sleep, and Pythagorean formulas are still used to calculate the areas of geometric shapes. And the geometry taught today is still Euclidean geometry, named for the fourth-century B.C.E. mathematician who enumerated its principles. Only in the last 200 years have other sorts of geometry—"non-Euclidean" systems—been imagined.

ANCIENT GREEK MOSAIC

There is geometry in the humming of the strings. There is music in the spacing of the spheres.." —PYTHAGORAS

VOICES

ARCHIMEDES WILL IT FLOAT?

ARCHIMEDES

“ *BOOK 1:* Basic principles of hydrostatics

“*Proposition 2:* *The surface of any fluid at rest is the surface of a sphere whose center is the same as that of the earth.*

“*Proposition 3:* *Of solids, those which, size for size, are of equal weight with a fluid will, if let down into the fluid, be immersed so that they do not project above the surface but do not sink lower.*

“*Proposition 6:* *If a solid lighter than a fluid is forcibly immersed in it, the solid will be driven upwards by a force equal to the difference between its weight and the weight of the fluid displaced.*

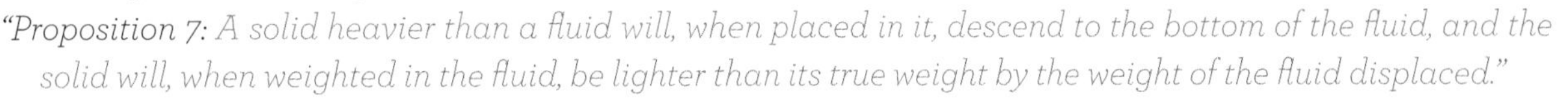

“*Proposition 7:* *A solid heavier than a fluid will, when placed in it, descend to the bottom of the fluid, and the solid will, when weighted in the fluid, be lighter than its true weight by the weight of the fluid displaced.*”

—FROM *ON FLOATING BODIES,* A TWO-VOLUME WORK ON FLUIDS AND BUOYANCY, THIRD CENTURY B.C.E.

SCIENCE EUREKA

THE TAKEAWAY: Much of Greek science was theory, but Archimedes put principles to use.

Greek philosophers who focused on the sciences rarely explored the practical implications of their insights. But occasionally a philosopher-scientist would turn what he had learned into something useful. Such a philosopher was Archimedes, born in the Greek colony of Syracuse, Sicily, around 287 B.C.E. His voice echoes down to us most famously in the single word “Eureka!” Legend has it that while in the bath he realized he could determine if an object was pure gold by measuring the amount of water it displaced; running naked into the streets, he shouted, “I have found it!” The story may be apocryphal, but Archimedes’ enthusiasm rings true. The scientist turned his understanding of mathematical principles into all sorts of inventions, many of which were used as instruments of war. He also advanced mathematical theory by approximating pi and describing the so-called golden ratio. Intent on a geometric drawing, he was killed by an invading Roman soldier in 212 B.C.E., reportedly saying as he fell, “Do not disturb my circles.”

Archimedes’ screw raised water from low-lying areas.

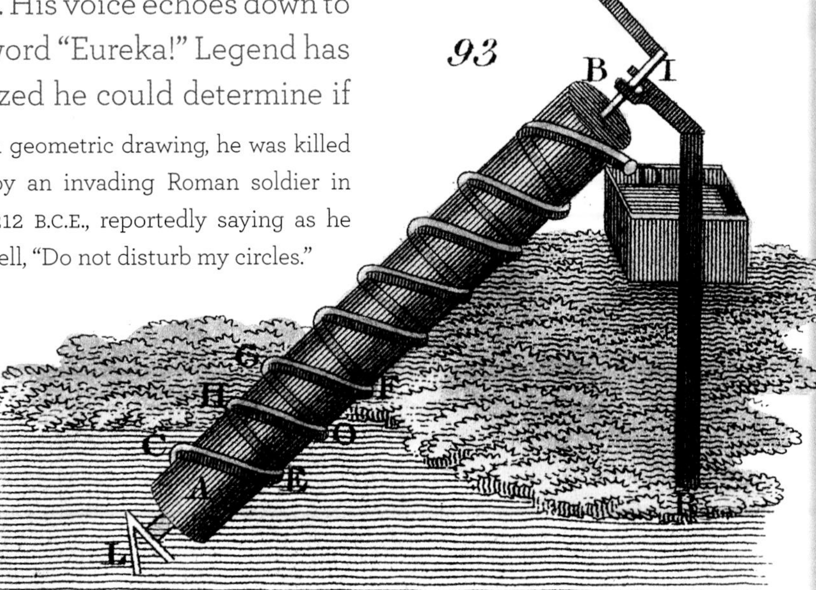

“ *Healing is a matter of time, but it is sometimes also a matter of opportunity.”* —HIPPOCRATES

SEE ALSO | EPIC JOURNEYS: PAGE 37

CULTURE THE HELLENISTIC WORLD

During his conquests, Alexander took pains to let local customs survive, but he also spread Greek culture by founding dozens of Greek-style cities throughout the lands of the eastern Mediterranean. The result was an amalgam of Eastern and Western traditions that defined the Hellenistic, or Greek-influenced, age. Greek merchants followed in the wake of Alexander's army, and Greek was soon the lingua franca of the whole region.

> In an effort to bind East and West together, Alexander ordered 80 close associates—and perhaps as many as 9,000 of his soldiers—to marry Eastern women.

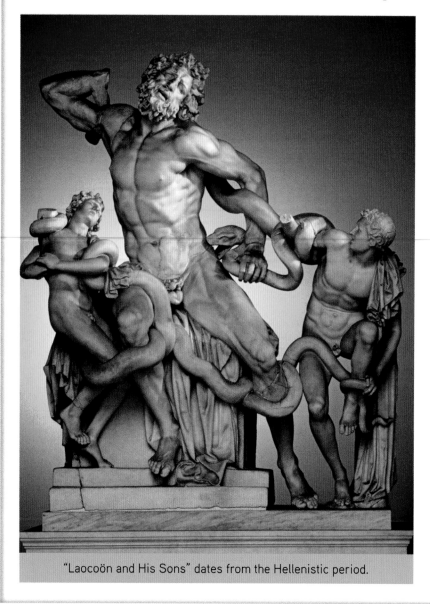

"Laocoön and His Sons" dates from the Hellenistic period.

Seleucis I established a dynasty after Alexander's death.

Persian wealth, now widespread, led to an economic boom that helped Hellenistic cities such as Asia Minor's Pergamon thrive. Its ruins include theaters, gymnasiums, baths, and other signs of the good life that could have been plucked right out of Athens.

The jewel in the crown of this Hellenistic world was Alexandria, which Alexander's general Ptolemy I Soter made the capital of his Egyptian Empire. Ptolemy fostered the Greek love of learning by founding the Royal Library of Alexandria, said to hold as many as 700,000 scrolls. Hellenistic influence faded as Roman power became ascendant, its death knell effectively sounding when the great library itself was destroyed by fire around 47 B.C.E.

THE TAKEAWAY: Alexander's successors spread Hellenism in the eastern Mediterranean.

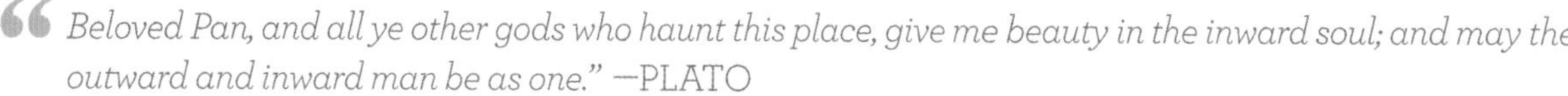

"Beloved Pan, and all ye other gods who haunt this place, give me beauty in the inward soul; and may the outward and inward man be as one." —PLATO

LEADERS

CLEOPATRA'S REIGN

Egyptian ruler Cleopatra fatally allied with Roman Mark Antony.

She had the feminine charms to beguile the greatest man in Rome, but Cleopatra VII was much more than a pretty face. Through her Ptolemaic forebears, Cleopatra was Greek, and her capital of Alexandria remained the epitome of Hellenism. Although she spoke Greek, she also cultivated her Egyptian roots by learning the local language—the first Ptolemaic pharaoh to do so—and worshiping Egyptian gods.

Cleopatra initially ruled with her brother Ptolemy XIII in 51 B.C.E., but she orchestrated his ouster and forthwith had coins stamped with her likeness alone. Plotters returned Ptolemy to the throne, but by seducing Julius Caesar—purportedly, she had herself delivered to him rolled up in a Persian rug—Cleopatra reclaimed power.

She had hoped that her son by Caesar would one day rule a united Rome and Egypt, but Caesar himself was soon dead, and her next attempt to woo Roman power in the form of Mark Antony ended disastrously: Rome's new ruler Octavian vanquished their joint fleets at Actium and invaded Egypt. As he approached Alexandria in 30 B.C.E., Cleopatra poisoned herself, possibly with a snakebite.

THE TAKEAWAY: Cleopatra was the last Greek ruler of Egypt; her death marked the end of an era.

VOICES

GELLIUS ANCIENT LIBRARIES

"The tyrant Pisistratus is said to have been the first to establish at Athens a public library of books relating to the liberal arts. Then the Athenians themselves added to this collection with considerable diligence and care; but later Xerxes, when he got possession of Athens and burned the entire city except the citadel, removed that whole collection of books and carried them off to Persia....

"At a later time an enormous quantity of books, nearly seven hundred thousand volumes, was either acquired or written in Egypt under the kings known as Ptolemies; but these were all burned during the sack of the city in our first war with Alexandria, not intentionally or by anyone's order, but accidentally by the auxiliary soldiers."

—FROM *ATTIC NIGHTS*, AULUS GELLIUS, SECOND CENTURY C.E.

LIBRARY OF ALEXANDRIA

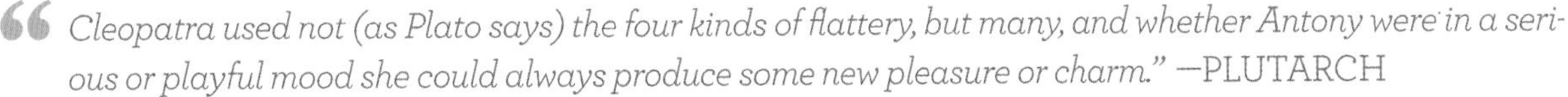

"Cleopatra used not (as Plato says) the four kinds of flattery, but many, and whether Antony were in a serious or playful mood she could always produce some new pleasure or charm." —PLUTARCH

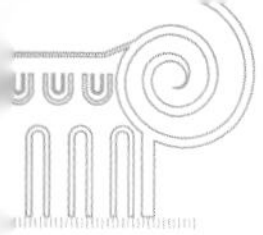

SEE ALSO | THE CLASSICAL AGE: PAGE 130

KEY DATES

753 B.C.E.
According to legend, Romulus and Remus found the city of Rome.

509 B.C.E.
The Roman Republic is established.

ca 450 B.C.E.
Romans codify the laws of the republic in the Twelve Tables.

264–146 B.C.E.
Rome fights a series of three wars, known as the Punic Wars, against Carthage.

THE MIGHT OF ROME

650 B.C.E.–476 C.E.

Above all else, Rome was about power, and Romans knew how to wield it to impose the people's will in republican times, or the tyrannical impulses of a single leader in the days of empire. Beyond the exploits of its armies, Rome showed its dominion in the countless structures it raised from Britain to the edges of Asia, as well as in the vast network of roads spanning thousands of miles that described the empire's physical extent. The power to fund such projects, control labor, and govern distant lands—to Romanize the world—is perhaps the best definition of Roman might. The origins of that power trace back to a community of farmers and shepherds living in the hills beside the Tiber River in the first half of the first millennium B.C.E. Among several ethnic groups, the Etruscans dominated, imposing a monarchy sometime around 650 B.C.E. In 509 B.C.E., the people rebelled, driving their Etruscan overlords from the city and establishing an early form of republicanism.

Over the next 250 years, Rome consolidated its hold over the Italian peninsula and then took on Carthage, battling its armies in a series of wars for the next 100 years. After a final victory in 146 B.C.E., Roman armies and warships turned their sights on the remnants of Alexander's empire in the east and eventually controlled the entire Mediterranean.

Relying on both military and administrative strengths, Rome ruled as a republic and as an empire for almost a thousand years. Its might finally gave way to internal weaknesses and external threats.

Rome became increasingly militaristic. After a period of turmoil, including clashes between rivals, Julius Caesar emerged. Returning from campaigns in Gaul, the general seized control of the government, setting in motion the downfall of the republic. His successors—beginning with his grandnephew Octavian, who became Augustus, the "revered one"—ruled as emperors.

The empire grew so extensive that it became unwieldy, so in 286 C.E. Diocletian split it into eastern and western halves; some 50 years later Constantine moved the capital to Byzantium in Asia Minor, renaming it Constantinople. Rome was on the way to becoming a backwater.

Its borders threatened by warrior peoples from the east and north, its own society racked by corruption and decadence, Rome fell from both within and without. The final blow came in 476 C.E., when the Germanic chieftain Odoacer, once a Roman soldier, deposed the last Roman emperor.

OPPOSITE: The Colosseum and the public baths of Titus and Trajan were gathering points for Roman citizens.

44 B.C.E.
Julius Caesar is assassinated after five years as dictator.

27 B.C.E.
Octavian becomes Augustus, first emperor of Rome.

286 C.E.
Diocletian divides the empire into eastern and western halves.

476 C.E.
Romulus Augustulus cedes power, ending the Western Roman Empire.

SEE ALSO | THE CLASSICAL AGE: PAGE 92

CLASS & SOCIETY

PATRICIANS AND PLEBES

The town of Pompeii was a popular vacation spot for wealthy Romans.

From its earliest days, Roman society consisted of two main groups, the patrician upper class and the common folk, or plebeians. Patricians were wealthy and politically powerful; most government positions and high military ranks belonged to them. The two consuls who led the republic were patricians, as initially were all the members of the senate, who advised the consuls. In the fifth century B.C.E., plebeians won the right to elect officials called tribunes, who served in separate assemblies, and plebeians eventually could be senators as well.

A young patrician could map out his future through what was known as the path of honor, rising from low magisterial offices up to consul. Plebeians gained status through military service or in one of several trade guilds. Some plebeian farmers owned their own land, but most were tenant farmers. Free women's power was usually limited to family management.

THE TAKEAWAY: Roman society was stratified, but even plebeians could rise to high positions.

THE MIGHT OF ROME

VIPs

Tiberius and Gaius Gracchus, 133–121 B.C.E.
Roman leaders who Instituted reforms

Marcus Tullius Cicero, 106–43 B.C.E.
Roman statesman, famous as an orator

Julius Caesar, 100–44 B.C.E.
General who conquered Gaul and Britain and became dictator

Augustus Caesar, 63 B.C.E.–14 C.E.
First emperor, initiated long period of stability

Constantine, 272–337 C.E.
Emperor who converted to Christianity, moved capital to Constantinople.

"*When you are at Rome live in the Roman style; when you are elsewhere live as they live elsewhere.*" —ST. AMBROSE

VOICES

POMPEII POLITICIANS, DRINKERS, AND LOVERS

"The worshipers of Isis as a body ask for the election of Gnaeus Helvias Sabinus as Aedile."

"The sneak thieves request the election of Vatia as Aedile."

"The whole company of late drinkers favor Vatia."

"Here slept Vibius Restitutus all by himself, his heart filled with longings for his Urbana."

"Health to you, Victoria, and wherever you are may you sneeze sweetly."

"Restitutus has many times deceived many girls."

"Romula kept tryst here with Staphylus."

—GRAFFITI FROM THE WALLS OF POMPEII

STATUE FROM POMPEII

DAILY LIFE ENTERTAINMENTS

With a suddenness that foiled escape, the volcano Vesuvius erupted in the summer of 79 C.E., burying Pompeii and Herculaneum in ash and mud—but preserving much of what we know about daily life in the Roman world. For patricians, it was a world of leisure and enjoyment. Rich families often had seaside villas as well as homes in town; the most lavish had private baths, but even city dwellings typically had enclosed garden courtyards called peristyles. Decorations abounded on walls and floors, but furnishings were sparse. The wealthy treated each other to lavish feasts and also ventured out, protected by bodyguards, to shop in the forum or attend the theater.

A fresco of frolicking cupids decorates a tomb in Pompeii.

{ Rome had both the Colosseum and the Circus Maximus, a chariot race track more than 2,000 feet from end to end. }

The lower classes, who lived in shoddy tenements or above shops, worked hard but also had their pleasures. Public baths with exercise yards were open to all, and bustling towns like Pompeii had taverns, wine bars, and brothels at almost every corner.

THE TAKEAWAY: Rich and poor alike enjoyed amusements ranging from soaks in the public baths to death matches in the coliseum.

"In Rome you long for the country; in the country—oh inconstant!—you praise the distant city to the stars." —HORACE

SEE ALSO | THE CLASSICAL AGE: PAGE 117

DAILY LIFE LIVES IN SERVITUDE

At its height, the city of Rome had a population of about a million—and more than 100,000 slaves. A wealthy landowner with a working estate might have several hundred slaves, but even a relatively poor householder might have two or three to help with menial chores. Slaves were both born and made. The child of slaves automatically entered servitude, but Roman armies boosted the ranks with captured enemies, warriors and civilians alike, and pirates also hauled in foreigners to sell at slave markets.

Bas-relief of gladiators

The life of a slave could be brutal or benign. Those who worked in mines and quarries, on building projects or as farm laborers were the worst off. Some powered treadmills; others served for years chained to their oars on galleys. Their diet was at subsistence levels, often doled out as feed was for livestock. Owners might brand their slaves or fit them with inscribed iron collars to identify them. One such collar read, "I have escaped from my post. Return me to Barbers' Street near the temple of Flora."

> Female slaves might work as maidservants to patrician women, but they were still subject to their master's sexual advances.

Gladiators were either slaves or criminals, and although they typically died gruesomely in the arena, they could also achieve a certain fame and perhaps win their freedom if they survived. Other slaves with special skills such as cooking or craftsmanship were in high demand and were treated well. Luckiest by far were the personal slaves of patrician masters, many of whom were educated and sometimes served as bookkeepers, secretaries, or even estate managers. Some earned the right to run their

COLUMELLA CHOOSING SLAVES FOR THE FARM

VOICES

ROMAN SLAVE MARKET

"The next point is with regard to slaves—over what duty it is proper to place each and to what sort of tasks to assign them. So my advice at the start is not to appoint an overseer from that sort of slaves who are physically attractive, and certainly not from that class which has busied itself with the voluptuous occupations of the city. The lazy and sleepy-headed class of servants, accustomed to idling, to the Campus, the Circus, and the theatres, to gambling, to cookshops, to bawdy-houses, never ceases to dream of these follies; and when they carry them over into their farming, the master suffers not so much loss in the slave himself as in his whole estate.... But be the overseer what he may, he should be given a woman companion to keep him within bounds."

—FROM *AGRICULTURE*, COLUMELLA, FIRST CENTURY C.E.

"Violence and injury enclose in their net all that do such things." —LUCRETIUS

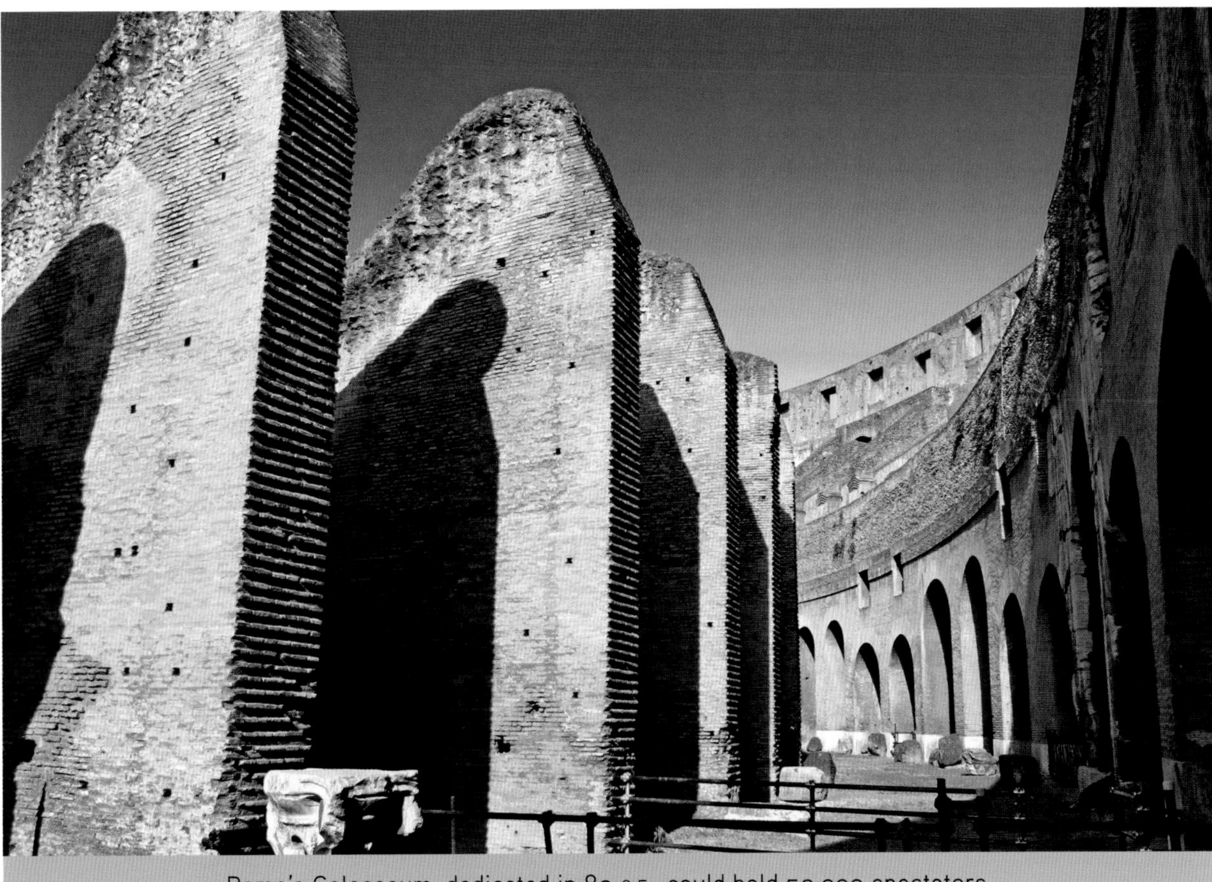

Rome's Colosseum, dedicated in 80 C.E., could hold 50,000 spectators.

own businesses, paying their owners a royalty for the privilege.

Slaves could buy their freedom, but the most devoted might be granted release as a gesture of gratitude. The bond was never completely broken, however; a freed slave owed his master the same devotions a son owed his father—plus perhaps several days or weeks of unpaid service every year. But freedom was freedom, especially since it included the right to Roman citizenship.

THE TAKEAWAY: Rome depended on slave labor at every level, from backbreaking toil to clerical work.

THUMBS UP / THUMBS DOWN

SPARTACUS ca 109–71 B.C.E.

SPARTACUS

CATO THE ELDER WROTE, "You have as many enemies as you have slaves." Indeed, Romans had long feared, and quashed, slave uprisings. But in 73 B.C.E., a slave gladiator named Spartacus led a two-year rebellion that shook Rome to its core. He and about 70 other slaves escaped from the gladiator school in Capua, seized weapons, and fled for the slopes of Vesuvius. After a stunning victory over an ill-prepared Roman troop, Spartacus attracted more followers, and soon his numbers swelled to 70,000, a ragtag army that for a time defeated every force sent against it. The senate finally ordered its best armies to return from foreign battlefields and eventually 40,000 Roman soldiers took on and defeated Spartacus, who, according to Plutarch, "was still defending himself when he was cut down." Roman general Crassus crucified 6,000 of the rebels as a warning, leaving their bodies to rot along the Appian Way. **CONCLUSION:** THUMBS UP.

"Slavery takes hold of few, but many take hold of slavery." —SENECA

SEE ALSO | THE WORLD AT WAR: PAGE 389

CONFLICTS THE ROMAN WAR MACHINE

If the quintessential Greek was a philosopher, the quintessential Roman was undoubtedly a soldier. Rome's centuries of dominating the world stage rested on the ability of its armies to subjugate foreign lands and impose order at home and abroad. Rome's first soldiers had to be landowners, a restriction that changed as the empire expanded. Recruits from the provinces swelled the ranks, and by the first century B.C.E., reforms instituted by the general and consul Gaius Marius covered landless plebeians. Long service, typically between 16 and 26 years, was rewarded: Foreigners gained citizenship after a full career, and retiring troops received grants of lands, usually in the provinces, a measure that helped ensure the spread of Roman culture throughout conquered territory. You didn't have to be from Rome to be Roman.

Organization was key to the army's many successes. The main unit was a legion of 4,000 to 6,000 infantry, or legionnaires, divided into 10 cohorts. Each of these cohorts consisted of several units, called centuries, with 80 to 100 men headed by a centurion. The whole legion attacked in three lines, with the youngest legionnaires in the front rank and the most experienced in the rear. Advancing on the enemy, legionnaires would either

Roman consul Decius Mus falls in the Battle of Sentium, 295 B.C.E.; painting by Rubens.

“I came, I saw, I conquered.” —JULIUS CAESAR

VOICES

ROMAN ARMY A SOLDIER'S OATH

"In the army of the consuls Gaius Laelius, son of Gaius, and Lucius Cornelius, son of Publius, and for ten miles around it, you will not with malice aforethought commit a theft, either alone or with others, of more than the value of a silver sesterce in any one day. And except for one spear, a spear shaft, wood, fruit, fodder, a bladder, a purse, and a torch, if you find or carry off anything there which is not your own and is worth more than one silver sesterce, you will bring it to the consul Gaius Laelius, son of Gaius, or to the consul Lucius Cornelius, son of Publius, or to whomsoever either of them shall appoint, or you will make known within the next three days whatever you have found or wrongfully carried off; or you will restore it to him whom you suppose to be its rightful owner, as you wish to do what is right."

—FROM *ATTIC NIGHTS*, AULUS GELLIUS, SECOND CENTURY C.E.

ROMAN SOLDIER

Roman-style chariots on a coin from Macedon.

hurl or thrust a six-foot javelin, then fight with a short, stabbing sword. Armor protected them, as did a heavy wood-and-leather shield with an iron rim, which legionnaires also used to knock down opponents.

In their many campaigns, the legions under Julius Caesar's generalship constructed massive ramps of wood and earth to breach defensive walls, built substantial bridges in as little as a day, and surrounded the army of Gallic leader Vercingetorix with a double-ringed wooden palisade more than 12 miles in circumference, forcing him to surrender. Roman forces also routinely built roads, aqueducts, defensive walls, and other structures.

> Terror was sometimes a Roman weapon: Julius Caesar ordered that all the Gauls of Uxellodunum who had fought against him have both their hands cut off.

Over several hundred years, Roman forces won territory from the moors of Scotland to the deserts of North Africa—but Roman against Roman was always the toughest fight.

THE TAKEAWAY: Rome's armies conquered with professionalism, organization, and strategy.

CONNECTIONS CROSSING THE RUBICON

WHEN MODERN ARMIES—OR MODERN INDIVIDUALS—travel past a point of no return, they are often said to have "crossed the Rubicon." The original Rubicon-crosser was Gaius Julius Caesar, whose success in foreign campaigns and popularity with the Roman people had made him a political threat to the Roman Republic's leadership. In 49 B.C.E., his army was fresh off its provincial conquests, which had subjugated some 300 Gallic tribes and caused the death of more than a million Gauls. Ordered to return to the city and disband his army, Caesar disobeyed, leading his men across northern Italy's Rubicon River, a natural boundary marking the border between Cisalpine Gaul and Roman Italy. His transgression started a bloody three-year civil war. With his powerful force of loyal veterans behind him, Caesar had by early 46 B.C.E. proclaimed himself dictator for life.

MODERN SOLDIERS ON THE MARCH

"Law stands mute in the midst of arms." —MARCUS TULLIUS CICERO

SEE ALSO | THE CLASSICAL AGE: PAGE 97

ARTS AFTER THE GREEKS

The arts were an everyday feature of life in ancient Rome. As the well-preserved ruins at Pompeii attest, the homes of the well-to-do were steeped in the visual arts. Virtually every wall bore murals depicting scenes from Greek mythology or views of nature, often enhanced with sophisticated techniques of perspective and shading to create a sense of depth. Floors were inlaid with complex mosaics consisting of thousands of multicolored tiles.

A Roman painting depicts Terpsichore, Greek muse of dance and song.

Comedic actors posture in a wall painting from Pompeii.

But there were feasts for other senses as well. Music was a constant companion, and women often performed on instruments such as the harp or kithara after banquets. Musicians playing flutes, drums, and cymbals plied the streets.

In both sculpture and literature, the Romans borrowed heavily from the Greeks, as in Virgil's epic poem *The Aeneid* or the histories of Livy and Tacitus. Roman poets could be both elegant and earthy, with Horace, Ovid, and the often bawdy Catullus leading the pack.

THE TAKEAWAY: Roman painters, writers, and musicians filled the everyday world with the arts.

Roman sculptors routinely reproduced the works of their Greek predecessors. In fact, many of the finest surviving examples of Greek sculpture are copies made in Roman times.

"I prefer that a boy should begin with the Greek language, because he will acquire Latin, which is in general use, even though we tried to prevent him." —QUINTILLIAN

RELIGION & PHILOSOPHY THE SPIRIT OF THE GODS

"We Romans owe our supremacy," wrote Cicero, "to our wisdom in believing that the spirit of the gods rules and directs everything." Indeed, the Romans filled their world with gods, from the Greek-borrowed pantheon to more exotic deities adopted from foreign cultures. Evil spirits were thought to be everywhere afoot, and children wore charms as protective talismans. The official state religion involved formal practices, including monthly festivals and sacrifices. Romans particularly revered Vesta, goddess of the hearth, and Vestal Virgins guarded her flame day and night in a temple situated prominently in the Forum. They also cared deeply about their household gods, some representing the spirits of ancestors, and worshiped them daily at a household shrine.

Cults arose in later years. Some worshiped living emperors as gods, but people seeking spiritual sustenance increasingly turned to foreign deities, such as the Egyptian goddess Isis. Mithras, a god with Persian roots who represented life after death, became a favorite of Roman soldiers.

THE TAKEAWAY: Official state gods, household gods, and foreign deities populated Roman beliefs.

Jupiter, in the form of a bull, carries off Europa in a Roman fresco.

CATULLUS ON A GIFT OF BAD POETRY

"If I did not love you more than my eyes, most delightful Calvus, for your gift I should hate you with Vatinian hatred. For what have I done or what have I said that you should torment me so vilely with these poets? . . . Great gods, what a horrible and accursed book which—if you please!—you have sent to your Catullus, that he might die of boredom the livelong day in the Saturnalia, choicest of days! No, no, my joker, you will not get off so easily: for at dawn I will haste to the booksellers' cases; the Caesii, the Aquini, Suffenus, every poisonous rubbish will I collect that I may repay you with these tortures. Meantime farewell! Be gone from here, where an ill foot brought you."

—FROM *CARMINA*, GAIUS VALERIUS CATULLUS, FIRST CENTURY B.C.E.

CATULLUS

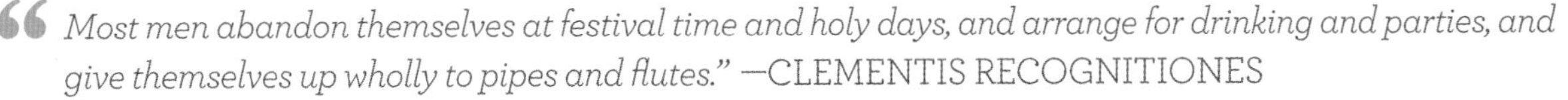

"Most men abandon themselves at festival time and holy days, and arrange for drinking and parties, and give themselves up wholly to pipes and flutes." —CLEMENTIS RECOGNITIONES

SCIENCE MARVELS OF ENGINEERING

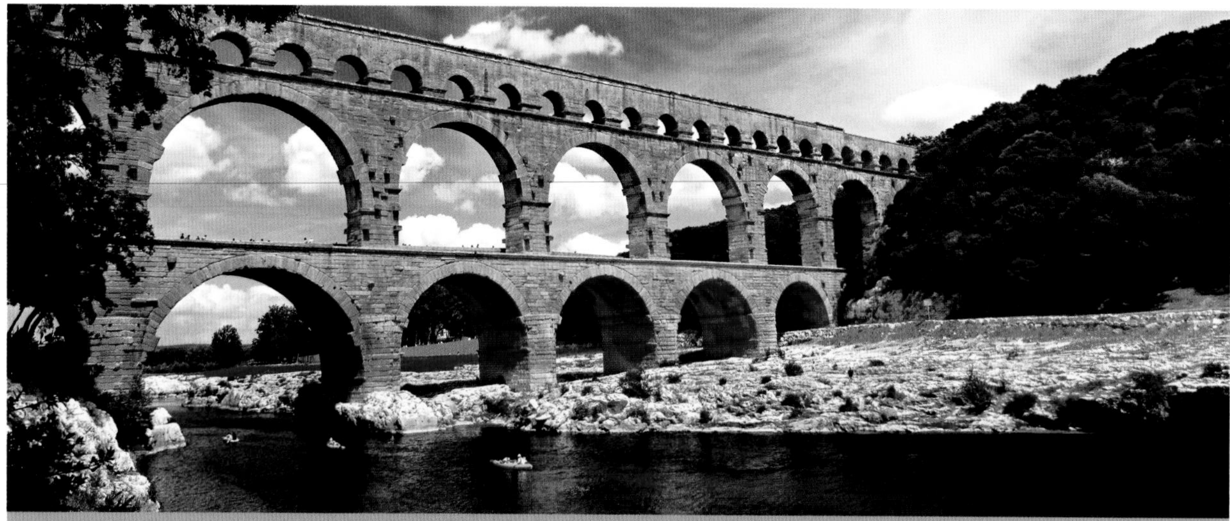

The Roman aqueduct Pont du Gard still stands near Nîmes in France.

Romans were master engineers, with a flair for both aesthetics and practicality. The aqueduct is a case in point. It took deft planning and surveying acumen to route a city's water supply from fresh sources miles away across elegant arched causeways in a steady downhill flow. Rome itself had 11 major aqueducts. Once it got to the city, water poured through underground pipes to reservoirs and cisterns, as well as baths, latrines, and fountains.

Romans used the arch everywhere, including in the massive 50,000-seat Colosseum, which had a water supply that could flood the arena for mock naval battles. The pinnacle of engineering, though, was the dome of Rome's Pantheon, temple to all the gods. The arched shape of the dome was an innovation that would be lost to subsequent builders for nearly 1,500 years. At 142 feet across, the Pantheon still boasts the world's largest unreinforced solid concrete dome.

THE TAKEAWAY: Rome's builders were masters of intelligent and innovative engineering.

CONNECTIONS A CONCRETE SOLUTION

To further their construction exploits, the Romans needed a building material that was more flexible than quarried stone. Experimenting with mixtures of volcanic ash, lime, rubble, and water, they came up with concrete sometime around 200 B.C.E. The lime and ash functioned like modern-day Portland cement and could also serve as mortar; mixing in fragments of rock, tile, brick, and other rubble and then adding water created the slow-hardening concrete. Its pliant quality and ability to be poured into molds made possible curved architectural shapes such as vault ceilings and domes. Concrete's waterproof nature also made it ideal for aqueduct channels and Rome's extensive roads.

KITT PEAK OBSERVATORY, BUILT FROM CONCRETE

“*I found Rome a city of bricks and left it a city of marble.*” —AUGUSTUS CAESAR

SEE ALSO | EPIC JOURNEYS: PAGE 36

VOICES

TACITUS REVOLT OF BOUDICCA IN BRITAIN

BOUDICCA

"Boudicca, in a [chariot], with her two daughters before her, drove through the ranks. She harangued the different nations in their turn: 'This,' she said, 'is not the first time that the Britons have been led to battle by a woman.' But now she did not come to boast the pride of a long line of ancestry, nor even to recover her kingdom and the plundered wealth of her family. She took the field, like the meanest among them, to assert the cause of public liberty, and to seek revenge for her body seamed with ignominious stripes, and her two daughters infamously ravished. From the pride and arrogance of the Romans nothing is sacred; all are subject to violation; the old endure the scourge, and the virgins are deflowered. But the vindictive gods are now at hand."

—FROM TACITUS, *ANNALS*, SECOND CENTURY C.E.

Portions of a Roman library remain in Ephesus, in present-day Turkey.

EMPIRES ROMAN BENEFITS

Rome conquered territory through military force, but the secret of its empire-building was to rule its provinces with a tolerant hand. Roman dominion came with benefits, including the rule of law within a province's borders and protection against barbarian incursions from without. Roman administrators allowed local customs, including religious practices, to survive. One carving in Gaul shows Cernunnos, the Celtic god of fertility, nestled between Apollo and Mercury.

> Rome's solidly built infrastructure helped the provinces thrive. One bridge in Spain is still in use.

The provinces paid hefty taxes but enjoyed the economic advantage of trade with Rome. The network of Roman roads kept goods flowing; by the turn of the millennium, postal stations along these routes improved communication.

Two things did the most to win provincial hearts and minds. One was the proffer of Roman citizenship to loyal provincials. The other was the raising of miniature Romes throughout the empire, complete with temples, forums, and theaters.

THE TAKEAWAY: Rome's culture lived on through the Romanization of its provinces.

"Whatever is unknown is taken for marvelous; but now the limits of Britain are laid bare."

—CORNELIUS TACITUS

SEE ALSO | POSTCLASSICAL ERA: PAGE 137

EMPIRES EAST LEAVES WEST

Diocletian, who split the empire, may never have seen Rome; Constantine ruled from Milan before heading east.

Under Augustus and a handful of later emperors, Rome ruled its burgeoning empire effectively, with little internal strife. But things soon changed. A series of emperors proved incompetent or unstable, and imperial affairs devolved to the point that, during one 50-year period in the third century C.E., 26 emperors and 40 usurpers trying to establish their own kingdoms rose to power—and fell. The empire was fracturing.

Constantinople held a crucial spot on the Bosporus Strait.

In Rome, as elsewhere, epidemics introduced along trade routes ravaged the population and disrupted harvest and shipments of grain on which cities depended. Out of this chaos emerged Diocletian, a cavalry commander who became emperor in a military coup in 284 C.E. He saved the empire by splitting it administratively into eastern and western halves and appointing a co-emperor. The plan brought stability but eventually helped precipitate the downfall of the west by elevating the importance of the east.

As the empire weakened, Christianity grew stronger, offering those in distress charity and a promise of eternal life. By 330, the emperor Constantine had embraced the new religion and moved the capital to Byzantium, on the Bosporus Strait. He renamed it Constantinople.

The empire's eastern half continued to thrive, stimulated by ongoing trade with peoples throughout the Near East and as far away as China. Eastern influences in the art and architecture of Constantinople and other cities, and the fact that Greek, not Latin, was the official language, confirmed that the eastern empire was a distinctly different world.

Emperor Constantine I ruled in the East.

THE TAKEAWAY: Waxing as the west waned, the eastern empire developed a different character.

“*It seems that when they show greatest reverence to the Deity, the greatest benefits accrue to the state.*” —CONSTANTINE I

CONFLICTS BARBARIANS BY OTHER NAMES

Waves of northerners invaded Rome for three centuries.

Known to this day as barbarians, the invading peoples who swept down on Rome were actually distinct societies lacking only written records. They had long threatened the empire's fringes; the Goths, a collection of eastern Germanic tribes, launched raids across the Danube as early as 150 C.E. Other Germanic tribes followed over the next three centuries, including the Burgundians, the Alemanni, and the Vandals from the north.

Weak at its core, Rome no longer could parry attacks. Emperor Valens was killed on the battlefield by Visigoth and Ostrogoth horsemen in 378, and Visigoth leader Alaric sacked Rome itself in 410. The next wave came from central Asia, when the Huns, skilled horsemen and archers, cut swaths through the provinces. Vandals followed two years later. The end came in 476, when Odoacer of the Germanic Scirii deposed the last emperor.

THE TAKEAWAY: Weakened internally, Rome couldn't thwart waves of invasion.

{ A 15-year epidemic, possibly smallpox, killed many Romans, including Emperor Marcus Aurelius in 180 C.E., leaving the empire vulnerable. }

VOICES

JORDANES THE ORIGIN OF THE HUNS

"We learn from old traditions that their [the Huns'] origin was as follows: Filimer, king of the Goths, . . . found among his people certain witches, whom he called in his native tongue Haliurunnae. Suspecting these women, he expelled them from the midst of his race and compelled them to wander in solitary exile afar from his army. There the unclean spirits, who beheld them as they wandered through the wilderness, bestowed their embraces upon them and begat this savage race, which dwelt at first in the swamps—a stunted, foul and puny tribe, scarcely human."

—FROM *THE ORIGIN AND DEEDS OF THE GOTHS*, SIXTH CENTURY C.E.

ATTILA THE HUN

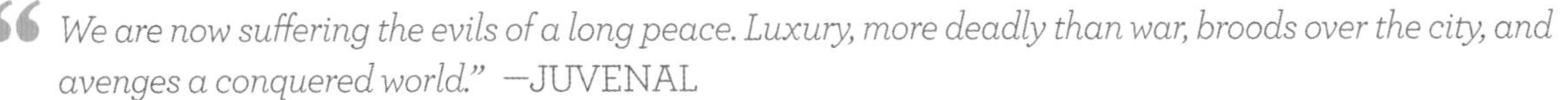

"We are now suffering the evils of a long peace. Luxury, more deadly than war, broods over the city, and avenges a conquered world." —JUVENAL

DEAD SEA SCROLLS

THE FIRST CENTURY C.E. was a turbulent time in the Roman province of Judea. One religious sect apparently felt the end so near that it took its most sacred texts into cliffside caves along a dry riverbed northwest of the Dead Sea, called the Wadi Qumran, and hid them away so well that they weren't found until a Bedouin shepherd boy stumbled upon them in 1947.

The Dead Sea Scrolls, more than 900 of them, include several copies of almost the entire Hebrew Bible, as well as other writings with an end-of-days flair reminiscent of an ascetic group known as the Essenes. Precisely who wrote and concealed the scrolls is unclear, but they confirm how crucial the texts were to the Jewish people.

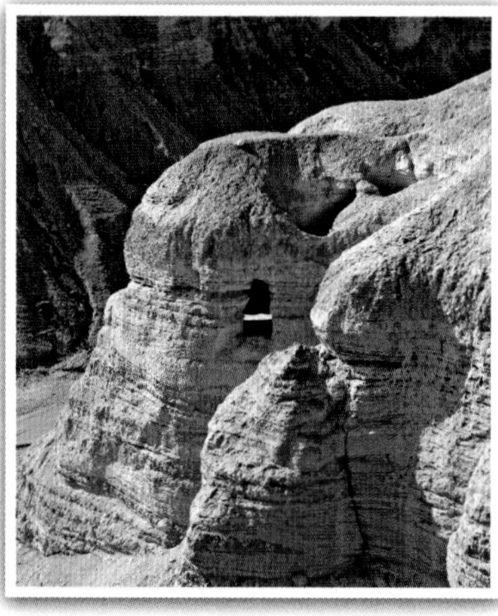

TREASURE TROVE The mouth of Cave 4, richest depository of scrolls, stands out against the forbidding limestone cliffs of the Wadi Qumran, now a national park. Fragments of more than 500 scrolls lay in this cave alone. The scrolls had been placed in pottery jars ranging from 18 to 25 inches in height.

“Hear O heavens and give ear O earth because YHWH declares: I have raised and matured sons and they have transgressed against me.”

“Your land is desolate, your cities burned with fire, your land, strangers devour it in your presence, and his desolation is upon her, as the overthrowing of strangers, and the daughter of Zion is left behind as a shed in a vineyard, and like a hut in a cucumber field, like a Nazarene city.”

ELEGANT SCRIPT The Isaiah Scroll (below), best preserved of all the scrolls, holds the text of Isaiah in neatly penned lines of Aramaic text, the common language of the area.

"Wash and make yourselves clean and turn away the evil of your habitual practices from before my eyes, stop doing evil."

ON-SITE RESEARCH Years after the initial discovery, archaeologists begin cataloging the scrolls and scroll fragments in the Qumran caves. Some pieces had to be recovered with tweezers.

"The voice said, Cry. And he said, What shall I cry? All flesh is grass, and all its beauty is as the flower of the field: The grass dries, the flower droops because the breath of YHWH blows on them: Surely the people are grass. The grass withers, the flower fades, but the word of our God will stand forever. Upon a mountain go, go up, with good news O Zion, raise up your voice in strength with good news; O Jerusalem, lift it up, do not be afraid; say to the cities of Judah, Behold your God. Behold, the Lord YHWH will come in strength, and his arm rules for him. Behold, his reward is with him, and his work before him. He shall feed his flock like a shepherd."

"Their land is full of silver and gold and there is no end to their wealth, also their land is full of horses and there is no end to their chariots. And their land is full of idols, the work of their hands, they worship that which their own fingers have made and humanity bows down and man is abased."

ANCIENT PAPER Most of the scrolls, including the one above, were written on parchment, some on papyrus, and a few on copper. The Temple Scroll is 27 feet long, divided into 66 columns of text.

DATES OF DISCOVERY

CAVE 1, 1947, contained two copies of Isaiah.

CAVE 2, February 1952, contained some 300 fragments.

CAVE 3, March 1952, included a copper scroll that listed hiding places of a treasure of gold, silver, and other valuables that has never been found.

CAVE 4, August 1952, contained 500 scrolls in some 15,000 fragments.

CAVES 5 AND 6 came to light shortly after Cave 4 and contain a few dozen of the texts.

CAVES 7, 8, AND 9, 1957, contained some Greek texts and copies of books of the Hebrew Bible.

CAVE 10, 1956, contained only a pottery fragment with two letters on it.

CAVE 11, 1956, included the Temple Scroll, which describes the Temple of Jerusalem's construction.

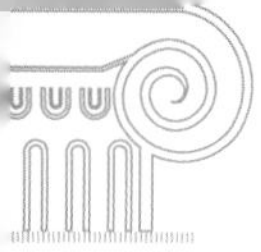

SEE ALSO | EPIC JOURNEYS: PAGE 49

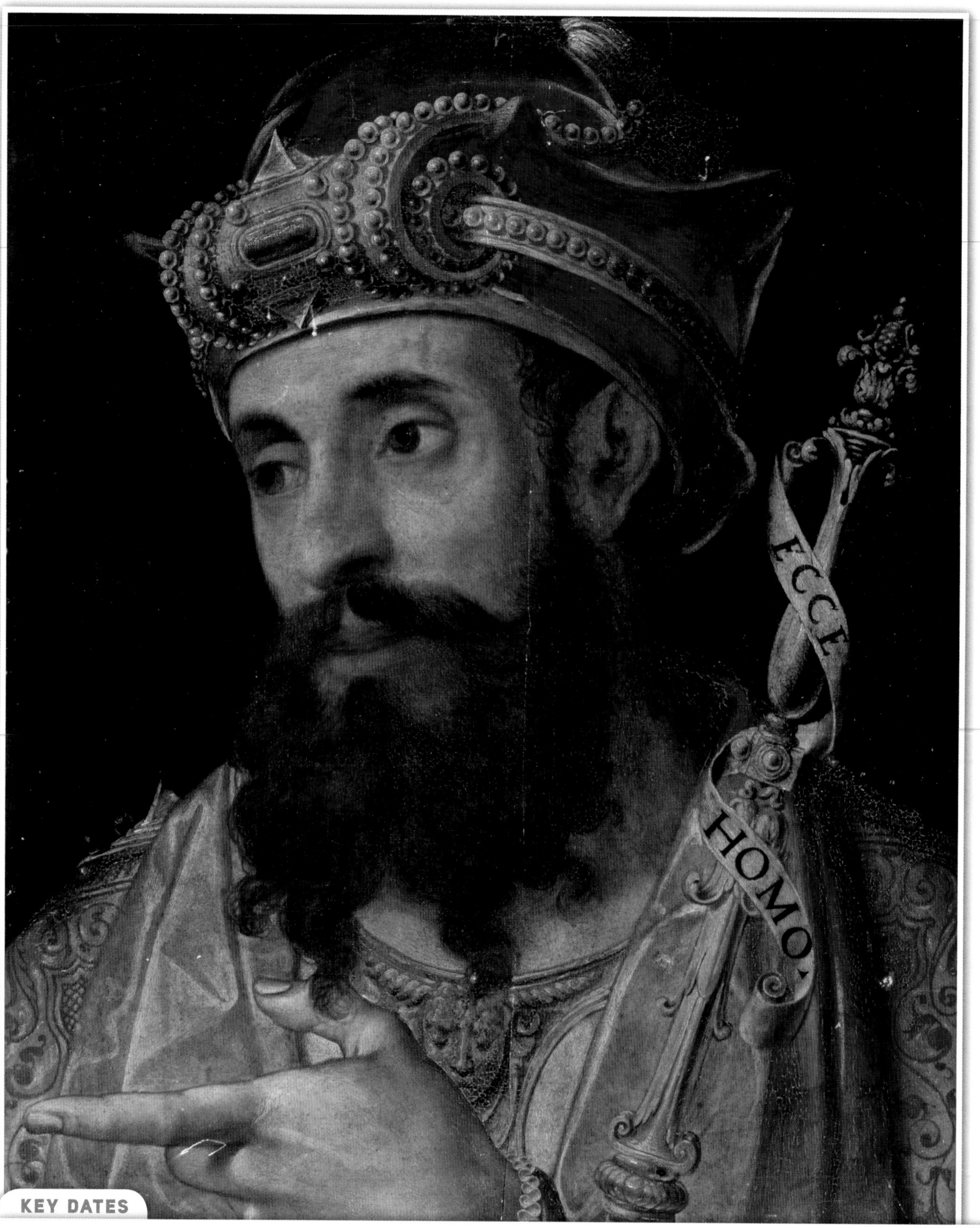

KEY DATES

539 B.C.E.
Israelites return from exile in Babylonia.

ca 520 B.C.E.
Second Temple is built in a recently restored Jerusalem.

444 B.C.E.
Jewish priests canonize the texts of the Torah.

164 B.C.E.
Hasmonean Revolt reestablishes Jewish authority in Jerusalem.

BIBLICAL LANDS

539 B.C.E.–70 C.E.

Both fertile and desolate, the area often referred to as the lands of the Bible—also known at various times as Canaan, Samaria, Judah, Judea, Palestine, and Israel—has throughout its history been a crossroads of cultures and a battleground of faith. Three of the world's great religions consider it sacred ground, especially the city of Jerusalem. During the classical age, when Greece and Rome flourished, the biblical lands saw conflict and oppression but also nurtured the new faith of Christianity, which would eventually spread across the globe. According to the Hebrew Bible—the Old Testament of the Christian Bible—God promised the lands of Canaan to his Chosen People, the Israelites, a Semitic tribe whose origins traced back to the patriarch Abraham. They founded the kingdom of Judah, with Jerusalem as its capital, sometime around 1000 B.C.E. Coveting the territory, the Babylonian king Nebuchadrezzar II sacked Jerusalem in 587 B.C.E., destroyed the sacred temple built by Solomon, and exiled the Jewish people to Babylon. But Babylon itself soon fell prey to the Persians, and in 539 B.C.E. the Israelites were allowed to return to Jerusalem, marking the beginning of a renewed Jewish presence.

The biblical lands of Palestine and Judea changed political hands time and again, but despite the conflicts, the region nurtured Judaism and gave birth to Christianity.

Judah and to the north, Samaria, later known as Palestine, would remain Persian provinces until the time of Alexander, but the Jewish people maintained a degree of religious autonomy. They rebuilt the temple and canonized their most sacred texts, the Torah. An uneasy peace held sway until the Ptolemaic king Antiochus plundered the temple in 168 B.C.E., installing an altar to Zeus. The Jews revolted under Judah Maccabee, head of a priestly family, and reclaimed the Temple, ushering in a 100-year period of Jewish rule.

Conflict was ever present, though, and in the first century B.C.E., Rome annexed the entire territory, which they called Judea. Concerned about uprisings, the Jewish establishment and their Roman overlords quashed all dissent, rounding up Jesus of Nazareth in the process. Some 40 years after his crucifixion, Roman forces sacked Jerusalem and razed the temple in response to another revolt. The last rebels died—either by their own hands or in a last-ditch fight—in the clifftop fortress of Masada in 73 C.E. Jews were later banned from Jerusalem and dispersed to other lands.

OPPOSITE: Pontius Pilate, Roman governor of Judea, earned the enmity of the Jewish population.

63 B.C.E.
Rome annexes the Judean state.

6 C.E.
Rome makes Judea an official province, with a governor.

ca 30 C.E.
Jesus of Nazareth is crucified for teachings deemed dangerous by authorities.

73 C.E.
The Great Jewish Revolt against Rome ends at Masada.

SEE ALSO | THE CLASSICAL AGE: PAGE 117

DAILY LIFE

TOWN AND COUNTRY

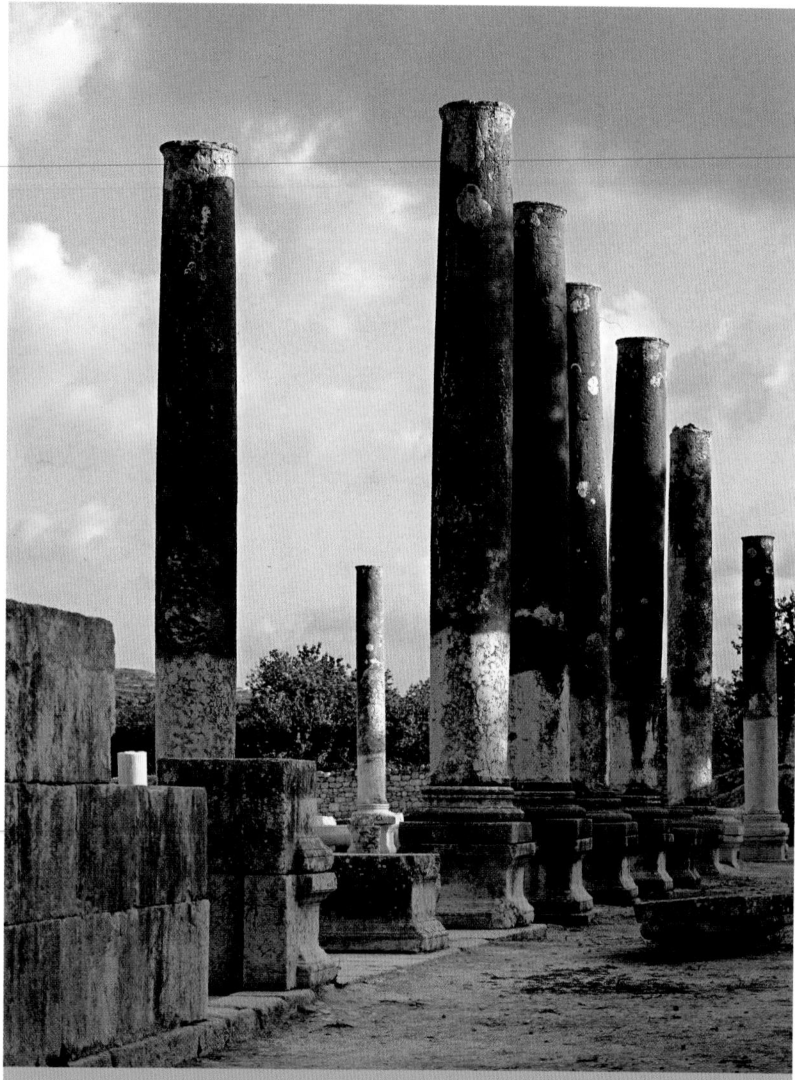

A colonnade marks the Roman forum in Samaria, present-day Israel.

The lands of the Bible were a study in contrasts, not least in the life of the people. For the most part agrarian, the society also had room for city dwellers engaged in commerce and trade with other parts of the classical world. Though there were harsh deserts to the south, most of the land was rich. In the second century B.C.E., a man named Aristeas noted that the country was heavily planted in olive trees, "with crops of corn and pulses, with vines too, and there is an abundance of honey."

Small rural communities had panels of judges who settled disputes and could impose taxes. Cities were managed by larger groups of elders from the priestly aristocracy. The common city folk included many artisans, those of Jerusalem being noted for their skill. Around the turn of the millennium, Hellenistic influences became increasingly apparent in architecture and in the lifestyles of the wealthier classes.

THE TAKEAWAY: Fruits of the land and skilled craftsmen supported thriving communities.

BIBLICAL LANDS

VIPs

Nehemiah, 445–413 B.C.E. Jewish leader who rebuilt Jerusalem, ended period of corruption

Judah Maccabee, 167–164 B.C.E. Jewish leader who led Hasmonean Revolt

Herod the Great, 73–4 B.C.E. King of Judea, productive but cruel

Herod Antipas, 21 B.C.E.–39 C.E. Son of Herod the Great, tetrarch of Galilee

Saul of Tarsus, c. 5 B.C.E.–67 C.E. Convert to Christianity who changed name to Paul and spread new faith

Jesus of Nazareth, ca 4 B.C.E.–ca 30 C.E. Religious leader many believed to be the Messiah

"They will leave you no grain, new wine or oil, nor any calves of your herds or lambs of your flocks until you are ruined." —BIBLE, DEUTERONOMY 28:51

Herod the Great's temple in Jerusalem was eventually destroyed during a Roman siege.

RELIGION YAHWEH'S PEOPLE

Nothing was more important to the Jews than their faith, which was founded on the concept of a covenant between themselves and God. They described the history of this relationship in the Torah—the first five books of the Hebrew Bible—which also detailed specific laws the people were to follow. Priests read from the Torah in synagogues that existed in virtually every Jewish community, reminding the people of their obligations; hardships were considered signs that their faithfulness had fallen short.

Toward the turn of the millennium, sects calling for a stricter adherence to the law began to emerge. One such group, the Pharisees, believed a Messiah foretold by scripture would deliver them from oppression. But they soon became members of the religious establishment, seeking accommodations with secular authorities. Others turned zeal into outright rebellion, which ended disastrously in the face of overwhelming Roman power.

> God's name, "I Am," represented by the four letters YHWH, or Yahweh, was considered too holy to utter.

THE TAKEAWAY: Many Jews saw oppression and persecution as a sign of God's displeasure.

THUMBS UP / THUMBS DOWN

HEROD THE GREAT ca 74–4 B.C.E.

HEROD THE GREAT

THE ROMAN PRACTICE of installing puppet rulers led the senate to name Herod, from a high-ranking Jewish family, king of the Jews in 40 B.C.E.. Herod began a building campaign that included expanding the Second Temple complex, raising fortresses at Masada and Herodium, and resurrecting the coastal city of Caesarea Maritima. But he was unpopular: Known for brutality and paranoia, Herod executed three sons on charges of conspiring against him. The Bible recounts that he ordered the slaughter of all male children in and near Bethlehem in an attempt to eliminate a rival king of the Jews. According to the historian Josephus, Herod died an excruciating death, possibly from kidney disease. **CONCLUSION: THUMBS DOWN**

> *"The Egyptians worship many animals and images of monstrous form; the Jews have purely mental conceptions of Deity, as one in essence."* —TACITUS

THE CLASSICAL AGE: BIBLICAL LANDS

SEE ALSO | POSTCLASSICAL AGE: PAGE 156

RELIGION

THE CHRISTIAN REVOLUTION

Early Christian bishops gathered at the Council of Nicaea in 325 C.E.

Turmoil was rampant in the world into which Jesus of Nazareth was born. Roman rule was an increasingly bitter pill for the common people, who were also losing faith in the religious establishment. Some sects called for returning to a strict adherence to Jewish law, but others hoped for a more dramatic turnaround. They looked to the scriptural prophecy that a savior would arise to free them. The most radical groups felt this Messiah would be a political leader who would overthrow Rome; others, such as a solitary preacher named John the Baptist, longed for a deliverer who would purify the faith.

Sometime around 26 or 27 C.E., Jesus came to John to be baptized and shortly thereafter began a three-year ministry. Gathering large crowds throughout his native

VOICES

PLINY LETTER TO EMPEROR TRAJAN ON THE CHRISTIANS

CHRISTIAN MARTYR

"This is the plan which I have adopted in the case of those Christians who have been brought before me. I ask them whether they are Christians, if they say 'Yes,' then I repeat the question the second time, and also a third—warning them of the penalties involved; and if they persist, I order them away to prison. . . . Those who denied that they were or had been Christians and called upon the gods with the usual formula, reciting the words after me, and those who offered incense and wine before your image —which I had ordered to be brought forward for this purpose, along with the regular statues of the gods—all such I considered acquitted—especially as they cursed the name of Christ, which it is said bona fide Christians cannot be induced to do."

—FROM PLINY THE YOUNGER, ca 112 C.E.

"What indeed has Athens to do with Jerusalem? What concord is there between the Academy and the Church? What between heretics and Christians?" —TERTULLIAN

VOICES

MARK THE HIGH PRIEST QUESTIONS JESUS

"They took Jesus to the high priest; and all the chief priests, the elders, and the scribes were assembled. Peter had followed him at a distance, right into the courtyard of the high priest; and he was sitting with the guards, warming himself at the fire. Now the chief priests and the whole council were looking for testimony against Jesus to put him to death; but they found none. For many gave false testimony against him, and their testimony did not agree. Some stood up and gave false testimony against him, saying 'We heard him say 'I will destroy this temple that is made with hands, and in three days I will build another, not made with hands.' But even on this point their testimony did not agree. Then the high priest stood up before them and asked Jesus, 'Have you no answer? What is it that they testify against you?' But he was silent and did not answer."

—BIBLE, BOOK OF MARK, 14:53–61

ST. MARK

Galilee, he preached a message of forgiveness, love, and renewal. He often talked about fulfilling the scriptures but stopped short of openly declaring himself the Messiah. But as he entered Jerusalem to celebrate Passover in about 30 C.E., adoring throngs greeted him as a liberating king. Religious authorities soon arrested him on charges of blasphemy and then turned him over to the Roman governor Pontius Pilate, who had him crucified as a political dissident.

{ The four Gospels of the New Testament are the sole source of information about the life of Jesus. Mark, the earliest, was probably written after the destruction of the temple in 70 C.E. }

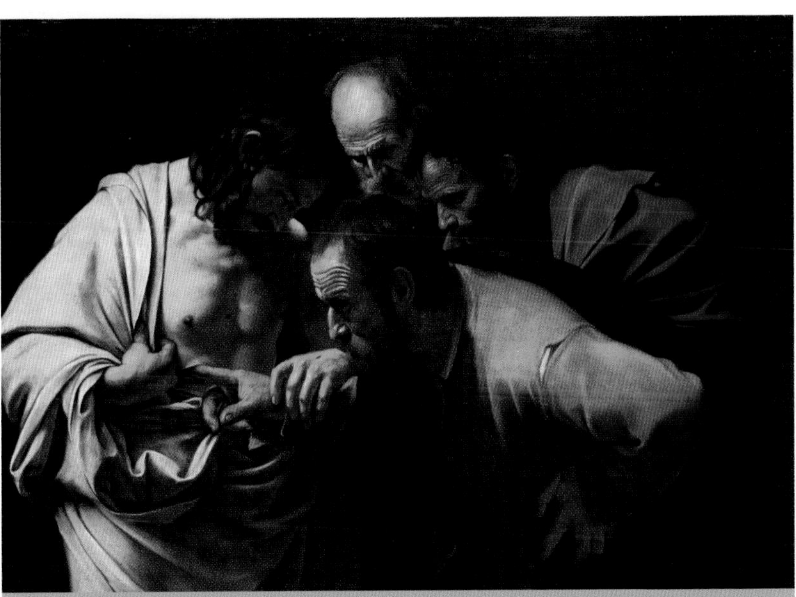

Jesus' apostle Thomas was said to doubt the resurrection.

The Bible says that Jesus rose from the dead two days after his crucifixion. His followers were inspired to spread the gospel, or "good news," of his life and ministry. They called him the Christ, or the "anointed one," and soon began referring to themselves as Christians. Despite persecution, they quickly gained adherents. One was a man named Saul, who had aggressively hunted down Christians until he had a conversion experience while traveling to Damascus. He changed his name to Paul and became the new faith's most vociferous advocate, traveling throughout the eastern Mediterranean and as far as Rome, spreading the word. The Christian revolution was under way.

THE TAKEAWAY: Beginning in turmoil, Christianity spread as far as Rome.

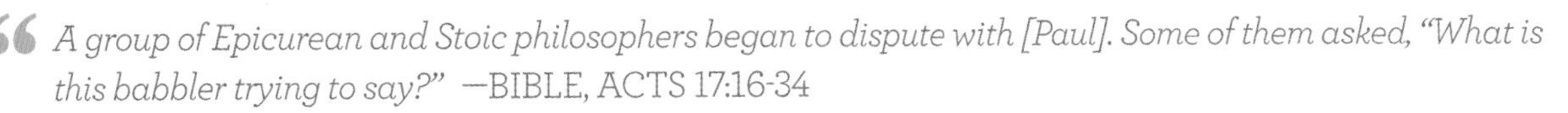

"A group of Epicurean and Stoic philosophers began to dispute with [Paul]. Some of them asked, "What is this babbler trying to say?" —BIBLE, ACTS 17:16-34

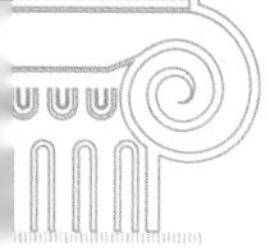

SEE ALSO | EPIC JOURNEYS: PAGE 31

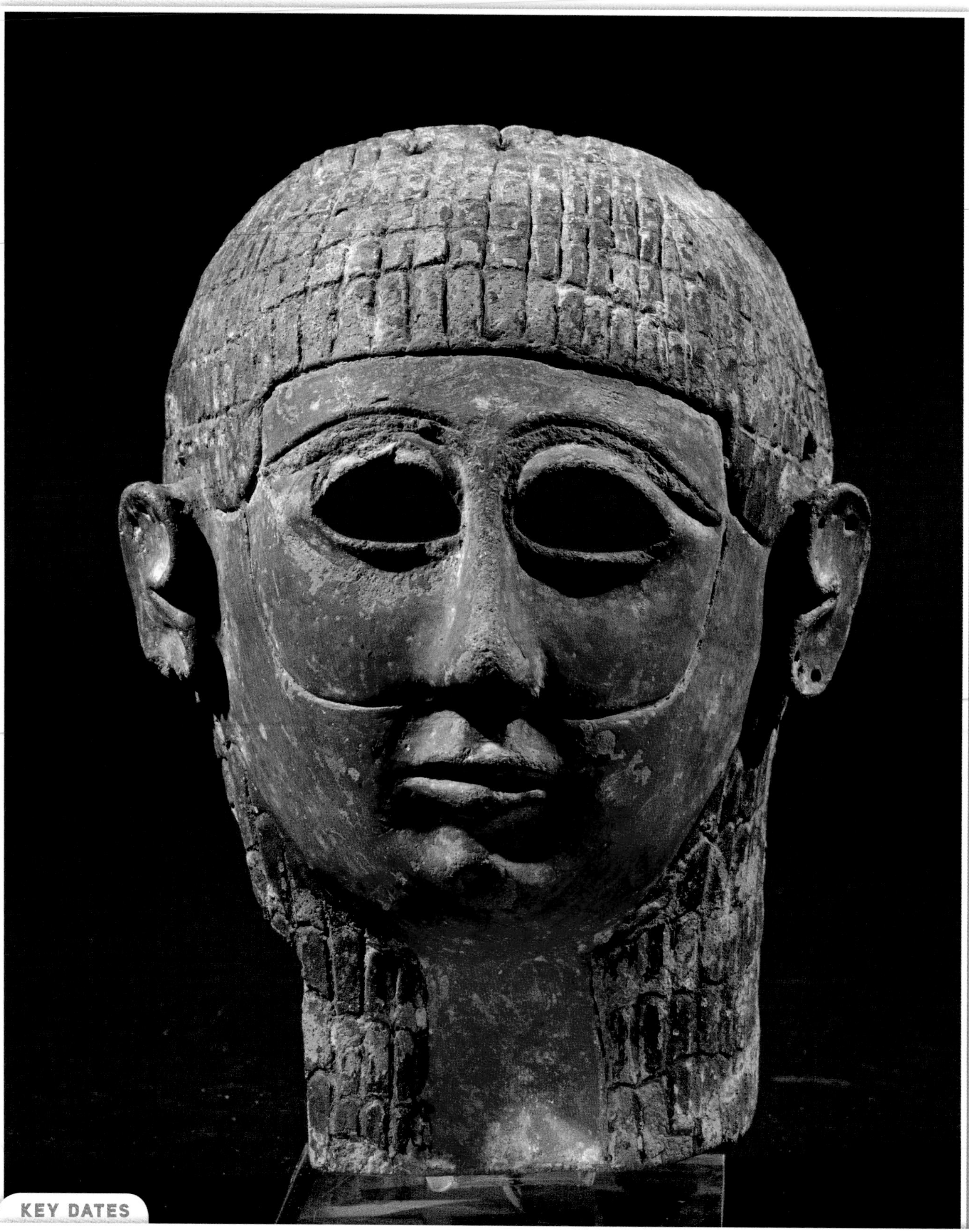

KEY DATES

530 B.C.E.
Kushite capital moves to Meroë.

ca 500 B.C.E.
Nok people begin making distinctive clay pots and sculpture.

ca 400–300 B.C.E.
Phoenician colony of Carthage dominates West Africa.

264 B.C.E.
First of three Punic Wars between Rome and Carthage begins.

NORTH AFRICA

500 B.C.E.–500 C.E.

In North Africa, civilization didn't stop with Egypt. Several cultures thrived to the south and west, both along the Mediterranean coast and farther inland. Their stories are little known to history primarily because, with one exception, they never developed written languages. But contemporary commentators from Egypt and Rome provide details, as do extensive artifacts. Some of the cultures of North Africa were colonies of Mediterranean societies, most notably Carthage. But others were distinct civilizations with roots tracing back to the second and third millennia B.C.E. Immediately to the south of Egypt lay the black African kingdom of Nubia, which achieved prosperity through agriculture, cattle herding, and gold mining. Nubians interacted with the pharaonic Egyptians for centuries, and were particularly noted for their archery skills, often serving in Egypt's armies.

Over time, a new kingdom called Kush took form in Nubian lands. Egypt often dominated Kush, but around the eighth century B.C.E., a Kushite king named Piye established a dynasty in Egypt that ruled for several centuries. The Kushites were eventually pushed back south, forming a new capital at Meroë, on the upper Nile's east bank. They retained many Egyptian customs but also developed their own form of writing, with a hieroglyphic alphabet that remains undeciphered. They also began smelting iron from rich ore deposits.

Trade was widespread across North Africa, and Nubian traders probably introduced iron smelting to the Nok people of present-day Nigeria. Around 500 B.C.E., Nok civilization blossomed as new iron tools, including axes and hoes, allowed more land to be turned to agriculture. The Nok also used their shallow-pit furnaces to fire clay, creating a unique style of terra-cotta pottery, as well as animal and human figurines. Unlike the idealized sculptures of Greece and Egypt, Nok figurines exhibit exaggerated features and expressions that heighten their emotional impact.

{ Egyptian influences blended with local customs in kingdoms along the Nile's upper reaches. To the west, the Nok people developed a distinct artistic style that spread to other West African cultures. }

South of Kush, a new kingdom arose in the first centuries C.E., centered on the town of Aksum in present-day Ethiopia. They defeated the Kushites, adopted Christianity, and became the most prosperous power in sub-Saharan Africa. By about 500 C.E., the Aksum kingdom stretched from southern Egypt to the southern Arabian Peninsula.

OPPOSITE: A bearded terra-cotta mask from Carthage dates to the fourth century B.C.E.

146 B.C.E. Rome defeats Carthage.

ca 30 C.E. Ethiopian kingdom of Aksum is founded.

331 C.E. Aksumite king Ezana converts to Christianity.

ca 350 C.E. Aksum defeats kingdoms in Meroë and southern Arabian Peninsula.

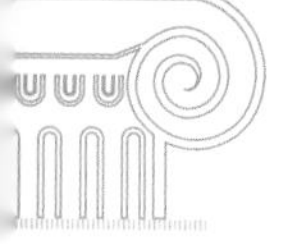

SEE ALSO | THE CLASSICAL AGE: PAGE 112

CONFLICTS THE RISE & FALL OF CARTHAGE

The Phoenician people of present-day Lebanon had a wanderlust. Excellent seafarers, they began establishing trading posts around the Mediterranean as early as 1000 B.C.E. By the middle of the millennium, their colony of Carthage, on the coast of present-day Tunisia, had risen to prominence, establishing colonies of its own in Sicily and on islands off the coast of Spain. Carthage was a thriving city, with a population that may have reached 700,000 at its height. A 20-mile-long wall girdled the city, which included buildings as tall as six stories. Its people retained many Phoenician practices, including worship of the god Baal Hammon and the lunar goddess Tanit.

> In its heyday, Carthage constructed a double-ringed harbor with trading vessels moored in the outer ring and military craft hidden from view in the inner ring.

Carthage's main interest was trade, but expansionist tendencies inevitably brought it into conflict with Greece and then Rome, both of whom had competing colonies in Sicily and elsewhere. Trading alliances ensured an uneasy peace for some three centuries, but when Rome took over the town of Messina in northeast Sicily in 264 B.C.E., open warfare broke out, launching the first of the three Punic Wars, a name derived from the Latin word for Phoenicia.

Riding the superior strength of its warships and legions, Rome was triumphant in the first Punic War, which dragged on for 23 years. Carthage abandoned its colonies in Sicily, but in 237 B.C.E., the Carthaginian general Hamilcar Barca established military outposts in Spain as a challenge to Rome. His son Hannibal, who as a boy had taken a pledge to destroy Rome, began the second Punic War with raids across the Ebro River in Spain in 218 B.C.E. His famous march on the Italian peninsula, complete with elephants, threatened Rome itself, but after 15 years of fighting he was forced to withdraw. Four years later, the Roman general Publius Cornelius Scipio—later known as Scipio Africanus—defeated Hannibal at Zama, southwest of Carthage.

The final end for Carthage came in 146 B.C.E. during the third

POLYBIUS THE DESTRUCTION OF CARTHAGE

VOICES

"At the sight of the city utterly perishing amidst the flames Scipio burst into tears, and stood long reflecting on the inevitable change which awaits cities, nations, and dynasties, one and all, as it does every one of us men. This, he thought, had befallen Ilium, once a powerful city, and the once mighty empires of the Assyrians, Medes, Persians, and that of Macedonia lately so splendid. And unintentionally or purposely he quoted—the words perhaps escaping him unconsciously—'the day shall be when holy Troy shall fall, And Priam, lord of spears, and Priam's folk.' And on my asking him boldly (for I had been his tutor) what he meant by these words, he did not name Rome distinctly, but was evidently fearing for her, from this sight of the mutability of human affairs."

—FROM POLYBIUS *HISTORIES*, SECOND CENTURY B.C.E.

POLYBIUS

"You know how to win a victory, Hannibal, but not how to use it." —MAHARBAL

VOICES

HANNO ON DISCOVERING GORILLAS

"We arrived at a bay called the Southern Horn; at the bottom of which lay an island like the former, having a lake, and in this lake another island, full of savage people, the greater part of whom were women, whose bodies were hairy, and whom our interpreters called Gorillae. Though we pursued the men we could not seize any of them; but all fled from us, escaping over the precipices, and defending themselves with stones. Three women were however taken; but they attacked their conductors with their teeth and hands, and could not be prevailed upon to accompany us."

—FROM ACCOUNTS OF CARTHAGINIAN HANNO THE NAVIGATOR, ca 500 B.C.E.

HANNO'S FLEET

{ Rome suffered the worst defeat in its history at Cannae in 216 B.C.E., when Hannibal trapped and killed some 50,000 legionnaires. }

and last Punic War. The city was utterly destroyed, and according to Roman historians the Roman conquerors plowed salt into the blasted soil so that nothing would ever grow there again.

THE TAKEAWAY: Carthage dominated the western Mediterranean for several centuries but ultimately fell to the power of Rome.

The ancient city of Carthage fell after more than a century of warfare with Rome.

"A lesson to posterity that in actual war it is better to have half the number of infantry, and the superiority in cavalry, than to engage your enemy with an equality in both." —POLYBIUS

CONNECTIONS TIME LINE

600 B.C.E.–500 C.E.

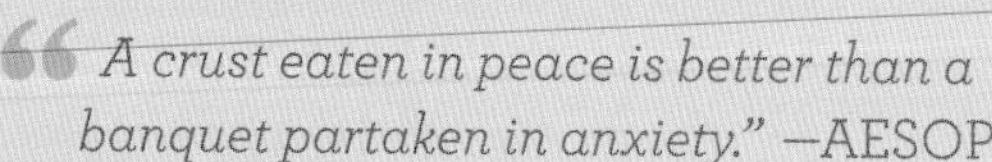

“A crust eaten in peace is better than a banquet partaken in anxiety.” —AESOP

149 B.C.E.
Carthaginians defend their city from the Romans in the third Punic War.

PUNIC WARS

500 B.C.E.
Buddhism begins to spread through northern India.

300 B.C.E.
The Anasazi of southwestern North America begin cultivating corn.

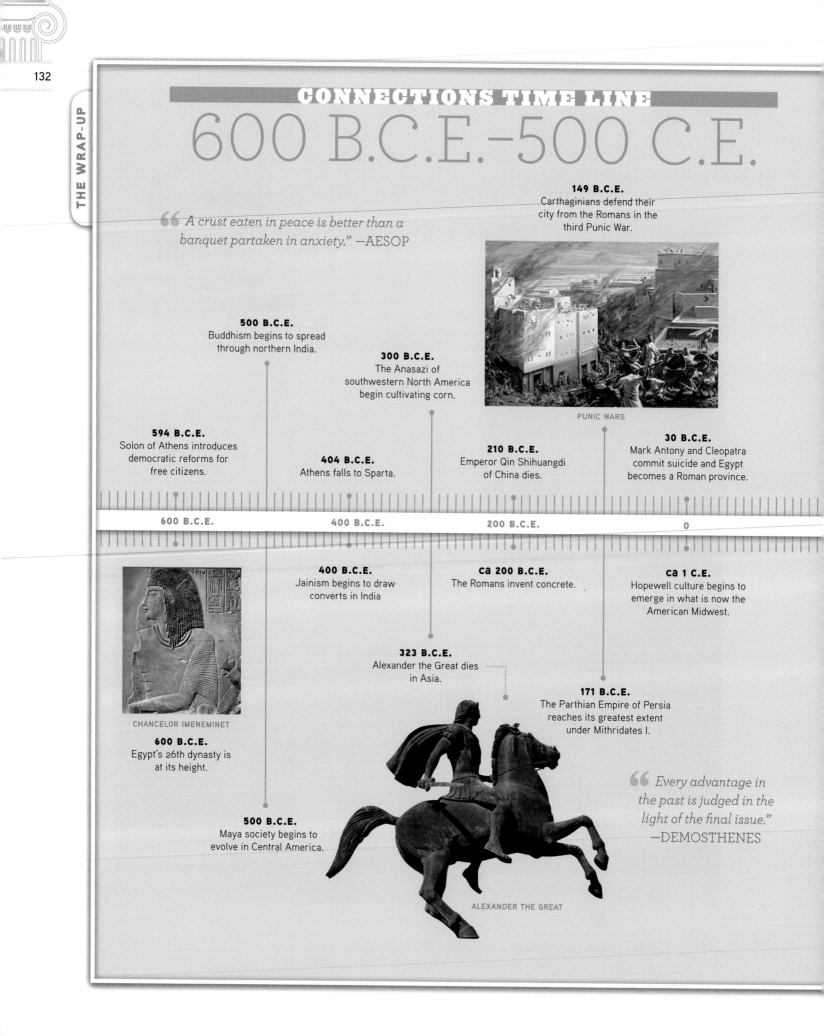

594 B.C.E.
Solon of Athens introduces democratic reforms for free citizens.

404 B.C.E.
Athens falls to Sparta.

210 B.C.E.
Emperor Qin Shihuangdi of China dies.

30 B.C.E.
Mark Antony and Cleopatra commit suicide and Egypt becomes a Roman province.

600 B.C.E. | 400 B.C.E. | 200 B.C.E. | 0

CHANCELOR IMENEMINET

600 B.C.E.
Egypt's 26th dynasty is at its height.

400 B.C.E.
Jainism begins to draw converts in India

ca 200 B.C.E.
The Romans invent concrete.

ca 1 C.E.
Hopewell culture begins to emerge in what is now the American Midwest.

323 B.C.E.
Alexander the Great dies in Asia.

171 B.C.E.
The Parthian Empire of Persia reaches its greatest extent under Mithridates I.

500 B.C.E.
Maya society begins to evolve in Central America.

ALEXANDER THE GREAT

“Every advantage in the past is judged in the light of the final issue.”
—DEMOSTHENES

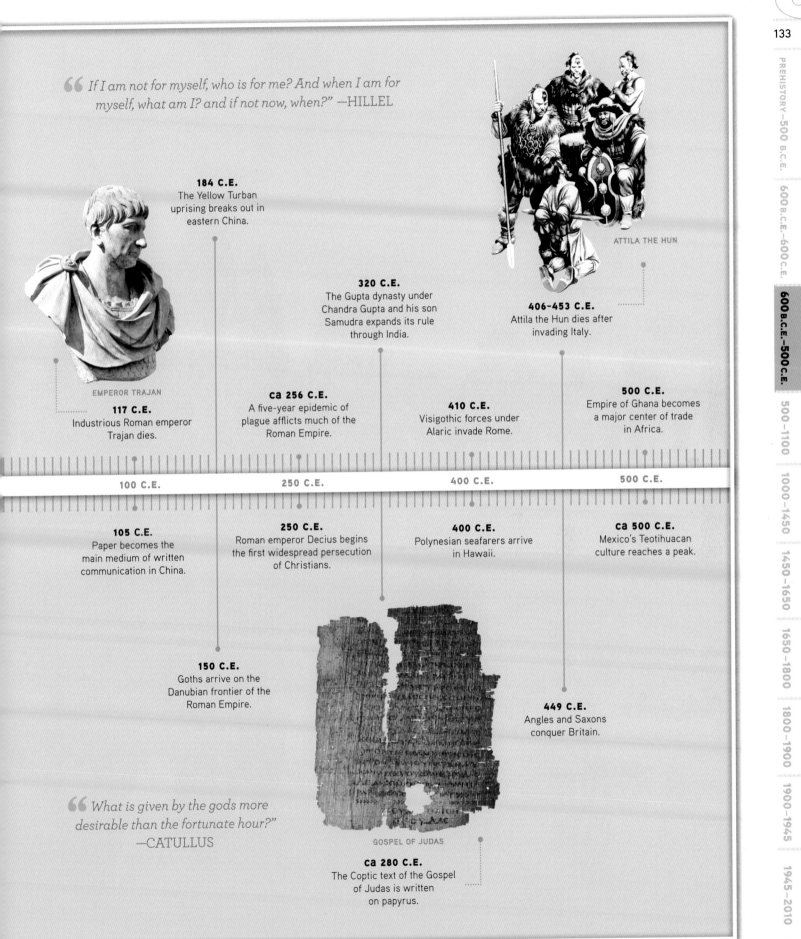

"If I am not for myself, who is for me? And when I am for myself, what am I? and if not now, when?" —HILLEL

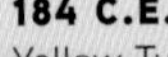

EMPEROR TRAJAN

117 C.E.
Industrious Roman emperor Trajan dies.

184 C.E.
The Yellow Turban uprising breaks out in eastern China.

ca 256 C.E.
A five-year epidemic of plague afflicts much of the Roman Empire.

320 C.E.
The Gupta dynasty under Chandra Gupta and his son Samudra expands its rule through India.

410 C.E.
Visigothic forces under Alaric invade Rome.

ATTILA THE HUN

406–453 C.E.
Attila the Hun dies after invading Italy.

500 C.E.
Empire of Ghana becomes a major center of trade in Africa.

100 C.E. | 250 C.E. | 400 C.E. | 500 C.E.

105 C.E.
Paper becomes the main medium of written communication in China.

250 C.E.
Roman emperor Decius begins the first widespread persecution of Christians.

400 C.E.
Polynesian seafarers arrive in Hawaii.

ca 500 C.E.
Mexico's Teotihuacan culture reaches a peak.

150 C.E.
Goths arrive on the Danubian frontier of the Roman Empire.

GOSPEL OF JUDAS

ca 280 C.E.
The Coptic text of the Gospel of Judas is written on papyrus.

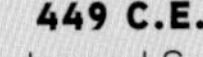

449 C.E.
Angles and Saxons conquer Britain.

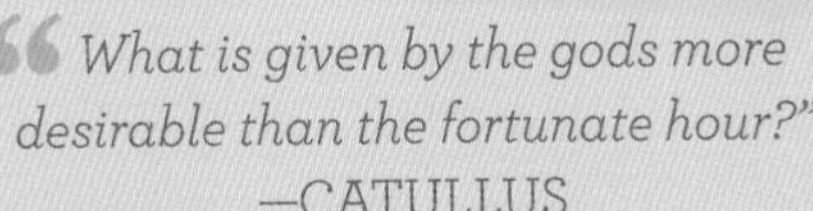

"What is given by the gods more desirable than the fortunate hour?" —CATULLUS

POSTCLASSI

CAL ERA

EMERGING VOICES

500–1100

CHAPTER

4

Angkor Wat was the heart of the Khmer capital for six centuries.

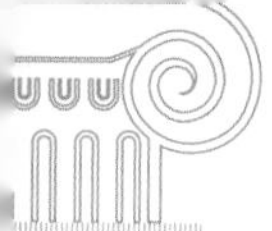

SEE ALSO | THE CLASSICAL AGE: PAGE 118

KEY DATES

527–565
Reign of Emperor Justinian, who codifies Roman law and rebuilds much of Constantinople.

532
Nika Riots cause widespread destruction and burning in the city.

550
Silk production begins in Constantinople after Christian emissaries bring silkworms back from China.

673
Byzantine warriors use "Greek fire" (combustible sulfur) for the first time.

BYZANTIUM

527–1054

The Western Roman Empire collapsed in the fifth century, but the eastern portion, known as the Byzantine Empire or simply Byzantium, was just beginning to shine. Citizens still considered themselves Romans, though their language, Romaic, was actually Greek. The center of Byzantine life was the great walled city of Constantinople (formerly called Byzantium), situated on a peninsula between the Black Sea and the Aegean and controlling much of the trade and traffic between Europe and the East. The empire reached its pinnacle under Justinian, emperor from 527 to 565, who expanded its boundaries and reclaimed some of the Roman territory lost to barbarians in preceding centuries. Counseled by his iron-fisted wife, Theodora, an erstwhile belly dancer and prostitute, Justinian quelled rioters protesting high taxes and food shortages. Though tens of thousands were killed, the emperor's rule was never seriously threatened again. Justinian orchestrated the writing of the Justinian Code, a compendium of civil laws that has formed the basis of most Western legal systems, and directed the construction of the Hagia Sophia cathedral, an enduring architectural masterpiece.

The Eastern Roman Empire, centered on Constantinople, held on long after the fall of Rome, its geographical location bringing both riches and troubles as neighboring states swelled their boundaries.

Justinian's successors lost control of Italy and other western holdings, in large part because Christians there recognized the pope rather than the Byzantine patriarch as their spiritual leader. Within the Byzantine world, a bitter dispute arose over iconoclasm—an eighth-century imperial effort to ban sacred images as idols. But by the next century, icons were restored in churches and the empire again thrived. Byzantium was able to reclaim several great cities the Arabs had taken, while in the north, it destroyed the Bulgarian army and defeated the Armenians, Georgians, and Normans. With Emperor Basil, the empire's borders were nearly those of its glory days.

In 1054 the pope excommunicated Constantinople's patriarch, finalizing the split between what we now know as the Roman Catholic and Eastern Orthodox churches. Byzantine leaders also faced opposition from within, as wealthy landowners refused to pay taxes. But nothing did more to weaken Byzantium than the spread of Islam by Muslim forces, who claimed or threatened Byzantine land to the south and east.

OPPOSITE: Emperor Justinian brought the Byzantine Empire to its height in the sixth century.

717–741
Reign of Emperor Leo III, who ignites the iconoclastic controversy with ban on icons.

842
Icons restored to Hagia Sophia on a day now known as the Feast of Orthodoxy

867
Emperor Basil I begins Macedonian dynasty which reestablishes much of the empire's former power.

1054
Final schism between eastern and western Christian churches.

SEE ALSO | THE CLASSICAL AGE: PAGE 108

CLASS & SOCIETY FARM AND CITY

Anastasius presides over Hippodrome games (left); a dish depicts a herdsman (right).

Seventh-century Byzantine culture suffered under constant attacks from Persia and Islam along the empire's eastern borders. Many cities became fortresses or were abandoned altogether. With a declining population in the Roman-style cities came an increasingly agrarian way of life. Most Byzantines were free or nearly free peasant farmers who kept livestock and tended orchards and small fields. Villagers lived according to country values—laws forbade marital infidelity and abortion. Meanwhile, Constantinople remained the hub of Byzantine culture. Classes ranged from slaves up to clergymen, courtiers, and, at the top, the emperor. People mixed freely in venues such as the Hippodrome, a sports stadium that rivaled Rome's Colosseum.

THE TAKEAWAY: Peasants with traditional values prevailed in the countryside, while the city had a more complex class structure.

BYZANTIUM

VIPs

Justinian, 483–565
Greatest emperor (527–565) of the Byzantine Empire

Theodora, c. 500–548
Actress and influential empress of Justinian

Belisarius, c. 505–565
General who overthrew Vandals in North Africa and Ostrogoths in Italy

Leo III, ca 680–741
Emperor (717–741) who outlawed icons, creating internal friction and rift with West

Basil II, ca 958–1025
Emperor (976–1025); expanded the empire

“*The safety of the state is the highest law.*” —JUSTINIAN

RELIGION ORTHODOX ORIGINS

The Byzantine church, which started out as the eastern branch of Roman Catholicism, began to develop its own practices. In the eighth century, many Byzantines began to think Islam prospered because it eschewed icons. Around 730, Emperor Leo III decreed that icon worship should stop. All over the empire, icons were removed or smashed, leading to riots among devout Christians.

Byzantines built Saint Catherine's Monastery on the Sinai Peninsula.

Iconoclasm was finally outlawed in 842, but the bitterness the controversy had caused created a rift between what would become two churches—Eastern Orthodox and Roman Catholic. Another point of contention lay in church doctrine: Rome insisted that the Holy Spirit proceeded from both Father and Son, not just the Father, as the Greeks believed. Because of this and other fine points of theology, the two branches of the Christian church parted ways in 1054 in what became known as the Great Schism.

> Leo III attempted to have all Jews in the empire forcibly baptized; most continued their worship in secret.

THE TAKEAWAY: After the fall of Rome, eastern and western branches of the Catholic Church began to follow separate paths until splitting completely in 1054.

Greek monk Theophanes the Confessor wrote an important history of the Byzantines.

VOICES

THEOPHANES AT THE HIPPODROME

"Herald: *You didn't come here to see the show, but only to insult the officials.*
Greens: *Yes, if anyone annoys us he will suffer the fate of Judas.*
Herald: *Shut up, you Jews, Manicheans, Samaritans!*
Greens: *You call us Jews and Samaritans; may the Mother of God protect us all equally!*
Herald: *I tell you, if you don't shut up, I'll have your heads cut off.*"

—A CONVERSATION BETWEEN A MEMBER OF THE GREENS RACING CLUB AND A HERALD OF JUSTINIAN, REPORTED BY GREEK CHRONICLER THEOPHANES

THEOPHANES THE CONFESSOR

"*Who can give law to lovers? Love is a greater law to itself.*" —BOETHIUS

SEE ALSO | KINGS AND NOMADS: PAGE 194

TRADE & ECONOMY CROSSROADS

Located at the meeting point of Asia and Europe, between the Black Sea and the Aegean, Constantinople was a main link in East-West trade routes. Through the city flowed Indian gems and spices, Chinese silks and porcelain, Persian rugs, and European textiles. From Russia and Scandinavia came furs, timber, honey, and slaves, which were then exported with the support of local banks. For about seven centuries, the bezant, the Byzantine currency, was accepted throughout the Mediterranean.

The city became one of the richest in the world, its gold and jewels the target of many would-be conquerors. Beyond the city walls, a large peasantry, which doubled as an army when necessary, produced such valuable trade goods as gold work, but it was agriculture upon which the Byzantine economy ultimately depended. The largest landholders were the church, the state, and a few wealthy individuals, but the work primarily fell upon the backs of the hardworking peasants. The olives, wines, grains, and other crops they turned out made the empire flourish.

{ The Silk Road from China through Constantinople, busy from 200 B.C.E. to 200 C.E., declined after Rome fell, then revived. }

Rich fabrics, as in this dalmatic robe (left), and golden coins (right) flowed through Byzantium on the Silk Roads.

The Byzantine trade network was widespread. Silk found in a Viking grave in Sweden probably originated in Byzantium. Despite occasional border skirmishes with Muslim opponents, trade was more common than war among Byzantium and its contemporaries.

THE TAKEAWAY: Byzantium grew rich from constant trade, but the empire's economy depended on agriculture.

"Rather let the crime of the guilty go unpunished than condemn the innocent." —JUSTINIAN

VOICES

JUSTINIAN

JUSTINIAN MIXED MARRIAGE

"We consider it ungodly that certain women are cheated of their liberty and, because slavery was introduced against natural liberty by the ferocity of the enemy, and this has been brought about by the depravity of the worst of men, . . . we desire to suspend from henceforth the Claudian senatus consultus *and all its observations about the declarations and sentences of judges, lest she who is by right free, but once seduced or taken* in flagrante delictu *or who was drawn down in any other way whatsoever from the free state of her ancestors to a condition of slavery, should fall under the rule of another."*

—FROM THE JUSTINIAN CODE, A CLAUSE PROTECTING WOMEN FROM SLAVERY, 534

LAW JUSTINIAN CODE

One of the greatest documents of western jurisprudence was created in sixth-century Byzantium. The Corpus Juris Civilis, or Justinian Code, was the collected work of Byzantium's greatest legal experts. Several years in the making, the code promoted equity and outlined procedures for judges to follow. The massive opus brought together from scattered sources imperial legislation from the second to sixth centuries and included more than 9,000 extracts from 39 imperial jurists. Most of the new laws were written in Greek; hence the Latin-speaking West remained unenlightened by the code for centuries.

The code's rediscovery in western Europe in the 11th century was a revelation. Until then, western legal systems were a jumble of Germanic folk law, Roman law, Old Testament law, and church law. Turning to the Justinian Code, the most comprehensive legal code ever recorded, newly emerging states were able to codify their laws upon the principle of natural law—principles of justice derived from reason. Under this system, the emperor was the final arbiter, and could determine a particular case based on ethical principles outside the written statutes. Though the system did not take into account the potential for corrupt jurists and emperors, it functioned well in most cases.

THE TAKEAWAY: The Byzantines under Justinian compiled legal statutes and precedents that served as a model set of laws for most of Europe.

Justinian's bejeweled reliquary cross

"He was too prone to listen to accusations; and too quick to punish. For he decided such cases without full examination." —PROCOPIUS

SEE ALSO | POSTCLASSICAL ERA: PAGE 147

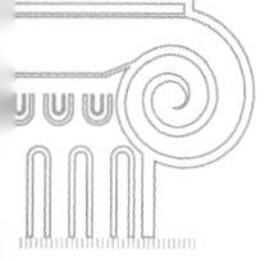

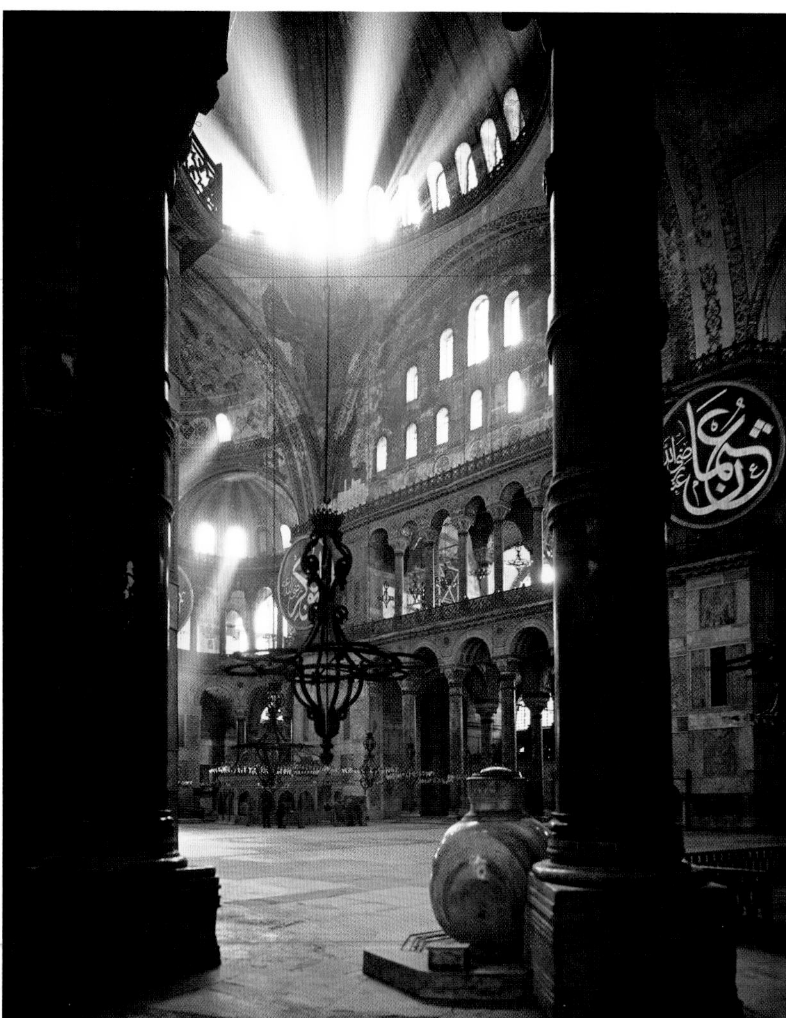

Sunlight beams through the windows of Hagia Sophia.

ART & ARCHITECTURE REBIRTH

The greatest work of Byzantine art, Hagia Sophia (Holy Wisdom) was rebuilt from an earlier church that had burned in fifth-century riots. Constructed in the 530s by Justinian's 10,000 hired laborers, the basilica was the largest enclosed space of the time, embellished with 20 tons of silver and surmounted by a gold-covered domed ceiling. Exquisite mosaics and icons graced the interior.

Following centuries of cultural stagnation, a time of relative peace in the late ninth century allowed for an artistic renaissance. Empress Theodora (wife of Theophilus), who had been a secret icon worshiper during the ban on icons, came to power in 842 and used her influence to resuscitate artistic tradition. Magnificent works of art soon began appearing, from icons and gilt-ornamented paintings to statuary and mosaics.

During this time, scholarship also enjoyed a revival. Translators brought to life many classical Greek texts on science and philosophy, and the art of illuminating manuscripts—decorating margins with colorful ornaments and illustrations—flourished.

THE TAKEAWAY: Hagia Sophia became a mosque in the 15th century and a museum in 1935.

A bronze horse from the Hippodrome

> *A spherical-shaped dome . . . does not appear to rest upon a solid foundation, but to cover the place beneath as though it were suspended from heaven by the fabled golden chain."* —PROCOPIUS

VOICES

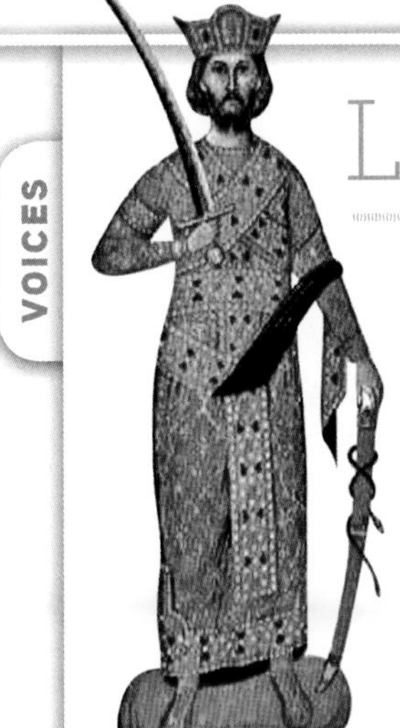

NICEPHORUS II

LIUTPRAND MISSION TO CONSTANTINOPLE

"In the palace which is called the crown hall, I was led before Nicephorus—a monstrosity of a man, a pygmy, fat-headed and like a mole as to the smallness of his eyes; disgusting with his short, broad, thick, and half hoary beard; disgraced by a neck an inch long; very bristly through the length and thickness of his hair; in color an Ethiopian; one whom it would not be pleasant to meet in the middle of the night; with extensive belly, lean of loin, very long of hip considering his short stature, small of shank, proportionate as to his heels and feet . . . bold of tongue, a fox by nature, in perjury and lying a Ulysses."

—LIUTPRAND, EMISSARY OF OTTO THE GREAT, ON BYZANTINE EMPEROR NICEPHORUS II

CONFLICTS WARS ON ALL SIDES

After subduing a riot in 532 and concluding a peace treaty with Persia the same year, Emperor Justinian was able to turn his attention to regaining some of the lost glory of Rome. His capable general Belisarius first wrested old Roman provinces in North Africa from the Vandals, then defeated the Visigoths in southeastern Spain. By mid-century much of Italy had been recaptured from the Ostrogoths and the Mediterranean was again dominated by the empire. But from out of the south came a powerful people, unified by a new religion. In 636 Muslims defeated the weakened Byzantines in a key battle in southwestern Syria, the first in a series of punishing losses for the empire. In later centuries Byzantium was involved in conflicts on its European borders, including the spectacular 1014 Battle of Kleidion in the Balkans, earning Emperor Basil II the title Bulgaroctonus, Bulgar Slayer.

THE TAKEAWAY: Byzantium was almost constantly at war, struggling to maintain its borders.

{ Constantinople was spared in the seventh century because of the use of an incendiary, "Greek fire," against the Arab fleet. }

General Belisarius begs for alms as an old man in this 1784 painting.

"He who would climb to a lofty height must go up by steps, not leaps." —POPE GREGORY I

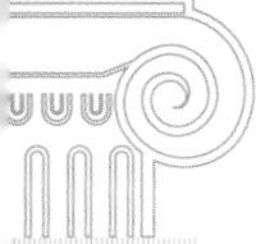

SEE ALSO | POSTCLASSICAL ERA: PAGE 146

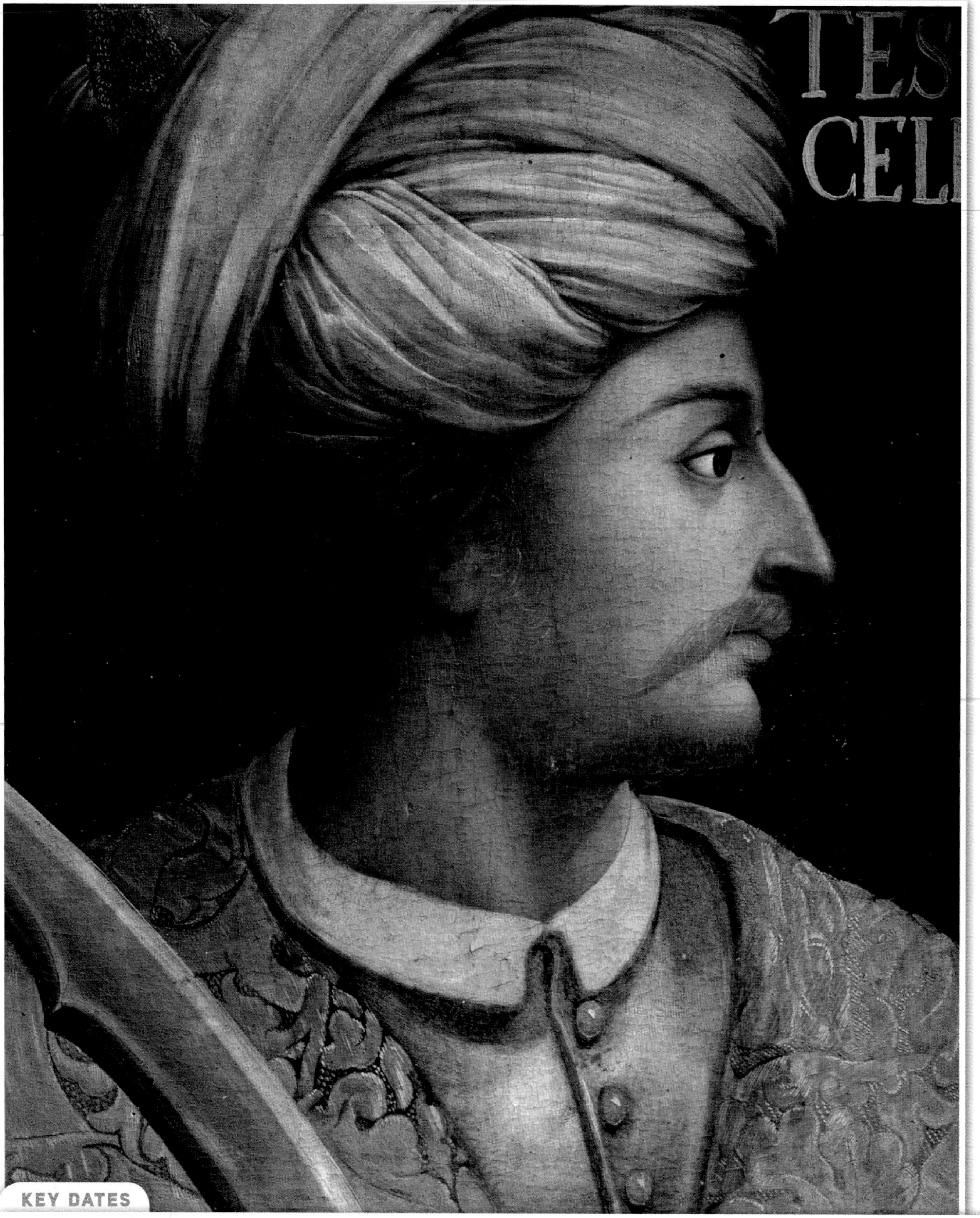

KEY DATES

ca 570–632
Muhammad lives and preaches.

ca 610
Muhammad undergoes a spiritual transformation.

ca 622
Muhammad and his followers flee Mecca in a journey called the Hegira.

632
Muhammad makes first hajj (pilgrimage) to Mecca. Abu Bakr becomes first caliph.

ISLAM

570–1055

The world's youngest major religion, Islam started in the Arabian Peninsula and rapidly mushroomed outward, its adherents driven to conquer by a religious duty known as jihad, or holy war. Islam's founder, Muhammad, was born in Mecca around 570, a period of political and religious instability in the region. Nomadic Bedouins ruled the peninsula by raiding trade caravans; they prayed to idols and nature gods. But Christians and Jews also lived in Arabia. When he was about 40, Muhammad began receiving messages from the angel Gabriel, which, according to tradition, became the basis for the Koran, Islam's holy book. He began preaching, and his devout following formed the nucleus of the new faith of Islam ("submission to Allah"). Supporting itself by caravan raiding, the movement gradually became so powerful that in 630, Muhammad led 30,000 soldiers to Syria, subduing tribes and forming alliances. Those who converted to Islam were granted mercy; the rest were killed. Christians and Jews, coming from the same tradition as Islam, were generally not forced into conversion—the tax they had to pay made them valuable. Many of the conquered, stung by years of Byzantine and Persian repression, welcomed the invaders.

From the Arabian Peninsula, the new religion of Islam sprang rapidly to life in the seventh century and burgeoned outward, its adherents spreading the word of Allah on the point of a sword.

The new religion offered Arabs hope for a glorious existence in paradise, although those who ignored the teachings of the Koran would burn in hell. Islam replaced idol worship with devotion to the needy, and while it condoned polygamy it also granted women property rights.

Between the years 633 and 718, the Islamic state subsumed Persia, Egypt, Morocco, and Spain, an unprecedented expansion. In the late seventh century, Islam split into two major factions, the Shiites (who believed caliphs, or leaders, should be descendants of Muhammad) and the majority Sunnis (who preferred able leadership over family connections).

The Sunni Umayyad clan established a dynasty in Damascus, ruling until being overthrown by the Abbasids in 750; the Abbasids moved their capital to Baghdad and remained in power until the 13th century. Around the year 1000 a Turkish people called Seljuks arrived on horseback in eastern Iran; by mid-century they had united with the Abbasid Sunni caliphate and had taken over eastern Islam.

OPPOSITE: Islam founder Muhammad displays a striking profile in an anonymous 18th-century painting.

ca 661–750
Umayyad dynasty builds an Islamic empire.

711
Berber Muslims of North Africa, known as Moors, invade Spain.

756
Córdoba breaks from the Abbasid dynasty.

786–809
Reign of Caliph Harun al-Rashid is pinnacle of Abbasid dynasty.

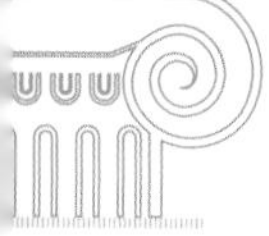

SEE ALSO | POSTCLASSICAL ERA: PAGE 150

LEADERS LIFE OF MUHAMMAD

An orphan at age six, Muhammad was raised by a grandfather and uncle. He became a camel driver and shepherd and at 25 received a marriage proposal from his 40-year-old cousin, a rich widow. The match gave Muhammad four daughters and time to retreat to a mountain cave to contemplate God. At around age 40 he began having prophetic visions, which led

Pilgrims circle the Kaaba, a shrine in the heart of Mecca.

to his preaching about the need for generosity and the coming of a judgment day. As his following grew, tribal leaders felt threatened; he decided to remove to Medina, an oasis to the north. In 630 he and 10,000 men marched on Mecca, which could give only token resistance; Muhammad entered his native city in triumph.

Later in 630 Muhammad led some 30,000 warriors northward to the border of Syria, along the way adding nomadic clans to the *ummah,* the community of the faithful. He died two years later; his father-in-law Abu Bakr was picked as his successor, or caliph.

THE TAKEAWAY: Muhammad's midlife visions had inspired thousands by the year 630.

ISLAM

VIPs

Muhammad, ca 570–632
Founder of Islam

Abu al-Abbas, 722–754
Founder of the Abbasid dynasty

Harun al-Rashid, 766–809
Caliph of the Abbasid dynasty

Muhammad al-Khwarizmi, ca 780–850
Pioneering mathematician

Caliph al-Mamun, 786–833
Intellectual Abbasid caliph

Abd al-Rahman, 891–961
Emir and caliph of Córdoba in Muslim-occupied Spain

Avicenna, 980–1037
Also known as Ibn Sina, an influential philosopher and scholar of medicine

CONNECTIONS SUNNIS VS. SHIITES

THE FOURTH CALIPH, Ali ibn Abi Talib (ca 600–661), was a cousin and son-in-law of Muhammad. He came to power during a coup that killed the third caliph, a kinsman of powerful Syrian military commander Muawiya (ca 602–680). In 657 the forces of Ali and Muawiya fought an indecisive battle; not long afterward, Ali was stabbed to death.

Those who favored Ali and the lineage of Muhammad came to be called the Shiites; the others, the Sunnis, went with Muawiya, who became caliph in 661. Today Sunnis make up about 80 percent of Muslims worldwide, though Shiites have a majority in Iran, Iraq, Bahrain, and Azerbaijan.

SUNNI-SHIITE RECONCILIATION, 2009

“*Surely God wrongs not men, but themselves men wrong.*” —THE KORAN, 10:44

Christians triumph over Muslims in the 732 Battle of Tours.

EMPIRES ISLAMIC EXPANSION

In the late seventh century, Islam's political power settled on the Umayyad dynasty, a Meccan merchant clan based in Damascus, Syria. The Umayyads carried the flag of Arabic Islam into Europe and Asia, but their wealth caused resentment among many of their subjects, including the Shiites. In 750 the Umayyads were toppled by the Abbasids, who moved the capital to Baghdad on the Tigris River and began promoting art and scholarship over imperial expansion.

In 711 Berber Muslims, known to Europeans as Moors, invaded Spain, thus initiating more than 700 years of Moorish rule in Iberia. In 756 an Umayyad ruler named Abd al-Rahman broke away from Abbasid control and named himself the governor of Córdoba in Spain.

{ Baghdad Caliph Harun al-Rashid sent a white elephant to Charlemagne as a present. }

The peninsula grew rich from trade, producing ceramics, jewelry, and crystal. Free schools, 70 libraries, and 700 mosques were sponsored in Córdoba alone.

Even with a breakaway dynasty, Islam established a cohesive culture in the Middle East and into Europe, with Arabic as the common language and the Koran as the holy book. Rebellions decreased the caliphs' power in the ninth century, but the Abbasids remained in place until the Mongol invasion of 1258.

THE TAKEAWAY: Cultural cohesion became more important than conquest under the Abbasids.

THUMBS UP / THUMBS DOWN: CALIPH HARUN AL-RASHID

HARUN AL-RASHID (R. 786–809), the caliph whose court inspired the Thousand and One Nights stories, fostered Baghdad's intellectual and cultural flowering. His scholars translated works from Greece and India into Arabic, and his writers created new forms of literature.

On the downside, he executed his close friend and adviser Jafar, and divided the empire among his sons. A civil war followed. Historians consider him a great patron of the arts, and a middling ruler. **CONCLUSION: THUMBS UP AND DOWN**

WATER JUG OF HARUN AL-RASHID

He who has a thousand friends has not a friend to spare, / And he who has one enemy will meet him everywhere." —ALI IBN ABI TALIB

SEE ALSO | POSTCLASSICAL ERA: PAGE 166

TRADE & ECONOMY DIVERSITY

From the eighth century until Islam began fracturing into multiple states in the ninth, Baghdad was the center of Islamic power. Though the power of the caliph began declining, that city, like Constantinople, continued to be of enormous importance as a major crossroads in a vast and exotic trade network. From India came rubies, ebony, sandalwood, coconuts, tigers, and elephants; China shipped silks, paper, porcelain, cinnamon, and peacocks; Arabia contributed ostriches and camels; Greece exported racing horses, female slaves, hydraulic engineers, and eunuchs; Egypt sent balsam, topaz, and donkeys.

As Islam expanded, it did not simply conquer and move on. Part of its success was based on establishing interconnected communities with thriving agricultural and commercial enterprises. The conquerors wisely left working trade networks alone. By the eighth century Arabic gold coins had become a standard throughout the Mediterranean. Though trade between Islamic countries and Europe was nearly cut off in the early days of Islam, mostly owing to Western suspicion of Muslims, by the mid-ninth century goods were flowing back and forth, undeterred by marauding Arab pirates.

THE TAKEAWAY: The spread of Islam was aided by the establishment of viable economic systems.

The Arabs cobbled together a workable economy by letting diverse peoples—Syrians, Egyptians, Persians, North Africans, and Jews—continue much as before.

Gilded brass astrolabe from Persia

ARAB COINS

AL-TANUKHI THE YELLOW DAY

VOICES

"[Caliph] Mutawakkil desired that every article whereon his eye should fall on the day of a certain drinking-bout should be colored yellow. Accordingly there was erected a dome of sandalwood covered and furnished with yellow satin, and there were set in front of him melons and yellow oranges and yellow wine in golden vessels; and only those slave-girls were admitted who were yellow with yellow brocade gowns. The dome was erected over a tessellated pond, and orders were given that saffron should be put in the channels which [gave] the water a yellow color as it flowed through the pond."

—ANECDOTE FROM AL-TANUKHI, A TENTH-CENTURY BAGHDAD JUDGE

"The best of rulers is he who keeps the company of men of learnng, and the worst of learned men is he who seeks the society of the king." —NIZAM AL-MULK

VOICES

AVICENNA ON MEDICINE

AVICENNA

"Medicine considers the human body as to the means by which it is cured and by which it is driven away from health. The knowledge of anything, since all things have causes, is not acquired or complete unless it is known by its causes. Therefore in medicine we ought to know the causes of sickness and health. And because health and sickness and their causes are sometimes manifest, and sometimes hidden and not to be comprehended except by the study of symptoms, we must also study the symptoms of health and disease . . . no knowledge is acquired save through the study of its causes and beginnings."

—FROM THE WRITINGS OF AVICENNA (IBN SINA), ca 1020

ART & SCIENCE INTELLECTS

Caliph al Mamun ushered in a new period of artistic and intellectual growth for Islam. He set up astronomical observatories and helped integrate Greek philosophy into Islamic thinking, freeing the latter from the mystical leanings of the past. Mathematician Muhammad ibn Musa al-Khwarizmi was the first to set down the principles of algebra and put his name to the term "algorithm." Scientist and philosopher Avicenna (Ibn Sina), Islam's most important early thinker, wrote some 200 works on philosophy, religion, science, and language, influencing Roger Bacon, Thomas Aquinas, and other Europeans. His *Canon of Medicine* was the world's most comprehensive medical compendium and served as Europe's principal medical text until the 17th century.

Star-shaped Umayyad stonework in Khirbat al-Mafjar, Israel

Arabic art become known for its intricate geometric designs and beautiful handwritten scripts. Tiled domes, exquisite paintings, and elaborately detailed tapestries and carpets spread far and wide. Brocades from the looms of Muslim Sicily clothed the wealthy of Europe; the pointed arch, developed in Persia, began appearing in European cathedrals.

THE TAKEAWAY: Islam's early medieval thinkers had a far-reaching influence on Western culture for centuries.

"The first essential in chemistry is that you should perform practical work and conduct experiments."

—JABIR IB HAIYAN

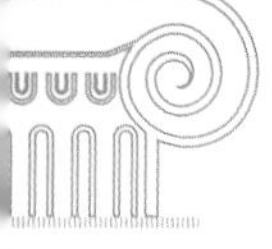

THE KORAN

IT WAS ONE OF ISLAM'S early leaders, Muhammad's son-in-law Uthman, who authorized a standard set of the Prophet's teachings. Compiled around 650, the Koran has become the sacred book of Islam. Considered the exact words of Allah, spoken to Muhammad through the angel Gabriel, the Koran forms the basis for Islamic law, doctrine, and social organization. It lays out not just a belief system but also a program for reforming and unifying society. The 114 chapters, or suras, consist of verses, or *ayat* (signs or miracles).

The Koran recognizes no distinctions between people. All are equally subject to the will of Allah, though the book does reinforce the notion of male superiority. More than one billion people around the world consider it a sacred text.

DEVOUT READER A young girl clutches a copy of the Koran in Sigli, Sumatra, Indonesia. Invaded by Arabs in the 13th century, Sumatra, like the rest of Indonesia, gradually became Islamic. Indonesia today holds more Muslims than any other nation: about 88 percent of the population, or 209 million people. As early as they learn to speak, Muslim children memorize sacred phrases in Arabic, such as the phrase beginning every chapter of the Koran: "In the name of God, the Merciful, the Compassionate."

"In the Name of Allah, the Compassionate, the Merciful,
Praise be to Allah, the Lord of the World,
The Compassionate, the Merciful,
Master of the Day of Judgment,
Only You do we worship, and only You."

"Those who spend their wealth in the Way of Allah are like a grain [of wheat] which grows seven ears, each carrying one hundred grains. Allah multiplies [further] to whom he wills. Allah is Munificent, All-Knowing."

ELEGANT EDITION These Koran manuscript pages from tenth-century Persia were written in the Kufic style, which originated in Kufa, near Babylon. The style was employed in creating deluxe copies of the Koran.

"A kind word and forgiveness are better than charity followed by injury. Allah is Self-sufficient and Forbearing."

"Oh believers, do not render vain your charities by taunts and injury, like him who spends his wealth for the sake of ostentation and does not believe in Allah and the Last Day. He is like a smooth rock covered by earth; when heavy rain falls on it, it leaves it completely bare. Such people get no reward for their works. Allah does not guide the unbelievers."

"In the name of Allah, the Gracious, the Merciful, say, 'I seek refuge in the Lord of mankind, the King of mankind, the God of mankind, from the evil of the sneaking whisperer, who whispers into the hearts of men, from among the Jinn and mankind.' "

SACRED TIME A spiritual leader in Fachi, Niger, writes prayers from the Koran on a wooden tablet as he teaches the 114 chapters to young boys.

"To orphans restore their property [when they reach their age], nor substitute [your] worthless things for [their] good ones; and devour not their substance [by mixing it up] with your own. For this is indeed a great sin."

"The sun and the moon run their courses according to a fixed reckoning. And the stemless plants and the trees humbly submit to His will. And the heaven He has raised high and set up a measure, that you may not transgress the measure. So weigh all things in justice and fall not short of the measure."

TRANSLATIONS

Since Arabic is considered the truest form of the Koran, translations are considered paraphrases unworthy of ritual use. Yet they exist.

LATIN: The first Latin translation was made in 1143 at the monastery of Cluny but not published until 1543.

ITALIAN, GERMAN, DUTCH: The Koran was first rendered into these languages from the original Latin version.

FRENCH: In 1647, André du Ryer came out with a French translation.

ENGLISH: Alexander Ross published the first English translation in the late 17th century. An English translation by George Sale appeared in 1734; numerous editions of his work followed. Several other English translations have come out, with various scholarly and literary attributes—one from 1861 arranges the suras in chronological order.

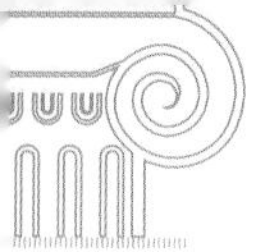

SEE ALSO | KINGS AND NOMADS: PAGE 182

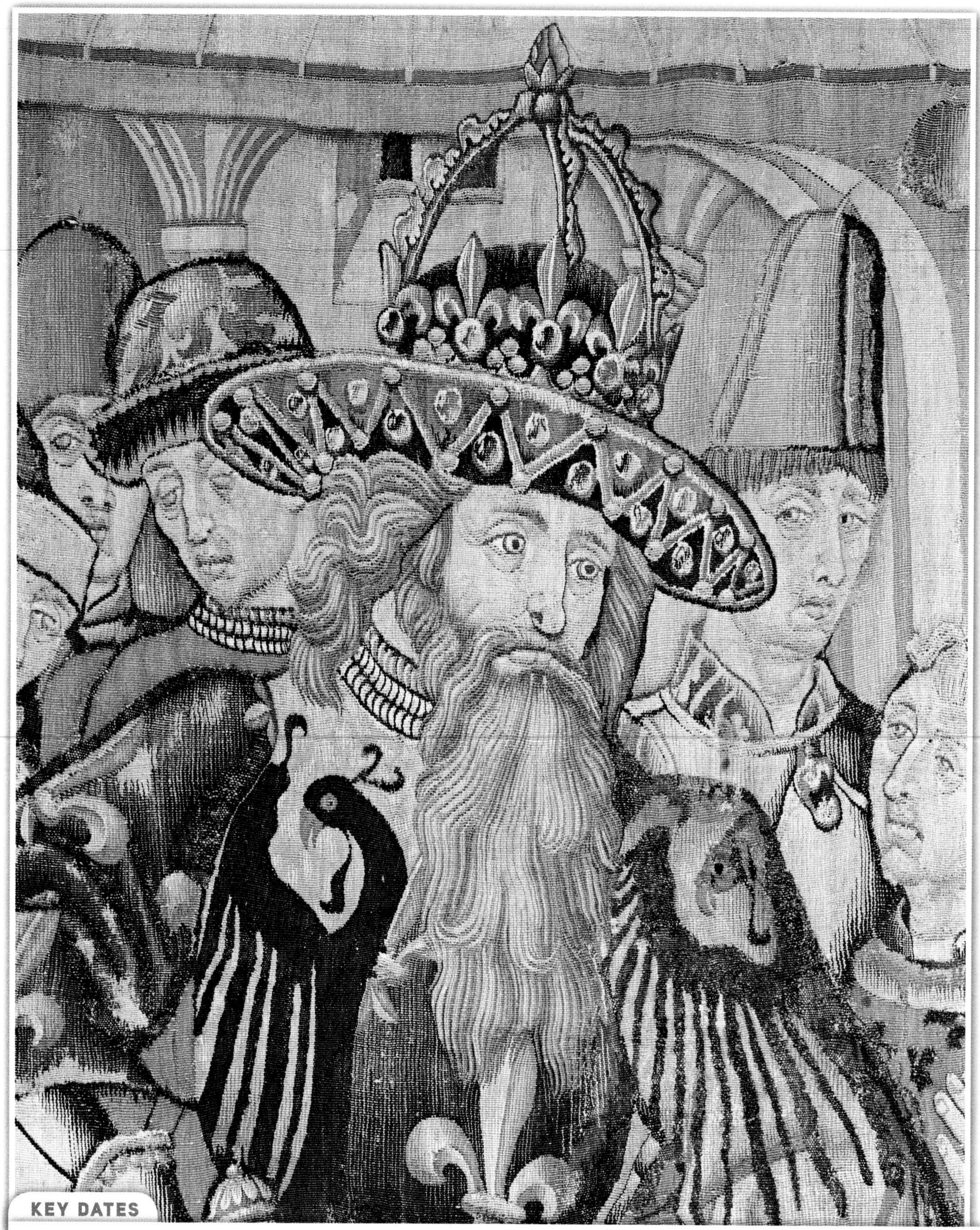

KEY DATES

732
Charles Martel defeats the Moors in the Battle of Tours.

768–814
Charlemagne reigns and helps establish feudalism by granting large estates to the nobility.

793
Danes sack the monastery of Lindisfarne in the first known Viking attack.

851
Viking forces begin taking over England.

VIKINGS, SLAVS, AND THE NORTH

500–1100

By the eighth century, Europe was just beginning to awaken from a long stagnation after the Roman pullout. Since the time of the mighty ruler Clovis, the Frankish kingdom—composed of today's France and western Germany—had been ruled by the Merovingian dynasty, but by the mid-600s that family line had weakened considerably. A new dynasty, though short-lived, would produce one of Europe's greatest rulers, Charlemagne. Under his strong and capable leadership, the Frankish kingdom grew, the arts flowered, and the Christian church spread across formerly pagan regions, uniting disparate tribes in a common culture.

The island of England was evolving on its own, with separate realms beginning to coalesce into a single kingdom by the ninth century. It was at this time that Scandinavian raiders began invading England and other parts of coastal Europe—the fearsome Vikings had just begun two centuries of seafaring dominance.

In the centuries after Rome, European nations began gradually emerging under strong leaders. The Christian church became Europe's dominant influence, often clashing with nascent monarchies.

Germany became a powerhouse in the next century under the redoubtable King Otto I, and in 962 the pope crowned him Holy Roman Emperor. His military prowess resulted in a major victory over invading Magyars of Hungary. Another invasion had more success: In 1066 the Normans under William the Conqueror took over England, putting an indelible French stamp on British history.

A loose confederation of ethnic groups living as farmers, hunters, and nomads ranged across what is now western Russia. The Scandinavians seized the region, subduing the Slavs and building cities along trading corridors. They established commercial ties with Byzantium and, accepting Byzantine missionaries, gradually converted to Orthodox Christianity. In the capital of Kiev, Prince Vladimir's conversion around 987 helped bring Byzantine influences to eastern European art.

Christianity was becoming the major force in European society. People believed that the political order of feudalism should mirror that ordained by God, with divine authority held by his earthly representatives—the church and the pope.

OPPOSITE: Frankish ruler Charlemagne brought land, culture, and the blessing of the church to his empire.

860
Vikings attack Constantinople with 200 ships.

955
Otto I of Germany defeats the Magyars at the Battle of Lechfeld.

987
Prince Vladimir of Kiev converts to Christianity.

1016
Danish regent Canute is crowned king of England.

SEE ALSO | THE CLASSICAL AGE: PAGE 119

CONFLICTS BARBARIAN INVASIONS

Most of the barbarians that migrated south of the Rhine in the fourth and fifth centuries were Germanic tribes, less interested in taking over than in simply finding better living conditions. A multiethnic tribe known as the Goths formed out of forest and steppe peoples living north of the Black Sea in today's Ukraine. The Roman Empire attempted to fight some of them, while allying with others; the end result was a massive influx of foreigners that hastened the empire's collapse. The eastern Goths, or Ostrogoths, were absorbed by the nomadic Huns of western Asia; the western Goths, or Visigoths, made inroads on Italy and eventually filtered into Spain.

Another large tribe, the Franks, gave rise to today's German and French peoples. Under Charlemagne, the Frankish kingdom reached from the Pyrenees in the south to Slavic lands north of the Rhine. In Britain, Anglo-Saxons—Angles, Saxons, and Jutes—began pushing out native Britons in the fifth century.

Seventh-century Anglo-Saxon helmet

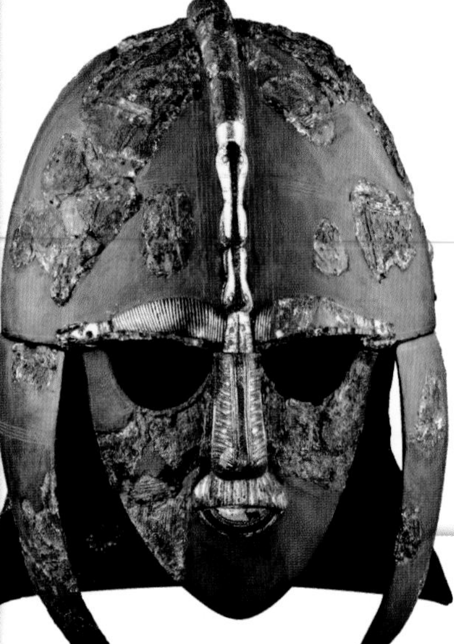

Germanic tribes brought their language to Britain, where it replaced the Celtic tongue of the native Britons.

THE TAKEAWAY: A variety of Germanic tribes spread out and populated Europe in the early middle ages.

LEADERS OF THE NORTH

VIPs

Clovis, 466–511
King who helped unify Franks

Benedict of Nursia, ca 480–547
Founder of Western monastic order; later canonized

Charlemagne, 742–814
King of the Franks (768-814)

Alfred the Great, 849–899
Learned king of Wessex who fought the Danes

Otto I, the Great, 912–973
King of Germany (936-973) and Holy Roman Emperor

Vladimir I, ca 956–1015
Grand Prince of Kiev who brought Christianity to Kievan Rus

ANGLO-SAXONS CRESS

VOICES

"1. In case a man's hair falls out, take juice of the wort which one names nasturtium and by another name cress, put it on the nose, the hair shall grow.

"2. This wort is not sown but it is produced of itself in springs and in brooks; also it is written that in some lands it will grow against walls.

"3. For a sore head, that is for scurf and for itch, take the seed of this same wort and goose grease, pound together, it draws from off the head the whiteness of the scurf."

—FROM ANGLO-SAXON MEDICAL MANUSCRIPTS

"God of Clotilda, if you grant me victory I shall become a Christian." —CLOVIS

VOICES

ERIK THE RED

ERIK THE RED THE NEW WORLD

“Then they came to land, and rowed along it in boats, and explored it, and found there flat stones, many and so great that two men might well lie on them stretched on their backs with heel to heel. Polar-foxes were there in abundance. This land they gave name to, and called it Helluland (stone-land). Then they sailed with northerly winds two half-days, and there was then land before them, and on it a great forest and many wild beasts. An island lay in the south-east off the land, and they found bears thereon, and called the island Bjarney (Bear Island); but the mainland, where the forest was, they called Markland (forest-land).”

—FROM *ERIK THE RED’S SAGA*; ERIK’S SON LEIF LANDS IN NORTH AMERICA

EXPLORATION THE NORTHMEN

The crumbling of Charlemagne’s empire in the late ninth century left its riches vulnerable to attack from outsiders. Norse seafarers from what are now Denmark, Sweden, and Norway swept down on monasteries and villages, spreading terror throughout Europe. The Vikings were driven to their bold, and often merciless, expeditions by the lack of good farmland at home. They ventured as far afield as Russia, Germany, and Constantinople, going wherever they could find a watery passage for their shallow-draft ships.

In addition to raiding, the Norsemen explored the North Atlantic, colonizing Iceland, then Greenland, and finally North America around the year 1000.

Though we know them mostly as brutal warriors, Vikings were also skilled artisans and they lived by a code of freedom, honor, and equality. Viking wives had rights belonging to few other medieval women. Many Vikings simply settled in the lands they raided, and eventually converted to Christianity. Their incursions in some ways strengthened disorganized states by forcing them to develop cohesive defenses.

THE TAKEAWAY: After Vikings terrorized coastal Europe, they were absorbed into local cultures.

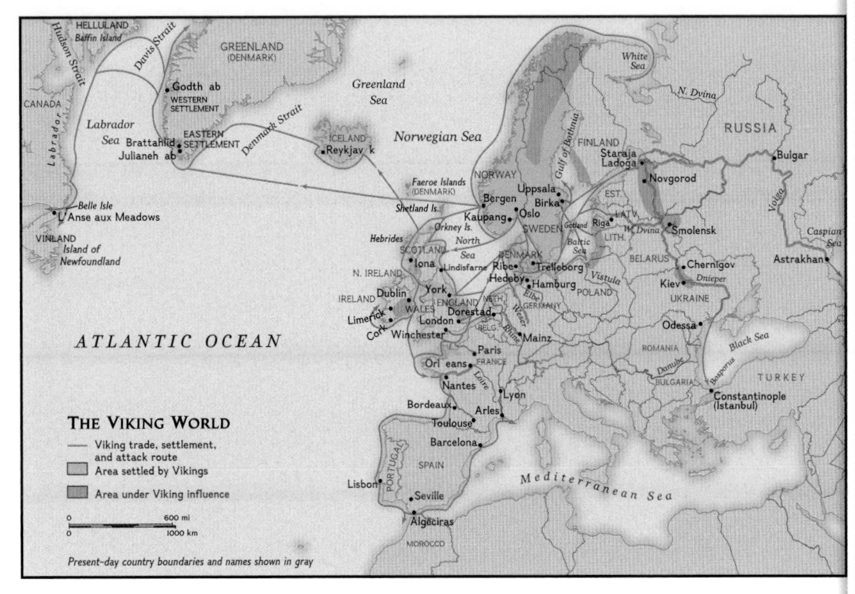

“Better ask for too little than offer too much / like the gift should be the boon.”

—VIKING POEM “HÁVAMÁL”

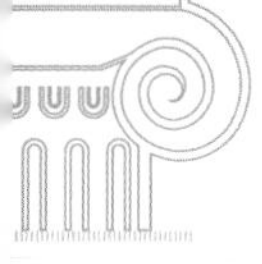

SEE ALSO | KINGS AND NOMADS: PAGE 186

RELIGION THE ROCK OF EUROPE

By the sixth century, Christianity had taken root in pockets of Europe and was slowly spreading across the land. The church was attracting and educating the smartest men. Though the lower clergy were often illiterate, the bishops and other high prelates—generally members of the nobility—were among the most influential members of society. Monasticism began to emerge as an important force in European culture.

Pope Gregory I the Great sent missionaries throughout Europe.

The early monastic movement was all about personal spiritual growth, the Eastern ascetics isolating themselves from society and its worldly temptations. In the more sparsely populated West, with its harsher climate, group monasticism made much more sense than solitary monasticism. Monastic communities began appearing in remote parts of France and Ireland, and these early monasteries, populated by devoted learners, became storehouses of intellectualism (and temporal wealth, making them targets for Viking raiders). Women joined orders as well, at first strictly cloistered, but in later centuries acquiring considerable spiritual and temporal power as the daughters of aristocratic families brought learning and wealth to their convents.

> In 597 Augustine and 40 monks established the first mission in England at Canterbury.

Monasteries became known for their extensive scriptoria, the rooms where monks labored over manuscripts of both religious and classical works. In this way, the medieval monasteries became schools and libraries, and it was not surprising that the elite turned to these institutions to find teachers for their children.

Monks began to take on a more

> *"God is that, the greater than which cannot be conceived."* —ST. ANSELM

Arches support the medieval cistern of France's Abbey of Cluny.

direct Christian outreach by sending missionaries to establish churches. One of the most prominent early missionizers, Pope Gregory I, was a Benedictine monk who zealously promoted Christianity, founded numerous monasteries, and became known as the "architect of the medieval papacy." As much politician as spiritual leader, Gregory beefed up the role of the pope by defending Rome from attack, ransoming hostages, enacting land reforms, and repairing aqueducts. The missionaries he sent all over Europe helped ally the Roman Catholic Church with the Frankish monarchy.

Five centuries later, Christianity had become the dominant force in Europe. A unifying religion and culture had spread across what was now called Christendom. The Holy Roman Empire, its loose boundaries roughly corresponding to central Europe, became an example of the alignment between church and state.

Yet differing objectives set up a polar tension between the papacy and the monarchies of such emerging nations as France, England, and Germany. Time and again the pope and a European monarch would challenge one another's authority. Though these conflicts rarely came to blows, they forced change and reform and helped to clear out corruption on both sides.

THE TAKEAWAY: Monasteries, missionaries, and the papacy Christianized Europe over the course of 500 years.

VOICES

RULE OF ST. BENEDICT RULES FOR SLEEP

"They shall sleep clothed, and girt with belts or with ropes; and they shall not have their knives at their sides while they sleep, lest perchance in a dream they should wound the sleepers. And let the monks be always on the alert; and, when the signal is given, rising without delay, let them hasten to mutually prepare themselves for the service of God with all gravity and modesty, however. The younger brothers shall not have beds by themselves, but interspersed among those of the elder ones. And when they rise for the service of God, they shall exhort each other mutually with moderation on account of the excuses that those who are sleepy are inclined to make."

—FROM A BOOK OF PRECEPTS COMPILED BY ST. BENEDICT OF NURSIA, ca 530

SAINT BENEDICT OF NURSIA

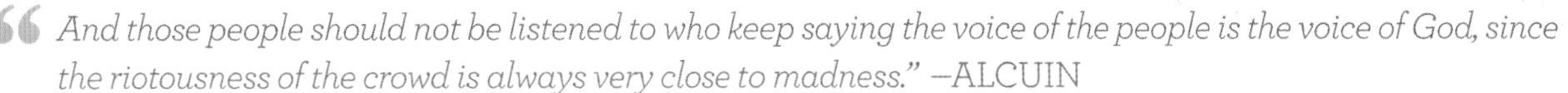
"And those people should not be listened to who keep saying the voice of the people is the voice of God, since the riotousness of the crowd is always very close to madness." —ALCUIN

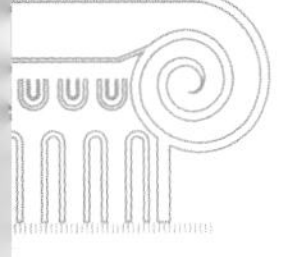

SEE ALSO | KINGS AND NOMADS: PAGE 191

CLASS & SOCIETY FEUDALISM

THE TAKEAWAY: Under the feudal system, peasants toiled for landholding lords, who owed allegiance to the king.

Between the eighth and eleventh centuries, the necessities of food production and military protection resulted in a class system called feudalism. At the top of the heap was the king, who gave land to nobles in return for armed support; at the bottom were the peasants, who toiled for their lords. Charlemagne and other rulers helped entrench feudalism by granting large estates to aristocrats. These powerful landowners then gave land to lesser lords—vassals—if they agreed to serve as knights during wars.

Though it provided security, the feudal system depended on inequality. The lowest of the peasants, the serfs, were little more than slaves, rarely working themselves clear of the debt they owed their lord for the privilege of cultivating a piece of land. But with political stability and the improvement of agricultural techniques in the 1000s, market towns began expanding and a new middle class developed. Peasants discovered they could sell their own produce and animals. Some moved to villages and became millers, bakers, brewers, and craftsmen.

{ A typical medieval vassal spent 40 days of the year in military service, and a lord often longer. }

Peasants labor on a 15th-century feudal estate.

"He decreed that, on the day on which they took care of the brethren, they should be refreshed with the bread of the brethren, for the laborer is worthy of his hire." —GEBHARD, BISHOP OF CONSTANCE

DAILY LIFE GRINDING AWAY

Life for most people in the feudal period was short and hard—oppressive labor, poor nutrition, war, and other violence limited the average lifespan to about 30 years. Most people rarely ventured more than ten miles beyond their birthplaces. Belief in superstition and magic was common in the countryside, blending in with the new Christian traditions; people prayed to local saints for miracles. The three major social institutions were the church, the monastery, and the castle. The first two were generally squat stone structures, while the castles were wooden forts. But in these secure havens, people could assemble for commerce and social activities. Though barter was the common means of exchange, silver coins were also used, the smallest of which could buy a cow.

Two classes of medieval women meet.

In Carolingian times, the church began to restrict the formerly relaxed conception of marriage. Until the 800s, many men had concubines as well as wives, and divorce was easily obtained. Under Louis the Pious, divorce was banned and concubinage condemned.

The early medieval diet leaned heavily on bread, cheeses, and vegetables in good times for peasants, with game meat added to the menu for the upper classes. All, including clerics, enjoyed copious quantities of alcohol, mainly wine and ale.

The dirt-grubbing existence of medieval Europe did harbor promise for a brighter future: Scholars and artists, supported by Charlemagne and others, were quietly working away, planting the seeds of a cultural efflorescence.

THE TAKEAWAY: A tough life was alleviated by the church and its promise of a better afterlife.

VOICES

ENGLAND THE PLOWMAN'S DAY

"Master: *What sayest thou, plowman? How do you do your work?*

"Plowman: *O my lord, I work very hard: I go out at dawn, driving the cattle to the field, and I yoke them to the plow. Nor is the weather so bad in winter that I dare to stay at home, for fear of my lord: but when the oxen are yoked, and the plowshare and coulter attached to the plow, I must plow one whole field a day, or more.*

"Master: *What more do you do in a day?*

"Plowman: *Certainly I do more. I must fill the manger of the oxen with hay, and water them and carry out the dung. . . . It is a great labor.*"

—FROM THE DIALOGUE BETWEEN MASTER AND DISCIPLE, ca 1000

CLERIC, KNIGHT, AND WORKMAN

"*Let me die in a tavern so that the wine may be near my dying mouth.*" —THE ARCHPOET

SEE ALSO | POSTCLASSICAL ERA: PAGE 164

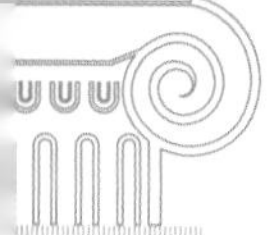

KEY DATES

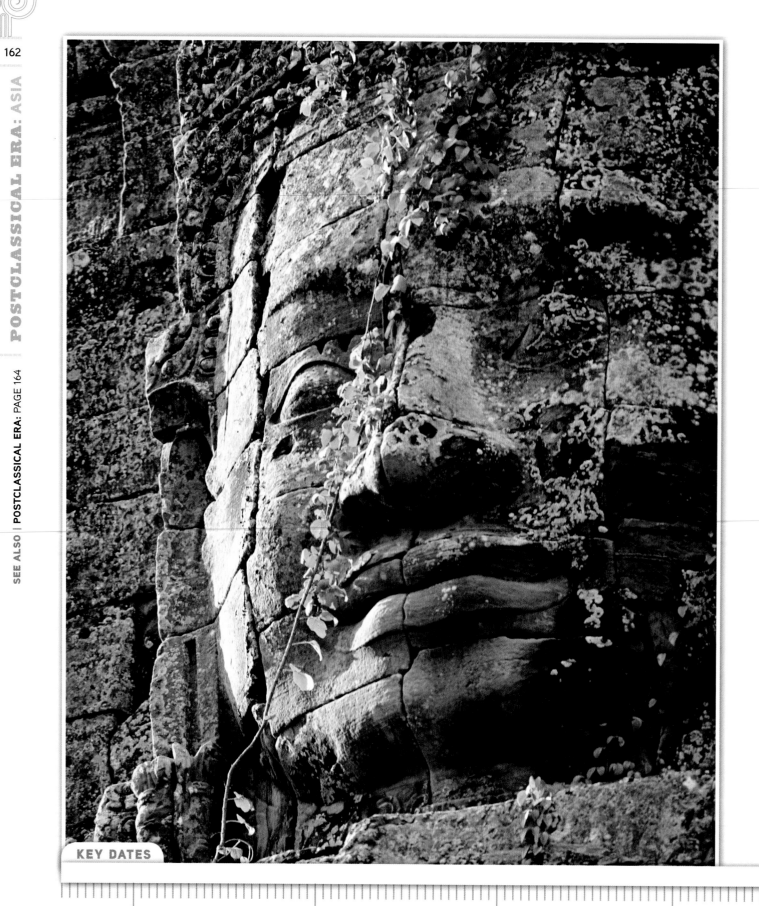

581
The Sui dynasty reunifies China after three dark centuries.

604
Yang Ti, the second Sui emperor, comes to power with plans to build a great canal.

610
The Grand Canal is completed, built by the forced labor of millions.

618–907
The Tang dynasty presides over a golden age for Chinese arts and society.

ASIA

581–1100

A dark age of disunity and turmoil befell China after the collapse of the Han dynasty in 220. But while it was similar to the condition of Europe after the Roman Empire, China's fragmentation was not followed by a massive change in its cultural complexion. Chinese customs and the ethical code of Confucianism continued to bind the people together even while conflicts flared between warring factions. In 581 the Sui dynasty came to power under the ruthless and ambitious Emperor Wendi. His accomplishments were many: He created a strong centralized government, declared a new law code, reduced taxes and the length of military service, established irrigation projects that increased food production, and expanded the empire by conquering southern and eastern China. His son and possible assassin, Yangdi, succeeded him in 604 and built the 1,240-mile Grand Canal system between the Yangtze and the Yellow rivers, a vital north-south link that helped unify China into the 20th century. Yet the enforced labor of millions turned his subjects against him and he was assassinated in 618.

China's early medieval period was marked by the rise of the Sui and Tang dynasties, unifying the land's warring kingdoms under a common banner. Japan and the Khmer states also prospered.

Into the power vacuum stepped one of China's greatest emperors, Taiyong, son of a Sui general. He seized power by ousting his father and killing his brothers, but he restored prosperity to the land and stemmed the rising might of the aristocracy by breaking the army into small units headed by commoners. The founder of the Tang dynasty, Taiyong also improved China's civil service, requiring an exam for bureaucrats that fewer than ten percent could pass. China was entering a golden age of culture and expansion. The powerful Empress Wu—China's only female sovereign—began as Taiyong's concubine, then after his death became his heir's mistress. Eventually, she became regent. She pushed the empire's borders from Mongolia to Vietnam. After the Tang dynasty's demise in 907, China split into ten regional kingdoms; rival warlords held sway until the beginning of the Song dynasty in 960.

Japan in the eighth and ninth centuries underwent rapid economic expansion. The Japanese began the manufacture of rice paper, and Nara became a key commercial city. Meanwhile, Khmer states united under King Jayavarman II, who established a capital at Angkor in today's Cambodia.

OPPOSITE: Vines and lichen cover a giant stone face at Bayon Temple in Angkor, capital of the Khmer Empire.

626–649
Emperor T'ai Tsung, one of China's most able leaders, rules.

690
Empress Wu usurps the throne from her son to become China's only female regent, ruling for 15 years.

800
In Cambodia, Jayavarman II unites his people into one kingdom, the Khmer Empire.

960
Chao K'uang founds the Song dynasty, reunifying China after the Tang dynasty's collapse.

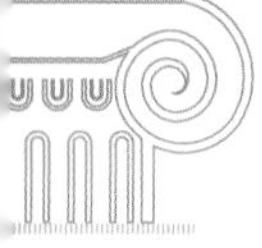

SEE ALSO | POSTCLASSICAL ERA: PAGE 160

NATIONS SUI AND TANG DYNASTIES

Renowned for her beauty, Yang Guifei was the concubine and downfall of Tang dynasty emperor Xuanzong.

The emergence of the Sui dynasty in the late 500s brought an end to some three centuries of strife within China. The massive Grand Canal project invigorated the Chinese economy by providing a north-south trading route. But the millions of Chinese conscripted to work on the canal and to wage an unsuccessful war against Korea revolted, and in 618 the Sui dynasty was toppled.

The Tang dynasty rose from the ashes, and a new period of benevolent rule began, with the Tang emperors promoting Confucian ideals of fair leadership. Enduring for nearly three centuries, the Tang made their capital in Chang'an, which swelled to a population of some two million.

The empire suffered a crisis when 60-year-old emperor Xuanzong neglected his duties to dally with a young courtesan, Yang Guifei. General An Lushan revolted in 755, and with 150,000 troops drove the emperor out. Turkish nomads known as Uighurs helped restore the Tang government.

THE TAKEAWAY: The Tang dynasty brought growth to China, but rebellion undermined it.

ASIA — VIPs

Yangdi, 569–618
Last Sui emperor, builder of China's Grand Canal

Taiyong, 599–649
Emperor who ruled over a golden age

Wu Zhao, 625–705
China's only female regent

An Lushan, 703–757
Chinese general who led a rebellion against the Tang

Du Fu, 712–770
Chinese poet who wrote of the natural world and the injustices of Chinese society

Jayavarman II, ca 770–835
Emperor who united Cambodia

Murasaki Shikibu, ca 973–1014
Author of *The Tale of Genji*

“*In the sky, there is no distinction of east and west; people create distinctions out of their own minds and then believe them to be true.*” —BUDDHIST SAYING

VOICES

TANG DYNASTY PASS AND FAIL

"One day, Wang Tsun . . . set out for the capital to take the imperial examination. As he was approaching the capital, he met Hsü T'ang, who was seeing some friends off at the outskirts of the city.

" 'Eh,' Hsü T'ang asked him, 'what are you doing here in the capital?'

" 'I have come to take the imperial examination,' answered the former functionary.

"Upon hearing this, Hsü T'ang angrily declared, 'How insolent you are, you lowly clerk!' Although they were now fellow candidates for the imperial examination Hsü T'ang treated him with contempt. But in the end, Wang Tsun passed the examination and became very famous. Hsü T'ang did not pass until five years later."

—FROM ANECDOTES OF THE TANG DYNASTY EXAMINATIONS

TANG-ERA TOMB FIGURE

CLASS & SOCIETY TANG LUXURY

The Tang nobility prized a life of luxury and sophistication. They imported musicians and acrobats to entertain in lavish homes that were furnished with bathrooms, water fountains, and ice-cooled fans. Handmade and printed silks adorned the well-to-do, as did elegant gold and silver jewelry. The newly arrived sport of polo became immensely popular among the aristocracy, who played it on imported Persian horses. Next on the ladder of China's highly stratified feudal society were the landed gentry, who held modest parcels of land, then the farmers and peasants, the poorest of whom were similar to Europe's serfs. Family life and indigenous religion were the glue that kept this mass of laborers from revolting—the seventh-century rebellion that brought down the Sui being a rare and spectacular exception.

Tang-era terra-cotta ox cart and attendants

China had more urban centers than Europe, and they were larger. To handle municipal affairs in these cities, an army of thousands of civil servants was needed, making up a large middle class. Entrance examinations during the Tang period were famously difficult—applicants had to demonstrate extensive knowledge of government, Confucian classics, and poetry.

{ A land tax in 780 caused provincial leaders to rebel, nearly destroying the Tang dynasty. }

THE TAKEAWAY: In China's top-down class system, the masses' hard work supported the nobles' lavish lifestyle.

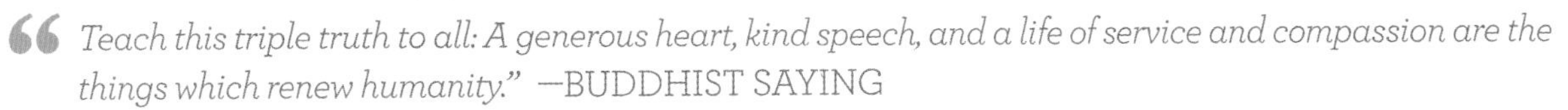

"Teach this triple truth to all: A generous heart, kind speech, and a life of service and compassion are the things which renew humanity." —BUDDHIST SAYING

SEE ALSO | KINGS AND NOMADS: PAGE 201

TRADE & ECONOMY SILK ROADS

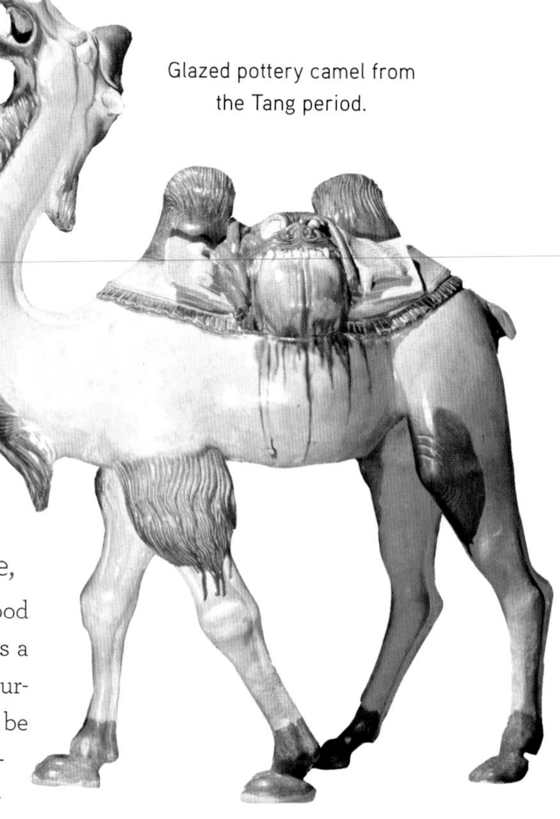

Glazed pottery camel from the Tang period.

In the seventh century, China's Tang dynasty established protectorates in the empire's far western regions, reaching them via the fabled Silk Road—a network of footpaths and caravan trails across rugged mountains and barren lands. The Silk Road was an east-west trading route for Chinese silks and porcelain, Roman glass, Bactrian gold jewelry, Persian bronze and silver vessels, and Indian precious stones. Also along this two-way road traveled religion, science, technology, artistic styles, and foods—a moving international bazaar that brought exotic influences from one culture to another.

During this period of power and stability, the Chinese made great strides in agricultural and other technologies. They invented an early method of printing by carving images and text onto blocks of wood and stamping them on pages. As a result, literature and the arts flourished, and paper money could be printed. A brilliant new three-color glaze made Chinese porcelains an even more sought-after commodity. Efficient blast furnaces allowed for the production of steel weapons and farming tools.

> Explorer Marco Polo (1254–1324) and Christian crusaders brought gunpowder back to Europe.

The Chinese also created gunpowder by accidentally mixing charcoal, sulfur, and saltpeter; loaded into bamboo, these early fireworks exploded in the sky—both to entertain people and to scare enemies.

The wealth of the Tang era led to a population boom both in the growing cities and in the countryside—and eventually, to unrest.

THE TAKEAWAY: In the Tang period, trade flourished and inventions helped fuel the economy.

CONNECTIONS FLYING CASH

THE CHINESE WERE THE FIRST PEOPLE KNOWN to use paper money. During a copper shortage in the ninth century, Emperor Hien Tsung issued the first paper money, which he considered a temporary measure. But the convenient, easily carried paper notes (known as flying cash) remained. Finance ministers found that they could help offset periods of inflation by reducing the amount of paper currency in circulation. Marco Polo's accounts of his 13th-century travels in China record his astonishment that printed paper could be exchanged for merchandise, a practice that did not reach Europe until the 17th century—and is now, of course, almost universal.

CURRENCY IN TIMES OF INFLATION

 *By copying, the ancient models should be perpetuated."* —XIE HE

VOICES

DU FU THE DESERTED WIFE

DU FU

> "I live concealed in mountain dell
> I call myself scion of a virtuous house,
> Though shrubs and trees are now my sole support.
> Trouble came upon us lately within the walls;
> My brothers were put to death.
> What matter that their rank was high?
> We could not recover their dead bodies.
> The age has no charms for me;
> All things are like the puffing-out of a candle."
>
> —FROM "ALONE IN HER BEAUTY," DU FU, EIGHTH CENTURY

RELIGION & ART PEACE AND POETRY

During the early medieval period, China incorporated elements of Confucianism with the mystical philosophy of Taoism and the religion of Buddhism, newly arrived with Indian traders. After centuries of turmoil, the Chinese welcomed a religion that promoted peaceful meditation and the hope of personal enlightenment. Tang rulers and nobility supported the building of Buddhist monasteries and temples; by the mid-sixth century, China held nearly 14,000 such places of worship. Buddhist pilgrims and missionaries began visiting sacred sites in India and spread their faith to Japan and Korea.

In addition to religion, the arts flowered during the Tang era. Pure white porcelains achieved a new brilliance. Painters Wu Daozi and Wang Wei's exquisite, delicate brushwork set a standard for later eras.

In literature, poetry in particular attained unequaled aesthetic beauty. Li Bai, Du Fu, and other poets wrote verses rich in imagery and feeling on the pleasures of fishing, the dishonor of failing the civil service exams, and the glories of the northern capital city of Ch'ang-an. A member of the reveling band of poets called the Eight Immortals of the Wine Cup, Li Bai reputedly drowned while leaning from a boat and trying to embrace the moon's reflection.

THE TAKEAWAY: Buddhism arrived and thrived under the Tang, as did poetry and painting.

Detail of a marble figure of the Bodhisattva Guanyin, Goddess of Mercy

> "*Resemblance reproduces the formal aspect of objects, but neglects their spirit; truth shows the spirit and substance like perfection.*" —JING HAO

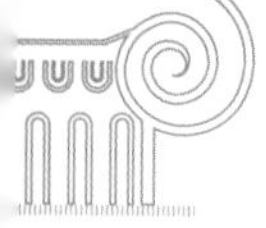

SEE ALSO | KINGS AND NOMADS: PAGE 203

NATIONS AN EARLY GOLDEN AGE

The early medieval era was a fertile time for Japanese civilization. Chinese culture, arriving via the Korean Peninsula, had been influencing the Japanese islands for centuries—wheel-turned pottery and cultivated rice had become staples of Japanese life. Now Chinese methods of weaving, irrigating, and writing—with ideographic script—took up residence in Japan.

Buddha statue, Todai-ji Temple, Nara

Chinese political systems began making their presence felt in Japan, and the mixture of Confucian and Buddhist religions fused with Japan's indigenous Shintoism, which emphasized the divinity in nature.

The militant Yamato clan rose to power in the fourth century, its armies taking control of much of the Japanese archipelago. The city of Nara, a center of Buddhism, served as the political capital for most of the eighth century. Then, in 794, the emperor relocated to Heian (modern Kyoto), inaugurating the Heian period (794–1185), notable among other things for its literature. Though the emperor was considered a deity, aristocrats held the real power, and in the ninth and tenth centuries that power was wielded by the Fujiwara clan.

{ Under the Taika Reforms of 645, Japan's land management and government organized along Chinese lines. }

THE TAKEAWAY: Influenced by China, the young nation of Japan became centralized and underwent a cultural renaissance.

SEI SHONAGON DETESTABLE THINGS

VOICES

“A visitor who tells a long story when you are in a hurry. If he is a person you are intimate with, you can pack him off, saying that you will hear it another time. But those whom you cannot treat in this way are very detestable.

“An exorcist who, when sent for in a case of sudden illness, recites his charms as if he were half asleep.

“Babies that cry or dogs that bark when you want to listen.

“The snoring of a man whom you are trying to conceal, and who has gone to sleep in a place where he has no business.

“People who interrupt your stories to show off their own cleverness. All interrupters, young or old, are very detestable.”

—FROM THE PILLOW BOOK OF SEI SHONAGON, ca 1002

SEI SHONAGON

“In those days people learned to recite sutras and practice austerities of religious observance after the age of seventeen or eighteen, but I could scarcely even think of such matters.” —MURASAKI SHIKIBU

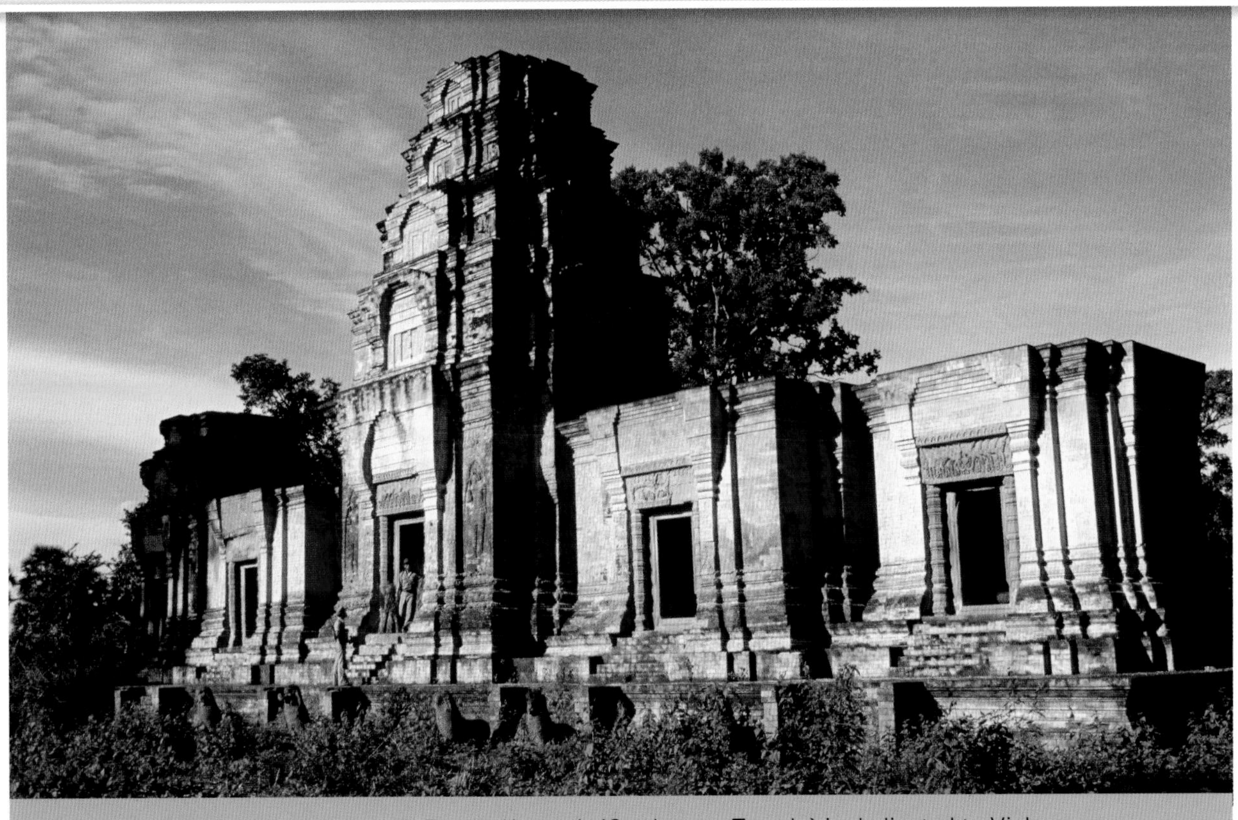

Angkor's 10th-century Prasat Kravanh (Cardamom Temple) is dedicated to Vishnu.

EMPIRES KHMER EMPIRE

The Hindu-Buddhist kingdom of the Khmer occupied what is now Cambodia from the seventh to the fifteenth centuries. Making their capital in Angkor, the Khmer constructed irrigation canals, reservoirs, roads, hospitals, and hundreds of stone temples. Their first great king, Jayavarman II, returned from exile in Java around 790 and by 802 had carved out an independent state. Each Khmer king constructed a pyramidal shrine known as a temple mountain, where sacred consecration ceremonies were held. The Khmer maintained that the king's temple mountain was the center of the universe; hence, their kingdom was above all others. Even so, a complex bureaucratic structure, including Brahmin priests and military leaders, kept a check on the king's absolute authority.

THE TAKEAWAY: The Khmer Empire came to power in the early 800s, its kings divine rulers.

KHMER DEITY

"With all our heart, revere the three treasures. The three treasures, consisting of Buddha, the Doctrine, and the Monastic Order, are the final refuge of the four generated beings." —PRINCE SHOTOKU

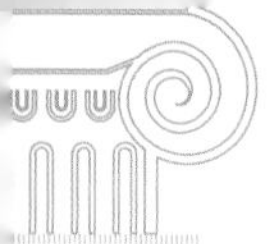

SEE ALSO | POSTCLASSICAL ERA: PAGE 172

KEY DATES

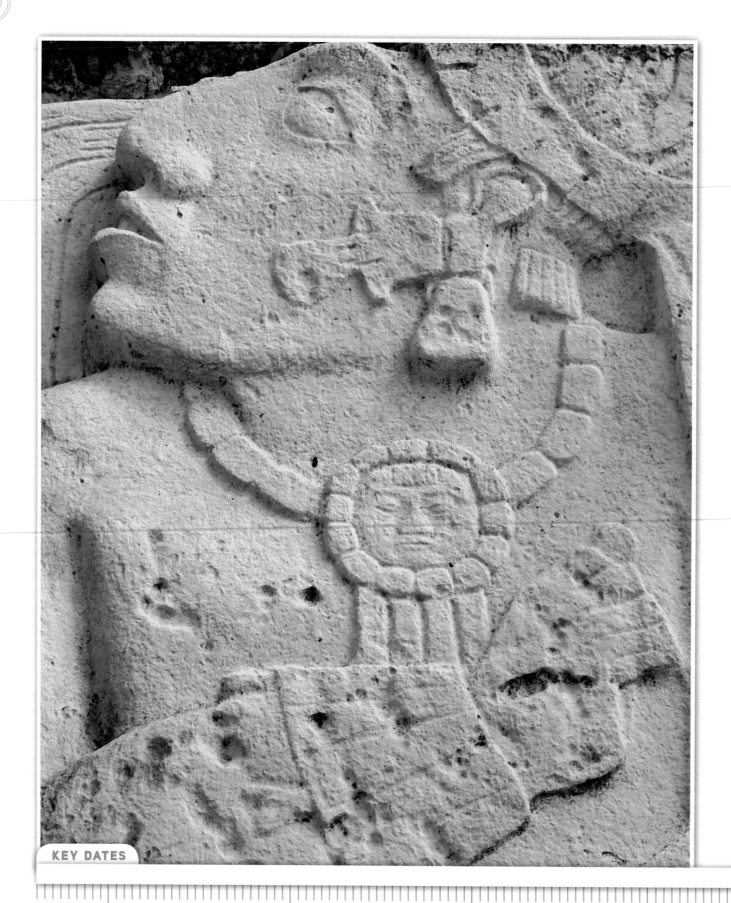

500
Teotihuacan rises to become the Valley of Mexico's first powerful city-state.

562
The Maya city-state of Tikal is devastated by an attack from a rival state, Calakmul.

ca 600
Tikal recovers, reaching its peak as the most powerful city-state on the Yucatán Peninsula.

615
Maya King Pacal, known as Sun Shield, begins his 68-year rule over the city-state of Palenque.

THE AMERICAS

500–1100

The first Americans to leave a detailed written record, the Maya flourished in and around the Yucatán Peninsula from 600 B.C.E. to 900 C.E., peaking in influence around 600 C.E. They put their hieroglyphs on stone monuments, pottery, bark paper, and deerskin. Once thought to be only astronomical data, these ancient writings tell quite a dramatic tale. Scholars in recent times have discovered a history dripping with blood—ritual sacrifices to the gods were an integral part of Maya life. Their blood sports were similar in violence to those of the Romans, who had captives killed by gladiators and animals in arenas. Like the ancient Greeks, the Maya had a common language and culture, spread over a wide sphere of influence but divided into city-states. Marriage alliances helped ease tensions between competing city-states, but open conflicts often broke out. One prominent Maya city-state, Tikal, held some 50,000 people and encompassed 50 square miles by the year 800. Tikal remained under one family dynasty for more than six centuries.

The soil of the Yucatán Peninsula was not fertile enough to support 500 people per square mile (the population density in places), so warriors had to push farther and farther out in search of provisions. Resentment in smaller villages erupted into revolts. In addition to endless wars, factors that may have helped bring on the ruin of the Maya include drought, deforestation, and depletion of natural resources.

Advanced civilizations dominated what is now southern Mexico, city-states wielding power and priests making careful observations of heavenly bodies for advice on war and agriculture.

By the year 900, power was shifting north to the Valley of Mexico, and jungle eventually enshrouded the Maya's splendid civilization.

To the north, the city-state of Teotihuacan became increasingly powerful in the sixth and seventh centuries. It was the first of several important urban centers in the Valley of Mexico, which would become Aztec country in the 13th century.

In what is now the United States, farming settlements began popping up along the southern Mississippi River between 800 and 1000. The Mississippian culture fanned out east and west. Typical villages included a central plaza, around which were large pyramid-shaped mounds with thatched-roof temples erected on the flat tops. Priests, nobles, and craftsmen inhabited these villages; beyond them were smaller villages occupied by farmers, hunters, and traders.

OPPOSITE: Mayan prisoners, such as the one in this ancient carving, often became the victims of ritual sacrifice.

ca 800
The Anasazi build stone pueblos in the North American southwest.

ca 900
Environmental stresses and warfare bring the downfall of the great Maya city-states.

ca 1000
The Aztec civilization flourishes in Teotihuacan.

ca 1050
The Cahokia of the Mississippi region build earthen mounds as bases for temples and other buildings.

EMPIRES WINNER TAKES ALL

The Maya had one of the most advanced civilizations in the Western Hemisphere before European contact. They dominated Mesoamerica, producing pyramid temples, elaborate gold and copper work, and hieroglyphics—and armies. Tikal and other Maya city-states studied the stars for propitious times to plant and wage war. One such "star war" in 562 resulted in a nearly fatal defeat for Tikal; indeed, it did not completely recover for more than a hundred years.

A reconstruction of a Mayan mural depicts a bloodletting ritual.

The attacking city-state might have been Calakmul, to the north. In 599, Calakmul warriors journeyed 150 miles west to successfully assault Palenque, which was ruled then by a queen named Lady Yohl Ik'nal, one of a very few female rulers. Yet Palenque regrouped under mighty King Pacal (Sun Shield), who ruled for 68 years, starting in 615 at age 12. Pacal provided protection to Tikal against the hostile Calakmul state, and he constructed Palenque's extensive palace, pyramid, and temple complex.

> One method of ritual bloodletting was to pull a thorn-studded rope through one's tongue.

A less glorious end awaited the king of Copan in 738—he was captured by rebels and beheaded. But a successor named Smoke Shell reasserted Copan's strength, aligning the state with Palenque by marrying a Palenque princess. His Copan Acropolis—a magnificent complex of temples and

CONNECTIONS THE MAYAN CALENDAR AND 2012

THE MAYA'S CAREFUL OBSERVATIONS OF THE PLANETS and stars allowed them to create a complex calendar consisting of two cycles—a solar year of 365 days and a ceremonial year of 260 days. These two cycles intermeshed to form a span of 52 years. Their Long Count system had a base of 20; there were 20 days in each of 18 months, with 5 unlucky days left over at the end of the year. According to Maya calculations, the universe was created in 3114 B.C.E. and a large cycle will end in 2012 C.E. Despite contemporary accounts claiming the Maya predicted an apocalypse on this date, for the Maya it was merely the start of a new cycle.

CHICHEN ITZA OBSERVATORY

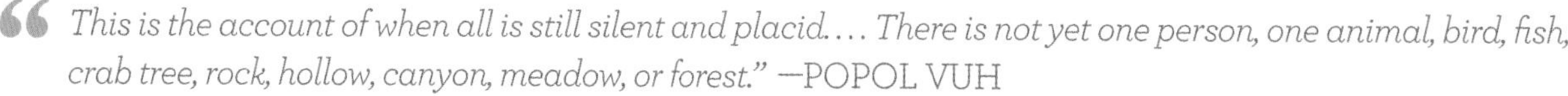

"This is the account of when all is still silent and placid.... There is not yet one person, one animal, bird, fish, crab tree, rock, hollow, canyon, meadow, or forest." —POPOL VUH

SEE ALSO | KINGS AND NOMADS: PAGE 209

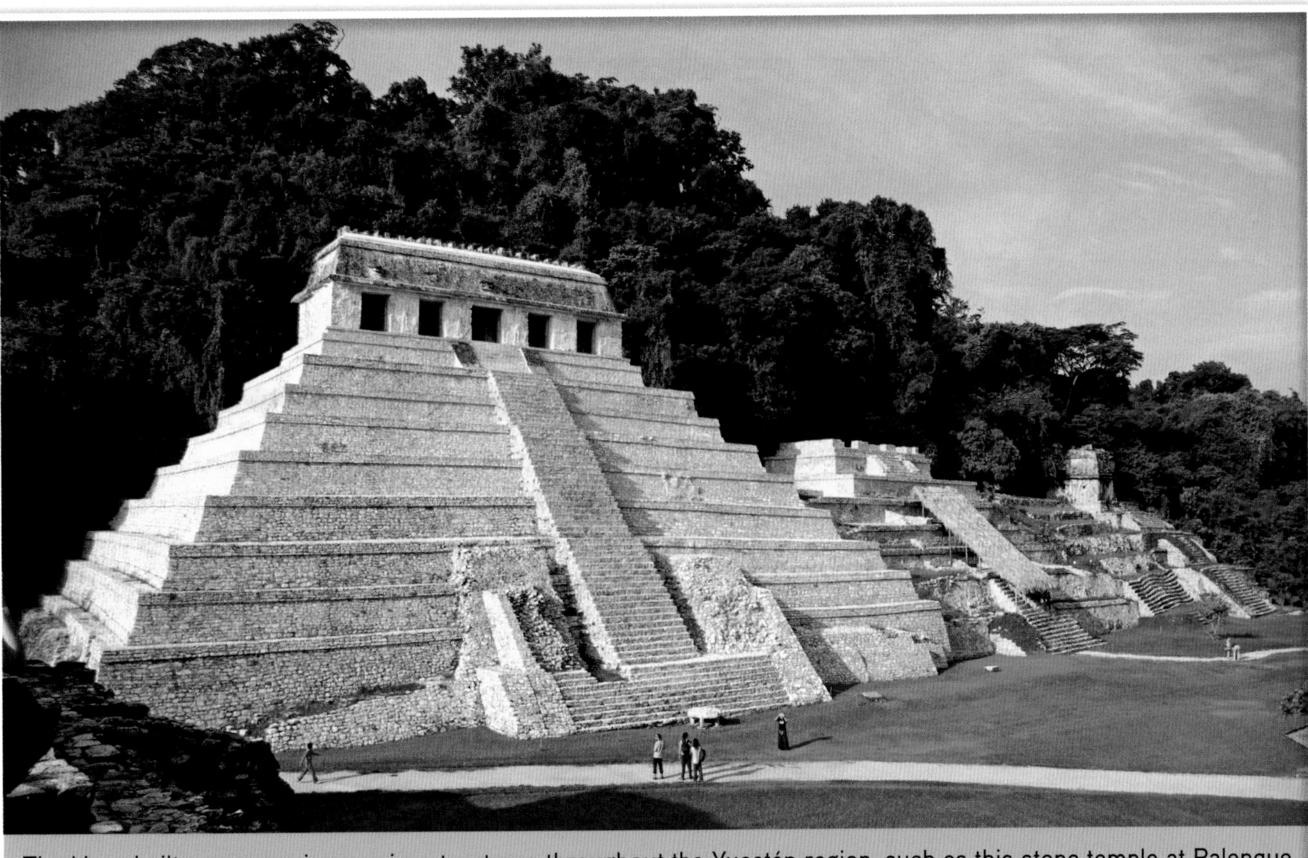

The Maya built numerous impressive structures throughout the Yucatán region, such as this stone temple at Palenque.

pyramids—was one of the final great Maya monuments.

Maya religious rituals, and even some of their games, often included blood. Sacrifices to the gods included killing prisoners of war or prisoners in ritualized combat. Royal blood was especially valuable, and it did not always come from captives—royals sometimes drew enough of their own blood to experience visions.

THE TAKEAWAY: Kings of Maya city-states erected stone temples and pyramids and readily made war on their neighbors.

VOICES

MAYA BEFORE THE EARTH APPEARED

"This is the account of how all was in suspense, all calm, in silence; all motionless, still, and the expanse of the sky was empty.

"This is the first account, the first narrative. There was neither man, nor animal, birds, fishes, crabs, trees, stones, caves, ravines, grasses, nor forests; there was only the sky.

"The surface of the earth had not appeared. There was only the calm sea and the great expanse of the sky."

—OPENING OF THE *POPUL VUH*, THE SACRED BOOK OF THE MAYA

VASE WITH MAYA DEITIES

"First the earth was created, the mountains and the valleys. The waterways were divided, their branches coursing among the mountains." —POPOL VUH

CONNECTIONS TIME LINE

500–1100

500
China enters a period of instability when divided into several warring kingdoms.

ca 500
The empire of Ghana becomes an important trading center for West African gold.

529
Saint Benedict establishes Monte Cassino Abbey in Italy.

THE BLIND BELISARIUS RESTING

533
Brilliant Byzantine general Belisarius destroys the Vandal kingdom in North Africa.

570
Byzantium and Persia establish a 50-year peace.

574
Crown Prince Shotoku of the Soga clan in Japan is born.

581
The Sui dynasty establishes a strong central government in China.

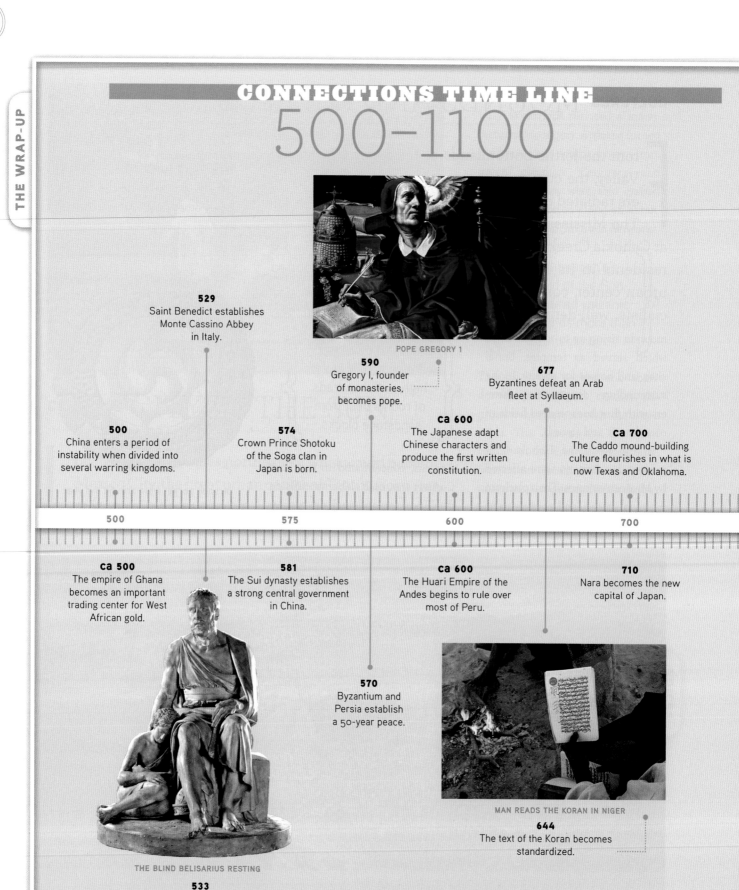

POPE GREGORY 1

590
Gregory I, founder of monasteries, becomes pope.

ca 600
The Japanese adapt Chinese characters and produce the first written constitution.

ca 600
The Huari Empire of the Andes begins to rule over most of Peru.

MAN READS THE KORAN IN NIGER

644
The text of the Koran becomes standardized.

677
Byzantines defeat an Arab fleet at Syllaeum.

ca 700
The Caddo mound-building culture flourishes in what is now Texas and Oklahoma.

710
Nara becomes the new capital of Japan.

500 575 600 700

> *"Never walk away from home ahead of your axe and sword."* —NORSE SAYING

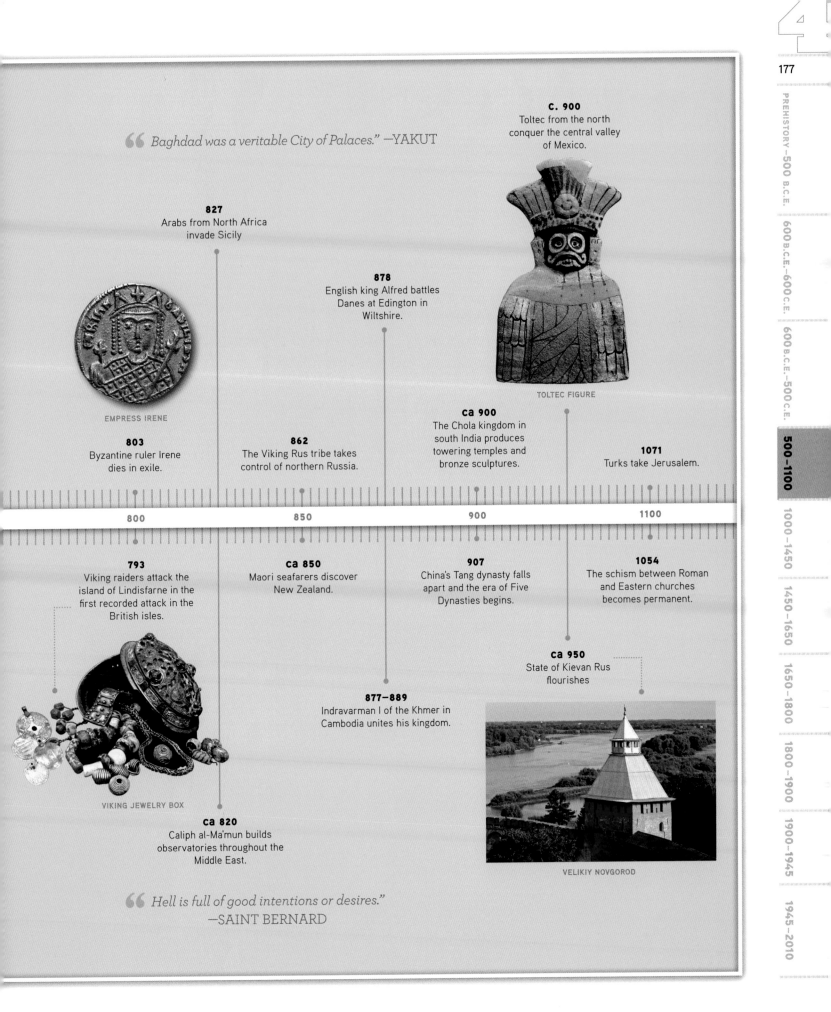

"Baghdad was a veritable City of Palaces." —YAKUT

c. 900
Toltec from the north conquer the central valley of Mexico.

TOLTEC FIGURE

827
Arabs from North Africa invade Sicily

EMPRESS IRENE

878
English king Alfred battles Danes at Edington in Wiltshire.

803
Byzantine ruler Irene dies in exile.

862
The Viking Rus tribe takes control of northern Russia.

ca 900
The Chola kingdom in south India produces towering temples and bronze sculptures.

1071
Turks take Jerusalem.

800 | 850 | 900 | 1100

793
Viking raiders attack the island of Lindisfarne in the first recorded attack in the British isles.

ca 850
Maori seafarers discover New Zealand.

907
China's Tang dynasty falls apart and the era of Five Dynasties begins.

1054
The schism between Roman and Eastern churches becomes permanent.

ca 950
State of Kievan Rus flourishes

VIKING JEWELRY BOX

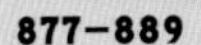

877–889
Indravarman I of the Khmer in Cambodia unites his kingdom.

VELIKIY NOVGOROD

ca 820
Caliph al-Ma'mun builds observatories throughout the Middle East.

"Hell is full of good intentions or desires."
—SAINT BERNARD

KINGS AND

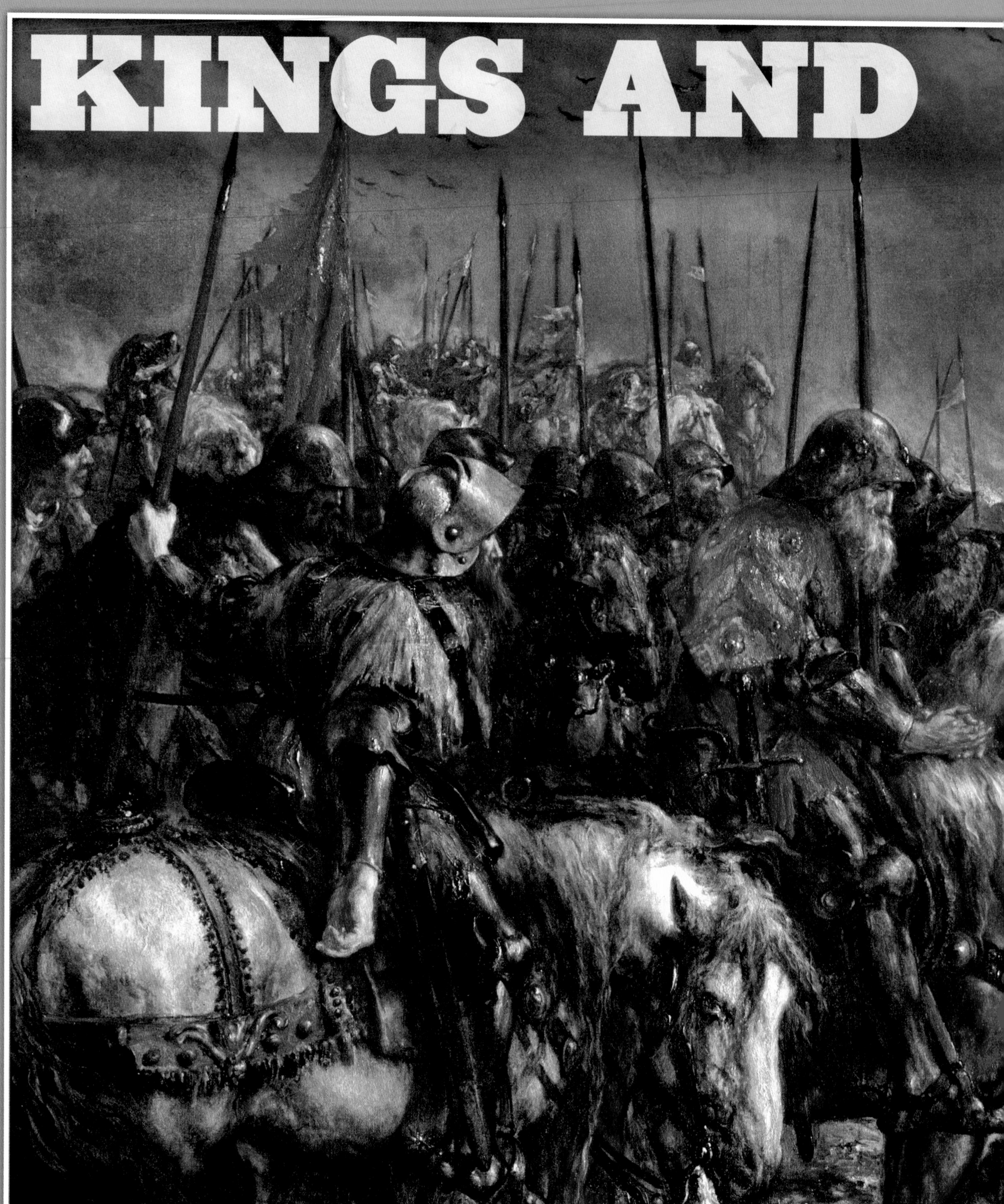

NOMADS

TALES OF CHIVALRY AND CONQUEST

1000–1450

CHAPTER

5

The English triumphed in the 1415 Battle of Agincourt.

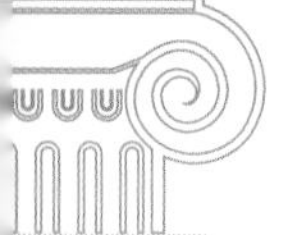

SEE ALSO | KINGS AND NOMADS: PAGE 185

KEY DATES

ca 1000
Christianity reaches Greenland and Iceland.

1066
William the Conqueror defeats Harold II of England at the Battle of Hastings

1095
Pope Urban II launches the first Crusade, calling Christian soldiers to take the Holy Land.

1160
Construction of the Notre Dame Cathedral begins.

EUROPE

1000–1453

By the turn of the millennium, the Dark Ages were beginning to give way to a period of greater prosperity and cultural refinement. Emerging European nations were unifying under central leadership, and the Christian Church was rapidly expanding its sphere of influence, becoming Europe's predominant cohesive force. With Viking and nomadic raids on the ebb, trade networks strengthened, cities grew, and the arts began flowering. The iron cannon and steel crossbow gave large armies new power, enabling monarchs to keep rebellious regions under firmer control; a sense of national identity began replacing regional allegiances. Other new technologies, including horse collars, horseshoes, and better plows allowed farmers a higher crop yield; new windmills and water mills served to grind grains and power machinery for clothmaking and metalworking. Merchants' and craftsmen's guilds fostered the rise of a powerful new middle class.

While the church unified much of Europe, it also butted heads with a competing institution—the state. Dramatic power struggles between the pope and rulers of Germany, France, and England defined much of the High Middle Ages. One of the flashpoints was lay investiture—the appointment of bishops by secular lords. The pope insisted that only the church held this authority; many secular rulers disagreed. One thing both sides agreed on was the need to bolster Christianity in the newly Islamized East.

Despite plagues and wars, Europe's economy and culture managed to thrive in the High Middle Ages, propelled by the Church, new technologies, and the emergence of powerful nation-states.

Beginning at the end of the 11th century, a series of Crusades sent European armies out to retake the Holy Lands conquered by the Muslims centuries earlier.

Cultural and economic progress was anything but steady in the late medieval period. Famines, plagues, and wars continued to ravage Europe, most notably in the 14th century. The Black Death devastated much of Europe's urban population in midcentury, and the Hundred Years' War exhausted the resources of France and England. The costly cross-channel dispute over territory actually lasted from 1337 to 1453, doing its part to impede international relations and slow Europe's march toward a cultural renaissance. But the seeds of that flowering had been sown in the High Middle Ages, as scholars and artists, benefiting from strong monarchies, left an enduring legacy in the form of philosophical works, epic poems, and Gothic cathedrals.

OPPOSITE: King Henry V reigned in England during the Hundred Years' War.

1187
Saladin reconquers Jerusalem for the Muslims.

1347
The Black Death, bubonic plague, devastates Europe's population.

1429
Joan of Arc saves the city of Orléans.

1440S
Johannes Gutenberg invents the printing press.

SEE ALSO | KINGS AND NOMADS: PAGE 192

Edward I of England pays homage to Philip IV of France.

NATIONS YOKED TO FRANCE

The working compromise between England's Anglo-Saxon and Viking-conquered territories vanished in 1066 when William the Conqueror, Duke of Normandy, invaded England and defeated King Harold at the Battle of Hastings. The powerful new ruler exerted an iron will over Britain—Anglo-Saxon language, literature, and traditions were replaced by French and other continental influences. William's great-grandson Henry II fought for control of the French provinces, even while struggling at home with Archbishop Thomas Becket, a conflict ending in Becket's murder in 1170.

In 1215 the English nobility forced the irascible King John to sign the Magna Carta, limiting the power of the king to the written law. By century's end, a nascent parliament was offering Europe an example of representative government. And with the onset of the Hundred Years' War in 1337, England and France began a struggle to finally divorce the two nations that William had forced into marriage.

THE TAKEAWAY: England's political link to France began with the Norman conquest and ended with the Hundred Years' War.

VIPs

EUROPE

William of Normandy (the Conqueror), 1028–1087
Conqueror of Anglo-Saxon England

Hildegard of Bingen, 1098–1179
Abbess and composer

Frederick I (Barbarossa), ca 1123–1190
Holy Roman emperor

Saladin, 1138–1193
Sultan who fought Richard the Lionheart in the Crusades

Edward III of England, 1312–1377
Molded his nation into a premier military power

Johannes Gutenberg, 1398–1468
Inventor of Europe's printing press

> *"[The Normans] are a race inured to war, and can hardly live without it; fierce in rushing against the enemy, and, where force fails of success, ready to use stratagem."* —WILLIAM OF MALMESBURY

VOICES

JOHN OF SALISBURY

"The martyr stood in the cathedral, before Christ's altar, as we have said, ready to suffer; the hour of slaughter was at hand. When he heard that he was sought—heard the knights who had come for him shouting in the throng of clerks and monks 'Where is the archbishop?'—he turned to meet them on the steps which he had almost climbed, and said with steady countenance: 'Here am I! What do you want?' One of the knight-assassins flung at him in fury: 'That you die now! That you should live longer is impossible.' . . . Steadfast in speech as in spirit, he replied: 'And I am prepared to die for my God, to preserve justice and my church's liberty.' "

—FROM A LETTER BY THOMAS BECKET'S SECRETARY, WHO WITNESSED HIS MURDER IN 1170

THOMAS BECKET

NATIONS A GROWING POWER

France's bickering duchies began to coalesce in the High Middle Ages, and by the end of the 13th century France was the richest and strongest country in Europe. King Philip Augustus used a subtle blend of war, diplomacy, and marriage alliances to expand his authority well beyond the traditional boundaries of the Ile de France (Paris and surrounds), advancing the crown's realm into the provinces of Normandy, Maine, Anjou, Artois, and Vermandois.

The Château de Vincennes outside Paris was built around 1360.

{ In 1358, French peasants revolted during the jacquerie against fees collected by the nobility. }

Philip's grandson, Louis IX, was the greatest of the Capetians, the dynasty that ruled France from 987 to 1328. Later known as St. Louis, he introduced popular reforms in government and law, and fostered achievements in learning and the arts. Notre Dame and Chartres cathedrals were among hundreds of magnificent Gothic churches built in 12th- and 13th-century France. By the time of the Hundred Years' War, the country had a vast treasury and an efficient bureaucracy capable of raising a mighty army.

THE TAKEAWAY: The French monarchy's growing power allowed it to build its treasury and take on England.

"We fluctuate long between love and hatred before we can arrive at tranquillity." —HÉLOISE

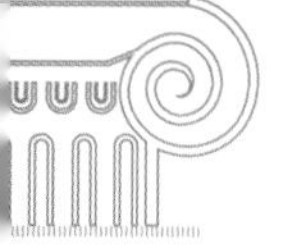

SEE ALSO | NEW WORLD ORDER: PAGE 272

JOAN OF ARC

VOICES

JOAN OF ARC TO HENRY VI

King of England, render account to the King of Heaven of your royal blood. Return the keys of all the good cities which you have seized, to the Maid. She is sent by God to reclaim the royal blood, and is fully prepared to make peace, if you will give her satisfaction; that is, you must render justice, and pay back all that you have taken.

". . . HEAR THE WORDS OF GOD AND THE MAID."

—FROM A LETTER BY JOAN OF ARC TO THE KING OF ENGLAND, 1429

CONFLICTS THE LONG WAR

In 1337 French king Philip VI began what would become the Hundred Years' War by laying claim to the English-held region of Gascony. But bad planning and over-confidence doomed France's initial efforts, and the English won a decisive victory in 1346 at Crécy, a town north of Paris. The English use of the longbow—quicker and easier to fire than the crossbow—was a key factor. But despite English king Henry V's stunning victory at Agincourt over 20,000 French soldiers in 1415, the French, with the help of the young visionary Joan of Arc, finally prevailed in 1453.

THE TAKEAWAY: After early British victories, France eventually won the war in 1453.

English and French armies meet in the 1346 Battle of Crécy.

"Whom once [Henry II] has esteemed, with difficulty he unloves them; whom once he has hated, with difficulty he receives into the grace of his familiarity." —PETER OF BLOIS

EMPIRES POWER STRUGGLES

Though the pope declared Charlemagne emperor of the new "Roman Empire," it was not until the crowning of Otto I of Germany in 962 that the Holy Roman Empire officially began. The church-state alliance gave the pope military strength and helped Otto maintain an image of moral superiority throughout an expanding empire that included Bohemia, Austria, and northern Italy. But the heads of church and state often clashed over policy issues. In the 11th century, the big issue was the right of the emperor to appoint church officials. Emperor Henry IV and Pope Gregory VII, both powerful figures, clashed over the problem—the emperor ultimately reduced to a show of begging forgiveness on his knees. The 1122 Concordat of Worms (in western Germany) ended the controversy.

When another Holy Roman emperor, Frederick I (Barbarossa, or "red beard"), invaded northern Italy in the late 1100s, the pope had to call on France and England to push him back. By the 13th century, emperors were selected by a council instead of the pope, and for 23 years during the "great interregnum" there was no emperor at all.

The gold crown of Otto I the Great, Holy Roman emperor

> Pope Gregory IX dubbed the brilliant, brutal Holy Roman Emperor Frederick II the Antichrist.

In 1273 Rudolf, of the Austrian Habsburg family, became emperor, inaugurating a nearly 500-year Habsburg reign in Central Europe. Yet the Holy Roman Empire gradually eroded, its candle going out in 1806.

THE TAKEAWAY: The Holy Roman Empire began as a confederation of the church and the German state, but often brewed internal conflict.

VOICES

FREDERICK I PEACE OF THE LAND

"If any one, within the term fixed for the peace, shall slay a man, he shall be sentenced to death, unless by wager of battle he can prove this, that he slew him in defending his own life.

"No one shall spread his nets or his nooses, or any other instruments for taking game, except for taking bears, boars and wolves.

"If any one shall have stolen 5 shillings, or its equivalent, he shall be hung with a rope; if less he shall be flayed with whips, and his hair pulled out with a pincers."

—LAWS ESTABLISHED BY FREDERICK BARBAROSSA, 1150s

FREDERICK I BARBAROSSA

> *"Law: an ordinance of reason for the commmon good, made by him who has care of the community."*
>
> —ST. THOMAS AQUINAS

SEE ALSO | POSTCLASSICAL ERA: PAGE 137

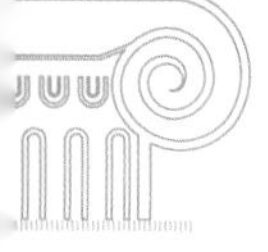

Notre Dame, one of the first Gothic cathedrals, was begun in the late 12th century in Paris.

RELIGION EUROPEAN BEDROCK

By the 11th century, Christianity had become the underpinning of European life. The social and political order of feudalism was intended to correspond to the order ordained by God. The ultimate fealty of man was to God and his earthly representatives in the church.

The Eastern Orthodox and Roman Catholic branches of the church had been diverging, and in 1054 they parted for good when the pope excommunicated the Byzantine patriarch over doctrinal differences. But both branches continued in their devotion to saints, relics, icons, and Mary, the mother of Jesus.

ST. FRANCIS

New monastic orders sprang to life in the High Middle Ages. In 1098, St. Robert of Molesme founded the austere Cistercian order in Citeaux, France. St. Francis of Assisi founded the Franciscans in 1209; his disciples lived in self-imposed poverty. In 1216, Spanish preacher Dominic founded another mendicant order, the Dominicans. Dedicated to preaching and charity, these new groups fanned out across Europe.

Twelfth-century Benedictine abbess Hildegard of Bingen composed more than 70 works of music.

THE TAKEAWAY: By the late Middle Ages, the Church was the foundation of European life.

“*Praise to thee, my Lord, for all thy creatures, / Above all Brother Sun / Who brings us the day and lends us his light.*” —ST. FRANCIS

CONFLICTS THE CRUSADES

When Seljuk Turks took over Palestine in the late 1000s, Christian pilgrims were no longer granted safe passage to the Holy Land. In 1095 Pope Urban II called for a holy war to take control of the region, thus igniting a series of Crusades over the next two centuries. Thousands of crusaders took up the cross and sword and marched eastward. In 1099 they wrested Jerusalem from the Muslims and thereby gained prestige for the church. But they were unable to hold the outposts they set up in the Holy Land; succeeding Crusades failed to accomplish what the first had, and crusading became a token rite of passage for Europe's devout young men.

Richard I the Lionheart journeys to Jerusalem in the Third Crusade.

Notable crusaders included Louis IX of France and Richard the Lionheart of England, the latter celebrated for his spirited battles with Kurdish sultan Saladin in the Third Crusade (1189–1192). Saladin had reconquered Jerusalem two years earlier, and Richard failed in his bid to retake it. In 1212 thousands of youngsters undertook the ill-fated Children's Crusade, many dying en route or ending up sold into slavery. With the fall of Acre in 1291, the crusading era ended.

Although the Crusades failed in their intended purpose, Europeans, at least, benefited from the cross-cultural exchange. Contact with the advanced civilizations to the East stimulated European culture and opened up trade routes.

{ St. Francis of Assisi joined the Fifth Crusade and negotiated with the Egyptian sultan. }

THE TAKEAWAY: From 1095 to 1291, Christian crusaders journeyed east to battle Muslims for control of the Holy Land.

THUMBS UP / THUMBS DOWN

SALADIN C. 1137–1193

THE MUSLIM COUNTERPART TO the western chivalric ideal was brilliant sultan Salah al-Din, or Saladin, the Mesopotamian commander who captured the Frankish-held kingdom of Jerusalem in 1187. Instead of massacring the inhabitants, as the Christians had done in 1099, he dealt with them generously. Brave, open-minded, and emotional, Saladin was easily moved to tears. His set-tos with Richard the Lionheart in the Third Crusade became the stuff of legend. Hearing of his adversary's troubles with ague, Saladin sent him fresh fruit and snow. But he was all business in war: He prevented the recapture of Jerusalem and solidified the Muslim hold on the Levant. **CONCLUSION:** THUMBS UP

SALADIN

"On the conquest of Jerusalem by the Christians in 1099 the Saracens were massacred in the streets and in the houses. Jerusalem had no refuge for the vanquished." —FRENCH ACCOUNT OF CRUSADES

TRADE & ECONOMY BOOM TIMES

The late medieval period saw a marked increase in trade between Asia and Europe, with Byzantium as the gateway. European economies rose with the stimulation of trade, as well as with new technologies, including water-driven clothmaking machines. The invention of gunpowder spread from China to Europe, further igniting the economy.

Europe's colorful marketplaces often included a money changer.

> The Hanseatic League established trading posts, built lighthouses, and defended merchants against piracy.

The growth of towns in the 12th century led to the rise of a middle class of merchants and artisans who formed guilds that established trade regulations and production standards. In the 13th century several cities in northern Germany created the Hanseatic League to protect trade in the Baltic, a network that stretched from England

The arms of the Hanseatic League of north German cities

to the hinterlands of Russia. Genoa and Venice cemented their importance as centers of Mediterranean commerce, with Flanders a counterpart in the North. Italian banking operations set a standard for Europe.

THE TAKEAWAY: Spurred by robust trade and new technology, most European economies expanded.

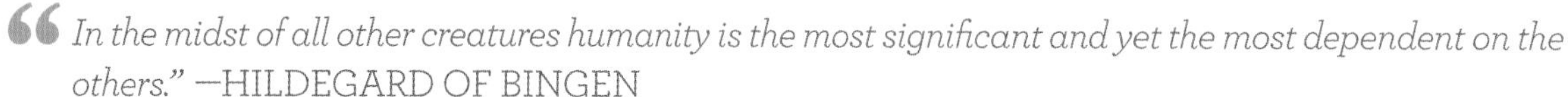

"In the midst of all other creatures humanity is the most significant and yet the most dependent on the others." —HILDEGARD OF BINGEN

SEE ALSO | KINGS AND NOMADS: PAGE 201

The plague devastated towns such as Tournai in the Middle Ages.

CLASS & SOCIETY PLAGUE YEARS

Following a time of relative calm, the 14th century brought calamity. Climate change caused by the Little Ice Age led to crop failures, famine, disease, and political instability. During the great famine of 1315–1322, food prices soared, as did crime and infanticide. More disaster was soon to come. Originating in China and carried by fleas on rats, bubonic plague began arriving on Mediterranean ships in 1347. Urban crowding and poor sanitation created the conditions for the worst pandemic in history. The highly contagious disease left people dead within three days of contact, often after terrible suffering. So fast-moving was the Black Death that within 20 years Europe's population was reduced by one-third. Entire villages were wiped out; the population decline led to labor shortages in both urban and rural areas, especially in hard-hit France and England.

{ Princess Joan of England died of the plague on the way to her wedding with Prince Pedro of Castile. }

Peasants began demanding higher wages, a move countered by local laws. Attempts to enforce such laws often created more civil unrest. Jews and other minorities became scapegoats in merciless pogroms as the populace looked for reasons for their misery.

THE TAKEAWAY: Following a famine, the Black Death swept like a scythe across the landscape.

CONNECTIONS ANIMAL ORIGINS OF EPIDEMICS

First recorded in 1000 B.C.E., bubonic plague, spread through bacteria-infested fleas, was a classic case of a zoonotic disease: one originating in animals. As early as 6000 B.C.E., with clustering human populations and the domestication of farm animals, microbes began to spread from animals to humans, with devastating effects. Trade routes such as the Silk Road and Mediterranean shipping lanes spread such plagues from Asia to Europe, and then from Europe to the New World with European settlers. Smallpox, measles, and AIDS are among the diseases that have made the deadly transition from animals to human-to-human transmission, as are various forms of influenza, including the modern forms of avian flu and swine flu.

MODERN DEFENSE AGAINST INFLUENZA

Had I been present at the creation, I would have given some useful hints for the better ordering of the universe." —ALFONSO X OF CASTILE

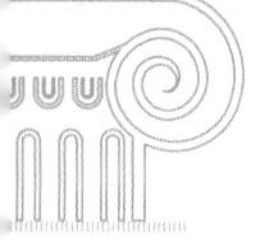

SEE ALSO | POSTCLASSICAL ERA: PAGE 160

GEOFFREY CHAUCER THE COOK'S TALE

GEOFFREY CHAUCER

"An apprentice dwelt once in our city
And of a craft of victuallers was he.
Gay he was as a goldfinch in the woods,
Brown as a berry, a proper short fellow,
With black, neatly combed hair.
He could so dance well and jollily
That he was called Perkin the Reveller."

—FROM *THE CANTERBURY TALES* (MODERNIZED TRANSLATION), 14TH CENTURY

DAILY LIFE TOWNFOLK

Everyday life for villagers and townspeople in the High Middle Ages revolved around home and church. Peasants formed a vast labor force, working the land in return for their lords' armed protection. Women could own land, though they were almost always subordinate to men; as an alternative to childbearing, they could choose the seclusion of the convent. For men, the clerical life often meant education, prestige, land, and money.

An urban middle class emerged in the 11th and 12th centuries, composed of merchants and craftsmen. Communities of former serfs developed into villages centered on a parish church and its cemetery, around which clustered farms, mills, breweries, and bake houses. Wheat was the main food crop, supplemented by dairy products and vegetables.

An intellectual flowering gave rise to universities. The university founded in Bologna in the late 11th century became renowned for its law faculty, while the best place to study theology was the University of Paris, founded around 1200.

A central part of a peasant's diet, bread was usually baked in a communal oven owned by the local lord.

Cooks prepare a meal in a 14th-century kitchen.

THE TAKEAWAY: Late medieval life for most centered on hearth, field, and church, while cities offered wider opportunities..

"I speak Spanish to God, Italian to women, French to men, and German to my horse."

—CHARLES V OF FRANCE

A detail from the "Trés Riches Heures" depicts a springtime engagement scene on a manor's grounds.

CLASS & SOCIETY

FEUDAL RIGHTS

By the High Middle Ages the feudal system was entrenched, with peasants working for their lords, who in turn served the king. Prelates and nobles had the most freedom and wealth, though a growing middle class enriched the cities. There were regional variations in Europe—Italy, for instance, was more urban than France and England, its city-states creating a more complex class structure. In Europe's small autonomous settlements, a lord's castle or manor was the focus of life and the scene of feasts and entertainment by bards and minstrels. Sports included hunting, falconry, jousting tournaments, and other military games.

When not at war, aristocratic men needed a code of conduct, thus the development of chivalry—the way of the chevalier, or knight. The main attributes of chivalry were bravery, honor, humility, and gallantry, especially toward women. Poems of courtly love from the time idealize women in a way not seen before in Europe. Thus while women were still second-class citizens, they were beginning to be appreciated as more than vessels for sex and childbearing.

{Early jousting tourneys were a violent business with few rules; in one bloody contest, 60 knights died.}

THE TAKEAWAY: Upper-class European society had the leisure for games and art.

"And Frenssh she spak ful faire and fetisly / After the scole of Stratford atte Bowe / For Frenssh of Parys was to hir unknowe." —CHAUCER

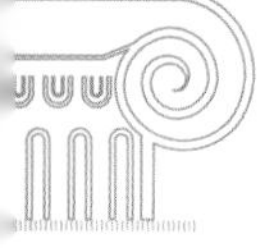

ARTS MASTERPIECES IN STONE

Europe's soaring Romanesque and Gothic buildings, particularly cathedrals, rank foremost among the masterworks of high medieval art. After the year 1000, the Romanesque style—characterized by symmetry and rounded arches—became ever more elaborate, until evolving into the Gothic. First appearing in France in the mid-12th century, the Gothic style was marked by pointed arches, ribbed vaults, flying buttresses, and brilliant stained glass. The style was the brainchild of Abbot Suger of St.-Denis, who believed that the best way to teach the Bible was through pictures. Cathedrals inside and out—from the cruciform shape to the sculptures of apostles—contained stories carved in stone, a benefit for a largely illiterate public.

Stained-glass window from Sainte-Chapelle, Paris

Other important visual art forms of the period included manuscript illumination and tapestry. The 231-foot-long Bayeux Tapestry, for instance, crafted in the late 11th century, doubled as a historical document containing more than 70 vividly detailed historical scenes.

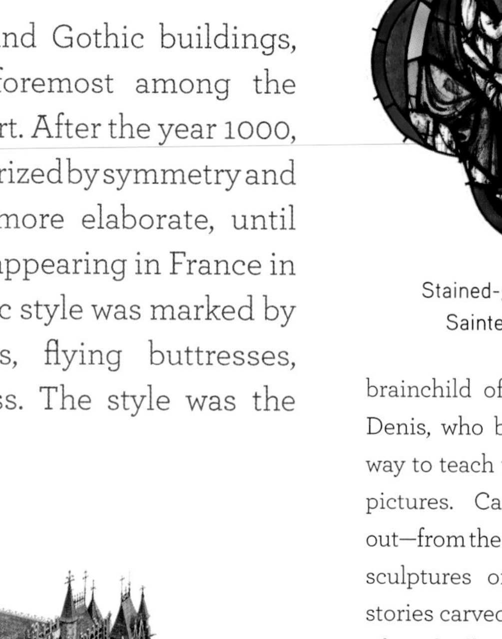

A cutaway shows the interior and exterior of Notre-Dame d'Amiens in northern France.

THE TAKEAWAY: Romanesque and Gothic architecture taught the faith through stories in stone.

CONNECTIONS "GOTHIC" ORIGINS

Architects in the Renaissance considered the work of their medieval predecessors excessive and labeled it for the barbarians who had overrun Rome. The term "Gothic," applied to the popular building style of the 12th to 16th centuries, was thus originally one of disdain. The term was later appropriated to describe literature with a gloomy setting and mysterious or macabre events, often with actual Gothic architecture in the background, as in Horace Walpole's *The Castle of Otranto* (1764). In recent years, this versatile word has evolved to distinguish a dark, post-punk fashion style.

GOTHIC MEMENTO MORI

> *"All by myself, wrapped in my thoughts, / and building castles in Spain and in France."*
>
> —CHARLES D'ORLÉANS

SEE ALSO | POSTCLASSICAL ERA: PAGE 166

TECHNOLOGY THE PRINTING PRESS

As early as the eighth century, the Chinese, Japanese, and Koreans were printing texts on paper with woodblocks. Movable, reusable clay type appeared in China around 1045 with clay characters, but the thousands of Chinese characters made the system impractical and it stagnated. When the printing press made its debut in Europe, it had an enormous impact on an increasingly well-educated European society.

In the 1440s German silversmith Johannes Gutenberg and his associates adapted wine-press mechanics to create the first printing press. Placing cast metal letters into composing sticks, they locked them into a metal form hanging above a press bed. The type was then inked, paper placed on the bed, and the form pressed down with a heavy handle-turned screw. The press could crank out 250 pages an hour.

The first Gutenberg Bibles were printed in about 1455, designed to look like manuscript Bibles, with illuminated initial letters. William Caxton turned out the first printed books in English, including *Recuyell of the Historyes of Troye* (1475).

> Johannes Gutenberg's partners became rich from sales of his Bible, while Gutenberg died in obscurity.

THE TAKEAWAY: The printing press brought books to the masses.

Johannes Gutenberg's invention of practical movable-type printing spread literacy across Europe.

> “*You will find something more in woods than in books. Trees and stones will teach you that which you can never learn from masters.*” —ST. BERNARD OF CLAIRVEAUX

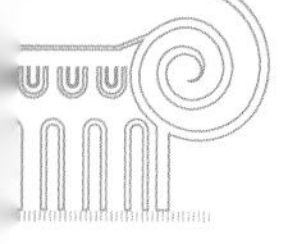

THE MAGNA CARTA

IN THE EARLY 1200S, England's unpopular King John broke with the nobility by refusing their choice for archbishop and using what they considered tyrannical means of collecting revenue.

By 1214 nobles were in open revolt, and after defeating the king's army at the 1214 Battle of Bouvines, they wrote up a list of grievances in the form of a contract between the crown and the nobility, guaranteeing the latter customary feudal rights. The Magna Carta has since become a model for other charters of democratic rights, including the Declaration of Independence.

FORCED HAND King John signs the Magna Carta on June 15, 1215. The erratic, disliked monarch quarreled with the English nobility over taxation, among other things. A group of barons drew up a "great charter" of their grievances; then, with an army of some 2,000 knights, the barons met the beleaguered king at Runnymede, a meadow on the Thames River 20 miles west of London. Here he signed and put his seal to the Magna Carta.

"FIRST, THAT WE HAVE GRANTED TO GOD, and by this present charter have confirmed for us and our heirs in perpetuity, that the English Church shall be free, and shall have its rights undiminished, and its liberties unimpaired."

"No free man shall be seized or imprisoned, or stripped of his rights or possessions, or outlawed or exiled. Nor will we proceed with force against him, except by the lawful judgement of his equals or by the law of the land. To no one will we sell, to no one deny or delay right or justice."

GET IT IN WRITING One of four extant copies of the Magna Carta issued over the great seal of King John on or after June 23, 1215, this original document is housed in the British Library in London.

"In future we will allow no one to levy an 'aid' from his free men, except to ransom his person, to make his eldest son a knight, and (once) to marry his eldest daughter."

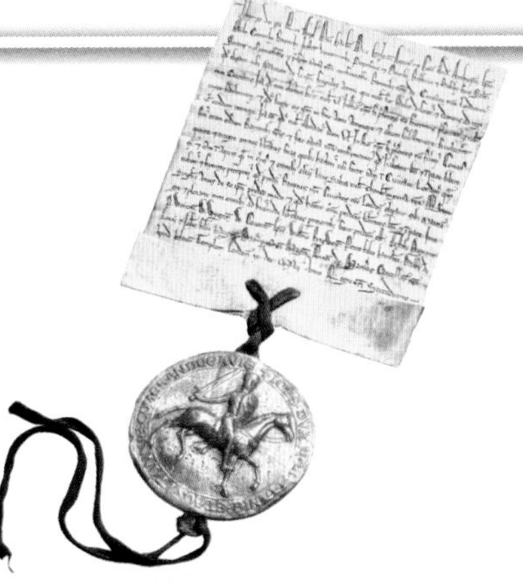

TOO LITTLE, TOO LATE The charter of King John (above) was issued on May 9, 1215, only a few weeks before the Magna Carta. The document grants Londoners the right to choose a mayor every year, "faithful, discreet and fit to govern the city." It did not go far enough to please rebellious barons, who cornered John into signing the much longer Magna Carta.

"It is accordingly our wish and command that the English Church shall be free, and that men in our kingdom shall have and keep all these liberties, rights, and concessions, well and peaceably in their fullness and entirety for them and their heirs, of us and our heirs, in all things and all places for ever."

MAGNA CARTA CLAUSES

The Magna Carta consists of a preamble and 63 clauses, which fall roughly into 9 categories.

THE CHURCH Freedom for the Church from crown interference

LANDHOLDERS Protection for nobles holding lands given by the king

TENANTS Protection for subtenants of landholders

MERCHANTS Guarantees for towns, merchants, and trade

ROYAL OFFICIALS Limits on overzealous officials

LEGAL REFORMS Overall matters of justice and legislation

ROYAL FORESTS Sharing of the crown's extensive holdings

CURRENT ISSUES Dropped in later versions, demands such as the firing of foreign mercenaries.

ASSURANCES Final clauses binding the king to the contract, on penalty of war.

"No widow shall be compelled to marry, so long as she wishes to remain without a husband. But she must give security that she will not marry without royal consent, if she holds her lands of the Crown, or without the consent of whatever other lord she may hold them of."

"In future it shall be lawful for any man to leave and return to our kingdom unharmed and without fear, by land or water, preserving his allegiance to us, except in time of war, for some short period."

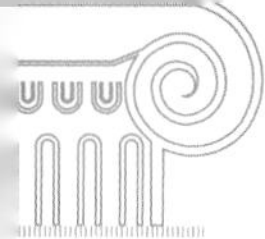

SEE ALSO | KINGS AND NOMADS: PAGE 200

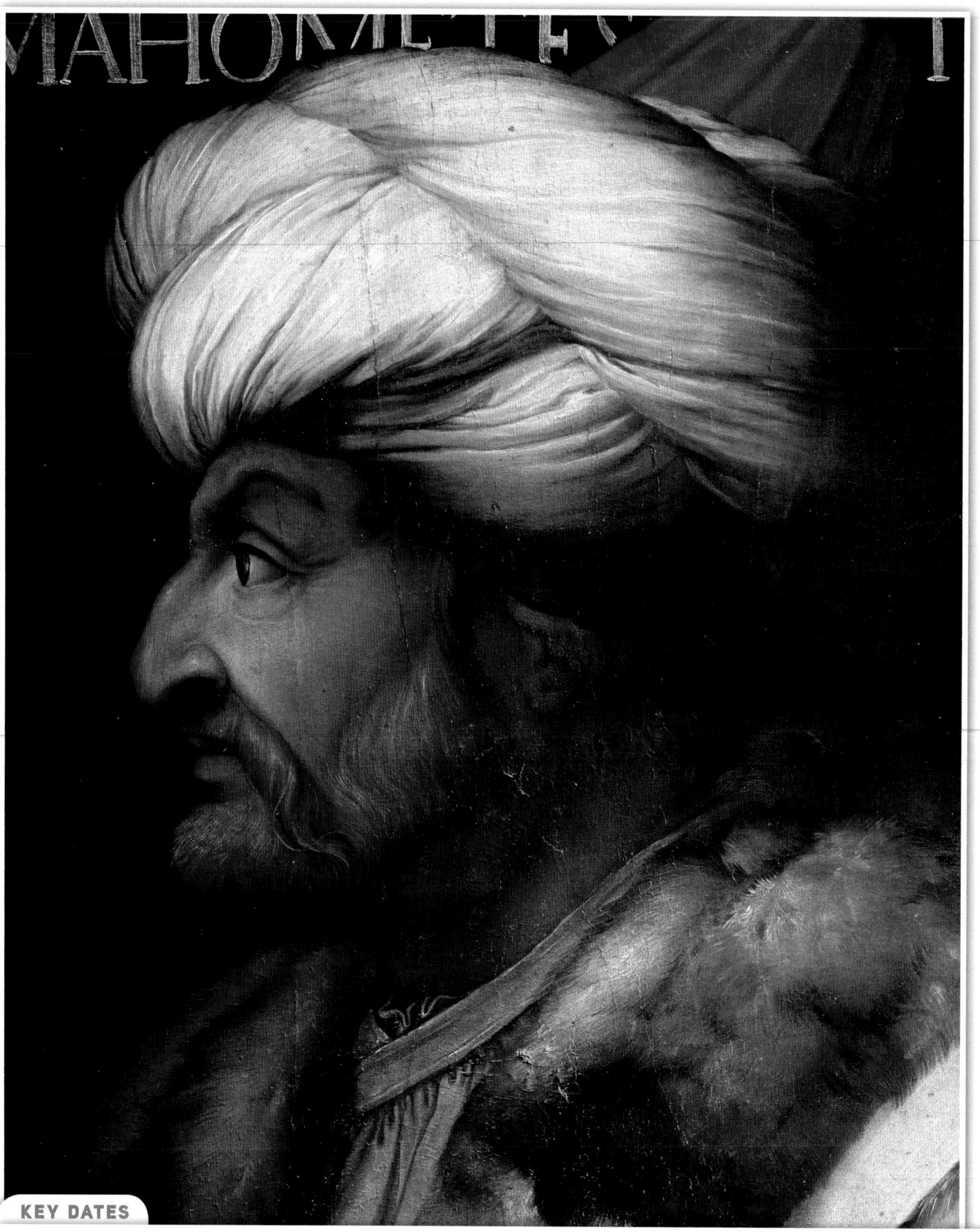

KEY DATES

1206–1227
Genghis Khan unifies the Mongols, conquers much of central and western Asia.

1237–1241
Mongols conquer Russia, where they are called the Golden Horde.

1258
Hulegu Khan conquers Baghdad, the Abbasid capital.

1260–1294
Kublai Khan rules China.

EMPIRES EAST & WEST

1000–1453

While the nations of western Europe were developing, the vast region of central Asia was in flux. Settled communities had for centuries endured raids from Huns and other nomadic warriors who swept down from the high country. In the 13th and 14th centuries these nomads coalesced into one spectacular empire. Ruled by the Mongols, the empire stretched from Hungary to the Sea of Japan. Hailing from the barren, windblown steppes of central Asia, in present-day Mongolia, the Mongols and their rivals, the Tatars, had long harassed the neighboring Chinese. The Mongols made up for their sparse numbers by their superior horsemanship, military tactics, endurance, and ferocity. Their greatest leader, Genghis Khan, ruled for some 21 years, during which he unified the Mongols and created an empire that, under his sons and grandsons would become the largest in history to that time.

At its height, the Mongol Empire encompassed four khanates: China, the richest and largest subkingdom; the Chaghatai khanate of central Asia; the Ilkhanate of Persia; and the Golden Horde of Russia. Mongol power waned after 1368, the year the Chinese drove the Mongols out of their lands.

The Mongol Empire swelled across central and eastern Asia in the 13th and 14th centuries, while, at nearly the same time, the Ottomans built a more enduring Muslim kingdom centered on Turkey.

At the end of the 13th century, another world-shaking empire arose, this one situated squarely between Europe and Asia. Named for their charismatic leader, Osman I, the Turkish nomads, called Ottomans, also originated in the central Asian steppes. Beginning in 1299 they rapidly expanded into southeastern Europe—the Balkans and Greece—crippling the Byzantine Empire. Under the inspired leadership of Sultan Murad I, Ottoman culture developed some of the institutions that would see it through nearly four centuries of expansion, including the elite fighting corps known as the Janissaries.

In the late 1300s, a final raider, a non-Muslim Turk who styled himself after the great khans, temporarily checked the Ottoman advance. Tamerlane was perhaps the greatest nomadic warrior of all—his brutal, lightning-fast raids won him territory in unimaginably short order. But Tamerlane's heirs were unable to hold the lands he'd conquered, and the Ottomans returned to their steadier advance. In 1453 they took the final and greatest Byzantine prize, Constantinople.

OPPOSITE: Mehmed II, the Conqueror, sultan of the Ottoman Empire, captured Constantinople in 1453.

1299
Osman I declares independence from Seljuk Turks, starts Ottoman dynasty in Turkey.

ca 1356
The Ottomans occupy Gallipoli, establishing a base for raids into Europe.

1402
Tamerlane's forces crush the Ottoman army, marking a brief low point for the empire.

1453
Ottoman forces capture Constantinople, ending the Byzantine Empire.

SEE ALSO | BREAKING BONDS: PAGE 241

EMPIRES THE OTTOMANS

In the late 13th century, a Turkish leader and devout Muslim named Osman declared independence from the Seljuk Turks and embarked on a campaign of conquest. In so doing he established the Ottoman Empire. By 1301, Osman had taken the ancient Anatolian city of Nicaea, and by the end of his reign he had captured the Byzantine city of Bursa. This stronghold would serve as the Ottoman capital from 1327 to 1361.

Tamerlane (Timur), a Turkish conqueror, swept across Eurasia.

After Osman's death, his heirs continued pushing westward into Byzantium and eastward against Turkish principalities. The Ottoman army's defeat by nomadic raider Tamerlane in 1402 was but a brief setback. By the 15th century, Mehmed II—dictator and patron of the arts—brought the 1,100-year-old Byzantine Empire to a close by conquering Constantinople in 1453. He renamed it Istanbul, and it became the Ottoman capital.

THE TAKEAWAY: Under strong rulers, the Ottoman Empire grew into a world power.

VIPs

EMPIRES EAST AND WEST

Genghis Khan, 1162–1227
Founder of the Mongol Empire

Rumi, 1207–1273
Sufi mystic and poet

Kublai Khan, 1215–1294
Mongol Emperor of China

Marco Polo, 1254–1324
Merchant whose travelogue brought Asia to the Europeans

Osman, 1258–1324
Founder of the Ottoman Empire in Turkey

Murad I, 1326–1389
Ottoman sultan and able administrator who presided over expansion of the empire

Tamerlane, 1336–1405
Founder of the Timurid Empire in Central Asia

> *"Anticipate charity by preventing poverty; assist the reduced fellowman . . . so that he may earn an honest livelihood, and not be forced to the dreadful alternative of holding out his hand."* —MAIMONIDES

VOICES

SULTAN MEHMED II

KRITOVOULOS SURPRISE ATTACK

"So the ships were dragged along very swiftly. And their crews, as they followed them, rejoiced at the event and boasted of it. Then they manned the ships on the land as if they were on the sea. Some of them hoisted the sails with a shout, as if they were setting sail, and the breeze caught the sails and bellied them out. Others seated themselves on the benches, holding the oars in their hands and moving them as if rowing."

—A GREEK HISTORIAN'S ACCOUNT OF MEHMED II'S CONQUEST OF CONSTANTINOPLE IN WHICH HIS SHIPS WERE PULLED OVER LAND

MILITARY JANISSARIES

THE TAKEAWAY: The Ottomans' elite fighters were Christian boys who were enslaved.

Under Murad I, the Ottomans developed their famous elite military unit, the Janissaries (from the Turkish for "new soldiers"). The first Janissaries were Christian youths drafted from conquered Balkan villages. Periodically, village boys from age seven to fourteen who showed physical and mental acumen were taken from their families; a seven-year training period honed them into zealous and disciplined Muslim warriors.

The Janissaries were ranked in three divisions and tattooed with their detachment numbers. Originally required to observe strict celibacy, they eliminated this rule in the 16th century. The lucrative positions began to be passed on to family members as time went by, but for the soldiers their comrades remained their family. They gained a fearsome reputation as warriors and later became a powerful political force as well.

Besides the Janissaries, many high-ranking officials were also former slaves. A Venetian ambassador to the Ottoman court found this arrangement extraordinary: "It is in the highest degree remarkable that the wealth, the administration, the force, in short the whole body politic of the Ottoman Empire reposes upon and is entrusted to men born in the Christian faith, converted into slaves, and reared up Muhammadans." The Janissary corps ended in 1826 after they mutinied and the sultan ordered their deaths.

{ In later centuries, the Janissaries were known for their involvement in palace coups. }

Janissaries, the Ottomans' premiere fighting corps, wore distinctive uniforms.

"There is a basket of fresh bread on your head, / and yet you go door-to-door asking for crusts." —RUMI

LEADERS THE MONGOLS

The Mongol Empire that emerged in central Asia in the early 1200s was the work of Temujin, known as Genghis Khan ("universal ruler"). Son of a minor Mongol chieftain, he seized power to avenge his father's death at the hands of Tatar tribesmen. After consolidating about 30 nomadic tribes, he began conquering Afghanistan, Persia, parts of Russia, and northern China.

Mongol warriors were famed for their horsemanship.

After Genghis Khan's death in 1227, his progeny continued expanding the empire. His grandson Kublai Khan brought down the Song dynasty and ruled China from 1260 to 1294. Kublai's brother Hulegu Khan captured the Abbasid capital of Baghdad in 1258, and another brother, Batu, established the Golden Horde khanate in Russia. Not until the 14th and 15th centuries were the Mongols defeated or absorbed by indigenous people.

{ Destroyer of Kiev, Genghis Khan's son Ogodei drank himself to death before he could launch an invasion of western Europe. }

THE TAKEAWAY: For a century and a half, the Mongols controlled most of central and northern Asia.

GENGHIS KHAN *THE GREAT YASA*

VOICES

GENGHIS KHAN

"An adulterer is to be put to death without any regard as to whether he is married or not.

"Whoever intentionally lies, or practices sorcery, or spies upon the behavior of others, or intervenes between the two parties in a quarrel to help the one against the other is also to be put to death.

"He ordered that all religions were to be respected and that no preference was to be shown to any of them. All this he commanded in order that it might be agreeable to Heaven.

"He forbade them to show preference for any sect, to pronounce words with emphasis, to use honorary titles; when speaking to the Khan or anyone else simply his name was to be used."

—FROM *THE MONGOL CODE OF LAW*, 13TH CENTURY, REPORTED BY AL-MAKRIZI

VICE

"One must magnify and pay honor to the pure, and the innocent, and the righteous, and to the learned, to whatsoever people they may belong; and condemn the wicked." —GREAT YASA

SEE ALSO | KINGS AND NOMADS: PAGE 204

VOICES

MARCO POLO

MARCO POLO MONGOL DAYS

"The women attend to their trading concerns, buy and sell, and provide everything necessary for their husbands and their families; the time of the men is devoted entirely to hunting, hawking, and matters that relate to the military life. They have the best falcons in the world, and also the best dogs. They live entirely upon flesh and milk, eating the produce of their sport, and a certain small animal, not unlike a rabbit, called by our people Pharaoh's mice." —FROM *THE TRAVELS OF MARCO POLO*, ca 1300

EXPLORATION MARCO POLO

In 1271, 17-year-old Marco Polo set off from Venice with his father and uncle for China. The older two men were traders who had already journeyed to the Mongol court, but this time they took with them a natural storyteller. After three and half years they reached Kublai Khan's summer capital at Shangdu (Xanadu). The khan took a liking to Marco and sent him on errands throughout his kingdom, from Tibet to India. The information he brought back would one day form the material of Europe's first great travel book.

When the Polos made their way back to Venice 17 years later, their own family did not recognize them. Three years later Marco was captured during a battle, and during his year in prison he dictated *The Travels of Marco Polo* to a professional writer. The adventure-filled chronicle became an instant bestseller.

THE TAKEAWAY: Marco Polo's travel account took European readers to the Far East.

Camel caravans still follow the Silk Road route that the Polos traveled through northwest China.

"As they do not count it any shame to run away in battle, they will sometimes pretend to do so, and in running away they turn in the saddle and shoot hard and strong at the foe." —MARCO POLO

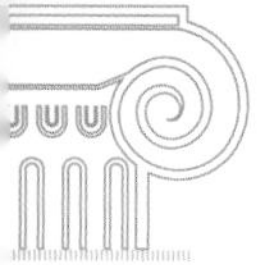

SEE ALSO | KINGS AND NOMADS: PAGE 206

KEY DATES

1006
Muslims settle in northern India.

1100
Chinese invent the magnetic compass.

1192
Yoritomo names himself ruler of Japan; founds the Kamakura shogunate.

1200–1300S
The Muslim Delhi sultanate rules in northern India.

ASIAN POWERS

1000–1450

Like Europe, Asia in medieval times was ruled by the dynasties that were most successful in seizing power, conquering neighboring lands, and administering efficient bureaucracies. China's Song dynasty, which ruled from 960 to 1279, arose after decades of warlord rivalry. The Song reunification of China did not take in as many provinces as did earlier dynasties, but it held strong in central and southern China until the incursions of nomadic Tatars and Mongols. During this time, the arts flourished, especially porcelains and landscape painting, and agriculture and commerce improved. Following a century of rule by the great Mongol khans, the Chinese reunited under rebel commander Zhu Yuanzhang and toppled the Mongol Yuan dynasty. The Ming ("brilliant") dynasty was born and lasted until 1644. Under the Mongols, China's population had dropped 40 percent to just over 60 million; under the Ming, it doubled. Chinese replaced Mongols in government posts, and civil service exams promoted people based on merit instead of influence. The Confucian philosophy returned, colleges flourished, slavery was outlawed, and taxes were levied in an equitable manner. In the early 1400s, the Great Wall was repaired and a new capital was built in the north—today's city of Beijing.

In Japan, Yoritomo, head of the Minamoto clan, grabbed power in 1192, inaugurating some 700 years of military rule. The country grew as a sea power and became more prosperous, though plagued from time to time with internal wars. Emperors were still nominal rulers, but real power lay in the hands of military leaders called shoguns, who presided over a feudal system of vassals and landed estates. Aided by typhoons, the shoguns foiled Mongol invasions. These warlords were served by a class of skilled warriors known as samurai, warrior aristocrats who embodied courage, obedience, and stoicism. The austere and meditative lifestyle of the samurai encouraged the spread of Zen Buddhism and stimulated such stylized arts as Noh theater and the tea ceremony.

Like Japan, India remained Mongol free, but by the 13th century, Islam had begun to exert influence over Indian society, especially in the north, while the religion of Jainism flourished in the Rajasthan region in northwest India.

China's Song and Ming dynasties, interrupted by the rule of Mongols, each reigned over China for three centuries. Meanwhile, Japan and India fended off the Mongols and developed distinct cultures.

OPPOSITE: Emperor Zhu Yuanzhang founded the Ming dynasty by defeating the Mongols in 1368.

1279
Mongols under Kublai Khan end the Song dynasty.

1333
Muromachi shogunate comes to power in Japan.

1405–1433
Admiral Zheng He voyages as far as Africa with China's great trading armada.

1421
Beijing becomes China's new capital.

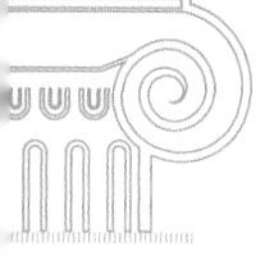

SEE ALSO | BREAKING BONDS: PAGE 258

Built by the Ming, Beijing's graceful Forbidden City housed the emperor.

EMPIRES PROSPEROUS TIMES

When General Zhao Kuangyin took power in 960, he became the first of China's Song emperors. Until the late 13th century, the Songs presided over central and southern China, making it productive and prosperous. They revived the civil service literary examinations and created an educated class of bureaucrats. Their capital, Hangzhou, peaking at more than one million citizens, was one of the world's great cities.

The Song dynasty's success eventually led to its downfall. To maintain the easy life to which they had become accustomed, landed gentry raised rents. Complacent bureaucrats let the military lapse into flabbiness. The country was now vulnerable to internal rebellion and outside encroachment. Mongol armies took advantage and overthrew the Song in 1279.

> The enormous Chinese ships of the Ming-era navy could carry up to 1,000 sailors.

In 1368, commander Zhu Yuanzhang forced the Mongols out,

ASIAN POWERS

VIPs

Zhao Kuangyin, 927–976
Emperor who reunified China after decades of power struggles

Zhu Xi, 1130–1200
Philosopher who pioneered neo-Confucianism

Yoritomo, 1147–1199
First shogun of Japan's Kamakura shogunate

Razia Sultana, 1205–1240
Mamluk sultan who was the first female Muslim ruler

Yongle, 1360–1424
Builder of the Forbidden City

Zheng He, 1371–1435
China's great admiral and diplomat

> *"The sage regards everything in the world as his own self. The mind that leaves something outside itself is not capable of uniting with Heaven."* —ZHU XI

giving rise to the Ming dynasty. Born a peasant, Zhu grew up resentful of the upper classes and he was quick to suppress any hint of rebellion. But China began enjoying a return of the good times, though with a twist: Land held by the rich was redistributed to the peasants; higher education proliferated, and not just to the elite; civil service exams, which had lapsed under the Mongols, were reinstituted.

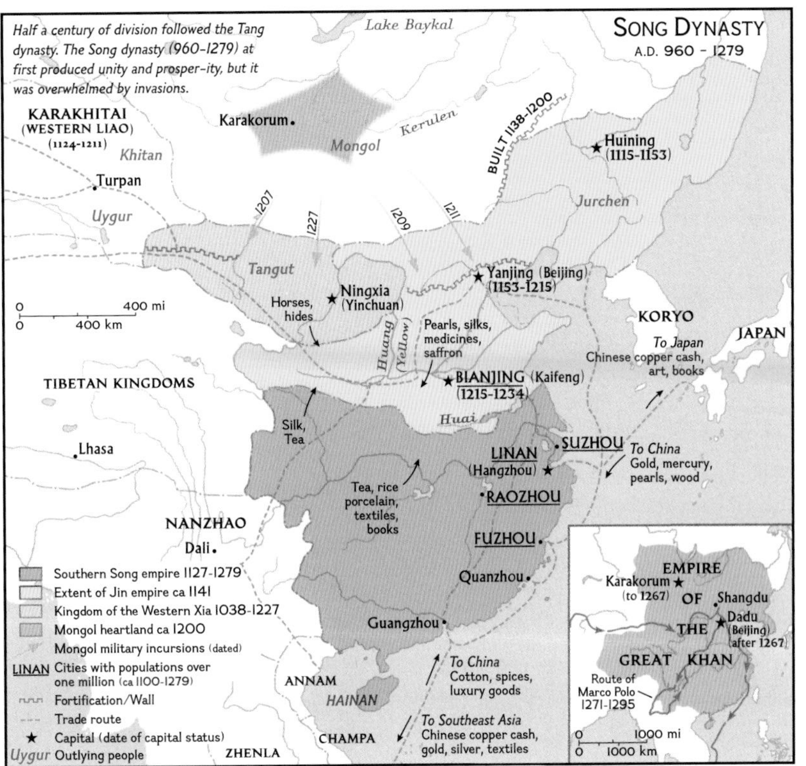

A Song-period bronze depicts the bodhisattva Manjushri riding a lion.

Zhu's son Emperor Yongle brought Chinese architecture to a pinnacle in the early 15th century. With hundreds of thousands of laborers, he began building what would become Beijing. Inside the walled city was the imperial square, which contained the Forbidden City. There, future emperors would construct beautiful gardens, pavilions, arched bridges, and pagodas.

The Ming also turned their attention outward, becoming masters of the Indian Ocean. Their huge navy was the envy of the world. Sailing fleets pushed into distant ports, opening up trade and demanding tribute. After the death of Yongle in 1424, the navy was scaled down as China became more isolationist.

THE TAKEAWAY: By the end of the Middle Ages, China was a powerful, but isolationist, empire.

THUMBS UP / THUMBS DOWN

ADMIRAL ZHENG ca 1371–1435

DECADES BEFORE THE GREAT European seafarers, Chinese admiral Zheng He was exploring the Indian Ocean. Born a commoner in Mongol territory around 1371, he was captured at age ten by Ming troops and made a eunuch slave. Working his way up the ranks, he quickly became trusted counselor. Between 1405 and 1433, he undertook a series of voyages covering more than 100,000 miles, journeying as far as the Persian Gulf and Kenya. Commanding an armada that could include more than 300 ships, he brought back exotic animals and even the Ceylonese monarch. **CONCLUSION: THUMBS UP**

ZHENG HE

> *"We have set eyes on barbarian regions far away hidden in a blue transparency of light vapors, while our sails loftily unfurled like clouds day and night."* —ZHENG HE

MILITARY THE SHOGUNATES

By the 12th century, Japan's imperial authority had declined to the point that bands of warriors ruled in a lawless, politically fractured landscape. Two warring bands, the Taira in the west and the Minamoto in the east, vied for supremacy. Under Yoritomo, the latter group finally gained the upper hand after winning a sea battle at Danno-ura, south of Honshu, in 1185. Following the emperor's death in 1192, Yoritomo declared himself supreme commander, thus creating the Kamakura shogunate, named for its location in central Japan.

The shogunate was at first interested primarily in military matters, leaving civil concerns to the Kyoto court. After crushing a 1221 rebellion, though, the shogunate assumed most of the government's authority.

Mongols attempted to invade in 1274 and 1281, but were repulsed by storms and an army of highly trained warriors known as samurai. The Kamakura period is also known for its promotion of the meditative version of Buddhism known as Zen and for the construction of temples. In 1333, the Muromachi shogunate took over, but by century's end, central authority was eroding; in the next century a civil war (1467–1477) led to increasing anarchy.

THE TAKEAWAY: The shogunate era originated as a military regime during a period of lawlessness.

A Japanese scroll depicts a warrior hero battling Mongol invaders.

THE JOEI CODE A WOMAN'S RIGHTS

"Whether when a wife or concubine, after getting an assignment from the husband, has been divorced, she can retain the tenure of the fief or not.

"–If the wife in question has been repudiated in consequence of having committed some serious transgression, even if she holds a written promise of the by-gone days, she may not hold the fief of her former husband. On the other hand, if the wife in question had a virtuous record and was innocent of any fault and was discarded by reason of the husband's preference for novelty, the fief which had been assigned to her cannot be revoked."

—FROM THE KAMAKURA SHOGUNATE'S LAW CODE, 1232

WOMAN AND ATTENDANT

VOICES

"To sit alone in the lamplight with a book spread out before you, and hold intimate converse with men of unseen generations—such is a pleasure beyond compare." —YOSHIDA KENKO

SEE ALSO | BREAKING BONDS: PAGE 262

Tamerlane (right), the Mongol-style conqueror, invaded India in 1398 and destroyed Delhi.

EMPIRES ISLAM ARRIVES

Qutb-ud-Din Aybak started as a slave to the Muslim Ghurid who controlled the region north of India. From his beginnings in charge of the royal stables, he rose to become a general in the early 1200s, winning important battles in northern India against the area's Hindu kings. Thus was launched the Delhi sultanate. This new Muslim sultanate continued into the 1300s under a succession of dynasties, from the slave sultans to the Afghan Khaljis to the Turkish Tughluqs. One so-called slave ruler, Razia, was the only female ruler of Muslim India. Daughter of a sultan, she was considered a judicious and forward-looking queen, but her reign was plagued by revolts; she was killed by Hindus.

In southern India, power revolved around a Muslim sultanate in the Vindhya Hills and the final great Hindu empire in Vijayanagara. Northern sultanates were able to staunch a Mongol invasion, but could not consolidate all of India—the south remained politically volatile through the 1400s.

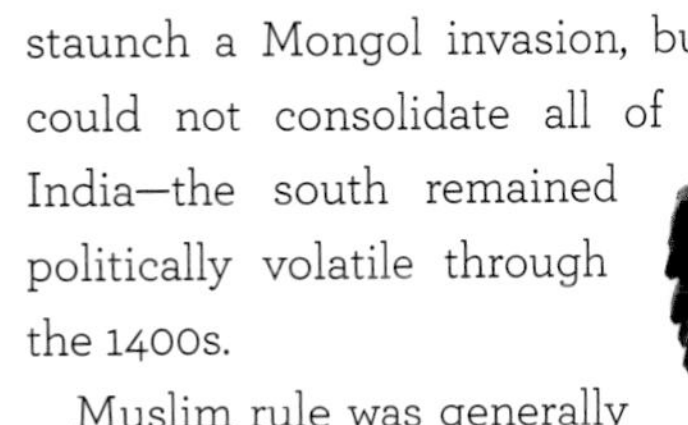

Muslim rule was generally tolerant. It did not come with forced conversion, though Hindus had to pay a special tax and lost some political status. Even so, the vastly different religious views of Muslims and Hindus and their divergent social structures kept the two populations frequently at odds.

THE TAKEAWAY: The Delhi sultanate established Muslim rule in northern India in the 13th century.

STONE CHARIOT AT VITTALA TEMPLE

> *"The sending down of the Book is from God the All-mighty, the All-wise. / We have sent down to thee the Book with the truth; / so worship God, making thy religion His sincerely."* —THE KORAN

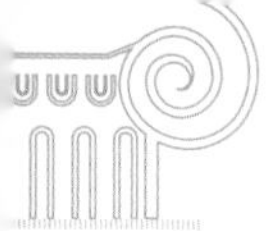

SEE ALSO | POSTCLASSICAL ERA: PAGE 171

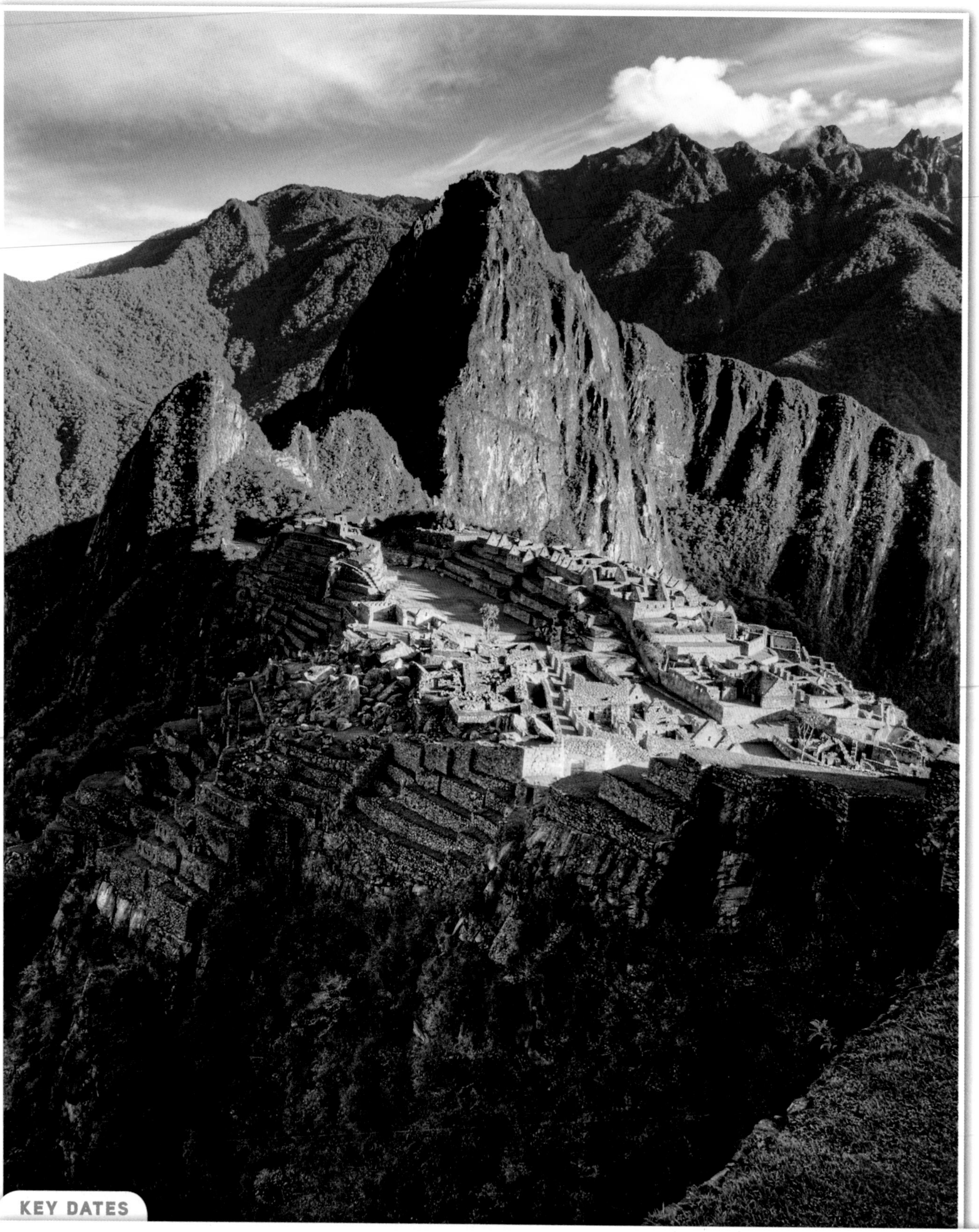

KEY DATES

ca 1000
Toltec civilization reaches its apex in central Mexico.

ca 1050
Central Mexican groups invade Maya settlements and influence Maya culture.

1170
Tula, the Toltec capital, falls to invaders, marking the empire's demise.

ca 1200
Drought drives the Anasazi to higher elevations, where they built cliff dwellings at Mesa Verde, Colorado.

THE AMERICAS

1000–1450

The late medieval period in the Americas was, like that in Europe, a time of empire building. Powerful rulers dominated weaker areas by force of arms, erected splendid cities, and, if they accumulated enough wealth, furthered the arts and learning. Dynasties rose and fell on the strength of individual rulers' talent for holding power. Appeasement of the gods through human sacrifice—usually of captives—was a Mesoamerican tradition that continued throughout the period. The Toltec civilization, which preceded the Aztec, arose in the 10th century and built a capital at Tula, just north of current Mexico City. By 1000, the Toltec had a population of some 30,000. A long drought in the 12th century brought intruders into the lake-rich Valley of Mexico. From the north came the Aztec, who were forced to compete with other migrant peoples for the valley's resources. In 1325 they founded Tenochtitlan, on the site of the future Mexico City. It would become one of the world's most splendid capitals. In the early 15th century, under Itzcoatl, the Aztec gained control of the entire valley and begin conquering neighboring territory. In the century before their downfall, they created the greatest of all early American empires under rulers Moctezuma I and II—a realm of 80,000 square miles and 6 million people. Yet in 1519 Spanish conquistador Hernán Cortés would destroy the Aztec with a small group of soldiers, smallpox, and the help of rebellious tribes.

The Toltec and Aztec in Mesoamerica, the Chimu and Inca in South America, and the Mississippians and Anasazi in North America built advanced civilizations before the arrival of Spanish conquerors in the 16th century.

Like the Aztec, the Inca of the Peruvian highlands established an empire on the back of an earlier civilization. The Chimu came to power around the year 1000, building reservoirs and canals for irrigation. Their magnificent capital, Chan Chan, held nearly 30,000 inhabitants. In the 15th century, the Inca gradually conquered the Chimu and established even greater sites—Cuzco and Machu Picchu, the latter possibly the palace of Inca ruler Pachacuti Inca Yupanqui.

Though not as magnificent as their counterparts to the south, the North American civilizations were similarly elaborate. The mound villages of the Mississippians in the east and the cliff dwellings and pueblos of the Anasazi in the west were the work of agricultural peoples with hierarchical social structures. Later Spanish explorers altered, but did not destroy, these civilizations.

OPPOSITE: The Inca built Machu Picchu, their ceremonial center, in the Peruvian highlands in the 15th century.

1325
Aztec found Tenochtitlán near today's Mexico City.

ca 1350
Aztecs begin to exact tribute from subjects.

1410
Peruvian ruler Viracocha Inca expands his empire.

1440
Moctezuma I becomes ruler of the Aztec.

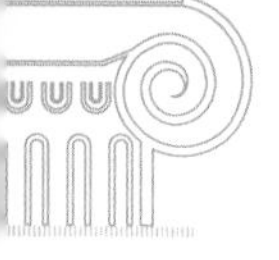

SEE ALSO | BREAKING BONDS: PAGE 247

Carvings show legendary Toltec ruler Topiltzin.

EMPIRES TOLTECS

The enterprising Toltec ruled the Valley of Mexico for some two centuries, starting around 1000. In their capital of Tula, they erected stone temples, pyramids, and ball courts similar to those of the earlier Maya to the south. Tall statues of warriors and bas-reliefs of battles and human sacrifices graced the city. Broken skulls littered the altar of at least one ball court, indicating that the ritual contests were brutal life-or-death struggles. Rulers were named for gods, such as Mixcoatl (Cloud Serpent) and Quetzalcoatl (Feathered Serpent). Legends have it that after Quetzalcoatl was forced out, he and his followers moved east to the Yucatán Peninsula, where they founded the city of Chichén Itzá.

The Toltec enriched themselves through trade and conquest. Their hoards of gold, silver, turquoise, coral, shells, and exotic feathers were fashioned into fine works of art. Weakened by drought, the once-powerful Toltec culture succumbed to northern invaders; in about 1170 the city of Tula was conquered and burned.

THE TAKEAWAY: The Toltec ruled the fertile Valley of Mexico from about 1000 to 1170.

VIPs — THE AMERICAS

Manco Cápac, r. ca 1200
First Sapa Inca, supreme ruler of the Inca empire

Tlacaelel, 1397–1487
Brother of Aztec emperor Moctezuma 1 and his key adviser

Moctezuma I, ca 1398–1469
Fifth Aztec emperor who built Aztec power through alliances

Pachacuti, 1438–ca 1472
Greatest Incan emperor, builder of Machu Picchu

Moctezuma II, 1466–1520
Aztec ruler who welcomed Cortés to Tenochtitlán

Hernán Cortés, 1485–1547
Explorer who conquered the Aztec for Spain

> *"Your Majesties may be fruitful and deserving in [God's] sight by causing these barbaric tribes to be enlightened and brought to the faith by Your hand."* —HERNÁN CORTÉS

EMPIRES AZTECS

AZTEC BRAZIER

THE TAKEAWAY: The Aztecs took bloodletting and empire-building to new heights.

The Aztec, or Mexica, migrated into the Valley of Mexico from the north in the 1200s and settled on a marshy island in Lake Texcoco, near current Mexico City. Hunters, fishers, and farmers, they had to become warriors in order to compete in a time of drought. In the 1300s they served in the armies of their more powerful neighbors, then in the 1400s turned their newfound might against their allies and embarked on their own campaign of conquest.

Eventually, the Aztec extended their empire from the Gulf of Mexico to the Pacific, a conquest attended by the traditional blood offerings. After one war, 20,000 captives were sacrificed on the Great Pyramid, with priests pulling out their hearts.

Also great builders, the Aztecs constructed the island city of Tenochtitlan and its canals, causeways, and grand central plaza. The city bedazzled Cortés when he arrived in 1519, and two years later, the Spaniard and his native allies toppled the mighty empire.

Musicians, artisans, and craftspeople enriched Aztec culture.

VOICES

DÍAZ DEL CASTILLO TENOCHTITLAN

"And when we saw so many cities and villages built in the water and other great towns on dry land and that straight and level causeway going towards Mexico, we were amazed and said that it was like the enchantments they tell us of in the legend of Amadis, on account of the great towers and temples and buildings rising from the water, and all built of masonry. And some of our soldiers even asked whether the thing that we saw were not a dream? It is not to be wondered at that I here write it down in this manner, for there is so much to think over that I do not know how to describe it . . . seeing things as we did that had never been heard of or seen before, not even dreamed about."

—DESCRIPTION OF TENOCHTITLAN FROM *THE TRUE HISTORY OF THE CONQUEST OF MEXICO*, BERNAL DÍAZ DEL CASTILLO, 1568

BERNAL DÍAZ DEL CASTILLO

"If I had known that you would have said such defamatory things I would not have shown you my gods."

—MOCTEZUMA II

SEE ALSO | BREAKING BONDS: PAGE 248

EMPIRES INCAN INFLUENCE

Inca Indians of the Andean plains herd vicuñas for shearing.

In about 1400 the Inca began expanding from the Cuzco Valley in the Andes, as kings sought better land and wider influence. Pachacuti (He Who Transforms the Earth) came to power in 1438, and quickly established a tradition of kings ruling for conquest. All subjects served the king periodically as soldiers, laborers, or farmers.

At its height, the Inca Empire stretched for 2,500 miles from current Ecuador to Chile, encompassing 100 ethnic groups. Pachacuti built the spectacular ceremonial center of Machu Picchu in the highlands, a complex that would remain hidden from 16th-century Spanish invaders. The nearby capital of Cuzco held temples, palaces, and fortresses. In 1471, Pachacuti abdicated in favor of his son, who completed the subjugation of the Chimu people.

INCAN CERAMIC JAR

THE TAKEAWAY: In just over a century, Inca rulers created a dominion spanning 2,500 miles.

CIEZA DE LEÓN THE INCAN ECONOMY

VOICES

PARTE PRIMERA

De la chronica del Peru, Que tracta la demarcacion de sus provincias: la descripcion dellas. Las fundaciones de las nuevas ciudades. Los ritos y costumbres de los indios. Y otras cosas estrañas dignas de ser sabidas. Fecha por Pedro d Cieça de Leon vezino de Sevilla. 1553.

CHRONICLES OF PERU

"At the beginning of the new year the rulers of each village came to Cuzco, bringing their quipus, which told how many births there had been during the year, and how many deaths. In this way the Inca and the governors knew which of the Indians were poor, the women who had been widowed, whether they were able to pay their taxes, and how many men they could count on in the event of war, and many other things they considered highly important. The Incas took care to see that justice was meted out, so much so that nobody ventured to commit a felony or theft. This was to deal with thieves, rapists, or conspirators against the Inca. As this kingdom was so vast, in each of the many provinces there were many storehouses filled with supplies and other needful things; thus, in times of war, wherever the armies went they drew upon the contents of these storehouses."

—FROM *CHRONICLES OF PERU*, PEDRO DE CIEZA DE LEÓN, 1540

"A continent more densely populated and abounding in animals than our Europe or Asia or Africa; and, in addition, a climate milder than in any other region known to us." —AMERIGO VESPUCCI

CLASS & SOCIETY EARTH MOVERS

A few centuries before the arrival of Europeans, people in the Mississippi Valley and the desert Southwest developed complex cultures. Advances in farming helped these complex societies thrive on a scale previously unknown in these regions. The cultivation of corn with beans, squash, and other crops gave the Mississippians relief from hunting and fishing. Thus settled, they could construct sprawling cities such as Etowah (Georgia), Moundville (Alabama), and Cahokia (near St. Louis), distinguished by giant earthen mounds used for burials, rituals, and temple sites. Cahokia held up to 20,000 residents, who lived in pole-and-thatch dwellings.

In today's Four Corners area, the Anasazi (Ancient Ones) constructed elaborate cliffside dwellings and multistory adobe apartments. New Mexico's Chaco Canyon and Colorado's Mesa Verde are two of the finest examples.

By the mid-13th century, climate change and other environmental stresses were hurting the Mississippians. Hernando de Soto's expedition across the Southeast in the 1540s would cause further dislocation and decline in these once-flourishing cultures.

> Sun-burnished pueblos fostered tales of golden cities, luring fortune hunters to the Southwest.

THE TAKEAWAY: Using earth, North American cultures built impressive structures.

Pueblo Bonito in New Mexico's Chaco Canyon was home to at least 5,000 people in the 11th century.

> *"Although they are not decorated with turquoises, nor made of lime or good bricks, nevertheless they are very good houses, three and four and five stories high."* —FRANCISCO VÁSQUEZ DE CORONADO

BREAKING

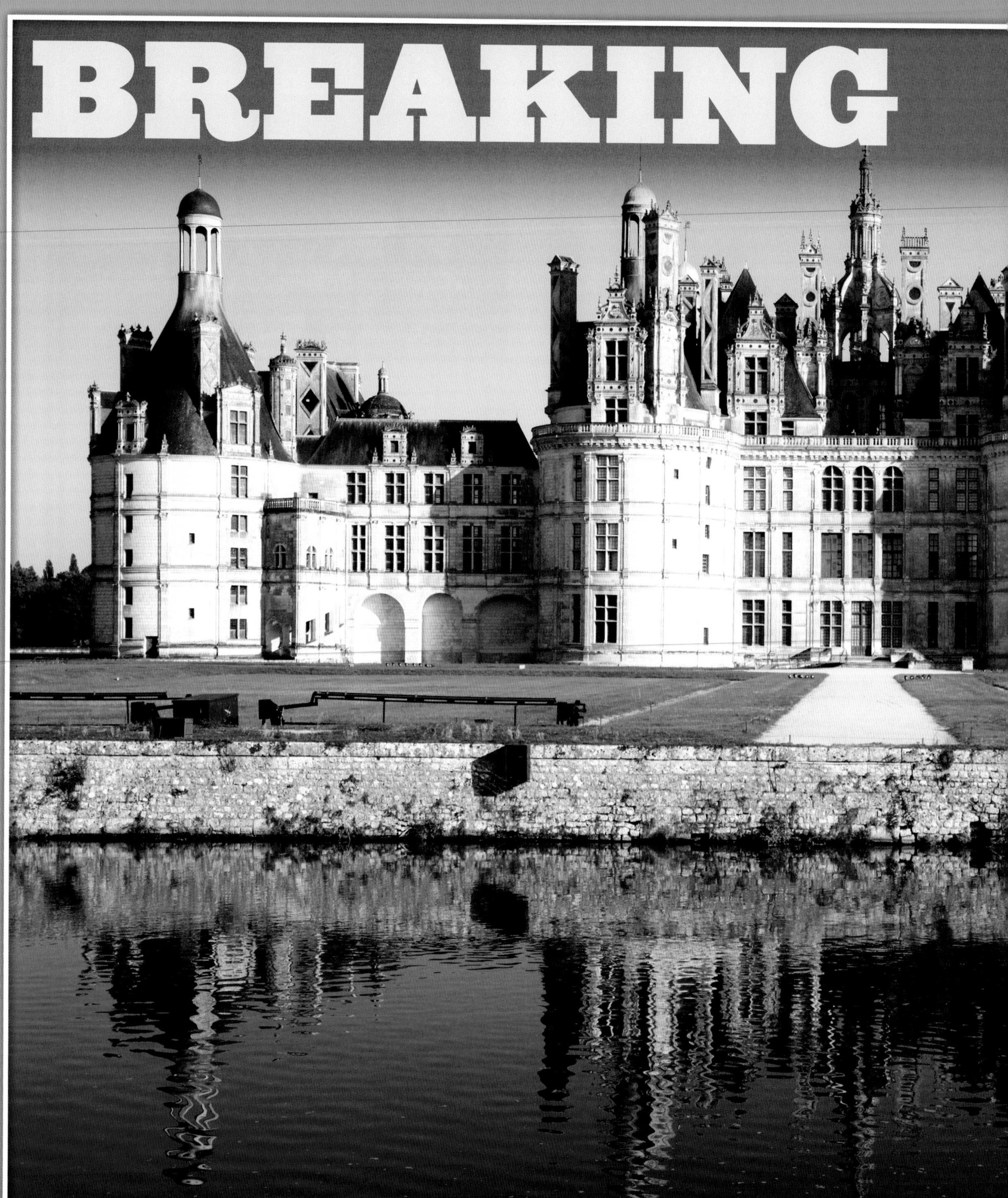

BONDS

DRAMAS OF TRANSFORMATION
1450–1650

CHAPTER
6

Castles like the Château de Chambord in France's Loire Valley flourished during the Renaissance.

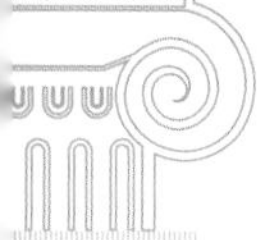

SEE ALSO | BREAKING BONDS: PAGE 242

KEY DATES

1420
Brunelleschi designs his architectural masterpiece Il Duomo in Florence.

1453
Turks convert Hagia Sophia Cathedral into a mosque.

1498
Vasco da Gama voyages around the Cape of Good Hope and reaches India.

1508–1512
Michelangelo paints the Sistine Chapel in Rome.

EUROPE

1450–1650

Though it became known as the Renaissance, or rebirth, the cultural flowering that spread across Europe from the 14th to 17th centuries was more of a gradual transition from the High Middle Ages. It was marked by a revival of humanism and the influence of classical Greece and Rome, which found rich expression in the arts and literature and the beginnings of modern science. The Renaissance began in Italy, where city-states fostered a predominantly urban culture, then gradually spread to northern Europe as Italian artists and teachers were brought to England, France, and Germany. It was in Germany in the early 16th century that a major religious movement took place that would shape the future course of political and social life for centuries to come. Initiated by Catholic scholar Martin Luther, the Reformation was a revolt against the power of the Roman Catholic Church, which until then had as strong an influence on communities and households as it did on the state. The rise of Protestant churches, tempering the heavy-handed doctrine and practice of the Catholic Church, furthered the ideals of humanism, a philosophy emphasizing individualism and secularism.

The revival of humanism and classical influences flowered into high artistic achievement during the Renaissance, a period in which Europe also reached the shores of distant continents.

The quest for knowledge espoused by the Renaissance resulted in spectacular leaps across the globe. Advances in geography and navigation enabled European nations, hungry for new trade routes, to send explorers farther afield. Funded by Spain, Christopher Columbus crossed the Atlantic in 1492 and chanced across some islands in the Caribbean, thus accidentally discovering the New World. Six years later, Vasco da Gama of Portugal rounded Africa and made landfall in India, opening an ocean route to Asia. More expeditions east and west continued to funnel riches and information to European shores. The remnants of Ferdinand Magellan's fleet, for example, returned in 1522 after completing the first circumnavigation of the globe.

The Renaissance was not without strife. Conflicts included the bitter Thirty Years' War, which pitted Protestants against Catholics from 1618 to 1648. But with European nations prosperous enough to reach out to new continents and to create enduring works of high art, the Renaissance was one of the greatest periods of achievement in history.

OPPOSITE: Elizabeth I was queen of England from 1558 to 1603, a time of prosperity and achievement.

1517
Martin Luther posts his 95 Theses and sparks the Protestant Reformation.

1532
Niccolò Machiavelli writes *The Prince*.

1588
Spanish Armada is sent to defeat Protestant England.

1618–1648
Thirty Years' War rages across the continent of Europe.

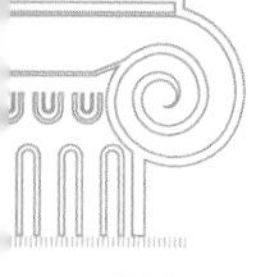

SEE ALSO | KINGS AND NOMADS: PAGE 197

Florentine statesman Lorenzo de' Medici holds court at his villa.

NATIONS FIRST BLOOM

By the 14th century, Italy was a patchwork of some 250 autonomous city-states. The largest and strongest—Florence, Milan, Rome, and Venice—were controlled by wealthy merchant families such as the Medicis and Borgias, who became patrons of the arts. Moving away from religious themes, Italian humanist writers such as Boccaccio and Petrarch began exploring the beauty of the human mind and body. And with the fall of Constantinople to the Turks in 1453, many Byzantine scholars packed up their classical manuscripts and fled to Italy, reviving an interest in classical learning.

THE TAKEAWAY: The Renaissance took root in the rich city-states of Italy.

VIPs

EUROPE

Copernicus, 1473–1543
Polish astronomer who discovered that planets orbit the sun

Martin Luther, 1483–1546
German theologian, famous for questioning Catholic practices

Henry VIII, 1491–1547
English king and head of Church of England

Charles V, 1500–1558
Ruler of Spain and Holy Roman Empire

William Shakespeare, 1564–1616
English playwright and poet

VOICES

MACHIAVELLI FEAR OR LOVE?

"Upon this a question arises: whether it be better to be loved than feared or feared than loved? It may be answered that one should wish to be both, but, because it is difficult to unite them in one person, it is much safer to be feared than loved, when, of the two, either must be dispensed with. . . . [M]en have less scruple in offending one who is beloved than one who is feared, for love is preserved by the link of obligation which, owing to the baseness of men, is broken at every opportunity for their advantage; but fear preserves you by a dread of punishment which never fails."

—FROM NICCOLÒ MACHIAVELLI, *THE PRINCE,* 1532

NICCOLÒ MACHIAVELLI

"We are much beholden to Machiavel and others, that write what men do, and not what they ought to do."

—FRANCIS BACON

NATIONS NEW IDEAS

From Italy the spirit of the Renaissance spread outward into northern Europe. After invading Italy in the late 15th century, the French took home new ideas about art and fashion. Italian diplomats further advanced the new ways of thinking throughout the continent, so that by the time the Renaissance was waning in Italy in the mid-16th century, it was peaking to the north. Rulers and nobles in France, England, Germany, and the Netherlands sponsored Italian painters and writers who enriched the walls of their churches and the minds of their countrymen. The development of movable type by Johannes Gutenberg around 1455 rapidly spread the new gospel of humanism.

Dutch scholar Erasmus was a leading intellect in the northern Renaissance.

Among widely read authors were such social critics as Sir Thomas More, whose 1516 fiction *Utopia* imagined a society governed by reason and concern for public welfare. His friend Desiderius Erasmus, born in the Netherlands, took aim at the corruption of the church in his 1511 book *The Praise of Folly*. And in France, physician-monk François Rabelais wrote adventure stories in the 1530s that mocked the church and other institutions.

It was Erasmus who wrote, "In the country of the blind, the one-eyed man is king."

THE TAKEAWAY: The art and philosophy of Renaissance Italy swept across Europe in the 15th and 16th centuries.

Artistic styles, such as that in Carpaccio's "Legend of St. Ursula," spread from Italy northward.

> *"Wisdom entereth not into a malicious mind, and science without conscience is but the ruin of the soul."*
>
> —FRANÇOIS RABELAIS

SEE ALSO | KINGS AND NOMADS: PAGE 189

Upper-class women busied themselves with the domestic and fine arts during the Renaissance.

CLASS & SOCIETY MOBILITY

While the plagues of the 14th century uprooted much of Europe's feudal structure, class divisions remained firmly in place. In cities and towns bankers, burghers, and guildsmen ranked over laborers; in the countryside, the declining feudal system left a mass of unskilled peasants from which would grow a middle class of small business- and landowners.

Peasant revolts beginning in the 14th century gradually led to the end of serfdom, a semi-slave system. The new manorial system was a looser arrangement, allowing the peasant class some freedom of social and economic mobility.

Emerging from the church-dominated past, the new age prompted reexamination of the individual's role in society. In 1528, for example, diplomat Baldassare Castiglione published *The Book of the Courtier*. Translated into many languages and circulated widely, the treatise on manners became a handbook for the newly risen classes on how to be a Renaissance gentleman.

During the Renaissance, some 80 percent of Europe's population lived in small rural villages.

THE TAKEAWAY: Aristocrats remained in power, yet serfdom was abolished and some peasants became landowners.

> *"They wonder much to hear that gold, which in itself is so useless a thing, should be everywhere so much esteemed."* —THOMAS MORE

VOICES

ENGLAND WHAT NOT TO WEAR

"None shall wear in his apparel:

"Any silk of the color of purple, cloth of gold tissue, nor fur of sables, but only the King, Queen, King's mother, children, brethren, and sisters, uncles and aunts; and except dukes, marquises, and earls, who may wear the same in doublets, jerkins, linings of cloaks, gowns, and hose; and those of the Garter, purple in mantles only. Cloth of gold, silver, tinseled satin, silk, or cloth mixed or embroidered with any gold or silver."

—FROM ELIZABETHAN STATUTES OF APPAREL, 1574

REVOLTING AGAINST SUMPTUARY LAWS

DAILY LIFE FOOD AND FINERY

For merchants and the middle and upper classes, daily life had a range of opportunities not available in earlier eras. The daughters of aristocrats had private tutors, some of whom were humanist scholars. Well-off merchants often sent daughters to convent schools for a better education than villages could provide.

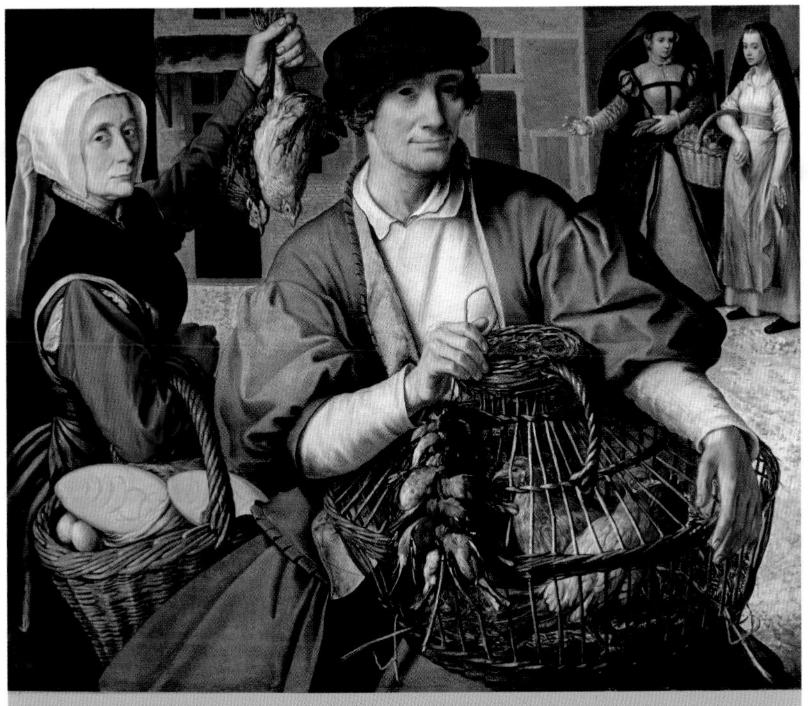

Country folk sold their products in town markets.

Marriage was a way for women to climb in social status; a man, likewise, could gain by marrying into wealth. Women not married by 21 usually entered convents.

Most people lived on two meals a day, the staple being vegetable

Lepers traditionally wore gray coats and red hats; prostitutes had to wear scarlet skirts.

soup and bread. Fowl and eggs supplemented the diet, but for peasants beef and pork were luxuries. Potatoes, of New World origin, were introduced in the late 1500s.

Sumptuary laws tried to enforce class distinctions through clothing. Lace and buttons were often forbidden to all but the nobility, yet members of the merchant class managed to flout the laws.

THE TAKEAWAY: Social status dictated a person's food, clothing, and housing.

"I want there to be no peasant in my realm so poor that he will not have a chicken in his pot every Sunday."

—HENRI OF NAVARRE

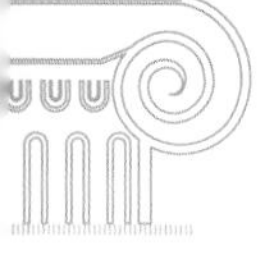

SEE ALSO | BREAKING BONDS: PAGE 220

The glorious dome of Brunelleschi's Santa Maria del Fiore caps the historic center of Florence.

ARTS THE AGE OF GENIUS

Renaissance painting, sculpture, and architecture gave dramatic new emphasis to the classics and the human form. Even by the early 1300s, painters like Giotto di Bondone were imbuing religious frescoes with realistic portraits. But the zenith of Italian Renaissance art arrived in the late 1400s and early 1500s, and was best exemplified in the work of three geniuses. Leonardo da Vinci was a painter, inventor, and prolific writer. His masterworks, "Mona Lisa" and "The Last Supper," are among the world's artistic treasures. He also left more than 4,000 pages of notes and drawings detailing human anatomy, mechanics, the principles of flight, hydraulics, optics, geology, and many other subjects.

Painter and sculptor Michelangelo Buonarroti was perhaps the greatest artist of his time, bringing the depiction of the human form to unsurpassed heights. His paintings on the Sistine Chapel in the Vatican and his sculptures—including the "Pieta" in Rome and the "David" in Florence—bring a majesty and emotion to the human experience.

Leonardo da Vinci's "Head of a Maiden" reveals his sure touch

Architecture flourished in the

> *"The power of one fair face makes my love sublime, for it has weaned my heart from low desires."*
> —MICHELANGELO BUONARROTI

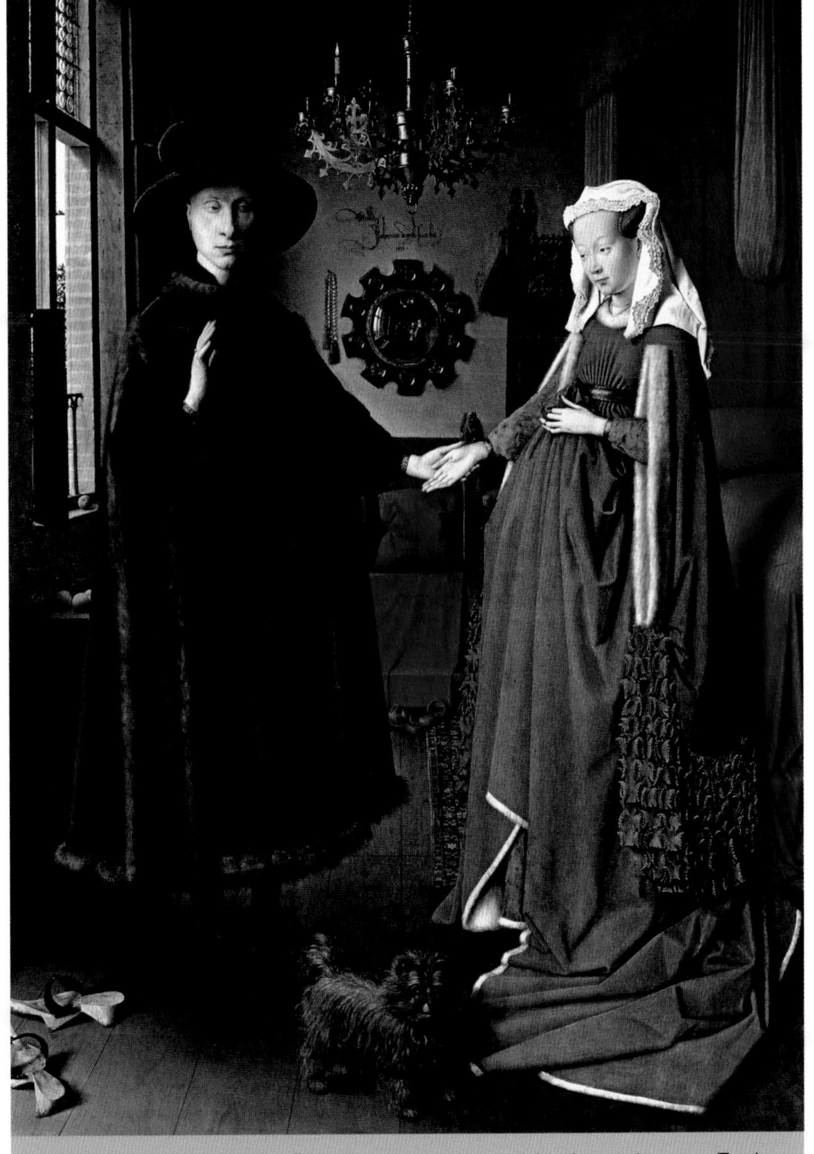
"The Arnolfini Marriage" shows the mastery of painter Jan van Eyck.

Michelangelo worked on a scaffold 80 feet high for four years in the Sistine Chapel.

era as well; masterpieces include the work of Filippo Brunelleschi, whose octagonal domed cathedral in Florence ranks as one of the greatest engineering feats of the Renaissance.

By the 15th and 16th centuries, Dutch, German, and French artists had begun combining Italian techniques with their own traditions. Jan van Eyck refined the use of oil as a medium, while Albrecht Dürer reigned as the greatest German painter of his era.

The period also nourished literary genius: William Shakespeare, born into the English Renaissance, and Spaniard Miguel de Cervantes wrote masterpieces of drama, poetry, and fiction.

THE TAKEAWAY: The Renaissance nourished multitalented artistic genius.

CONNECTIONS SHAKESPEARIAN PHRASES

Borrowing from Shakespeare is so common that almost every writer is guilty, even if unconsciously. When Arthur Conan Doyle's Sherlock Holmes cries to Watson, "The game is afoot" (*The Return of Sherlock Holmes,* 1904), he steals from Henry V. But well-known phrases such as "all's well that ends well," "to play fast and loose," or "pomp and circumstance" are not Shakespeare's only contributions to the language. Dictionaries credit him with inventing over 1,000 now-familiar words, including "outbreak," "vulnerable," "bedazzle," "fashionable," "employer," "sanctimonious," "negotiate," "obscene," "tranquil," "jaded," "bedroom," and "zany."

POMP AND CIRCUMSTANCE

"Drink to me only with thine eyes, / And I will pledge with mine; / Or leave a kiss but in the cup / And I'll look not for wine." —BEN JONSON

SEE ALSO | NEW WORLD ORDER: PAGE 280

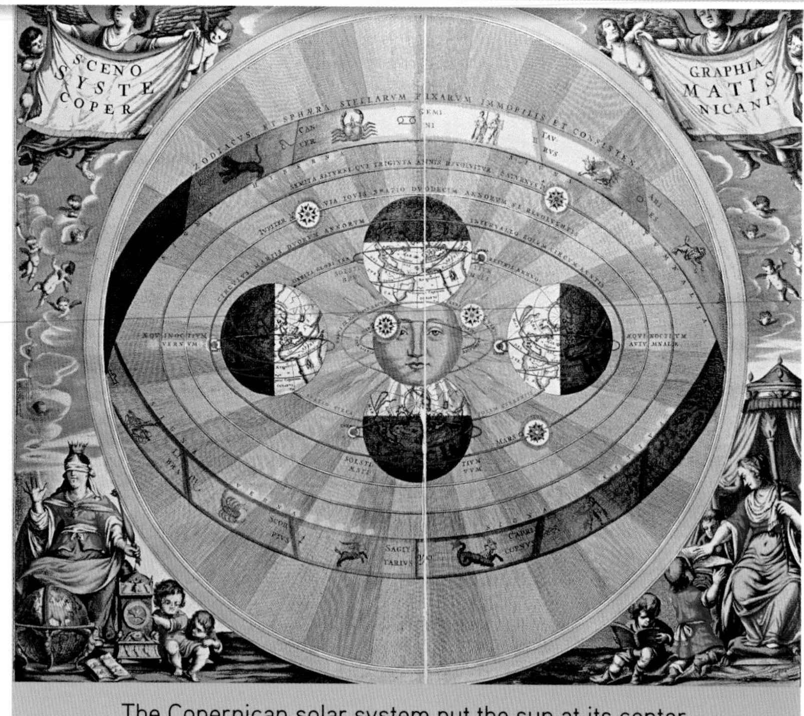

The Copernican solar system put the sun at its center.

SCIENCE TAKING A NEW LOOK

It was natural that the skeptical and energetic attitudes of the Renaissance would burst forth in advances in science and technology. Daring to break faith with the ancient idea of an Earth-centered, unchanging universe, Polish astronomer Nicolaus Copernicus discovered that planets orbit the sun—an observation so controversial that he did not publish the concept until 1543, just before his death.

Such great observational astronomers as Tycho Brahe of Denmark and Johannes Kepler of Germany clarified the size and the clockwork mechanisms of the universe. In 1609 Italian physicist and astronomer Galileo Galilei became the first scientist to turn a telescope to the heavens—his numerous discoveries, including the four large moons of Jupiter, and his probing experiments helped move science toward modern methods.

> Astronomer Johannes Kepler had to devote six years of his life to clearing his mother of charges of witchcraft.

Investigations into the smallest corners of the natural world were under way by the mid-1400s, when natural philosophers began using one-lens microscopes to examine insects. In 1590, Dutch spectacle maker Zacharias Janssen invented the compound microscope, opening up new worlds for discovery.

The revolution in medicine was

HORKEY GALILEO'S "FICTITIOUS" PLANETS

VOICES

GALILEO GALILEI

"Galileo Galilei, the mathematician of Padua, came to us in Bologna and he brought with him that spyglass through which he sees four fictitious planets. On the twenty-fourth and twenty-fifth of April I never slept, day and night, but tested that instrument of Galileo's in innumerable ways, in these lower as well as the higher [realms]. On Earth it works miracles; in the heavens it deceives, for other fixed stars appear double.... [D]ejected, he took his leave from Mr. Magini very early in the morning. And he gave no thanks for the favors and the many thoughts, because, full of himself, he hawked a fable."

—LETTER FROM SKEPTICAL GERMAN SCIENTIST MARTIN HORKEY TO JOHANNES KEPLER, 1610

"O speculators about perpetual motion, how many vain chimeras have you created in the like quest? Go and take your places with the seekers after gold." —LEONARDO DA VINCI

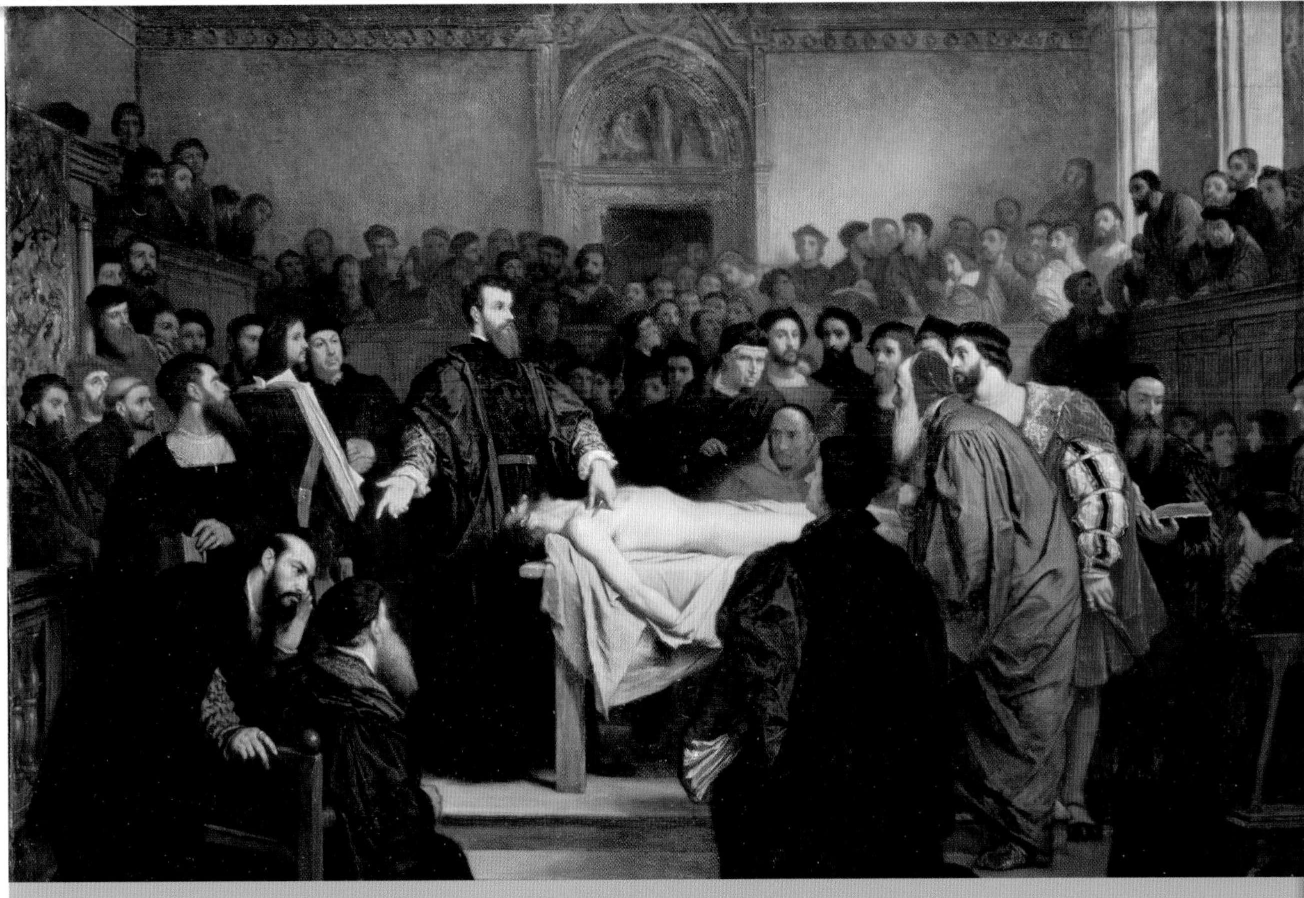

Belgian anatomist Andreas Vesalius teaches at Padua using a cadaver.

led by German-Swiss physician Paracelsus, an outspoken thinker who contested the ancient idea that diseases were caused by imbalances in the humors—the four fluids (blood, phlegm, yellow bile, and black bile) said to determine the body's health and temperament. Instead, he proposed external factors as disease vectors. The 16th-century Belgian anatomist Vesalius was among the first to dissect human cadavers, a practice previously forbidden by the church. English physician William Harvey became the first to propound the theory of blood circulation in 1628.

English philosopher and author Francis Bacon expounded ideas on the scientific method itself in such groundbreaking works as *Advancement of Learning* (1605), a survey of the state of knowledge, and *Novum Organum* (1620), an analysis of his inductive method of investigation. French mathematician and philosopher René Descartes laid the foundations for modern philosophy in his *Discourse on the Method* (1637), an attempt to unify all knowledge as the result of reasoning from self-evident premises.

In *De Homine Figuris*, French philosopher René Descartes expounded his theories of the body.

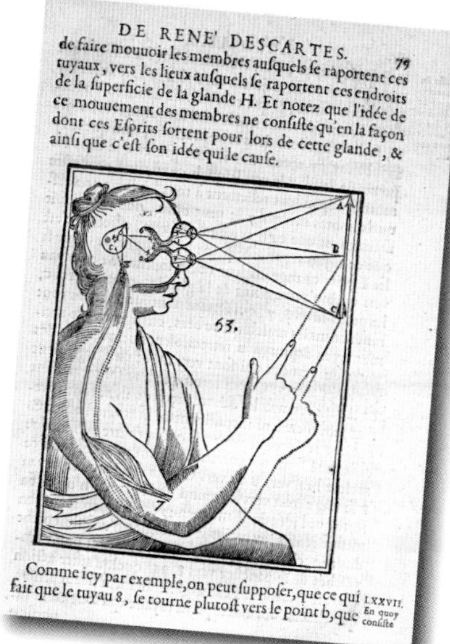

DE RENE' DESCARTES. 79

de faire mouuoir les membres aufquels fe raportent ces tuyaux, vers les lieux aufquels fe raportent ces endroits de la fuperficie de la glande H. Et notez que l'idée de ce mouuement des membres ne confifte qu'en la façon dont ces Efprits fortent pour lors de cette glande, & ainfi que c'eft fon idée qui le caufe.

Comme icy par exemple, on peut fuppofer, que ce qui fait que le tuyau 8, fe tourne plutoft vers le point b, que

LXXVII. En quoy confifte

THE TAKEAWAY: Logical investigation during the Renaissance laid the groundwork for the scientific revolution.

> *Finally we shall place the Sun himself at the center of the Universe. . . . if only we face the facts, as they say, 'with both eyes open.'"* —NICOLAUS COPERNICUS

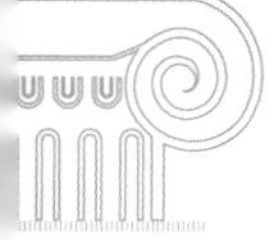

SEE ALSO | BREAKING BONDS: PAGE 242

RELIGION A BRANCHING CHURCH

When German religious scholar Martin Luther wrote a letter of protest to his archbishop in 1517, he did not know that he was igniting a revolution. His long list of grievances—in all, 95 theses—criticized, among other things, the church practice of selling indulgences to forgive sins, past and future. These official pardons struck Luther as a particularly corrupt way for a supposedly Christian institution to extract money from the masses. Meant merely to spark an academic debate, Luther's ideas shot across northern Europe, thanks to the new printing press. Within 50 years, Lutheranism and other dissenting Christian sects had torn a gaping hole in the fabric of Roman Catholic life. The Reformation was born.

Europe was not new to such dissenting ideas. The practices Luther boldly opposed were ones that had long troubled even devout church supporters. They and humanists alike were alarmed at the increasingly large role the church had taken in secular affairs. The church had long allowed lucrative clerical positions to be bought by wealthy

> Geneva preacher John Calvin founded Calvinism in the 1540s, insisting on a literal reading of the scriptures.

Martin Luther and Huldrych Zwingli hold a discussion in Marburg with Saxon religious reformers in 1529.

> *"When Luther at first appeared, he merely touched, with a gentle hand, a few abuses of the grossest description, now grown intolerable."* —JOHN CALVIN

VOICES

MARTIN LUTHER SELLING ABSOLUTION

MARTIN LUTHER

"Papal indulgences for the building of St. Peter's are circulating under your most distinguished name, and as regards them, I do not bring accusation against the outcries of the preachers, which I have not heard, so much as I grieve over the wholly false impressions which the people have conceived from them; to wit, – the unhappy souls believe that if they have purchased letters of indulgence they are sure of their salvation; again, that so soon as they cast their contributions into the money-box, souls fly out of purgatory; furthermore, that these graces are so great that there is no sin too great to be absolved, even, as they say—though the thing is impossible—if one had violated the Mother of God."

—FROM A LETTER TO THE ARCHBISHOP OF MAINZ, 1517

families. Some popes themselves were not above outright hypocrisy, raising money not only for wars but for embellishing the Vatican and holding lavish banquets.

Luther's message was that salvation was a gift directly from God that could not be bought and did not require the intercession of a church official. He and other reformers simplified church doctrine and rituals; their leaders, known as ministers instead of priests, preached the Bible and held services in local languages instead of Latin.

Protestant sects sprang up across Europe, their views more radical than Luther's. Followers of Huldrych Zwingli's Reformed Church in Zurich created a church-state that banned the Catholic mass and prohibited music during services. Another radical group, the Anabaptists, separated from Zwingli over their opposition to infant baptism; they also refused to hold office or bear arms, for which they were persecuted by both Catholics and Protestants. The English church, more conservative, nonetheless broke from the pope in 1534 when Henry VIII declared himself and his heirs the rightful heads of the Church in England.

THE TAKEAWAY: Starting in 1517, the Protestant Reformation swept across Europe.

"The king's majesty justly and rightfully is and ought to be supreme head of the Church of England."

—THE ACT OF SUPREMACY

SEE ALSO | BREAKING BONDS: PAGE 229

Imperial forces storm the town of Magdeburg in 1631 during the Thirty Years' War.

CONFLICTS THE PRICE OF REFORMATION

Europe was far from peaceful during the Renaissance and Reformation—a number of conflicts, religious and territorial, flared up around the continent. Charles V, grandson of Ferdinand and Isabella of Spain, inherited lands that made him Holy Roman Emperor of a region that included Spain, Austria, Germany, the Netherlands, and Italy. From 1521 to 1544 he waged a brutal war against France under Francis I, taking the king himself prisoner after a victory at Pavia in 1525. The Reformation divided Germany and other countries into rival Protestant and Roman Catholic factions, weakening Charles's grip on the empire.

Charles's son, Philip II, was an aggressive empire builder, annexing Portugal in 1580 and the Philippine Islands (named in his honor) in the late 1500s. But he was powerless in the face of the new Protestantism, and in the 1560s the Netherlands rebelled against his rule. When the British sided with the Dutch, Philip launched an attack on England by sea in 1588. The mighty Spanish Armada of some 130 ships met its match in the British navy and North

A Huguenot, Henry of Navarre survived the St. Bartholomew's Day massacre and became King Henry IV in 1589.

 *There shall be a Christian and Universal Peace, and a perpetual, true, and sincere Amity, between his Sacred Imperial Majesty, and his most Christian Majesty."* —TREATY OF WESTPHALIA

Atlantic weather; storms destroyed much of the retreating fleet.

Wars of religion raged across Europe between 1545 and 1650. The Huguenots, French Protestants, gained so much power and influence that Henry II, son of Francis, began to persecute them. After his death a civil war erupted, the most serious consequence of which was the 1572 St. Bartholomew's Day massacre, when thousands of Huguenot citizens were killed by Catholic forces.

Perhaps the bitterest of the religious wars, the Thirty Years' War (1618–1648) was fought mostly on German soil, involving the Holy Roman Empire, Sweden, and the Netherlands, though side conflicts swirled throughout Europe. To defeat Protestantism, the Catholic Church had reinvigorated the Inquisition, trying to root out opponents. As a countermeasure, Lutherans, Calvinists, and other denominations formed defense leagues. Clashes were inevitable. The war took a heavy toll on Germany's population, agriculture, commerce, and industry.

The Treaty of Westphalia, an important step toward religious toleration, brought peace: Catholics and Protestants recognized the right of the others to exist in their own states.

{ In the Defenestration of Prague, 1618, three Catholics were thrown from the windows of Prague Castle. }

Elizabeth I appears triumphant after the defeat of the Spanish Armada.

Yet the Thirty Years' War fragmented the Holy Roman Empire into some 300 states, a development that would bring about economic and social changes to Europe.

THE TAKEAWAY: Spurred by the divisions of the Reformation, European religious wars lasted more than a century.

THUMBS UP / THUMBS DOWN

THE IRON DUKE 1507–1582

SPANISH SOLDIER AND STATESMAN Fernando Álvarez de Toledo, Duke of Alba, was a patrician who proved himself a brilliant soldier as a young man. His victories placed him high in the court of King Philip II, and in 1567 the king sent Alba to the Netherlands to suppress a rebellion. The duke arrested the leaders and established a reign of terror with the infamous Council of Troubles (or Council of Blood), which overrode local laws and condemned more than 12,000 rebels to death. Philip called Alba home in 1573 and placed him under house arrest, though seven years later he led a successful invasion of Lisbon. After his death in 1582 his reputation remained strong in Spain, but in Portugal and the Netherlands his name is synonymous with cruelty and terror. **CONCLUSION: THUMBS DOWN.**

THE DUKE OF ALBA

"The signal to commence the massacre should be given by the bell of the palace." —DE THOU

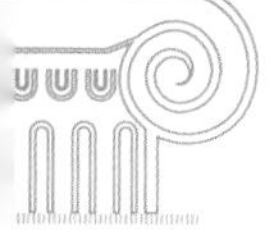

SEE ALSO | BREAKING BONDS: PAGE 246

EXPLORATION VOYAGES WEST

While France, England, Germany, and Italy were dominating Europe, Spain and Portugal were quietly reaching out for new worlds to conquer. With its face to the Atlantic and its feet practically on the African coast, Portugal was perfectly situated for launching expeditions. In the late 1400s Portugal began exploring Africa's west coast. With Italy having a hegemony over Mediterranean routes and the Ottomans now controlling trade to the

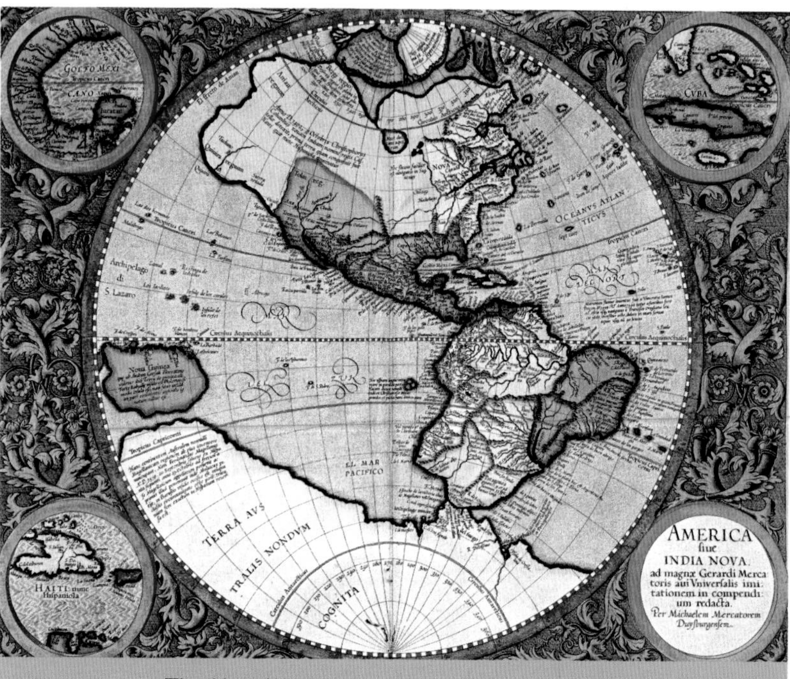

The New World takes shape on a 1595 map.

Orient (after the 1453 fall of Constantinople), Portugal was desperately in need of alternate trade routes.

Gold and slaves imported from the African coast only whetted explorers' appetites. One by one, the Portuguese occupied the steppingstones off the coasts of Portugal and Africa: the Azores, Madeira, and the Canary and Cape Verde Islands. The explorers' maneuverable, three-masted caravels kept pushing their way south.

With Portugal making headway in the new enterprise of exploration, Spain took notice. So when a Genoese sailor named Christopher Columbus (Cristoforo Colombo) wanted funding for a trip to Japan and was turned down by the king of Portugal, Ferdinand and Isabella gave the matter some thought. Columbus's idea of sailing due west to reach the Orient was, if not wholly original, still unusual. It took him nearly a decade to get his plan approved, which included a

Christopher Columbus appears in profile in a medal from the 15th or 16th century.

promise to spread Christianity abroad. Finally, mostly thanks to Isabella, Columbus's proposed venture was funded and launched.

In October 1492, Columbus's three ships made landfall in the Bahamas, although for the rest of his life he believed that he had in fact landed on the eastern reaches of Asia. Columbus had optimistically underestimated the ocean's width and the size of the Earth. It remained for a later navigator, Italian Amerigo Vespucci, to prove

{ English explorer Henry Hudson vanished after being set adrift by mutineers in Hudson Bay, 1611. }

that Columbus had bumped into a new continent. A published version of Vespucci's accounts led to the new land being named "America" in his honor. In 1497 Venetian John Cabot (Giovanni Caboto), sailing

Journey over all the universe in a map, without the expense and fatigue of traveling, without suffering the inconveniences of heat, cold, hunger, and thirst." —MIGUEL DE CERVANTES

John Cabot departs from Bristol, England, in 1497.

> Magellan's voyages were so difficult that at times the crew was reduced to eating leather from the yardarms.

under English patronage, took a northern route across the Atlantic and explored areas of the North American coast that had been discovered by the Vikings nearly 500 years before.

Crowning this age of exploration was the expedition that began in 1519, when a Spanish fleet led by Ferdinand Magellan of Portugal set out to find the western passage to the Indies that had eluded Columbus. In 1520 the ships rounded the icy tip of South America and entered the Pacific. Magellan died in 1521, but Juan Sebastián de Elcano took command, continuing west in one ship, and circumnavigated the globe, returning to Spain in 1522.

THE TAKEAWAY: Expeditions from Iberia reached and explored the New World in the late 1400s and early 1500s.

Spanish explorer Juan Ponce de León reached Florida in 1513.

VOICES

AMERIGO VESPUCCI IGUANAS

AMERIGO VESPUCCI

"Thus went we on through their houses, or rather tents, and found many of those serpents alive, and they were tied by the feet and had a cord around their snouts, so that they could not open their mouths, as is done [in Europe] with mastiff-dogs so that they may not bite: they were of such savage aspect that none of us dared to take one away, thinking that they were poisonous: they are of the bigness of a kid, and in length an ell and a half: their feet are long and thick, and armed with big claws: they have a hard skin, and are of various colours: they have the muzzle and face of a serpent: and from their snouts there rises a crest like a saw which extends along the back as far as the tip of the tail."

—FROM A LETTER TO THE GONFALONIER OF FLORENCE, ABOUT HIS FIRST VOYAGE TO SOUTH AMERICA

"The tempest was terrible and separated me from my [other] vessels that night, putting every one of them in desperate straits, with nothing to look forward to but death." —CHRISTOPHER COLUMBUS

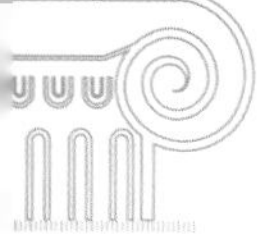

EXPLORATION VOYAGES EAST

No matter which way they headed, the explorers' aim was to get to the Orient and its precious metals, jewels, and, especially, spices, prized by Europeans because they made meat palatable even when it was close to spoiling. With a new route to Asia, the jewels, silks, pepper, cloves, and cinnamon of the Far East could flow into western markets without a Mediterranean middleman. Portugal and Spain took the lead in financing these expeditions, investments that would soon pay off handsomely, making titans of these formerly ignored countries.

The Spice Islands were known for their nutmeg, mace, and cloves.

The prime mover of Portugal's maritime outreach was Prince Henry the Navigator, founder of a school devoted to navigation and sponsor of expeditions of discovery. After capturing the Moroccan port of Ceuta in 1415, he became governor of the Algarve, the southernmost province of Portugal, and began attracting cartographers, shipbuilders, instrument makers, and astronomers. No aspect of seamanship was left unstudied in his explorers' laboratory.

The ships of Portuguese navigator Vasco da Gama sailed to India in 1498.

Henry's aim was to send a voyage around Africa to India for the purposes of trade and missionizing. Expeditions began in 1420s, and by the 1440s Henry's sailors had rounded Cape Verde, some 1,500 miles away, bravely overcoming superstitions about boiling water

> *"This may seem strange, that [West African] princes and noblemen used to . . . raise their skins with pretty knots in diverse forms, as it were branched damask."* —RICHARD EDEN

SEE ALSO | NEW WORLD ORDER: PAGE 295

and sea monsters. Though Henry himself never sailed on these voyages, he was so keen on financing them that he went into heavy debt to do so.

Later in the century, Columbus's expedition westward yielded little of tangible value to the Spanish monarchs. Of much more immediate commercial interest was the Portuguese explorer Vasco da Gama's sensational accomplishment in 1498. He sailed around the Cape of Good Hope, the tip of Africa, and went on to Calicut, on the southwest coast of India. Here finally was the long-hoped-for feat that promised real wealth. Portuguese admiral Alfonso da Albuquerque established a base at Goa, on India's west coast, in 1510. The high cost of spices plummeted, and Venice and other established centers of trade saw their monopolies disappear.

On Vasco de Gama's second voyage (1502-1503), he founded a Portuguese colony in Mozambique.

Henry the Navigator launched voyages from Portugal in the 1400s.

Along with the opportunities opened up by world exploration, however, came the abuse of native populations, giving pause to Isabella and other leaders who believed that serving God was their highest duty. Yet whether under the guise of Christianization or expansion, the new colonial urge overwhelmed any moral qualms.

THE TAKEAWAY: Early voyages to the East opened trade routes and started the colonial era.

VOICES

VASCO DA GAMA CHRISTIANS AND SPICES

VASCO DA GAMA

"On the following day [May 22] these same boats came again alongside, when the captain-major [da Gama] sent one of the convicts to Calicut, and those with whom he went took him to two Moors from Tunis, who could speak Castilian and Genoese. The first greeting that he received was in these words: 'May the Devil take thee! What brought you hither?' They asked what he sought so far away from home, and he told them that we came in search of Christians and of spices. They said: 'Why does not the King of Castile, the King of France, or the Signoria of Venice send thither?' He said that the King of Portugal would not consent to their doing so, and they said he did the right thing."

—FROM A JOURNAL BY A MEMBER OF DA GAMA'S 1498 EXPEDITION

"The reception was friendly, as if the people were pleased to see us, though at first appearances looked threatening, for they carried naked swords in their hands." —VASCO DE GAMA

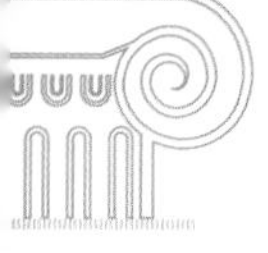

SEE ALSO | BREAKING BONDS: PAGE 229

NATIONS ENGLAND IN UPHEAVAL

In 1455 a dispute within the long-reigning Plantagenet family broke out into the War of the Roses, named for the emblems of the family branches—the red rose of the Lancasters and the white of the Yorks. Though the Yorkists finally won, a Lancastrian named Henry Tudor seized the throne in 1485 and became Henry VII. By marrying Elizabeth of York, he united the two houses. His burly, red-haired son Henry VIII inherited a stable kingdom in 1509.

Mostly remembered as a royal rogue who married six times, Henry VIII used his political strength to increase the throne's power. Thus when the pope refused to grant him a divorce from Catherine of Aragon, he was able to dissolve ties with Rome and establish himself as the head of the church in his own country. This independent church gradually transformed itself into the Church of England.

Henry's son Edward VI reigned only six years until his death in 1553, when his half-sister Mary, daughter of the Catholic Catherine of Aragon, became England's ruler. In attempting to return the country to Catholicism, she killed so many Protestants she became known as Bloody Mary. On her death in 1558, her half-sister Elizabeth took the throne.

> Henry VIII divorced two wives and executed two others. One died naturally and one outlived him.

Queen Elizabeth I was smart and politically savvy; she conducted England through a long period of exploration and artistic creativity. Elizabeth sponsored English settlements in the New World, promoted trade with Asia, and successfully fought off an invasion by the Spanish Armada. She also laid the foundation for religious tolerance in England, permitting Catholicism as long as it respected the crown. English literature became world-class during the reign of

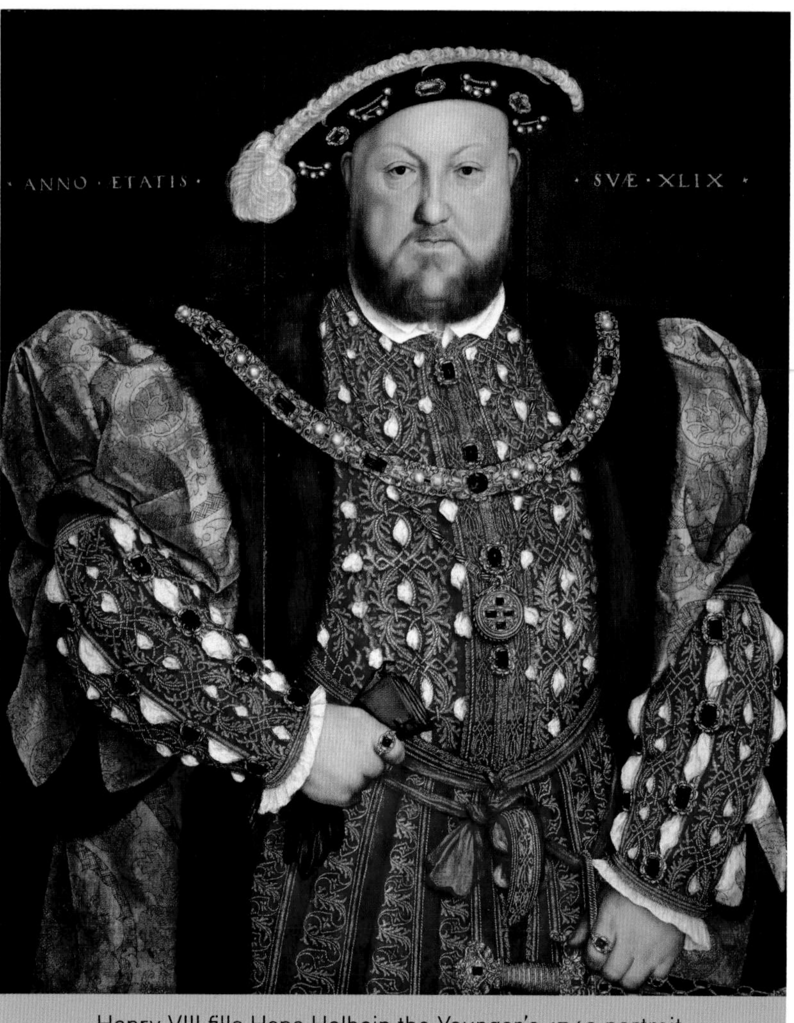

Henry VIII fills Hans Holbein the Younger's 1540 portrait.

> "O Jesu my dearest one, / now set me free. / In prison's oppression, in sorrow's obsession / I weary for thee."
> —MARY, QUEEN OF SCOTS

VOICES

WYNKFIELDE READY TO BE GONE

"[The executioners], with her two women, helping her up, began to disrobe her of her apparel: then she, laying her crucifix upon the stool, one of the executioners took from her neck the Agnus Dei, which she, laying hands off it, gave to one of her women, and told the executioner he should be answered money for it. Then she suffered them, with her two women, to disrobe her of her chain of pomander beads and all other her apparel most willingly, and with joy rather than sorrow, helped to make unready herself, putting on a pair of sleeves with her own hands which they had pulled off, and that with some haste, as if she had longed to be gone."

—FROM AN ACCOUNT BY ROBERT WYNKFIELDE OF QUEEN MARY'S EXECUTION, 1587

EXECUTION OF MARY, QUEEN OF SCOTS

the Virgin Queen: William Shakespeare, Christopher Marlowe, and Edmund Spenser gloried in the richness of Elizabethan English.

Elizabeth's one rival was Mary Stuart, queen of the Scots and a descendant of Henry VII. Forced to abdicate her throne, she fled to England in 1567, where Elizabeth imprisoned her for 18 years; convicted of conspiracy, she was beheaded. Nevertheless, Mary's only son was next in line for the throne, and on Elizabeth's death in 1603 he became King James I.

James's son Charles I struggled with Parliament over its right to limit his powers, and in 1629 he dissolved that governing body. When Charles tried to reconvene Parliament to raise money for a war against rebellious Scotland, hard feelings escalated into civil war. In 1649 Charles was tried for treason and executed, and in 1653 a member of Parliament, Oliver Cromwell, was named Lord Protector. Two years of anarchy followed Cromwell's death in 1658, and in 1660 Charles's son was installed as King Charles II.

{ Scots rebelled when Charles I attempted to impose upon them the English Book of Common Prayer. }

King Charles I receives a rose on the way to prison in 1647.

THE TAKEAWAY: The long, strong reign of Elizabeth was the highlight of a difficult period for England.

"Though God hath raised me high, yet this I count the glory of my crown: that I have reigned with your loves."

—QUEEN ELIZABETH I

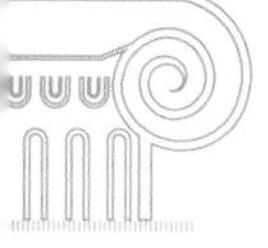

SEE ALSO | BREAKING BONDS: PAGE 249

Built by the Moors in the 14th century, the Alhambra became a Christian stronghold at the end of the 15th.

EMPIRES SAILING TO GLORY

In 1469 the largest of the Spanish states were united with the marriage of Ferdinand of Aragon and Isabella of Castile. Their combined forces drove the Muslims out of their last Iberian stronghold, Granada, in 1492, the same year that Spain sponsored Columbus's voyages. The dark side of Ferdinand and Isabella's Christian zeal expressed itself in the notorious Spanish Inquisition, a deviant variation on the Roman Catholic court of inquiry. In addition to Muslims and other so-called heretics, wealthy Jewish converts were selected for persecution during a period of anti-Semitic fervor. Some 2,000 suspected heretics were tortured and burned under the auspices of Dominican priest Tomás de Torquemada. The grand inquisitor also helped spur the expulsion of 160,000 Jews from Spain in 1492.

{ One of Ferdinand and Isabella's daughters, Catherine of Aragon, became Henry the VIII's first wife. }

With both Spain and Portugal vying for a monopoly on the new Asian trade routes, the pope had to settle the matter. The 1494 Treaty of Tordesillas decreed that Spain had rights to everything west of a longitudinal line through the Atlantic, while Portugal got everything to the east up to the Asian coast. Since the line cut through the bulge on South America's eastern coast, eastern

Ferdinand and Isabella united two Spanish states when they married.

> *"If it were an art to overcome heresy with fire, the executioners would be the most learned doctors on earth."*
> —MARTIN LUTHER

Brazil belonged to the Portuguese. By the 1550s, Spain was raking in boatloads of silver and gold from the New World; these riches, as well as a series of royal marriages, made Spain the greatest of European powers. Portugal, with its eastern trade, had also become a force to be reckoned with.

In 1556 Philip II, a member of the powerful Habsburg family, became king of an empire that extended over Spain, the Netherlands, and part of Italy, and he sought to expand it.

{ By the late 1600s, Portuguese Brazil was the world's largest sugar producer, its plantations worked by slave labor. }

Over the next four decades he took the Philippines, annexed Portugal, and defeated the Ottoman fleet in the Battle of Lepanto (1571). Meanwhile, the treasure-laden Spanish galleons proved too tempting for English and Dutch sailors. To punish England's piracy, Philip tried attacking the island nation with his famous armada. His humiliating loss in 1588 marked a turning point, though it did not spell the end of Spain's might.

For several more decades, Spain maintained its world-dominating status, even while hemorrhaging money to pay off debts to foreign bankers. During this time the arts flourished, producing the novelist Miguel de Cervantes and such painters as El Greco and Velázquez.

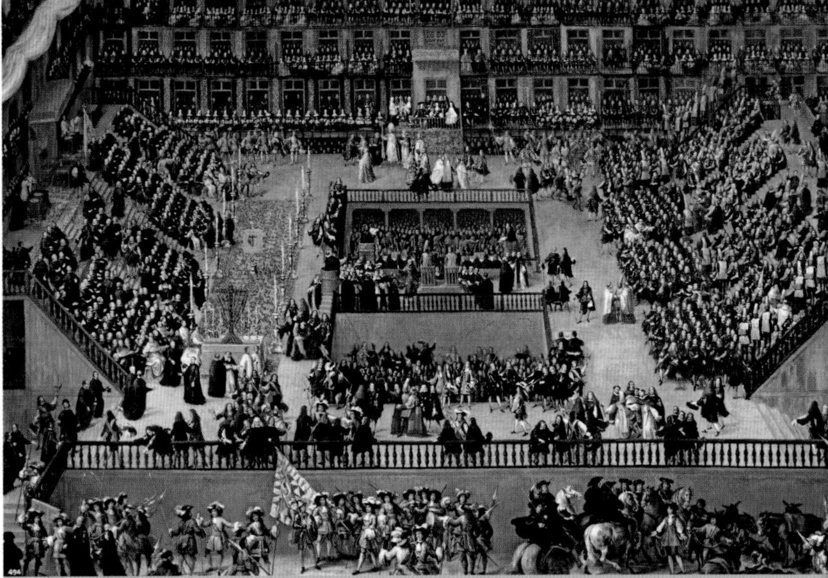

Witnesses gather in Madrid's Plaza Mayor to condemn heretics.

THE TAKEAWAY: Lifted by riches from exploration, Spain and Portugal became world powers.

VOICES

SPAIN INTO THE HANDS OF PIRATES

"When the edict of expulsion became known in the other countries, vessels came from Genoa to the Spanish harbors to carry away the Jews. The crews of these vessels, too, acted maliciously and meanly toward the Jews, robbed them, and delivered some of them to the famous pirate of that time who was called the Corsair of Genoa. To those who escaped and arrived at Genoa the people of the city showed themselves merciless, and oppressed and robbed them, and the cruelty of their wicked hearts went so far that they took the infants from the mothers' breasts. ❧ Many ships with Jews, especially from Sicily, went to the city of Naples on the coast. The King of this country was friendly to the Jews."

—FROM AN ACCOUNT OF THE EXPULSION OF JEWS FROM SPAIN, 1492

EXPULSION OF JEWS FROM SPAIN

"O how small a portion of earth will hold us when we are dead, who ambitiously seek after the whole world while we are living." —PHILIP II

SEE ALSO | POSTCLASSICAL ERA: PAGE 158

Tsar Ivan the Terrible captures a Livonian fortress.

NATIONS THE FIRST TSARS

In the 15th century the Tatar Mongols controlled Russia and exacted tribute from its populace. Then in 1480 Ivan III (Ivan the Great) freed the Moscow region from their iron grip. Calling himself "tsar" (caesar), he expanded the Kremlin and expanded Russia's holdings up to the Arctic Ocean. His grandson, Ivan IV, was one of the most feared and powerful of the early tsars. Known as Ivan the Terrible, he came to power at age 16 and became infamous for arresting, torturing, and executing suspected traitors. Yet as a ruler, Ivan centralized the government, increased trade with Europe, and pushed Russia's borders to the east and south.

After the death of Ivan's son Fyodor in 1598, Russia fell into a 15-year period known as the Time of Troubles, despite the efforts of a nobleman named Boris Godunov who took the throne. Poland occupied Moscow in 1608, but a popular backlash reinstalled a new Russian tsar, Michael Romanov, in 1613.

{ Ivan III was said to be descended from Rurik, the legendary Norse founder of Kievan Russia. }

BORIS GODUNOV ca 1551–1605

BORIS GODUNOV

AN ADVISER TO IVAN IV'S WEAK-MINDED SON tsar Fyodor I, Boris Godunov became the de facto ruler of Russia during Fyodor's reign. In the 1590s he waged a successful war against Sweden, retaking land along the Gulf of Finland; turned back a Tatar attack on Moscow; bolstered foreign trade; and built several fortresses and defensive towns. On the death of Fyodor, an assembly elected Godunov to the throne. As tsar, he instituted a number of popular reforms, including reorganizing the judicial system, permitting the building of Lutheran churches, and negotiating with foreign powers for land. **CONCLUSION: THUMBS UP**

THUMBS UP / THUMBS DOWN

Russian aristocrats, or boyars, held political power in the 17th century.

THE TAKEAWAY: Tsarist Russia threw off Mongol dominion and expanded far beyond Moscow.

> *"If you kiss someone in Christ's name, you should kiss him or her holding your breath, without sputtering."*
> —THE DOMOSTROI, RULES FOR RUSSIAN HOUSEHOLDS

EMPIRES OTTOMAN EMPIRE

Suleyman the Magnificent was one of the greatest Ottoman rulers.

After taking Constantinople in 1453, the Ottomans pushed farther into Europe, conquering Athens, then Serbia, Bosnia, and Albania. With formidable forces on both land and sea, the empire grew fat on plundered wealth. As Sunni Muslims, the Ottoman Turks thought it their sacred duty to fight Christians, yet they also clashed with Iranian Shiites, whom they considered heretics. Under Sultan Selim the Grim, they took Syria and Cairo from the Mamluks who had ruled Egypt for more than 250 years.

By the mid-1500s, Sultan Suleyman I (the Magnificent) expanded the empire to its largest extent yet, its boundaries reaching from Algiers to Bahrain, and from Yemen to Hungary. The Ottomans also controlled most of the Mediterranean coast and the Black Sea. Yet they were finally checked at the port of Lepanto (in present-day Greece) in 1571 when naval forces from Spain, Venice, and the papal states of Italy captured more than 100 Ottoman ships. Despite this, the empire prospered until the late 17th century, when military setbacks and weak rulers led to a decline.

> Ottoman men could have up to four official wives, who lived in a section of the house called the harem.

THE TAKEAWAY: The Ottoman juggernaut continued rolling east and west well into the 1600s.

At the Battle of Lepanto in 1571, the galleys of the Holy League defeated the Turkish fleet.

> *"My woman of the beautiful hair, my love of the slanted brow, my love of eyes full of mischief/... I'll sing your praises always."* —SULEYMAN THE MAGNIFICENT

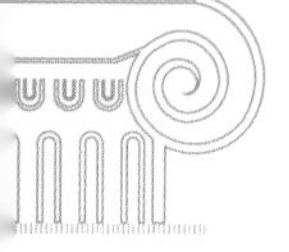

LUTHER'S 95 THESES

To help fund the rebuilding of St. Peter's in Rome, Pope Leo X pushed the sale of indulgences into German provinces in 1517. Originally issued to relieve sinners from church penalties, their reach broadened to expunge penalties imposed by God in purgatory. To 34-year-old monastic scholar Martin Luther, versed in law, philosophy, and theology, these certificates smacked not only of corruption but of outright blasphemy. Arguing that only God could forgive sins, Luther wrote a set of 95 Theses disputing the power of indulgences and the authority of the pope. The Reformation had begun.

HAMMER OUT FREEDOM Luther wrote his 95 Theses on October 31, 1517, but whether the scholar actually nailed a placard to the door of the Castle Church at Wittenberg, Germany, is disputed. Regardless, Luther's theses rapidly spread across the land. A papal agent called Luther "a leper with a brain of brass and a nose of iron." Some were in favor of burning him, yet he survived for decades to write, hold debates, marry a former nun, and father five children.

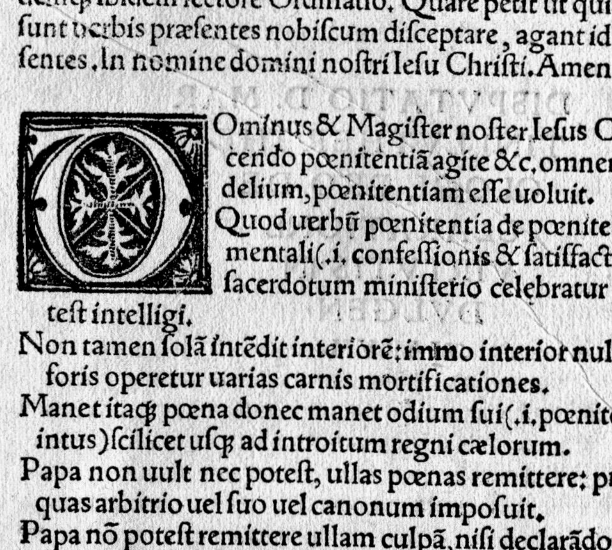

AMORE ET STVDIO ELVCIDANDAE ueritatis hæc ſubſcripta diſputabunt Vuittenbergæ, Præſidēte R.P. Martino Luther, Artiū & S. Theologiæ Magiſtro, eiuſdemqꝫ ibidem lectore Ordinatio. Quare petit ut qui non poſſunt uerbis præſentes nobiſcum diſceptare, agant id literis abſentes. In nomine domini noſtri Ieſu Chriſti. Amen.

i Dominus & Magiſter noſter Ieſus Chriſtus, dicendo pœnitentiā agite &c. omnem uitam fidelium, pœnitentiam eſſe uoluit.

ij Quod uerbū pœnitentia de pœnitentia ſacramentali (.i. confeſſionis & ſatiſfactionis quæ ſacerdotum miniſterio celebratur) non poteſt intelligi.

iij Non tamen ſolā intēdit interiorē: immo interior nulla eſt, niſi foris operetur uarias carnis mortificationes.

iiij Manet itaqꝫ pœna donec manet odium ſui (.i. pœnitentia uera intus) ſcilicet uſqꝫ ad introitum regni cælorum.

v Papa non uult nec poteſt, ullas pœnas remittere: præter eas, quas arbitrio uel ſuo uel canonum impoſuit.

vj Papa nō poteſt remittere ullam culpā, niſi declarādo & approbando remiſſam a deo. Aut certe remittēdo caſus reſeruatos ſibi, quibus contēptis culpa prorſus remaneret.

vij Nulli prorſus remittit deus culpam, quin ſimul eum ſubijciat humiliatum in omnibus ſacerdoti ſuo uicario.

viij Canones pœnitentiales ſolū uiuentibus ſunt impoſiti: nihilqꝫ morituris, ſecundū eoſdem debet imponi.

ix Inde bene nobis facit ſpirituſſanctus in Papa: excipiēdo in ſuis decretis ſemper articulum mortis & neceſſitatis.

x Indocte & male faciūt ſacerdotes ij, qui morituris pœnitētias canonicas in purgatorium reſeruant.

xj Zizania illa de mutanda pœna Canonica in pœnā purgatorij, uidentur certe dormientibus Epiſcopis ſeminata.

xij Olim pœnæ canonicæ nō poſt, ſed ante abſolutionem imponebantur, tanqꝫ tentamenta ueræ contritionis.

"1. Our Lord and Master Jesus Christ, when He said 'Repent,' willed that the whole life of believers should be repentance."

"5. The pope has neither the will nor the power to remit any penalties other than those which he has imposed either by his own authority or by that of canon law."

DEBATABLE POINTS Luther's 95 Theses (propositions for debate) were probably posted in public view, thus meant for academic discussion.

“10. Ignorant and wicked are the actions of those priests who impose canonical penances on the dead in purgatory.”

DISPVTATIO DE VIRTVTE INDVLGEN.

xiij Morituri,per mortem omnia ſoluunt, & legibus canonũ mor/
tui iam ſunt,habentes iure earũ relaxationem.
xiiij Imperfecta ſanitas ſeu charitas morituri, neceſſario ſecum fert
magnũ timorem,tãtoq; maiorẽ,quãto minor fuerit ipſa.
xv Hic timor & horror,ſatis eſt,ſe ſolo(ut alia taceam) facere pœ/
nam purgatorij,cum ſit proximus deſperationis horrori.
xvj Videntur,infernus,purgatorium, cælum differre;ſicut deſpe/
ratio,prope deſperatio,ſecuritas differunt.
xvij Neceſſarium uidetur animabus in purgatorio ſicut minui hor
rorem,ita augeri charitatem.
xviij Nec probatũ uidetur ullis,aut rationibus,aut ſcripturis, ꝙ ſint
extra ſtatum meriti ſeu augendæ charitatis.
xix Nec hoc probatũ eſſe uidetur, ꝙ ſint de ſua beatitudine certæ
& ſecuræ,ſaltem oẽs,licet nos certiſſimi ſimus.
xx Igit Papa per remiſſionẽ plenariã omniũ pœnarũ,non ſimpli
citer omniũ intelligit,ſed a ſeipo tm̃modo impoſitarũ.
xxj Errant itaq; indulgentiarũ prædicatores ij, qui dicunt per Pa/
pæ indulgentias,hominẽ ab omni pœna ſolui & ſaluari.
xxij Quin nullam remittit animabus in purgatorio, quã in hac ui/
ta debuiſſent ſecundum Canones ſoluere.
xxiij Si remiſſio ulla omniũ omnino pœnarũ pōt alicui dari: certũ
eſt eam nõ niſi perfectiſſimis.i.pauciſſimis dari.
xxiiij Falli ob id neceſſe eſt,maiorem partẽ populi: per indifferentẽ
illam & magnificam pœnæ ſolutæ promiſſionem.
xxv Qualẽ poteſtatẽ habet Papa ĩ purgatoriũ gñaliter talẽ habet
qlibet Epiſcopus & curat⁹ in ſua dioceſi,& parochia ſpãliter.
j Optime facit Papa, ꝙ nõ poteſtate clauis (quã nullam habet)
ſed per modum ſuffragij,dat animabus remiſſionem.
ij Hominẽ prædicant,qui ſtatim,ut iactus nũmus in ciſtam tin/
nierit,euolare dicunt animam.
iij Certũ eſt nũmo in ciſtam tinniente,augeri quæſtum & auari/
ciam poſſe:ſuffragiũ aũt eccleſiæ eſt in arbitrio dei ſolius.
iiij Quis ſcit ſi omnes animæ in purgatorio uelint redimi, ſicut de
ſancto Seuerino & paſchali factum narratur?
v Nullus ſecurus eſt de ueritate ſuæ contritionis; multo minus

a ij

“16. Hell, purgatory, and heaven seem to differ as do despair, almost-despair, and the assurance of safety.

LATIN TO GERMAN The “Disputation on the Power and Efficacy of Indulgences,” or the 95 Theses, was originally written in Latin, but was soon translated into German and printed in multiple copies.

WRITTEN IN BRONZE The original wooden doors of the Schlosskirche (Castle Church) on which Luther is said to have posted his 95 Theses burned in 1760. In 1858 the church replaced them with these bronze portals (below) inscribed with the Latin text of the theses.

“28. It is certain that when the penny jingles into the money-box, gain and avarice can be increased, but the result of the intercession of the Church is in the power of God alone.”

“45. Christians should be taught that he who sees a person in need, and passes him by, and then purchases pardons, purchases not the indulgences of the pope, but the indignation of God.”

“75. It is folly to think that the papal pardons are so powerful that they could absolve a man even if he had committed an impossible sin and violated the Mother of God.”

IMPORTANT DATES

OCTOBER 1517 Luther makes public his 95 Theses.

DECEMBER 1517 Outraged, the archbishop of Mainz forwards a copy to Rome.

OCTOBER 7, 1518 Luther is summoned by a cardinal to Augsburg to defend his theses; fearing imprisonment, he later flees.

1520s Lutheranism as a branch of Christianity spreads in Germany.

JANUARY 1521 For attacks on the papacy and such church practices as pilgrimages and devotion to saints, Luther is excommunicated.

1534 Luther publishes a landmark German translation of the Bible.

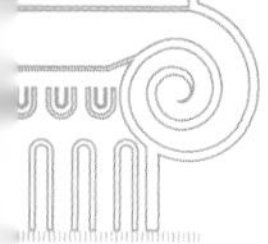

SEE ALSO | BREAKING BONDS: PAGE 246

KEY DATES

1492
Explorer Christopher Columbus reaches the shores of Hispaniola.

1521
Cortés defeats the Aztecs and takes Tenochtitlan.

1539
De Soto leads an expedition across the American southeast.

1540
Coronado travels the American southwest in search of gold.

THE AMERICAS

1450–1650

Starting in the late 1400s, European nations spent nearly three centuries sending their tendrils out across the globe in one of history's greatest periods of conquest and colonization. The first New World colony was established by Columbus on behalf of Spain less than three months after he made landfall in the Caribbean in 1492. On an island-hopping expedition, his flagship *Santa Maria* ran aground off the large island of Hispaniola (shared today by Haiti and the Dominican Republic). Taino Indians helped rescue the men, and Columbus took it as a sign from God that he should settle there. When Columbus returned the following year, however, he found the colony destroyed, likely by antagonized Indians. He built another, bigger fort, and became the first governor of Hispaniola. He urged kind treatment of the natives, and he and the colony profited from the cotton the Indians produced and the gold they acquired, mostly through island trade. Indians who resisted working as virtual serfs for their new masters were dealt with harshly. The indigenous people had little defense against the newcomers' muskets and swords, but even more destructive were the new diseases unwittingly spread throughout the local populations.

Columbus sent Indian slaves back to Spain, but most died on the way. Eventually the practice was halted; instead, African slaves were brought to the Caribbean to raise sugarcane and other crops. By 1511 there were additional Spanish colonies on Puerto Rico, Jamaica, and Cuba.

With Europe's discovery of the New World, a busy era of colonialism was under way. Spanish conquistadors took the lead, enslaving local populations and sending booty home to enrich the empire.

Colonists finally found the mineral wealth they were seeking by probing the interior of Mexico and South America. Spearheaded by conquistadors, most of whom were noblemen with little or no inheritance, these Spanish and Portuguese expeditions brought down the Aztec and Inca Empires. Most conquistadors supplemented their own forces with local troops who bore old resentments against the ruling authorities, but the only ones sharing the profits were the European adventurers, who were paid in land grants and money.

With the Spanish making inroads in Florida and New Mexico, competition for North America grew heated, and by the mid-16th century France had colonies in Canada, while the British and Dutch began colonizing the Atlantic coast from Virginia to Massachusetts.

OPPOSITE: Christopher Columbus reached the Americas in 1492, opening up a new world to colonization.

1565
The Spanish establish a colony at St. Augustine, Florida.

1585
England sets up the ill-fated Roanoke colony.

1607
The English establish a permanent colony at Jamestown in Virginia.

1620
Puritans cross the Atlantic on the *Mayflower* and reach Massachusetts Bay.

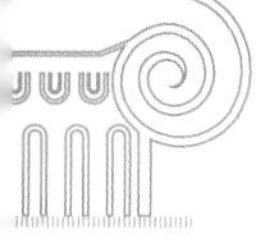

SEE ALSO | KINGS AND NOMADS: PAGE 211

EXPLORATION COLUMBUS

An expert sailor, Christopher Columbus honed his skills in the waters near his Genoa home. With funding from Spain, he set out to cross the Atlantic in 1492 in three ships, holding the latest instruments, including an astrolabe that enabled him to find his latitude. Longitude was a matter of guesswork and the use of a compass, hourglass, and a rope with knots that could measure ship speed.

From Spain, Columbus sailed to the Canary Islands, then west for seven weeks without sighting land, his worried crews growing ever more mutinous. On October 12, 1492, they made landfall, possibly on the Bahamian island of San Salvador.

In all, Columbus made four treks from Spain to the Caribbean, convinced to the end that he was exploring islands of Asia. He died in poverty, his accomplishments overlooked in the mad rush for discovery and colonization.

The *Pinta*, the *Nina*, and the *Santa Maria* sail toward the West Indies.

THE TAKEAWAY: Thinking he'd found a shortcut to Asia, Columbus opened up a new world.

VIPs

THE AMERICAS

Christopher Columbus, 1451–1506
Italian explorer who sought the Orient by sailing westward

Francisco Pizarro, 1475–1541
Spanish conquistador who defeated the Inca in South America

Hernán Cortés, 1485–1547
Spanish conquistador who led an expedition to conquer Aztecs in Mexico

Jacques Cartier, 1491–1557
French mariner who explored Gulf of St. Lawrence in Canada

John Winthrop, 1588–1649
First governor of the Massachusetts Bay Colony

CONNECTIONS COLUMBIAN EXCHANGE

WITH COLUMBUS, THE AMERICAN-EUROPEAN exchange began. Animals, foods, diseases, and ideas crossed the ocean from one world to another. Tobacco, potatoes, pumpkins, corn, manioc, tomatoes, cacao beans, and turkeys were new to Europe; most would become staples. The Europeans brought with them livestock, including horses, pigs, sheep, and cattle; crops such as rice, wheat, and apples; and African products such as bananas, coffee beans, and sugarcane. Less beneficial imports to the New World included muskets, gunpowder, smallpox, measles, and unintentional passengers such as dandelions and chickweeds.

TOMATOES CAME FROM SOUTH AMERICA

> *"Your Highnesses have an Other World here, by which our holy faith can be so greatly advanced and from which great wealth can be drawn."* —CHRISTOPHER COLUMBUS

Cuauhtémoc, last Aztec emperor, was taken prisoner by troops of Cortés; he was later tortured and hanged.

CONFLICTS AZTECS

The 200-year-old Aztec civilization of southern Mexico was at its height when Spanish conquistador Hernán Cortés came calling. As a 19-year-old, brash and quarrelsome, he had sailed to the Caribbean in 1504. After helping colonize Cuba, he was authorized to lead an expedition to Mexico in 1519. Well schooled in how to dominate native populations, he sailed to the land of the Aztecs with 600 men in 11 ships. Landing in the new port of Veracruz, he burned his ships to impress on his men that they were not turning back.

The army marched inland, cannons and horses intimidating locals, who had never seen either. With the help of his mistress and interpreter, Malinche, Cortés befriended Aztec ruler Moctezuma II, who believed at first that the Spaniard was an incarnation of Quetzalcoatl, the feathered serpent god. But Cortés then took the king hostage, and the Aztecs, under Moctezuma's brother, attacked the Spaniards. Moctezuma was mortally wounded and Cortés retreated from the capital of Tenochtitlan. After recruiting some 200,000 Indians who were disaffected by the Aztec demands for tribute and sacrificial victims, Cortés returned the next year. Moctezuma had died, and Cortés found a revolt—and a smallpox epidemic—under way. Following a four-month siege, he took and destroyed the capital in 1521. In its place he founded Mexico City.

> In Aztec legend, the deity Quetzalcoatl had departed Mexico with a promise that he would return some day.

THE TAKEAWAY: Using subterfuge and political manipulation, Cortés conquered Mexico in 1521.

> *"Cortés replied in his strange and savage tongue, speaking first to La Malinche, 'Tell Moctezuma that we are his friends. There is nothing to fear.'"* —AZTEC ACCOUNT

SEE ALSO | KINGS AND NOMADS: PAGE 212

CONFLICTS INCAS

Like Cortés, Spanish conqueror Francisco Pizarro used trickery to overcome an empire. Pizarro accompanied explorer Vasco Núñez de Balboa in 1513, crossing Panama to reach the Pacific. Arriving in Peru in 1531 with fewer than 200 men, he could hardly expect to overtake Inca leader Atahualpa's army of thousands. Instead, he lured Atahualpa into the Spanish camp, imprisoned him, and killed his unarmed contingent.

The last king of the Incas, Atahualpa ruled for eight years.

A ceremonial Inca knife takes the shape of Naylamp, a mythical ruler who arrived by sea from the north.

Receiving a huge ransom in gold, Pizarro executed Atahualpa anyway on trumped-up charges. Within five years he had captured the Inca capital of Cuzco, driven out its rulers, and founded the new capital of Lima.

As in Mexico, the Spaniards recruited locals to overthrow the empire and then demanded labor and tribute. Huge quantities of silver flowed back to Spain from South America and Mexico in the 1500s, along with large amounts of gold from Central America.

> Atahualpa questioned the legitimacy of Christianity and flung a Bible he was offered to the ground.

As for Pizarro, he stayed in Peru and became engaged in a war with his comrade Diego de Almagro, whom he killed; Almagro's followers then killed Pizarro in 1541.

THE TAKEAWAY: Pizarro conquered Peru in the 1530s, sending home vast amounts of loot.

"*In all these capitals the Incas had temples of the Sun, mints, and many silversmiths who did nothing but work rich pieces of gold or fair vessels of silver.*" —PEDRO DE CIEZA DE LÉON

The Spanish attack and plunder an Indian village in a search for gold.

EMPIRES IBERIAN COLONIES

As in Mexico and Peru, the rest of Latin America yielded to Spanish incursion in the 1500s. Spanish adventurer Pedro de Valdivia journeyed in 1540 into what is now Chile and founded the city of Santiago. The local Araucanians destroyed it, but the Spanish rebuilt and established several other cities. Without a centralized empire, the Indians here were able to resist settlement for some three centuries. Settlers also poured into Argentina from Peru and by 1580 had established Buenos Aires. By treaty, Brazil went to the Portuguese, who began settling there in the 1530s.

> The Dutch gained control of northeastern Brazil in 1630, but were pushed out in 1654.

With the first settlements established, Spanish and Portuguese colonists flooded into South America and, once the easy gold and silver were gone, set up plantations. Battle and disease killed many Indians; others were enslaved in a serf system called *encomienda*. The harsh suppression killed millions; to replace them, settlers imported large numbers of African slaves.

THE TAKEAWAY: Spanish and Portuguese took over South America in the 16th century.

VOICES

AGUIRRE SEARCHING FOR EL DORADO

"[The Marañon] is very deep, and for 800 leagues along its banks it is deserted, with no towns, as your majesty will see from the true report we have made. Along the route we took there are more than 6,000 islands. God only knows how we escaped from such a fearsome lake! I advise you, King and lord, not to attempt nor allow a fleet to be sent to this ill-fated river, because. . . . in this river there is nothing but despair."

—FROM A LETTER BY LOPE DE AGUIRRE TO KING PHILIP OF SPAIN, 1561

EL DORADO

"The Spaniards still do nothing save tear the natives to shreds, murder them and inflict upon them untold misery, suffering and distress." —BARTOLOME DE LAS CASAS

SEE ALSO | NEW WORLD ORDER: PAGE 310

Reaching the Mississippi River in 1541, Hernando de Soto plants a cross to mark the territory for Spain.

EXPLORATION SPANISH INROADS

Turning to North America, the Spanish found little gold but plenty of fiercely resistant Indians. Itinerant explorer Juan Ponce de León explored Puerto Rico from 1508 to 1509 and reached the coast of a lush region he named Florida in 1513, searching in part for a legendary fountain of youth. He failed to find the fountain, and upon his return in 1521 was mortally wounded by local Indians.

Eighteen years later, Hernando de Soto made a four-year, 4,000-mile trek through the Southeast (1539–1543) with 700 men, stirring up resentment in his wake. He sickened and died along the Mississippi, leaving a legacy of disease, mistrust, and turmoil among the indigenous people. In the same manner, Francisco Vásquez de Coronado marched north from Mexico in 1540, wreaking chaos among the Pueblos in a futile search for the fabled Seven Cities of Cibola.

Though destructive, the early explorers gained for Europe a huge store of geographical knowledge, as well as the notion that permanent settlement was more likely to pay off than quick strikes for gold. Spanish colonization of Florida began in 1565, when Pedro Menéndez de Avilés founded the town of St. Augustine and destroyed a French settlement just north. Though Franciscans put up dozens of missions in Florida, missionizing had more permanent success in the West.

> The Spanish established Santa Fe in 1609, two years after the British founded Jamestown.

THE TAKEAWAY: The Spanish settled Florida and New Mexico in the 16th and 17th centuries.

"They gave us to understand that very far from here was a province called Apalachen, where was much gold and plenty of everything we wanted." —CABEZA DE VACA

EXPLORATION NEW FRANCE

French exploration of the New World got seriously under way in 1534 when Jacques Cartier sailed up the Gulf of St. Lawrence. He returned the following year, searching unsuccessfully for a northwest passage to the Indies. Like other Europeans, he caused resentment among the Indians by capturing some and taking them home. But by 1600, the French had created a European market for hats made of beaver pelts. The profitable trade helped spur the development of New France, or Canada.

In 1608 Samuel de Champlain founded a permanent French settlement in Canada at Quebec, forging alliances with many tribes, particularly the Huron. Jesuit missionaries soon arrived, and with the spread of European diseases, the Huron became vulnerable to attacks by their rivals, the Iroquois, who lived in present-day New York State. Despite flare-ups of violence, fur traders known as voyageurs founded Montreal in 1642 and ranged far to the west by canoe.

> Explorers sought the Northwest Passage—a sea route between the Atlantic and Pacific—for more than 300 years

Longhouses and palisades mark a Susquehanna Indian village.

THE TAKEAWAY: The French began claiming Canada in 1534.

VOICES

CHAMPLAIN VERY APT TO TURN OVER

"In this place were a number of savages who had come for traffic in furs, several of whom came to our vessels with their canoes, which are from eight to nine paces long, and about a pace or pace and a half broad in their middle, growing narrower toward the two ends. They are very apt to turn over, in case one does not understand managing them, and are made of birch bark, strengthened on the inside by little ribs of white cedar, very neatly arranged. They are so light that a man can easily carry one. Each can carry a weight equal to that of a pipe."

—FROM *THE FOUNDATION OF QUEBEC*, SAMUEL DE CHAMPLAIN, 1608

SAMUEL DE CHAMPLAIN

"I am rather inclined to believe that this is the land God gave to Cain." —JACQUES CARTIER

SEE ALSO | NEW WORLD ORDER: PAGE 312

COLONIES DISSENTING VOICES

In 1585 colonists from England arrived at what seemed like a promising site for settlement on Roanoke Island, off the coast of North Carolina. After clashes with Indians, the settlers abandoned this first English colony in North America. But in 1587 a second expedition brought a larger party of 117. With the colony suffering from lack of supplies, leader John White returned to England for help. War between England and Spain prevented him from returning to Roanoke for three years, whereupon he found it deserted. The fate of the Lost Colony remains a mystery.

For preaching religious freedom, Anne Hutchinson was banished from Massachusetts.

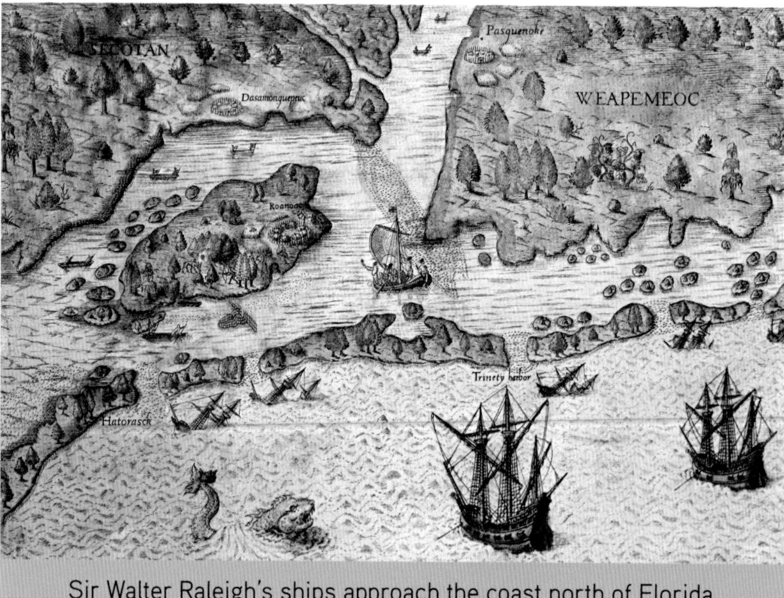

Sir Walter Raleigh's ships approach the coast north of Florida.

The next English attempt at colonization was also beset with trials. Founded in Virginia in 1607, Jamestown was located on a marshy island along the James River. Hostile Indians, malaria, and starvation nearly destroyed it, but fresh arrivals from England kept this toehold on the continent alive. Colonist John Rolfe

{ The letters "CROATOAN" carved on a palisade post were among the few clues left by the Lost Colonists. }

JOHN WINTHROP A CITY ON A HILL

VOICES

"[W]ee must be knitt together, in this worke, as one man. Wee must entertaine each other in brotherly affection. Wee must be willing to abridge ourselves of our superfluities, for the supply of other's necessities. Wee must uphold a familiar commerce together in all meekeness, gentlenes, patience and liberality. Wee must delight in eache other; make other's conditions our oune; rejoice together, mourne together, labour and suffer together, allwayes haueving before our eyes our commission and community in the worke, as members of the same body. Soe shall wee keepe the unitie of the spirit in the bond of peace. . . . For wee must consider that wee shall be as a citty upon a hill. The eies of all people are uppon us."

—FROM "A MODELL OF CHRISTIAN CHARITY," WRITTEN ABOARD THE *ARBELLA*, 1630

"As one small candle may light a thousand, so the light here kindled hath shone unto many, yea in some sort to our whole nation." —WILLIAM BRADFORD

In 1620, separatist Puritans, or Pilgrims, landed at Plymouth Rock in Massachusetts.

introduced West Indian tobacco to the soil in 1612, and Jamestown had a cash crop.

Virginia developed a tobacco plantation economy, worked mostly by indentured servants. A similar economy developed in the colony of Maryland, founded in 1634 by the Calverts, aristocrats seeking a refuge for their fellow Catholics.

Among other religious dissidents seeking refuge in America were the Puritans—Protestants at odds with the Church of England. One such group migrated to Holland in 1608 and then to the New World aboard the *Mayflower* in 1620. Calling themselves Pilgrims, they settled at Plymouth, where they met Indians who, fortunately, wanted to avoid hostilities and taught them how to plant corn and other native crops.

A larger group of Puritans reached Massachusetts Bay in 1630 and founded Boston. One notable dissenter against the colony's version of Puritanism—Roger Williams—was ousted; he founded the adjacent colony of Rhode Island in 1636. By befriending the Narragansett Indians he helped the colonists defeat and nearly wipe out the Pequots in 1637.

{ Roger Williams wrote "A Key into the Language of America," the first English study of Indian languages. }

THE TAKEAWAY: The British gained an American foothold with Jamestown in 1607, then focused on New England.

Expedition artist John White painted a Pomeiooc villager in North Carolina.

"Authority without wisdom is like a heavy axe without an edge, fitter to bruise than polish."
—ANNE BRADSTREET

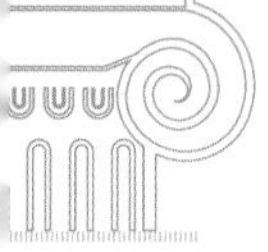

SEE ALSO | BREAKING BONDS: PAGE 260

KEY DATES

1368–1644
The Ming dynasty thrives in China.

1400s
Timbuktu is the center of the Songhai trading empire that crossed the Sahara.

1510
The Portuguese under Alfonso de Albuquerque take over Goa.

1523
Babur invades India and begins the Mughal Empire.

ASIA AND AFRICA

1450–1650

The decline of the Mongols in the East left Asia relatively stable. China's Ming dynasty fostered a period of peace and prosperity in which the country established trade with Japan, relocated the capital to Beijing, and fortified the Great Wall. By 1500 the 132-year-old Ming empire was the most powerful and advanced state of its time. Italian missionaries, arriving in the 1580s from the tattered towns and religious wars of Europe, thought the Chinese cities with their colored tiles and curved roofs represented a highly civilized nation. But rebellions in the 17th century sparked by wars and famine brought down the splendid Ming dynasty. In India, a Mongol descendant named Babur invaded from Afghanistan in 1523, inaugurating more than three centuries of rule by the Mughals, the Indian name for people descended from Turks and Mongols. It was Babur's grandson Akbar who, with a half century of rule, consolidated the Mughal Empire's grip on northern India. The empire created a melting pot of Arab and Persian thought in India.

Great empires in Asia continued to build splendid cities and public works, while African kingdoms were exploited by Muslim traders and a growing European slave trade.

Japan at the time was nominally ruled by an emperor, though for several centuries real power had lain in the hands of the shogun (the military leader), the daimyos (the shogun's warlord followers), and the samurai (the daimyos' elite warrior corps). The Japanese lived in a feudal system, with the reigning dynasty and its supporters holding vast amounts of land. Becoming fearful of outside influences, the Japanese began expelling foreign missionaries in the early 1600s, and in the 1630s the nation shut its doors completely, remaining isolated for more than 200 years.

African kingdoms and Asian empires were increasingly linked to each other and to Europe through growing trade networks. Before the 15th century, Muslim traders had created commercial ties across the Indian Ocean with India and China. Then in the 15th century, Portuguese adventurers began setting up outposts on the Gold Coast (current Ghana). They also started exporting African slaves to Europe, a market that expanded with the discovery of the New World and that led to the decline of rich cultural centers such as Timbuktu. By the 17th century the Dutch had taken control of west African ports, founding Cape Town in southern Africa in 1652.

OPPOSITE: Indian ruler Shah Jahan embraces his favorite wife, Arjumand Banu Begum.

1603
Japan is dominated by the shogunate, founded by Togukawa Ieyasu.

1630s
Japan shuts its doors to all foreigners except Dutch and Chinese traders.

1632
Construction of the Taj Mahal begins in Agra, India.

1644
Manchus overrun China and found the Qing dynasty.

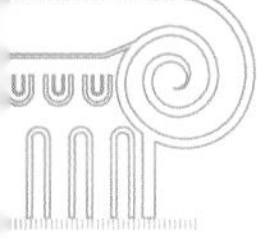

SEE ALSO | NEW WORLD ORDER: PAGE 289

TRADE AFRICAN CROSSROADS

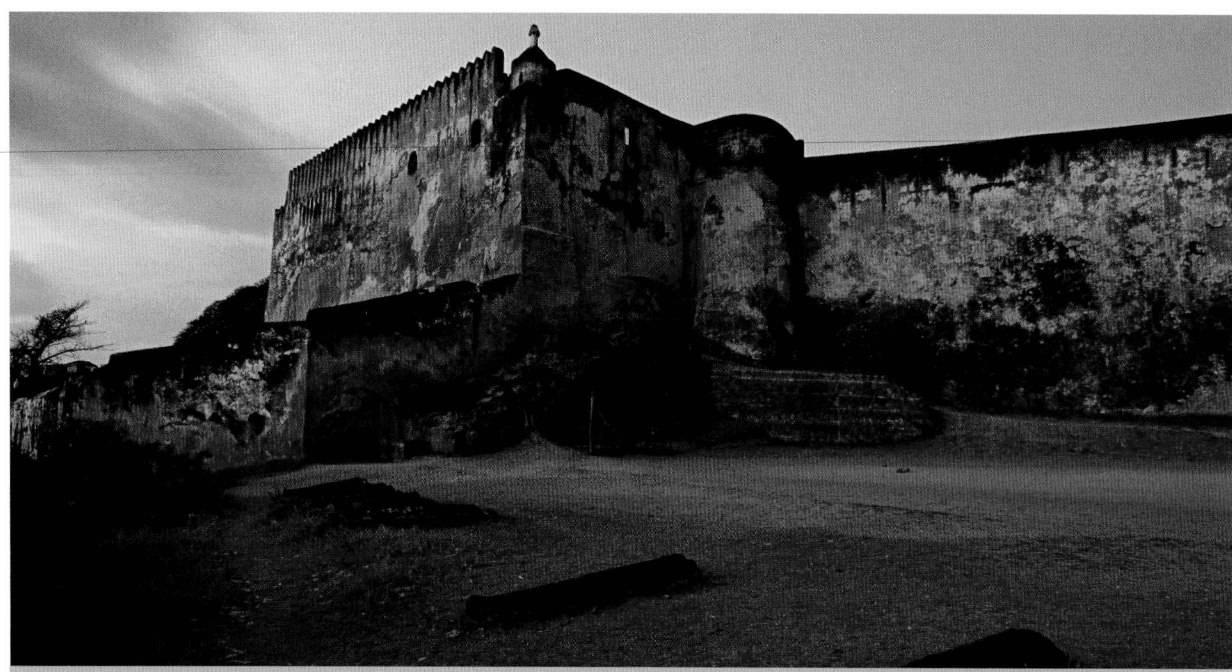

Fort Jesus was erected by the Portuguese in 1593 to protect the vital trade port of Mombasa, Kenya.

By the end of the 15th century, Africa had become a crossroads of trade for the expanding European-Asian network. Portuguese explorers had rounded the Cape of Good Hope and crossed the Indian Ocean to establish a link with Asia. In the early 1500s Portuguese soldier Francisco de Almeida set up a number of forts on the coast of east Africa and Malaysia. He also took the precaution of burning competing port towns, including the strategic port of Mombasa, on the Kenyan coast. When opposed by Arab and Egyptian interests, he destroyed their coastal towns and defeated their fleets off India in 1509.

In southeastern Africa, the Mwene Matapa dynasty had ruled the region between the Zambezi and Limpopo rivers from the 14th century and presided over a lucrative gold trade. The locals, known as the Shona, also traded ivory and copper in exchange for porcelain from China and beads and cloth from India and Indonesia. The Portuguese invaded the area in the 1530s, finally toppling the regime in 1629 and gaining rights to the region's valuable mines.

VIPs

ASIA AND AFRICA

Nyatsimba Mutota, reigned 1400s Semi-legendary first ruler of the Mwene Matapa dynasty of southeastern Africa

Babur, 1483–1530
First Mughal ruler of India

Toyotomi Hideyoshi, 1536–1598
Powerful Japanese daimyo who became regent

Akbar, 1542–1605
Grandson of Babur and great ruler of Mughals

Tokugawa Ieyasu, 1543–1616
Shogun, leader of unified Japan

Matteo Ricci, 1552–1610
Jesuit missionary to China

Shah Jahan, 1592–1666
Builder of the Taj Mahal

"*He told the Christians to go away and that Mombasa was not like Kilwa: they would not find people with hearts that could be eaten like chickens.*" —HANS MAYR

VOICES

AFRICANUS TIMBUKTU

"The inhabitants are very rich, especially the strangers who have settled in the country; so much so that the current king has given two of his daughters in marriage to two brothers, both businessmen, on account of their wealth. There are many wells containing sweet water in Timbuktu; and in addition, when the Niger is in flood canals deliver the water to the city. Grain and animals are abundant, so that the consumption of milk and butter is considerable. But salt is in very short supply because it is carried here from Tegaza, some 500 miles from Timbuktu."

—FROM AN ACCOUNT BY LEO AFRICANUS (EL HASAN BEN MUHAMMED EL-WAZZAN-EZ-ZAYYATI), 1600

SANKORE MOSQUE, TIMBUKTU

By the early 1500s Portugal had also established trading outposts in Mozambique on Africa's east coast and Angola on its west. In the next century Angola became a key supplier of slaves for the Portuguese colony of Brazil. In 1641 the Dutch elbowed in on the slave trade, briefly pushing the Portuguese out of Angola. But by the end of the decade the Portuguese had returned and would remain there for some two centuries, planting the New World crops of sugarcane, corn, and tobacco. The Portuguese struggled in Mozambique, however, where they faced local rebellions in the late 1600s.

In most of North Africa the Muslims remained strong through the period. The Songhai people from the west took over Timbuktu in the late 1400s and brought the trade and commercial center to its zenith of prosperity, its population reaching around one million. Timbuktu was a cosmopolitan center. Moroccan merchants traveled there to exchange gold and slaves for Saharan salt and North African cloth and horses. Scholars from Mecca and Egypt taught classes in law, theology, and science. Morocco took the city in 1591, but was ineffective in defending the city against constant attacks from Tuaregs and other groups.

{ The king of the Songhai, Sonni Ali the Great, is remembered in oral tradition as a great magician. }

At Timbuktu's market stalls, traders haggle over slaves and spices.

THE TAKEAWAY: The Portuguese created new trade routes, while in North Africa, Muslim influence spread.

"There are in Timbuktu numerous judges, teachers and priests, all properly appointed by the king. He greatly honors learning." —LEO AFRICANUS

NEW WORLD

REVOLUTIONARY WORDS

1650–1800

CHAPTER

7

French Enlightenment intellectuals gather in Madame Geoffrin's salon.

SEE ALSO | NEW WORLD ORDER: PAGE 274

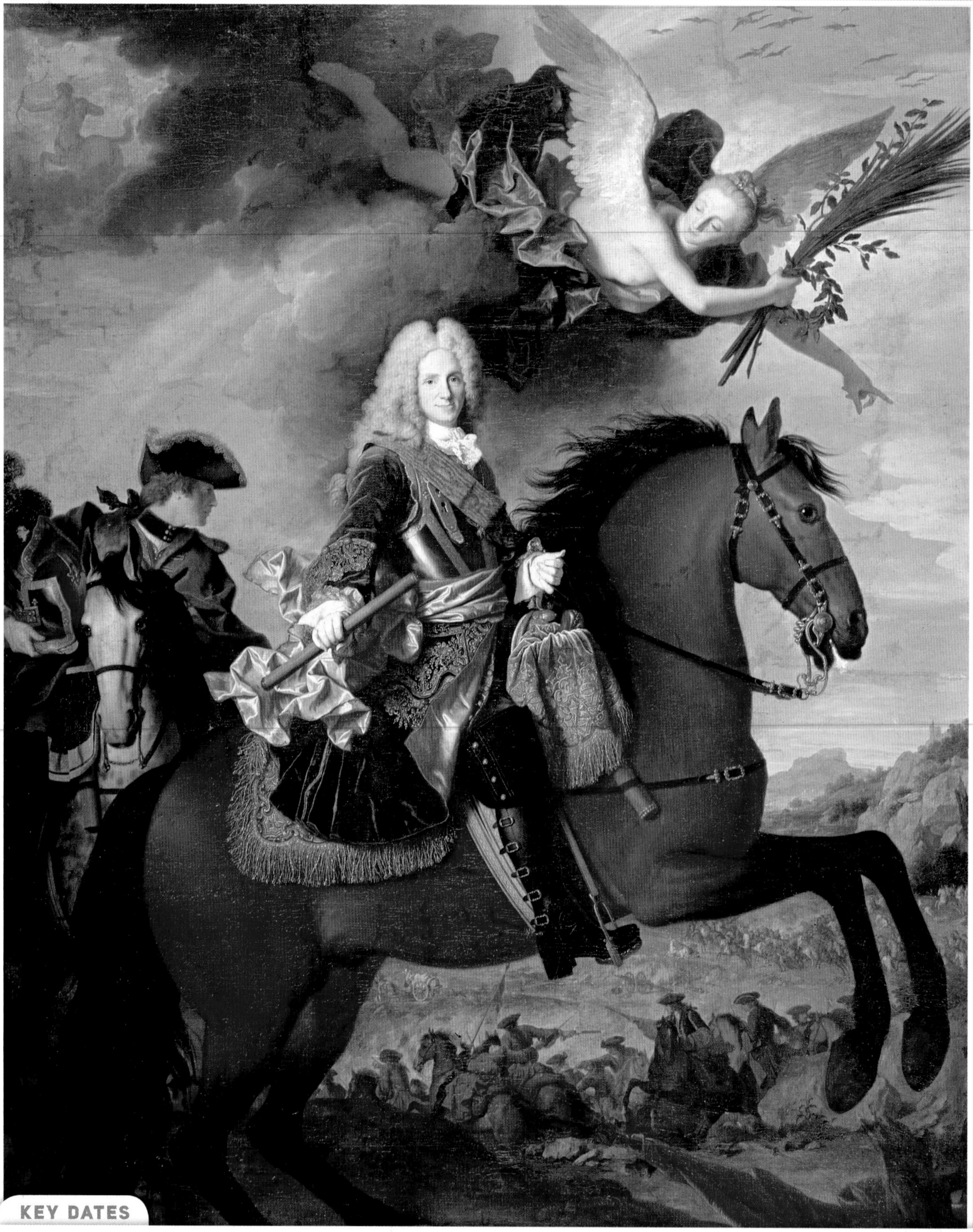

KEY DATES

1648
The Treaty of Westphalia ends the Thirty Years' War.

1649
English King Charles I is executed by Oliver Cromwell and his rebel followers in Parliament.

1687
Sir Isaac Newton publishes *Philosophiae Naturalis Principia Mathematica.*

1688
The Glorious Revolution begins after William and Mary accept a bill of rights to limit royal power.

EUROPE

1650–1800

During the Enlightenment that dawned in Europe in the late 1600s, reason, skepticism, and self-interest took precedence over faith. Now as before, people prayed and trusted in God, but the fierce contests between opposing creeds that had plagued Europe during the Reformation gave way to political debates and power struggles. As religious warfare subsided, kingdoms across the continent grew stronger and better organized. In England, Parliament placed constitutional limits on the power of the monarch. In France and other European countries, however, rulers claimed absolute authority. Monarchs laid down laws, imposed taxes, and waged wars as they saw fit, imposing their will on councils that lacked the power of the British Parliament. Such absolutism was summed up by a statement attributed to King Louis XIV of France: *"L'état c'est moi."* (I am the state.)

Even as monarchs grew prouder and mightier, scientists and philosophers were advancing new ideas and theories that would revolutionize Europe and topple kingdoms. Writing in 1784, as the Enlightenment (also known as the Age of Reason) reached its peak, the German philosopher Immanuel Kant offered this motto for the age: "Have the courage to use your own understanding." Scholars took nothing on faith and called everything into question. That bold spirit of inquiry and innovation nurtured not only the scientific revolution and the industrial revolution, but also political uprisings as reformers proposed ways of reorganizing society for the good of the populace rather than a privileged few.

Monarchs across the European continent reached the height of their powers in the same century that produced the French Revolution and sent the French king and queen to the guillotine.

Rulers like Frederick the Great of Prussia and Catherine the Great of Russia responded to that challenge by seeking to modernize and rationalize their realms. But such enlightened despots could not prevent the great upheaval that loomed as prolonged warfare between the major powers of Europe exhausted the great French kingdom and drained its treasury.

It may not be true that King Louis XV declared, *"Après moi, le deluge"* (After me, the flood), but in 1789 his successor, Louis XVI, indeed faced a torrent of opposition and was later executed in the tumultuous French Revolution. The revolution marked the beginning of the end for the old regime in Europe, dominated by absolute monarchs and haughty aristocrats.

OPPOSITE: Philip V was the first Bourbon king of Spain and a key figure in the War of the Spanish Succession.

1690
John Locke publishes his "Essay Concerning Human Understanding."

1756
Britain challenges France and other nations in the Seven Years' War.

1775
The American Revolution begins, as the colonies fight for their independence from Great Britain.

1789
The French Revolution begins with the fall of the Bastille.

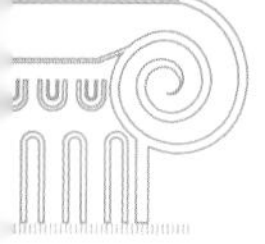

SEE ALSO | EMPIRES RISING: PAGE 326

NATIONS THE LIMITS OF RULE

England did not become a true constitutional monarchy until it tried doing without a monarch and found that having half a king—or one significantly reduced in authority by Parliament—was better than none. The man who taught the English that lesson was Oliver Cromwell, leader of the rebels in Parliament who executed King Charles I in 1649 and formed a republic. As Lord Protector of the Commonwealth, he transformed that republic into a virtual dictatorship and imposed his strict Puritan views on the populace.

After Cromwell died in 1658, many in England welcomed the

The Great Fire of London, 1666, destroyed a large part of the city.

VIPs

EUROPE

Oliver Cromwell, 1599–1658
Leader who turned England into a republican commonwealth

Isaac Newton, 1642–1727
English physicist and mathematician who revolutionized science

Peter I, 1672–1725
Tsar of Russia, reformer and statesman

Frederick II, 1712–1786
King of Prussia who made his country into a military power

Louis XVI, 1754–1793
King of France who reigned at the time of the French Revolution

VOICES

SAMUEL PEPYS THE GREAT FIRE

"So I down to the water-side, and there got a boat and through bridge, and there saw a lamentable fire.... Everybody endeavouring to remove their goods, and flinging into the river or bringing them into lighters that layoff; poor people staying in their houses as long as till the very fire touched them, and then running into boats, or clambering from one pair of stairs by the water-side to another. And among other things, the poor pigeons, I perceive, were loth to leave their houses, but hovered about the windows and balconys till they were, some of them burned, their wings, and fell down."

—FROM THE DIARY OF SAMUEL PEPYS, SEPTEMBER 2, 1666

SAMUEL PEPYS

"New opinions are always suspected, and usually opposed, without any other reason but because they are not already common." —JOHN LOCKE

VOICES

WILLIAM AND MARY

PARLIAMENT NEW RIGHTS

"That it is the right of the subjects to petition the king, and all commitments and prosecutions for such petitioning are illegal;

"That the raising or keeping a standing army within the kingdom in time of peace, unless it be with consent of Parliament, is against law;

"That the subjects which are Protestants may have arms for their defence suitable to their conditions and as allowed by law;

"That election of members of Parliament ought to be free;

"That the freedom of speech and debates or proceedings in Parliament ought not to be impeached or questioned in any court or place out of Parliament."

—FROM THE BRITISH BILL OF RIGHTS, 1689

restoration of the monarchy under King Charles II. But he and his successor, King James II, were Catholic sympathizers who so antagonized Parliament that it invited the Dutch Protestant leader, William of Orange, and his wife, Mary, daughter of James II, to seize the throne. That bloodless coup in 1688, known as the Glorious Revolution, saw William and Mary accept a Bill of Rights that limited the monarchy's powers.

{ Parliament added to the Bill of Rights in 1689 by passing the Toleration Act, which allowed Protestants freedom of worship. }

The Glorious Revolution gave England—or Great Britain, as it was known following its union with Scotland in 1707—a strong parliamentary system that helped it become one of the most powerful nations on earth. British colonists fanned out to North America, Australia, and other distant lands, carrying with them the belief that rulers should respond to the will of the people. The American colonists who defied King George III and seceded from Britain in 1776 were following the lead of earlier English dissidents like the political philosopher John Locke, who opposed Charles II and inspired the Declaration of Independence.

Britain's political progress was matched by its commercial advances. The Industrial Revolution began in Great Britain in the late 1700s with the invention of the steam engine. Commercial and industrial development swelled London, which rapidly recovered from the devastation of the Great Fire of 1666 to become the world's most populous city by the early 1800s.

English bracket clock, circa 1700.

THE TAKEAWAY: Rulers came and went in England as Parliament limited the monarchy.

"How comes it to pass, then, that we appear such cowards in reasoning, and are so afraid to stand the test of ridicule?" —ANTHONY ASHLEY COOPER

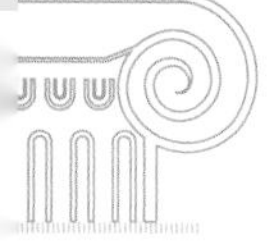

SEE ALSO | EMPIRES RISING: PAGE 328

Empress Maria Theresa of Austria leads a quadrille in celebration of the retreat of foreign troops.

EMPIRES RISING POWERS

By 1650 the Holy Roman Empire, which once covered a large swath of central Europe, had been shattered. The Treaty of Westphalia, which ended the ruinous Thirty Years' War in 1648, confirmed the independence of Switzerland and left Germany divided into some 300 principalities, many of them ruled by Protestants who upheld their faith in what was once an exclusively Catholic domain. Most of those states were small and weak. Two major powers, however, emerged from the debris of the old empire—one based in Berlin, the future capital of Prussia, and the other in Vienna, seat of the Habsburg dynasty, whose possessions embraced Austria, Hungary, and surrounding lands.

The Habsburgs were Roman Catholics and heirs to what remained of the Holy Roman Empire. Their subjects were people of various faiths, including Muslims in the northern Balkan Peninsula, conquered in part by Habsburg forces after they repelled the Turkish troops in Vienna in 1683.

A new threat emerged in 1740 when Emperor Charles VI died, leaving the throne to his 23-year-old daughter Maria Theresa. Frederick II of Prussia, supported by states whose various royal families laid claim to the Austrian throne, then invaded the Habsburg province of Silesia, hoping to ignite a revolt against the young, untested empress. She held her realm together and blocked further Prussian advances by making concessions to nobles in Hungary, which

> *"Peace is not an absence of war, it is a virtue, a state of mind, a disposition for benevolence, confidence, justice."* —BARUCH SPINOZA

VOICES

FREDERICK I AN OBSTINATE BOY

"A bad, obstinate boy, who does not love his father. . . . You know very well that I cannot stand an effeminate fellow who has no manly tastes, who cannot ride or shoot (to his shame be it said!), is untidy about his person, and wears his hair curled like a fool instead of cutting it; and that I have condemned all these things a thousand times, and yet there is no sign of improvement. For the rest, haughty, offish as a country lout, conversing with none but a favored few instead of being affable and popular, grimacing like a fool, and never following my wishes out of love for me."

—FROM A LETTER BY FREDERICK I TO HIS 16-YEAR-OLD SON, LATER FREDERICK II

FREDERICK II

would achieve equal status with Austria in the Habsburg Empire. After the war, Maria Theresa reigned skillfully, overshadowing her husband, Emperor Francis I, and adding to the glory and refinement of Vienna, which became the musical capital of Europe.

Maria Theresa's archrival, Frederick II, became known as Frederick the Great for his efforts to make Prussia both a great military power and a modern, well-organized state. His kingdom had been forged after the Thirty Years' War by his cunning ancestor Frederick William, known as the Great Elector. (Electors were German princes who chose the Holy Roman emperor.) Like Frederick William, Frederick the Great commanded the services of militant aristocrats called Junkers, who led Prussian troops in the wars he waged. But he also earned a reputation as an enlightened ruler by tolerating Catholics and Jews in his officially Protestant kingdom and establishing a merit system for civil servants.

{ Maria Theresa bore 16 children by her husband, Francis I, who died in 1765, and remained co-ruler afterward with their son, Joseph II. }

"I am the first servant of the state," Frederick declared modestly. Yet he was also the absolute master of Prussia, a rising European power that would one day forge a united Germany.

THE TAKEAWAY: By 1800, Prussia and Austria, the heart of the Habsburg Empire, were the two major powers in central Europe.

Empress Maria Theresa and other Habsburgs lived in Vienna's Schönnbrunn Palace.

"This agglomeration which was called and which still calls itself the Holy Roman Empire is neither holy, nor Roman, nor an Empire." —VOLTAIRE

SEE ALSO | EMPIRES RISING: PAGE 324

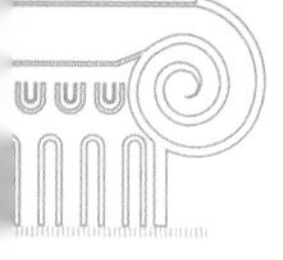

Robespierre and Louis de Saint-Just being taken to the guillotine.

CONFLICTS

REVOLUTION

As the exalted ruler of one of Europe's greatest kingdoms, Louis XIV of France, who reigned from 1643 to 1715, felt entitled to live in grand style. His predecessors had resided in Paris, but he distanced himself from its teeming masses and transformed a royal hunting lodge outside the city into the magnificent palace of Versailles. "In the presence of the absolute monarch the great become the small," wrote one observer. Known as the Sun King, Louis XIV dazzled followers, but beyond the glittering halls of Versailles, large parts of France remained cloaked in medieval gloom. Peasants lived much as they had for centuries, laboring under obligations to their landlords. The population grew faster than the food supply, causing bread riots in Paris and other cities. Protestants known as Huguenots once again faced persecution by Catholics when Louis revoked the tolerant Edict of Nantes, insisting that France must have only "one king, one law, one faith."

> The palace of Versailles had 1,400 fountains and a stable large enough to hold 10,000 horses.

Despite such unrest, Louis's successors might have preserved the monarchy had they kept their

FRANCE THE RIGHTS OF MAN

VOICES

"1. Men are born and remain free and equal in rights. Social distinctions may be founded only upon the general good.

"2. The aim of all political association is the preservation of the natural and imprescriptible rights of man. These rights are liberty, property, security, and resistance to oppression.

"3. The principle of all sovereignty resides essentially in the nation. No body nor individual may exercise any authority which does not proceed directly from the nation." —FROM THE DECLARATION OF THE RIGHTS OF MAN, 1789

DECLARATION OF THE RIGHTS OF MAN

"The tree of liberty only grows when watered by the blood of tyrants." —BERTRAND BARÈRE DE VIEUZAC

Queen Marie Antoinette antagonized the French populace.

financial house in order. But long and costly conflicts with Britain, Prussia, and other powers emptied their coffers. In 1789 an assembly convened by Louis XVI to approve new taxes instead presented him with a list of grievances. When he threatened to use troops to disband a subsequent National Assembly, Parisians on July 14 stormed a royal fortress called the Bastille, striking the first blow in the tumultuous French Revolution. A few months later, women marched from Paris to Versailles with weapons in hand, prompting the king to yield to the assembly and ratify its Declaration of the Rights of Man and the Citizen, which promised citizens equality under the law.

Unappeased, radicals called Jacobins, led by Maximilien de Robespierre, resolved to abolish the monarchy and establish a republic. In 1793 they launched the Reign of Terror, during which Louis XVI and his queen, Marie Antoinette, were among thousands executed by guillotine. The extreme measures of the radicals, including an attempt to replace Catholic rituals with a Cult of the Supreme Being, led to a violent reaction in which Robespierre and many others were in turn executed. France remained in turmoil until Napoleon Bonaparte took power as first consul of the French republic in 1799.

THE TAKEAWAY: The revolution overthrew the old regime but did not provide a stable new one.

THUMBS UP / THUMBS DOWN

MAXIMILIEN DE ROBESPIERRE 1758–1794

HAD MAXIMILIEN DE ROBESPIERRE DIED IN 1792, when the French Republic was founded, he would have been remembered like Thomas Jefferson as a champion of liberty and equality. As a young lawyer from a wealthy family, he dedicated himself to defending the poor, protesting religious persecution, and opposing cruel punishments. After Britain and other kingdoms declared war on the French Republic, however, Robespierre advocated the use of terror. "Terror is nothing but prompt, severe, inflexible justice," he declared. As director of the Committee of Public Safety, he oversaw the unleashing of a Reign of Terror, executing not only royalty and royalists but also fellow republicans like Georges-Jacques Danton who opposed his extreme measures. **CONCLUSION:** **THUMBS DOWN**

"At length I recollected the thoughtless saying of a great princess, who, on being informed that the country people had no bread, replied, 'Let them eat cake.'" —VOLTAIRE

SEE ALSO | THE WORLD AT WAR: PAGE 386

EMPIRES FACING WEST

In 1682, when Tsar Peter I of the Romanov dynasty took power, Russia lagged far behind France and other European countries economically and militarily. Much of its territory lay in Asia, but Peter was determined to make Russia a dynamic Western power. Drawing on his experiences of touring Europe and inspecting factories and shipyards, he proceeded to westernize his government by moving his capital from Moscow to St. Petersburg, whose location on the Gulf of Finland gave the Russian Navy he was building access to the Baltic Sea and the Atlantic Ocean. Like Louis XIV of France, he summoned proud aristocrats called boyars to his new capital, where they lived in European-style town houses and paid court to their monarch at his handsome Winter Palace. Boyars and other prominent men had to cut off their long beards and appear clean-shaven like European gentlemen or pay a steep beard tax he imposed. Like Frederick II of Prussia, he earned a new title, Peter the Great, by strengthening his administration and bolstering his armed forces, which expanded westward into the Baltic States and southward to the Black Sea. Under his rule, Russians founded new industries and built factories, canals, and roads. He died at the age of 53 as dramatically as he had lived, becoming ill after diving into

Peter I would at times take part in his subjects' daily work—for instance, taking up a laborer's tools in a shipyard.

A portrait of Peter I highlights his clean-shaven countenance.

PETER THE GREAT CUTS A BEARD

ROUSSET DE MISSY BEARDS

VOICES

"The tsar . . . ordered that gentlemen, merchants, and other subjects, except priests and peasants, should each pay a tax of one hundred rubles a year if they wished to keep their beards; the commoners had to pay one kopek each. Officials were stationed at the gates of the towns to collect that tax. . . . There were many old Russians who, after having their beards shaved off, saved them preciously, in order to have them placed in their coffins, fearing that they would not be allowed to enter heaven without their beards."

—FROM *LIFE OF PETER THE GREAT*, JEAN ROUSSET DE MISSY, ca 1730

"I have conquered an empire but I have not been able to conquer myself." —PETER THE GREAT

the Neva River in winter to rescue drowning sailors.

Peter's successors failed to live up to his strong example until his feeble grandson, Peter III, was murdered in 1762 with the connivance of a German-born wife, who ruled Russia with a firm hand until 1796 and became known as Catherine the Great. The fact that she had many lovers, one of whom helped do away with her husband, gave her an unsavory reputation. But her behavior was not unusual among European royalty, who seldom married for love. Catherine was as ambitious for Russia as she was for herself. Her troops wrested Crimea from the Ottoman Empire, occupied Ukraine, and menaced Poland, which was partitioned among Russia, Austria, and Prussia. Influenced by Enlightenment ideals, Catherine improved Russia's administration and took steps to ease the plight of its downtrodden serfs, but she feared losing the support of their noble masters and punished those peasants harshly when they rebelled. Appalled by the French Revolution, she abandoned efforts to reform the old regime, which would endure for more than a century until it was swept away in the Russian Revolution.

{ St. Petersburg was called "the city built on bones" because some 100,000 serfs died constructing it. }

Catherine the Great, dressed in legislative regalia

THE TAKEAWAY: Russia modernized and became a major military power in Europe by 1800.

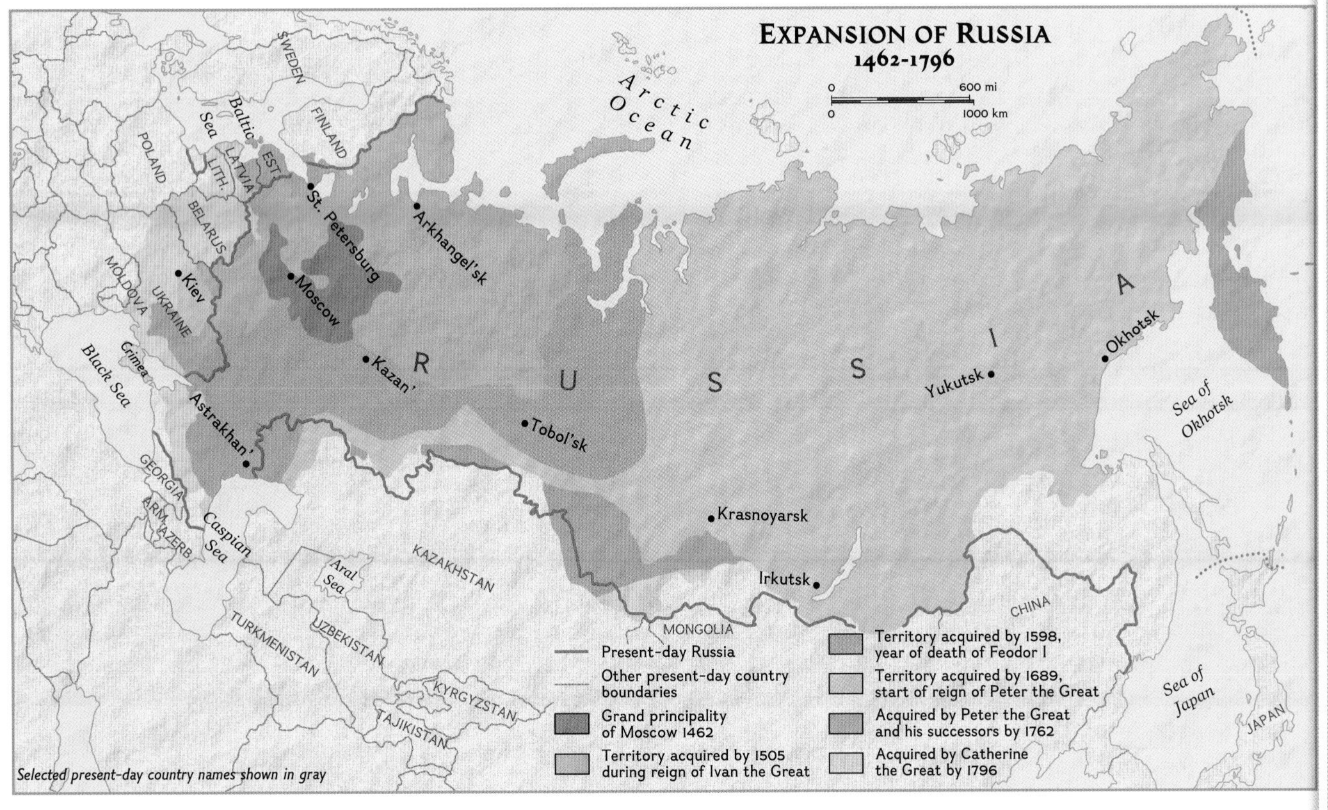

"I may be kindly, I am ordinarily gentle, but in my line of business I am obliged to will terribly what I will at all." —CATHERINE THE GREAT

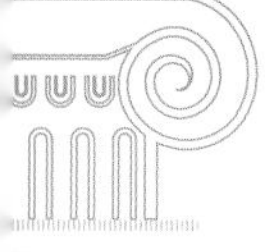

CONFLICTS EUROPE AT WAR

During the 18th century, Europe was convulsed by three sprawling conflicts. The War of the Spanish Succession (1701–1714) began when a French prince, Philip of Anjou, took the vacant Spanish throne, prompting hostile kingdoms to oppose France's claim to Spain, which was no longer a great power in Europe but still had vast colonies overseas. The War of the Austrian Succession (1740–1748) was triggered when Frederick the Great of Prussia challenged Maria Theresa of Austria and threatened her hold on the far-flung Habsburg Empire. And the explosive Seven Years' War (1756–1763) ignited when Prussia and Austria forged competing alliances with other European countries. In each of these conflicts, France and Britain were on opposing sides, with Britain supporting Prussia in the Seven Years' War while France joined Russia in backing Austria. The combined forces of Prussia and Britain proved too much for their opponents, but after its defeat in the Seven Years' War, France reemerged as a military power with the rise of Napoleon Bonaparte at century's end.

{ The Seven Years' War, which extended beyond Europe to colonies in the New World, anticipated the global conflicts of the 20th century. }

THE TAKEAWAY: Alliances shifted during the 1700s, but bitter hostility between France and Britain remained constant.

The Battle of Vigo Bay, 1702, took place in the early years of the War of the Spanish Succession.

"Men are not hanged for stealing horses, but that horses may not be stolen." —GEORGE SAVILE

SEE ALSO | EMPIRES RISING: PAGE 324

VOICES

THOMAS MILBURN TRANSPORTED TO BOTANY BAY

"[We were] chained two and two together and confined in the hold during the whole course of our long voyage. . . . [W]e were scarcely allowed a sufficient quantity of victuals to keep us alive, and scarcely any water; for my own part I could have eaten three or four of our allowances. . . . [W]hen any of our comrades that were chained to us died, we kept it a secret as long as we could for the smell of the dead body, in order to get their allowance of provision, and many a time have I been glad to eat the poultice that was put to my leg for perfect hunger."

—FROM A LETTER BY MILBURN, 1790

BOTANY BAY TRANSPORTEES

SOCIETY THE IDEA OF JUSTICE

Enlightenment reformers denounced harsh legal practices that had changed little since the Middle Ages, including torturing suspects to make them confess and imposing the death penalty for nonviolent crimes. In his 1764 essay "On Crimes and Punishments," Italian philosopher Cesare Beccaria laid out principles of justice that were later embraced by many nations. No defendant should be treated as a criminal until found guilty, he declared, and punishments should be proportional to the offense. Such enlightened thinking did not bring a swift end to harsh practices. In 18th-century England, more than 200 offenses were punishable by death, including stealing goods worth more than 40 shillings. Judges often commuted the death sentence, however. Those found guilty of their first capital offense might be branded on the thumb or transported to colonies in North America or in Australia, claimed for Britain by explorer James Cook in 1770. By leading productive new lives in the colonies, many of those convicts demonstrated that condemned criminals could be rehabilitated.

THE TAKEAWAY: Enlightenment thinkers bequeathed to the modern world the idea that punishment should fit the crime.

Four men held in a pillory are taunted by a British crowd.

"Laws are like cobwebs, which may catch small flies, but let wasps and hornets break through."

—JONATHAN SWIFT

SEE ALSO | BREAKING BONDS: PAGE 226

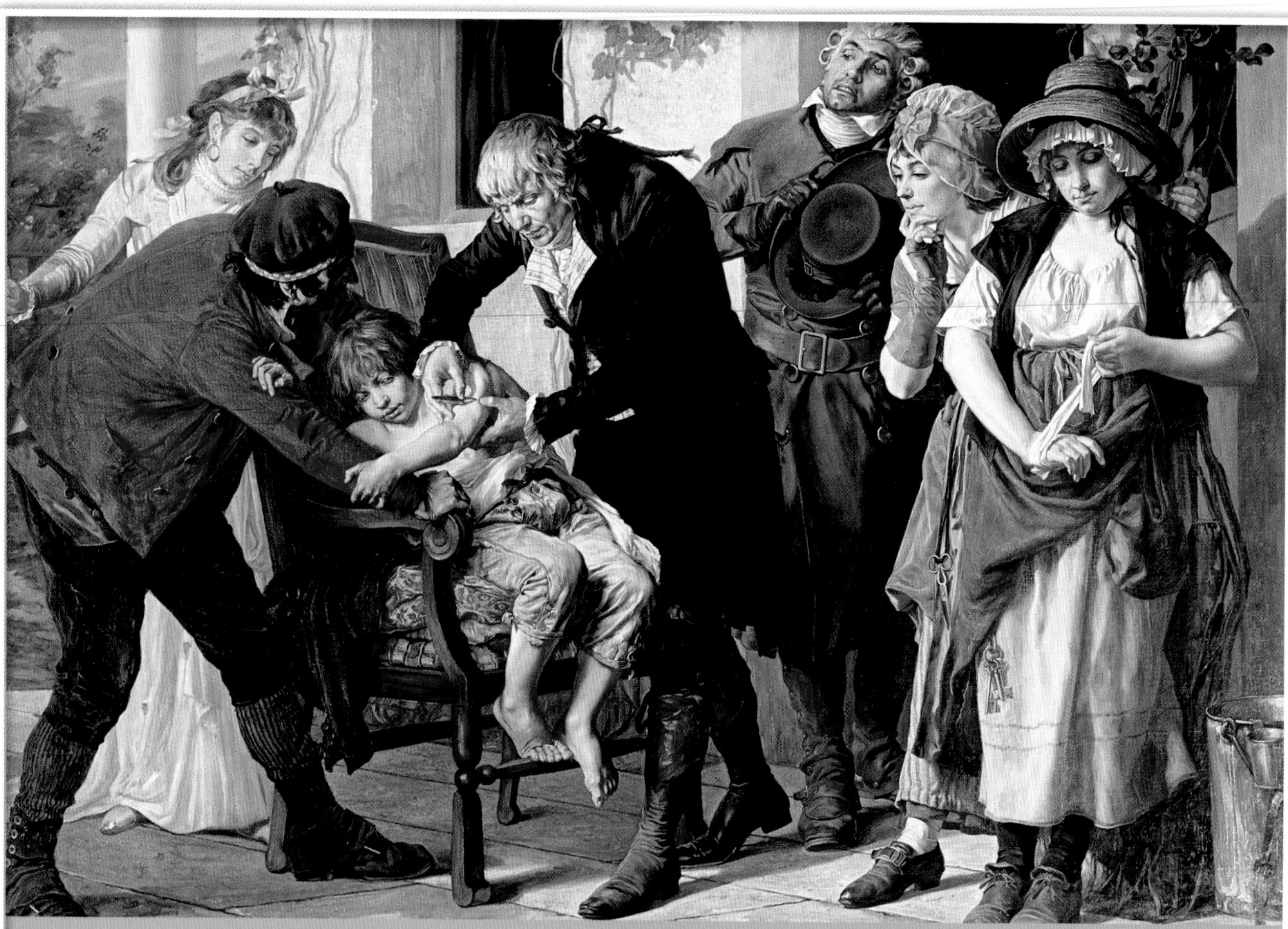

English surgeon Edward Jenner performs the first smallpox vaccination in 1796.

SCIENCE THE QUANTIFIABLE WORLD

The scientific revolution began in Europe, when those seeking to understand nature discarded theories that could not be confirmed by experience or experiments and based their conclusions strictly on what they could observe and measure. Astronomers such as Copernicus and Galileo had set the stage for this revolution by overturning the old geocentric view of the universe. But the great pioneer of modern science was English physicist Isaac Newton, who in 1687 defined the laws of motion and demonstrated mathematically that the orbits of planets and moons are determined by gravity, a force that varies inversely with the distance between two objects. By showing that nature operates according to quantifiable principles, Newton made observation, measurement, and mathematics the basis for proposing and testing scientific theories.

New or improved tools and better techniques allowed scientists to examine previously unseen or unmeasurable phenomena. Newton, for instance, developed his theory of optics by using a glass prism to split a beam of light into a rainbowlike spectrum of colors. He also invented the first successful reflecting telescope, using mirrors rather than lenses to focus captured light. His colleague

> *"To myself I seem to have been only like a boy playing on the seashore . . . finding a smoother pebble or a prettier shell than ordinary, whilst the great ocean of truth lay all undiscovered before me."* —NEWTON

Robert Hooke and fellow Englishman Robert Boyle devised an air pump, which they used to compress gases and arrive at Boyle's law, stating that the pressure of a gas varies inversely with its volume. The microscope was perfected in the 1660s by the Dutch scientist Antonie van Leeuwenhoek, who peered through its lens to observe microorganisms. German astronomer William Herschel fled French troops who invaded his homeland during the Seven Years' War, settling in England, where he built the most powerful telescope yet devised and with it discovered the planet Uranus in 1781—the first planet discovered since prehistory. He and Caroline Herschel, his sister and colleague, went on to look beyond the solar system and discover star clusters and nebulae.

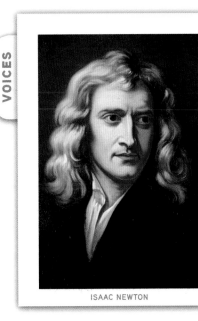

Isaac Newton's reflecting telescope

Institutes such as the Royal Society of London and the French Academy of Sciences helped publicize such findings, but their members were not always honored by the public. One of the luminaries of the French Academy, Antoine-Laurent Lavoisier, who shared credit with Englishman Joseph Priestly for identifying oxygen, was guillotined during the French Revolution for having profited as a landlord. "It took them only an instant to cut off that head," an admirer lamented, "and a hundred years may not produce another like it."

> Isaac Newton was a legend in his own time, elected president of London's Royal Society and buried in Westminster Abbey.

French physicist Denis Papin and English chemist Robert Boyle

THE TAKEAWAY: The scientific revolution emphasized observation and experimentation.

VOICES

ISAAC NEWTON

NEWTON SINS OF MY YOUTH

"*Using the word (God) openly*
Making a feather while on Thy day
Denying that I made it.
Putting a pin in John Keys hat on Thy day to pick him.
Refusing to go to the close at my mothers command.
Threatning my father and mother Smith to burne them and the house over them
Wishing death and hoping it to some
Setting my heart on money learning pleasure more than Thee"

—SELECTED ENTRIES FROM ISAAC NEWTON'S "FITZWILLIAM NOTEBOOK," A DIARY HE KEPT IN HIS YOUTH

"*The sweetest and most inoffensive path of life leads through the avenues of science and learning.*"
—DAVID HUME

SEE ALSO | NEW WORLD ORDER: PAGE 286

CLASS & SOCIETY COUNTRY LIFE

Despite the growth of cities such as London and Paris, Europe remained a largely rural society in the 18th century. More than three-quarters of the population were country dwellers, most of them mired in poverty and subject to periodic plagues and famines. Worst off were the serfs in Russia, owned outright by their landlords. Wealthy merchants and professionals such as lawyers and doctors gained prominence in European towns and cities, but this rising middle class remained politically subordinate to the aristocracy until the French Revolution and the industrial revolution transformed society.

THE TAKEAWAY: Many people who worked the land in Europe were little better than slaves.

Women negotiate the price of fish in a scene from the British countryside.

NORMANDY FAMINE IN THE PROVINCES

VOICES

BREAD DISTRIBUTION DURING FAMINE

"Of the 450 sick persons whom the inhabitants were unable to relieve, 200 were turned out, and these we saw die one by one as they lay on the roadside. A large number still remain, and to each of them it is only possible to dole out the least scrap of bread. We only give bread to those who would otherwise die. The staple dish here consists of mice, which the inhabitants hunt, so desperate are they from hunger. They devour roots which the animals cannot eat."

—FROM "REPORT OF THE ESTATES OF NORMANDY," 1651

"A brave world, sir, full of religion, knavery, and change: we shall shortly see better days." —APHRA BEHN

VOICES

WOLLSTONECRAFT

WOMEN'S RIGHTS

"I view, with indignation, the mistaken notions that enslave my sex. I love man as my fellow; but his sceptre, real or usurped, extends not to me, unless the reason of an individual demands my homage; and even then the submission is to reason, and not to man. In fact, the conduct of an accountable being must be regulated by the operations of its own reason; or on what foundation rests the throne of God?"

—FROM *A VINDICATION OF THE RIGHTS OF WOMAN*, MARY WOLLSTONECRAFT, 1792

MARY WOLLSTONECRAFT

PHILOSOPHY WOMEN SPEAK UP

When Enlightenment philosophers spoke of the rights of man, they did not have women in mind. Jean-Jacques Rousseau, for example, a leading French exponent of liberty, declared that women had an important role to play only within the home. Yet women fostered the Enlightenment and its reforms by hosting philosophical salons, and they demonstrated by their accomplishments that they were as qualified as men for the rights of citizenship. Some achieved distinction in the arts or as scientists, like Caroline Herschel or Margaret Cavendish, the first woman admitted to a meeting of the Royal Society.

Women, here making straw hats, often worked out of their homes.

In 1792, British author Mary Wollstonecraft published *A Vindication of the Rights of Woman,* in which she chided Rousseau and others for portraying women as "useless members of society." In France a year earlier, Olympe de Gouges composed a Declaration of the Rights of Woman, based on the Declaration of the Rights of Man and the Citizen. She opposed the Jacobins, who banned revolutionary women's societies, and denounced the Reign of Terror, to which she herself fell victim in 1793.

THE TAKEAWAY: In the late 1700s, women inspired by the Enlightenment began pressing for equal rights.

"Woman is born free and lives equal to man in her rights. Social distinctions can be based only on the common utility." —OLYMPE DE GOUGES

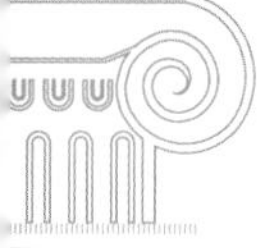

SEE ALSO | BREAKING BONDS: PAGE 224

VOICES

J. S. BACH MORE MONEY, PLEASE

"For some years, and up to the present time, I have had the direction of the music in the two principal churches in Leipzig; but I have had to suffer, though in all innocence, from one or another vexatious cause, at different times a diminution of the fees connected with this function, which might be withheld altogether unless your kingly Majesty will show me grace and confer upon me a predicate of your Majesty's Court Capelle, and will issue your high command to the proper persons for the granting of a patent to that effect."

—FROM A LETTER TO KING AUGUST III, 1733

J. S. BACH

An 18th-century string quartet in Austria.

ARTS MUSICAL MASTERS

Europe's intricate baroque style of the 17th and 18th centuries was summed up musically by the dazzling works of German composer Johann Sebastian Bach, who began his career as a church organist and, like many baroque composers, divided his talents between sacred and secular music. Along with such composers as Antonio Vivaldi—a Catholic priest and violin virtuoso—and George Frideric Handel, baroque composers devised such sacred masterworks as Bach's *St. Matthew Passion* and Handel's *Messiah.*

Classical composers of the 1700s owed much to their baroque predecessors but favored melodic clarity over complexity and gave a larger role to instruments than to the voice. Obliging geniuses like the Viennese composers Joseph Haydn and Wolfgang Amadeus Mozart, a prodigy who began performing when he was five, brought music into the secular world.

{ Johann Sebastian Bach had 20 children, four of whom, including C.P.E Bach, became composers as well. }

THE TAKEAWAY: The transition from baroque to classical reflected a movement from piety to pleasure.

"Music has charms to soothe a savage breast, / To soften rocks, or bend a knotted oak."

—WILLIAM CONGREVE

ARTS BEYOND BAROQUE

The baroque style in art was rich, ornate, and uplifting. Often inspired by biblical themes—as in works by the 17th-century Flemish painter Peter Paul Rubens and the Italian sculptor Gian Lorenzo Bernini, who helped adorn St. Peter's Basilica—baroque art was embraced by the Catholic Church as a way of competing with Protestantism, which discouraged artistic images in churches. In the early 18th century, however, baroque gave birth to a new style of painting and ornamentation, called rococo, which was lighter, brighter, and less devout, making it well suited for decorating theaters and residences. Like classical composers, French painter Jean-Antoine Watteau and other rococo artists produced elegant works that reflected the tastes of their wealthy patrons, often portrayed in handsome salons and country estates. In the late 1700s the neoclassical French artist Jacques-Louis David turned away from that lavish style and celebrated the austerity and heroism of republican Rome in paintings that made him the artistic champion of the French Republic.

THE TAKEAWAY: Baroque art gave way to new styles expressing the worldly interests of artists and their patrons.

Rococo-era painter Canaletto was famous for his landscapes, such as this one of Venice's Grand Canal.

"The soft complaining flute, / In dying notes, discovers / The woes of hopeless lovers." —JOHN DRYDEN

SEE ALSO | NEW WORLD ORDER: PAGE 307

BARON DE GRIMM MADAME GEOFFRIN'S SALON

VOICES

MADAME GEOFFRIN

"However deficient the poor man [Madame Geoffrin's husband] was, he was permitted to sit down to dinner, at the end of the table, upon condition that he never attempted to join in conversation. A foreigner who was very assiduous in his visits to Madame Geoffrin, one day, not seeing him as usual at table, enquired after him: 'What have you done, Madam, with the poor man whom I always used to see here, and who never spoke a word?'–'Oh, that was my husband–he is dead.'"

—EXCERPT FROM THE MEMOIR OF BARON DE GRIMM, 1815

PHILOSOPHY NATURAL RIGHTS

Enlightenment philosophers concerned themselves with all branches of knowledge and inquiry, including religion, politics, economics, and the natural sciences. One of the pioneers of the Enlightenment was political philosopher John Locke, whose treatises on government, written in the late 1600s, refuted the idea that rulers were like fathers, entitled to command and punish their childish subjects as they saw fit. Instead, he defined government as a contract between people endowed with natural rights and their rulers. Locke favored England's constitutional monarchy, but other Enlightenment thinkers like Thomas Jefferson and Jean-Jacques Rousseau, in his book *The Social Contract* (1762), argued that only a republic could embody the will of the people.

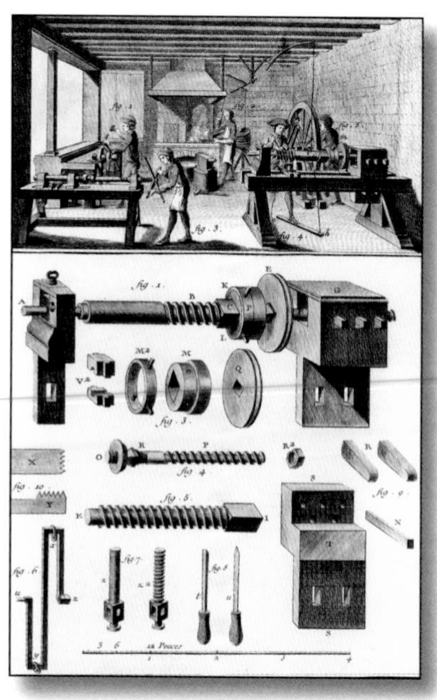

The Enlightenment produced Diderot's *Encyclopedia* (above right, an illustration on tools), and *The Wealth of Nations* by Adam Smith (left).

In France, the intellectual center of the Enlightenment, the leading light was François-Marie Arouet, who took the pen name Voltaire and wrote plays and novels such as his satirical masterpiece *Candide* (1759) as well as philosophical treatises. His French colleague, Denis Diderot, opposed racial and religious bias, criticizing Europeans for enslaving people of other lands. Such ideas were considered

"Thought depends absolutely on the stomach, but in spite of that, those who have the best stomachs are not the best thinkers." —VOLTAIRE

French philosopher Voltaire was a great admirer of Isaac Newton and wrote a book explaining his work.

dangerous, and parts of Diderot's *Encyclopedia,* a great compendium of knowledge he edited, were censored. He and his fellow philosophers had influential defenders, however, including prominent women such as Marie Thérèse Geoffrin, who subsidized the *Encyclopedia* and hosted its authors at her Paris salon.

Enlightenment philosophers advocated not only political and religious freedom but also free trade and enterprise, extolled by the pioneering British economist Adam Smith in his book *The Wealth of Nations* (1776).

THE TAKEAWAY: Enlightenment philosophers laid out core principles of civil and religious liberty and intellectual freedom.

Frederick the Great of Prussia converses with Voltaire.

VOICES

ROUSSEAU REGAINING LIBERTY

"Man is born free; and everywhere he is in chains. One thinks himself the master of others, and still remains a greater slave than they. How did this change come about? I do not know. What can make it legitimate? That question I think I can answer. If I took into account only force, and the effects derived from it, I should say: 'As long as a people is compelled to obey, and obeys, it does well; as soon as it can shake off the yoke, and shakes it off, it does still better; for, regaining its liberty by the same right as took it away, either it is justified in resuming it, or there was no justification for those who took it away."

—FROM *THE SOCIAL CONTRACT,* JEAN-JACQUES ROUSSEAU, 1762

"I have tried too in my time to be a philosopher; but I don't know how, cheerfulness was always breaking in."

—OLIVER EDWARDS

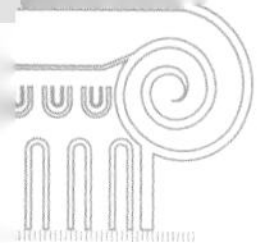

SEE ALSO | BREAKING BONDS: PAGE 234

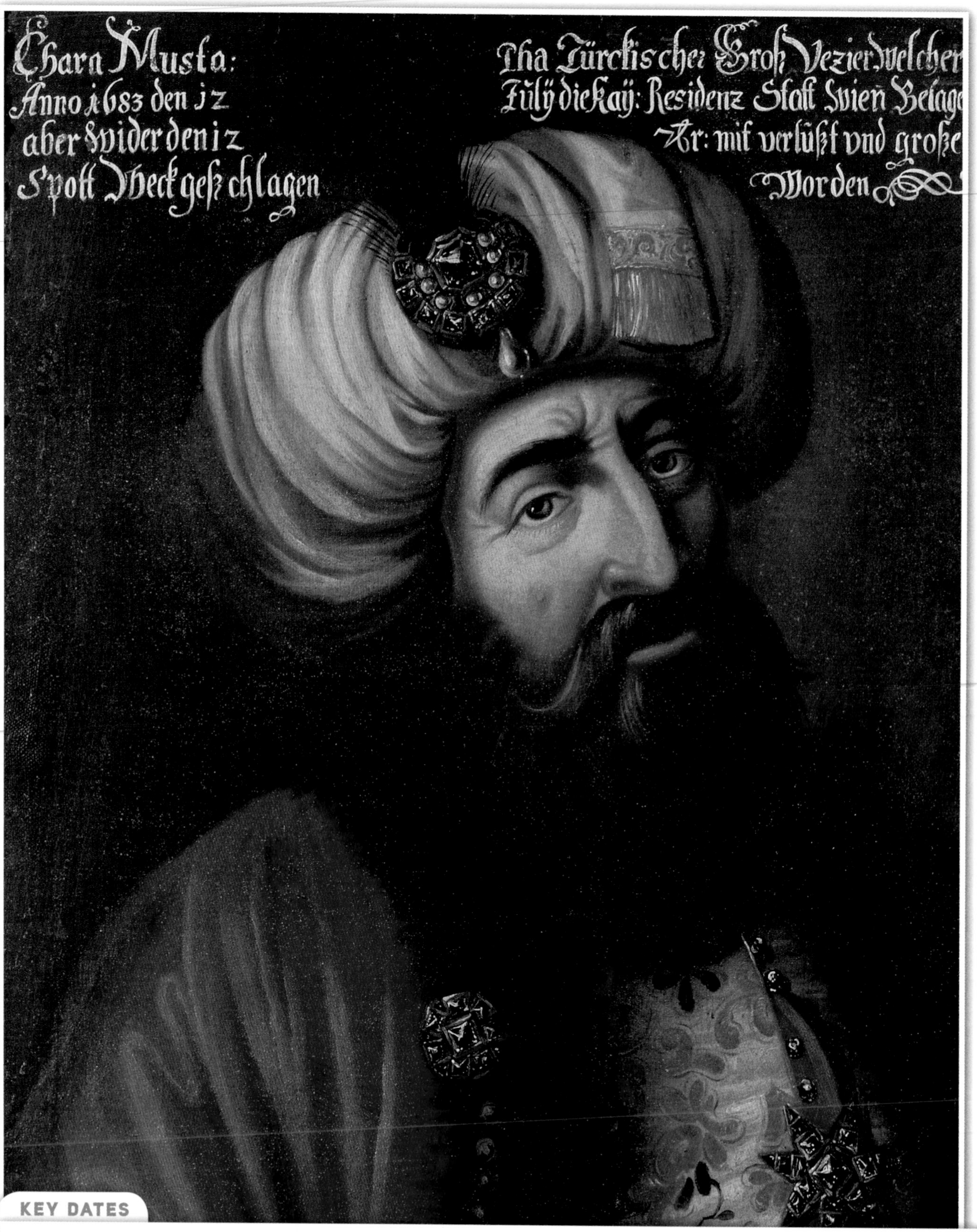

KEY DATES

1648
Sultan Mehmed IV succeeds to the Ottoman throne after his father is assassinated.

1652
Through the Dutch East India Company, Europeans begin colonization of South Africa.

1670
Asante clans unify on the Gold Coast of West Africa.

1683
Ottoman forces are driven back from Vienna.

MIDDLE EAST & AFRICA

1648–1800

As European nations grew stronger through advances in trade, navigation, and technology, they challenged rival empires and remote kingdoms that were once superior to them or safely beyond their reach. Even the vast and formidable Ottoman Empire, which extended around the Mediterranean from the Balkan peninsula through the Middle East and across North Africa, began to decline in the 17th century as it came under military and economic pressure from Europeans. The Turks who dominated that empire had once prospered as middlemen in the lucrative trade between Europe and the Far East, but they lost that advantage as venturesome Europeans sailed around Africa or South America to reach the Orient. Sultans in Constantinople found it harder to raise revenue and pay their troops. Ottoman forces overreached when they besieged Vienna in 1683 and were beaten back. By 1800, the Turks were losing their grip on the Balkans and Egypt, occupied briefly in the late 1790s by French troops under Napoleon, whose intervention brought in rival British forces and inaugurated an era of European imperialism in Africa.

The decline of the once-great Ottoman Empire and the growth of the transatlantic slave trade in the 18th century set the stage for European nations to dominate Africa and the Middle East.

Before 1800, much of Africa remained beyond the direct control of either the Ottoman Empire or the major European powers. Large parts of the continent, however, were deeply affected by the transatlantic slave trade, which reached its peak in the 18th century, when more than 50,000 slaves were exported annually from Africa to European colonies in the Americas. Many tribal societies were devastated in the process. But African kingdoms such as Asante, located in what is now Ghana, enhanced their power and wealth, traditionally measured in gold and other precious materials, by dealing in slaves, which they captured in raids and sold to European merchants for shipment to the New World. Few Europeans involved in the slave trade or other pursuits in Africa ventured far inland from the coast, with the notable exception of Dutch colonists called Boers, who occupied what is now South Africa.

OPPOSITE: Grand Vizier Kara Mustafa Pasha led the Ottoman armies that were defeated in Vienna.

1703
Ottoman Sultan Ahmed III introduces European culture to the empire.

1718
The tulip era begins amid a relatively peaceful Ottoman Empire.

1769
Local troops wrest control of Egypt from the Ottomans.

1795
British forces occupy the South African colony, seizing control from the Dutch.

SEE ALSO | BREAKING BONDS: PAGE 241

EMPIRES SULTANS AND VIZIERS

Imperial forces rescue Vienna from Ottoman invasion in 1683.

The Ottoman Empire was past its peak in 1648 when Sultan Mehmed IV succeeded his deranged father, known as Ibrahim the Crazy, who was murdered by palace officials when Mehmed was just six years old. The young ruler remained under the guardianship of his mother and grandmother until he matured, and even then his authority was limited. Gone were the days when a figure like 16th-century sultan Suleyman the Magnificent steered the empire with a strong hand. Power now lay largely with the Janissaries—an elite corps of officers recruited as boys—and with the grand vizier, who managed affairs of state while the sultan engaged in more pleasurable pursuits. Mehmed took an interest in warfare and sometimes joined his forces in the field. But he did not control the army and failed to prevent his overzealous grand vizier from launching a risky campaign in the 1680s to crush the Habsburg dynasty in Austria and seize Vienna, which ended in a bitter defeat for Ottoman forces.

Ultimately, Mehmed paid for

MIDDLE EAST & AFRICA

VIPs

Kara Mustafa Pasha, 1634–1683
Grand vizier who led Ottoman troops to defeat in Vienna

Mehmed IV, 1642–1693
Ottoman sultan who presided over losses and instability in the empire

Suleyman II, 1642–1691
Ottoman sultan who reestablished order in the empire after Mehmed IV was deposed

Osei Tutu, ca 1660–ca 1712
Founder of the Asante empire, formed from a union of smaller states

Ahmed III, 1673–1736
Ottoman sultan and patron of the arts

“*Allah! Lord who liv'st for aye! O Sole! O King of Glory's Ray! Monarch who ne'er shalt pass away! show thou to us thy bounties fair.*” —SULTAN MUSTAFA II

VOICES

MONTAGU TURKISH WOMEN'S BATHS

"They generally take this diversion once a week, and stay there at least four or five hours, without getting cold by immediate coming out of the hot bath into the cool room, which was very surprising to me. The lady that seemed the most considerable amongst them entreated me to sit by her and would fain have undressed me for the bath. I excused myself with some difficulty, they being however all so earnest in persuading me, I was at last forced to open my shirt, and show them my stays, which satisfied them very well, for I saw they believed I was so locked up in that machine, that it was not in my own power to open it, which contrivance they attributed to my husband."

—FROM LADY MARY WORTLEY MONTAGU'S TURKISH EMBASSY LETTERS, 1763

LADY MARY

that and other setbacks by losing the throne to his brother, Suleyman II, who repaired some of the damage done to the empire. During the reign of Ahmed III, which began in 1703, European dress and ornaments became popular among the elite and a craze developed for tulips. During the so-called tulip era, wealthy Turks were influenced by European customs, but Ottoman authorities were slow to adopt European technology and weaponry and fell behind military rivals such as Russia. Economically, rulers in Constantinople depended on revenues collected by tax farmers, whose corruption ignited uprisings in the Balkans and elsewhere.

> Traditionalists who disdained technology forced Ottoman leaders to shut down their printing press in 1742.

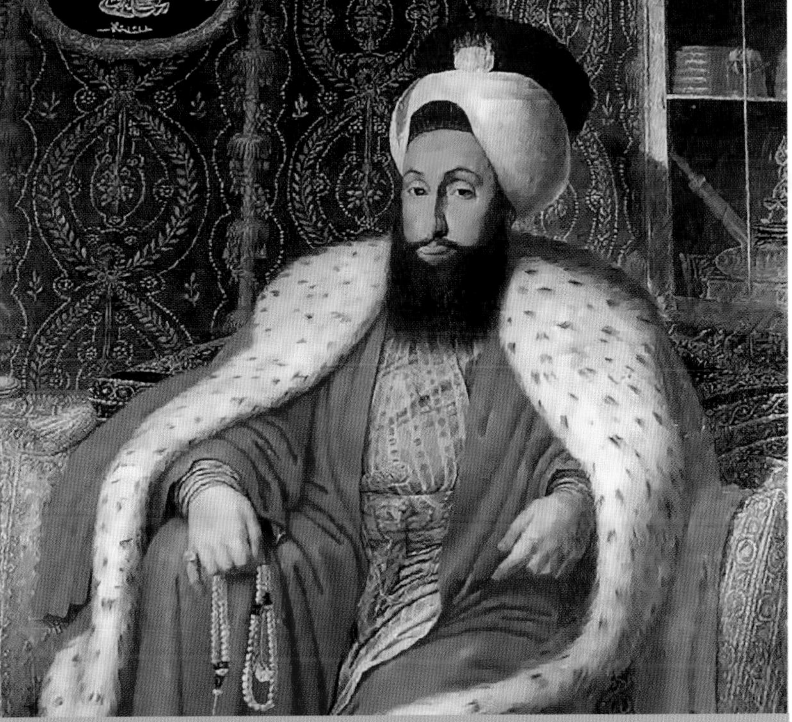

Ottoman sultan Selim III attempted to modernize the empire.

The Ottoman Empire's Sunni Muslim rulers tolerated Christians and Jews but persecuted Shiite Muslims and opposed Shiite-dominated Persia (Iran). In that country, religious leaders called *ulama* grew more powerful than shahs of the faltering Safavid dynasty. In the 1720s, the Safavid dynasty was toppled, and Persia entered a long period of unrest.

THE TAKEAWAY: Ottoman rulers became increasingly detached from affairs of state as their empire declined.

"Being's the bounty of the Lord; and Life, the gift Divine / The Breath, the present of his love; and Speech his Grace's sign." —YUSEF NABI

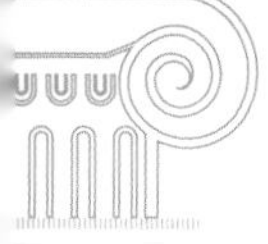

SEE ALSO | EMPIRES RISING: PAGE 336

COLONIES SOUTH AFRICA

European colonization of South Africa began in 1652, when the Dutch East India Company founded Cape Town near the tip of the continent as a supply station for ships rounding Africa on their way to and from India and other Asian lands. The first settlers there were company employees, including farmers who raised crops and livestock to feed the town's inhabitants and provision ships that docked there. The company imported slaves from other regions rather than enslave black South Africans, called Khoikhoi, hoping to avoid conflict with them.

By 1700, however, venturesome Boers, most of them Dutch settlers, were trekking inland from Cape Town with herds of cattle and clashing with various tribes, which were decimated by smallpox, communicated by the colonists. By the 1780s some 20,000 Europeans were living in South Africa. Cape Town grew into an important way station between Europe and Asia, housing both Europeans and their slaves.

The Dutch remained in control of the South African colony until 1795, when British forces occupied the colony to acquire vital sea routes to Asia and to prevent rival France from seizing it. Great Britain annexed South Africa a decade later and sent in its own colonists, who would later contend violently with Boers as well as Zulus and other defiant tribal groups.

THE TAKEAWAY: European powers wrestled for control of South Africa and its shipping routes.

A porcelain plate portrays four ships flying the Dutch flag off the Cape of Good Hope.

JAN VAN RIEBEECK RUNAWAY SLAVES

VOICES

JAN VAN RIEBEECK

“The freeman Jan Reijnierssen came to complain early in the morning that during the night all his male and female slaves had run away, taking with them 3 or 4 blankets, clothing, rice, tobacco, etc. We thereupon called the new interpreter Doman, now called Anthony, who had returned from Batavia with the Hon. Cuneus, and asked him why the Hottentots [Khoikhoi] would not search for the runaway slaves, to which he coolly replied that he did not know. The Commander, not trusting him, then called the interpreter Eva alone into his office and privately asked her whether our blacks were not being harboured by the Hottentots. . . . She (speaking good Dutch) said these words, namely: “I tell you straight out, Mijnheer Van Riebeeck, Doman is no good.”

—FROM THE 1758 JOURNAL OF VAN RIEBEECK, THE COMMANDER AT CAPE TOWN

“That execrable sum of all villainies, commonly called the Slave Trade.” —JOHN WESLEY

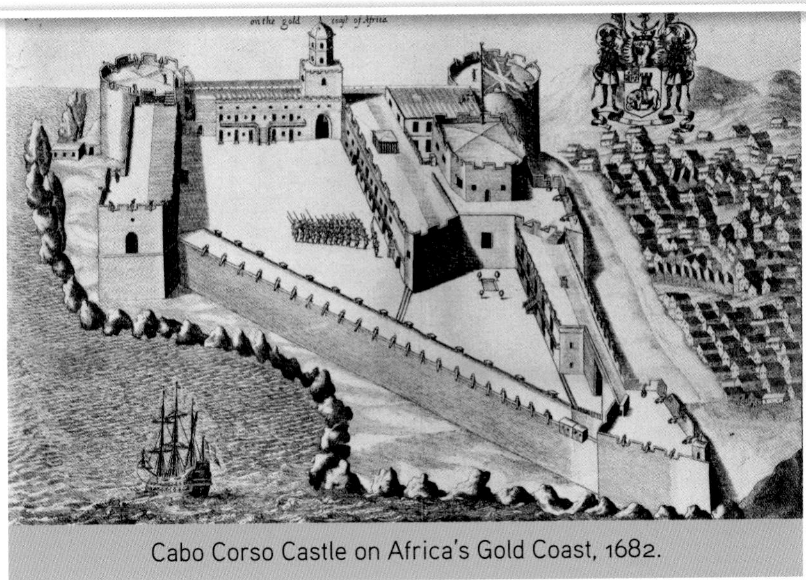

Cabo Corso Castle on Africa's Gold Coast, 1682.

EMPIRES ASANTE KINGDOM

The Asante kingdom was forged in the interior of present-day Ghana in the late 1600s by an imposing ruler named Osei Tutu. He was aided by his shrewd adviser, Okomfo Anokye, a priest who helped him assert authority over other Asante chieftains and impress his majesty on the people. The chief emblem of Tutu's kingship was the Golden Stool, which served as his throne in his capital, Kumasi. According to legend, it descended from heaven, signaling that he was blessed with power by the spirits above, much like European kings who claimed they had a divine right to rule. Gold, produced in Asante territories, was the traditional standard for measuring wealth and prestige in Asante society. Another status symbol was kente cloth, a colorful fabric woven of cotton or silk obtained through trade.

> While a prince, Osei Tutu escaped from the court of a powerful Denkyera overlord where he was held hostage.

Once a loose collection of separate states and clans, in the 17th century, the Asante peoples began to cooperate. Reinforcing this new unity through centralized authority, military reforms, and an Asante council, King Tutu and his forces gained access to the coast by defeating their neighbors and longtime foes the Denkyera. There, slaves the Asante had captured were offered to European merchants in exchange for firearms. By the close of the 17th century, slaves formed the largest part of the Asante trade.

Such trade proved a mixed blessing for the Asante, strengthening them initially in relation to their African rivals, but exposing them in the 19th century to colonization by the British.

THE TAKEAWAY: Africans such as the Asante had their own traditions of kingship, conquest, and imperialism, which were heightened by the slave trade.

Asante gold mask (left); terra-cotta memorial head from Ghana (below)

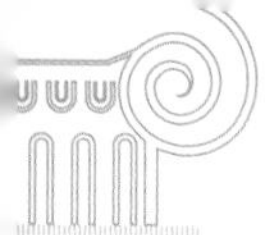

SEE ALSO | NEW WORLD ORDER: PAGE 297

KEY DATES

1637
Japanese shogun Iemitsu bans the Christian religion and expels all missionaries and most traders.

1644
The Qing dynasty is founded when Manchus seize Beijing.

1658–1707
Reign of Aurangzeb, last of the great Mughal emperors.

1688–1704
Literature, art, and drama flourish during a golden age of culture in Japan known as the Genroku period.

ASIA

1644–1800

In Asia, as in Africa and the Middle East, societies that had long been ignorant of Europeans or little influenced by them were exposed to Western pressures during the 17th and 18th centuries and responded to that challenge in various ways. The Tokugawa shoguns who ruled Japan, fearing that their country might be colonized like the Spanish-ruled Philippines, banned Christian missionaries and restricted trade with foreigners to the port of Nagasaki, where small numbers of Chinese and Dutch merchants were allowed access. Japan's self-imposed isolation caused it to lag behind Europe technologically, but helped it preserve its independence and its distinct culture. Literature and the arts flourished at the capital, Edo (modern-day Tokyo), where shoguns pacified the country's warlords and transformed hard-fighting samurai into gentlemen and scholars, handier with their pens than they were with their swords.

China and Japan restricted trade and other contacts with foreigners in the 1700s, maintaining their sovereignty while India's Mughal Empire came under increasing British economic control.

Similar policies toward Westerners were pursued by emperors of China's Qing dynasty, founded in the mid-1600s when Manchurian invaders overthrew the Ming dynasty, weakened by internal rebellions. The Qing barred Catholic missionaries from proselytizing in China in the early 1700s, and foreign trade was conducted under tight supervision at the port of Guangzhou (Canton). By controlling trade, China's rulers protected domestic productions such as silk, tea, and porcelain, purchased by foreigners at Guangzhou with silver that enriched Chinese manufacturers and the imperial treasury. Here as in Japan, this was an era of prosperity and high artistic achievement.

Rulers of India found it harder to hold their diverse society together and resist foreign incursions. The Mughal emperor Aurangzeb, who reigned for nearly a half century beginning in 1658, extended his realm through conquest from what is now Pakistan to southern India. In the process, he spread Islam and alienated the Hindu majority in the south. To raise revenue, he and his successors imposed heavy taxes and allowed European companies to maintain fortified trading posts in Mumbai (Bombay), Calcutta, and other ports. The British East India Company gained power in the mid-1700s as the Mughal Empire declined, allowing Britain to dominate India.

OPPOSITE: "Ohisa of the Takashima Tea-Shop" was one of Japanese printmaker Utamaro's masterworks.

1756
The nawab of Bengal punishes the British there for violating trade restrictions.

1760
The British defeat the French at the Battle of Wandiwash, increasing British power in India.

1791
A masterpiece of the Chinese language, *The Dream of the Red Chamber*, is published.

1796
Qing emperor Qianlong steps down in favor of his son, and the White Lotus Rebellion erupts.

SEE ALSO | THE WORLD AT WAR: PAGE 403

EMPIRES FROM MUGHALS TO THE BRITISH

The nawab of Bengal meets with Col. Robert Clive.

The Mughal emperor Aurangzeb left a tainted legacy to his heirs when he died in 1707. In expanding the empire to its greatest extent and imposing his iron will and strict Muslim beliefs on India, he had bitterly antagonized large segments of its population. His successors rescinded some of his harshest measures, such as placing a punitive tax on non-Muslims and ordering the destruction of Hindu temples. But many people who had rebelled against Aurangzeb, including Hindu Marathas living along India's west coast and Sikhs inhabiting the northwest province of Punjab, remained sharply at odds with the later Mughal rulers.

To add insult to injury, invaders swept down from Persia in 1739 and sacked Delhi, the Mughal capital, carrying off the splendid Peacock Throne on which Aurangzeb and other emperors had perched. Having taxed their disgruntled subjects to the limit, Mughal rulers were no longer able to raise enough revenue to keep their realm intact and became mere figureheads, to whom India's various nawabs, or provincial governors, paid lip service and little else.

Meanwhile, European powers were beginning to take an interest in the wealth of India, and the British, French, Portuguese, Dutch, and Danish set up trading posts along the coast, sometimes battling each other for supremacy. Finding India politically divided, British traders and troops proceeded to conquer the country by playing one nawab off against another. Such tactics enabled the British East India Company to foil the rival French East India Company and make the thriving port of Calcutta, in the province of Bengal, a base for British expansion.

British businessmen wanted to acquire wealth, not territory. But over time, one aim led to the

ASIA

VIPs

Aurangzeb, 1618–1707
Mughal emperor, skillful but ruthless

Kangxi, 1654–1722
Second emperor of the Qing (Manchu) dynasty

Tokugawa Yoshimune, 1684–1751 Eighth Tokugawa shogun of Japan, able administrator

Cao Zhan, ca 1715–1763
Author of the Chinese masterpiece, *Dream of the Red Chamber*

Robert Clive, 1725–1774
British administrator of Bengal

> “*Bengal is called, by way of distinction, the paradise of the earth.... The silver of the west and the gold of the east have for many years been pouring into that country.*” —ROBERT CLIVE

VOICES

J. Z. HOLWELL THE BLACK HOLE OF CALCUTTA

"I called aloud for Water for God's sake. . . . But from the water I had no relief; my thirst was rather increased by it; so I determined to drink no more, but patiently wait the event; and kept my mouth moist from time to time by sucking the perspiration out of my shirt sleeves, and catching the drops as they fell, like heavy rain, from my head and face; you can hardly imagine how unhappy I was if any of them escaped my mouth."

—FROM A FIRSTHAND ACCOUNT, 1756; PROBABLY EXAGGERATED

BLACK HOLE OF CALCUTTA

other. The turning point came in 1756 when the nawab of Bengal punished the British there for violating trade restrictions. Their garrison was seized and prisoners were incarcerated in a stifling cell, known to posterity as the Black Hole of Calcutta, where many of them died. The British retaliated by sending a relief expedition led by Col. Robert Clive, who secured Calcutta and went on to seize all of Bengal, replacing its defiant nawab with a compliant one who served as Clive's puppet.

> By the late 1700s the once-vast Mughal domain was confined to Delhi and vicinity, which came under British control in 1803.

Although Bengal remained technically independent, it was required to make large, regular payments to the British. Much of the money went to individuals, including Clive himself. The term "nawab, "or "nabob," was soon applied to British officials like Clive who, with the help of local recruits called sepoys, took charge of one province after another and became India's real governors.

In effect, India came under the control not just of Britain, but of the East India Company. The resentment this engendered among the populace would build over the next century.

THE TAKEAWAY: Mughal emperors lost India because they could not command its diverse populace; British commerce moved into the power vacuum.

THUMBS UP / THUMBS DOWN

EMPEROR AURANGZEB 1618–1707

AURANGZEB AT PRAYER

THE THIRD SON of Emperor Shah Jahan, Aurangzeb defeated his eldest brother, the heir, in battle and killed other kinsmen before taking the throne. Such ruthlessness could be an asset for Mughal emperors, who often contended with plots and rebellions. A devout Muslim, Aurangzeb also refrained from leading a dissolute life like some earlier rulers. His religious fervor became a liability, however, when he abandoned the tolerant policies of his predecessors and began to suppress other faiths. When the spiritual leader of the Sikhs, Guru Tegh Bahadur, refused to convert to Islam, Aurangzeb had him executed. Such measures divided the empire even as it expanded. **CONCLUSION:** **THUMBS UP and DOWN**

"Our conquest there, after twenty years, is as crude as it was the first day. . . . Every rupee of profit made by an Englishman is lost for ever to India." —EDMUND BURKE

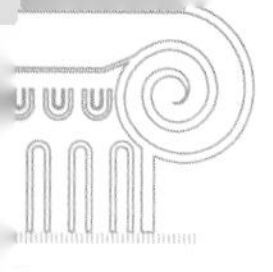

SEE ALSO | BREAKING BONDS: PAGE 258

Mongol envoys present horses to Emperor Qianlong.

EMPIRES THE QING DYNASTY

The Manchus who took control of China in the 17th century were among many invaders who swept down from the north during the long and turbulent history of that country. The Great Wall, rebuilt and extended by emperors of the Ming dynasty, proved no more effective in preventing Manchu advances against Ming-era warriors than it had been earlier in keeping Mongols from overrunning China. Unlike the nomadic Mongols, Manchus had settled as farmers in southern Manchuria and had long been exposed to Chinese culture through trade and other contacts. That helped them to form alliances with Chinese rebels as the Ming dynasty collapsed.

Rulers of the Qing dynasty, founded in 1644 when Manchus seized Beijing, readily adopted customs of the Chinese they governed while remaining distinct from them. The dynamic Qing emperor Kangxi, who reigned from 1661 to 1722, continued in the expansive tradition of his Manchu predecessors by subjugating Tibet and seizing the island of Taiwan, which served as a refuge for Ming loyalists. More than just a conqueror, he was a dedicated scholar who embodied the Confucian ideal of the cultivated and benevolent ruler by lowering taxes, endowing schools, and publishing encyclopedias and other scholarly books. His cordial relations with

KANGXI SACRED EDICTS

VOICES

KANGXI EMPEROR

"1. Esteem most highly filial piety and brotherly submission, in order to give due importance to human moral relations.

"2. Behave with generosity toward your kindred, in order to illustrate harmony and benignity.

"3. Cultivate peace and concord in your neighborhoods, in order to prevent quarrels and litigations.

"4. Give importance to agriculture and sericulture, in order to ensure a sufficiency of clothing and food."

—FROM A SET OF MORAL INSTRUCTIONS PROMULGATED BY THE KANGXI EMPEROR, 1670

"From the earliest times great attention has been given to the improvement of agriculture. Indicate the arrangements adopted for that purpose by the several dynasties." —CHINESE EXAM QUESTION

Catholic missionaries turned chilly after the pope prohibited ancestor worship by Chinese converts in 1704. Christian mission work dwindled in China and did not revive until the 19th century.

During the long reigns of Kangxi and his grandson Qianlong, the country remained prosperous and Manchu authorities commanded the obedience if not the affection of their Chinese subjects. But in 1796, when the elderly Qianlong abdicated in favor of his son, the White Lotus Rebellion erupted. Fueled by famine and official abuses in rural areas, it was led by Buddhists who denounced the Manchus as foreign oppressors and promised followers that the Buddha would return. The uprising was poorly organized, but corrupt imperial officers siphoned off funds for troops and supplies, allowing the unrest to continue until authorities resorted to starving peasants into submission. The rebellion signaled that the Qing dynasty was losing moral authority in China and heralded larger and bloodier revolutions to come.

> Refined 18th-century Manchu emperor Qianlong was credited with composing some 40,000 poems.

Qing dynasty plate

THE TAKEAWAY: Manchu rulers were often enlightened leaders, but they did not end the corruption that doomed their predecessors.

A detail of a silk painting captures the Kangxi emperor's visit to the south.

> *"Give an account of the circulating medium under different dynasties, and state how the currency of the Sung dynasty corresponds with our use of paper money."* —CHINESE EXAM QUESTION

SEE ALSO | GOLDEN AGES: PAGE 70

CLASS & SOCIETY FAMILY TIES

Most Chinese, whether they were Buddhists or members of other faiths, subscribed to Confucian doctrines that governed civic and family life. A philosophy more than a religion, Confucianism taught that rulers and elders should act benevolently toward those under their care and should receive respect and reverence in return. Fathers were lords and masters of the household, to whom their children owed filial piety.

Mothers were honored as well and sometimes wielded power behind the scenes, as when an emperor died, leaving a young heir who ruled under the guidance of the empress dowager.

Courtesans might sing or dance in public places, but respectable women were expected to remain at home. Under the Qing dynasty, it became common among the wealthy for a girl's feet to be bound so that they remained small and dainty, leaving her unable to walk properly as an adult and confined to the house.

China's clan organization and bureaucratic merit system provided some opportunities for social advancement. Wealthy people might support promising young men from poor families within their clan as they studied for the grueling civil service exam.

Female attendants

THE TAKEAWAY: In imperial China, families were sacred.

An 18th-century gouache painting for the European market shows Chinese women arranging water lilies.

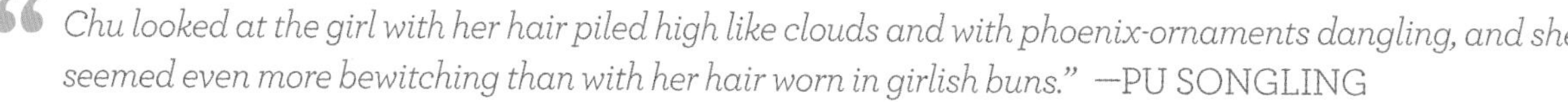

"Chu looked at the girl with her hair piled high like clouds and with phoenix-ornaments dangling, and she seemed even more bewitching than with her hair worn in girlish buns." —PU SONGLING

VOICES

CAO ZHAN A QING MAIDEN

"While wrapped in these thoughts, he felt much annoyance at not being able to recognize who she was. But on further minute inspection, he noticed that this maiden, with contracted eyebrows, as beautiful as the hills in spring, frowning eyes as clear as the streams in autumn, a face, with transparent skin, and a slim waist, was elegant and beautiful and almost the very image of Lin Tai-yu. Pao-yu could not, from the very first, make up his mind to wrench himself away."

—FROM *DREAM OF THE RED CHAMBER*, ca 1759

CHINESE MAIDEN

ARTS EXPRESSIVE MASTERY

Traditionally, arts in China such as painting, calligraphy, and poetry were pastimes of the elite, including members of the imperial family and scholars who served the emperor. Two of the finest painters of the early Qing period, Zhu Da and Shi Tao, were descendants of the ousted Ming dynasty who entered Buddhist monasteries, which often served as refuges for those who suffered personal or political misfortune.

The collapse of the Ming may have contributed to the eccentric behavior of Zhu Da and influenced his artistic style, which was more expressive and individualistic than that of earlier masters. In other respects, Chinese culture during this era reflected the country's prosperity and the growing importance of merchants and their finely crafted merchandise. Qing China was known for its lustrous silk fabric with intricately woven designs. The era's elegant porcelain gained new fame with its exquisite glazes; the pottery became known to English speakers as china, for the country that produced it.

Members of China's expanding commercial class were literate and read popular novels like *Dream of the Red Chamber*, dealing with forbidden love between cousins. Like bestsellers today, such novels were romantic and sometimes erotic but often informed readers in the process of entertaining them.

{ Painter Zhu Da attached the character "ya," meaning "dumb," to his door and then refused to speak. }

THE TAKEAWAY: China developed a vibrant culture as its merchants produced fine goods for export and read fiction.

Qing porcelain lion

"If a man is true and honest, rainbow-colored clouds will spread under his feet. If he is wicked and malicious, the clouds will be black." —LI RUZHEN

SEE ALSO | NEW WORLD ORDER: PAGE 302

CLASS & SOCIETY THE WAY OF THE WARRIOR

A print depicts the attack of the 47 ronin on a lord's house.

During the Tokugawa era, also known as the Edo period, Japan evolved from a feudal society governed by force into an orderly, centralized state, governed by enlightened shoguns like Tokugawa Yoshimune, who ruled peacefully from 1716 to 1745 and promoted education and respect for the law. Under such tranquil conditions, many samurai laid down their swords and became scholars and bureaucrats, dedicated to preserving peace rather than disturbing it.

But not all men raised in the old warrior tradition adapted to the new regime. Wandering samurai called *ronin,* who no longer had warlords to support them, posed a threat to public order. In 1651 the government foiled a plot by ronin to overthrow the shogun. Although feared as outlaws, ronin were also admired for adhering strictly to Bushido, the old warrior's code. The story of 47 ronin who avenged their slain master became legendary and inspired many Japanese novels and plays.

THE TAKEAWAY: Tokugawa shoguns brought law and order to Japan but had to contend with stubborn samurai.

TSUNETOMO THE BOOK OF THE SAMURAI

VOICES

"Above all, the Way of the Samurai should be in being aware that you do not know what is going to happen next, and in querying every item day and night. Victory and defeat are matters of the temporary force of circumstances. The way of avoiding shame is different. It is simply in death. ✤ Even if it seems certain that you will lose, retaliate. Neither wisdom nor technique has a place in this. A real man does not think of victory or defeat. He plunges recklessly towards an irrational death. By doing this, you will awaken from your dreams. ✤ There are two things that will blemish a retainer, and these are riches and honor. If one but remains in strained circumstances, he will not be marred."

—FROM *HAGAKURE,* A GUIDE TO THE CODE OF BUSHIDO, ca 1700

EDO PERIOD SAMURAI ARMOR

"It is essential that one say not of a thing that 'it is sad,' but that it be sad of itself."

—CHIKAMATSU MONZAEMON

VOICES

BASHO THREE HAIKU

A cicada shell;
it sang itself
utterly away

She wraps up rice cakes
while one hand
restrains her hair

On a leafless branch
a crow sits—
autumn evening

BASHO

ARTS THE FLOATING WORLD

In Japan as in China, the rise of a wealthy merchant class seeking entertainment helped create a market for novels and other popular art forms. The most prolific author of the Edo period was Ihara Saikaku, who made his name churning out thousands of short, humorous poems called haikai. This verse form gave birth to haiku—evocative poems of three lines and 17 syllables perfected by Saikaku's gifted contemporary, Matsuo Basho, a former samurai. In the late 1600s, Saikaku took up fiction; his erotic novels told of a subculture where women figured not just as geishas but as actresses in kabuki, a form of theater from which female performers were later banned. Artists also portrayed the "floating worlds" of pleasure houses, depicting them expertly in woodblock prints.

THE TAKEAWAY: Many Edo period artists portrayed the seductive underworld of entertainers.

Four actors of the Kabuki theater, in full character and costume.

"When one knows poetry well, one understands also without explanation the reasons governing order and disorder in the world." —KAMO MABUCHI

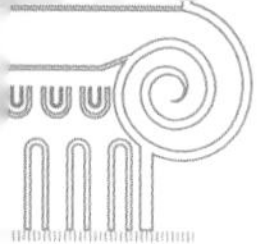

SEE ALSO | NEW WORLD ORDER: PAGE 278

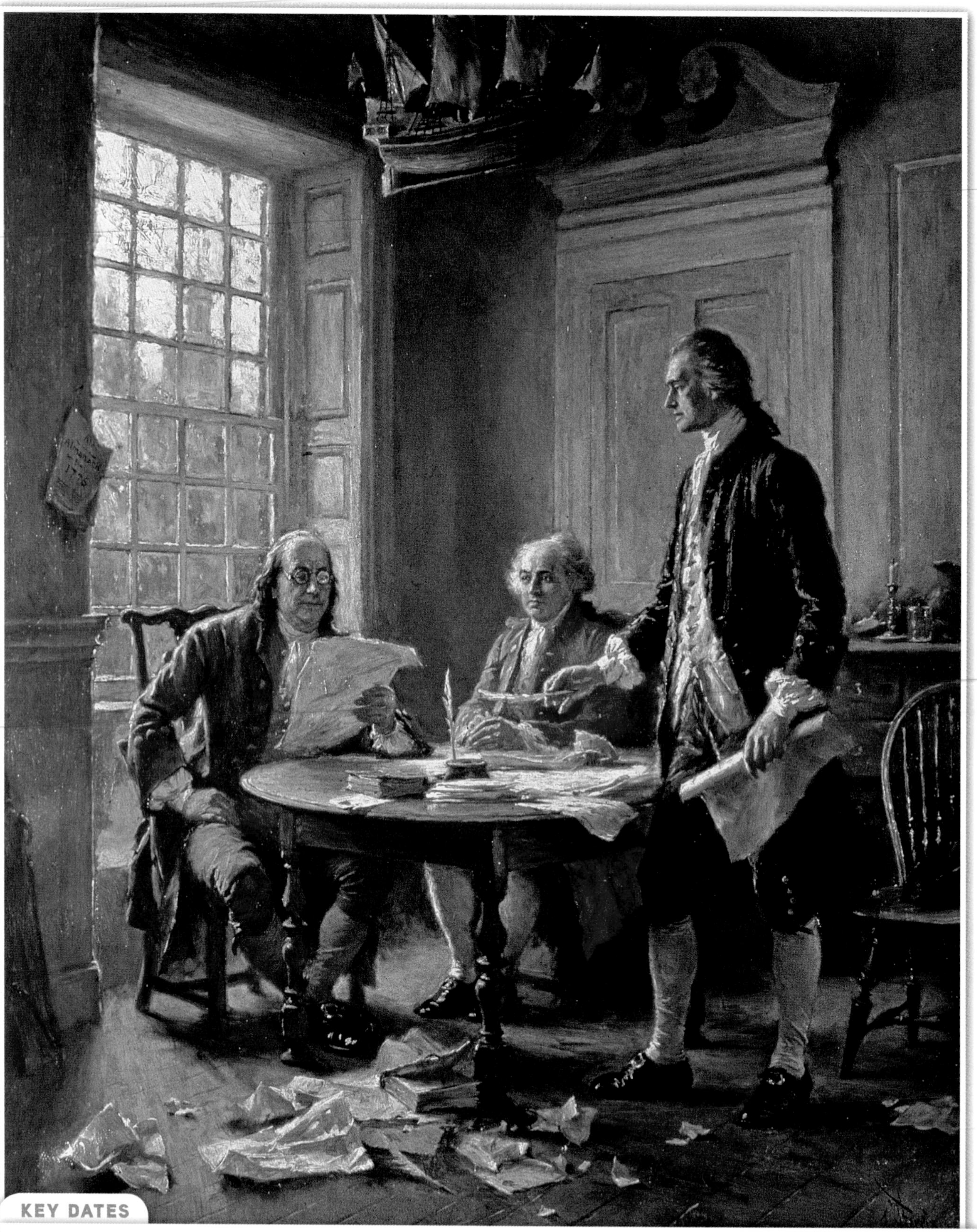

KEY DATES

1675
Chief Metacomet, also known as King Philip, leads Indians to fight against colonists.

1682
William Penn, proprietor of Pennsylvania, arrives in the town of Philadelphia.

1759
Brazil expels Jesuits from its lands.

1765
The British Parliament passes the Stamp Act, triggering colonial protests.

THE NEW WORLD

1650–1800

The Old World had a wrenching impact on the New in the late 17th and 18th centuries as European powers vied fiercely for control of colonies. In the process, they overwhelmed Native American societies by introducing their own settlers and millions of African slaves. Spain's empire remained the largest in the New World, with colonies that encompassed most of South America—with the notable exception of Portuguese Brazil—and extended northward through Mexico to Texas, New Mexico, and California. Spain no longer derived as much wealth as it once did from its American possessions, however, and faced sharp competition from the British and French in the Caribbean and Florida. Further challenges to the Spanish empire came from the Portuguese, whose enterprising colonists pushed westward beyond the original border of Brazil, and from Indians of various tribes that stoutly resisted advances by Spanish missionaries and troops.

Costly struggles among European colonial powers at home and abroad helped loosen the grip on their possessions in the New World and led to the American Revolution and other uprisings.

In North America, France and Britain engaged in a struggle for supremacy that culminated in the French and Indian War (1754–1763), an extension of the Seven Years' War in Europe. The British had far more settlers in their thriving colonies along the Atlantic coast than the French did in Canada. But French explorers and traders forged alliances with Indian tribes extending from the St. Lawrence River valley and the Great Lakes region southward along the Mississippi River to the port of New Orleans. Those tribes joined the French in opposing British colonists when they advanced into northern New England or pushed westward beyond the Appalachian Mountains. In 1763, however, the British defeated the French and forced them to give up their Canadian lands.

Anglo-American colonists then turned against Britain after it imposed taxes on them to recover the heavy expenses of the French and Indian War. During the American Revolution (1775–1783), France and its ally Spain backed the rebellious colonists against the British, hoping to advance their own imperial interests at Britain's expense. In the long run, however, no European power benefited from the victory of the fledgling United States, whose successful struggle for independence encouraged uprisings against colonial rulers elsewhere.

OPPOSITE: Benjamin Franklin, John Adams, and Thomas Jefferson work on the Declaration of Independence.

1774–1775
The First Continental Congress convenes in Philadelphia.

1781
General George Washington, aided by French forces, wins a decisive victory over the British at Yorktown, Virginia.

1788
The states ratify the U.S. Constitution.

1789
Americans elect George Washington as the nation's first president.

SEE ALSO | NEW WORLD ORDER: PAGE 310

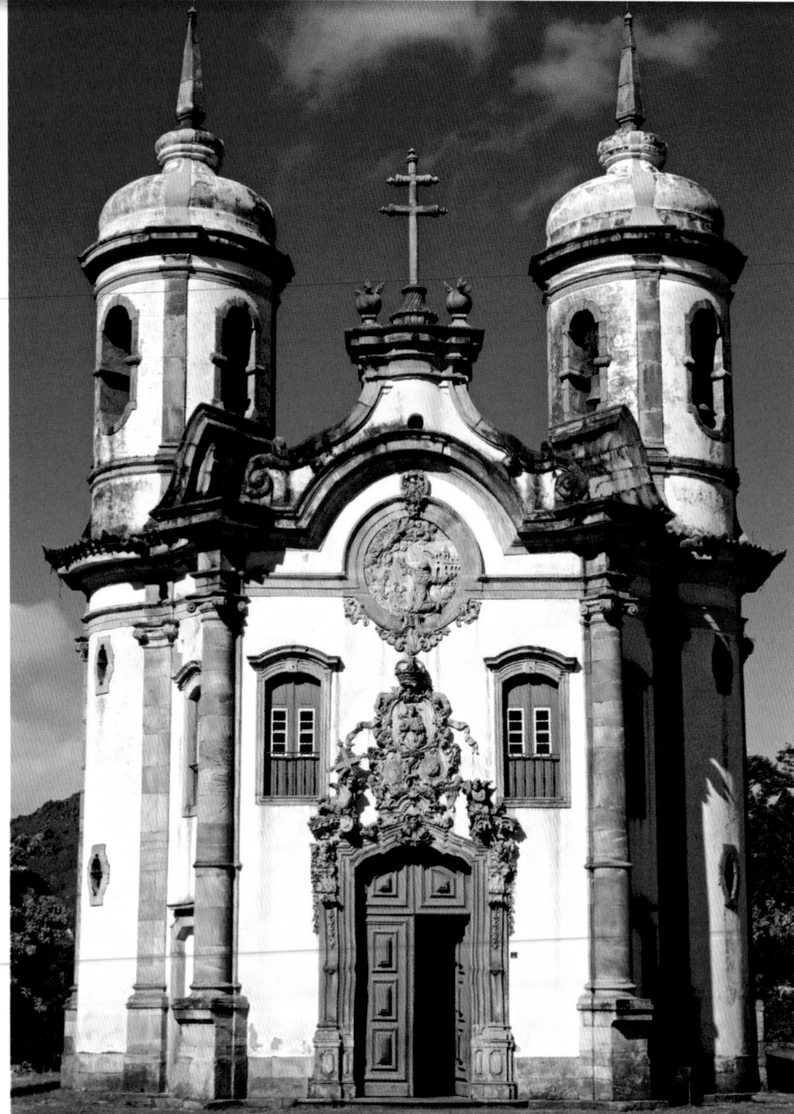
The 18th-century church of Sao Francisco de Assis, Ouro Preto, Brazil

COLONIES NEW SOCIETIES

Unlike British colonists, many of whom immigrated to the New World as families, early Spanish and Portuguese colonists were predominantly male and often took as partners Indian or African women, producing offspring of mixed race known as mestizos (part Indian) or mulattos (part African). Some wealthy planters, merchants, or officials brought wives with them from Europe or were joined by their wives after they became established in the colonies. Their offspring were known as criollos and formed the elite of Latin American society.

No country in the region had a more diverse population than Brazil, where nearly four million Africans were imported as slaves during colonial times. Many worked originally on sugarcane plantations near the coast, but others later toiled in gold or diamond mines operated by Portuguese prospectors who pushed inland during the 1700s. Indians were also enslaved by the Portuguese

> The last Spanish colony established in the New World was Alta California, founded in 1769 and annexed by the United States in 1848.

THE NEW WORLD — VIPs

Benjamin Franklin, 1706–1790
Scientist, writer, and a founding father of the United States

Chief Pontiac, 1720–1769
Ottowa leader of Indian rebellion

George Washington, 1732–1799 Commander of the Continental Army and first president of the United States

John Adams, 1735–1826
Statesman who backed the Declaration of Independence

James Madison, 1751–1836
Fourth president of the United States and one of the drafters of the U.S. Constitution

> *"The inhabitants of Lima are composed of whites, or Spaniards, Negroes, Indians, Mestizos, and other castes, proceeding from the mixture of all three."* —JORGE JUAN AND ANTONIO DE ULLOA

VOICES

SOR JUANA HAIR VS. LATIN

"I began to study Latin grammar, in which I believe I had fewer than twenty lessons. And so intense was my interest, that although in women (and especially in the very flowering of youth) the natural adornment of the hair is so valued, I would cut off four to six finger-lengths of my hair, measuring how long it had been before. And I made myself a rule that if by the time it had grown back to the same length I did not know this or that thing that I intended to study, then I would cut my hair off again to punish my dullness."

—FROM A 1691 LETTER BY MEXICAN NUN AND POET SOR JUANA INÉS DE LA CRUZ TO THE BISHOP OF PUEBLA, WHO HAD CRITICIZED HER FOR PURSUING SECULAR STUDIES

SOR JUANA INÉS DE LA CRUZ

in raids called *bandeiras*. Jesuit missionaries tried to shield Indians under their care from exploitation, but growing resentment of their power led to their expulsion from Brazil in 1759. Catholicism continued to loom large in colonial Latin America. Friars of other orders took over Jesuit missions, and a Catholic church or cathedral dominated nearly every town or city square from Cuba to Peru.

THE TAKEAWAY: Interaction between European colonists, Africans, and Indians produced new societies in Latin America.

Portugal's powerful minister, the Marques de Pombal, took control of Brazil's lucrative trade.

"We have seen Indians in immense numbers, and all those on this coast of the Pacific contrive to make a good subsistence on various seeds, and by fishing." —FATHER JUNIPERO SERRA

SEE ALSO | BREAKING BONDS: PAGE 252

COLONIES BRITISH NORTH AND SOUTH

William Penn makes a treaty with the Delaware Indians in November 1683.

The colonies founded in North America by English settlers varied greatly in climate, terrain, and culture. New England was defined by its harsh winters and rugged landscape—which favored small farms rather than large plantations—and by its stern Puritan traditions. Puritanism made New Englanders diligent and studious, leading to the founding of colleges intended primarily to educate ministers, such as Harvard (established 1636) and Yale (1701). But they also lived in a time of considerable superstition and weren't above falling prey to rumor and hysteria, leading to the execution of suspected witches in Salem, Massachusetts, and other towns in the late 1600s.

Colonies along the mid-Atlantic coast were defined by broad estuaries such as the Hudson and Delaware Rivers and Chesapeake Bay, which favored maritime commerce and attracted large populations to the region's ports. New York, seized by England from Dutch colonists in 1664, developed into one of the largest cities in British America. It was surpassed only by Philadelphia, founded in 1682 by William Penn, an English Quaker who welcomed to his colony people of other faiths and nationalities. Philadelphia's tradition of open-mindedness was epitomized by Benjamin Franklin, who set up shop there as a printer in the 1720s and became a celebrated author, wit, scientist, and Enlightenment philosopher.

Colonies in the South were defined by their semitropical

"Any government is free to the people under it where the laws rule and the people are a party to the laws."

—WILLIAM PENN

climate and marshy coastal areas that favored a plantation economy based on cash crops like rice, cotton, and tobacco. In the late 1600s, plantation owners shifted from employing white indentured servants to purchasing slaves from Africa or the West Indies, favored because they remained the property of their owners and were relatively immune to malaria and other diseases. Slave owning planters dominated the southern coast, but the mountainous interior was home to poor, land-hungry white settlers who ventured beyond the Appalachians in defiance of Indian tribes and colonial authorities. Bacon's Rebellion, an uprising by frontiersmen against Virginia's governor in 1676, was one of many disturbances triggered by the determination of Anglo-Americans to expand westward.

By 1750, there were more than a million British colonists in North America but only about 20,000 French colonists in Canada.

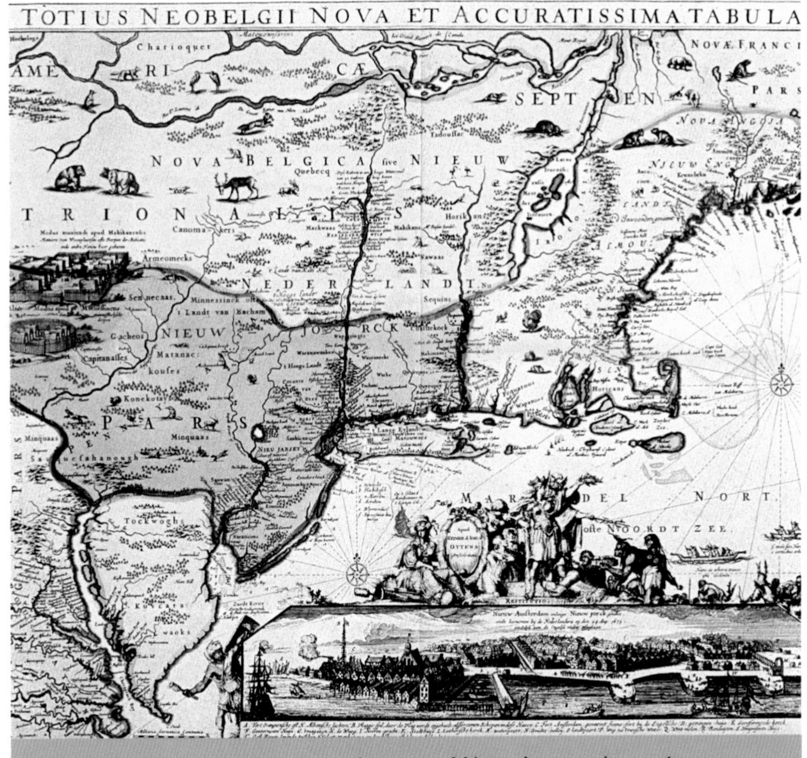

A map of the Dutch settlement of New Amsterdam, 1673.

THE TAKEAWAY: America's colonies had differences that lingered even after nationhood.

VOICES

ANN PUTNAM WITCH TRIALS

"The Deposition of Ann Putnam junior who testifieth and saith that on the 13'th March 1691/92 I saw the Apparition of Goody Nurse: and she did immediately afflict me but I did not know what her name was then: tho I knew where she used to sit in our Meeting house: but since that she hath greviously afflicted me by biting pinching and pricking me: urging me to write in her book and also on the 24'th of March being the day of her examination I was greviously tortured by her during the time of her examination and also several times since and also during the time of her examination I saw the Apparition of Rebekah Nurse go and hurt the bodies of Mercy Lewes Mary Wolcott Elizabeth Hubbard and Abigail Williams."

—TESTIMONY AGAINST REBECCA NURSE, 1692 (SOME SPELLING MODERNIZED)

ACCUSED WITCH, SALEM

"Here individuals of all nations are melted into a new race of men, whose labors and posterity will one day cause great changes in the world." —JOHN HECTOR ST. JOHN

SEE ALSO | EMPIRES RISING: PAGE 342

CONFLICTS INDIAN WARS

Chief Pontiac incites other Indian tribes to fight the British.

European colonists throughout North America faced determined opposition from the Indians they imposed on, including Pueblos in New Mexico, who ousted Spanish settlers there temporarily in the late 1600s. New Englanders faced a similar challenge in 1675 when Chief Metacomet, also known as King Philip, led Indians against settlers. Hundreds of colonists died before the English won King Philip's War with the help of Iroquois allies.

{ Many Acadians—French from Nova Scotia—moved to Louisiana and became known as Cajuns. }

Many tribes turned against the British in the French and Indian War, which began in 1754 when British troops and Virginia militia, led by George Washington, were routed at Fort Necessity by a mixed force of French soldiers and tribal warriors.

BRITISH GENERAL BRADDOCK

Even after the French abandoned Canada in 1763, Indians led by Chief Pontiac of the Ottawa tribe carried on the fight. But the British forced Pontiac to come to terms and tried to avoid further conflict by limiting westward settlement—a boundary scorned by colonists.

THE TAKEAWAY: The taking of tribal lands spurred most Indian wars in North America.

"No one has a right to remove us, because we were the first owners. The Great Spirit above has appointed this place for us, on which to light our fires, and here we shall remain." —TECUMSEH

VOICES

WILLIAM BYRD

WILLIAM BYRD A DAY IN JUNE

"June 10, 1709. I rose at 5 o'clock this morning but could not read anything because of Captain Keeling, but I played at billiards with him and won half a crown of him and the Doctor. George B-th brought home my boy Eugene. . . . In the evening I took a walk about the plantation. Eugene was whipped for running away and had the [bit] put on him. I said my prayers and had good health, good thought, and good humor, thanks be to God Almighty."

—ENTRY FROM VIRGINIA PLANTER WILLIAM BYRD'S DIARY

CLASS & SOCIETY A FLUID SOCIETY

Unlike Europe, British colonies in America had few aristocrats of ancient pedigree. Even the lofty Calverts who founded Maryland owed their royal charter to a gentleman without rank, George Calvert, who earned a knighthood and the title First Baron of Baltimore by serving the crown. Some leading families in Maryland, Virginia, and other southern colonies were of aristocratic origins, but others achieved distinction through their own efforts. For instance, middle-class adventurer William Byrd, the son of a London goldsmith, obtained a grant of 1,200 acres in Virginia and founded a dynasty of prominent slave owners and politicians. Southern planters formed an elite distinct from the upper class in the North, where some merchants owned slaves but most prospered by hiring free labor for low wages.

Quakers had communities in Rhode Island, North Carolina, Pennsylvania, and western New Jersey.

Poor people could hope for advancement in the fast-growing colonies. Free people of all ranks could give thanks that they were not slaves, whose plight was publicized in compelling narratives like that of Olaudah Equiano, captured in Africa as a boy and sold to one master after another before he purchased his liberty in Philadelphia in 1766 with his earnings as a clerk.

> In large parts of the South, blacks came to outnumber whites and developed a distinct and separate culture.

TOBACCO LABEL

THE TAKEAWAY: Colonial classes were fluid, enabling some at the bottom to rise.

"Surely this traffic cannot be good, which spreads like a pestilence, and taints what it touches! Which violates that first natural right of mankind, equality and independency!" —OLAUDAH EQUIANO

U.S. CONSTITUTION

James Madison, "father of the U.S. Constitution," agreed with Federalist leader Alexander Hamilton that the United States needed a government strong enough to raise taxes, pay debts, and keep the nation secure. But unlike Hamilton's plan, which called for a government resembling Britain's constitutional monarchy, the U.S. Constitution limited the president to a four-year term but allowed him to run for reelection.

GEORGE WASHINGTON Two years before he was chosen first president of the United States, George Washington was unanimously elected to become the president of the Philadelphia Constitutional Convention.

Madison worried that defining citizens' liberties might limit them. But fervent protests from Antifederalists that the president or Congress might trample on their rights led Madison and other Founders to propose the Bill of Rights, enacted as the first ten amendments to the Constitution. These guaranteed Americans freedom of religion and expression, the right to bear arms, and other legal protections.

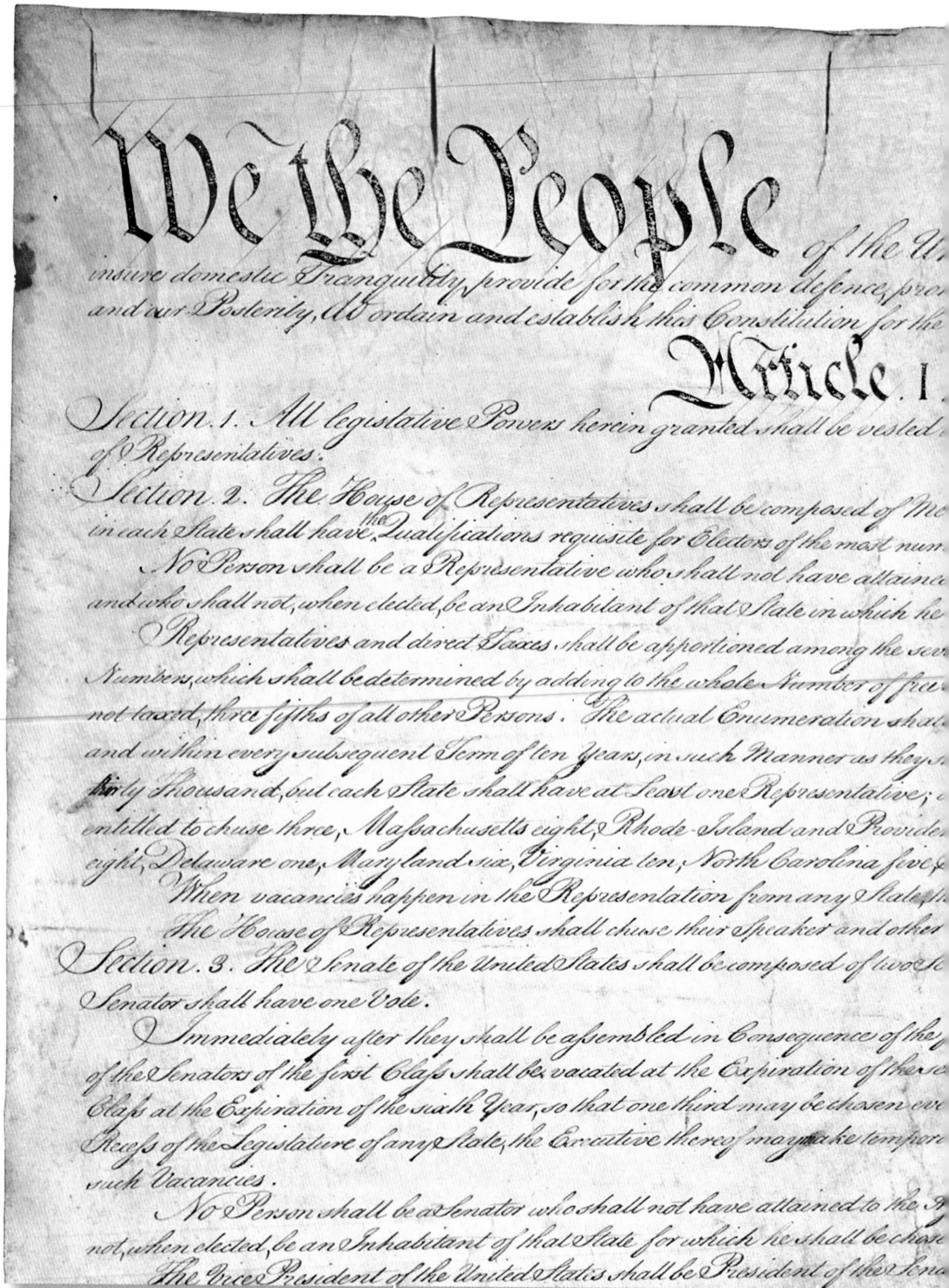

We the People

"The President, Vice President and all civil Officers of the United States, shall be removed from Office on Impeachment for, and Conviction of, Treason, Bribery, or other high Crimes and Misdemeanors."

"The Congress shall have Power to lay and collect Taxes, Duties, Imposts and Excises, to pay the Debts and provide for the common Defence and general Welfare of the United States; but all Duties, Imposts and Excises shall be uniform throughout the United States."

ORIGINAL DRAFT Handwritten on parchment by Pennsylvania general assembly clerk Jacob Shallus, the original draft of the Constitution has weathered the centuries well.

> "The Senate of the United States shall be composed of two Senators from each State, chosen by the Legislature thereof for six Years; and each Senator shall have one Vote."

d States, in Order to form a more perfect Union, establish Justice,
the general Welfare, and secure the Blessings of Liberty to ourselves
ited States of America.

Congress of the United States, which shall consist of a Senate and House

rs chosen every second Year by the People of the several States, and the Electors
s Branch of the State Legislature.
the Age of twenty five Years, and been seven Years a Citizen of the United States,
ll be chosen.
States which may be included within this Union, according to their respective
ons, including those bound to Service for a Term of Years, and excluding Indians
made within three Years after the first Meeting of the Congress of the United States,
by Law direct. The Number of Representatives shall not exceed one for every
until such enumeration shall be made, the State of New Hampshire shall be
Plantations one, Connecticut five, New York six, New Jersey four, Pennsylvania
th Carolina five, and Georgia three.
ecutive Authority thereof shall issue Writs of Election to fill such Vacancies.
ers; and shall have the sole Power of Impeachment.
ons from each State, chosen by the Legislature thereof, for six Years; and each

t Election, they shall be divided as equally as may be into three Classes. The Seats
d Year, of the second Class at the Expiration of the fourth Year, and of the third
econd Year; and if Vacancies happen by Resignation, or otherwise, during the
Appointments until the next Meeting of the Legislature, which shall then fill

thirty Years, and been nine Years a Citizen of the United States, and who shall

ut shall have no Vote, unless they be equally divided.

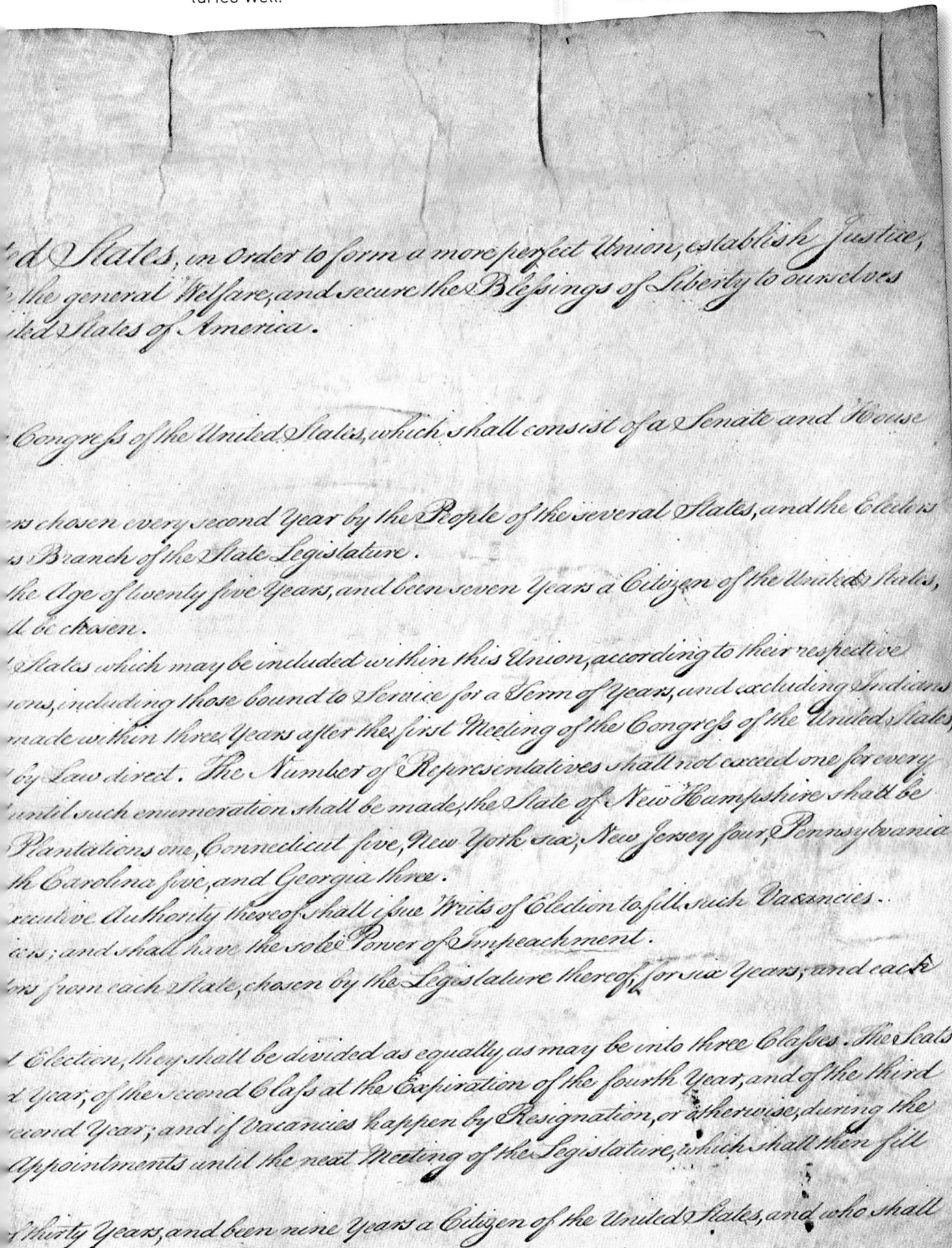

> "Treason against the United States, shall consist only in levying War against them, or in adhering to their Enemies, giving them Aid and Comfort. No Person shall be convicted of Treason unless on the Testimony of two Witnesses to the same overt Act, or on Confession in open Court."

SIGNED AND RATIFIED The four-page document was signed on September 17, 1787, by 39 of the constitutional convention's delegates. The constitution was ratified by the required nine states on June 21, 1788.

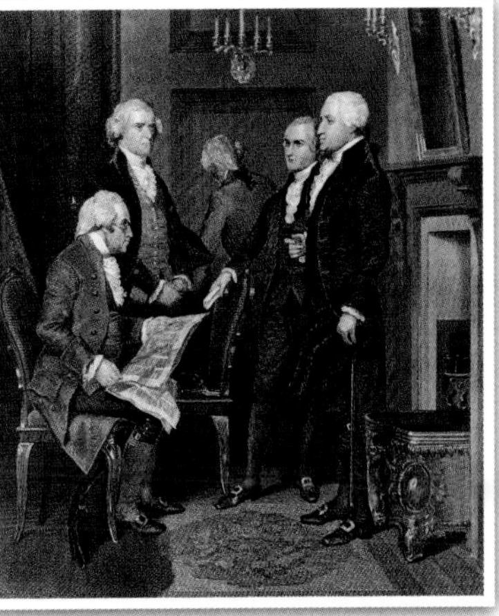

THE FIRST CABINET George Washington's first presidential Cabinet consisted of Henry Knox, Secretary of War; Thomas Jefferson, Secretary of State; Edmund Jennings Randolph, Attorney General; and Alexander Hamilton, Secretary of the Treasury. Article Two of the Constitution states that the president may appoint "public Ministers and Consuls," with the advice and consent of the Senate.

THE PREAMBLE The Constitution begins with a statement of purpose: "We the People of the United States, in Order to form a more perfect Union, establish Justice, insure domestic Tranquility, provide for the common defence, promote the general Welfare, and secure the Blessings of Liberty to ourselves and our Posterity, do ordain and establish this Constitution for the United States of America."

BILL OF RIGHTS

Twelve amendments were originally proposed for the Constitution in 1789; two, which concerned constituents and compensation, were not approved, but the other ten became the Bill of Rights. Among them:

Amendment I Congress shall make no law respecting an establishment of religion, or prohibiting the free exercise thereof; or abridging the freedom of speech, or of the press; or the right of the people peaceably to assemble, and to petition the Government for a redress of grievances.

Amendment X The powers not delegated to the United States by the Constitution, nor prohibited by it to the States, are reserved to the States respectively, or to the people.

CONFLICTS AMERICAN REVOLUTION

The American Revolution stemmed from many grievances, among them the British practice of forcing colonists to serve as soldiers and to house troops in their homes during the French and Indian War. American anger mounted in 1765 when Parliament passed the Stamp Act, which taxed newspapers to cover war debts—a bill denounced by orator Patrick Henry as taxation without representation. The hotbed of resistance was Massachusetts, where rebels drew deadly fire from British troops in 1770, dumped tea into Boston Harbor to protest taxation in 1773, and ignited the Revolutionary War in 1775 at Concord, Lexington, and Bunker Hill. Urged on by John Adams of Massachusetts, the Continental Congress approved the Declaration of Independence in Philadelphia on July 4, 1776. After initial setbacks, American forces achieved a stunning triumph at Saratoga, New York, in October 1777. Aided by French forces, in October 1781, Commander in Chief George Washington won a decisive victory at Yorktown, Virginia, leading Britain to recognize American independence in 1783.

BEN FRANKLIN

THE TAKEAWAY: Stretched thin by other wars, Britain knew defeat at the hands of rebellious American colonists.

American troops fire on the British at the Battle of Lexington, 1775; painting by Wollen.

"The basis of our political system is the right of the people to make and to alter their constitutions of government." —GEORGE WASHINGTON

SEE ALSO | NEW WORLD ORDER: PAGE 314

VOICES

ABIGAIL ADAMS

ABIGAIL ADAMS REJOICING

"When Col. Crafts read from the Belcona of the State House the Proclamation, great attention was given to every word. As soon as he ended, the cry from the Belcona, was God Save our American States and then 3 cheers which rended the air, the Bells rang, the privateers fired, the forts and Batteries, the cannon were discharged, the platoons followed and every face appeard joyfull. . . . After dinner the kings arms were taken down from the State House and every vestage of him from every place in which it appeard and burnt in King Street." —FROM A LETTER TO JOHN ADAMS, JULY 21, 1776

NATIONS NEW RULES

After defying King George III, Americans were wary of rulers and approved Articles of Confederation that left the country with a weak legislature and no chief executive. Tasks such as paying off the nation's war debt, however, required a stronger federal government, advocated by Federalists like Alexander Hamilton. They pushed for the Constitutional Convention that met in Philadelphia in 1787 to form "a more perfect union." With the help of Benjamin Franklin, Federalists and Antifederalists—who sought to limit federal power—compromised by drawing up a Constitution that balanced the tripartite powers of the president, the Congress, and the Supreme Court. The first U.S. Congress—convened in 1789, the same year that the country's first president, George Washington, was elected—added a Bill of Rights.

Almanac featuring George Washington

THE TAKEAWAY: The new government was founded on a balance of powers.

CONNECTIONS THE U.S. CONSTITUTION

In its original form, the U.S. Constitution did not guarantee each citizen a vote. But this remarkable document created a republic based on the principle that government should do what the public demands, not what a monarch decrees. Its language inspired the revolutionary French Republic in the 1790s and served as a model for the constitutions of many republics to the present day, including Poland, Mexico, and the Cherokee nation, which formed its own constitutional government in the 1820s, but lost its independence when the U.S. Supreme Court ruled that it lacked the status of foreign nations.

CEREMONY HONORING SPANISH CONSTITUTION

"Our Constitution is in actual operation; everything appears to promise that it will last; but in this world nothing is certain but death and taxes." —BENJAMIN FRANKLIN

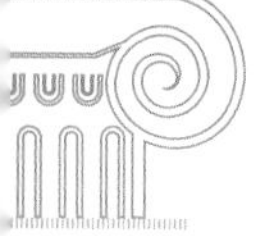

CONNECTIONS TIME LINE

1650–1800

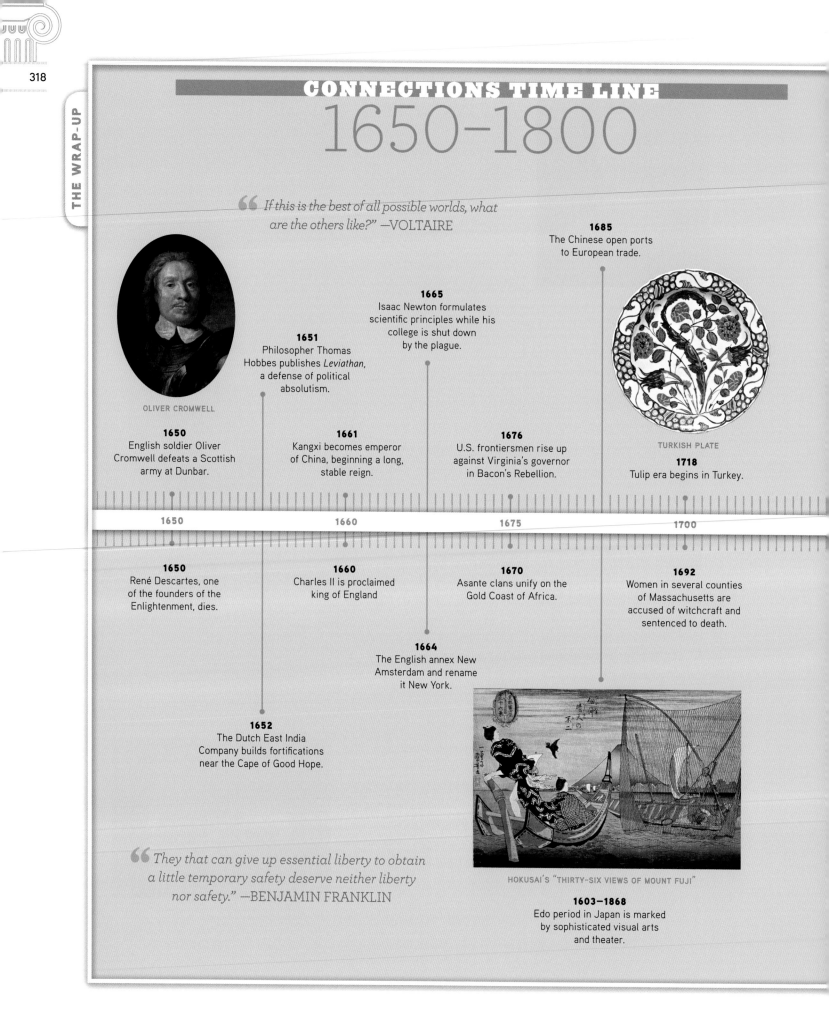

"If this is the best of all possible worlds, what are the others like?" —VOLTAIRE

OLIVER CROMWELL

1650
English soldier Oliver Cromwell defeats a Scottish army at Dunbar.

1651
Philosopher Thomas Hobbes publishes *Leviathan,* a defense of political absolutism.

1661
Kangxi becomes emperor of China, beginning a long, stable reign.

1665
Isaac Newton formulates scientific principles while his college is shut down by the plague.

1676
U.S. frontiersmen rise up against Virginia's governor in Bacon's Rebellion.

1685
The Chinese open ports to European trade.

TURKISH PLATE

1718
Tulip era begins in Turkey.

1650 · 1660 · 1675 · 1700

1650
René Descartes, one of the founders of the Enlightenment, dies.

1652
The Dutch East India Company builds fortifications near the Cape of Good Hope.

1660
Charles II is proclaimed king of England

1664
The English annex New Amsterdam and rename it New York.

1670
Asante clans unify on the Gold Coast of Africa.

1692
Women in several counties of Massachusetts are accused of witchcraft and sentenced to death.

HOKUSAI'S "THIRTY-SIX VIEWS OF MOUNT FUJI"

1603–1868
Edo period in Japan is marked by sophisticated visual arts and theater.

"They that can give up essential liberty to obtain a little temporary safety deserve neither liberty nor safety." —BENJAMIN FRANKLIN

QING PORCELAIN BUDDHA

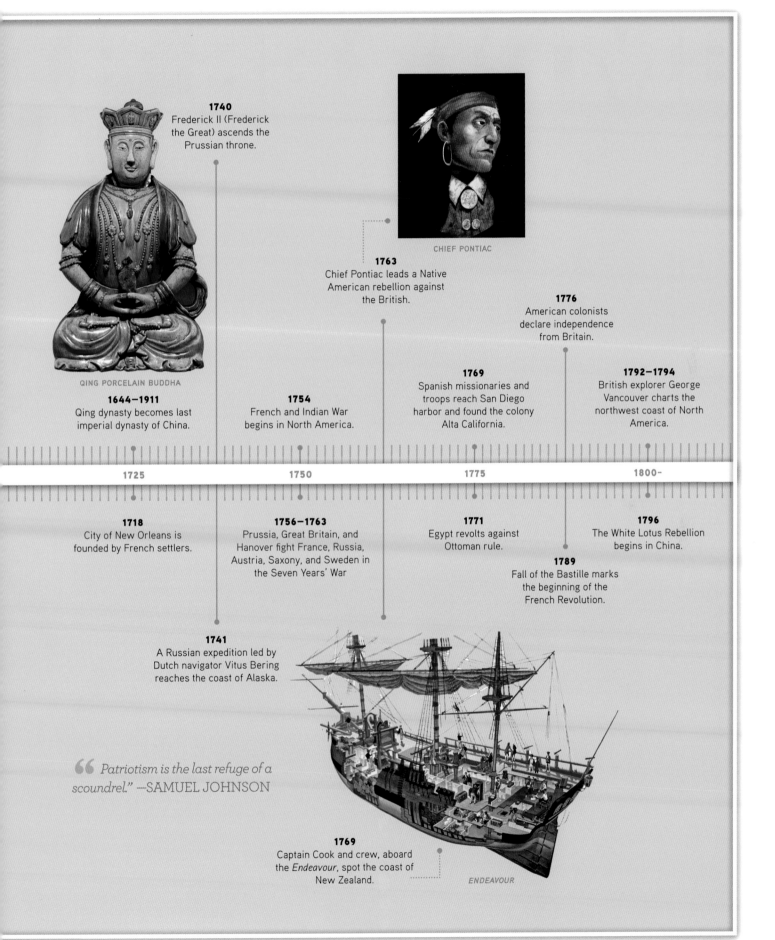

1740
Frederick II (Frederick the Great) ascends the Prussian throne.

CHIEF PONTIAC

1763
Chief Pontiac leads a Native American rebellion against the British.

1776
American colonists declare independence from Britain.

1644–1911
Qing dynasty becomes last imperial dynasty of China.

1754
French and Indian War begins in North America.

1769
Spanish missionaries and troops reach San Diego harbor and found the colony Alta California.

1792–1794
British explorer George Vancouver charts the northwest coast of North America.

1725 | 1750 | 1775 | 1800–

1718
City of New Orleans is founded by French settlers.

1756–1763
Prussia, Great Britain, and Hanover fight France, Russia, Austria, Saxony, and Sweden in the Seven Years' War

1771
Egypt revolts against Ottoman rule.

1796
The White Lotus Rebellion begins in China.

1789
Fall of the Bastille marks the beginning of the French Revolution.

1741
A Russian expedition led by Dutch navigator Vitus Bering reaches the coast of Alaska.

"Patriotism is the last refuge of a scoundrel." —SAMUEL JOHNSON

1769
Captain Cook and crew, aboard the *Endeavour*, spot the coast of New Zealand.

ENDEAVOUR

EMPIRES RI

SING

CHRONICLES OF THE MACHINE AGE

1800–1900

CHAPTER

Delacroix's "Liberty Leading the People" commemorates an 1830 uprising.

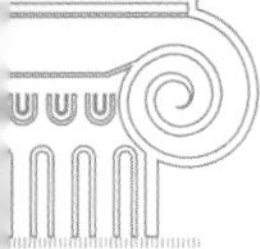

SEE ALSO | **EMPIRES RISING:** PAGE 324

KEY DATES

1804
Napoleon becomes emperor of France.

1815
Napoleon is defeated for the last time at Waterloo.

1848
Marx and Engels write *The Communist Manifesto.*

1853–1856
Crimean War is fought between Russia and a British and French alliance.

EUROPE

1800–1900

During the 19th century, European nations grew stronger economically and politically and brought much of the rest of the world under their control or influence. The Enlightenment that spread across Europe in the 1700s had encouraged people to think of themselves not as subjects but as citizens. That concept helped ignite the French Revolution, which in turn spawned the regime of Napoleon Bonaparte, who proclaimed himself emperor in 1804 but affirmed the legal rights of French citizens in his Napoleonic Code. Napoleon was the first modern ruler to fully exploit nationalism and assemble a great citizen army. His troops were devoted to him but even more devoted to France, demonstrating their patriotism in one punishing battle after another. Yet ultimately, Napoleon the conqueror asked too much of his troops and went down to defeat. At the Congress of Vienna in 1815, the victorious powers that crushed Napoleon tried to restore the old order in Europe and prop up imperial dynasties like the Habsburgs in Austria and the Romanovs in Russia, who opposed the national aspirations of ethnic groups within and along their borders. Nationalistic fervor could not long be suppressed, however. Over the next century, the map of Europe would be radically redrawn as those old empires declined and new nations such as Italy and Germany (embracing Prussia and other Germanic states that it absorbed) emerged to rival France and Great Britain.

European power reached around the globe in the 19th century as Great Britain, France, Germany, and other nations industrialized and flexed their muscles in Africa and Asia.

Nationalism, along with industrialism and imperialism, transformed Europe and the world at large. The advantage Britain gained as the first country to industrialize was enhanced by political reforms that gave British citizens a greater say in their government and greater pride in their empire. Spreading out around the globe as merchants, engineers, soldiers, and settlers, they brought large parts of Africa and Asia under their authority, more than offsetting the loss of colonies in the Americas.

France took longer to industrialize and stabilize politically, but by the mid-1800s it too was a major imperial power. Germany and other industrialized nations envied the sprawling British and French empires and sought their own colonies and spheres of influence, fueling global rivalries that led to the devastating world wars of the 20th century.

OPPOSITE: English scientist Michael Faraday's discoveries about electricity fed the industrial revolution.

1857
Britain takes complete control of India after the Sepoy Rebellion.

1870
Kingdom of Italy is finally united under Victor Emmanuel II.

1871
German Empire declared at Versailles by King William I of Prussia.

1902
Britain defeats Boer republics in South Africa.

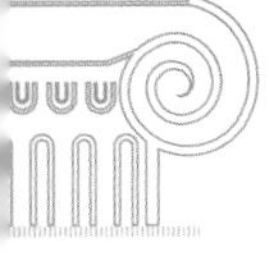

LEADERS NAPOLEON'S LEGACY

Born on the French island of Corsica, Napoleon Bonaparte launched his military career as a defender of the revolutionary French Republic before seizing power in a coup in 1799. Weary of turmoil and terror, French citizens welcomed his dictatorial regime and in 1804 voted to approve Napoleon as their emperor by a huge margin. He retained their loyalty by promising them equality under the law, promoting public education, and leading his Grand Army to smashing victories over Austria, Prussia, and Russia. The British remained defiant, however, and were secure against invasion after shattering the French fleet at Trafalgar in 1805.

When Tsar Alexander I turned against France and sided with Britain, Napoleon invaded Russia in 1812 and advanced on Moscow. The Russians abandoned and burned their capital, depriving French troops of food and shelter as winter closed in. More than 500,000 of Napoleon's 600,000 men perished

VIPs

EUROPE

Napoleon Bonaparte, 1769–1821
French general who conquered much of Europe

Klemens von Metternich, 1773–1859
Powerful Austrian minister

Giuseppe Mazzini, 1805–1872
Champion of Italian unity and founder of Young Italy society

Karl Marx, 1818–1883
German revolutionary and economist

Louis Pasteur, 1822–1895
French biochemist who discovered that microorganisms cause disease.

The Battle of Waterloo, in 1815, ended 23 years of war between Napoleonic France and other European nations.

> *"I have heard Madame Bonaparte say that her husband was in the constant habit of poring over the list of what are called the cadres of the army at night before he slept."* —MADAME DE RÉMUSAT

SEE ALSO | EMPIRES RISING: PAGE 320

VOICES

VICTOR HUGO PURSUED BY DEATH

VICTOR HUGO

"The massacre radiated—a word horribly true—from the boulevard into all the streets. It was a devil-fish stretching out its feelers. Flight? Why? Concealment? To what purpose? Death ran after you quicker than you could fly. In the Rue Pagevein a soldier said to a passer-by, 'What are you doing here?' 'I am going home.' The soldier kills the passer-by. In the Rue des Marais they kill four young men in their own courtyard. Colonel Espinasse exclaimed, 'After the bayonet, cannon!' Colonel Rochefort exclaimed, 'Thrust, bleed, slash!' and he added, 'It is an economy of powder and noise.'"

—FROM *THE HISTORY OF A CRIME*, VICTOR HUGO, 1852

in that disastrous campaign. After fleeing to the island of Elba in 1814, he returned a year later to rally his forces, but was finally defeated at Waterloo by Britain's Duke of Wellington.

When Napoleon fell, the French monarchy was restored but failed to gain broad support. In 1830 Parisians took to the streets to denounce the repressive King Charles X, forcing him to abdicate in favor of his cousin, Louis-Philippe, whose modest constitutional reforms did not satisfy them either. In 1848 revolutionaries overthrew Louis-Philippe and established the Second Republic. Louis-Napoleon Bonaparte, nephew of the conqueror, was elected president of France. Barred from running for reelection, he carried out a coup in December 1851.

{ Author Victor Hugo went into exile after Louis-Napoleon's coup and did not return until he was deposed. }

Louis-Philippe of France leaves the Tuileries Palace in 1848.

Like his uncle before him, Louis-Napoleon dispensed with republicanism and proclaimed himself emperor, reigning as Napoleon III.

Napoleon III's regime ended in disgrace in 1870 when German forces, under Prussian leadership, invaded France and captured him and his army. From that debacle emerged the enduring Third Republic, equipped with a new constitution that placed power firmly in the hands of elected leaders. Like Britain, France began forcefully expanding its overseas empire, which grew to include Algeria, Tunisia, French West Africa, Indochina, Tahiti, and other colonies.

THE TAKEAWAY: France struggled to reconcile its longing for Napoleonic glory with its republican principles.

"I go, but you, my friends, will continue to serve France. Her happiness was my only thought. It will still be the object of my wishes." —NAPOLEON BONAPARTE

SEE ALSO | EMPIRES RISING: PAGE 332

ECONOMY BRITAIN INDUSTRIALIZES

Britain's navy (shown here fighting a French ship in 1801) helped establish the country's power.

By defeating Napoleon, Britain surpassed its longtime rival France and went on to become the world's leading imperial power. Britain's dominant position rested on its naval might and its vast industrial output. Few people living in the British Isles benefited from the industrial revolution in its early stages, however. Working conditions in factories and coal mines were so dismal and dangerous that acts of Parliament prohibiting labor by children under the age of nine and limiting the workweek to six 12-hour days were considered major reforms. Many rural people remained poor and subject to natural disasters like the ruinous potato blight that caused famine in Ireland in the mid-1800s, claiming up to a million lives and leading perhaps two million to emigrate.

In the long run, however, industrialization and investment in businesses at home and abroad raised the standard of living in Britain substantially and bolstered the British Empire. Firms like the British East India Company and British South Africa Company dominated foreign countries economically and cleared the way for the British government to take over those colonies, some of which later became self-governing dominions or commonwealths. By the late 1800s, the British had colonies or commonwealths on every continent except Antarctica and could boast that the sun never set on their empire.

THE TAKEAWAY: Britain's industrial and military supremacy won it colonies around the globe.

“*In the Manufacture of Woollens, the Scribbling Mill, the Spinning Frame, and the Fly Shuttle, have reduced manual Labour nearly One third.*” —LEEDS CLOTH MERCHANTS

VOICES

BURRITT LIFE DURING THE POTATO FAMINE

"We entered a stinted den by an aperture about three feet high, and found one or two children lying asleep with their eyes open in the straw. Such, at least, was their appearance, for they scarcely winked while we were before them. The father came in and told his pitiful story of want, saying that not a morsel of food had they tasted for 24 hours. He lighted a wisp of straw and showed us one or two more children lying in another nook of the cave. Their mother had died, and he was obliged to leave them alone during most of the day."

—FROM "A JOURNAL OF A VISIT TO SKIBBEREEN AND ITS NEIGHBOURHOOD," ELIHU BURRITT, 1847

POTATO FAMINE RIOT

EMPIRES BRITISH INDIA

In 1857, Indian troops called sepoys rebelled against the East India Company. Among their grievances were suspicions that their powder cartridges—which they had to bite open to load their rifles—were greased with fat from cows and pigs, violating dietary laws of Hindus and Muslims. Many civilians joined the rebellion, which prompted Britain to intervene and take direct control of India.

British troops and officials poured into the country to put down the revolt and impose order, and British engineers oversaw the construction of extensive roads, railways, and telegraph lines.

Advances in communications, education, and medicine helped modernize India, but the British served their own interests as colonizers by extracting cotton and other raw materials from India and using the colony as a market for British goods. Vast amounts of cloth manufactured in Britain were exported to India, for example, stifling that country's production of handwoven textiles in the process.

England's King George V at the head of the 1st Bengal Irregular Cavalry.

{ Britain's Queen Victoria was crowned empress of India in 1876; her son, Edward VII, became emperor. }

Indians were barred from high positions in the army and the civil service, and many resented the suggestion that the British were civilizing them, when their own culture went back thousands of years. The Indian National Congress Party, organized in the 1880s, became a powerful voice for independence in decades to come. Yet Britain would long resist pressure to grant India commonwealth status: As the British Empire's crown jewel, India was too valuable to let go.

THE TAKEAWAY: The populous colony of India remained under British rule for nearly a century.

"(Indians) cannot enter into an Englishman's desire for venting his high spirits on a fine day by killing game of some kind. 'Live and let live' is their rule of conduct." —MONIER MONIER-WILLIAMS

SEE ALSO | THE WORLD AT WAR: PAGE 382

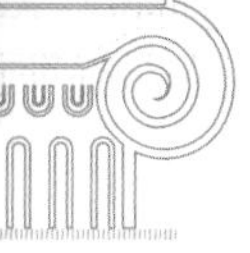

European rulers reorganize territory at the Congress of Vienna following the Napoleonic wars.

EMPIRES GERMANIC NATIONS

At the Congress of Vienna in 1815, Prince Klemens von Metternich of Austria tried to create a balance of power within Europe and prevent the rise of new nations that might threaten the diverse Austrian Empire, made up Germans, Italians, Slavs, and other ethnic groups. He did not want Italians to form their own republic, for example, or Germans to seek union with Austria's old rival, Prussia.

Metternich's plan began to unravel in 1848 when revolutions erupted in many European countries, including Austria and Prussia, which resisted demands for a German republic and set out instead to forge a German Reich (empire). Leading that effort was the ruthless statesman Otto von Bismarck. Drawing on Prussia's industrial and military might, Bismarck engineered wars of expansion that allowed the country to annex other German states and strip France of Alsace and Lorraine. King William I of Prussia crowned his victory over France in 1871 by becoming kaiser (emperor) of Germany, an imposing new nation.

THE TAKEAWAY: Prussia built a new German Empire in the 1800s.

TOWLE BISMARCK RISES TO THE ATTACK

VOICES

OTTO VON BISMARCK

"Irritable, imperious, yet thin-skinned and sensitive, Bismarck never seems to care to conceal the annoyance or anger so easily aroused in his breast by opposition. At such a time you will see him contract his bushy brows, look rapidly around the chamber as if to take stock of his enemies, and finally rise to his feet amid a sudden hush and breathless attention. In a delivery broken, abrupt; spasmodic, with a voice husky and apparently always finding its breath with difficulty,—except at certain moments of high passion, when it rings out strong, clear, and defiant,—with his big hands clutching the shining buttons of his military tunic, or savagely twirling and twisting a paper or a pencil, he proceeds to reply to the attack."

—FROM "BISMARCK IN THE REICHSTAG AND AT HOME," GEORGE TOWLE, 1880

"Union between the monarchs is the basis of the policy which must now be followed to save society from total ruin." —PRINCE KLEMENS VON METTERNICH

Revolutionaries in Milan fight Austrian troops in the streets in 1848.

NATIONS ITALY UNITES

Unlike Germany, hammered together by the conservative monarchist Bismarck, Italy owed its unification partly to the efforts of republicans and revolutionaries like Giuseppe Mazzini and Giuseppe Garibaldi. Exiled in 1831 for opposing Austrian domination of northern Italy, Mazzini formed an organization called Young Italy, dedicated to transforming that politically fractured country, made up of various small kingdoms and papal states, into an Italian republic. In 1848 Mazzini returned to his homeland and joined Garibaldi and other rebels in proclaiming a republic.

Like other European revolutions of the time, that Italian uprising faltered. Garibaldi and others later threw their support to King Victor Emmanuel II of Sardinia-Piedmont and his prime minister, Camillo di Cavour. In 1860, Garibaldi landed in Sicily with a thousand volunteers and eventually met up in Naples with Victor Emmanuel, who was proclaimed Italy's king in 1861. Victor Emmanuel completed Italy's unification in 1870 by seizing the papal states around Rome.

{ After Rome was seized, the Roman Catholic Church was homeless until the Vatican City was established in 1929. }

THE TAKEAWAY: Italy took shape when revolutionaries joined with moderates to unify their country.

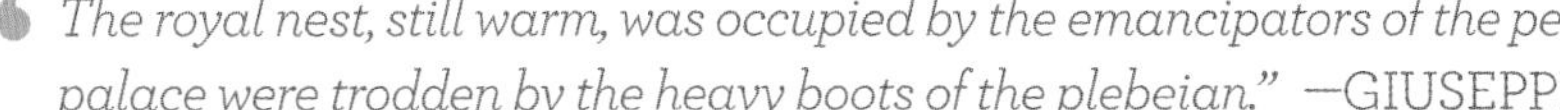

"The royal nest, still warm, was occupied by the emancipators of the people, and the rich carpets of the royal palace were trodden by the heavy boots of the plebeian." —GIUSEPPE GARIBALDI

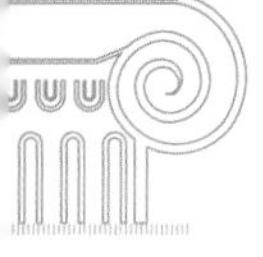

SEE ALSO | EMPIRES RISING: PAGE 325

NATIONS RUSSIA IN TURMOIL

Under Tsar Alexander I, the grandson of Catherine the Great, Russia repulsed Napoleon and expanded its already vast empire by incorporating Poland and Finland. The Russian economy remained backward, however, with little industry and a huge gap between the country's aristocratic elite and its impoverished serfs. When Alexander died in 1825, officers loyal to his brother Constantine—who renounced his claim to the throne but was favored by those seeking reform—rebelled against Alexander's reactionary successor, Tsar Nicholas I. Nicholas crushed the Decembrist Revolt; not until 1861 did his reform-minded son and heir, Alexander II, free Russia's hard-toiling serfs. That emancipation was just one of several steps the new emperor took in order to modernize his realm and catch up with rivals such as Britain and France, which had defeated Russia in the costly Crimean War (1853–1856).

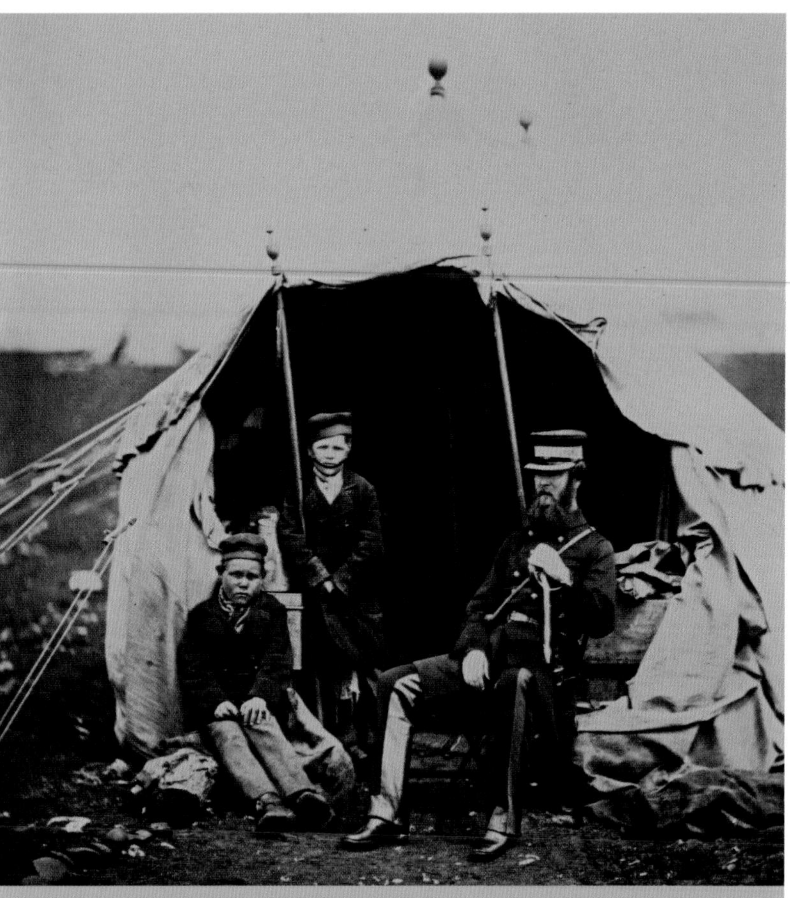

A British officer and two Russian boys at rest in the Crimean War.

Alexander II was considering a constitutional government when he was assassinated by radicals in 1881.

Russian literature flourished in the 19th century with writers such as Leo Tolstoy.

Despite reforms, Russia made slow progress. Its culture reached new heights with the achievements of artists such as author Anton Chekhov and composer Pytor Ilyich Tchaikovsky. But its society was torn by discord; some Russians concluded that their country would never achieve its full potential until the tsarist regime was abolished.

THE TAKEAWAY: After ousting Napoleon, Russia struggled to modernize like western nations.

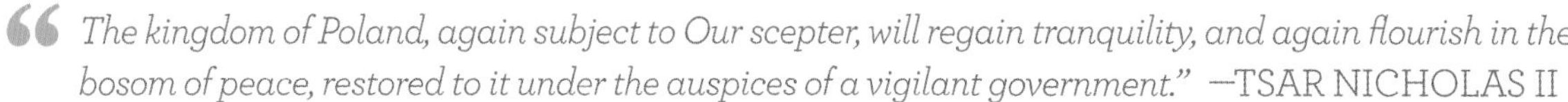

"The kingdom of Poland, again subject to Our scepter, will regain tranquility, and again flourish in the bosom of peace, restored to it under the auspices of a vigilant government." —TSAR NICHOLAS II

CONFLICTS WARFARE EXPANDS

Warfare grew deadlier in the 19th century as armies grew larger and weapons more powerful. In one battle between Napoleon's Grand Army and the Russians at Borodino in 1812, 75,000 men were killed or wounded. The Crimean War—which began when Russia invaded the Ottoman Empire and escalated when France and Britain intervened to block the move—claimed nearly 750,000 lives, many lost to hunger, disease, or infection.

Florence Nightingale modernized nursing after her wartime service.

British and French troops besieged Sevastopol during the Crimean War.

Appalled by the filthy hospital wards, British nurse Florence Nightingale introduced new standards of sanitation.

Advances such as using railroads to carry troops made European armies more efficient later in the 19th century, helping German forces achieve rapid victory over France in the Franco-Prussian War (1870–1871).

THE TAKEAWAY: European warfare shifted from contests between professional soldiers to struggles between nations.

THUMBS UP / THUMBS DOWN

NAPOLEON III 1808–1873

NAPOLEON III

EMPEROR NAPOLEON III OF FRANCE lacked the military genius of his uncle, Napoleon I, but that did not stop him from seeking glory through conquest. By forging an alliance with Britain, long hostile to France, he prevailed over Russia in the Crimean War. His penchant for foreign intrigue later alienated the British, however, and antagonized the strengthening empire of Prussia. In 1870, with his popularity fading, Napoleon III tried to regain his prestige and restore French glory by accompanying his forces into battle against Prussia. Surrounded at Sedan by more than 200,000 German troops, he surrendered along with 83,000 French soldiers. That humiliating defeat caused his downfall and left France and Germany bitter enemies, a rivalry that would later fuel two world wars. **CONCLUSION: THUMBS DOWN.**

It may seem a strange principle to enunciate as the very first requirement in a hospital that it should do the sick no harm." —FLORENCE NIGHTINGALE

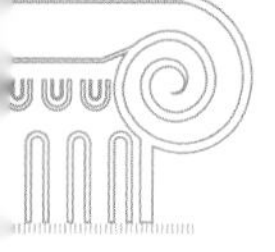

SEE ALSO | THE WORLD AT WAR: PAGE 369

ECONOMY THE INDUSTRIAL REVOLUTION

Factories, such as these ironworks in eastern Europe, spread quickly in the industrial revolution.

The industrial revolution that spread from Great Britain to other nations in the 19th century replaced traditional sources of energy such as water, wind, and horsepower with far more efficient sources. The steam engine, refined by British inventor James Watt in 1769, powered factories, locomotives, and steamships, increasing the speed at which goods were produced and distributed and making industrialists and investors rich. In 1831 another form of energy was harnessed when Michael Faraday of Britain generated electricity by moving a magnet through a coiled wire. That made possible communication by telegraph—using a code devised by American Samuel Morse in 1837—and by telephone, patented in 1876 by Morse's countryman Alexander Graham Bell. Another American, Thomas Alva Edison, helped illuminate the world by perfecting the incandescent lightbulb and forming a company that brought electric power to cities.

In the late 1800s Italian Guglielmo Marconi also used electricity to generate radio waves and send wireless messages to distant receivers. Meanwhile, German engineers Gottlieb Daimler and Rudolf Diesel were devising internal combustion engines fueled by petroleum, revolutionizing transportation at the turn of the century.

At first, many people found the

> Nations that industrialized grew stronger militarily by producing advanced weaponry such as iron battleships.

> *"The blessings which physio-mechanical science has bestowed on society, and the means it has still in store for ameliorating the lot of mankind, have been too little dwelt upon."* —ANDREW URE

industrial revolution and its technologies alarming. Some artisans lost their jobs as their crafts were mechanized. Those who found employment in factories toiled monotonously from dawn to dusk, operating heavy machinery that

Paul Daimler drives his father in the first four-wheeled Daimler car, 1886.

maimed so many laborers in Manchester, England, that one observer likened the city to a war zone. As bad as working conditions were, living conditions in crowded, crime-plagued, disease-ridden industrial slums were worse. The wealthy and powerful had little sympathy for protesting laborers. Strikers were treated as outlaws, and dissidents called Luddites, who sabotaged machinery, were subject to the death penalty.

Some blamed the ills of industrial society on capitalism and advocated socialism, or collective ownership of the means of production by workers or by society as a whole. Utopian socialists urged owners to establish model communities like New Lanark in Scotland, where industrialist Robert Owen raised the wages of cotton-mill workers and improved their housing and schools. Radical socialists argued that capitalists as a class would never willingly give up their power and insisted that only through revolution would workers own the wealth they produced.

In 1848 German-born radicals Karl Marx and Friedrich Engels published *The Communist Manifesto,* which called on workers to unite against capitalist bosses, forecasting a class struggle between the bourgeoisie and the oppressed proletariat. What Marx and Engels did not foresee was that reforms such as allowing laborers to form unions and bargain collectively would permit them to share in the benefits of industrialization, easing class tensions. Over time, that process enabled many members of the working class or their children to join an expanding middle class.

> Communism was a radical branch of the socialist movement, which included those who sought reform, not revolution.

THE TAKEAWAY: The industrial revolution accelerated the pace and productivity of modern life.

VOICES

MARX AND ENGELS THE CLASS STRUGGLE

"The history of all hitherto existing society is the history of class struggles. Freeman and slave, patrician and plebeian, baron and serf, guild master and journeyman, in one word, oppressor and oppressed, standing constantly in opposition to each other, carried on an uninterrupted warfare, now open, now concealed; a warfare which always ended either in a revolutionary transformation of the whole of society or in the common ruin of the contending classes. . . . Modern bourgeois society, springing from the wreck of feudal society, had not abolished class antagonisms. It has but substituted new classes, new conditions of oppression, new forms of warfare, for old."

—FROM *THE COMMUNIST MANIFESTO,* KARL MARX AND FRIEDRICH ENGELS, 1848

FRIEDRICH ENGELS AND KARL MARX

"If any one wishes to see in how little space a human being can move, how little air—and such air!—he can breathe. . . it is only necessary to travel [to Manchester]." —FRIEDRICH ENGELS

SEE ALSO | THE WORLD AT WAR: PAGE 400

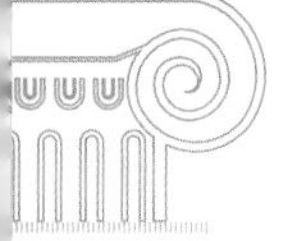

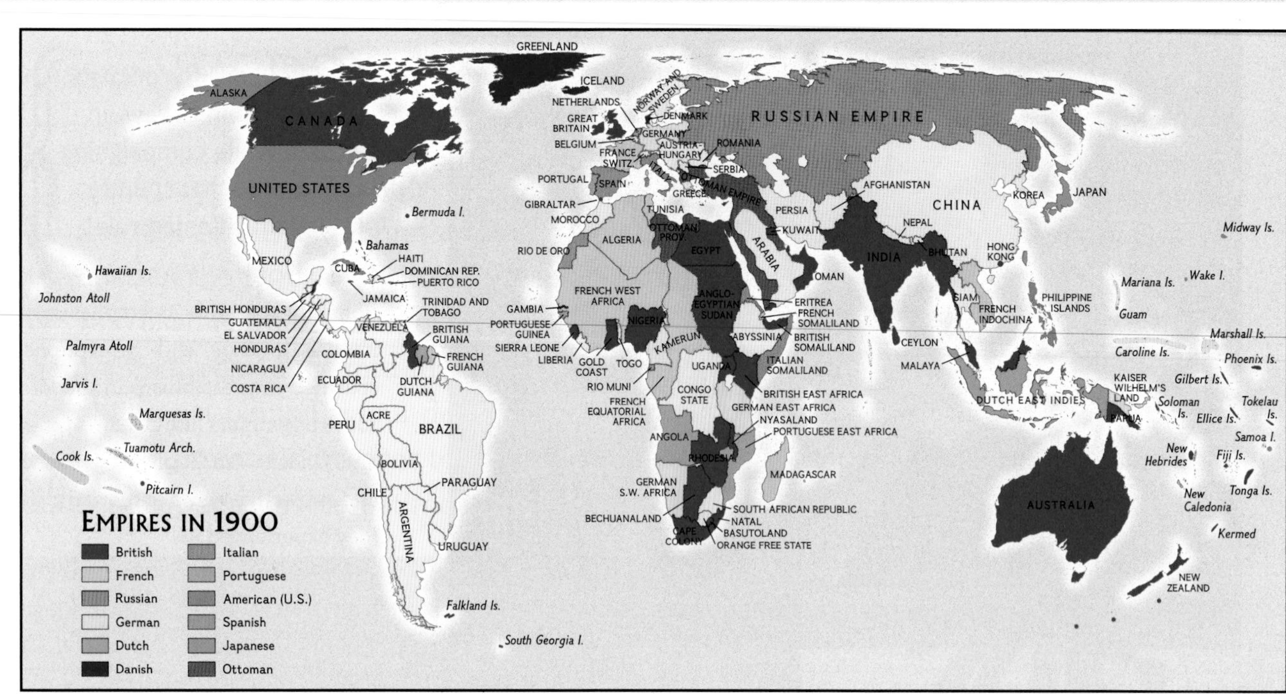

EMPIRES THE IMPERIALIST AGE

European imperialism in the 1800s differed from European colonialism in earlier times, which depended on settlement by colonists, who created societies in the New World much like those they left behind in the Old. During the 19th century, industrial and military advances gave developed nations a huge advantage over less developed countries in Africa, Asia, and the Pacific, allowing Europeans to dominate those lands economically and politically without always settling there in large numbers or imposing their culture on the society.

Private enterprise played a large part in the spread of the mighty British Empire, which grew to embrace 400 million people and nearly one-fourth of the world's territory by 1900. Traders brought India under British influence before it was acquired as a colony, and commercial interests there led Britain to intervene in Burma and other Asian lands. When China's rulers tried to stop Britain from exporting Indian opium to their country, British forces bullied them into legalizing the trade and surrendering

CONNECTIONS THE LEGACY OF COLONIALISM

One consequence of imperialism was to aggravate tensions between ethnic groups in countries under foreign rule. The rivalry between the Hutu majority and the Tutsi minority that resulted in genocide in Rwanda was longstanding, but the two groups were not bitterly at odds until they were colonized first by Germans and later by Belgians, who administered Rwanda from 1918 to 1962. Those early colonizers favored Tutsis. Hutu militants who later took control of Rwanda turned on their former oppressors, massacring nearly one million opponents in 1994.

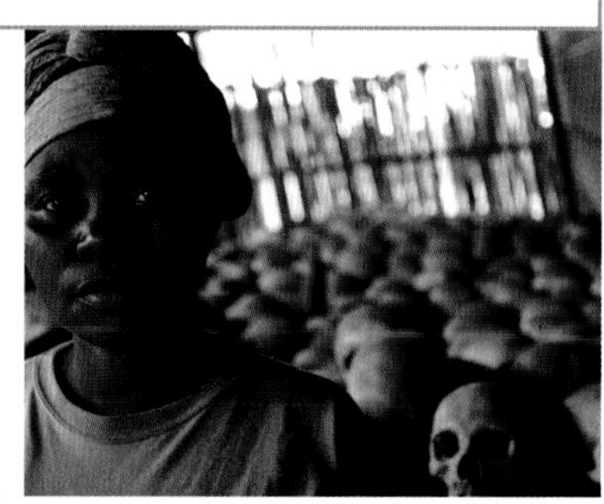

SURVIVOR AT MEMORIAL, RWANDA

> *"Take up the White Man's burden—/ Send forth the best ye breed—/ Go bind your sons to exile / To serve your captives' need."* —RUDYARD KIPLING

Hong Kong. Completion of the Suez Canal in 1869 greatly facilitated trade between Britain and India. To protect their access to the canal, the British suppressed a nationalist uprising in Egypt in 1882.

Meanwhile, diamond magnate Cecil Rhodes of the British South Africa Company was forging a commercial empire that extended British rule from the Cape Colony to the new colony he established, Rhodesia. Boers (descendants of Dutch and other European colonists) defied the British and fought a long and bitter war against them that ended in 1902, when they yielded to Britain but won some concessions.

{ More than 150,000 French soldiers died in campaigns to secure Algeria and other African colonies. }

Modern weaponry, such as this Maxim machine gun, aided imperialist efforts.

France, Britain's closest imperial rival, meanwhile exploited the decline of the Ottoman Empire in North Africa by colonizing Algeria and claiming Tunisia as a protectorate.

By the late 1800s many nations were engaged in the scramble for Africa. In 1884 delegates from more than a dozen countries met in Berlin to carve up control of Africa. By the end of the century, emerging European powers such as Germany and Italy and industrialized nations elsewhere like the United States and Japan joined in the quest for profitable acquisitions.

THE TAKEAWAY: Imperial powers used military and economic superiority to expand worldwide.

Ships under steam and sail make the first crossing of the Suez Canal in 1869.

"Thus the African is really helpless against the material gods of the white man, as embodied in the trinity of imperialism, capitalistic exploitation, and militarism." —EDWARD MOREL

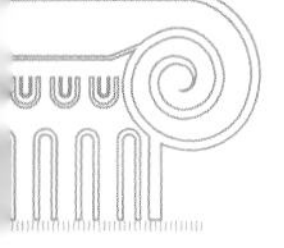

THE ORIGIN OF SPECIES

In 1859, British naturalist Charles Darwin laid out the principles of evolution in his masterwork, *On the Origin of Species by Means of Natural Selection*. His theory of natural selection—that species evolve through random variations in their physical characteristics that make individuals better able to survive and reproduce in certain environments—was inspired by his voyage around the world in the 1830s aboard the ship *Beagle*. Research he conducted in the Galapagos uncovered separate species of finch, each with a beak adapted to its environmental conditions. His conclusion that all species, including humans, evolved through such adaptations challenged the biblical account of creation.

CHARLES DARWIN, portrayed here at the age of 31, studied religion and biology at Cambridge University. Following his five-year voyage aboard the *Beagle*, he married his cousin Emma Wedgwood and fathered ten children while developing his theories. Learning that Alfred Russel Wallace was proposing similar ideas, Darwin finally published his masterwork in 1859 to both acclaim and controversy. Having suffered from ill health much of his life, he died of a heart attack in 1882.

488 CONCLUSION. CHAP. XIV.

others; it follows, that the amount of organic change in the fossils of consecutive formations probably serves as a fair measure of the lapse of actual time. A number of species, however, keeping in a body might remain for a long period unchanged, whilst within this same period, several of these species, by migrating into new countries and coming into competition with foreign associates, might become modified; so that we must not overrate the accuracy of organic change as a measure of time. During early periods of the earth's history, when the forms of life were probably fewer and simpler, the rate of change was probably slower; and at the first dawn of life, when very few forms of the simplest structure existed, the rate of change may have been slow in an extreme degree. The whole history of the world, as at present known, although of a length quite incomprehensible by us, will hereafter be recognised as a mere fragment of time, compared with the ages which have elapsed since the first creature, the progenitor of innumerable extinct and living descendants, was created.

In the distant future I see open fields for far more important researches. Psychology will be based on a new foundation, that of the necessary acquirement of each mental power and capacity by gradation. Light will be thrown on the origin of man and his history.

Authors of the highest eminence seem to be fully satisfied with the view that each species has been independently created. To my mind it accords better with what we know of the laws impressed on matter by the Creator, that the production and extinction of the past and present inhabitants of the world should have been due to secondary causes, like those determining the birth and death of the individual. When I view all beings not as special creations, but as the lineal descendants of some few beings which lived long before the

“These facts seemed to me to throw some light on the origin of species—that mystery of mysteries, as it has been called by one of our greatest philosophers.”

“It may be said that natural selection is daily and hourly scrutinizing, throughout the world, every variation, even the slightest.”

BEST SELLER The first print run of Darwin's 502-page, 15-shilling book by John Murray of London was a modest 1,250 copies, but the book was an immediate success.

“New and improved varieties will inevitably supplant and exterminate the older, less improved and intermediate varieties.”

CHAP. XIV. CONCLUSION. 489

first bed of the Silurian system was deposited, they seem to me to become ennobled. Judging from the past, we may safely infer that not one living species will transmit its unaltered likeness to a distant futurity. And of the species now living very few will transmit progeny of any kind to a far distant futurity; for the manner in which all organic beings are grouped, shows that the greater number of species of each genus, and all the species of many genera, have left no descendants, but have become utterly extinct. We can so far take a prophetic glance into futurity as to foretel that it will be the common and widely-spread species, belonging to the larger and dominant groups, which will ultimately prevail and procreate new and dominant species. As all the living forms of life are the lineal descendants of those which lived long before the Silurian epoch, we may feel certain that the ordinary succession by generation has never once been broken, and that no cataclysm has desolated the whole world. Hence we may look with some confidence to a secure future of equally inappreciable length. And as natural selection works solely by and for the good of each being, all corporeal and mental endowments will tend to progress towards perfection.

It is interesting to contemplate an entangled bank, clothed with many plants of many kinds, with birds singing on the bushes, with various insects flitting about, and with worms crawling through the damp earth, and to reflect that these elaborately constructed forms, so different from each other, and dependent on each other in so complex a manner, have all been produced by laws acting around us. These laws, taken in the largest sense, being Growth with Reproduction; Inheritance which is almost implied by reproduction; Variability from the indirect and direct action of the external con-

Y 3

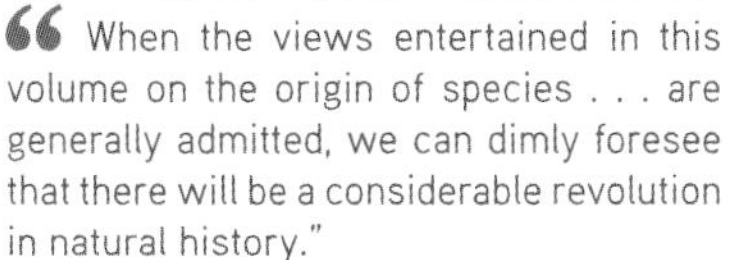

“When the views entertained in this volume on the origin of species . . . are generally admitted, we can dimly foresee that there will be a considerable revolution in natural history.”

FAMOUS PHRASE The phrase “survival of the fittest,” credited to Herbert Spencer, did not appear in the book until its fifth printing.

DARWIN'S FINCHES Darwin collected and observed a variety of finches while in the Galapagos. Noting that finches from different islands had distinctively different beak shapes, each suitable for the food on that island—insects, seeds, or flowers, for instance—he began to develop his theory of natural selection, suggesting that animals who were best fitted for survival in their environment were more likely to pass on their traits to many offspring.

“As many more individuals of each species are born than can possibly survive; and as, consequently, there is a frequently recurring struggle for existence, it follows that any being, if it vary however slightly in any manner profitable to itself, under the complex and sometimes varying conditions of life, will have a better chance of surviving, and thus be naturally selected.”

OTHER BOOKS BY DARWIN

1839: *Journal of Researches into the Geology and Natural History of the Various Countries Visited by H.M.S. Beagle*

1846: *Geological Observations on South America*

1862: *On the Various Contrivances by which British and Foreign Orchids Are Fertilised by Insects*

1868: *The Variation of Animals and Plants under Domestication*

1871: *The Descent of Man, and Selection in Relation to Sex*

1872: *The Expression of the Emotions in Man and Animals*

1875: *Insectivorous Plants*

1881: *The Formation of Vegetable Mould, through the Action of Worms, with Observations on Their Habits*

SEE ALSO | EMPIRES RISING: PAGE 346

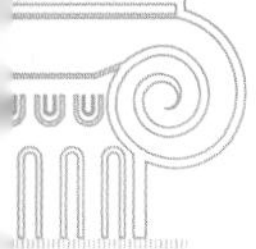

KEY DATES

1803
United States purchases the Louisiana Territory from France.

1804
Revolution in Haiti leads to independence from France.

1812–1815
War of 1812 is fought between the United States and Britain.

1822
Brazil gains independence from Portugal.

THE AMERICAS

1800–1900

Following the example of the United States, many countries in the Americas rebelled against European colonial rule in the 19th century. Haitians won independence from France in 1804, and Mexicans rose up against Spain in 1810. By the mid-1820s most Latin American countries were free, including the former Portuguese colony of Brazil. Achieving prosperity and political stability, however, proved to be a challenge for those new nations. Former colonies in Central and South America lacked the advantages of the United States, which despite its rebellion had profited under British rule by engaging in maritime trade and governing through colonial assemblies. Mindful of those benefits, Canadians chose to remain under British rule until their country became a self-governing British dominion in 1867.

Latin American nations had no preparation for self-rule and few sources of wealth other than agricultural products and precious metals, much of which had been extracted in colonial times. Many fell under the control of military rulers, or caudillos, and became economically dependent on European nations or the United States, which emerged as the leading power in the hemisphere.

After gaining independence, nations in both North and South America, including the United States, struggled politically; the United States became a great world power only after the Civil War.

The United States did not become a great nation without a struggle. As Americans advanced westward, they faced determined resistance from Indian tribes with ancient ties to the land and confronted settlers from other nations. Victory in the Mexican-American War (1846–1848) enlarged the United States at Mexico's expense. But that triumph caused turmoil as Southerners dependent on slave labor clashed with Northerners over whether to allow slavery in western territories ceded by Mexico and Indian tribes.

The election in 1860 of President Abraham Lincoln, committed to containing slavery, led southern states to secede from the Union, resulting in the Civil War (1861–1865). Aptly described as the Second American Revolution, that wrenching conflict settled two outstanding national issues by ending slavery and placing states firmly under federal authority. The triumph of federal might over states' rights strengthened the nation's hand as its industrial capacity increased in the late 1800s and it competed with powers around the world.

OPPOSITE: Simón Bolívar, known as the Liberator, led revolutions against Spanish rule in South America.

1846–1848
Mexican War leads to U.S. expansion and acquisition of Mexican territory.

1861–1865
American Civil War ends slavery and gives the federal government authority over the states.

1867
Canada is declared a self-governing dominion of the British Empire.

1876
Sitting Bull and Native American forces defeat General Custer at Battle of Little Bighorn.

SEE ALSO | EMPIRES RISING: PAGE 344

EXPLORATION

WESTERN EXPANSION

All but two Texas defenders were killed in the battle of the Alamo.

No one did more to promote America's westward expansion than President Thomas Jefferson, who concluded the momentous Louisiana Purchase in 1803 by offering France $15 million for territory that included New Orleans, St. Louis, and a vast area between the Mississippi Valley and the Rocky Mountains that France claimed but did not control. Jefferson sent explorers Meriwether Lewis and William Clark on a transcontinental trek that brought them to the mouth of the Columbia River in 1805. Their dealings with western Indians, who were not yet threatened by white settlers, were largely peaceful.

Other tribes living between the Appalachian Mountains and the Mississippi feared being overrun by Americans, however, and sided with Britain against the United States in the War of 1812. General Andrew Jackson of Tennessee won renown in that conflict by crushing defiant Creek Indians in Alabama and defeating British troops at New Orleans in January 1815.

Elected president in 1828, Jackson cleared ground for white settlers by completing removal of the Cherokee and other tribes from the Southeast to the Indian Territory (present-day Oklahoma). Farther south, in 1836, Americans in Texas rebelled against Mexico and won independence in a struggle that included a ferocious battle at the Alamo in

INDIAN PEACE MEDAL

THE AMERICAS

VIPs

Thomas Jefferson, 1743–1826
Third president of the U.S.

José de San Martín, 1778–1850
Argentine revolutionary and statesman

Simón Bolívar, 1783–1830
South American revolutionary, president of Gran Colombia, and dictator of Peru

Robert E. Lee, 1807–1870
Confederate general and commander of the Army of Northern Virginia

Abraham Lincoln, 1809–1865
Sixteenth president of the United States

John D. Rockefeller, 1839–1937
Founder of the Standard Oil Company

"In its magnificent domain of space and time, the nation of many nations is destined to manifest to mankind the excellence of divine principles." —JOHN O'SULLIVAN

VOICES

LEWIS CHASED BY A GRIZZLY

"Set out this morning at the usual hour; the wind was moderate; I walked on shore with one man. About 8 A. M. we fell in with two brown bear; both of which we wounded; one of them made his escape, the other after my firing on him pursued me seventy or eighty yards, but fortunately had been so badly wounded that he was unable to pursue so closely as to prevent my charging my gun; we again repeated our fir and killed him. It was a male not fully grown, we estimated his weight at 300 lbs, not having the means of ascertaining it precisely."

—FROM THE JOURNALS OF MERIWETHER LEWIS, APRIL 29, 1805

GRIZZLY BEAR DRAWING FROM EXPEDITION

San Antonio. By annexing Texas in 1845, the United States became involved in a border dispute with Mexico that soon led to war. After invading Mexico and seizing Mexico City, Americans secured a treaty that gave them possession of New Mexico and California, where gold was discovered at war's end in 1848. The ensuing Gold Rush brought hundreds of thousands of people to California, which entered the Union as a state in 1850.

Settlement of the West slowed during the Civil War but resumed in earnest when the conflict ended. Completion of the transcontinental railroad to California in 1869 linked the East to the West just four years after the defeated South rejoined the North. The coast-to-coast route signaled that the United States, once loosely confederated, had coalesced as a nation.

THE TAKEAWAY: After breaking away from Britain, the United States forged its own empire.

About 12,000 settlers followed the 2,000-mile Oregon Trail west in the 1840s.

"The existence of an area of free land, its continuous recession, and the advance of American settlement westward, explain American development." —FREDERICK JACKSON TURNER

SEE ALSO | NEW WORLD ORDER: PAGE 306

NATIONS INDIANS OF THE EAST

Seminole Indian leader Osceola was captured in 1837.

Although American settlers justified depriving tribes of their territory by claiming that they were not making good use of the land, many Indians in the East were in fact efficient farmers. Particularly successful as cultivators were the so-called Five Civilized Tribes of the Southeast—Seminole, Creek, Choctaw, Chickasaw, and Cherokee. Prominent members of those tribes learned English and lived in frame houses but retained their tribal identity.

{ Tribes removed to Indian Territory lost much of their land there before it became the state of Oklahoma in 1907. }

Some, like the scholar Sequoyah, who devised the Cherokee alphabet, moved west voluntarily to avoid assimilation. Others, like Cherokee chief John Ross, stood fast. Although the U.S. Supreme Court ruled that the Cherokees had a right to their lands, Andrew Jackson evicted them from their homes in Georgia and forced their removal to Indian Territory. Thousands died on the ensuing journey, known as the Trail of Tears.

THE TAKEAWAY: The Cherokee built a prosperous society before they were driven west.

JONES DRAGGED FROM THEIR HOUSES

VOICES

TRAIL OF TEARS

"The Cherokees are nearly all prisoners. They have been dragged from their houses, and encamped at the forts and military posts, all over the nation. In Georgia, especially, multitudes were allowed no time to take any thing with them except the clothes they had on. Well-furnished houses were left prey to plunderers, who, like hungry wolves, follow in the trail of the captors. These wretches rifle the houses and strip the helpless, unoffending owners of all they have on earth."

—FROM A REPORT BY REV. EVAN JONES TO *BAPTIST MISSIONARY MAGAZINE*, SEPTEMBER 1838

"The Indians are acknowledged to have an unquestionable and, heretofore, unquestioned right to the lands they occupy." —JOHN MARSHALL

NATIONS INDIANS OF THE WEST

American expansion brought confinement and calamity to Indians who had long moved freely across the Great Plains, hunting buffalo on horseback. Some found life on government reservations unbearable and fled. In 1864, Cheyenne fugitives led by Chief Black Kettle agreed to return to the dismal Sand Creek Reservation in Colorado, where troops then attacked their camp and slaughtered more than 150 people. Black Kettle survived, only to die in 1868 in a similar assault led by Colonel George Armstrong Custer. Angry Cheyennes later joined Lakota Sioux—whose reservation in the Black Hills of South Dakota was overrun by prospectors—in defying the U.S. Army and hunting freely in Montana. Led by Chief Sitting Bull, they repulsed a rash attack by Custer at the Little Bighorn River in August 1876 and killed the colonel and many of his men.

Sitting Bull later yielded to the government but died in a clash with reservation police in 1890, shortly before troops of Custer's old regiment massacred more than 200 of his fellow Sioux at Wounded Knee. He would be remembered as one of the last great Indian resistance leaders, along with Geronimo of the Apache and Chief Joseph of the Nez Percé, who eluded pursuing soldiers and led his followers on an epic 1,300-mile odyssey before surrendering in 1877.

Chief Joseph of the Nez Percé evaded U.S. troops for months.

THE TAKEAWAY: Western tribes often resisted confinement to reservations.

General George Armstrong Custer led his troops into a disastrous rout at Little Bighorn in 1876.

"*The white men are bad school-masters; they carry false looks, and deal in false actions; they smile in the face of the poor Indian to cheat him.*" —BLACK HAWK

SEE ALSO | NEW WORLD ORDER: PAGE 310

CONFLICTS THE CIVIL WAR

Abraham Lincoln was assassinated soon after the Civil War ended.

Abraham Lincoln proved prophetic when he declared in 1858 that the nation could not endure "half slave and half free." The political balance between the slaveholding South and the free-labor North shifted in the 1850s when California, Oregon, and Minnesota were admitted as free states. Southerners hoped to restore the balance by legalizing slavery in western territories destined for statehood. Democratic senator Stephen Douglas of Illinois backed a compromise allowing the residents of each territory to decide whether to permit slavery there. Opposed to any measure that would extend slavery, Lincoln debated and nearly defeated Douglas as the Republican senatorial candidate in 1858 and then defeated him in the 1860 presidential race. Lincoln faced an immediate crisis as southern states seceded and chose Jefferson Davis of Mississippi as president of the newly formed Confederacy.

The Civil War began in April 1861 when Confederates in Charleston, South Carolina, bombarded Fort Sumter and forced Unionists holding it to surrender. Though the South seemed to be at a disadvantage to the more populous and productive North, Southerners were defending their own ground and were well commanded. In June 1862 Robert E. Lee of Virginia took charge of Confederate forces and repulsed a massive assault on their capital, Richmond. Lee's invasion of Maryland that September led to a furious battle at Antietam, with 23,000 casualties—the bloodiest

President Lincoln and members of his Cabinet read the Emancipation Proclamation.

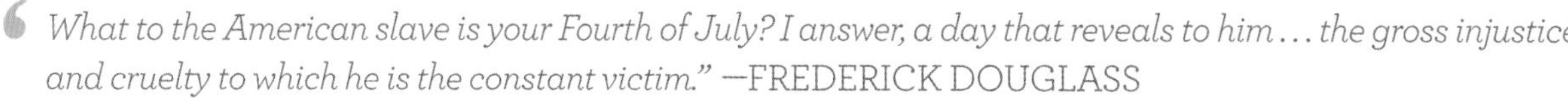
"What to the American slave is your Fourth of July? I answer, a day that reveals to him ... the gross injustice and cruelty to which he is the constant victim." —FREDERICK DOUGLASS

day of fighting in American history. When Lee's battered army withdrew, Lincoln issued the Emancipation Proclamation, declaring slaves in the Confederacy free and encouraging them to seek refuge with Union forces, which were enhanced by the enlistment of black troops.

In July 1863, Federals defeated Lee's resurgent army at Gettysburg, Pennsylvania, and won control of the Mississippi by capturing Vicksburg. Ulysses Grant, who took Vicksburg, went on to defeat Confederates at Chattanooga, Tennessee, after they had routed Union troops at nearby Chickamauga. Named general in chief in 1864, Grant pinned down Lee's dwindling army at Petersburg while William Sherman claimed Atlanta for the Union and swept triumphantly through Georgia and the Carolinas. The war ended when

{ The tide of the war turned on July 4, 1863, when Grant claimed Vicksburg and Lee's army retreated from Gettysburg. }

Lee surrendered at Appomattox on April 9, 1865, one day after the U.S. Senate passed the 13th Amendment, abolishing slavery, and less than a week before Lincoln was assassinated by Confederate sympathizer John Wilkes Booth.

THE TAKEAWAY: The Civil War started in 1861 over the issue of whether to allow slavery in American territories.

Casualties on the third day of the battle of Gettysburg, July 1863.

OLIPHANT FLAMES OF CHICKAMAUGA

"The firing of the guns had set fire to the high sedge grass of the field. The fence was on fire and the tall dead trees in the field were blazing high in the air. Dead and wounded men were lying there in great danger of being consumed and the federals occupying the opposite side of the field were pouring a deadly shower of shot and shell through the smoke and flames. Bowing our heads and grasping our guns firmly we plunged into this vortex of hell. On emerging from the fire and smoke, yelling like demons, we dashed at the federals and soon had them flying. It was a fearful place. The heartrending appeals of the wounded, some of whom were scorching, the hissing bullets and screeching shells, made it an experience never to be forgotten."

—FROM AN ACCOUNT BY PRIVATE WILLIAM OLIPHANT, SIXTH TEXAS INFANTRY

PRIVATE W. J. OLIPHANT

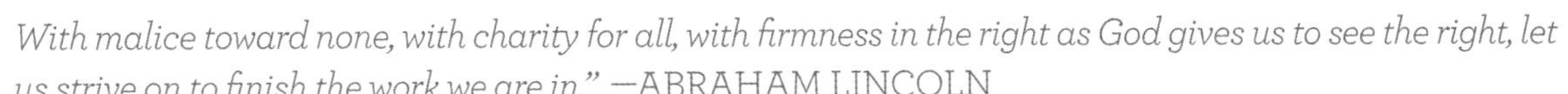

"With malice toward none, with charity for all, with firmness in the right as God gives us to see the right, let us strive on to finish the work we are in." —ABRAHAM LINCOLN

SEE ALSO | THE WORLD AT WAR: PAGE 376

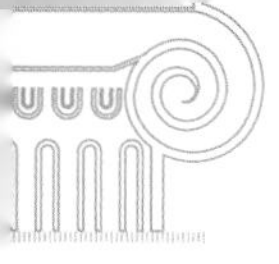

Cartoons skewered tycoons such as Vanderbilt, Gould, and Field.

ECONOMY WEALTH AND WORK

After the Civil War, the United States industrialized rapidly. New York, Chicago, and other cities boomed as European immigrants arrived by the millions in search of employment, keeping the cost of labor down. Shrewd capitalists used those profits to expand operations and dominate entire industries, such as petroleum. John D. Rockefeller's Standard Oil Corporation gained control of 90 percent of that business, while Andrew Carnegie's U.S. Steel Company overwhelmed its competitors by acquiring mines, factories, and railroads that carried its product. Rising public concern over such monopolies or trusts (combining many companies under one board of trustees) led Congress to pass the Sherman Antitrust Act in 1890.

The right of workers to form unions and go on strike had been affirmed by a ruling of the Massachusetts Supreme Court in 1842, which set a precedent for other states. National organizations like the Knights of Labor and the American Federation of Labor emerged to give workers greater bargaining power as they demanded higher wages and a shorter workweek. Owners, in turn, tried to break strikes by replacing strikers with nonunion laborers or using police to force them back to work.

Economic crises like the Panic of 1893, which left one in five workers unemployed, affected farmers as well as industrial laborers and led Populists to urge reforms that would distribute wealth more equitably. Their People's Party did not last long, but some of their proposals—including a graduated income tax—were later adopted.

> The need to coordinate railroad schedules led to the adoption of standard time in the United States in 1883.

THE TAKEAWAY: Industrial growth concentrated wealth in the hands of a few corporations.

Italian immigrants search for lost baggage at Ellis Island.

> *"This coal side of our civilization has . . . little children of all ages, from six years upward, at work in the coal breakers, toiling in dirt, and air thick with carbon dust."* —HENRY DEMAREST LLOYD

EMPIRES THE U.S. EXTENDS ITS GRASP

The United States followed the path of other imperial powers in the late 1800s by acquiring territories overseas, including Hawaii, where American missionaries and planters had gained influence over the royal family. When Queen Liliuokalani took the throne in 1891, she vowed to maintain independence. Two years later, Americans in Hawaii rebelled against her, and U.S. Marines came ashore to support them. Reluctantly, she abdicated, clearing the way for U.S. annexation of Hawaii in 1898.

In the same year, President William McKinley asked Congress to declare war on Spain following the mysterious explosion of the battleship U.S.S. *Maine* off Cuba, where rebels were seeking freedom from Spain. No evidence linked Spain to the explosion, but newspapers whipped up a war frenzy. Among those who welcomed the Spanish-American War as an opportunity for the United States to enter the world stage was Theodore Roosevelt. Stepping down as Under Secretary of the Navy, he commanded volunteers called Rough Riders against Spanish forces in Cuba, emerging as a national hero and McKinley's choice for vice president in 1900.

Theodore Roosevelt as a cavalry officer in 1898

Cuba gained independence when Spain was defeated, but it remained subject to American intervention. The United States also won control of other former Spanish colonies, including Puerto Rico, Guam, and the Philippines, where insurgents who had been fighting Spanish troops soon became opponents of American occupiers. What began as a "splendid little war" against Spanish imperialism, in the words of Secretary of State John Hay, turned into a brutal struggle against Filipinos seeking independence.

THE TAKEAWAY: The Spanish-American War made the United States a world power.

VOICES

THE CALL THE WORK OF FIENDS

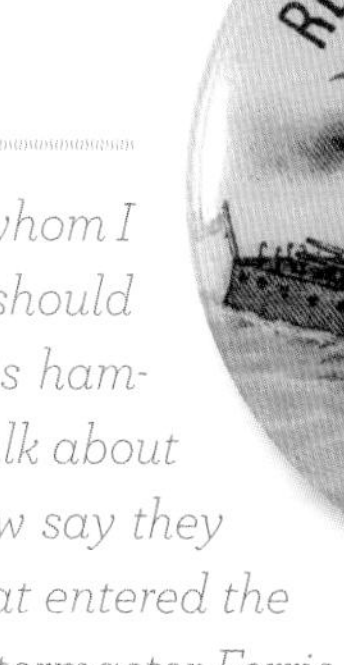

PATRIOTIC PIN

"What appeared to have made the deepest impression on all with whom I have conversed in relation to the matter is the fact that the explosion should have occurred after the 9 o'clock 'tattoo,' when every man was in his hammock asleep and the lamps put out. Another singular feature is the talk about mysterious boats and other floating objects some of the Maine's crew say they saw immediately preceding the explosion. They say a small black boat entered the harbor and circled the Maine several times during the evening. 'Quartermaster Ferris,' Thompson states, 'hailed this mysterious boat twice as she approached the Maine on the port side, but received no response.'" —FROM "THE WORK OF FIENDS MAY LEAD TO WAR," THE *SAN FRANCISCO CALL*, FEBRUARY 19, 1898

"[The Spanish-American War] has been a splendid little war, begun with the highest motives, carried on with magnificent intelligence and spirit." —JOHN MILTON HAY

EMPIRES RISING: THE AMERICAS

LEADERS LATIN AMERICA

Long before Spain lost Cuba, its American empire began to crumble. In 1808 Napoleon Bonaparte placed his brother Joseph on the Spanish throne, a move that undermined Spanish authority overseas and encouraged rebellions in its colonies. Two commanding figures appeared who helped liberate South America—Simón Bolívar of Venezuela, an ambitious, aristocratic soldier, and José de San Martín of Argentina, at one time a loyal Spanish officer. Their paths converged in Peru, where San Martín yielded, allowing Bolívar to take Lima, the old Spanish imperial capital.

Already ruler of Gran Colombia (embracing Colombia, Venezuela, Ecuador, and Panama), Bolívar became master of Peru and of a new nation that was carved out of its interior, called Bolivia in his honor. His hopes for a union of these Hispanic countries were dashed, however, when Gran Colombia broke apart in the late 1820s. "America is ungovernable," Bolívar concluded.

Brazil achieved freedom from Portugal with less upheaval and avoided fragmentation. In 1807 Prince Regent João (John) left Portugal to escape Napoleon and set up court in Rio de Janeiro. Aided by the British, his son Pedro became regent when João returned to Portugal in 1821, but he resisted efforts by Portugal to hold on to the colony. In 1822, he declared independence for Brazil, which adopted a constitution in 1824.

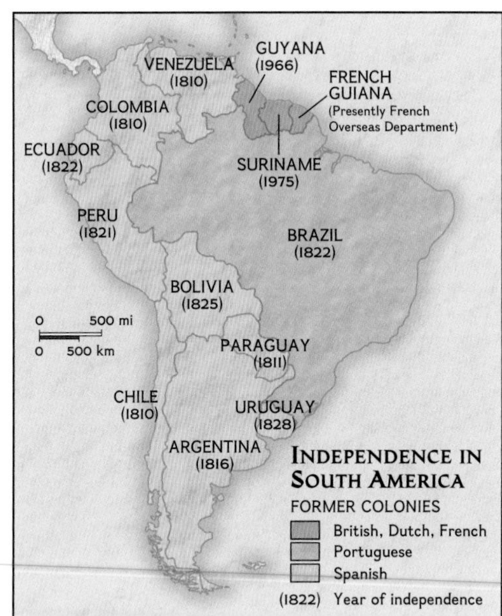

José de San Martín created the national flag of Peru.

THE TAKEAWAY: Many nations emerged when South America achieved independence from Spain and Portugal in the early 1800s.

SIMÓN BOLÍVAR A DUAL CONFLICT

VOICES

SIMÓN BOLÍVAR

"We are not Europeans; we are not Indians; we are but a mixed species of aborigines and Spaniards. Americans by birth and Europeans by law, we find ourselves engaged in a dual conflict: we are disputing with the natives for titles of ownership, and at the same time we are struggling to maintain ourselves in the country that gave us birth against the opposition of the invaders. Thus our position is most extraordinary and complicated."

—FROM THE MESSAGE TO THE CONGRESS OF ANGOSTURA, 1819

"A Latin-American revolution, to be successful, must originate with, or be supported by, the soldiery. The conspirators begin with bribing a portion of the garrison of an important post." —FRIEDRICH HASSAUREK

SEE ALSO | EMPIRES RISING: PAGE 325

NATIONS MEXICO

Mexico's war for independence began in 1810 when a Catholic priest, Miguel Hidalgo y Costilla, launched an uprising by poor Mexicans against the Spanish ruling class. Though he was captured and executed by Spanish troops in 1811, the struggle continued. Mexico did not achieve independence until Agustín de Iturbide, an officer who had opposed the uprising, switched sides and proclaimed himself emperor in 1821, only to be deposed by those favoring representative government.

The Mexican Republic, which emerged in 1824 under a liberal constitution, proved unstable. A decade later, Antonio López de Santa Anna defied that constitution and staged a military coup. Discredited when rebellious Texans defeated him at San Jacinto in 1836, he later regained power—only to suffer an even greater loss in 1847 when invading American troops forced Mexico to cede its northern territories. Even so, Mexico managed to hold on to its independence after a failed takeover by France in the 1860s.

{ Mexican president Benito Juárez, who fought the French occupation, was born to Indian parents. }

THE TAKEAWAY: Mexico threw off Spanish rule in 1821 but still had to contend with foreign powers.

Antonio López de Santa Anna defies the Spanish troops of Ferdinand VII.

"Mexico is the country of inequality. No where does there exist such a fearful difference in the distribution of fortune, civilization, cultivation of the soil, and population." —ALEXANDER VON HUMBOLDT

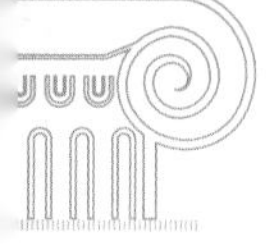

Revolutionaries burned the town of Cap-Français, Haiti, in 1791.

LEADERS HAITI

Haiti's war for independence was a struggle not just against French rule but against slavery. Inhabited largely by slaves of African heritage, Haiti also had a small population of free blacks, among them a dedicated revolutionary, Toussaint L'Ouverture. When France failed to grant slaves citizenship as promised in the 1790s, L'Ouverture led a rebellion. After making peace with France when it abolished slavery, he invaded Spanish-ruled Santo Domingo (now the Dominican Republic) and ended slavery there. Seized in 1802 by Napoleon's forces, he died in captivity a year later. But his legacy was fulfilled when Napoleon abandoned his American empire, leaving Haiti free in 1804.

THE TAKEAWAY: Haiti became the first American country to throw off slavery.

LECLERC SHOW NO MERCY

VOICES

CHARLES LECLERC

"I have received, Citizen General, your letter with the list of the troubling subjects with which you contend. Show no mercy with anyone that you suspect. . . . One must be unflinching and inspire great terror; it is the only thing that will suppress the blacks. . . . This insurrection is in its last crisis. By the first month of the revolutionary calendar, with a month of campaigning, all will be over. . . . Frequently inform me about your position. I need to be informed as often as possible. Use examples of severity to inspire terror."

—FROM A LETTER ABOUT THE HAITIAN REBELLION BY GENERAL CHARLES VICTOR EMMANUEL LECLERC, 1802

"In overthrowing me, you have done no more than cut down the trunk of the tree of the black liberty in St. Domingue—it will spring back from the roots." —TOUSSAINT L'OUVERTURE

SEE ALSO | EMPIRES RISING: PAGE 324

NATIONS CANADA

Unlike the rebellious American colonies that formed the United States, Canadian colonies remained loyal to Britain and served as a refuge for Americans who wished to remain under British rule. Tens of thousands of those loyalists fled to Canada during and after the American Revolution. Most were English-speaking Protestants who settled in Nova Scotia, New Brunswick, or Ontario (known originally as Upper Canada).

Meanwhile, Quebec (or Lower Canada) remained predominantly French and Roman Catholic. French fur traders known as voyageurs continued to venture west from Montreal in canoes and intermarry with Indians of various tribes, fostering communities of mixed-race Métis. But the firms those voyageurs worked for, including the Hudson's Bay Company and the rival North West Company, were now led by men of British heritage, including explorers David Thompson and Simon Fraser, who followed the Columbia and Fraser Rivers to the Pacific Coast in the early 1800s.

{ Four provinces confederated in 1867, but Newfoundland and Labrador did not join Canada until 1949. }

John A. Macdonald, a lawyer and businessman, is known as the founding father of Canada.

Canada had to overcome ethnic and political divisions before it became one nation. Scottish immigrant John Macdonald, leader of Canada's Conservative Party, favored maintaining close ties with Britain. "A British subject I was born," he said; "a British subject I will die." He recognized that Canada would not achieve unity, however, until its English-speaking and French-speaking inhabitants reached a political accommodation. In 1854 he formed a coalition with George-Étienne Cartier of Quebec, head of the Liberal Party. Their alliance helped pave the way for the confederation of Canada as a self-governing British dominion in 1867, with Macdonald as its first prime minister.

Not everyone welcomed confederation. Métis living in Manitoba, led by Louis Riel, fought the Canadian government in 1869 and again in 1885, when it encroached on their settlements. Troops crushed the second, armed uprising and Riel was convicted of treason. Shortly before he was executed in November 1885, the Canadian Pacific was completed, linking the nation from Montreal in the East to British Columbia in the West.

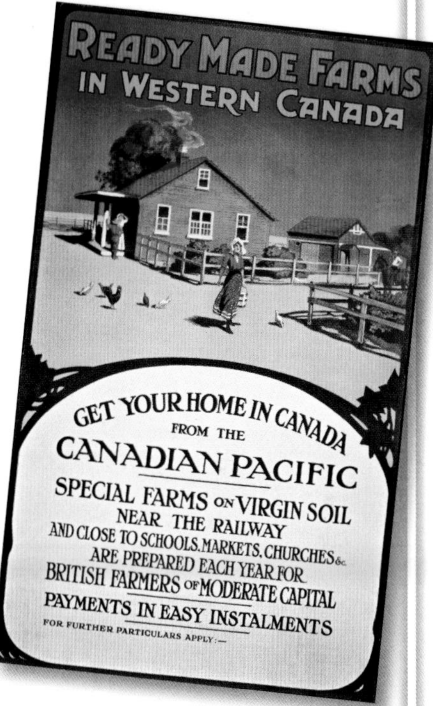

CANADIAN POSTER

THE TAKEAWAY: Canada reached nationhood peacefully and united its English- and French-speaking regions without civil war.

> *"We may be a small community and a Half-breed community at that—but we are men, free and spirited men and we will not allow even the Dominion of Canada to trample on our rights."* —LOUIS RIEL

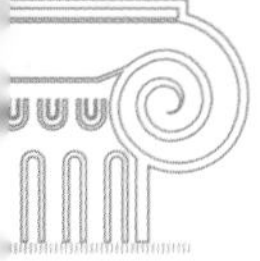

SEE ALSO | EMPIRES RISING: PAGE 358

KEY DATES

1807
Protestant missionaries enter China.

1839–1842
Opium War leads China to a major defeat at the hands of the British.

1840
Maoris of New Zealand reach accommodation with Britain in the Treaty of Waitangi.

1850–1864
Taiping Rebellion in China leads to 20 million deaths.

ASIA & THE PACIFIC

1800–1900

In 1800 China and Japan remained powers unto themselves, largely isolated from the West and the emerging forces of industrialism and nationalism that would transform the world. Both countries were forced to abandon their isolationism during the 19th century. But Japan was quick to adopt Western technology and reform its political system while imperial China had to endure defeat, humiliation, and revolution before modernizing in the 20th century and reconstituting itself as a nation. China's Manchu rulers lost prestige when British gunboats destroyed their antiquated fleet during the first Opium War (1839–1842). The Manchus were then nearly toppled by the tumultuous Taiping Rebellion (1850–1864), a movement inspired partly by Christianity that sought to create a new order where all property was shared in common. Foreign troops helped China's imperial forces crush that uprising and later intervened to put down the Boxer Rebellion (1899–1900), aimed at ridding the country of "foreign devils." Empress Dowager Cixi, who encouraged the Boxers, bowed to foreign powers afterward by allowing them to station troops in China.

China, long dominant in Asia, failed to modernize and lost power in the 1800s to Britain and other imperial nations, including the more adaptable, newly industrialized Japan.

Japan's course diverged from China's in 1853 when American warships entered Tokyo Bay and demanded trading rights. Shocked, the Japanese proceeded to open their doors to foreign goods and technology and eventually reorganized their government. Japan's long-standing shogunate gave way to a constitutional monarchy under Emperor Meiji. The emperor and his advisers launched a rapid program of industrialization and militarization, which allowed Japan to occupy territory overseas, including Korea and Taiwan, seized from China in 1894.

Japan's ascent brought it into competition not just with China but with Western imperial powers. France took charge of Indochina, while Britain colonized Malaya and Singapore and sent so many settlers to Australia and New Zealand that the indigenous Aborigines and Maoris in those countries were nearly overwhelmed. Another rival to Japan emerged in the Pacific at century's end when the United States annexed Hawaii and occupied the Philippines. Here as elsewhere, imperial expansion in the 19th century set the stage for explosive conflict in the 20th century.

OPPOSITE: The powerful Empress Dowager Cixi of China opposed foreign influences in her country.

1853
Commodore Perry forces Japan to open doors to foreign trade.

1867
Meiji Restoration brings back an emperor as supreme ruler of Japan.

1899–1900
Chinese rise up against foreign powers in the Boxer Rebellion.

1901
Australia becomes a self-governing British Commonwealth.

SEE ALSO | EMPIRES RISING: PAGE 336

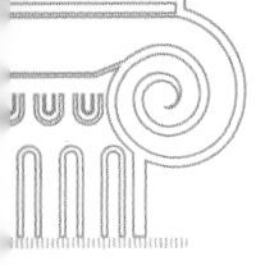

Europeans forced access to Chinese ports, such as this one at Whampoa.

CONFLICTS OPIUM WARS

In 1838 Chinese authorities tried to halt the ruinous trade in opium, which British merchants smuggled into China from India. Shipments would be seized, they declared, and anyone caught peddling the drug would be put to death. But China did not in fact have the power to stop the drug traffic. To sustain that profitable trade, Britain went to war and forced China not only to legalize the drug but also to cede Hong Kong and renounce its claims to Korea, Indochina, and Burma. This defeat was the beginning of the end for the troubled Qing dynasty and its Manchu rulers. Leaders of the Taiping Rebellion that erupted in 1850 denounced those Manchurian overlords and set much of the populace against them.

THE TAKEAWAY: China's imperial regime proved no match for British imperial power.

ASIA & THE PACIFIC — VIPs

Matthew C. Perry, 1794–1858
U.S. naval officer who forced Japan to open to trade

Hong Xiuquan, 1814–1864
Chinese visionary and leader of the Taiping Rebellion

Charles George Gordon, 1833–1885
British general who helped suppress the Taiping Rebellion

Empress Cixi, 1835–1908
Regent and unofficial ruler of China for almost 50 years

Meiji Tenno, 1852–1912
Emperor and modernizer of Japan

LIN ZEXU

LIN ZEXU OVERFLOWING WITH POISON — VOICES

"Some [British merchants] . . . have . . . caused every province of the land to overflow with that poison. These then know merely to advantage themselves, they care not about injuring others! This is a principle which heaven's Providence repugnates; and which mankind conjointly look upon with abhorrence! Moreover, the great emperor hearing of it, actually quivered with indignation."

—FROM A LETTER BY COMMISSIONER LIN ZEXU TO QUEEN VICTORIA, 1839

"I began to go to school at six. I studied first the three primers: the 'Trimetrical Classic,' the 'Thousand-words Classic,' and the 'Incentive to Study.'" —YAN PHOU LEE

CONFLICTS TAIPING REBELLION

In 1837 Hong Xiuquan, a poor young schoolteacher anguished by his failure to pass China's civil service exam, experienced visions that led him to espouse a revolutionary gospel derived from Christianity and from Chinese prophesies. He and his followers, known as the God Worshipers' Society, promised that those who did good would enter a heavenly kingdom on earth, where all would share equally in God's blessings. Their message appealed to China's long-suffering peasants, who enlisted by the millions when Hong proclaimed the coming of the Heavenly Kingdom of Great Peace (Taiping) and launched a rebellion. Women were promised equality with men and formed their own regiments in the rebel army, which captured Nanjing in 1853. More than 20 million people died during the rebellion, one of the deadliest conflicts in history.

Hong squandered his gains, however, by feuding with his commanders while his opponents rallied. In 1864 Hong committed suicide, shortly before government forces reclaimed Nanjing.

Taiping rebels storm a town in this contemporary painting.

{ The Chinese government was aided by foreigners like British officer Charles George "Chinese" Gordon. }

France joined Britain in campaigns against China in the 19th century.

THE TAKEAWAY: The Taiping Rebellion was fueled by poverty and despair in rural China.

> “*We must establish elementary and high schools, colleges and universities, in accordance with those of foreign countries.*” —EMPEROR KUANG HSU

SEE ALSO | NEW WORLD ORDER: PAGE 302

Commodore Perry gave a miniature railway to the Japanese in 1854.

NATIONS JAPAN MODERNIZES

Japan's self-imposed isolation ended abruptly on July 8, 1853, when a fleet of American warships commanded by Commodore Matthew Perry steamed uninvited into Edo Bay. Japanese authorities had long resisted contact with foreigners, allowing only a few Dutch and Chinese merchant ships to enter its waters periodically. But Japan had no naval vessels to match Perry's heavily armed warships, and its government felt compelled to accept the proposal he delivered from President Millard Fillmore, who requested a treaty that would grant American vessels access to Japanese ports. That agreement was followed by treaties with Britain, France, and other European powers, exposing the country to Western ideas and technology.

Many Japanese blamed the Tokugawa dynasty, whose shoguns had long ruled the country, for yielding to foreign demands. Under the shogunate, Japan's aristocratic daimyo and the samurai who waged war for them had largely been peaceful. But daimyo and samurai now rebelled against the dynasty and threw their support to Emperor Komei, who, unlike his predecessors, was no mere figurehead, and denounced the shogun for bowing to foreign "barbarians." Foes of the Tokugawa took up the slogan: "Revere the

Meiji ivory carving of falconer in traditional clothing

"The land bordering the head of the bay was gay with a long stretch of painted screens of cloth, upon which was emblazoned the arms of the Emperor." —MATTHEW PERRY

VOICES

FILLMORE TRADE—OR ELSE!

"The United States of America reach from ocean to ocean, and our Territory of Oregon and State of California lie directly opposite to the dominions of your imperial majesty. Our steamships can go from California to Japan in eighteen days. Our great State of California produces about sixty millions of dollars in gold every year, besides silver, quicksilver, precious stones, and many other valuable articles. Japan is also a rich and fertile country, and produces many very valuable articles. . . . I am desirous that our two countries should trade."

—FROM A LETTER BY PRESIDENT MILLARD FILLMORE TO THE EMPEROR OF JAPAN, 1852

MILLARD FILLMORE

Emperor! Expel the barbarians!"

When samurai failed to expel foreigners, rebel leaders concluded that Japan would first have to master the techniques of Westerners before competing with them. After defeating the Tokugawa, they restored imperial rule under Komei's heir, Mutsuhito, who took the name Meiji ("Enlightened Rule") at his coronation in 1868 and went on to modernize Japan with his advisers' help. Instead of restoring daimyo and samurai to prominence, the new government offered them titles but stripped them of any real power. And instead of adopting Britain's liberal political system, Meiji adopted a constitution like imperial Germany's and made the nation's legislators and prime minister subject to him and his heirs.

{ Japan's constitution was described as a gift to avoid any suggestion that the emperor was yielding to reform. }

Generous government concessions to industrialists like Mitsubishi Shokai spurred the production of steel and armaments. By the 1890s, Japan's armed forces were ready to carry their imperial flag, emblazoned with the rising sun, overseas to Taiwan, Korea, and other countries and bid for supremacy in Asia and the Pacific.

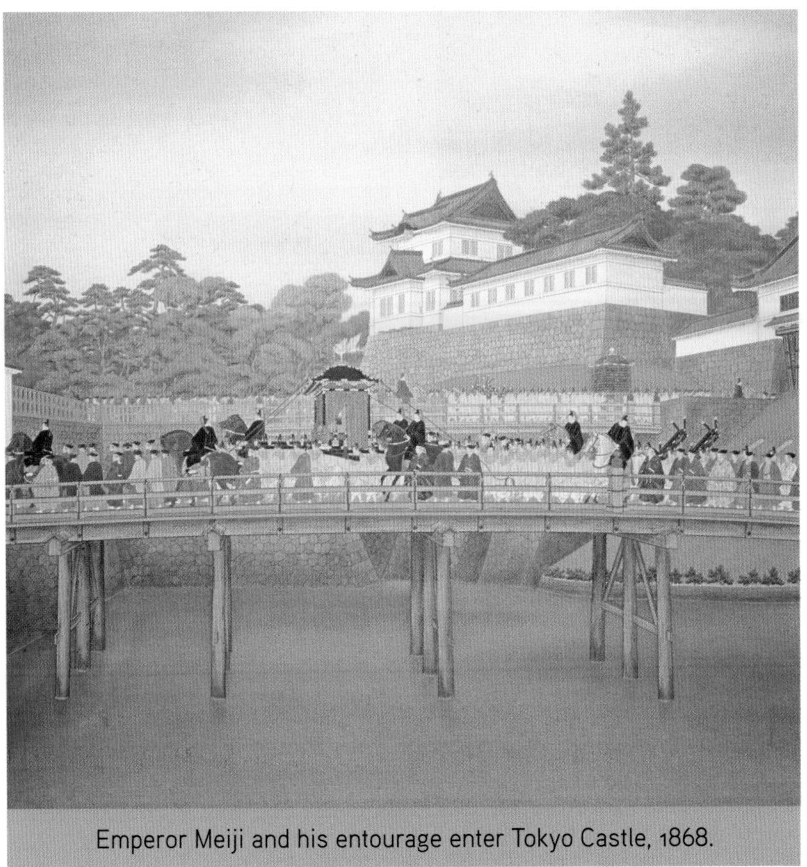

Emperor Meiji and his entourage enter Tokyo Castle, 1868.

THE TAKEAWAY: Japan could not exclude foreign powers from its shores, but it later used their technology to compete with them.

"At Mitsui's, the largest silk store in Tokyo, one will see crowds of clerks sitting upon the matted floors, each with his soroban, or adding machine, by his side." —ALICE BACON

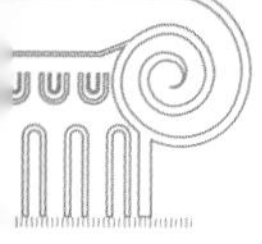

SEE ALSO | NEW WORLD ORDER: PAGE 279

NATIONS AUSTRALIA

Claimed for Great Britain by Captain Cook in 1770 and founded as a penal colony under military rule, Australia became a free society in the 1800s and offered opportunity to millions of settlers. The first colonizing expedition arrived on Australia's east coast in 1787 with more than 700 convicts, 160 of them women, and settled at what is now Sydney. Convicts who completed their sentences received land grants of 30 to 50 acres.

Australian settlers read the news from Britain.

Soldiers and officers obtained larger grants when they left service, and some became wealthy by selling rum. A more constructive trade began when sheep were introduced to Australia. By 1830 free settlers, many of whom came to raise sheep and harvest wool, outnumbered the country's convicts.

The discovery of gold, copper, and other minerals in the mid-1800s lured fortune hunters far beyond the original colony of New South Wales. Prospectors seeking gold in Victoria on Australia's southeastern tip rebelled against colonial authorities there. Demanding voting rights and an end to taxation without representation, in 1854 they holed up in the Eureka Stockade and defied lawmen. The ensuing battle made heroes of the rebels and advanced the cause of democratic government in Victoria.

For the most part, Australians resolved their differences without bloodshed, except when dealing with the country's Aborigines, many of whom perished in clashes or epidemics as settlers infringed on their domain. By 1901, when Australia's colonies confederated to form a self-governing British commonwealth, there were fewer than 100,000 Aborigines left in a nation of more than three million people.

{ More than 160,000 convicts were shipped to Australia before transportation of prisoners ended in 1868. }

Miners flocked to Victoria, looking for gold, in the mid-1800s.

THE TAKEAWAY: Australia grew from a tiny colony at Sydney Cove to an independent nation spanning the continent.

> *"Soldiers and the Inhabitants die very quick here, what with drinking & being exposed to the sudden changes of the weather."* —WILLIAM COKE

Maori chiefs and Lieutenant-Governor William Hobson sign the Treaty of Waitangi in 1840.

NATIONS NEW ZEALAND

New Zealand's early British settlers confronted a formidable native society, made up of Polynesians called Maoris, who were adept both at waging war and at making peace. Conflict and disease reduced their population, but there were still about 100,000 Maoris in New Zealand in 1840—50 times the number of colonists—when their chiefs agreed to the Treaty of Waitangi, recognizing British sovereignty in exchange for a pledge to protect their property rights. The country was granted self-rule in the 1850s, but the Maori continued to fight for their land until the 1870s, as more than 200,000 settlers arrived.

THE TAKEAWAY: Maoris used diplomacy as well as warfare to reckon with British colonization.

VOICES

TE RAUPARAHA HAKA

“*I die! I die! I live! I live!*
I die! I die! I live! I live!
This is the hairy man
Who has caused the sun to shine again
The Sun shines!!”

—THE 1820 HAKA (CHANT AND DANCE) OF MAORI CHIEF TE RAUPARAHA, WHOSE FELLOW CHIEF (THE HAIRY MAN) HID HIM FROM HIS ENEMIES AND SAVED HIS LIFE

HAKA DANCE

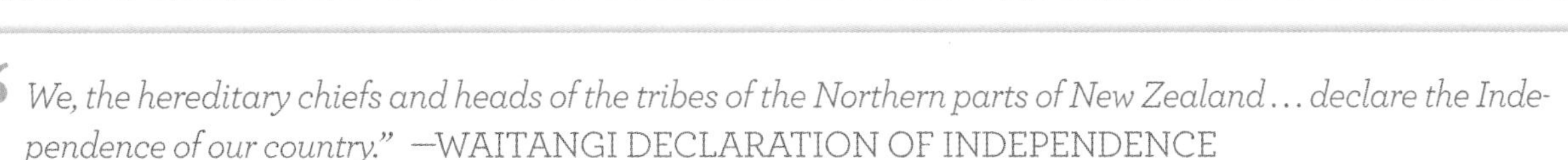
“*We, the hereditary chiefs and heads of the tribes of the Northern parts of New Zealand . . . declare the Independence of our country.*” —WAITANGI DECLARATION OF INDEPENDENCE

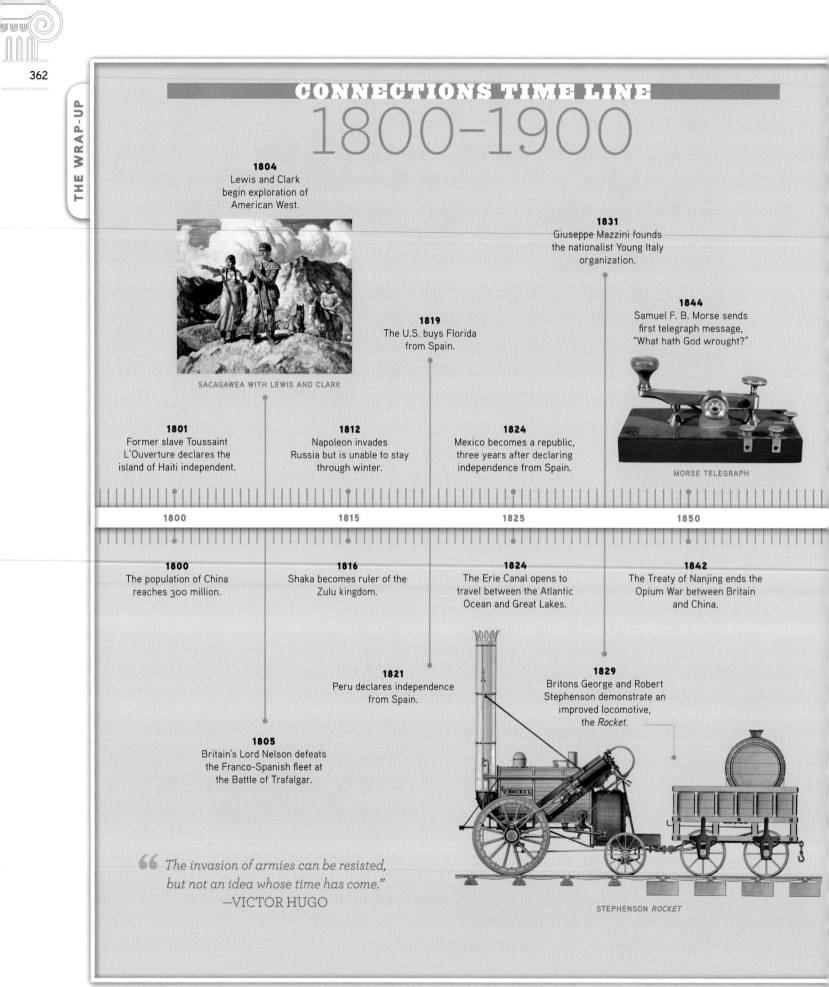

CONNECTIONS TIME LINE

1800–1900

1804
Lewis and Clark begin exploration of American West.

SACAGAWEA WITH LEWIS AND CLARK

1831
Giuseppe Mazzini founds the nationalist Young Italy organization.

1819
The U.S. buys Florida from Spain.

1844
Samuel F. B. Morse sends first telegraph message, "What hath God wrought?"

MORSE TELEGRAPH

1801
Former slave Toussaint L'Ouverture declares the island of Haiti independent.

1812
Napoleon invades Russia but is unable to stay through winter.

1824
Mexico becomes a republic, three years after declaring independence from Spain.

1800 — 1815 — 1825 — 1850

1800
The population of China reaches 300 million.

1816
Shaka becomes ruler of the Zulu kingdom.

1824
The Erie Canal opens to travel between the Atlantic Ocean and Great Lakes.

1842
The Treaty of Nanjing ends the Opium War between Britain and China.

1821
Peru declares independence from Spain.

1829
Britons George and Robert Stephenson demonstrate an improved locomotive, the *Rocket*.

1805
Britain's Lord Nelson defeats the Franco-Spanish fleet at the Battle of Trafalgar.

> "*The invasion of armies can be resisted, but not an idea whose time has come.*"
> —VICTOR HUGO

STEPHENSON *ROCKET*

1865
U.S. Civil War ends as Robert E. Lee surrenders the Confederate Army of Northern Virgina to Ulysses S. Grant.

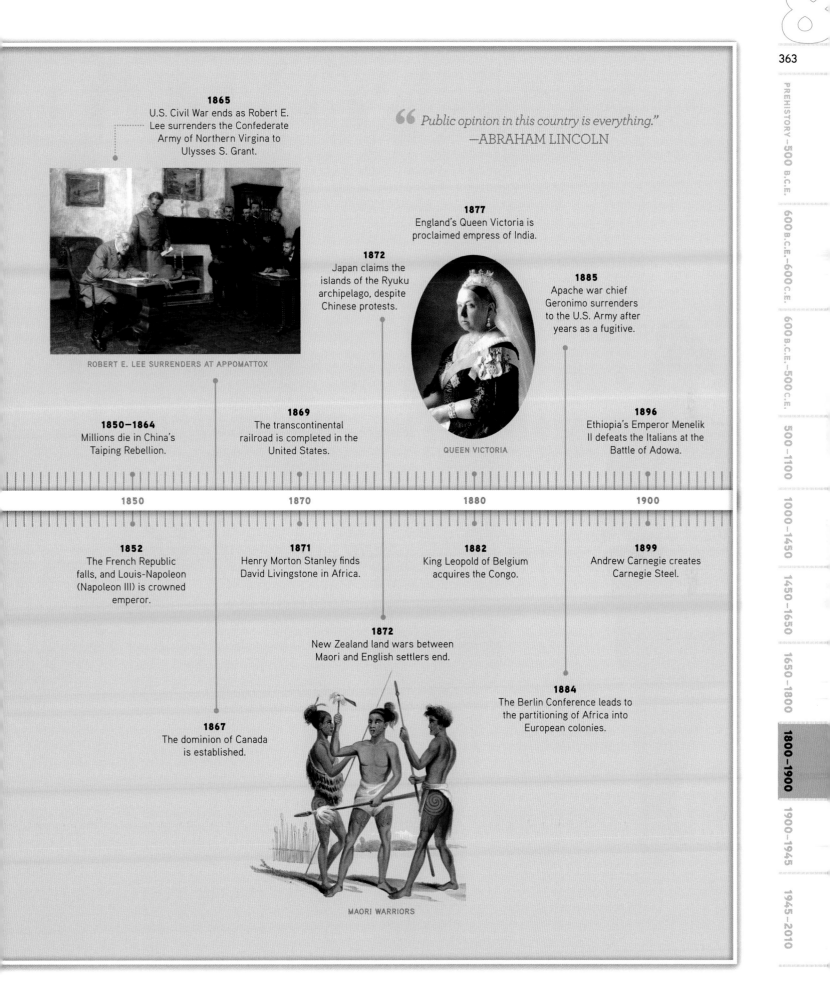

"Public opinion in this country is everything."
—ABRAHAM LINCOLN

ROBERT E. LEE SURRENDERS AT APPOMATTOX

1877
England's Queen Victoria is proclaimed empress of India.

1872
Japan claims the islands of the Ryuku archipelago, despite Chinese protests.

QUEEN VICTORIA

1885
Apache war chief Geronimo surrenders to the U.S. Army after years as a fugitive.

1850–1864
Millions die in China's Taiping Rebellion.

1869
The transcontinental railroad is completed in the United States.

1896
Ethiopia's Emperor Menelik II defeats the Italians at the Battle of Adowa.

1850 | 1870 | 1880 | 1900

1852
The French Republic falls, and Louis-Napoleon (Napoleon III) is crowned emperor.

1871
Henry Morton Stanley finds David Livingstone in Africa.

1882
King Leopold of Belgium acquires the Congo.

1899
Andrew Carnegie creates Carnegie Steel.

1872
New Zealand land wars between Maori and English settlers end.

1884
The Berlin Conference leads to the partitioning of Africa into European colonies.

1867
The dominion of Canada is established.

MAORI WARRIORS

THE WORLD

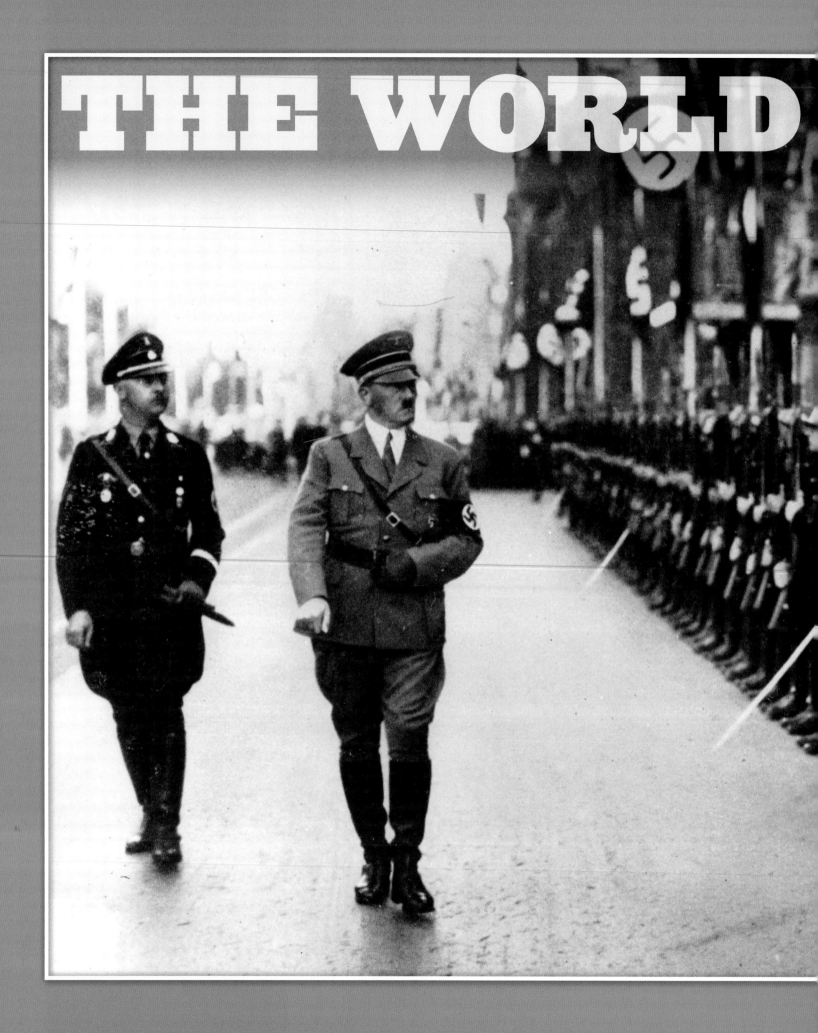

AT WAR

ACCOUNTS OF CRISIS AND HEROISM

1900–1945

CHAPTER

German dictator Adolf Hitler and Chief of Police Heinrich Himmler inspect the SS Guard.

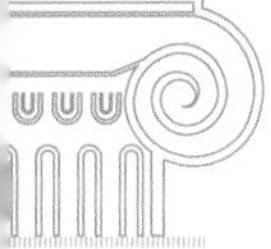

SEE ALSO | THE WORLD AT WAR: PAGE 371

KEY DATES

1901
Guglielmo Marconi transmits the world's first Morse code signals across the Atlantic.

1903
The Wright brothers complete the first successful test flight of their engine-powered airplane.

1905
Albert Einstein publishes his special theory of relativity.

1909
Pablo Picasso and Georges Braque begin to develop a style of painting known as cubism.

AGE OF SCIENCE

1900–1945

By 1900 the world had entered an era of rapid technological advances. This age of science, which began with the industrial revolution, saw more innovation in two centuries than had occurred in the past two thousand years. Transportation, for example, changed little between the time of Alexander the Great and Napoleon Bonaparte, whose troops still moved on foot or horseback, hauled supplies in carts drawn by animals, and went to sea in ships that moved under sail. By 1939, however, when Adolf Hitler unleashed German forces on campaigns of conquest that rivaled Napoleon's, warfare had been revolutionized by the introduction of submarines, aircraft, tanks, and trucks. No less important to the modern world and its warriors were advances in communications such as radio. Using such technologies, Germany and its ally Japan made quick gains in the early stages of the Second World War, only to be driven back and defeated as their opponents brought superior technology to bear.

Scientific breakthroughs made the 20th century a time of both phenomenal progress and unprecedented peril, marked by advances in transportation and communication and two devastating world wars.

Any doubt that scientific advances shaped history was dispelled in August 1945 when the United States ended the war by obliterating the Japanese cities of Hiroshima and Nagasaki with a single atomic bomb dropped on each. Those blasts served as stunning confirmation of a theoretical breakthrough made by physicist Albert Einstein in the early 1900s, when he demonstrated mathematically that a tiny amount of mass could be converted into an enormous amount of energy.

For those caught up in the two catastrophic world wars of the 20th century and the campaigns of terror and genocide waged by Hitler and other dictators, these were the worst of times. But where peace and justice prevailed, these were also the best of times. Advances in medicine and public health eliminated age-old plagues; radio and motion pictures delighted vast audiences; and automobiles and airplanes carried people farther, faster, and higher than ever before. Invention was embodied in new forms of expression, including jazz—which became so popular in the 1920s that the decade was known as the Jazz Age—and cubism, summed up by the startling works of Pablo Picasso, whose paintings were as radical a departure from classical artistic tradition as Einstein's theories were from the classical physics of Isaac Newton.

OPPOSITE: Brilliant physicist Albert Einstein helped to lead a revolution in modern science.

1914
The construction of the Panama Canal is completed.

1922
James Joyce's *Ulysses* is published, making famous the technique of stream-of-consciousness.

1928
Scottish biologist Alexander Fleming discovers penicillin.

1939
A team of German scientists split the atom.

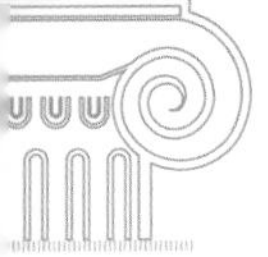

SEE ALSO | GLOBAL CULTURES: PAGE 439

Three passengers enjoy a Model T Ford, 1913.

TECHNOLOGY TRANSPORTATION

Transportation transformed the early 20th century. American industrialist Henry Ford made autos affordable to millions, reducing to hours journeys that once took days. Ocean voyages grew shorter as well when the Panama Canal opened in 1914 and passenger ships approached speeds of 30 knots. Gas-filled airships, like that unveiled in 1900 by Ferdinand von Zeppelin of Germany, were soon outpaced by airplanes. The first such flight, made in 1903 by Orville and Wilbur Wright, spanned 120 feet. In 1927 Charles Lindbergh flew nonstop from New York to Paris at over 100 miles an hour. By World War II, planes with jet engines surpassed 500 miles an hour.

THE TAKEAWAY: The world grew smaller with the automobile and aircraft.

VIPs

AGE OF SCIENCE

Marie Curie, 1867–1934
Polish-French physicist who helped decipher radioactivity and won two Nobel prizes

Orville and Wilbur Wright, 1871-1948 & 1867–1912
Builders of the first successful powered airplane

Albert Einstein, 1879–1955
German-American physicist who revolutionized thinking on space and time

Edwin Hubble, 1889–1953
American astronomer who helped measure the universe

VOICES

WILBUR AND ORVILLE WRIGHT

WRIGHT THE FIRST FLIGHT

“*I found the control of the front rudder quite difficult on account of its being balanced too near the center and thus had a tendency to turn itself when started so that the rudder was turned too far on one side and then too far on the other. As a result the machine would rise suddenly to about 10 ft. and then as suddenly, on turning the rudder, dart for the ground. A sudden dart when out about 100 feet from the end of the tracks ended the flight. Time about 12 seconds (not known exactly as watch was not promptly stopped).*”

—FROM ORVILLE WRIGHT'S DIARY, DECEMBER 17, 1903

“*Isn't it astonishing that all these secrets have been preserved for so many just so that we could discover them!!*” —ORVILLE WRIGHT

TECHNOLOGY COMMUNICATIONS

An early Thomas Edison phonograph

Electronic communication, which began in the 1800s with the invention of the telegraph and telephone, went wireless at the turn of the century when Guglielmo Marconi and other inventors devised techniques for using radio waves to send messages. Confounding predictions that radio signals sent long distance would be lost in space, Marconi succeeded in transmitting messages in Morse code by radio across the Atlantic in 1901.

The invention of vacuum tubes allowed radio waves to be amplified and made possible the first broadcast of voice and music in 1906. By the 1920s commercial radio stations were operating in many countries, bringing news and entertainment to the homes of millions.

The development of radio coincided with the emergence of motion pictures, based on techniques developed in the late 1800s by the Edison Company and the French inventors Louis and Auguste Lumière. By the early 1900s directors were using that technology to make dramatic films. Stage actors like British comedian Charlie Chaplin, who began his career in vaudeville, gained international fame in movies and soon were among the most popular figures on the planet. Cinema, phonographs, radio, and television—first used to broadcast news and entertainment in the 1930s—combined to produce a pop culture based on mass communications.

THE TAKEAWAY: Like motorized vehicles, radio and other electronic media shrank the world.

Actor and director Charlie Chaplin works the gears in his 1936 film, *Modern Times*.

> *"Just because something doesn't do what you planned it to do doesn't mean it's useless."*
> —THOMAS EDISON

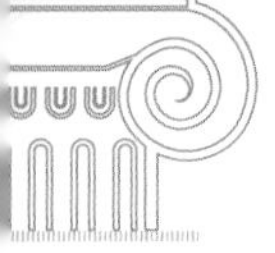

SEE ALSO | THE WORLD AT WAR: PAGE 395

Bacteriologist Alexander Fleming at his microscope.

SCIENCE BREAKTHROUGHS

Scientific breakthroughs in medicine and other fields brought the world great benefits in the 20th century and made societies as a whole healthier, wealthier, and more productive. But many scientific advances were subject to the law of unintended consequences. Penicillin, for example, discovered in 1928 by Alexander Fleming, a British physician and bacteriologist, saved countless lives by curing bacterial infections, but it was used so widely during and after the Second World War that some bacteria developed resistance to it and other antibiotics. Freon, developed by American chemist Thomas Midgley in 1930, made refrigeration and air-conditioning practical. Not until the 1970s did scientists identify Freon, also used as an aerosol propellant, as a threat to the atmosphere's ozone layer.

In no field were the unforeseen consequences of discoveries greater than in nuclear physics. Albert Einstein had no intention of launching a nuclear arms race when he arrived at his special theory of relativity in 1905 and produced the equation $E=mc^2$, meaning that the energy within the nucleus of an atom is equal to its mass times the speed of light squared. The initial impact of his discovery was to help explain such natural phenomena as the release of nuclear energy in the form of radioactivity, as heavy elements like uranium gradually decay. Research in radioactivity by scientists like Marie and Pierre Curie of France led to the use of x-rays to diagnose and treat illnesses.

Powder compact made of Bakelite, a versatile early plastic

Drawing on the theories of Einstein and other physicists, astronomers traced the vast amounts of energy emitted by stars to nuclear reactions produced in their cores under pressure. In 1929 American astronomer Edwin Hubble used

> In 1907, chemist Leo Baekeland invented the first multipurpose plastic, which he called Bakelite.

> *"After all, science is essentially international, and it is only through lack of the historical sense that national qualities have been attributed to it."* —MARIE CURIE

VOICES

EINSTEIN VAST AMOUNTS OF POWER

"Over the course of the last four months it has been made probable through the work of Joliot in France as well as Fermi and Szilard in America—that it may be possible to set up a nuclear chain reaction in a large mass of uranium, by which vast amounts of power and large quantities of new radium-like elements would be generated. Now it appears almost certain that this could be achieved in the immediate future. ∞ This new phenomenon would also lead to the construction of bombs."

—FROM A LETTER BY ALBERT EINSTEIN TO PRESIDENT ROOSEVELT, AUGUST 2, 1939

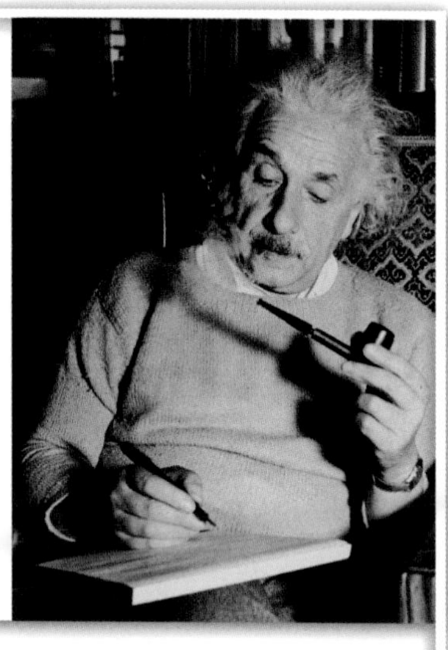

ALBERT EINSTEIN

measurements of starlight to show that the universe is expanding and calculated the rate of expansion. His finding led to the big bang theory, proposing that the universe originated more than ten billion years ago with a cosmic expansion of densely compressed matter.

The frightening possibility that scientists might produce their own big bang on Earth, powerful enough to level cities, became real in January 1939 when a team of German scientists split the atom by breaking uranium down into lighter elements and converting part of its mass into energy. That breakthrough, made as war loomed in Europe, raised fears in other countries that Adolf Hitler might one day possess a nuclear weapon. Einstein, born in Germany but now residing in the United States, wrote a letter to President Franklin Roosevelt in August urging him to fund an American nuclear research program to counter the German threat. From that warning came the top-secret Manhattan Project, a massive, nationwide effort to produce the first atomic bomb. Scientists tested such a weapon successfully on July 16, 1945, near Los Alamos, New Mexico, less than a month before it was used against Japan to end World War II.

{ Ernest Rutherford of New Zealand showed in 1911 that the atom consists of electrons orbiting a nucleus. }

Marie and Pierre Curie in their laboratory in Paris.

THE TAKEAWAY: Breakthroughs in physics brought great risks and great rewards.

"We cannot control atomic energy to an extent which would be of any value commercially, and I believe we are not likely ever to be able to do so." —ERNEST RUTHERFORD

ARTS MODERNISM

In the early 1900s a movement called modernism, which broke sharply with tradition, came to dominate painting, literature, music, and other arts. Modernists rejected conventional standards of beauty, proportion, harmony, and realism. The calamitous First World War seemed to confirm their view that things were falling apart and had to be reassembled in new ways.

Backed by his paintings, Pablo Picasso takes his own picture, 1916.

Ragtime music, like that of Scott Joplin, influenced both the jazz and classical worlds

One of the forerunners of modernism was French painter Paul Cézanne, who moved beyond impressionism and painted landscapes that were increasingly abstract and geometrical. "Everything in Nature is modeled after the sphere, the cone, and the cylinder," he wrote. That approach was taken up in Paris in the early 1900s by Georges Braque of France and Pablo Picasso of Spain, who developed a style known as cubism because they portrayed objects in fragments, often reducing them to geometrical shapes.

> Modern literature was influenced by psychoanalyst Sigmund Freud, who stated that the subconscious mind harbors repressed desires.

Modern art influenced modern

> *"For me, a painting is a dramatic action in the course of which reality finds itself split apart. For me, that dramatic action takes precedence over all other considerations."* —PABLO PICASSO

SEE ALSO | THE WORLD AT WAR: PAGE 382

architects like Swiss designer Le Corbusier (born Charles-Edouard Jenneret), whose influential designs were spare and geometrically precise. In literature, modernists such as James Joyce of Ireland and Virgina Woolf of England departed from the realism and objectivity of 19th-century novelists and explored the hidden thoughts and yearnings of their characters.

Composers and performers created their own musical streams of consciousness by abandoning conventional tonality and meter. Even popular music like jazz was modernist in allowing artists, like New Orleans trumpeter Louis Armstrong, to improvise and go beyond the conventional limits of standard meter and melody.

THE TAKEAWAY: Arts in the early 20th century mirrored the dramatic changes in society and technology.

Manhattan's Flatiron Building (1902) was one of the first skyscrapers.

VOICES

VALÉRY THE LIMIT OF MODERNISM

PAUL VALÉRY

"Europe in 1914 had perhaps reached the limit of modernism in this sense. Every mind of any scope was a crossroads for all shades of opinion; every thinker was an international exposition of thought. There were the works of the mind in which the wealth of contrasts and contradictory tendencies was like the insane displays of light in the capitals of those days: eyes were fatigued, scorched. . . . How much material wealth, how much labor and planning it took, how many centuries were ransacked, how many heterogeneous lives were combined, to make possible such a carnival, and to set it up as the supreme wisdom and the triumph of humanity?"

—FROM "THE CRISIS OF THE MIND," PAUL VALÉRY, 1919

"The beauty of the world has two edges, one of laughter, one of anguish, cutting the heart asunder."

—VIRGINIA WOOLF

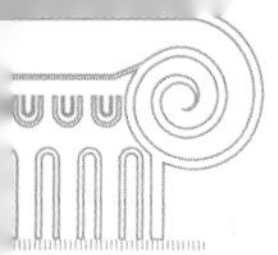

SEE ALSO | THE WORLD AT WAR: PAGE 378

KEY DATES

1901
President William McKinley is assassinated by an anarchist.

1908
Ford Motor Company produces the first Model T.

1910
The Mexican Revolution begins.

1917
The United States enters World War I.

THE AMERICAS

1900–1945

The United States, which had just begun to emerge as a world power in the late 1800s, achieved such prominence globally during the 1900s that this was labeled the American Century. The chief sources of America's strength were its stable political system—based on an evolving Constitution whose amendments made the nation increasingly democratic—and its hugely productive economy. Industrially, it surpassed Great Britain and other European countries. And unlike Britain, which had to import food, the United States with its vast agricultural areas more than met the demands of its fast-growing population. It could recruit and equip a huge army, if the need arose, and was potentially the greatest power on Earth. As the 20th century dawned, however, it remained unclear whether the country would fulfill that potential. Politically, it had far to go before it reached the goal of "liberty and justice for all" set forth in 1892's Pledge of Allegiance. Women were not allowed to vote in federal elections until 1920, and most African-Americans were effectively barred from polling places in the South until the 1960s. Economically, this wealthy nation was still riddled with poverty, and many people in rural areas lived without electricity or plumbing. Not until the Great Depression gripped the country in the 1930s and President Franklin D. Roosevelt introduced his New Deal did the government take strong measures to relieve poverty and avert greater social and political turmoil.

{ Relying on its political stability and economic vigor, the United States entered the 20th century as the strongest nation in the Americas and emerged during the 1900s as the greatest power in the world. }

Latin American countries lacked the political stability and economic resources to weather storms like the Great Depression and were overshadowed by U.S. wealth and power. By intervening in Cuba during the Spanish-American War and annexing Puerto Rico, the United States demonstrated that it had the potential to dominate Latin America militarily as well as economically. The Mexican Revolution, which erupted in 1910, spilled across the border in 1916 and drew American troops into that country. By ending that intervention, however, and joining the war in Europe in 1917, the United States made clear that it had larger concerns overseas. The question it faced in years to come was how to use its strength internationally not just to respond to conflicts like World War I but to prevent them from occurring.

OPPOSITE: President Franklin D. Roosevelt led the United States through the Depression and war.

1923
Mexican bandit Pancho Villa is killed by gunmen.

1929
Black Tuesday in New York signals a stock market crash and the beginning of the Great Depression.

1935
President Roosevelt signs the U.S. Social Security Act.

1941
The United States enters World War II after the bombing of Pearl Harbor.

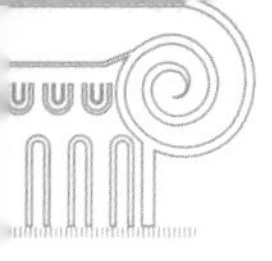

SEE ALSO | EMPIRES RISING: PAGE 348

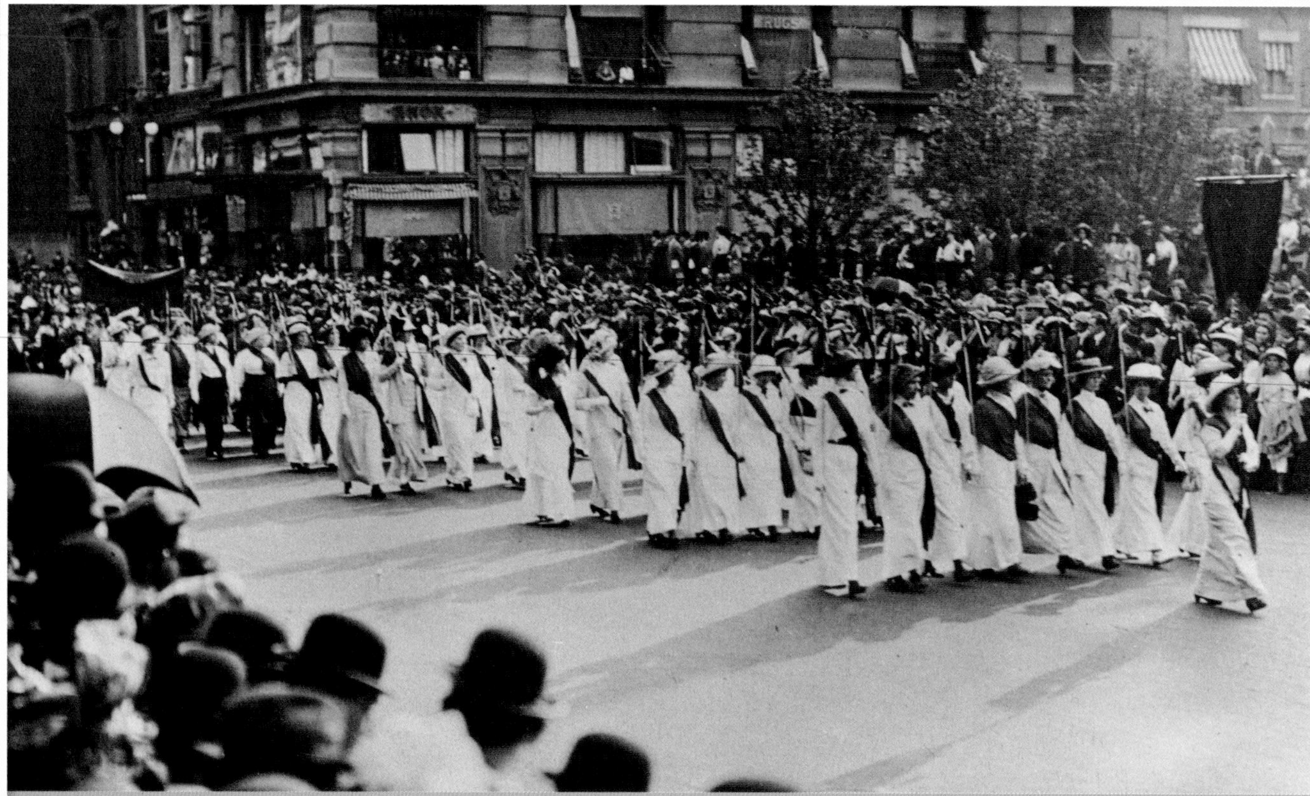

Women's suffrage demonstrators march for the vote, 1910.

CLASS & SOCIETY PROGRESSIVISM

The early 20th century became known as the Progressive Era in America because reformers committed to causes such as women's rights and the defeat of political corruption made major advances. Progressives took charge of political parties and pushed for change from the White House. Republican Theodore Roosevelt, thrust into office in 1901 by the assassination of William McKinley, was the first president to use the Sherman Antitrust Act to bust trusts, forcing monopolies to break up into smaller companies. He also proposed an eight-hour day for American workers and conserved forests and wildlife by protecting public land from private development. Democrat Woodrow Wilson, elected president in 1912, furthered progressive causes by backing constitutional amendments that allowed for a graduated federal income tax and direct election of U.S. senators—chosen previously by state legislatures and their political bosses.

Other important social changes were begun by people with little political power. The National Asso-

THE AMERICAS

VIPs

John D. Rockefeller, 1839–1937 Oil magnate, founder of Standard Oil Company, and philanthropist

Woodrow Wilson, 1856–1924 The 28th president of the United States, advocate of League of Nations

Theodore Roosevelt, 1858–1919 The 26th president of the United States; regulator of trusts

W.E.B. Du Bois, 1868–1963 American sociologist, protest leader, and one of the founders of the NAACP

Franklin D. Roosevelt, 1882–1945 The 32nd president of the United States and proponent of New Deal

“*No man is above the law and no man is below it; nor do we ask any man's permission when we require him to obey it.*” —THEODORE ROOSEVELT

VOICES

SHEPHERD TRIANGLE SHIRTWAIST FIRE

"On the sidewalk lay heaps of broken bodies. A policeman later went about with tags, which he fastened with wires to the wrists of the dead girls, numbering each with a lead pencil, and I saw him fasten tag no. 54 to the wrist of a girl who wore an engagement ring. A fireman who came downstairs from the building told me that there were at least fifty bodies in the big room on the seventh floor. . . . I looked upon the heap of dead bodies and I remembered these girls were the shirtwaist makers. I remembered their great strike of last year in which these same girls had demanded more sanitary conditions and more safety precautions in the shops. These dead bodies were the answer."

—FROM "EYEWITNESS AT THE TRIANGLE" BY WILLIAM SHEPHERD, *MILWAUKEE JOURNAL*, MARCH 27, 1911

TRIANGLE FIRE

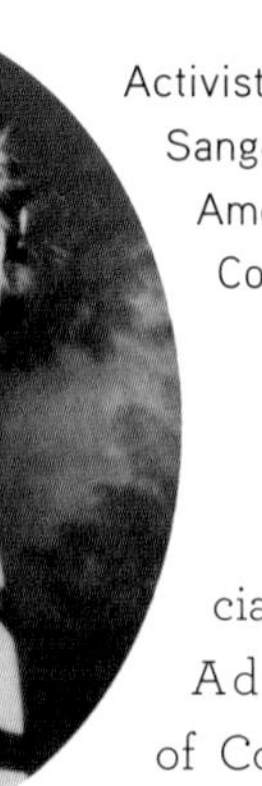

Activist Margaret Sanger founded the American Birth Control League

ciation for the Advancement of Colored People (NAACP), founded in 1909 by African-American historian W.E.B. Du Bois and other activists, challenged racial segregation in court. The National American Woman Suffrage Association grew from barely 10,000 members in 1890 to over two million in 1917; in 1920, the adoption of the 19th Amendment gave women the vote.

Women also made economic gains as labor unions sought better conditions for those who toiled in trades like the garment industry, notorious for its dismal sweatshops. In 1911, 146 employees died in a fire in New York's Triangle Shirtwaist Factory, where the owners had locked the emergency exits. Protests from labor unions and the public led to tough new safety regulations in New York factories.

The Progressive Era ended in the 1920s as Americans wearied of moralistic reforms like Prohibition (1920–1933), easily violated by bootleggers. Fears that foreigners were spreading radical ideas and might overwhelm the nation's Anglo-American population led to severe restrictions on immigration. Meanwhile, as the economy boomed, investors on Wall Street borrowed heavily to buy stocks, trusting that prosperity was here to stay.

THE TAKEAWAY: Reformers sought to transform American society early in the century.

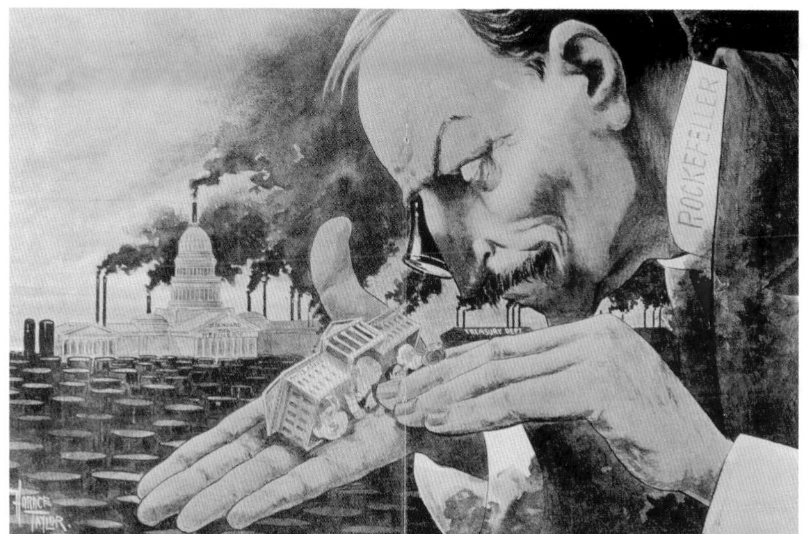

A cartoon lampoons the influence of Standard Oil founder Rockefeller.

"When I sell liquor, it's called bootlegging; when my patrons serve it on Lake Shore Drive, it's called hospitality." —AL CAPONE

SEE ALSO | EMPIRES RISING: PAGE 351

ECONOMY

THE GREAT DEPRESSION

In October 1929 the great stock market boom went bust. Soon businesses were laying off workers by the thousands and banks were calling in loans at home and abroad, transforming a recession into a global catastrophe known as the Great Depression. By 1932 the U.S. unemployment rate had reached 25 percent. Homeless people camped in shantytowns, known as Hoovervilles after the increasingly unpopular President Herbert Hoover. As the Depression deepened, Hoover lost his bid for reelection to Franklin Roosevelt, who promised "a new deal for Americans." Roosevelt restored faith in the banking system and promoted economic recovery through New Deal agencies such as the Civilian Conservation Corps.

Cartoon showing New Deal programs dancing around President Roosevelt

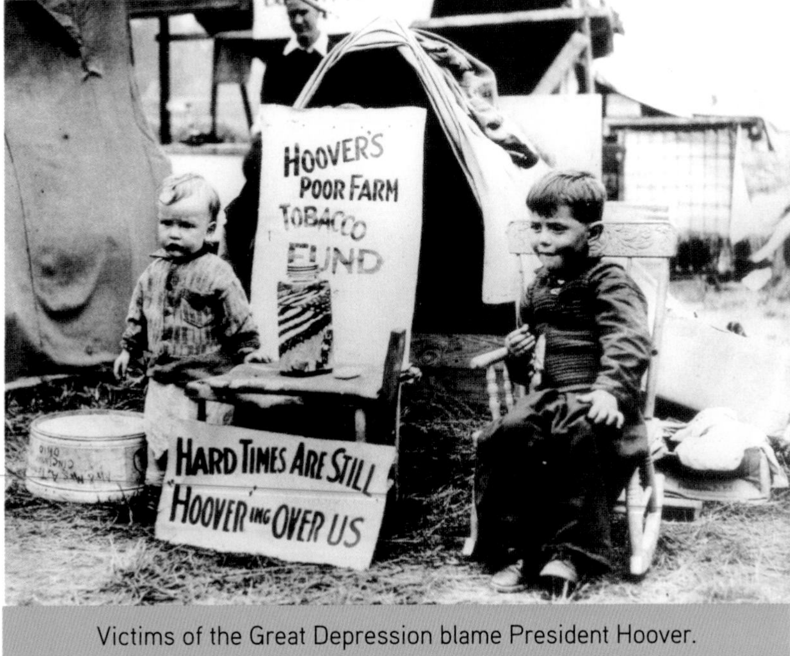

Victims of the Great Depression blame President Hoover.

THE TAKEAWAY: The U.S. stock market crash of 1929 propelled the world into the Great Depression.

U.S. SENATE LIVING ON DANDELIONS

VOICES

"One woman went along the docks and picked up vegetables that fell from the wagons. Sometimes the fish vendors gave her fish at the end of the day. On two different occasions this family was without food for a day and a half. . . .

"Another family did not have food for two days. Then the husband went out and gathered dandelions and the family lived on them."

—FROM HEARINGS BEFORE A SUBCOMMITTEE OF THE SENATE COMMITTEE ON MANUFACTURES, 1932

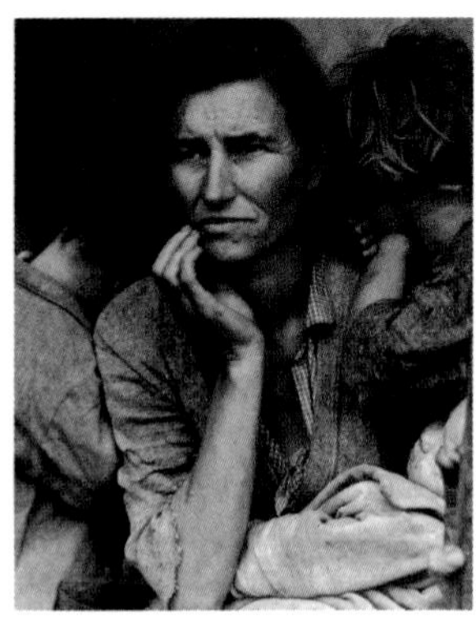

MOTHER OF SEVEN, CALIFORNIA

"We are moving forward to greater freedom, to greater security for the average man then he has ever known before in the history of America." —FRANKLIN DELANO ROOSEVELT

REVOLUTIONS MEXICO TRANSFORMED

In 1910, a century after it rebelled against Spain, Mexico once again experienced violent revolutionary upheaval. Among those who took up arms were Indians and mestizos toiling for wealthy landowners who held them in peonage, or debt servitude. Mexicans also resented foreign ownership of their resources and felt they had not yet achieved true independence. The Mexican Revolution erupted in November 1910 after President Porfirio Díaz had his presidential opponent, Francisco Madero, arrested. Rebel leaders Pancho Villa and Emiliano Zapata raised troops in support of Madero and helped install him as president. In 1913 he was killed in a coup encouraged by the U.S. ambassador to Mexico, acting without the knowledge of President Wilson.

In 1916 Villa raided a U.S. army camp in New Mexico, prompting Wilson to send forces led by General John Pershing deep into Mexico in pursuit. That nearly set the United States at war with Mexico before Wilson withdrew Pershing in 1917 to prepare for combat in Europe. The Mexican Revolution ended in 1920 when Alvaro Obregon became president, endorsing a new constitution that promised reform.

Mexican president Lázaro Cárdenas addresses a crowd.

THE TAKEAWAY: The Mexican Revolution was fueled by widespread poverty.

Bandit and revolutionary leader Francisco (Pancho) Villa attacked both Mexican and U.S. targets.

“*Men of the South! It is better to die on your feet than to live on your knees!*” —EMILIANO ZAPATA

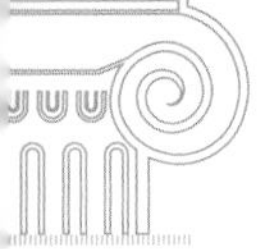

SEE ALSO | THE WORLD AT WAR: PAGE 384

KEY DATES

1901
The Social Revolutionary Party is founded in Russia.

1905
Greeks in Crete revolt against the Turks.

1912
The alliance of Germany, Austria-Hungary, and Italy is renewed.

1914
World War I begins after Austrian archduke Francis Ferdinand is assassinated.

EUROPE & THE WORLD WARS

1900–1945

European imperial rivalries originating in the 1800s ignited explosive world wars in the 1900s. The German Reich that emerged in 1871 faced rival empires on either side in France and Russia and sought to strengthen its position by forging the Triple Alliance with Austria-Hungary (as the former Austrian empire was now known) and Italy. In response, France formed the Triple Entente with Britain and Russia. Those entangling alliances threatened to drag all the major European powers into war if anyone broke the peace.

World War I was triggered in the Balkans on June 28, 1914, when Archduke Franz Ferdinand, heir to the Austro-Hungarian throne, was assassinated in the Bosnian capital of Sarajevo by a member of a terrorist group organized in neighboring Serbia. Austria-Hungary blamed Serbia and declared war on that country on July 28 despite Russia's pledge to defend Serbia.

When Russia began mobilizing its forces, Germany set out to defeat France before Russian troops were ready. Within days, Europe was engulfed in a massive conflict that soon spread to other continents. The Turkish-ruled Ottoman Empire sided with the Central Powers (Germany and its partners) while Italy joined the opposing Allies, who emerged triumphant in 1918 after the United States entered the fray.

Billed as the war to end all wars, World War I left chaos in its wake instead, leading to the rise of aggressive new regimes in Europe that launched World War II 21 years later.

This ruinous conflict and the Versailles Treaty that concluded it failed to end imperial rivalries. Though several emperors were toppled during the war, menacing new regimes emerged afterward, notably Hitler's Third Reich.

Germany launched World War II in 1939 by invading Poland and went on to use its tanks and bombers to wage blitzkrieg, or lightning war, against France and Britain. Those Allies faced an even greater challenge now than in the last war. In 1941, however, the aggressive Axis powers set the stage for their ultimate defeat with attacks on the Soviet Union and the United States that drew those two future superpowers into the conflict on the Allied side.

OPPOSITE: An illustration dramatizes the German bombing of London during World War II.

1920
The Russian Civil War ends in victory for the Bolsheviks.

1926
Benito Mussolini takes control in Italy.

1933
Adolf Hitler is elected chancellor in Germany.

1939
World War II begins in Europe as Hitler invades Poland.

CONFLICTS WORLD WAR I

Germany might have avoided war had its leaders discouraged their ally Austria-Hungary from avenging the assassination of Archduke Franz Ferdinand by attacking Serbia. Once the die was cast and Russia began mobilizing to defend Serbia, German generals forged ahead, hoping to deliver a decisive blow against the Allied nations of Russia, France, and Britain. In August 1914 they sent most of their army into France, intending to overwhelm French forces and leave Russia alone to be defeated by the Central Powers.

After advancing rapidly, German forces lost momentum as they neared Paris and were pushed back in the First Battle of the Marne. A stalemate ensued in northern France as the opposing forces dug trenches, shielded by barbed wire and machine guns. Massive battles in 1916 at Verdun and the Somme resulted in more than two million casualties. Poison gas attacks made trench warfare all the more horrific.

The Central Powers fared better against Russia, where the tsarist regime suffered humiliating defeats and collapsed in March 1917. Communist leader Vladimir Lenin took power in November and soon pulled out of the war. By then, Germany's allies were faltering as

> World War I was intensely destructive, claiming the lives of nearly 15 million soldiers and civilians.

French soldiers take a break in the trenches of Verdun, 1917.

EUROPE — VIPs

Vladimir Lenin, 1870–1924
Russian leader of Bolsheviks and first head of the U.S.S.R.

Winston Churchill, 1874–1965
British prime minister who led Great Britain in World War II

Joseph Stalin, 1879–1953
Successor to Lenin and premier of the U.S.S.R.

Benito Mussolini, 1883–1945
Fascist dictator and prime minister of Italy

Adolf Hitler, 1889–1945
Founder of the German Nazi Party, chancellor of the Third Reich, and instigator of genocide during World War II

"The United States must be neutral in fact as well as in name. . . . We must be impartial in thought as well as in action." —WOODROW WILSON

SEE ALSO | THE WORLD AT WAR: PAGE 386

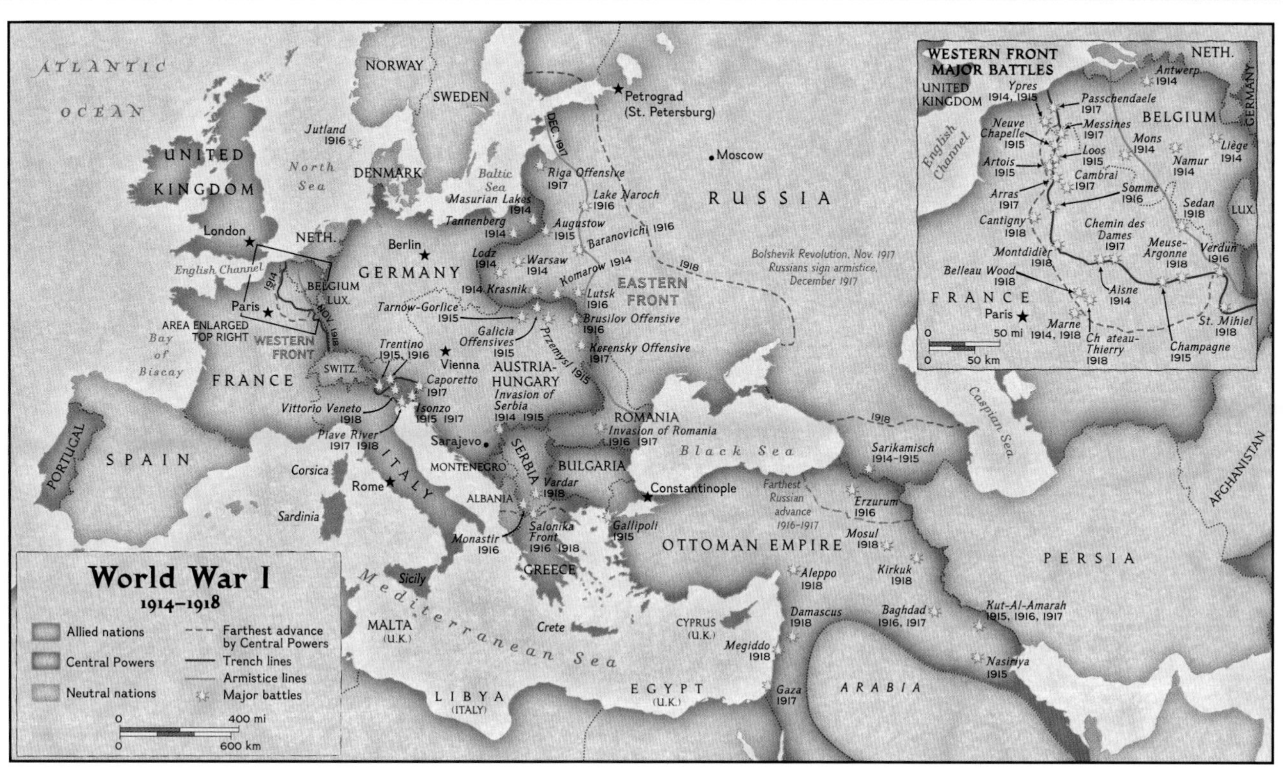

well. After being repulsed by Turks at Gallipoli in 1915 with terrible losses, the Allies rebounded and joined Arabs in the Middle East in shattering the Ottoman Empire. Austria-Hungary, meanwhile, had been attacked by Italy—which went over to the Allies in 1915—and was losing control of its empire.

Hurt by a British naval blockade, Germany struck back in February 1917 by declaring unrestricted submarine warfare in the Atlantic. That placed American ships at risk and helped induce the U.S. to join the Allies in April. By 1918 more than a million American troops had arrived in France. Bolstered by their presence and the introduction of tanks, which helped puncture enemy defenses, the Allies broke through and forced Germany and its allies to capitulate in November.

THE TAKEAWAY: The entry of the U.S. into World War I helped the Allies prevail over the Central Powers.

VOICES

EMPEY GAS ATTACK IN THE TRENCHES

"German gas is heavier than air and soon fills the trenches and dugouts, where it has been known to lurk for two or three days, until the air is purified by means of large chemical sprayers. We had to work quickly, as Fritz generally follows the gas with an infantry attack. A company man on our right was too slow in getting on his helmet; he sank to the ground, clutching at his throat, and after a few spasmodic twistings, went West [died]."

—FROM *OVER THE TOP*, ARTHUR GUY EMPEY, 1917

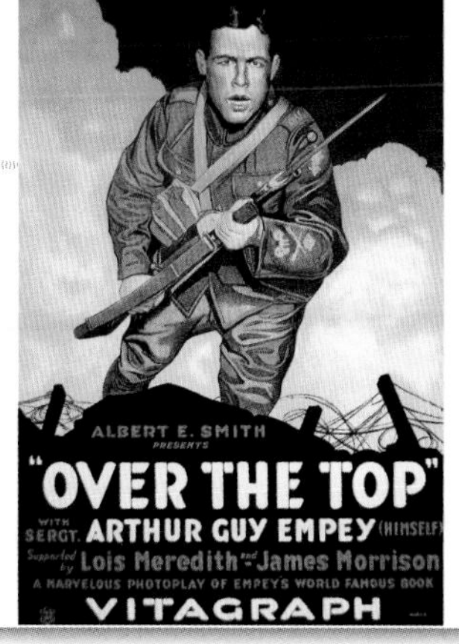

POSTER FOR *OVER THE TOP* FILM

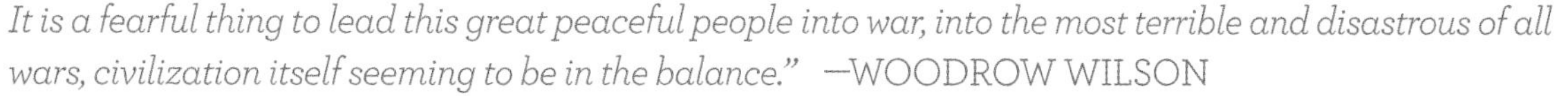

"It is a fearful thing to lead this great peaceful people into war, into the most terrible and disastrous of all wars, civilization itself seeming to be in the balance." —WOODROW WILSON

TREATY OF VERSAILLES

IN 1919, delegates met at the Paris Peace Conference to draw up a treaty that would end the war and restructure Europe. Leading the talks was President Woodrow Wilson, whose hopes for a lasting peace, enforced by a newly established League of Nations, were not fulfilled. By blaming the war on Germany, forcing it to pay reparations to the Allies, and reducing its territory, the Treaty of Versailles undermined Germany's postwar government, the Weimar Republic. Newly recognized nations such as Czechoslovakia struggled to reach self-determination. The league lacked enforcement powers and lost crucial support when the U.S. Senate voted not to join the league. In the end, the treaty may have only led to a new, bitter conflict.

32 TREATY OF PEACE WITH GERMANY.

caring for or erecting suitable memorials over the said graves and to facilitate the discharge of its duties.

Furthermore they agree to afford, so far as the provisions of their laws and the requirements of public health allow, every facility for giving effect to requests that the bodies of their soldiers and sailors may be transferred to their own country.

ARTICLE 226.

The graves of prisoners of war and interned civilians who are nationals of the different belligerent States and have died in captivity shall be properly maintained in accordance with Article 225 of the present Treaty.

The Allied and Associated Governments on the one part and the German Government on the other part reciprocally undertake also to furnish to each other:

(1) A complete list of those who have died, together with all information useful for identification;

(2) All information as to the number and position of the graves of all those who have been buried without identification.

PART VIII.

REPARATION.

SECTION I.

GENERAL PROVISIONS.

ARTICLE 231.

The Allied and Associated Governments affirm and Germany accepts the responsibility of Germany and her allies for causing all the loss and damage to which the Allied and Associated Governments and their nationals have been subjected as a consequence of the war imposed upon them by the aggression of Germany and her allies.

ARTICLE 232.

The Allied and Associated Governments recognize that the resources of Germany are not adequate, after taking into account permanent diminutions of such resources which will result from other provisions of the present Treaty, to make complete reparation for all such loss and damage.

The Allied and Associated Governments, however, require, and Germany undertakes, that she will make compensation for all damage done to the civilian population of the Allied and Associated Powers and to their property during the period of the belligerency of each as an Allied or Associated Power against Germany by such

WOODROW WILSON Although President Wilson succeeded in creating the League of Nations, the Versailles Treaty was more punitive than he had hoped. After returning to the United States in 1919, he suffered a stroke while campaigning for public acceptance of the league.

"The Members of the League undertake to respect and preserve as against external aggression the territorial integrity and existing political independence of all Members of the League."

"The tutelage of [former colonies] should be entrusted to advanced nations who by reason of their resources, their experience or their geographical position can best undertake this responsibility."

FRENCH AND ENGLISH The original copy of the final treaty, which was published in French and English, was placed in French archives.

“Germany renounces in favour of the Principal Allied and Associated Powers all her rights and titles over her oversea possessions.”

“Germany shall pay in such installments and in such manner (whether in gold, commodities, ships, securities or otherwise) as the Reparation Commission may fix, during 1919, 1920 and the first four months of 1921, the equivalent of 20,000,000,000 gold marks.”

TREATY OF PEACE WITH GERMANY. 33

aggression by land, by sea and from the air, and in general all damage as defined in Annex I hereto.

In accordance with Germany's pledges, already given, as to complete restoration for Belgium, Germany undertakes, in addition to the compensation for damage elsewhere in this Part provided for, as a consequence of the violation of the Treaty of 1839, to make reimbursement of all sums which Belgium has borrowed from the Allied and Associated Governments up to November 11, 1918, together with interest at the rate of five per cent. (5%) per annum on such sums. This amount shall be determined by the Reparation Commission, and the German Government undertakes thereupon forthwith to make a special issue of bearer bonds to an equivalent amount payable in marks gold, on May 1, 1926, or, at the option of the German Government, on the 1st of May in any year up to 1926. Subject to the foregoing, the form of such bonds shall be determined by the Reparation Commission. Such bonds shall be handed over to the Reparation Commission, which has authority to take and acknowledge receipt thereof on behalf of Belgium.

ARTICLE 233.

The amount of the above damage for which compensation is to be made by Germany shall be determined by an Inter-Allied Commission, to be called the *Reparation Commission* and constituted in the form and with the powers set forth hereunder and in Annexes II to VII inclusive hereto.

This Commission shall consider the claims and give to the German Government a just opportunity to be heard.

The findings of the Commission as to the amount of damage defined as above shall be concluded and notified to the German Government on or before May 1, 1921, as representing the extent of that Government's obligations.

The Commission shall concurrently draw up a schedule of payments prescribing the time and manner for securing and discharging the entire obligation within a period of thirty years from May 1, 1921. If, however, within the period mentioned, Germany fails to discharge her obligations, any balance remaining unpaid may, within the discretion of the Commission, be postponed for settlement in subsequent years, or may be handled otherwise in such manner as the Allied and Associated Governments, acting in accordance with the procedure laid down in this Part of the present Treaty, shall determine.

ARTICLE 234.

The Reparation Commission shall after May 1, 1921, from time to time, consider the resources and capacity of Germany, and, after giving her representatives a just opportunity to be heard, shall have discretion to extend the date, and to modify the form of payments, such as are to be provided for in accordance with Article 233; but not to cancel any part, except with the specific authority of the several Governments represented upon the Commission.

68340—S. Doc. 70, 67-1——3

“The Allied and Associated Powers publicly arraign William II of Hohenzollern, formerly German Emperor, for a supreme offence against international morality and the sanctity of treaties.”

RULES FOR THE CONQUERED The 440 articles of the treaty covered a wide range of political and economic issues, including prisoners of war, ports and railways, and air rights over Germany.

CRUSHING BURDEN A German lithograph from the 1930s depicts Germany crushed under the weight of the treaty. Angered by the war reparations clause and the treaty's "dictated peace," Germans also suffered under runaway inflations in the 1920s, followed by the Great Depression in the 1930s.

NEW NATIONS

The final peace settlement included four treaties besides the one with Germany. Together, the five treaties created new nations from the former Austro-Hungarian Empire, Germany, and Russia. They included:

FINLAND: From Russia

LATVIA: From Russia

ESTONIA: From Russia

LITHUANIA: From Russia

POLAND: From Russia and Germany

CZECHOSLOVAKIA: From Austria-Hungary

AUSTRIA: Split off from Austria-Hungary

HUNGARY: Split off from Austria-Hungary

SEE ALSO | THE WORLD AT WAR: PAGE 330

Painting by Vladimirov of Bloody Sunday fighting at the Winter Palace, 1905.

CONFLICTS

END OF THE TSARS

The collapse of Russia's Romanov dynasty began in January 1905 when troops guarding Tsar Nicholas II at the Winter Palace in St. Petersburg gunned down more than 100 unarmed protesters. The Bloody Sunday attack provoked a revolution by Russians opposed to imperial rule. Troops loyal to Nicholas eventually put down the rebellion, but the tsar lacked the military power to cope with rival nations like Japan, whose navy destroyed the Russian Baltic fleet in 1905. His forces met with further disasters in World War I, resulting in uprisings that led him to abdicate in March 1917.

Members of the Duma legislature then formed a provisional government, but this body was short-lived; it was toppled in November by communists called Bolsheviks, led by Vladimir Lenin.

THE TAKEAWAY: Weakened internally and externally, Russia's imperial regime collapsed in 1917.

VOICES

REED STORMING THE WINTER PALACE

JOHN REED

"We penetrated at length to the gold and malachite chamber with crimson brocade hangings where the Ministers had been in session all that day and night and where the shveitzari *had betrayed them to the Red Guards. The long table covered with green baize was just as they had left it, under arrest. Before each empty seat was pen and ink and paper; the papers were scribbled over with beginnings of plans of action, rough drafts of proclamations and manifestos. Most of these were scratched out, as their futility became evident, and the rest of the sheet covered with absent-minded geometrical designs."*

—FROM *TEN DAYS THAT SHOOK THE WORLD*, JOHN REED, 1922

"When we say 'the state,' the state is we, it is the proletariat, it is the advance guard of the working class."

—VLADIMIR LENIN

LEADERS # LENIN TO STALIN

Lenin's rise to power in 1917 was made possible by Germany, which offered him safe passage from Switzerland, where he was living in exile, to the Russian frontier. The Germans expected Lenin to withdraw from World War I if his Bolsheviks took charge, and he did, hoping to regain lost territory if Germany fell to the Allies. But first he had to contend with Russians hostile to his new regime. In July 1918 he ordered the execution of Nicholas II; his wife, Alexandra; and other members of the imperial family in order to prevent White Russians opposed to his Reds (as Bolsheviks were known) from rallying around the Romanovs. Undeterred, the Whites kept up their civil war until 1921, when the Reds emerged triumphant. Lenin proceeded to reconstitute the old Russian Empire as the Union of Soviet Socialist Republics. Like the tsars of old, he used secret police to track down dissidents, eliminating opposition to his Communist Party.

Farmworkers put on a brave front at Russia's Klishevo collective farm.

> The Soviet Communist Party promoted revolution abroad through the Communist International, or Comintern.

Although ruthless, Lenin stopped short of imposing one-man rule on the Communist Party and its Politburo—the supreme council. Following his death in 1924, however, Joseph Stalin fixed an iron grip on the Communist Party and terrorized Soviet society. In 1928 he launched a wrenching Five-Year Plan to collectivize agriculture and increase industrial production. Peasants who resisted the plan were killed or imprisoned, and others were forced to provide so much food for the state that they starved. Through brutal methods, industrial output rose sharply. To silence his critics, Stalin launched murderous purges in the mid-1930s that spread beyond the top ranks of the Communist Party and the Red Army and claimed millions of victims, who were executed or sent to labor camps, where many perished.

A 1932 poster touts Stalin's first five-year plan.

THE TAKEAWAY: Under Stalin, the Marxist goal of rule by the masses became a one-man dictatorship.

> *"We must gradually, but systematically and persistently, place our agriculture on a new technical basis, the basis of large-scale production, and bring it up to the level of socialist industry."* —JOSEPH STALIN

SEE ALSO | EMPIRES RISING: PAGE 329

CONFLICTS SPANISH CIVIL WAR

Like Russia, Spain suffered upheaval as its imperial order collapsed. Little remained of the Spanish Empire after the United States defeated Spain in 1898 and stripped away Cuba, the Philippines, and other possessions. But the Spanish monarchy endured until 1931, when King Alfonso XIII was forced to flee the country. Elections in 1936 brought to power a left-wing coalition of Republicans,

Spanish dictator Primo de Rivera ruled in the 1920s.

including democratic socialists and communists. Opposing them were right-wing Nationalists, led by Gen. Francisco Franco, who feared a Soviet-style revolution in Spain and rebelled against the Republican government in a civil war that soon involved forces from other nations.

Franco, who sympathized with the fascist regimes of Benito Mussolini and Adolf Hitler, received military aid from Italy and Germany.

> Franco launched his rebellion in Spanish Morocco and used Moroccan troops against Republicans in Spain.

Germany used the conflict to test its air force, developed in violation of the Versailles Treaty. A German bombing raid on the Spanish village of Guernica in 1937 killed or wounded more than 1,500 people and inspired a memorable protest from Pablo Picasso, whose painting "Guernica" showed tortured figures looking skyward in horror.

Spain's Republicans were aided by the Soviet Union and volunteers from various countries opposed to what they saw as fascist aggression. Britain and France withheld aid to the Republicans, hoping to avoid a wider European war. Franco's victory in early 1939, however, increased that threat by placing Spain under a dictator beholden to Hitler and Mussolini, encouraging them to proceed with war plans.

THE TAKEAWAY: Franco's Nationalists won the Spanish Civil War with strong support from Nazi Germany and fascist Italy.

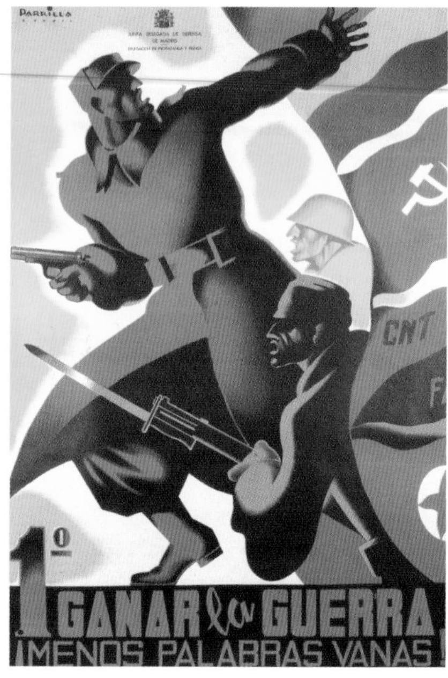

A Spanish Civil War poster exhorts: "Win the war, not with empty words!"

> *Everyone believes in the atrocities of the enemy and disbelieves in those of his own side, without ever bothering to examine the evidence."* —GEORGE ORWELL

Italian dictator Benito Mussolini leads militia in a goose-stepping parade, 1928.

LEADERS MUSSOLINI'S RISE

Fascism arose in Italy in the chaotic aftermath of World War I when Benito Mussolini, a former socialist who swung to the far right, organized paramilitary forces to battle leftists. In 1922 those forces, known as Blackshirts, marched on Rome and induced Italy's constitutional monarch, King Victor Emmanuel III, to appoint Mussolini prime minister. Armed with emergency powers, he cracked down on political opponents and became dictator. Mussolini built up the armed forces and invaded Ethiopia in 1935, but by the time he reached a pact with Hitler in 1939 Italy was far behind Germany militarily.

THE TAKEAWAY: Mussolini's fascist regime failed to bring Italy imperial glory.

CONNECTIONS ORIGINS OF FASCISM

THE TERM "FASCIST" DERIVES FROM *FASCES:* bundles of rods that ancient Roman rulers carried as symbols of authority. By adopting this as their party emblem and hailing Mussolini like a Roman emperor with stiff-armed salutes, Italian fascists showed their fascination with power. Favoring the nation over the individual and the mighty over the weak, they despised communists, who promised to end social distinctions. Fascist and communist proponents were alike, however, in seeking to impose a one-party rule. Today, the term "fascist" is often loosely applied to any people who force their views on others.

SYMBOLS OF AUTHORITY

War alone brings up to its highest tension all human energy and puts the stamp of nobility upon the peoples who have courage to meet it." —BENITO MUSSOLINI

LEADERS HITLER'S GERMANY

An embittered veteran of World War I, Adolf Hitler set out to avenge Germany's defeat and punish those he held responsible for that humiliation. He fixed the blame not just on the Allies and the punitive Versailles Treaty but on German revolutionaries who forced Kaiser Wilhelm II to abdicate shortly before Germany surrendered. By the time that uprising began, the war was already lost. But Hitler and other demagogues claimed that loyal troops could have saved Germany from defeat had they not been stabbed in the back by communists and Jews. Although many Jews had supported the war effort and served in the army, Hitler made them all scapegoats for Germany's downfall.

Heinrich Himmler speaks at the town hall in Linz, Austria, 1938.

Hitler found an outlet for his venomous views in the early 1920s as leader of a small party of right-wing extremists known as National Socialists, or Nazis. Mimicking Mussolini and his Blackshirts, he sent Nazi Brownshirts, or storm troopers, out to create havoc at a time when runaway inflation was destabilizing Germany's democratic Weimar Republic. In 1923 Hitler was convicted of treason for attempting to overthrow the Bavarian state government in Munich, Germany. He ended up serving less than a year in prison, where he began dictating his manifesto, *Mein Kampf* (*My Struggle*).

Hitler emerged from prison determined to play by the political rules until he gained power. By 1930 the Great Depression had descended on Germany and the Nazis were on the rise, increasing their number of seats in the Reichstag (parliament) from 12 to 107. In 1933 Hitler became chancellor—the equivalent of prime minister—and used an arson attack on the Reichstag by a former communist to obtain emergency powers and arrest political opponents, making the Nazi party supreme. In 1934 he became Germany's unchallenged führer (leader), with absolute power over the state.

{ Inflation was so severe in Germany during the 1920s that workers were paid with actual truckloads of cash. }

An original edition of Adolf Hitler's *Mein Kampf*

"The name of Germany is dishonoured for all time if German youth does not finally rise, take revenge, smash its tormentors. Students! The German people look to us." —GERMAN RESISTANCE PAMPHLET

SEE ALSO | THE WORLD AT WAR: PAGE 384

VOICES

HITLER THE GERMAN CONCEPT OF PERSONALITY

"Internationalization today means only Judaization. We in Germany have come to this: that a sixty-million people sees its destiny to lie at the will of a few dozen Jewish bankers. This was possible only because our civilization had first been Judaized. The undermining of the German conception of personality by catchwords had begun long before. Ideas such as 'Democracy,' 'Majority,' 'Conscience of the World,' 'World Solidarity,' 'World Peace,' 'Internationality of Art,' etc., disintegrate our race-consciousness."

—FROM A SPEECH BY ADOLF HITLER IN MUNICH, SEPTEMBER 18, 1922

ADOLF HITLER

Hitler proceeded to build a new empire called the Third Reich and persecute those he accused of betraying the Kaiser's old empire. In 1935 he repudiated the Versailles Treaty and prepared for war by enlarging Germany's armed forces, which had already expanded far beyond the treaty's limits. His storm troopers had helped him seize power, but to deal with communists, Jews, and other targeted groups he relied on a more disciplined security force, the SS, led by Heinrich Himmler, who had already begun to set up the first concentration camps, beginning with Dachau in 1933.

{ Nazis tried to lure German workers away from socialism to fascism, which in fact favored owners over laborers. }

THE TAKEAWAY: Hitler seized power in the 1930s, vowing to restore German prestige lost in World War I.

Jews in Baden-Baden are rounded up following Kristallnacht, 1938.

"The street free for the brown battalions, / The street free for the Storm Troopers. / Millions, full of hope, look up at the swastika; / The day breaks for freedom and for bread." —THE NAZI ANTHEM

SEE ALSO | THE WORLD AT WAR: PAGE 390

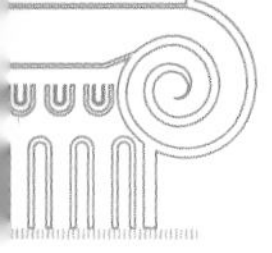

American troops hit the beaches at Normandy, June 6, 1944.

CONFLICTS WORLD WAR II

Hitler's first aggressive moves in Europe went unopposed by French and British leaders, who tried to appease him and avoid war. In 1936 Hitler reoccupied the Rhineland, bordering France, and went on to annex Austria in 1938 and occupy the German-speaking Sudetenland in Czechoslovakia. When Hitler seized the rest of Czechoslovakia in early 1939, Britain's Neville Chamberlain finally saw the light and joined France in pledging to oppose Germany if it attacked Poland.

World War II began in September 1939 when Germany did, in fact, invade Poland. France and Britain declared war but were not ready to fight, leaving Poland to be carved up by Hitler and Stalin, whose nonaggression pact postponed hostilities between them while they practiced aggression on others. In May 1940 Hitler unleashed a blitzkrieg against France, which fell in June. That left Britain isolated, but newly appointed Prime Minister Winston Churchill stood firm as the Luftwaffe bombed Britain. That blitz was countered by the Royal Air Force with the help of radar, dashing Hitler's hopes for quick victory.

The war widened in 1941 as German forces landed in North Africa to aid Italian troops against the British and conquered the Balkans before invading the Soviet Union in June. After making huge gains, the Germans stalled that winter near Moscow and barely withstood

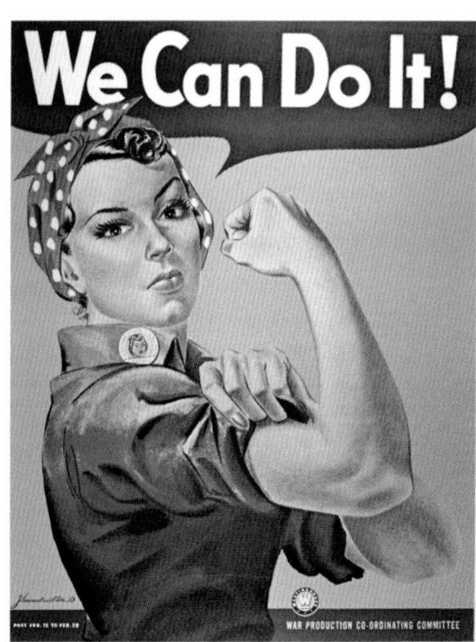

A World War II poster encourages the effort on the home front.

"The experience of the past two years has proven beyond doubt that no nation can appease the Nazis. No man can tame a tiger into a kitten by stroking it." —FRANKLIN D. ROOSEVELT

a Soviet counterattack. In 1942 they renewed their offensive but were sucked into a furious battle for Stalingrad that fall and were eventually driven back toward their border in 1943.

Germans suffered another major defeat when British armor in North Africa smashed their lines at El Alamein in October 1942. The British went on to link up with American troops, who had entered the war in 1941. Together they invaded Italy in 1943 and ousted Mussolini. By 1944 Allied Supreme Commander Dwight D. Eisenhower had forces ready in Britain to retake France. Landing in Normandy in June, they liberated Paris in August and repulsed a German counteroffensive at year's end in the Battle of the Bulge. In early 1945 they poured into Germany from the west as the Red Army advanced from the east. The fall of Berlin to the Soviets on April 30 led to Hitler's suicide and Germany's surrender on May 7.

> Nearly 60 million soldiers and civilians perished during World War II, the most destructive conflict in history.

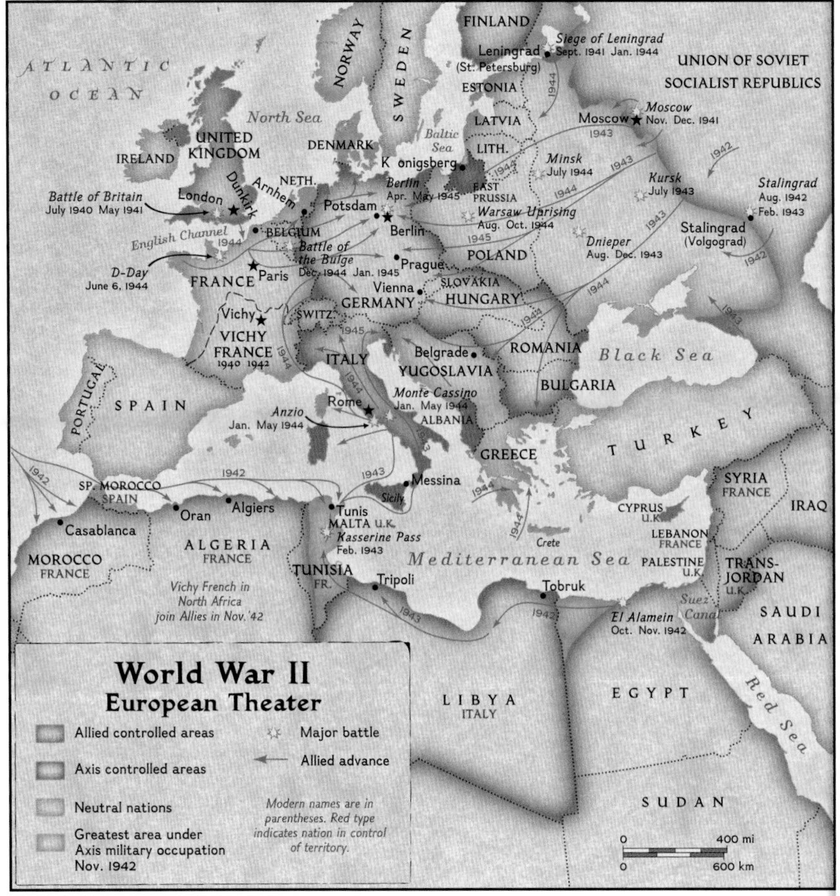

THE TAKEAWAY: Hitler lost World War II when the Soviets and Americans were drawn into the conflict against him.

VOICES

CHURCHILL OUR POLICY

WINSTON CHURCHILL

"I say to the House as I said to ministers who have joined this government, I have nothing to offer but blood, toil, tears, and sweat. We have before us an ordeal of the most grievous kind. We have before us many, many months of struggle and suffering. You ask, what is our policy? I say it is to wage war by land, sea, and air. War with all our might and with all the strength God has given us, and to wage war against a monstrous tyranny never surpassed in the dark and lamentable catalogue of human crime. That is our policy."

—FROM A SPEECH BY WINSTON CHURCHILL, MAY 13, 1940

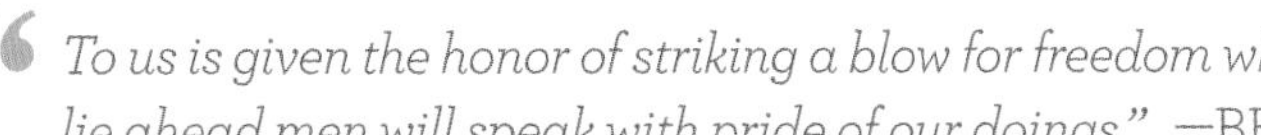

"To us is given the honor of striking a blow for freedom which will live in history, and in the better days that lie ahead men will speak with pride of our doings." —BERNARD MONTGOMERY

SEE ALSO | THE WORLD AT WAR: PAGE 391

Inhabitants of the Warsaw ghetto are deported to concentration camps, 1943.

CONFLICTS THE HOLOCAUST

On the night of November 9, 1938—Kristallnacht, or the Night of Broken Glass—Nazis burned synagogues, wrecked stores, killed nearly 100 Jews, and arrested thousands more. It was a grim preview of the holocaust awaiting Jews and other ethnic groups defined by Nazis as subhuman. In the early years of World War II, Jews were imprisoned in Polish ghettoes and shot by Nazi death squads in the Soviet Union. In 1922 SS officials devised the "final solution." All Jews would be sent either to concentration camps—where they would labor as slaves or die in gas chambers—or to extermination camps, where they would be put to death. Six million Jews, as well as other victims, were murdered before the war ended.

THE TAKEAWAY: Nazis systematically killed Jews and others they considered inferior.

RUDOLF HESS DEATH CHAMBERS

VOICES

RUDOLF HESS

"The Camp Commandant at Treblinka told me that he had liquidated 80,000 in the course of one half year. He was principally concerned with liquidating all the Jews from the Warsaw Ghetto. He used monoxide gas and I did not think that his methods were very efficient. So when I set up the extermination building at Auschwitz, I used Cyclon B, which was a crystallized Prussic Acid which we dropped into the death chamber from a small opening. It took from 3 to 15 minutes to kill the people in the death chamber depending upon climatic conditions."

—FROM THE TESTIMONY OF NAZI LEADER RUDOLF HESS, NUREMBERG WAR TRIALS, 1946

"I was to be sent to Auschwitz but I traded places with a woman who wanted to be with relatives. . . . Nobody knew that they were to be gassed when they returned to Auschwitz." —ANNA W., SURVIVOR

CONFLICTS WAR IN THE PACIFIC

Having seized French Indochina, and planning further Pacific conquests, Japan anticipated American retaliation by launching a preemptive strike on December 7, 1941, against the U.S. Pacific Fleet at Pearl Harbor and attacking American bases on the Philippines. Gen. Douglas MacArthur had to abandon those islands to the Japanese but vowed to return.

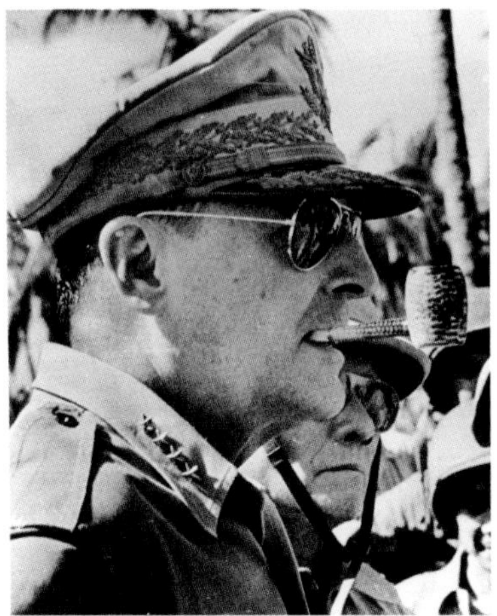

Gen. Douglas MacArthur commanded in the Southwest Pacific.

The U.S. Navy rebounded in May 1942 when vital intelligence helped it win the Battle of Midway and sink four Japanese aircraft carriers. But it took American forces three years of brutal island fighting to retake the Philippines and seize Japanese strongholds such as Iwo Jima and Okinawa, where some 50,000 Americans were killed or wounded in the spring of 1945. A bloody invasion of Japan was averted when atomic bombs shattered Hiroshima and Nagasaki in August, killing more than 120,000 people and prompting Japan to surrender.

General MacArthur returned to the Philippines in October 1944 when he landed on the island of Leyte with American forces.

U.S. fighter planes soar in formation over the Midway Atoll.

THE TAKEAWAY: Japan's leaders attacked the United States and saw their empire destroyed.

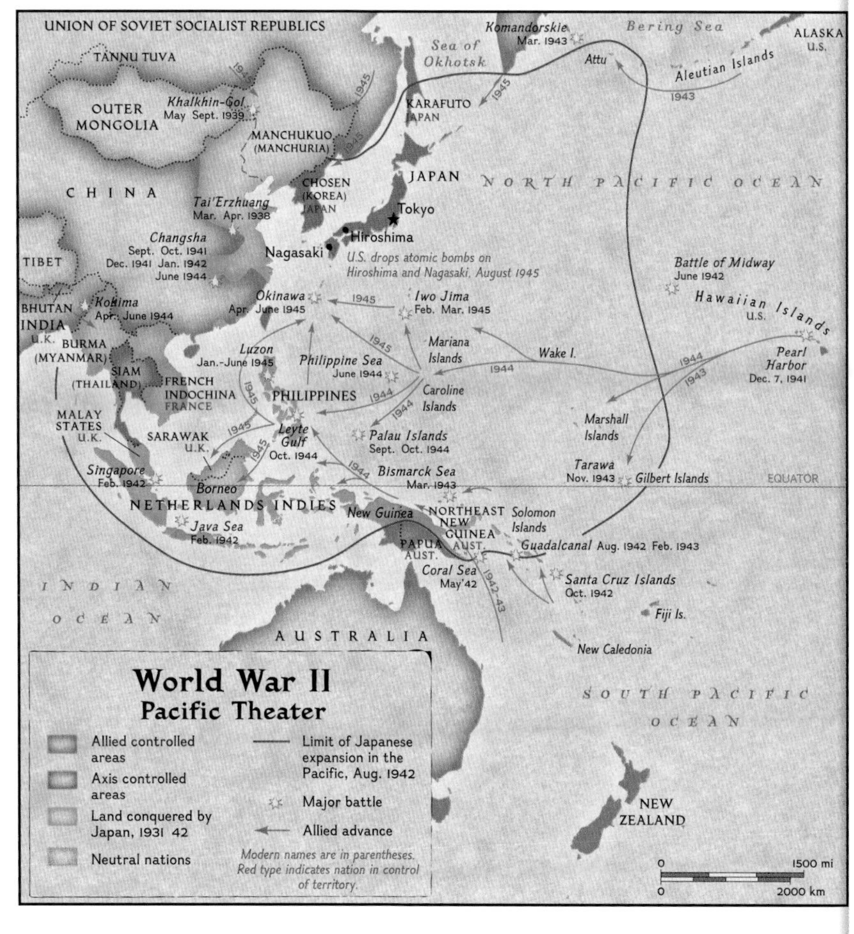

> "I felt the city of Hiroshima had disappeared all of a sudden. Then I looked at myself and found my clothes had turned into rags due to the heat." —AKIHIRO TAKAHASHI

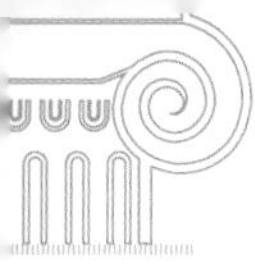

SEE ALSO | THE WORLD AT WAR: PAGE 403

KEY DATES

1905
Sun Yat-sen founds the Revolutionary Alliance, dedicated to expelling the Manchus.

1910
Japan annexes Korea.

1912
The Republic of China is officially proclaimed with Sun Yat-sen as president.

1922
Egypt declares independence under King Fuad.

UNREST IN THE EAST

1900–1945

Like Europe, the Middle East and Far East underwent massive convulsions in the first half of the 20th century as empires weakened or collapsed under the stress of war and revolutions and new regimes emerged. Nowhere was this process more traumatic than in China. Once a great imperial power, China had declined in the 1800s as the country's impoverished masses turned against its emperors. The greatest threat came from Japan, which surged ahead of China by industrializing and modernizing its armed forces. Japanese military leaders gained increasing influence over Emperor Yoshihito and his successor, Hirohito, and expanded their empire at China's expense. In 1912 the last Chinese emperor was forced to abdicate by revolutionaries led by Sun Yat-sen, who established the Chinese republic. That new government proved no stronger than the imperial regime it replaced. Warlords took control of large areas, and the Chinese Communist Party vied with the Nationalist People's Party (Kuomintang) of Sun Yat-sen and his successor, Chiang Kai-shek. Chiang and Communist leader Mao Zedong reached a truce in 1937 and joined in opposing Japanese forces, who occupied their country until 1945, when the Nationalists and Communists resumed their civil war. Mao's victory in 1949 led to China's resurgence as a great power.

Asia and the Middle East underwent profound identity shifts in the early 20th century as citizens of China, Japan, India, and elsewhere overthrew old regimes and colonial overlords.

India broke free from imperial domination by using moral pressure rather than military force. When Britain failed to reward India for its contributions to the Allied cause in World War I by granting it dominion status, Mohandas Gandhi organized nonviolent resistance to British rule. His campaign helped India gain independence after World War II, but he could not prevent bloody strife between Hindus and Muslims, who separated from India to form Pakistan in the north.

It took some independent countries decades to achieve real autonomy. Egypt, for example, remained under British influence long after it became officially independent in 1922. Turkey, on the other hand, recovered quickly from the collapse of its empire during World War I and reached an accommodation with the West. Like their European neighbors, Turkish leaders separated church from state by distancing their government and its laws from Sharia, or the rules of Islam.

OPPOSITE: Mao Zedong led China's communist revolution in the 1930s and 1940s.

1929
The All-India Congress claims independence.

1934
The Red Army begins the Long March toward China's northwest.

1941
The Japanese attack the American base at Pearl Harbor, bringing the United States into World War II.

1945
The United States drops atomic bombs on the Japanese cities of Hiroshima and Nagasaki.

SEE ALSO | GLOBAL CULTURES: PAGE 428

NATIONS THE ARAB WORLD

During World War I, Britain and France encouraged Arabs to rebel against the Ottoman Empire and seek freedom. British officer T. E. Lawrence won fame as Lawrence of Arabia by campaigning against the Turks with Feisal, son of Emir Hussein of Mecca. After helping the British take Damascus in 1918, Feisal hoped that Arabs there would be rewarded with their own state. Instead, Syria and Lebanon were handed to the French as mandates—countries administered by foreign powers until they were deemed ready for independence—while Iraq and Palestine became British mandates. Arab nationalists felt betrayed. Their resentments increased when the British admitted Jewish settlers to Palestine in keeping with the Balfour Declaration of 1917, which advocated "a national home for the Jewish people" in what was once Israel and soon would be again.

King Farouk of Egypt and Franklin Roosevelt meet in 1945.

> Vast oil reserves found in Saudi Arabia and Iraq in the early 1900s made the Middle East vital to the West.

Egypt gained independence shortly after World War I, but its monarch, King Fuad I, clashed with nationalists in parliament. He and his successor, King Farouk, were also opposed by the Muslim Brotherhood, whose members wanted their society to be governed by the teachings of the Koran. The Brotherhood gained considerable support in Egypt because that nation remained subject to British intervention. During World War II, Britain reoccupied Egypt to prevent Germany from seizing it.

A jug depicts Lord Kitchener, an early British administrator of Egypt

THE TAKEAWAY: After World War I, Arab countries came under Western influence, causing tensions in the Middle East.

MIDDLE EAST & ASIA — VIPs

Sun Yat-sen, 1866–1925
Chinese politician who became provisional president of the republic

Mohandas Gandhi, 1869–1948
Indian spiritual leader and nationalist

Kemal Ataturk, 1881–1938
Founder of modern Turkey and president of the Turkish republic

Chiang Kai-shek, 1887–1975
Chinese Nationalist leader who fought Communist forces

Hirohito, 1901–1989
Emperor of Japan who reigned before and during World War II

> *"The only time that we might have been absorbed by Europe was when we were . . . possessed of the notion that the hat was superior to the turban and the fez."* —TAHA HUSSEIN

An Irish soldier taunts Turkish snipers during the World War I battle of Gallipoli.

NATIONS MODERN TURKEY

The modern nation of Turkey was fostered by liberal reformers called Young Turks, who created a secular state where courts, schools, and other public institutions were not governed by Islamic laws or customs. In 1908 they restored a constitution suspended by their sultan, whom they replaced with a figurehead. As Turkish nationalists, they opposed efforts by non-Turks to break free of the Ottoman Empire. When some Armenians joined with Russians during World War I to fight against Turks the Turks retaliated by rounding up Armenians and deporting them to Syria and Mesopotamia. More than a half million Armenians died in transit or were killed by Turkish guards. The Ottoman Empire collapsed at war's end, but Turkey emerged intact under Mustafa Kemal Ataturk, who won recognition of Turkey's borders in 1923.

THE TAKEAWAY: Although it was largely a Muslim country, Turkey remained a secular state.

VOICES

ATATURK MOVING AT 20TH-CENTURY SPEED

ATATURK

"We shall raise our country to the level of the most prosperous and civilized nations of the world. We shall endow our nation with the broadest means and sources of welfare. We shall raise our national culture above the contemporary level of civilization. ∾ Therefore, we should judge the measure of time not according to the lax mentality of past centuries, but in terms of the concepts of speed and movement of our century. Compared to the past, we shall work harder. We shall perform greater tasks in a shorter time."

—FROM A SPEECH BY MUSTAFA KEMAL ATATURK, 1933

"New Turkey, the people of New Turkey, have no reason to think of anything else but their own existence and their own welfare. She has nothing more to give away to others." —MUSTAFA KEMAL ATATURK

SEE ALSO | GLOBAL CULTURES: PAGE 433

Italian troops move through the high grass in Ethiopia after the invasion.

NATIONS SOUTH AFRICA & ETHIOPIA

Most African countries remained under European colonial rule until after World War II. Two notable exceptions were Ethiopia and South Africa. South Africa became a self-governing British dominion in 1910, controlled by Afrikaners (whites descended from the Boers), who discriminated against the nation's black majority. Ethiopia, by contrast, was ruled by its own black imperial dynasty until Italy invaded the country in 1935. Under Mussolini, Italy employed weapons that Ethiopia's ruler, Emperor Haile Selassie, could not match, including poison gas and bombs. Forced into exile, Haile Selassie returned to power in 1941 after British troops helped Ethiopians oust the Italians. In later years, he served as an inspiration to other black African leaders.

> Once known as Ras (Prince) Tafari, Haile Selassie was hailed as a messiah by Jamaica's Rastafari movement.

HAILE SELASSIE 1892–1975

THUMBS UP / THUMBS DOWN

HAILE SELASSIE

THE REIGN OF ETHIOPIAN EMPEROR Haile Selassie, lasting from 1930 to 1974, resembled that of Europe's Enlightenment monarchs. Selassie worked to modernize Ethiopia and improve its educational system, and he introduced a constitution that established a parliament—although he could and did override that legislature and rule by decree at times. In 1974 he was overthrown by an army officer, Mengistu Haile Mariam. In contrast with Mengistu and his harsh regime, Selassie served as a model for Africans struggling to end colonialism and gain independence. **CONCLUSION:** **THUMBS UP**

THE TAKEAWAY: By regaining control of Ethiopia, Emperor Haile Selassie became a symbol of self-determination in Africa.

> *"There are good men and wicked. The former should be made use of and the latter punished, without attempting to understand why the ones are good and the others wicked."* —HAILE SELASSIE

NATIONS CHANGE IN CHINA

Chiang Kai-shek faced two big challenges after taking power in China in 1928. As the successor to Sun Yat-sen, who ended imperial rule in 1912 and founded the Nationalist People's Party, Chiang had recently ousted communists from that ruling party. Communists then reconstituted and found refuge in the southeastern province of Jiangxi, where they gained support among peasants by redistributing land to the poor.

Chiang's other challenge came from Japan, whose forces overwhelmed Chinese troops in 1931 and took control of Manchuria. Chiang did little to stop them and focused instead on defeating communists and their leader, Mao Zedong, who fled Jiangxi in 1934 and led his troops on the Long March, a grueling 6,000-mile trek to northwestern China. The survivors of that ordeal formed a dedicated cadre in years to come as Mao organized peasants to fight the Japanese, who occupied China from 1937 to 1945. Chiang suspended hostilities with Mao to join that fight, but his party was ineffective and plagued by corruption. Mao emerged from World War II with a formidable army and drove Chiang and his Nationalists into exile on Taiwan in 1949.

{ Mao Zedong built the Chinese Communist Party by focusing on the peasant masses in the countryside. }

Chiang Kai-shek stands behind Sun Yat-sen, 1924.

THE TAKEAWAY: China slipped from Nationalist to Communist hands in the 1940s.

Chinese communists marched 6,000 miles over 18 mountain ranges in 1934's Long March.

“*A revolution is not the same as inviting people to dinner, or writing an essay, or painting a picture . . . A revolution is an insurrection, an act of violence by which one class overthrows another.*” —MAO ZEDONG

SEE ALSO | EMPIRES RISING: PAGE 355

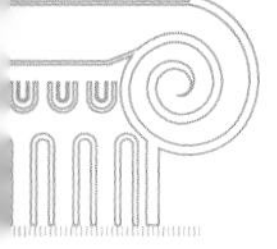

Japanese students mobilized for factory work stand by their machines in 1939.

NATIONS JAPAN MILITARIZES

Japan forged its 20th-century empire by seizing territory from faltering imperial regimes, including China's Qing dynasty and Russia's Romanovs. Victories over China in 1895 and Russia in 1905 brought the Japanese Taiwan and Korea, where they crushed an independence movement in 1919. They also acquired the Lioadong Peninsula, west of Korea, and a Russian-built railroad in Manchuria, where China was losing its grip. During World War I, Japan also grabbed the Marshall Islands and other German territories in the Pacific after siding with the Allies.

As Japan's empire grew, so did the power of its military chiefs, who faced little opposition after the Great Depression struck Japan in 1930 and undermined its weak constitutional government. Through acts of violence like the assassination of Prime Minister Hamaguchi Osachi—who had agreed to a treaty with Western powers limiting Japan's naval buildup—Japanese militarists gained the upper hand.

Japanese officers then provided a pretext for the conquest of Manchuria in 1931 by sabotaging the railroad there and blaming Chinese forces. In 1937 commander in chief Emperor Hirohito authorized an invasion of China that devastated the city of Nanjing, where Japanese troops went wild, raping and murdering civilians. Overconfident Japanese commanders responded to American efforts to curb Japanese expansion by targeting U.S. bases when they entered World War II in 1941, exposing Japan to a shattering defeat in 1945.

> By appointing Gen. Tojo Hideki prime minister in 1941, Emperor Hirohito chose an officer committed to war.

THE TAKEAWAY: As Japan acquired an empire, its military leaders took control.

The Japanese empire is a manifestation of morality and its special characteristic is the propagation of the Imperial Way." —JAPANESE GOVERNMENT DOCUMENT

LEADERS INDIAN SELF-RULE

During World War I, India contributed more than a million troops to the Allied cause, but it still was not granted independence from Britain. In protest, Mohandas Gandhi launched a nonviolent resistance movement called satyagraha. Despite the massacre of demonstrators by British troops at Amritsar in 1919, Gandhi remained committed to passive resistance and suspended his campaign in 1922 when protests turned violent. He renewed demonstrations in 1930 in a march with followers to the sea.

Gandhi and Jawaharlal Nehru pressed for independence as leaders of India's Congress Party. Both were imprisoned during World War II for refusing to support the Allies unless India was granted self-rule, which it finally achieved in 1947. Gandhi decried violent clashes between his fellow Hindus and rival Muslims that led to the partition of India and Pakistan. Slain in 1948 by a Hindu extremist, he was hailed as Mahatma (great soul).

{ Gandhi first used nonviolent resistance to protest racial discrimination against Indians in South Africa. }

Jawaharlal Nehru speaks to a crowd from his balcony in Simla, India.

THE TAKEAWAY: Gandhi and his followers exerted moral force to gain independence for India.

VOICES

GANDHI FIGHTING FOR THE SPIRIT

"I would like to give you and your readers just this assurance that our non-cooperation is not intended to promote isolation or exclusiveness, but it is but a prelude to real cooperation with the rest of the world not excluding the West. Nor would I have your readers to think that in fighting the British government I am fighting western civilisation, but I am endeavouring to fight modern civilisation as distinguished from the ancient which India has not happily yet discarded. Modern civilisation as represented by the West of today, in my opinion, has given Matter a place which by right belongs to Spirit."

—FROM A LETTER BY MOHANDAS GANDHI TO *THE SURVEY* MAGAZINE, MARCH 5, 1922

MOHANDAS GANDHI

"I want nothing to do with any religion concerned with keeping the masses satisfied to live in hunger, filth, and ignorance." —JAWAHARLAL NEHRU

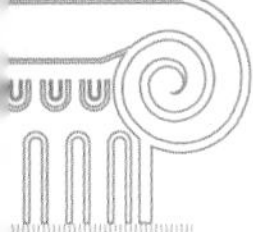

CONNECTIONS TIME LINE
1900–1945

SINKING OF THE *LUSITANIA*

MARCONI DETECTOR

1901
Inventor Guglielmo receives a transatlantic signal on his radio.

1901
Queen Victoria of England dies and is succeeded by her son, Edward VII.

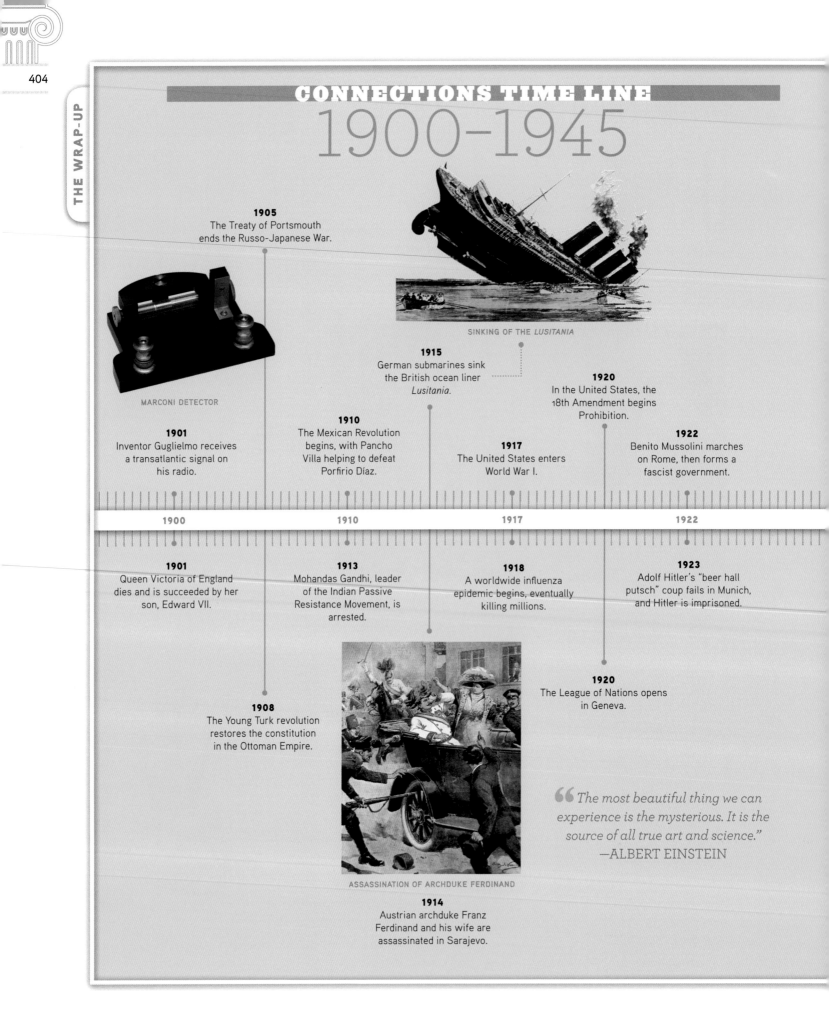

1905
The Treaty of Portsmouth ends the Russo-Japanese War.

1908
The Young Turk revolution restores the constitution in the Ottoman Empire.

1910
The Mexican Revolution begins, with Pancho Villa helping to defeat Porfirio Díaz.

1913
Mohandas Gandhi, leader of the Indian Passive Resistance Movement, is arrested.

1914
Austrian archduke Franz Ferdinand and his wife are assassinated in Sarajevo.

ASSASSINATION OF ARCHDUKE FERDINAND

1915
German submarines sink the British ocean liner *Lusitania*.

1917
The United States enters World War I.

1918
A worldwide influenza epidemic begins, eventually killing millions.

1920
In the United States, the 18th Amendment begins Prohibition.

1920
The League of Nations opens in Geneva.

1922
Benito Mussolini marches on Rome, then forms a fascist government.

1923
Adolf Hitler's "beer hall putsch" coup fails in Munich, and Hitler is imprisoned.

1900 — 1910 — 1917 — 1922

> *"The most beautiful thing we can experience is the mysterious. It is the source of all true art and science."*
> —ALBERT EINSTEIN

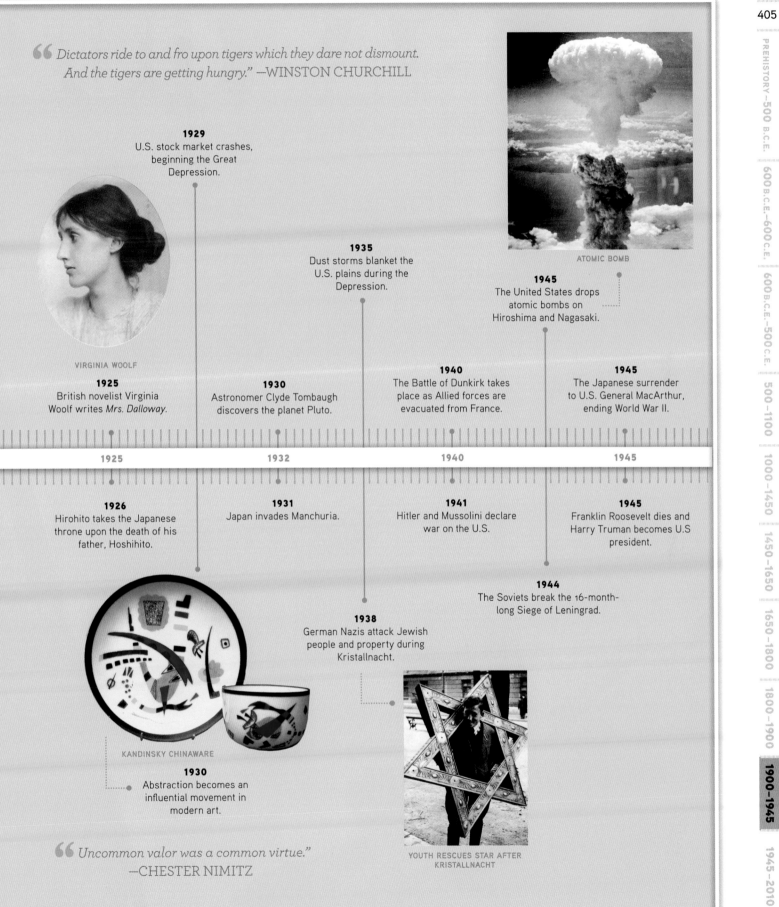

“Dictators ride to and fro upon tigers which they dare not dismount. And the tigers are getting hungry.” —WINSTON CHURCHILL

ATOMIC BOMB

1929
U.S. stock market crashes, beginning the Great Depression.

VIRGINIA WOOLF

1925
British novelist Virginia Woolf writes *Mrs. Dalloway.*

1930
Astronomer Clyde Tombaugh discovers the planet Pluto.

1935
Dust storms blanket the U.S. plains during the Depression.

1940
The Battle of Dunkirk takes place as Allied forces are evacuated from France.

1945
The United States drops atomic bombs on Hiroshima and Nagasaki.

1945
The Japanese surrender to U.S. General MacArthur, ending World War II.

1925 1932 1940 1945

1926
Hirohito takes the Japanese throne upon the death of his father, Hoshihito.

1931
Japan invades Manchuria.

1941
Hitler and Mussolini declare war on the U.S.

1945
Franklin Roosevelt dies and Harry Truman becomes U.S president.

1944
The Soviets break the 16-month-long Siege of Leningrad.

1938
German Nazis attack Jewish people and property during Kristallnacht.

KANDINSKY CHINAWARE

1930
Abstraction becomes an influential movement in modern art.

YOUTH RESCUES STAR AFTER KRISTALLNACHT

“Uncommon valor was a common virtue.” —CHESTER NIMITZ

GLOBAL CUL

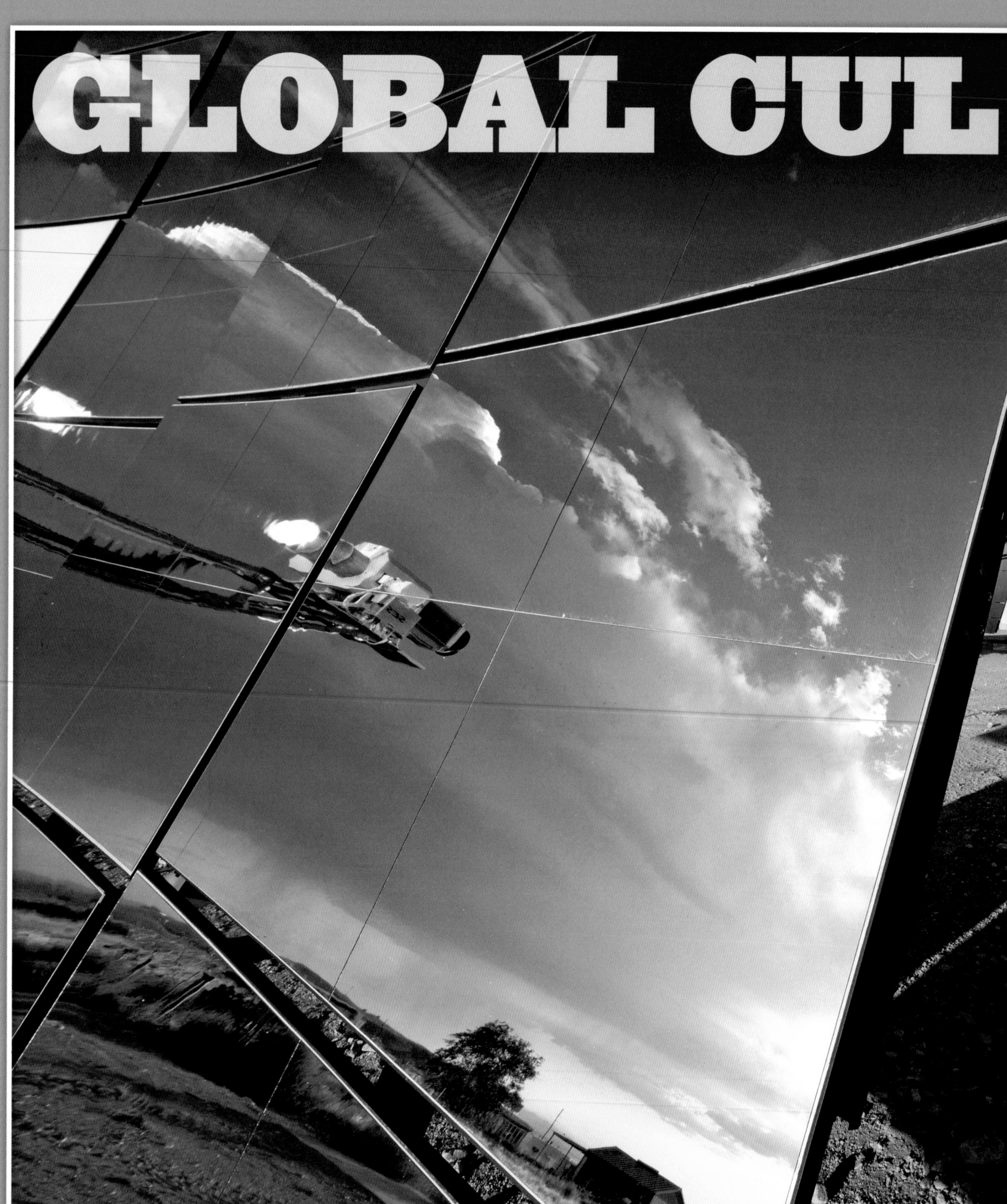

POSTWAR EUROPE

1945–2010

At the end of World War II, a deep rift opened between the Soviet Union and its Western allies. Meeting at Yalta in February 1945 as their armies were on the verge of defeating Germany, Franklin Roosevelt, Winston Churchill, and Joseph Stalin agreed that the Soviets would occupy East Germany and East Berlin and that free elections would be held in Allied-occupied European countries after the war to form "governments responsive to the will of the people." It soon became clear that Stalin had no intention of honoring that pledge. East Germany, Poland, Czechoslovakia, Hungary, and other countries occupied by the Red Army during the war became satellites of the Soviet Union, ruled by communists obedient to Moscow. As Churchill declared in 1946, an "iron curtain" had descended on Europe, separating the democratic West from the communist East. This ideological struggle between East and West, known as the Cold War, threatened to ignite a firestorm in Europe but never reached the flash point. The divided city of Berlin was a hot spot where tensions ran high. But the prospect of nuclear warfare between the Western allies—led by the United States, Britain, and France—and the Soviet Union, which developed nuclear weapons in 1949, served as a deterrent to violence in Europe even while countries like Korea and Vietnam became battlegrounds for communist forces and their foes. The United Nations (UN) did little to ease tensions between the United States and Soviet Union, both of which had veto power over actions of the UN Security Council.

A marriage of opposites, the pact between the Soviets and their democratic allies ended in divorce after they defeated Germany in 1945, resulting in a Cold War that lasted more than 40 years.

Ultimately, the Soviets lost the Cold War because their costly arms race with the West crippled their inefficient, government-run economy and made the Western alternative of free enterprise and free elections increasingly attractive. Beginning with Poland in 1989, one nation after another in the Soviet bloc broke away from Moscow. In 1991 the Soviet Union dissolved, and Ukraine, Georgia, and other countries gained independence from a reorganized Russian Republic. Several of these nations later joined the European Union (EU), designed to end destructive rivalries between member nations and form a political and economic unit capable of competing peacefully with the United States, Russia, China, and other great powers.

OPPOSITE: Russian prime minister Vladimir Putin was an intelligence officer for the KGB during the Cold War.

1985
Mikhail Gorbachev becomes the new leader of the Soviet Union.

1989
Poland and Hungary become independent and the Berlin Wall in Germany is demolished.

1991–1995
Deadly Yugoslav wars take place between Serbs, Croats, and Bosnians.

1999
Vladimir Putin becomes president of Russia.

SEE ALSO | GLOBAL CULTURES: PAGE 413

REGIONS EASTERN EUROPE TO 1989

When Stalin died in 1953, Nikita Khrushchev soon succeeded him as premier and eased repression within the Soviet Union by releasing political prisoners from labor camps. But neither Khrushchev nor his successor, Leonid Brezhnev, loosened Moscow's grip on Eastern European countries, which were bound to the Soviet Union by the Warsaw Pact. Soviet troops entered Budapest in 1956 to force Hungary back into that alliance, erected the Berlin Wall in 1961 to contain East Germans, and invaded Czechoslovakia in 1968 to crush democratic reforms there.

By 1985, when Mikhail Gorbachev became premier, Soviet power was declining. The new premier promoted reforms across the Soviet bloc. His attempt to salvage communism through perestroika (restructuring) failed. But by allowing Warsaw Pact countries to leave the alliance without reprisals, he brought Soviet control of Eastern Europe to a largely peaceful end.

The Brandenburg Gate once stood just past the Berlin Wall.

THE TAKEAWAY: The struggle to control countries in the Soviet bloc proved too much for Moscow.

POSTWAR EUROPE

VIPs

Winston Churchill, 1874–1965
British prime minister

Joseph Stalin, 1878–1953
Soviet politician and dictator

Nikita Khrushchev, 1894–1971
Soviet politician during the Cold War

Alexander Dubcek, 1921–1992
Slovak politician famous for his attempt to achieve socialism in Czechoslovakia, known as The Prague Spring

Margaret Thatcher, 1925–
British prime minister and conservative political force

Mikhail Gorbachev, 1931–
Political leader of the Soviet Union who helped end the Cold War

CONNECTIONS THE ORIGINS OF AL QAEDA

In 1979 the Soviets invaded Afghanistan, where they were opposed by Muslim insurgents called mujahideen (holy warriors). Among the foreigners in their ranks was Osama bin Laden, who returned home to Saudi Arabia in 1989 and turned against his own government and its American allies. Although Americans had aided the mujahideen, bin Laden blamed them for exploiting Muslim countries and declared a jihad (holy war) against the United States. His terrorist network, al Qaeda, was granted refuge in Afghanistan by the Taliban—Islamic fundamentalists who were now in control.

MUJAHIDEEN IN AFGHANISTAN IN 1987

> *"The idea of restructuring . . . combines continuity and innovation, the historical experience of Bolshevism and the contemporaneity of socialism."* —MIKHAIL GORBACHEV

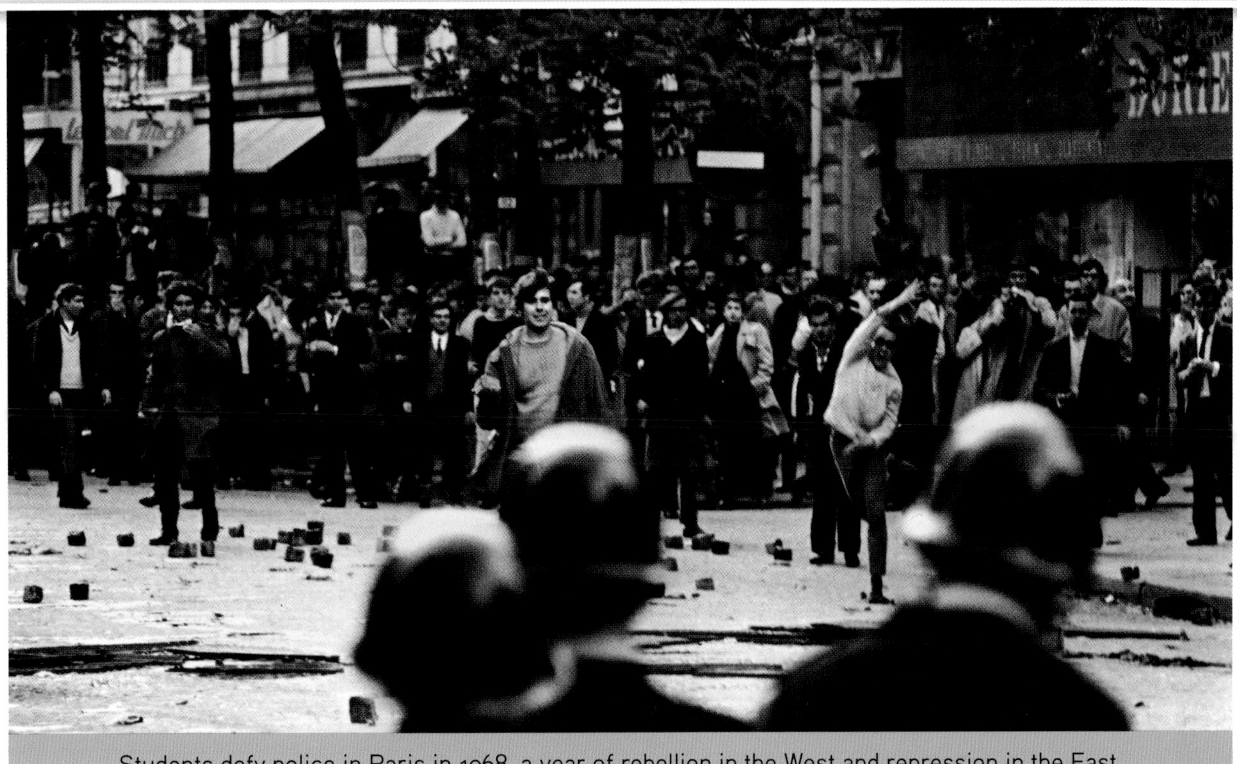
Students defy police in Paris in 1968, a year of rebellion in the West and repression in the East.

REGIONS WESTERN EUROPE TO 1989

As leader of the Western alliance, the United States sought to prevent the Soviets from expanding beyond Eastern Europe. President Harry Truman launched that containment policy in 1947 when he offered aid to prevent communist insurrection in Greece and Soviet intervention in Turkey. Secretary of State George Marshall then offered a plan for economic assistance to most European nations outside the Soviet bloc. Bolstered by this aid, West Germany and Italy overcame defeat and the bitter legacy of fascism to join the United States and other democratic nations in the North Atlantic Treaty Organization (NATO).

Western Europe did not always follow America's lead. In the 1960s French president Charles de Gaulle defied a nuclear test ban treaty so that his country, like Britain, could develop its own nuclear arsenal. Left-wing parties and protesters in Europe denounced America for going to war in Vietnam. But optimism was widespread when the Soviet bloc collapsed in 1989. East and West Germans celebrated by shattering the Berlin Wall and went on to reunify Germany in 1990.

A German poster for the Marshall Plan promises aid to countries in need.

THE TAKEAWAY: Western European nations were aided by the United States after World War II but remained independent.

> *"You have a row of dominoes set up, you knock over the first one, and what will happen to the last one is the certainty that it will go over very quickly."* —DWIGHT D. EISENHOWER

SEE ALSO | THE WORLD AT WAR: PAGE 384

Russian soldiers patrol Grozny, the capital of Chechnya, after battling rebels there.

CONFLICTS ETHNIC DIVISIONS

The end of the Cold War unleashed hostilities in previously repressed trouble spots. In 1990, ethnically divided Yugoslavia broke up; fighting erupted among Serbians, Bosnians, and Croatians. Serbian forces murdered thousands of Bosnian Muslims and drove others from their homes. International pressure induced them to make peace, and commanders were put on trial. And nearly 100,000 people were killed in a decade-long struggle between Russia and Chechnya, which declared independence in 1991.

THE TAKEAWAY: As communism collapsed, conflicts flared in Yugoslavia and Chechnya.

UN TRIBUNAL DEATH IN BOSNIA AND HERZEGOVINA

VOICES

MILAN LUKIC

"Evidence . . . shows that Milan Lukić and other armed men forced a group of approximately 70 Muslim civilians into Meho Aljić's house, locking them inside. All the exits had been blocked by heavy furniture and a garage door was also placed against a door to prevent escape. Gunshots were fired at the house and grenades were thrown inside, setting the house on fire."

—FROM THE JUDGMENT SUMMARY FOR MILAN LUKIĆ BY THE INTERNATIONAL CRIMINAL TRIBUNAL FOR THE FORMER YUGOSLAVIA, JULY 20, 2009

"I would like to say to you that what we have just heard, this tragic text, is a supreme absurdity. I should be given credit for peace in Bosnia, not war." —SLOBODAN MILOSEVIC

REGIONS EUROPEAN UNION

After the Cold War, many European nations joined the European Union. All EU nations except Britain adopted a common currency, the Euro. And in 2009 the EU's 27 members, including ten former communist countries, ratified a constitution providing for a European president, parliament, and court of justice. This reversed a trend in which many small states had broken away from larger nations or empires. Ireland, for example, had won independence from Britain in a long struggle by the Irish Republican Army, which spilled over into Northern Ireland before British prime minister Tony Blair helped negotiate a peace accord in 1998. Irish voters initially rejected the EU constitution, but in 2009 they approved the plan overwhelmingly amid a global financial crisis.

The EU's expansion posed a challenge to Russian leader Vladimir Putin, who succeeded Boris Yeltsin in 1999 and who sought to restore strength and stability to a nation undergoing a hectic transition from communism to capitalism. Putin cracked down on Russian oligarchs suspected of corruption, placed restrictions on the press, sent troops back to Chechnya to suppress acts of terror by separatists, and pressured Georgia, Ukraine, and other neighboring countries to stay out of the EU.

{ Immigrants from former colonies have poured into some countries, including Algerians into France and Pakistanis into Britain. }

British prime minister Tony Blair helped bring peace to Northern Ireland.

THE TAKEAWAY: The Cold War was replaced by competition between Russia and the EU.

Catholic youths at odds with Protestant loyalists in Northern Ireland confront troops there in 1981.

"Give me a lever long enough and a firm place and I will move the world. The European Union is a firm place to stand." —BERTIE AHERN

GLOBAL CULTURES: COMPUTER AGE

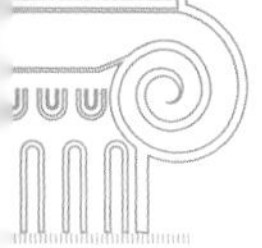

SEE ALSO | GLOBAL CULTURES: PAGE 417

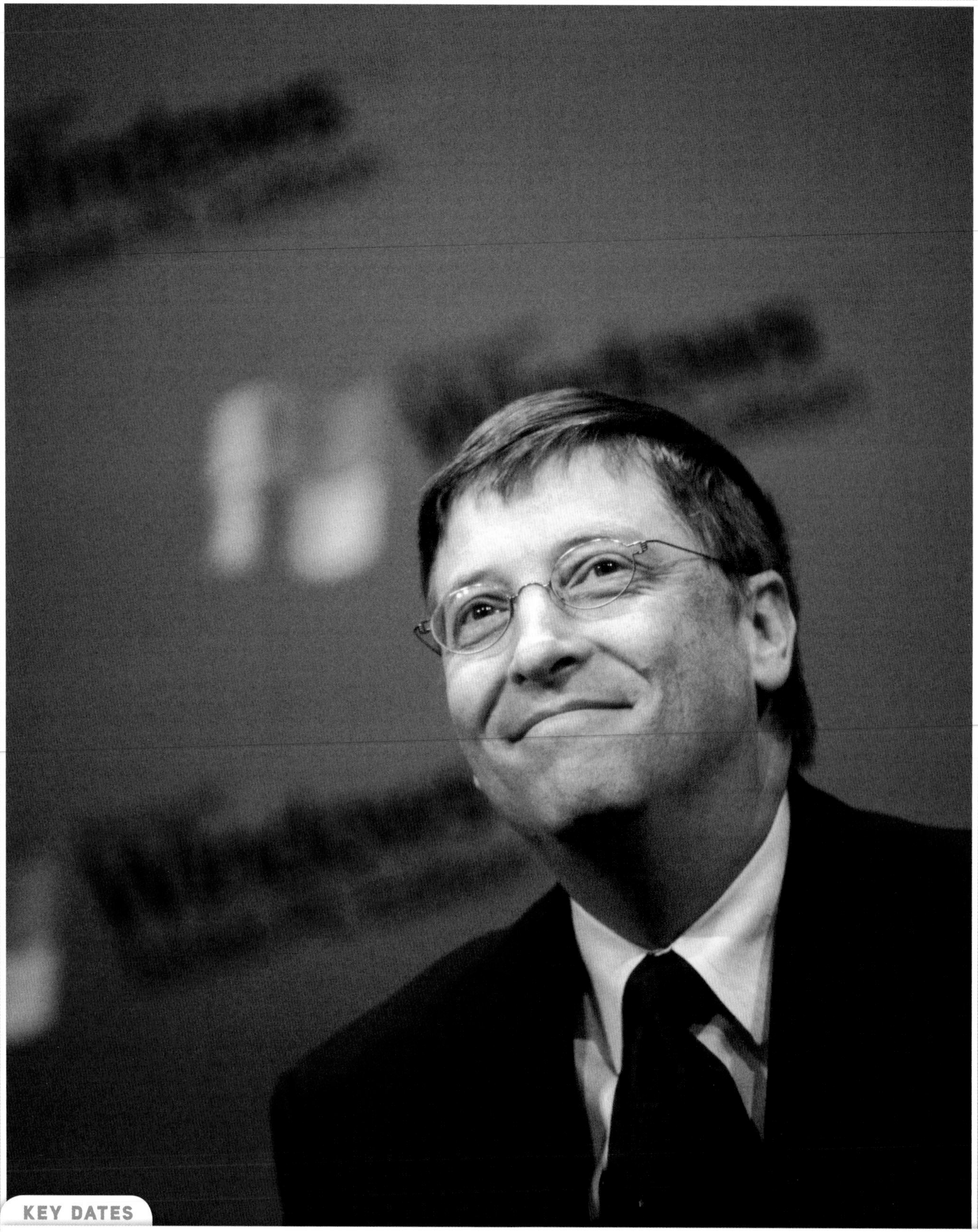

KEY DATES

1962
Silent Spring, written by Rachel Carson, is published and begins the modern environmental movement.

1957
The Soviet Union sends the world's first satellite, Sputnik, into space.

1970
Millions of Americans celebrate the first Earth Day, an event to increase awareness of the fragility of the environment.

1981
IBM introduces the first generation of personal computers.

COMPUTER AGE

1945–2010

Fierce international rivalries during World War II and the Cold War spurred major scientific advances, including the development of computers and rockets capable of reaching outer space. Scientist Wernher von Braun, who developed missiles for Germany during World War II, went on to direct American efforts as the United States vied with the Soviet Union in the nuclear arms race and the space race. The Soviets launched the first satellite, Sputnik I, in 1957 and went on to put the first person in orbit. Intent on closing the gap, Americans made a massive investment and landed astronauts on the moon in 1969. By the 1990s, with the Cold War behind them, Americans and Russians were working together to create the International Space Station. Like rocketry, computer science received a big boost from military research but had peaceful applications that were of even greater significance. Among the pioneers of digital technology was British mathematician Alan Turing, who helped develop specialized computers to break German military codes during World War II.

Computers and other technology developed in the mid-1900s for military purposes ended up fostering a revolution in productivity and global communication in the post–Cold War world.

In 1946 scientists at the University of Pennsylvania developed ENIAC (Electronic Numerical Integrator and Computer), first used to perform calculations for physicists developing the hydrogen bomb. Early computers like ENIAC were huge, containing thousands of bulky vacuum tubes, which later gave way to tiny transistors on microchips. That led to the development of personal computers and worldwide communication on the Internet, developed by the Pentagon in 1969 to link military researchers. Computers became big business, and leaders of those businesses—such as Bill Gates, whose company, Microsoft, came to dominate the market for operating-system software—became modern captains of industry.

Computers proved indispensable to research in many scientific fields. The Human Genome Project, launched in 1990 to map the more than 20,000 genes contained in human DNA, was completed two years ahead of schedule in 2003, a feat unthinkable without computers capable of processing vast amounts of data at superhuman speeds. Computer models also established a link between emissions of greenhouse gases and global warming, leading environmentalists to press for worldwide reductions.

OPPOSITE: Bill Gates dominated the computer industry with the software produced by his company, Microsoft.

1984
Scientists discover the retrovirus that causes AIDS.

1990
NASA launches the Hubble Space Telescope into orbit.

1997
Two Stanford students introduce a new search engine, Google, as a research project.

2003
The Human Genome Project sequences all human genes.

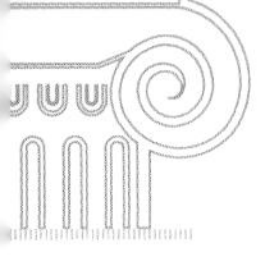

SEE ALSO | GLOBAL CULTURES: PAGE 439

SCIENCE THE SPACE AGE

The space race between the United States and Soviet Union offered a welcome contrast to the nuclear arms race. Satellites launched by the two superpowers beginning in the late 1950s were used for peaceful purposes like tracking storms and detecting the Earth's Van Allen belts as well as for military surveillance. After placing the first satellite in orbit in 1957, the Soviets maintained their lead by sending the first man, Yuri Gagarin, into space in 1961. President John F. Kennedy responded by launching the spectacular Apollo program, which achieved its goal on July 20, 1969, when astronaut Neil Armstrong stepped from the lunar module *Eagle* onto the moon's surface in a feat televised around the world.

The Apollo 13 insignia bears the motto "From the Moon, Knowledge."

A versatile new vehicle for space flight appeared in 1981 with the launching of *Columbia,* a reusable American space shuttle that glided gently back to Earth after being rocketed into orbit. Like the Apollo missions, these flights were risky, resulting in the loss of the shuttle *Challenger* and its crew in 1986 and *Columbia* and its crew in 2003.

The future of space exploration may lie with versatile robotic vehicles like the rovers that landed on Mars in 2004. But crews on the International Space Station have demonstrated that humans can function well in outer space for long periods and might one day occupy a station on the moon or on Mars.

The space shuttle *Atlantis* lifts off from Cape Canaveral in Florida.

THE TAKEAWAY: In the space race, unlike the arms race, each side tried to outshine their opponents, not annihilate them.

"I believe that this nation should commit itself to achieving the goal, before this decade is out, of landing a man on the moon and returning him safely." —JOHN F. KENNEDY

VOICES

BILL GATES YOU STEAL OUR SOFTWARE

"The feedback we have gotten from the hundreds of people who say they are using [Altair] BASIC has all been positive. Two surprising things are apparent, however, 1) Most of these "users" never bought BASIC (less than 10% of all Altair owners have bought BASIC), and 2) The amount of royalties we have received from sales to hobbyists makes the time spent on Altair BASIC worth less than $2 an hour.

"Why is this? As the majority of hobbyists must be aware, most of you steal your software."

—FROM AN OPEN LETTER TO HOBBYISTS BY A 20-YEAR-OLD GATES, 1976

BILL GATES

TECHNOLOGY THE SILICON AGE

Until the 1970s, computers were used mainly by government agencies, universities, and businesses. Most cost hundreds of thousands of dollars and took up an entire room. The development of microprocessors in the mid-1970s changed all that by compressing first thousands and later millions of transistors onto a tiny silicon chip. Compared with monster computers of the past like ENIAC, whose 18,000 vacuum tubes gave it a memory of 18,000 bits (binary digits), microprocessors stored millions of bits of information in a microcomputer at a fraction of the cost.

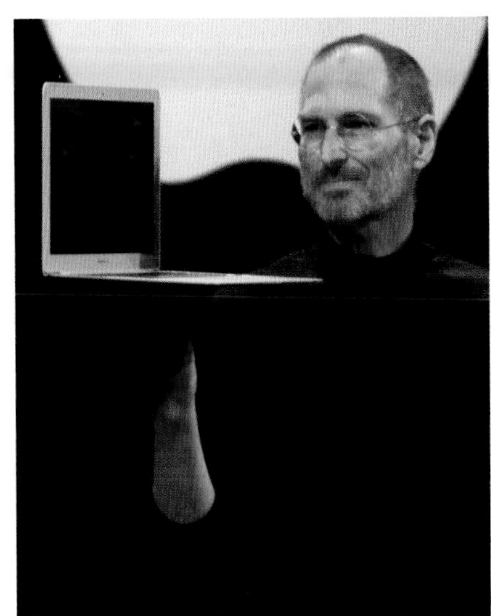

Steve Jobs of Apple holds the company's MacBook laptop computer.

This breakthrough was a bonanza not just for industry leaders like IBM, which introduced its first personal computer (PC) in 1981, but for young entrepreneurs like Bill Gates and Paul Allen of Microsoft, which provided the operating systems for most PCs. Stephen Wozniak and Steven Jobs of Apple gave IBM a run for its money with features—such as icons and the mouse—that made computers easier to use.

By the 1990s, the Internet had given birth to the World Wide Web, conceived by the British software engineer Tim Berners-Lee. Computers became essential, used not just to exchange e-mails but to teach classes, make purchases, and play games. Companies integral to the Internet like search engine Google soared in value as newspapers and other businesses tied to the printed page struggled to adapt.

Punch cards were once widely used to store data.

THE TAKEAWAY: By loading more power into a small package, engineers made computers indispensable.

"Anyone who has lost track of time when using a computer knows the propensity to dream, the urge to make dreams come true and the tendency to miss lunch." —TIM BERNERS-LEE

SEE ALSO | GLOBAL CULTURES: PAGE 445

SCIENCE GENETIC TOOLS

The secrets of heredity were revealed in 1953 when British physicist Francis Crick and American biologist James Watson identified the molecular structure of DNA as a double helix, consisting of intertwined strands that separate and recombine with other strands when cells replicate. That discovery led to genetic engineering, or techniques for recombining DNA to produce a clone or new genetic hybrids.

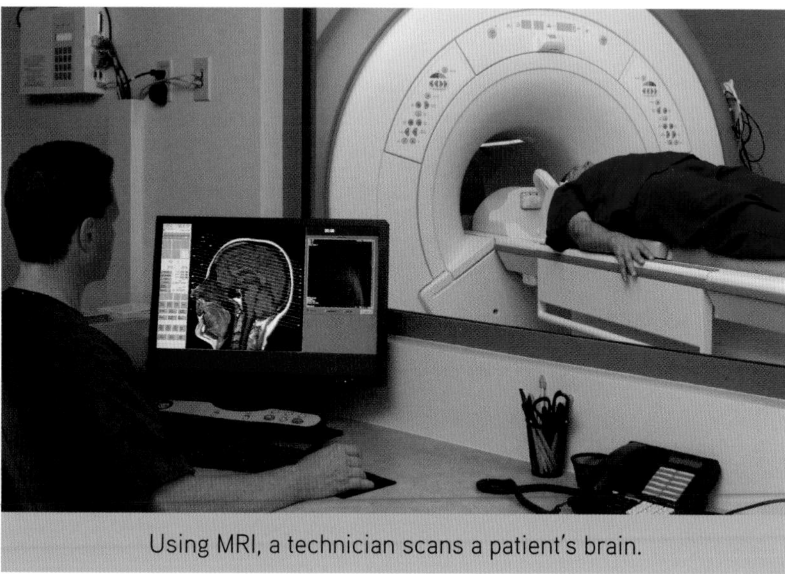

Using MRI, a technician scans a patient's brain.

DNA analysis is now used for many purposes, including identifying criminals and tracing ancestry.

Researchers are now using genetic engineering and the findings of the Human Genome Project to diagnose and treat genetic diseases and seek vaccines for viral diseases such as AIDS, which became widespread in the early 1980s and afflicts some 50 million people worldwide. Those advances and modern diagnostic tools like magnetic resonance imaging (MRI) may soon significantly reduce the toll of some diseases and add others to the list of scourges no longer to be feared, like smallpox, eradicated in the 20th century.

THE TAKEAWAY: Genetic engineering is used not only to save lives but to create new forms of life.

JAMES WATSON THE SECRET OF LIFE

VOICES

JAMES WATSON

"The question then became whether the A-T and G-C base pairs would easily fit the backbone configuration devised during the previous two weeks. At first glance this looked like a good bet.... However, we both knew that we would not be home until a complete model was built in which all the stereochemical contacts were satisfactory. There was also the obvious fact that the implications of its existence were far too important to risk crying wolf. Thus I felt slightly queasy when at lunch Francis winged into the Eagle to tell everyone within hearing distance that we had found the secret of life."

—FROM *THE DOUBLE HELIX*, JAMES D. WATSON, 1968

"DNA is essentially not capable of doing anything; it's just the instruction book. Having printed out the instruction book doesn't make the house come into being." —FRANCIS COLLINS

Polluted rivers like this one in Calcutta, India, pose risks for many species within their ecosystems.

SOCIETY GOING GREEN

The modern environmental movement grew out of earlier efforts by conservationists to preserve habitat for endangered species by creating parks and wildlife refuges. Environmentalists like Rachel Carson, an American naturalist whose book *Silent Spring* (1962) helped define this new movement, were concerned not just with protecting threatened species but with shielding entire ecosystems from the harmful impact of human activity, pollution, and toxins such as DDT.

America's newly energized environmentalists hailed the passage of the Clean Air Act of 1970, the Clean Water Act of 1972, and the Endangered Species Act of 1973, which authorized federal authorities to deny permits for logging, mining, and other activities on land deemed critical habitat for threatened species. Critics of that bill complained that it removed large areas from economic develop-ment to protect a single species. Environmentalists also backed the development of wind turbines, solar power cells, and other alternatives to both coal-burning and nuclear power plants. The latter were opposed by those who feared accidents like the meltdown at a Soviet plant in Chernobyl in 1986 that killed dozens and exposed millions to harmful radiation.

THE TAKEAWAY: The environmental movement gained momentum starting in the 1960s.

Koalas, native to Australia, are threatened by habitat destruction.

> *"As crude a weapon as the cave man's club, the chemical barrage has been hurled against the fabric of life."*
> —RACHEL CARSON

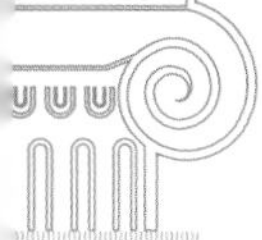

SEE ALSO | GLOBAL CULTURES: PAGE 435

KEY DATES

1950
U.S. senator Joseph McCarthy charges that the State Department is infiltrated by communists.

1955
Rosa Parks refuses to relinquish her seat on a bus in Alabama to a white man.

1963
U.S. President John F. Kennedy is assassinated in Dallas.

1973
A coup in Chile ousts President Salvador Allende.

THE AMERICAS

1945–2010

When World War II ended and the nuclear age dawned, the United States and its neighbors in the Western hemisphere found they could no longer distance themselves from dangers abroad. Determined now to play a leading role in global affairs, American officials helped organize the UN, which drew up its charter in 1945 and later made its headquarters in New York. In 1948 the United States and 20 other nations formed the Organization of American States (OAS), based in Washington, D.C. Although founded to promote peace and security, those international bodies were soon caught up in the Cold War. The UN authorized military action by the United States and other nations when communist North Korea invaded South Korea in 1950. And the OAS ousted Cuba in 1962 after its leader, Fidel Castro, embraced communism and accepted Soviet aid.

Long wary of foreign entanglements, the United States became involved with other nations in the Americas and elsewhere after World War II. Changing demographics at home, meanwhile, altered the face of politics.

The Cold War brought the United States challenges abroad and disturbances at home, including the Red Scare of the early 1950s, when Senator Joseph McCarthy and others tried to root out suspected communists. Protestors in the 1960s opposed the Vietnam War, intended to prevent a communist takeover there. Political tensions eased when the conflict in Vietnam ended in the 1970s and the Cold War drew to a close. But Americans still confronted a dangerous world as their heavy reliance on Middle Eastern oil and deep involvement in that troubled region exposed them to economic stress, terrorist attacks, and renewed conflict overseas.

Closer to home, trade agreements with Mexico and other Latin American nations and increased immigration from those countries raised concerns that by lowering such barriers the United States might lose its industrial capacity and cultural identity. By 2005 nearly a third of the nation's population was Hispanic, African American, or Asian. The country was undergoing a social transformation as groups formerly excluded from leadership positions, including women and minorities, used rights secured in the past century to make gains in the new century.

Diversity was on display in the 2008 U.S. presidential race, which saw one woman run for president, another woman nominated for vice president, and the son of an immigrant from Kenya elected to the country's highest office.

OPPOSITE: Fidel Castro defied the United States when he allowed Soviets to deploy nuclear weapons in Cuba.

1998
Augusto Pinochet, charged by Spain with murdering Spanish citizens while dictator of Chile, is arrested in London.

2005
Hurricane Katrina strikes the southern United States, resulting in about 1,800 deaths.

2007
A financial crisis sends the U.S. economy into a deep recession.

2008
Barack Obama is elected as the first African-American president of the United States.

SEE ALSO | GLOBAL CULTURES: PAGE 410

Reporter Edward R. Murrow challenged McCarthyism in the 1950s.

CLASS & SOCIETY COLD WARS

Fear of communism increased in the United States when, in 1949, the Soviet Union used stolen American nuclear secrets to develop an atomic bomb and communists took control of mainland China. Senator Joseph McCarthy heightened the Red Scare in the 1950s with sweeping accusations of communist subversion in the State Department and U.S. Army. But he lost public support when he badgered witnesses during televised hearings. No less controversial were proceedings by the House Un-American Activities Committee (HUAC), which looked into the suspected communist ties of cultural figures like singer Paul Robeson.

THE TAKEAWAY: The Red Scare mushroomed in the early 1950s.

THE AMERICAS — VIPs

Harry Truman, 1884–1972
33rd president of the United States, co-founder of the UN

Juan Perón, 1895–1974
President of Argentina whose oppressive regime ended in turmoil

Joseph McCarthy, 1908–1957
Republican senator from Wisconsin who led a movement against supposed communist infiltration

Fidel Castro, 1926–
Leader of Cuba who led that country's communist revolution

Martin Luther King, Jr., 1929–1968 U.S. civil rights leader who organized protests in the 1950s and '60s

PAUL ROBESON SECOND-CLASS CITIZENS — VOICES

PAUL ROBESON

"I am not being tried for whether I am a Communist, I am being tried for fighting for the rights of my people, who are still second-class citizens in this United States of America. My mother was born in your state, Mr. Walter, and my mother was a Quaker, and my ancestors in the time of Washington baked bread for George Washington's troops when they crossed the Delaware, and my own father was a slave. I stand here struggling for the rights of my people to be full citizens in this country. And they are not."

— FROM TESTIMONY BEFORE HUAC, JUNE 12, 1956

"I have here in my hand a list of 205 . . . a list of names that were made known to the Secretary of State as being members of the Communist Party." —JOSEPH MCCARTHY

CLASS & SOCIETY SOCIAL PROTEST

The gravest crisis of the Cold War occurred in October 1962 when Fidel Castro, angered by American efforts to overthrow him, allowed the Soviets to station nuclear weapons in Cuba. The superpowers stood at the brink of World War III until each side made concessions and the missiles were withdrawn. The threat of nuclear holocaust helped foster an American peace movement that opposed the Vietnam War, which began in earnest after President Kennedy was assassinated in 1963 and succeeded by Lyndon Johnson. Many who protested that war were baby boomers, born after 1945. This group also backed the civil rights movement, led by Martin Luther King, Jr., who drew on Gandhi's philosophy of nonviolent resistance. The movement protested racial segregation and rallied support for the Civil Rights Act. Pushed through Congress by Johnson in 1964, that bill guaranteed African Americans voting rights and other constitutional liberties. Social issues of the sixties also included women's liberation, which sought equal rights for women at home and at work.

> Presidents Lyndon Johnson and Richard Nixon waged war in Vietnam for ten years but failed to prevent a communist victory.

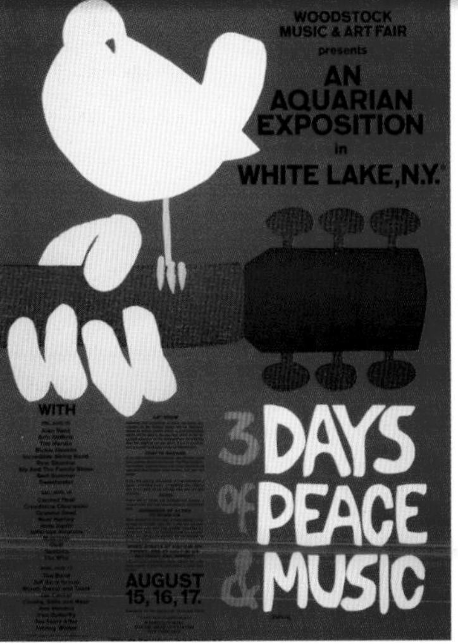

A poster touts the 1969 rock music festival Woodstock.

THE TAKEAWAY: Social protest movements of the 1960s and '70s were bolstered by the young.

The March on Washington in 1963, led by Martin Luther King, Jr., helped win passage of the Civil Rights Act.

"Nonviolence is the answer to the crucial political and moral question of our time."
—MARTIN LUTHER KING, JR.

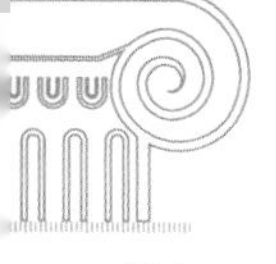

BARACK OBAMA

OBAMA HARD CHOICES AHEAD

"Our nation is at war against a far-reaching network of violence and hatred. Our economy is badly weakened, a consequence of greed and irresponsibility on the part of some, but also our collective failure to make hard choices and prepare the nation for a new age. Homes have been lost, jobs shed, businesses shuttered."

—FROM BARACK OBAMA'S INAUGURAL ADDRESS, 2009

NATIONS GLOBAL TIES

As the 20th century waned, Americans were deeply affected by global events. President Nixon's trip to China in 1972 led to diplomatic ties with that country. Soaring gas prices were linked to conflicts in the Middle East, including a revolution in Iran, where the seizure of the U.S. Embassy contributed to President Jimmy Carter's loss to Ronald Reagan in 1980. U.S. power and wealth increased with the collapse of the Soviet bloc and then the lowering of trade barriers under President Clinton.

Terrorist attacks on September 11, 2001, caused conflict overseas and controversy at home. Public doubts about the war in Iraq launched in 2003 by President George W. Bush, dismay over the slow government response to Hurricane Katrina that ravaged New Orleans in 2005, and disgust with financial maneuvers that triggered a stock market crash set the stage for the election of President Barack Obama in 2008.

THE TAKEAWAY: Globalization tied the United States to other nations at the turn of the century.

President George Bush views wreckage left by Hurricane Katrina, which claimed more than 1,800 lives.

"It took a Nixon to go to China, and it may take a Democrat to balance the budget." —THOMAS FOLEY

SEE ALSO | GLOBAL CULTURES: PAGE 445

REGIONS LEFT AND RIGHT IN LATIN AMERICA

During the Cold War, Latin American leaders had to walk a fine line if they wanted to avoid becoming too closely linked with the United States or the Soviet Union. One man who took an independent stance was President Juan Perón of Argentina. An army officer by training, he used strong-arm tactics to achieve power in 1946 but also relied on his keen political instincts and those of his

Chilean dictator Augusto Pinochet salutes parading cadets in 1986.

popular wife, Eva (Evita), who secured voting rights for women in Argentina. Although he echoed Marxist rhetoric, the president avoided alignment with either the Soviets or the Americans.

Fidel Castro started out on a similar path when he took power in Cuba in 1959, but he soon antagonized the United States by nationalizing American-owned sugar plantations, canceling elections, and

> President Hugo Chávez of Venezuela used oil revenues to promote a socialist agenda like that of Fidel Castro.

reaching out to the Soviet Union. A U.S.-backed invasion of Cuba by anti-Castro rebels failed in 1961, and President Kennedy later halted efforts to depose the Cuban leader.

That did not prevent the United States from going after other left-wing regimes, including backing a coup in Chile in 1973 by General Augusto Pinochet against President Salvador Allende, or funneling aid in the 1980s to right-wing rebels seeking to topple Nicaragua's socialist government.

Chilean president Bachelet practiced medicine before entering politics.

The end of the Cold War diminished both outside interference and internal strife in Latin America and fostered new leaders trained not as military officers but as lawyers, doctors, or labor leaders. Emblematic of the new generation was Michelle Bachelet—the daughter of a Chilean officer who was tortured for opposing the Pinochet coup—who practiced medicine before being elected Chile's president in 2006.

THE TAKEAWAY: Latin American countries have become more stable since the Cold War.

> *"Is the U.S. going to forbid revolution to take place in Latin America? That's absolutely impossible! Even the U.S. had its revolutionary era."* —FIDEL CASTRO

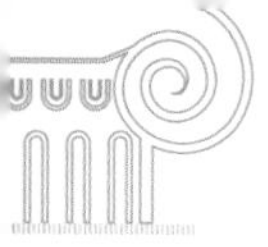

SEE ALSO | THE WORLD AT WAR: PAGE 400

KEY DATES

1947
Palestine divides into two provisional states under the UN's Partition Plan.

1948
The Jewish state in Palestine is proclaimed as Israel.

1948
The South African parliament formally institutes apartheid.

1960
Over 15 former colonies recognized as independent countries in Africa.

MIDDLE EAST AND AFRICA

1945–2010

After World War II, nationalism surged in Africa and the Middle East as Europeans gradually gave up their colonies. Decolonization was often chaotic, even when colonial administrators were eager to leave. The British, for example, had no desire to retain their troublesome mandate over Palestine, where Arabs were clashing with Jewish settlers in Jerusalem and other sites sacred to both groups. In 1947 Britain turned Palestine over to the UN, which called for dividing the country into two states. Arabs, who outnumbered Jews in Palestine roughly two to one, rejected that proposal. In 1948 the first Arab-Israeli war erupted, leading many Palestinians to flee territory lost to the newly founded nation of Israel.

Weakened by the world wars it helped produce, European imperialism came to a turbulent end in Africa and the Middle East after 1945, but the regions remained wracked by internal conflicts.

The long-lasting Arab-Israeli dispute was not the only source of tension in the Middle East. Oil brought emerging nations wealth but also exposed them to Western pressure, and Islamic fundamentalists opposed pro-Western rulers like Shah Mohammad Reza Pahlavi, who was ousted in the Iranian revolution of 1979. Oil-producing countries gained bargaining power by forming OPEC (Organization of the Petroleum Exporting Countries). But economic cooperation did not prevent conflict, as happened in 1990 when Iraqi dictator Saddam Hussein invaded oil-rich Kuwait. The United States and its allies defeated his forces in the Gulf War of 1991 and later toppled him in the Iraq War that began in 2003.

Decolonization in Africa was particularly difficult in countries with sizable European populations. A bitter struggle between French troops and Algerian insurgents claimed hundreds of thousands of lives before Algeria won independence from France in 1962. Although South Africa was no longer under British rule, it was still dominated by whites who kept the country's black majority separate and unequal through a rigid policy of apartheid. Liberation came peacefully when Nelson Mandela, leader of the African National Congress (ANC), was released from prison in 1990, negotiated an end to apartheid, and won South Africa's first truly democratic presidential election in 1994.

OPPOSITE: Nelson Mandela offers a winning smile shortly before being elected president of South Africa.

1964
Lawyer Nelson Mandela begins a life sentence for plotting to overthrow South Africa's government.

1980
A long series of border disputes erupts after Iraq invades Iran.

1990–1993
More than two million Rwandans flee the country to escape genocide.

2003
The United States invades Iraq, beginning the Iraq War.

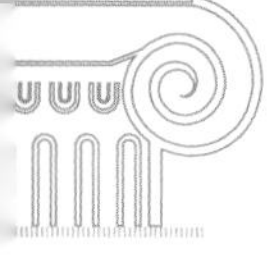

SEE ALSO | GLOBAL CULTURES: PAGE 427

A Palestinian woman sits in a battle-scarred house in Gaza.

CONFLICTS ISRAEL & PALESTINE

From its inception, Israel was at odds with neighboring Arab countries and with Palestinians living in Gaza and the West Bank, seized when Israeli forces defeated Egypt and Syria in the Six Day War in 1967. The fate of the occupied territories remained a point of contention. In 1978 Prime Minister Menachim Begin reached an accord with Egypt's president Anwar Sadat, mediated by President Jimmy Carter at Camp David. That left unresolved Israel's dispute with the Palestine Liberation Organization (PLO), which later gave way to the Palestinian Authority. The building of Israeli settlements in occupied territory and the emergence of Palestinian militant group Hamas complicated peace efforts.

THE TAKEAWAY: Israel's victory in 1967 led to conflict with Palestinians in occupied territories.

Prime Minister Golda Meir helped to found Israel in 1948.

ABBA EBAN AFTER 3,000 YEARS, THE TIME HAS ARRIVED

VOICES

ABBA EBAN

"The situation to be constructed after the cease-fire must depend on certain principles. The first of these principles surely must be the acceptance of Israel's statehood and the total elimination of the fiction of her non-existence. It would seem to me that after 3,000 years the time has arrived to accept Israel's nationhood as a fact, for here is the only State in the international community which has the same territory, speaks the same language and upholds the same faith as it did 3,000 years ago."

—FROM A SPEECH BY ISRAELI FOREIGN MINISTER ABBA EBAN TO THE UN DURING THE SIX DAY WAR, 1967

"Can we, from now on—all of us—turn a new leaf and, instead of fighting with each other, can we all, united, fight poverty and disease and illiteracy?" —GOLDA MEIR

CONFLICTS HOT SPOTS

Conflicts in the Middle East were fueled and sometimes ignited by the world's major powers. In 1956 British, French, and Israeli forces invaded Egypt after President Gamal Abdel Nasser nationalized the Suez Canal. The United States helped bring that intervention to an end, but it later aided Israel while the Soviets backed Egypt and Syria in the inconclusive 1973 Yom Kippur War.

A soldier drapes a flag over Saddam Hussein's statue.

Another hot spot in the Middle East was the Persian Gulf region, from which much of the world's oil flowed. Alarmed by the Iranian revolution in 1979, the United States helped Iraq's Saddam Hussein avoid defeat by Iran in the 1980s. His use of chemical weapons earned U.S. distrust, however, and the United States led a coalition against him after he seized Kuwait's oil fields in 1990. American and British forces ousted him in 2003 but failed to find weapons of mass destruction in Iraq as some expected.

> The presence of U.S. military bases in Saudi Arabia helped set terrorist Osama bin Laden against America.

THE TAKEAWAY: The Middle East's oil reserves drew global powers into its conflicts.

An Israeli convoy passes a truckload of captured Egyptian troops during the Six-Day War in 1967.

"We are determined to knock out Saddam Hussein's nuclear bomb potential. We will also destroy his chemical weapons facilities." —GEORGE H. W. BUSH

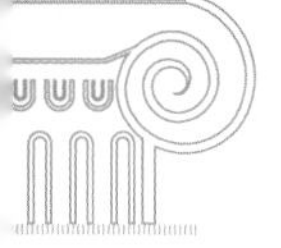

SEE ALSO | THE WORLD AT WAR: PAGE 400

VOICES

JOMO KENYATTA THIS IS OUR LAND

"We are here in this tremendous gathering under the K.A.U. flag to find which road leads us from darkness into democracy. In order to find it we Africans must first achieve the right to elect our own representatives. That is surely the first principle of democracy. We are the only race in Kenya which does not elect its own representatives in the Legislature and we are going to set about to rectify this situation. We feel we are dominated by a handful of others who refuse to be just. God said this is our land. Land in which we are to flourish as a people. We are not worried that other races are here with us in our country, but we insist that we are the leaders here, and what we want we insist we get. We want our cattle to get fat on our land so that our children grow up in prosperity; we do not want that fat removed to feed others."

—JOMO KENYATTA, SPEECH AT NYERI, KENYA, 1952

REGIONS SUB-SAHARAN AFRICA

The first country in sub-Saharan Africa to achieve independence after World War II was Ghana in 1957, led by Kwame Nkrumah, who had been jailed for protesting British rule. Resistance leader Jomo Kenyatta had also been a political prisoner before taking charge of the former British colony Kenya in 1963. But ethnic and tribal tensions made emerging nations politically unstable and prey to dictators. The region was also plagued by AIDS, which claimed twice as many victims here as in all of the rest of the world, and drought in areas like Darfur, where desertification contributed to a massive refugee crisis in the early 2000s.

THE TAKEAWAY: The transition to independence was traumatic in sub-Saharan Africa.

Crowded markets like this one in Lagos, Nigeria, help sustain the African economy in hard times.

"The test of the future will be the amount of purchasing power we put into the hand of our workers and farmers." —KWAME NKRUMAH

NATIONS SOUTH AFRICA IN TRANSITION

Racial segregation had long been an unfortunate fact of life in South Africa. But it became the law of the land in 1948 when the National Party, committed to preserving white supremacy, was elected and enacted apartheid, a policy designed to isolate and intimidate nonwhites. All South Africans were registered by race as white, black, Asian, or Coloured (mixed race), and interracial marriage was prohibited. To discourage blacks from developing a common identity and seeking political power, white leaders tribalized them by dividing them into ten groups of Bantu (the language family to which most black South Africans belonged) and assigning each to its own reserve, or Bantustan.

President Nelson Mandela and F. W. de Klerk shake hands in 2004.

The removal of blacks to reserves left nearly four-fifths of South Africa's territory in the hands of its white minority. Nonwhites were required to show passes to enter restricted areas, confined to certain jobs, and denied voting rights. Those who opposed the government and its policies were subject to arrest.

Despite such restrictions, the African National Congress (ANC) waged a long campaign against apartheid. ANC leader Nelson Mandela used his skills as a lawyer to organize nonviolent protests until police killed dozens of unarmed demonstrators at Sharpeville in 1960 and the ANC was outlawed. Mandela concluded that he would have to fight apartheid in earnest and helped form the ANC's covert military wing. Arrested in 1962, he was sentenced to life in prison.

The longer the government held him, the larger Mandela's reputation grew among the country's black majority. In 1990, faced with mounting opposition to his party's policies at home and abroad, South Africa's reform-minded President F. W. de Klerk released the 71-year-old Mandela and reached an agreement with him that ended apartheid and led to free elections. As president from 1994 to 1999, Mandela worked to preserve the interracial accord that brought him to power.

{ Mandela and de Klerk received the Nobel Peace Prize in 1993 for making South Africa a multiracial democracy. }

THE TAKEAWAY: Nelson Mandela's example inspired South Africans to defeat apartheid.

"South Africa is starved of the great things many of her children can create and do, because of artificial barriers, and the refusal to let people develop to their fullest potential." —DESMOND TUTU

SEE ALSO | THE WORLD AT WAR: PAGE 401

KEY DATES

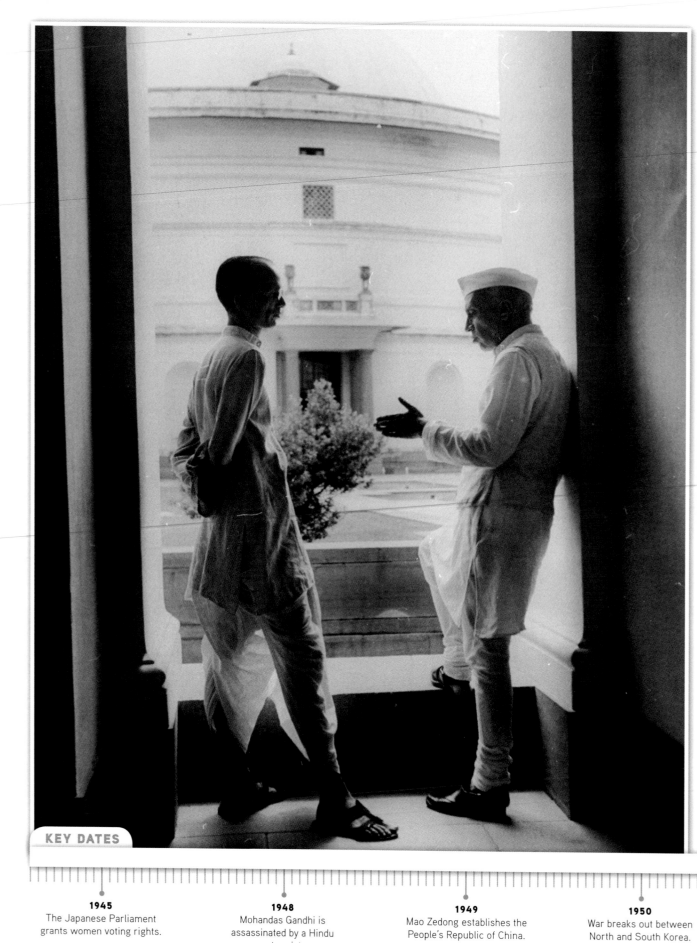

1945
The Japanese Parliament grants women voting rights.

1948
Mohandas Gandhi is assassinated by a Hindu extremist.

1949
Mao Zedong establishes the People's Republic of China.

1950
War breaks out between North and South Korea.

ASIA'S REVIVAL

1945–2010

Asian countries, which were overshadowed by Western powers during the industrial revolution and the age of imperialism, regained prominence globally in the late 1900s. The resurgence was sudden and dramatic. Nationalist drives after World War II spurred political change in Southeast Asia and Cold War anxieties in the West. For China, Japan's defeat meant the end of one war and the resumption of another great struggle—a civil war that brought communist leader Mao Zedong to power in 1949 and left China in revolutionary upheaval for decades to come. Korea and Vietnam faced similar ordeals from the 1950s to the '70s as each was divided between communists in the north and anticommunists in the south and became battlegrounds in the Cold War, which caused far more bloodshed in Asia than anywhere else. The Vietnam War spilled over into Laos and Cambodia, where a genocidal communist regime, the Khmer Rouge, took power.

Once home to some of the world's most industrious societies, Asia has reclaimed that honor in recent times. The booming economies of many countries have led to the phrase "the Asian miracle."

Rising from the ashes of destruction, one Asian country after another reached new heights of prosperity. The revival began in Japan, which benefited from America's policy of rebuilding nations it defeated. By the 1970s Japan was exporting so many appliances and automobiles that their recovery was called a miracle. Mao's successors in China retained a communist government but successfully retooled the economy along capitalist lines in the late 1900s.

For India, triumph mingled with tragedy as it won independence from Britain in 1947 but lost Pakistan in a violent partition that cost the lives of more than a million people. The two leaders who dominated India politically from 1947 to the mid-1980s—Jawaharlal Nehru and his daughter, Indira Gandhi—tried to steer a course between capitalism and communism. India remained a democracy, however, and flourished in the global capitalist system that developed after the Cold War, emerging as one of the world's fastest-growing economies.

Some countries lagged far behind, however, notably North Korea, where communist dictators Kim Il Sung and his son, Kim Jong Il, sought nuclear weapons while their people starved. But Asia as a whole entered the 21st century ready to match Europe and America stride for stride.

OPPOSITE: Indian prime minister Jawaharlal Nehru (right) was hailed as pandit (teacher).

1975
The North Vietnamese Army captures Saigon, marking the end of the Vietnam War.

1979
China establishes full diplomatic relations with the United States.

1988
Benazir Bhutto becomes the first female prime minister of Pakistan.

2008
The Taj Mahal Palace Hotel in Mumbai is attacked and destroyed by terrorists.

NATIONS CHINA LEAPS FORWARD

Chinese workers inspect a solar cell in a factory in Taizhou.

Mao Zedong's revolution did not end in 1949. In the late 1950s he formed communes where thousands of peasants worked collectively. Billed as a Great Leap Forward, this chaotic program contributed to a famine that claimed millions of lives. To suppress dissent among officials and intellectuals, Mao launched the Cultural Revolution in 1966, during which time suspected counterrevolutionaries were sentenced to "reeducation," often meaning hard labor.

Not until the 1980s, when Chairman Deng Xiaoping loosened restraints on business, did China truly leap forward economically.

{ China, the most populous country in the world, passed the one billion mark in population in 1980. }

Deng used deadly force in Beijing's Tiananmen Square in 1989 to crush a pro-democracy movement, but economic reforms continued, making China an industrial giant exporting goods around the globe.

THE TAKEAWAY: China suffered political turmoil but experienced economic success.

UNITED STATES TIANANMEN SQUARE, JUNE 3, 1989

VOICES

TIANANMEN SQUARE DEMONSTRATORS

"*TROOPS USING AUTOMATIC WEAPONS ADVANCED IN TANKS, APC'S AND TRUCKS FROM SEVERAL DIRECTIONS ON TIANANMEN SQUARE JUNE 3. THERE WAS CONSIDERABLE RESISTANCE BY DEMONSTRATORS, AND THE NUMBER OF CASUALTIES APPEARS HIGH. THE EMBASSY ESTIMATES THAT THE 50-70 REPORTED DEAD IN FOREIGN MEDIA IS PROBABLY MUCH TOO LOW. HOSPITALS ARE SAID TO BE OVERFLOWING WITH CASUALTIES.*"

—CABLE FROM THE U.S. DEPARTMENT OF STATE TO THE U.S. EMBASSY IN BEIJING, JUNE 3, 1989

"*Yellow cat, black cat, as long as it catches mice, it is a good cat.*" —DENG XIOPING

SEE ALSO | GLOBAL CULTURES: PAGE 423

CONFLICTS DIVIDED NATIONS

Korea, a former Japanese colony, was divided in 1945 when American troops occupied the zone below the 38th parallel and Soviets occupied the zone above that line. In June 1950, communist North Korea invaded South Korea. Armed with a UN resolution authorizing the use of force, the United States led the fight against North Korea, which was nearly defeated before communist China entered the war on its side. A cease-fire in 1953 restored the original boundary between the two Koreas.

Vietnam won independence from France in 1954 through an agreement that temporarily divided the noncommunist South from the communist North, led by Ho Chi Minh. Intent on containing communism, the United States backed the South in conflicts against North Vietnam and its Viet Cong allies in the South. Some three million Vietnamese and 58,000 American soldiers died in the war before the United States withdrew in 1973 and the South fell to the North in 1975.

Soldiers in a South Korean poster attack Communists.

THE TAKEAWAY: Colonialism gave way to war in Korea and Vietnam in the 1950s and '60s.

A U.S. Navy airman fires an M-60 from a helicopter during the Vietnam War.

> *If the Americans do not want to support us anymore, let them go, get out! Let them forget their humanitarian promises!"* —NGUYEN VAN THIEU

SEE ALSO | THE WORLD AT WAR: PAGE 403

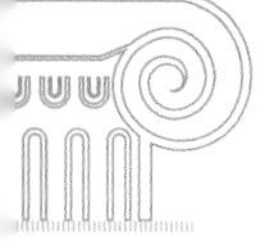

Indira Gandhi campaigns in 1979 for reelection as India's prime minister.

NATIONS A DIVIDED SUBCONTINENT

Unlike other conflict-ridden Asian countries after World War II, India was divided largely by religion. Bloody clashes between Hindus and Muslims led British authorities to grant the request of India's Muslim League to create a separate Muslim state, Pakistan, when they left India in 1947. This partition caused further chaos as millions fled to either side of the India-Pakistan border.

In 1948 Prime Minister Nehru sent Indian troops to oppose Pakistani forces in the disputed province of Kashmir. Prime Minister Indira Gandhi waged another war against Pakistan in 1971 and forced it to grant independence to Bangladesh, a predominantly Muslim country.

Gandhi also opposed Sikhs in India who were demanding their own state. After ordering troops to attack Sikh militants in a shrine, she was assassinated in 1984 by two of her Sikh bodyguards. Many Sikhs renounced separatism, however—among them Manmohan Singh, who became India's first non-Hindu prime minister in 2004.

THE TAKEAWAY: Religious differences among Muslims, Hindus, and Sikhs have shaped India.

JAWAHARLAL NEHRU 1889–1964

THUMBS UP / THUMBS DOWN

JAWAHARLAL NEHRU

NEHRU, WHO LED INDIA from independence in 1947 until his death in 1964, was a complex figure. He preached peaceful coexistence but used armed force against Pakistan and other countries. He proclaimed neutrality in the Cold War but accepted aid first from the Soviet Union and later from the United States. He was consistent, however, in seeking to make India a strong secular state. A brahman by birth who stood atop the Hindu social scale, he denounced India's caste system. And he backed legislation that prohibited polygamy and protected the inheritance rights of women. **CONCLUSION:** THUMBS UP

> *"The Hindus and Muslims belong to two different religious philosophies, social customs, literatures. They . . . belong to two different civilizations."* —MUHAMMAD ALI JINNAH

ECONOMY ASIAN TIGERS

Japan entered a new era in 1945 when it was defeated and occupied by U.S. forces. General Douglas MacArthur took charge of the country and offered a new constitution that reduced Emperor Hirohito to a figurehead. Hirohito would no longer appoint Japan's prime minister, who would be chosen instead by the Diet, the country's legislature. Nor would he command the armed forces, which were disbanded. Women gained the right to vote, and the public education system was expanded. Factories destroyed during the war were rebuilt and retooled. By relying on the United States for defense, Japan found it could concentrate on modernizing its economy, and by 1952, when the occupation ended, it had surpassed prewar production levels.

Compact discs are among Japan's many high-tech exports.

By the 1960s Japanese companies faced competition from firms elsewhere in Asia with lower labor costs. Japan was king of the jungle, but it had to contend with "four little tigers": Hong Kong, Taiwan, South Korea, and Singapore. As those new manufacturing centers developed, they in turn faced competition from China and other emerging industrial powers. By the 1990s Japan's economic bubble—inflated by a steep rise in housing prices in its fast-growing cities—had burst. Like many Western nations, Japan also had to cope with problems created by its own prosperity, including a declining birth rate as young professionals had fewer children.

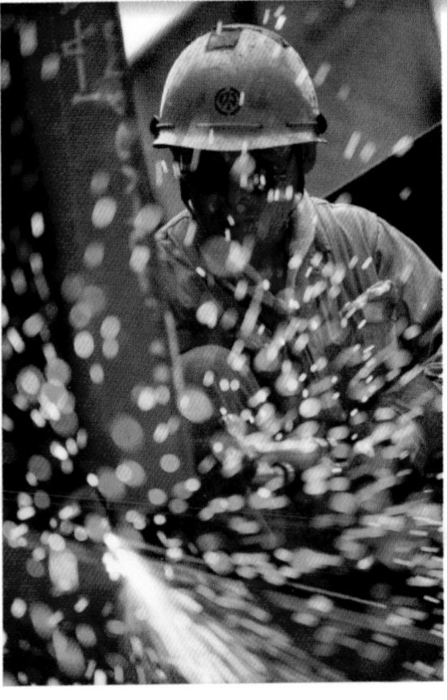

Sparks fly as a shipbuilder in Osaka, Japan, works on a tanker.

THE TAKEAWAY: Without the need to provide its own armed forces, Japan prospered.

The Singapore Flyer offers a bird's-eye view of that fast-growing city.

"Perhaps the best advice to give to a young American is: 'Go East, Young Man.'" —KISHORE MAHBUBANI

SEE ALSO | GLOBAL CULTURES: PAGE 445

KEY DATES

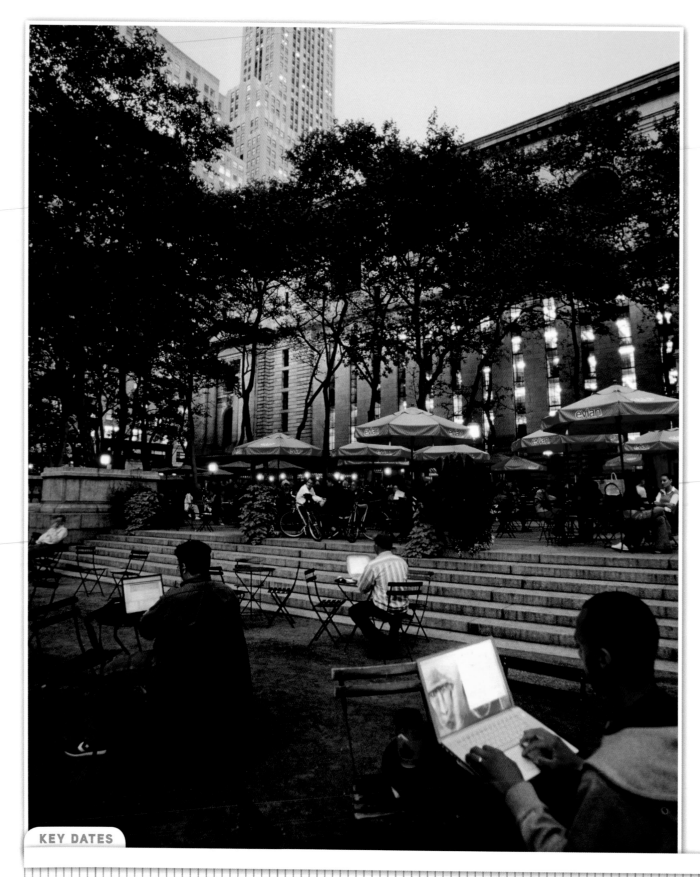

1956
The green revolution in agriculture allows Mexico to become self-sufficient for its wheat supply.

1962
Telstar, the first telecommunications satellite, goes into orbit.

1969
The microprocessor is invented, spurring computer development.

1977
The first cell phones are tested in Chicago.

SMALL WORLD

1945–2010

When terrorists hijacked commercial jets and crashed them into the World Trade Center and the Pentagon on September 11, 2001, journalists were quick to compare the shocking attacks to the Japanese assault on Pearl Harbor 60 years earlier. In one respect, however, those two disasters were not at all alike. Photographs showing the explosive attack on Pearl Harbor were not published in the United States for more than a year after the event because government censors feared they would demoralize the public. On 9/11, by contrast, much of the nation and the world saw the terrible events unfold live on television. The distance that once separated people from catastrophes and their victims had been obliterated by new modes of communication, including cell phones, used by those aboard one of the hijacked jets to speak with loved ones before the plane went down.

Globalization in the form of instantaneous transmission of words and images around the world magnified the impact of the 9/11 attacks. But those assaults were also a violent reaction to globalization and the worldwide power and influence of the United States and its economic system, as symbolized by the Pentagon and the World Trade Center.

> *Globalization, fostered by worldwide networks of communication and commerce, has increased international cooperation and development as well as threats to the new, interconnected world.*

Since the end of the Cold War, the prospect of a new international order in which countries around the globe would follow the Western model of political and economic development, guided by agencies such as the World Trade Organization (WTO), has been welcomed in many places and dreaded in others. Critics of globalization, including some Westerners, see it as a new form of imperialism, in which multinational corporations and organizations are imposing their terms on the world and homogenizing its cultures. But even people opposed to that process make use of computers and the Internet to recruit followers and form international networks. In that sense, globalization appears irreversible.

Global problems such as human-induced climate change require global solutions. And no solution to the world's problems, however radical, can be implemented without making use of technologies that are shrinking the planet. For many people, an increasingly interconnected world is not a threat but an opportunity, allowing a free exchange of ideas and information to everyone's benefit.

OPPOSITE: Glowing computer screens link wireless Internet surfers in New York City to Web sites worldwide.

1994
The North American Free Trade Agreement (NAFTA) goes into effect.

2001
Suicide bombers belonging to the al Qaeda terrorist group attack the Pentagon and World Trade Center.

2002
Wal-Mart has its biggest day of sales in history, reaching \$1.43 billion in revenue on the day after Thanksgiving.

2009
The 2009 United Nations Climate Change Conference is held in Copenhagen, Denmark.

SEE ALSO | GLOBAL CULTURES: PAGE 442

SOCIETY POPULATION GROWTH

British economist Thomas Malthus proposed in 1798 that population naturally increases at a faster rate than food production, resulting in wars, famines, and other disasters. In recent times, the so-called green revolution in agriculture has allowed food production to keep pace with population growth even in fast-growing countries like India. But the world's population may soon exceed the Earth's carrying capacity.

Between 1960 and 2010, the world's population grew from three billion to nearly seven billion. It is expected to reach nine billion by 2045. Most of that growth occurs in developing countries, poorly equipped to provide for a population heavily skewed toward youth. About half the world in 2010 lived in poverty, earning the equivalent of $2 a day on average. Unless checked, population growth may have positively Malthusian effects on world health and stability.

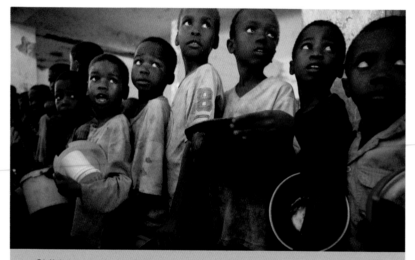

Children await food at a relief agency in famine-stricken Somalia.

THE TAKEAWAY: Modern population growth occurs primarily in less developed countries.

SMALL WORLD

VIPs

Norman Borlaug, 1914–2009
American agronomist and humanitarian; father of the green revolution

James Hansen, 1941–
American climatologist who helped raise awareness of global climate change

Osama bin Laden, 1957–
Saudi terrorist leader behind the September 11, 2001, bombings

Sergey Brin and Larry Page, 1973– and 1973–
Creators of the Internet search engine Google and founders of the company of that name

CONNECTIONS THE GREEN REVOLUTION

THE FIRST AGRICULTURAL REVOLUTION occurred some 10,000 years ago when humans domesticated wheat, barley, rice, and other grains. The second, "green" revolution came about in the mid-20th century when scientists developed new grain varieties with higher yields. These hybrid crops fended off starvation in countries such as India and Pakistan in the 1960s and have since accounted for record harvests around the world. However, these life-saving crops require large amounts of pesticides and fertilizers; in the long run, their environmental harm may outweigh their benefits.

CROP DUSTER IN TEXAS

> *"The environmentalist vision . . . sees humanity entering a bottleneck unique in history, constricted by population and economic pressures."* —E. O. WILSON

A hijacked jet hits the doomed World Trade Center on 9/11.

SOCIETY TERRORISM

Many terrorist groups in the late 20th century had local objectives, such as gaining independence for their state. Al Qaeda, organized in the late 1980s by Osama bin Laden, was exceptional in that its goals were global. Although bin Laden wanted to overthrow the U.S.-backed monarchy in Saudi Arabia and end the American presence there, his larger aim was to lead Muslims from many countries in a holy war against the United States and its allies around the world. Al Qaeda operatives bombed U.S. embassies in Kenya and Tanzania in 1998 and attacked the destroyer U.S.S. *Cole* at a port in Yemen in 2000 before launching the devastating September 11 assaults that leveled the twin towers of the World Trade Center, shattered part of the Pentagon, and killed nearly 3,000 people in 2001.

> The size of al Qaeda is hard to determine, but it ranges from hundreds to thousands of members.

Al Qaeda's operations were disrupted late that year when the United States and its allies ousted the Taliban regime in Afghanistan that was harboring bin Laden and his associates; the terrorists went into hiding in mountains along the Pakistan border. It was unclear what role al Qaeda played in subsequent attacks by terrorists who had similar goals. Train bombings that killed nearly 200 people in Madrid in 2004—originally blamed on ETA, a Basque terrorist group—were later attributed to terrorists inspired by al Qaeda, as were bombings on London's transit system in 2005 that killed more than 50 people.

THE TAKEAWAY: Terrorist tactics enable small groups like al Qaeda to disrupt powerful nations like the United States.

> "Buildings Burn and Fall as Onlookers Search for Elusive Safety"
> —*NEW YORK TIMES* HEADLINE, 9/12/2001

9/11 COMMISSION REPORT

In 2002, a national commission was established to determine who was responsible for the 9/11 attacks, why the U.S. government failed to foresee them, and what could be done to prevent further terrorist acts. The 9/11 Commission Report, issued in 2004, concluded that all 19 terrorists involved were members of al Qaeda and found no evidence linking foreign governments to the plot. The attacks "should not have come as a surprise," the report stated, but lack of coordination within and among federal agencies like the FBI and CIA fatally hampered efforts to uncover al Qaeda's plans.

IN MEMORIAM President and First Lady George and Laura Bush bow in memory of those who died aboard a jetliner that crashed in Pennsylvania on 9/11, when passengers tried to wrest control of the plane from hijackers. President Bush's decision to attack the Taliban in Afghanistan for harboring al Qaeda won broad public support.

EXECUTIVE SUMMARY

We present the narrative of this report and the recommendations that flow from it to the President of the United States, the United States Congress, and the American people for their consideration. Ten Commissioners—five Republicans and five Democrats chosen by elected leaders from our nation's capital at a time of great partisan division—have come together to present this report without dissent.

We have come together with a unity of purpose because our nation demands it. September 11, 2001, was a day of unprecedented shock and suffering in the history of the United States. The nation was unprepared.

A NATION TRANSFORMED

At 8:46 on the morning of September 11, 2001, the United States became a nation transformed.

An airliner traveling at hundreds of miles per hour and carrying some 10,000 gallons of jet fuel plowed into the North Tower of the World Trade Center in Lower Manhattan. At 9:03, a second airliner hit the South Tower. Fire and smoke billowed upward. Steel, glass, ash, and bodies fell below. The Twin Towers, where up to 50,000 people worked each day, both collapsed less than 90 minutes later.

At 9:37 that same morning, a third airliner slammed into the western face of the Pentagon. At 10:03, a fourth airliner crashed in a field in southern Pennsylvania. It had been aimed at the United States Capitol or the White House, and was forced down by heroic passengers armed with the knowledge that America was under attack.

More than 2,600 people died at the World Trade Center; 125 died at the

"Since well before 9/11—and continuing to this day—the intelligence community is not organized well for joint intelligence work. . . . The structures are too complex and too secret."

"None of the measures adopted by the U.S. government from 1998 to 2001 disturbed or even delayed the progress of the al Qaeda plot. Across the government, there were failures of imagination, policy, capabilities, and management."

EXECUTIVE SUMMARY The Executive Summary of the lengthy 9/11 Commission Report encapsulates the commission's findings and recommendations.

"In the words of one official, no analytic work foresaw the lightning that could connect the thundercloud to the ground."

2 THE 9/11 COMMISSION REPORT

Pentagon; 256 died on the four planes. The death toll surpassed that at Pearl Harbor in December 1941.

This immeasurable pain was inflicted by 19 young Arabs acting at the behest of Islamist extremists headquartered in distant Afghanistan. Some had been in the United States for more than a year, mixing with the rest of the population. Though four had training as pilots, most were not well-educated. Most spoke English poorly, some hardly at all. In groups of four or five, carrying with them only small knives, box cutters, and cans of Mace or pepper spray, they had hijacked the four planes and turned them into deadly guided missiles.

Why did they do this? How was the attack planned and conceived? How did the U.S. government fail to anticipate and prevent it? What can we do in the future to prevent similar acts of terrorism?

A Shock, Not a Surprise

The 9/11 attacks were a shock, but they should not have come as a surprise. Islamist extremists had given plenty of warning that they meant to kill Americans indiscriminately and in large numbers. Although Usama Bin Ladin himself would not emerge as a signal threat until the late 1990s, the threat of Islamist terrorism grew over the decade.

In February 1993, a group led by Ramzi Yousef tried to bring down the World Trade Center with a truck bomb. They killed six and wounded a thousand. Plans by Omar Abdel Rahman and others to blow up the Holland and Lincoln tunnels and other New York City landmarks were frustrated when the plotters were arrested. In October 1993, Somali tribesmen shot down U.S. helicopters, killing 18 and wounding 73 in an incident that came to be known as "Black Hawk down." Years later it would be learned that those Somali tribesmen had received help from al Qaeda.

In early 1995, police in Manila uncovered a plot by Ramzi Yousef to blow up a dozen U.S. airliners while they were flying over the Pacific. In November 1995, a car bomb exploded outside the office of the U.S. program manager for the Saudi National Guard in Riyadh, killing five Americans and two others. In June 1996, a truck bomb demolished the Khobar Towers apartment complex in Dhahran, Saudi Arabia, killing 19 U.S. servicemen and wounding hundreds. The attack was carried out primarily by Saudi Hezbollah, an organization that had received help from the government of Iran.

Until 1997, the U.S. intelligence community viewed Bin Ladin as a financier of terrorism, not as a terrorist leader. In February 1998, Usama Bin Ladin and four others issued a self-styled fatwa, publicly declaring that it was God's decree that every Muslim should try his utmost to kill any American, military or civilian, anywhere in the world, because of American "occupa-

"The 9/11 attacks were a shock, but they should not have come as a surprise. Islamist extremists had given plenty of warning that they meant to kill Americans indiscriminately and in large numbers."

FULL REPORT In addition to the summary, the ten-member 9/11 commission, headed by former New Jersey governor Thomas Kean, produced a 585-page report on the attacks.

RESCUERS LOST Debris from the shattered World Trade Center covers a New York City Fire Department vehicle. More than 300 firefighters lost their lives on 9/11 when the towers collapsed.

PENTAGON ON FIRE A rescue helicopter circles the smoldering Pentagon, where more than 180 people perished.

OPERATIONAL FAILURES

The 9/11 Commission identified several operational failures that allowed terrorists to enter the United States and carry out the attacks:

Not discovering false statements on visa applications;

Not recognizing passports manipulated in a fraudulent manner;

Not expanding no-fly lists to include names from terrorist watchlists;

Not searching airline passengers identified by the computer-based CAPPS screening system; and

Not strengthening aircraft cockpit doors or taking other measures to prepare for the possibility of suicide hijackings.

SEE ALSO | GLOBAL CULTURES: PAGE 439

Demonstrators urge action against global warming.

SOCIETY GLOBAL WARMING

Scientists have connected the amount of carbon in the atmosphere to changes in global climate since Swedish chemist Svante Arrhenius made the link more than 100 years ago. But the possibility that the Earth might be warming up at a destructive rate was not taken seriously until the 1980s, when NASA scientist James Hansen and others began to warn that human activities such as burning oil, raising cattle (which produce methane), and clearing land of trees and plants (which absorb carbon dioxide) were already raising average global temperatures. Between 1990 and 2010, yearly emissions of carbon dioxide rose by 20 percent. Evidence of melting glaciers, thawing permafrost, and vanishing Arctic ice pointed to damage already done.

> The extent of Arctic sea ice coverage reached record lows in the first decade of the 21st century.

Talks in Copenhagen between world leaders in 2009 failed to yield a binding agreement about how to combat the problem—an issue needing worldwide cooperation.

THE TAKEAWAY: Unchecked human energy consumption may make the world too hot for many species to handle.

INKLEY JUST TOO FAR TO SWIM

VOICES

POLAR BEAR

"The rapid decline in summer sea ice poses a very serious threat to the polar bear. [New] studies led government scientists to the conservative conclusion that fully two-thirds of the world's polar bears, including all polar bears in the United States, will disappear by 2050, due to ice loss. Although excellent swimmers, the projections for retreat of ice 300 to 500 miles from the coast by 2050 will be just too far for polar bears to swim."

—TESTIMONY BY SCIENTIST DOUGLAS INKLEY TO THE U.S. SENATE, 2008

"We are dumping so much carbon dioxide into the Earth's environment that we have literally changed the relationship between the Earth and the Sun." —AL GORE

SOCIETY GLOBALIZATION

Globalization is nothing new. When Columbus and other mariners fanned out around the globe in the 15th and 16th centuries, they drew distant continents and remote islands into a worldwide web of commerce and colonization—a network in which ideas and beliefs were exchanged along with goods, germs, and people. That process accelerated in the 20th century when advances in transportation and communications such as jet aircraft and the Internet overcame barriers of time and space and reduced a vast planet to what some call a global village.

Google developed the world's most widely used Internet search engine.

Now as before, globalization is not a one-way street. U.S. companies like Nike, Google, and McDonald's are among the most recognized brands in the world; European financial firms have connections worldwide. But developing countries have acquired a huge stake in foreign economies and now produce many of the goods bought by Europeans and Americans, whose ethnic makeup increasingly resembles that of the world at large.

> Financial globalization means that shocks like the U.S. credit crisis in 2008 spread quickly around the world.

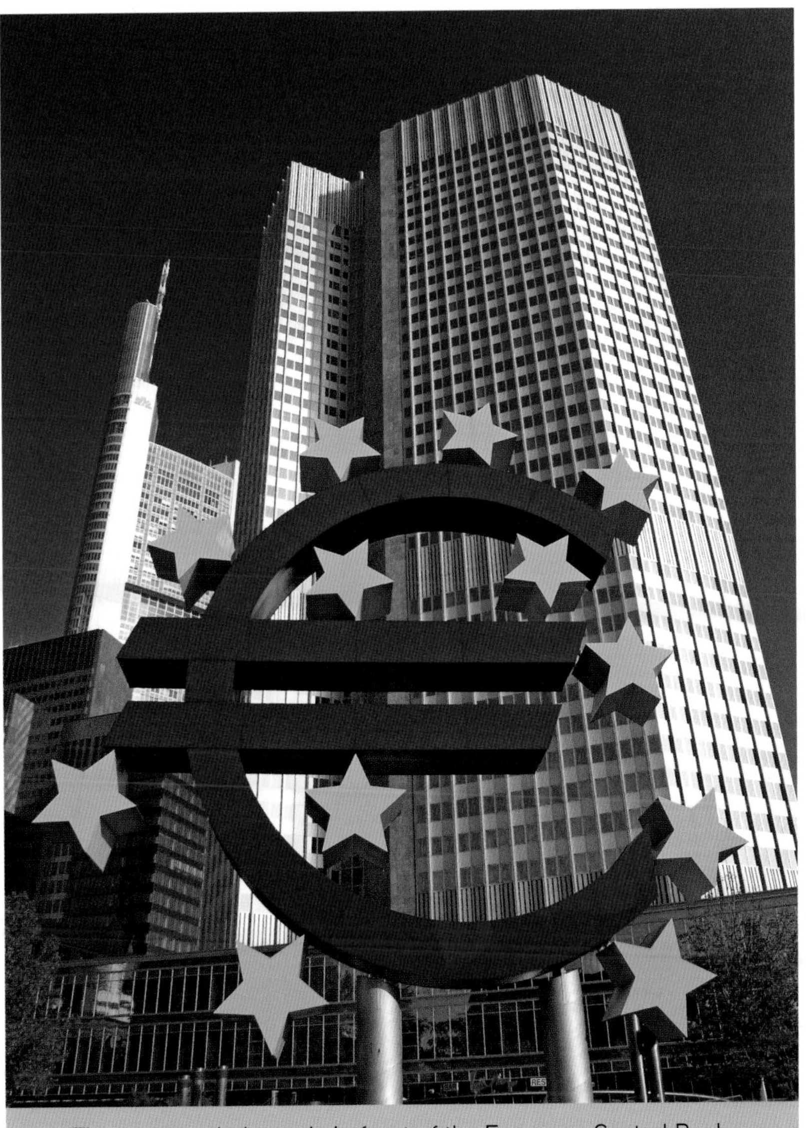

The euro symbol stands in front of the European Central Bank.

THE TAKEAWAY: Modern technology has brought distant countries closer together, culturally and economically.

> *"Once we open India up by allowing these chains, dozens more will be eagerly waiting to come in. . . . Is that what we want for India?"* —MANEKA GANDHI

CONNECTIONS TIME LINE

1945–2010

1949
Mao Zedong declares his country the People's Republic of China.

1970
Students in Washington, D.C. protest killings at Kent State University.

WASHINGTON PROTEST

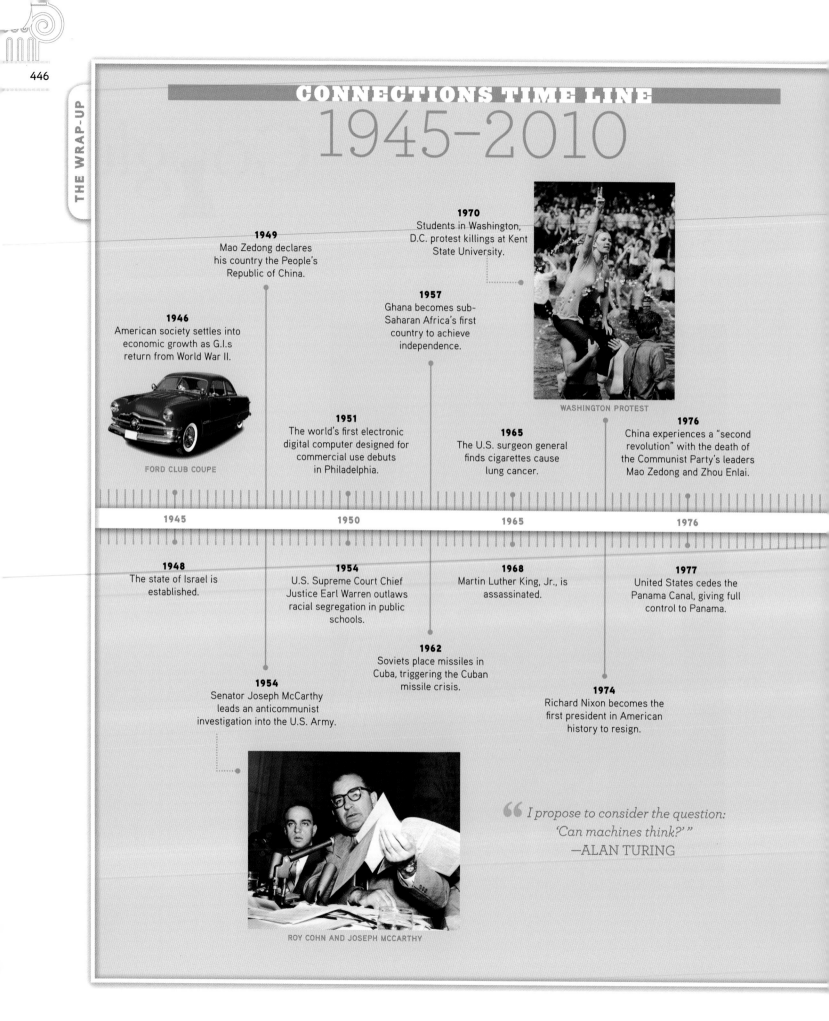

1946
American society settles into economic growth as G.I.s return from World War II.

FORD CLUB COUPE

1957
Ghana becomes sub-Saharan Africa's first country to achieve independence.

1951
The world's first electronic digital computer designed for commercial use debuts in Philadelphia.

1965
The U.S. surgeon general finds cigarettes cause lung cancer.

1976
China experiences a "second revolution" with the death of the Communist Party's leaders Mao Zedong and Zhou Enlai.

1945 1950 1965 1976

1948
The state of Israel is established.

1954
U.S. Supreme Court Chief Justice Earl Warren outlaws racial segregation in public schools.

1968
Martin Luther King, Jr., is assassinated.

1977
United States cedes the Panama Canal, giving full control to Panama.

1962
Soviets place missiles in Cuba, triggering the Cuban missile crisis.

1954
Senator Joseph McCarthy leads an anticommunist investigation into the U.S. Army.

1974
Richard Nixon becomes the first president in American history to resign.

ROY COHN AND JOSEPH MCCARTHY

"I propose to consider the question: 'Can machines think?'"
—ALAN TURING

"A moment comes, which comes but rarely in history, when we step out from the old to the new." —JAWAHARLAL NEHRU

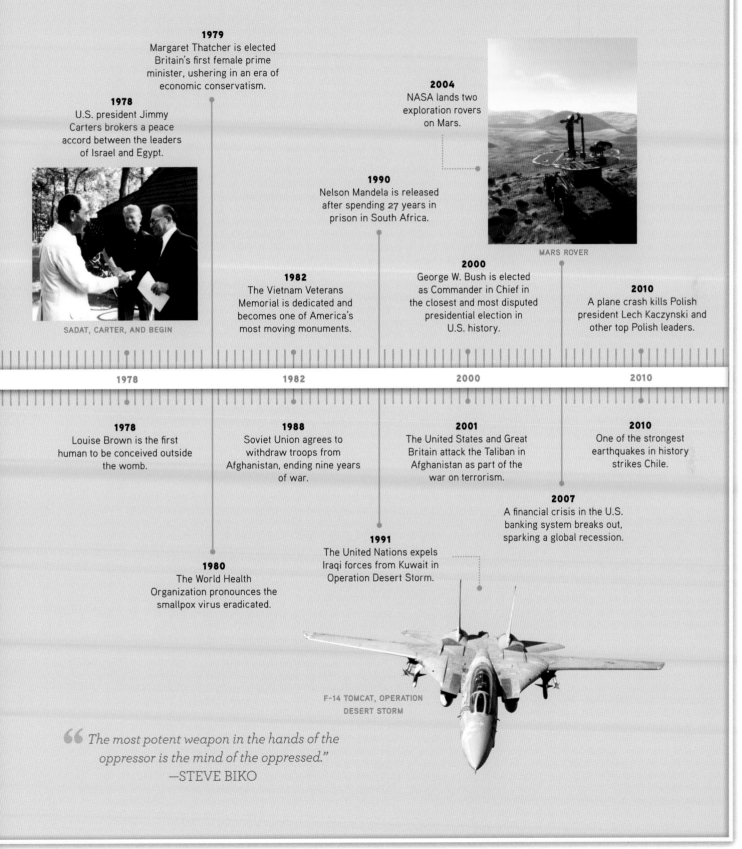

1979
Margaret Thatcher is elected Britain's first female prime minister, ushering in an era of economic conservatism.

1978
U.S. president Jimmy Carters brokers a peace accord between the leaders of Israel and Egypt.

SADAT, CARTER, AND BEGIN

2004
NASA lands two exploration rovers on Mars.

MARS ROVER

1990
Nelson Mandela is released after spending 27 years in prison in South Africa.

1982
The Vietnam Veterans Memorial is dedicated and becomes one of America's most moving monuments.

2000
George W. Bush is elected as Commander in Chief in the closest and most disputed presidential election in U.S. history.

2010
A plane crash kills Polish president Lech Kaczynski and other top Polish leaders.

1978 | 1982 | 2000 | 2010

1978
Louise Brown is the first human to be conceived outside the womb.

1988
Soviet Union agrees to withdraw troops from Afghanistan, ending nine years of war.

2001
The United States and Great Britain attack the Taliban in Afghanistan as part of the war on terrorism.

2010
One of the strongest earthquakes in history strikes Chile.

2007
A financial crisis in the U.S. banking system breaks out, sparking a global recession.

1991
The United Nations expels Iraqi forces from Kuwait in Operation Desert Storm.

1980
The World Health Organization pronounces the smallpox virus eradicated.

F-14 TOMCAT, OPERATION DESERT STORM

"The most potent weapon in the hands of the oppressor is the mind of the oppressed." —STEVE BIKO

ILLUSTRATIONS CREDITS

Key to credits abbreviations:
t=top, b=bottom, l=left, r=right, c=center
Art Resource,NY=AR; The Bridgeman Art Library International=BAL

Cover: Fly/Shutterstock; 2-3, Carla Cioffi/NASA; 6, Private Collection/BAL.

CHAPTER 1: 10-11, Robert Clark/NGS Image Collection; 12, pamspix/iStockphoto; 14 (t), Jane McIlroy/Shutterstock; 14 (b), Wikipedia (Venus_of_Brassempouy.jpg); 15 (t), Ekaterina Starshaya/iStockphoto; 15 (b), AR; 16 (l), Peter V. Bianchi/NGS Image Collection; 16 (r), Ashmolean Museum, University of Oxford, UK/BAL; 17 (l), David L. Brill/NGS Image Collection; 17 (t), Bill Doyle; 17 (b), Private Collection/Look and Learn/BAL; 18 (t), AR; 18 (b), Dave Barnard/Shutterstock; 19, James L. Stanfield/NGS Image Collection; 20, zebra0209/Shutterstock; 22, Erich Lessing/AR; 23 (t), British Museum/AR; 23 (c), Erich Lessing/AR; 23 (b), Marie-Lan Nguyen/Wikipedia; 24 (l), James L. Stanfield/NGS Image Collection; 24 (r), Bernard D'Andrea/NGS Image Collection; 26 (t), Erich Lessing/AR; 25 (b), Louvre, Paris, France /BAL; 26 (t), Musee de Picardie, Amiens, France/Giraudon/BAL; 26 (b), Gordon Gahan/NGS Image Collection; 27 (t), Museum of Fine Arts, Boston, Massachusetts, USA/Henry Lillie Pierce Fund/BAL; 27 (l), Wikipedia (PhoenicianCoin2A.jpg); 27 (b), Lynn Abercrombie/NGS Image Collection; 28, Erich Lessing/AR; 28-29, Réunion des Musées Nationaux/AR; 29, Réunion des Musées Nationaux/AR; 30, Vanni/AR; 32, Kenneth Garrett/NGS Image Collection; 33 (t), Erich Lessing/AR; 33 (c), Kenneth Garrett/NGS Image Collection; 33 (b), Diego Cervo/Shutterstock; 34 (t), Kenneth Garrett/NGS Image Collection; 34 (b), Louvre, Paris, France / BAL; 35 (t), Werner Forman/AR; 35 (b), O. Louis Mazzatenta/NGS Image Collection; 36, Kenneth Garrett/NGS Image Collection; 37 (t), H. Tom Hall/NGS Image Collection; 37 (b), Hunter Yeary; 38, James P. Blair/NGS Image Collection; 40, James P. Blair/NGS Image Collection; 41 (t), India Office Library, London/Ann & Bury Peerless Picture Library/BAL; 41 (c), Randy Olson/NGS Image Collection; 41 (b), William Albert Allard/NGS Image Collection; 42, Bridgeman-Giraudon/AR; 44, Pete Oxford/Minden Pictures/NGS Image Collection; 45 (t), O. Louis Mazzatenta/NGS Image Collection Picture; 45 (bl), The Trustees of the British Museum/AR; 45 (br), Royal Ontario Museum/Corbis; 46 (t), Zhang Zhang Hong Nian/NGS Image Collection; 46 (b), Artshots/Shutterstock; 47 (t), Free Library, Philadelphia, PA, USA/BAL; 47 (b), Bibliotheque Nationale, Paris, France/BAL; 48, Scala/AR; 50, Jesús Eloy Ramos Lara/Dreamstime; 51 (t), Herbert Kane/NGS Image Collection; 51 (b), Kenneth Garrett/NGS Image Collection; 52 (tl), Musee des Antiquites Nationales, St. Germain-en-Laye, France/Lauros/Giraudon/BAL; 52 (tr), The Trustees of the British Museum/AR; 52 (b), James L. Stanfield/NGS Image Collection, 53 (t), Kenneth Garrett/NGS Image Collection; 53 (bl), Randy Olson/NGS Image Collection; 53 (br), David Blossom/NGS Image Collection.

CHAPTER 2: 54-5, James P. Blair/NGS Image Collection; 56, Simon Norfolk/NGS Image Collection; 58, Scala/AR; 59 (t), Bildarchiv Preussischer Kulturbesitz/AR; 59 (b), Bettmann/Corbis; 60 (t), Erich Lessing/AR 60 (b), Wikipedia (Navjote_Yazdi.jpg); 61 (t), HIP/AR; 61 (b), Private Collection/Ann & Bury Peerless Picture Library/BAL; 62 (l), Erich Lessing/AR; 62 (r), Erich Lessing/AR; 63 (t), Musee Rolin, Autun, France /BAL; 63 (b), Simon Norfolk/NGS Image Collection; 64 (l), Réunion des Musées Nationaux/AR; 64 (r), Private Collection/Bonhams, London, UK/BAL; 65, Erich Lessing/AR; 66, O.Louis Mazzatenta/NGS Image Collection; 68 (l), Bibliotheque Nationale, Paris, France /BAL; 68 (r), Erich Lessing/AR; 69 (t), Wikipedia (Ban_Zhao.jpg); 69 (b), Bildarchiv Preussischer Kulturbesitz/AR; 70 (t), Private Collection/Archives Charmet/BAL; 70 (b), Wikipedia (Laozi_002.jpg); 71 (l), Réunion des Musées Nationaux/AR; 71 (r), Réunion des Musées Nationaux/AR; 72 (t), Bibliotheque Nationale, Paris, France/Archives Charmet/BAL; 72 (b), Réunion des Musées Nationaux/AR; 73 (t), Erich Lessing/AR; 73 (b), Craig Hanson/Shutterstock, 74 (t), Michael S. Yamashita/NGS Image Collection, 74 (b), Hsien-Min Yang/NGS Image Collection; 75 (t), Private Collection/BAL; 75 (b), Wiris/Shutterstock; 76 (t), Erich Lessing/AR; 76 (b), Michael S. Yamashita/NGS Image Collection; 77 (t), Asian Art & Archaeology, Inc./Corbis; 77 (c), Clive Streeter/Getty Images; 77 (b), Anyka/Shutterstock; 78, Stephen Webel/iStockphoto; 78-79, Tohoku University Library; 79, Institut des Hautes Etudes Chinoises, Paris/Archives Charmet/BAL; 80, James P. Blair/NGS Image Collection; 82, Jodi Cobb/NGS Image Collection; 83 (t), The Trustees of the British Museum/AR, 83 (b), World Religions Photo Library/BAL; 84 (l), Museum Associates/LACMA/AR; 84 (r), eROMAZe/IStockphoto; 85 (l), Carlos Neto/Shutterstock; 85 (tr), Borromeo/AR; 86 (t), National Gallery, London, UK/BAL; 86 (bl), HIP/AR; 86 (br), Yan Vugenfirer/BigStock; 87 (tl), Kimbell Art Museum, Fort Worth, Texas/AR; 87 (tr), Vanni/AR; 87 (b), Erich Lessing/AR.

CHAPTER 3: 88-89, Bart Parren/Shutterstock; 90, Erich Lessing/AR; 92 (l), Réunion des Musées Nationaux/AR; 92 (r), Galina Barskaya/Shutterstock; 93 (t), The Metropolitan Museum of Art/AR; 93 (b), Vatican Museums and Galleries, Vatican City, Italy/BAL; 94 (t), Louvre, Paris, France/Giraudon/BAL; 94 (b), bkp/Shutterstock; 95 (t), Erich Lessing/AR; 95 (b), Alinari/AR; 96 (t), ollirg/iStockphoto; 96 (b), Museo Archeologico Nazionale, Taranto, Puglia, Italy/Giraudon/ BAL; 97 (t), Nottingham City Museums and Galleries (Nottingham Castle)/BAL; 97 (b), Bildarchiv Preussischer Kulturbesitz/AR; 98, Scala/AR; 99 (t), Walters Art Museum, Baltimore, USA/BAL; 99 (b), Réunion des Musées Nationaux/AR; 100 (t), estelle75/iStockphoto; 100 (b), Henning Janos/Shutterstock; 101 (t), NYPublic Library; 101b, HIP/Art Resource; 102, Alfio Ferlito/ Shutterstock; 103 (t), Vladimir Korostyshevskiy/ Shutterstock; 103 (b), NG Books; 104 (l), James L. Stanfield/NGS Image Collection; 104 (r). British Museum, London, UK/BAL; 105 (t), Erich Lessing/AR; 105 (b), Wikipedia (Ancientlibraryalex.jpg); 106, Scala/AR; 108, Bryan Busovicki/Shutterstock; 109 (t), Alfio Ferlito/Shutterstock; 109 (b), O. Louis Mazzatenta/NGS Image Collection; 110 (t), Clara/Shutterstock; 110 (b), Art Museum, Baltimore, USA/BAL; 111 (t), Michael Effler/Shutterstock; 111 (b), Archive Timothy McCarthy/AR; 112, Erich Lessing/AR; 113 (l), Fitzwilliam Museum, University of Cambridge, UK/BAL; 113 (t), Private Collection/The Stapleton Collection/BAL; 113 (b), Rafal Olkis/Shutterstock; 114 (l), Réunion des Musées Nationaux/AR; 114 (r), Erich Lessing/AR; 115 (t), Scala/AR; 115 (b), Schorle/Wikipedia; 116 (t), Elena Elisseeva/Shutterstock; 116 (b), Robert Sisson/NGS Image Collection; 117 (t), Private Collection/BAL; 117 (b), Melissa Farris; 118 (l), Biblioteca Nacional, Madrid, Spain/AISA/BAL; 118 (r), The Metropolitan Museum of Art/AR; 119 (t), Musee des Beaux-Arts, Dunkirk, France/Giraudon/BAL; 119 (b), Private Collection/DACS/Archives Chamet/BAL; 120, Francesco Dazzi/Shutterstock; 120-121, John C. Trever, PhD, digital image by James E. Trever; 121, David Boyer/NGS Image Collection; 122, Cameraphoto Arte, Venice/AR; 124, Erich Lessing/AR; 125 (t), Brooklyn Museum of Art, New York, USA/BAL; 125 (b), Wikipedia (HerodtheGreat2.jpg); 126 (t), Scala/AR; 126 (b), HIP/AR; 127 (t), Scala/Ministero per i Beni e le Attività culturali/AR; 127 (b), Bildarchiv Preussischer Kulturbesitz/AR; 128, Erich Lessing/AR; 130, Alinari/AR; 131 (t), Private Collection/Look and Learn/BAL; 131 (b), Tate, London/AR; 132 (t), Peter V. Bianchi/NGS Image Collection; 132 (bl), Scala/AR; 132 (br), Netfalls/Shutterstock; 133 (tl), fotoecho/Shutterstock; 133 (tr), Private Collection/Look and Learn/BAL; 133 (b), Kenneth Garrett/NGS Image Collection.

CHAPTER 4: 134-135, Luciano Mortula/Shutterstock; 136, Scala/AR; 138 (l), Bibliotheque Nationale, Paris, France/Lauros/Giraudon/BAL; 138 (r), Hermitage, St. Petersburg, Russia /BAL; 139 (l), Erich Lessing/AR; 139 (r), The Orthodox Church in America, www.oca.org <http://www.oca.org/; 140 (l), Bibliotheque des Arts Decoratifs, Paris, France/Archives Charmet/BAL; 140 (r), Private Collection/BAL; 141 (t), Bildarchiv Preussischer Kulturbesitz/AR; 141 (b), Scala/AR; 142 (t), Erich Lessing/AR; 142 (b), Aleister Crowley/Wikipedia; 143 (t), Wikipedia (Nikiphoros_Phokas.jpg); 143 (b), Erich Lessing/AR; 144, Bildarchiv Preussischer Kulturbesitz/AR; 146 (t), Reza/NGS Image Collection; 146 (b), Ahmad Al-Rubaye/AFP/Getty Images; 147 (t), Réunion des Musées Nationaux/AR; 147 (b), Treasury of the Abbey of Saint-Maurice, Valais, Switzerland/Lauros/Giraudon/BAL; 148 (l), Historiska Museet, Stockholm, Sweden/Ancient Art and Architecture Collection Ltd./BAL; 148 (r), National Maritime Museum, London, England/NGS Image Collection; 149 (t), Bibliotheque Nationale, Paris, France/BAL; 149 (b), Scala/AR; 150, James L. Stanfield/NGS Image Collection; 150-151, V&A Images,

London/AR; 151, George Steinmetz/NGS Image Collection; 152, Musee des Beaux-Arts, Dijon, France/Lauros/Giraudon/ BAL; 154, The Trustees of the British Museum/AR; 155 (t), Private Collection/BAL; 155 (b), NG Books; 156, Scala/White Images/AR; 157 (t), Patricia Hofmeester/Shutterstock; 157 (b), Wikipedia (Fra_Angelico_031.jpg); 158 (t), Ceboksary Art Museum, Russia/ BAL; 158 (b), izold/iStockphoto; 159; Aachen Cathedral Treasury, Aachen, Germany/Bildarchiv Steffens/BAL; 160, Musee Conde, Chantilly, France/ Giraudon/BAL; 161 (t), HIP/AR; 161 (b), Wikipedia (Cleric-Knight-Workman. jpg); 162, David Alan Harvey/NGS Image Collection; 164, The Trustees of the British Museum/AR; 165 (t), Werner Forman/AR; 165 (b), Allen Memorial Art Museum, Oberlin College, Ohio, USA/R.T. Miller, Jr. Fund/BAL; 166 (t), Werner Forman/AR; 166 (b), James P. Blair/NGS Image Collection; 167 (t), British Library, London, UK/British Library Board. All Rights Reserved/BAL; 167 (b), Werner Forman/AR; 168 (t), Thomas J. Abercrombie/NGS Image Collection; 168 (b), Musee des Beaux-Arts, Angers, France/Giraudon/BAL; 169 (t), David Alan Harvey/NGS Image Collection; 169 (b), Erich Lessing/AR; 170, Dave Rock/Shutterstock; 172 (t), Doug Stern/NGS Image Collection; 172 (b), Curtis Kautzer/Shutterstock; 173 (t), Yvan/Shutterstock; 173 (b), Museum of Fine Arts, Boston, Massachusetts, USA/Gift of Landon T. Clay/BAL; 174 (t), Luis Acosta/AFP/Getty Images; 174 (b), Kenneth Garrett/NGS Image Collection; 175 (t), Werner Forman/AR; 175 (b), Richard Schlecht/NGS Image Collection; 176 (t), Scala/AR; 176 (bl), Réunion des Musées Nationaux/AR; 176 (br), James L. Stanfield/NGS Image Collection; 177 (tl), Erich Lessing/AR; 177 (tr), Michel Zabe/AZA INAH/BAL; 177 (bl), Sisse Brimberg/NGS Image Collection; 177 (br), Dmitriy Yakovlev/iStockphoto.

CHAPTER 5: 178-179, Guildhall Art Gallery, City of London/BAL; 180, Private Collection/© Philip Mould Ltd, London/BAL; 182, Wikipedia (Hommage_of_Edward_I_to_Philippe_le_Bel.jpg), 183 (t), HIP/AR; 183 (b), St. Nick/Shutterstock; 184 (t), Réunion des Musées Nationaux/AR; 184 (b), Bibliotheque Nationale, Paris, France/BAL; 185 (t), Kunsthistorisches Museum, Vienna, Austria/BAL; 185 (b), Private Collection/Ken Welsh/BAL; 186 (t), Cardaf/Shutterstock; 186 (b), Alinari/AR; 187 (t), Private Collection/Bonhams, London, UK/BAL; 187 (b), Scala/Ministero per i Beni e le Attività culturali/AR; 188 (l), Scala/AR; 188 (r), Museum of London, UK/BAL; 189 (t), Musee des Beaux-Arts, Tournai, Belgium/BAL; 189 (b), Frontpage/Shutterstock; 190 (t), Private Collection/BAL; 190 (b), Osterreichische Nationalbibliothek, Vienna, Austria/Alinari/BAL; 191, Réunion des Musées Nationaux/AR; 192 (t), Réunion des Musées Nationaux/AR; 192 (c), Private Collection/Giraudon/BAL; 192 (b), Anyka/Shutterstock; 193, Private Collection/Archives Charmet/BAL; 194, Private Collection/The Stapleton Collection/BAL; 194-195, HIP/AR; 195, HIP/ AR; 196, Bildarchiv Preussischer Kulturbesitz/AR; 198, HIP/AR; 199 (t), National Gallery, London, UK/BAL; 199 (b), Snark/AR; 200 (t), Bibliotheque Nationale, Paris, France/BAL; 200 (b), James L. Stanfield/NGS Image Collection; 201 (t), Biblioteca Nazionale, Turin, Italy/BAL; 201 (b), Wikkiss/Dreamstime, 202, National Palace Museum, Taipei, Taiwan/BAL; 204, iPhotos/Shutterstock; 205 (t), NG Books; 205 (c), Kimbell Art Museum, Fort Worth, Texas/AR; 205 (b), Michael S. Yamashita/NGS Image Collection; 206 (t), HIP/AR; 206 (b), The Trustees of the British Museum/AR; 207 (t), Stanisław Chlebowski/Wikipedia; 207 (b), yellowcrestmedia/iStockphoto; 208, Alexey Stiop/Shutterstock; 210, Museo Arqueologico, Mexico City, Mexico/BAL; 211 (t), Michel Zabé/AR; 211 (c), Biblioteca Medicea-Laurenziana, Florence, Italy/BAL; 211 (b), Private Collection/Ken Welsh/BAL; 212 (tl), Ned M. Seidler/NGS Image Collection, 212 (tr), Stephen Alvarez/NGS Image Collection; 212 (b), Pedro de Cieza de León/Wikipedia, 213 Ira Block/NGS Image Collection, 214 (tl), Bridgeman-Giraudon/AR; 214 (tr), Peter38/Shutterstock; 214 (b), Chateau de Versailles, France/Giraudon/BAL; 215 (t), H. Tom Hall/NGS Image Collection; 215 (bl), Scala/White Images/AR; 215 (br), LijuanGuo/Shutterstock.

CHAPTER 6: 216-217, Richard Schmidt-Zuper/iStockphoto; 218, Alinari/ AR; 220 (t), Erich Lessing/AR; 220 (b), Scala/AR; 221 (t), Fitzwilliam Museum, University of Cambridge, UK/BAL; 221 (b), Cameraphoto Arte, Venice/AR; 222, British Library, London, UK/British Library Board. All Rights Reserved/ BAL; 223 (t), Museo de Bellas Artes, Valencia, Spain/BAL; 223 (b), Erich Lessing/AR; 224 (t), James L. Amos/NGS Image Collection; 224 (b), Alinari/ AR; 225 (t), National Gallery, London, UK/BAL; 225 (b), Jodi Cobb/NGS Image Collection; 226 (t), British Library, London, UK/British Library Board. All Rights Reserved/BAL; 226 b; Biblioteca Marucelliana, Florence, Italy/ BAL; 227 (t), Bridgeman-Giraudon/AR; 227 (b), Bibliotheque de l'Institut de France, Paris, France/ Archives Charmet/BAL; 228, Bildarchiv Preussischer Kulturbesitz/AR; 229 (t), The Metropolitan Museum of Art/AR; 229 (b), Allen Carroll, NGS; 230, Bildarchiv Preussischer Kulturbesitz/AR; 231 (t), Wikipedia (Elizabeth_I_Armada_Portrait_British_School.jpg); 231 (b), Erich Lessing/AR; 232 (l), Biblioteca Universidad, Barcelona, Spain/Paul Maeyaert/BAL; 232 (r), Victor R. Boswell, Jr/NGS Image Collection; 233 (t), Ernest Board/NGS Image Collection; 233 (cr), Library of Congress; 233 (b), Atwater Kent Museum of Philadelphia/ Courtesy of Historical Society of Pennsylvania Collection,/BAL; 234 (l), Bridgeman-Giraudon/AR; 234 (r), The Pierpont Morgan Library/AR; 235 (t), Bildarchiv Preussischer Kulturbesitz/AR; 235 (b), Royal Geographical Society, London, UK/BAL; 236, Scala/Ministero per i Beni e le Attività culturali/AR; 237 (t), Bibliotheque Nationale, Paris, France/Giraudon/BAL; 237 (b), Réunion des Musées Nationaux/AR; 238 (t), S.Borisov/Shutterstock; 238 (b), Wikipedia (Losreyescatolicos.jpg); 239 (t), Erich Lessing/AR; 239 (b), Bettmann/Corbis; 240 (t), State Russian Museum, St. Petersburg, Russia/ BAL; 240 (r), Wikipedia (Russian_boyar_from_XVII_century.JPG); 240 (bl), Bildarchiv Preussischer Kulturbesitz/AR; 241 (t), Bibliotheque Nationale, Paris, France/Archives Charmet/BAL; 241 b; Wikipedia (Battle_of_Lepanto_1571. jpg); 242, Foto Marburg/AR; 242-243, Ralph W. Klein/Lutheran School of Theology at Chicago; 243, JackJelly/iStockphoto; 244, The Metropolitan Museum of Art/AR; 246 (t), Private Collection/Index/BAL; 246 (b), Agisilaou & Spyrou/iStockphoto; 247, Museo de Bellas Artes, Zaragoza, Spain/BAL; 248 (l), Bildarchiv Preussischer Kulturbesitz/AR; 248 (r), Museo del Oro, Lima, Peru/BAL ; 249 (t), Bildarchiv Preussischer Kulturbesitz/AR; 249 (b), British Museum, London, UK/BAL; 250, The Historic New Orleans Collection/ BAL; 251 (t), Private Collection/Peter Newark American Pictures/BAL; 251 (b), Private Collection/BAL; 252 (l), British Museum, London, UK/BAL; 252 (r), Schlesinger Library, Radcliffe Institute, Harvard University/BAL; 253 (t), Bridgeman-Giraudon/AR; 253 (b), The Trustees of The British Museum/AR; 254, Private Collection/Dinodia/BAL; 256, James L. Stanfield/NGS Image Collection; 257 (t), Mark Hannaford/AWL/Aurora Photos; 257 (b), Michael Hampshire/NGS Image, 258 (t), The Metropolitan Museum of Art/AR; 258 (b), Gesu, Rome, Italy/BAL; 259 (t), Musee du Berry, Bourges, France/ Lauros/Giraudon/BAL; 259 (b), Private Collection/Paul Freeman/BAL; 260 (l), Luciano Mortula/iStockphoto; 260 (r), Erich Lessing/AR; 261 (t), Réunion des Musées Nationaux/AR; 261 (b), Private Collection/Dinodia/BAL; 262 (t), Jarno Gonzalez Zarraonandia/Shutterstock; 262 (b), Scala/AR; 263 (t), Private Collection/Index/BAL; 263 (b), Private Collection/Peter Newark Military Pictures/BAL; 264 (t), Réunion des Musées Nationaux/AR; 264 (b), Bjorn Landstrom/NGS Image Collection; 265 (tl), James L. Stanfield/NGS Image Collection; 265 (tr), The Metropolitan Museum of Art/AR; 265 (bl), Tretyakov Gallery, Moscow, Russia/BAL; 265 (br), Scala/AR.

CHAPTER 7: 266-267, Musee Nat. du Chateau de Malmaison, Rueil-Malmaison, France/Lauros/Giraudon/BAL; 268, Prado, Madrid, Spain/ Giraudon/BAL; 270 (t), Guildhall Library, City of London/BAL; 270 (b), Wikipedia (Samuel_Pepys.jpg); 271 (t), The Granger Collection, New York; 271 (b), Victoria & Albert Museum, London, UK/BAL; 272, Erich Lessing/AR; 273 (t), Bildarchiv Preussischer Kulturbesitz/AR; 273 (b), Razvan Stroie/ Shutterstock; 274 (t), Galerie Dijol, Paris, France/BAL; 274 (b), Bridgeman-Giraudon/AR; 275, Private Collection/BAL; 276 (l), HIP AR; 276 (r), Réunion des Musées Nationaux/AR; 277 (t), Scala/AR; 277 (b), NG Books; 278, Wikipedia (Bakhuizen,_Battle_of_Vigo_Bay.jpg); 279 (t), Private Collection/ BAL; 279 (b), HIP/AR; 280, Academie Nationale de Medecine, Paris, France/ Archives Charmet/BAL; 281 (tr), HIP/AR; 281 (tl), Royal Society, London, UK/BAL, 281 (b), Bridgeman-Giraudon/AR; 282 (t), The Fleming-Wyfold Art Foundation/BAL; 282 (b), Bibliotheque Nationale, Paris, France/Archives Charmet/BAL; 283 (t), Wikipedia (Marywollstonecraft.jpg); 283 (b), Luton Museum, Bedfordshire, UK/BAL; 284 (r), Stadtische Museum, Erfurt, Germany/BAL; 284 (l), Mozart Museum, Prague, Czech Republic/Giraudon/ BAL; 285, Museum of Fine Arts, Houston, Texas, USA/Robert Lee Blaffer Memorial Collection Gift of Sarah Campbell Blaffer/BAL; 286 (t), Tokyo Fuji Art Museum, Tokyo, Japan/BAL; 286 (bl), Wikipedia (AdamSmith.jpg); 286 (r), Scala/White Images/AR; 287, Private Collection/Roger-Viollet, Paris/BAL; 288, Erich Lessing/AR; 290, Erich Lessing/AR; 291 (t), Chawton House Library, Hampshire, UK/BAL; 291 (b), Wikipedia (Konstantin_Kapidagli_002.jpg); 292 (t), Private Collection/Paul Freeman/BAL; 292 (b), Wikipedia (Jan_van_ Riebeeck.png); 293 (t), Private Collection/BAL; 293 (bl), Private Collection/ Boltin Picture Library/BAL, 293 (br), Private Collection/Heini Schneebeli/BAL; 294, Erich Lessing/AR; 296, Erich Lessing/AR; 297 (t), Private Collection/ Peter Newark Historical Pictures/BAL; 297 (b), Bibliotheque Nationale, Paris, France/BAL; 298 (t), Réunion des Musées Nationaux/AR; 298 (b), Wikipedia (Portrait_of_the_Kangxi_Emperor_in_Court_Dress.jpg); 299 (t), Réunion des

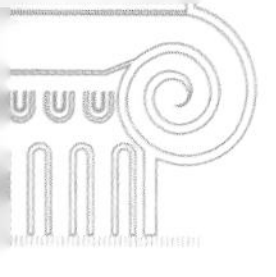

Musées Nationaux/AR; 299 (b), Réunion des Musées Nationaux/AR; 300 (t), Private Collection/Paul Freeman/BAL; 300 (b), National Trust Photo Library/AR; 301 (t), Wikipedia (Hongloumeng1.jpg); 301 (b), Private Collection/Heini Schneebeli/BAL; 302 (l), Werner Forman/AR; 302 (r), Werner Forman/AR; 303, Erich Lessing/AR; 304 (t), Werner Forman/AR; 304 (b), Scala/AR; 305 (t), HIP/AR; 305 (b), Scala/AR; 306, Private Collection/BAL; 308, OSTILL/iStockphoto; 309 (t), Schalkwijk/AR; 309 (b), Wikipedia (Louis-Michel_van_Loo_003.jpg); 310, Pennsylvania Academy of the Fine Arts, Philadelphia, USA/BAL; 311 (t), Museum of the City of New York, USA/BAL; 311 (b), Collection of the New-York Historical Society, USA/BAL; 312 (l), Private Collection/Peter Newark American Pictures/BAL; 312 (r), The New York Public Library/AR; 313 (t), Virginia Historical Society, Richmond, Virginia, USA/BAL; 313 (bl), Private Collection/The Stapleton Collection/BAL; 313 (r), Virginia Historical Society, Richmond, Virginia, USA/BAL; 314, The Metropolitan Museum of Art/AR; 314-315, National Archives; 315, AR; 316 (t), Réunion des Musées Nationaux/AR; 316 (b), National Army Museum, London/BAL; 317 (t), Massachusetts Historical Society, Boston, MA, USA/BAL; 317 (c), National Portrait Gallery, Smithsonian Institution/AR; 317 (b), Pedro Armestre/AFP/Getty Images; 318 (tl), Réunion des Musées Nationaux/AR; 318 (tr), V&A Images, London/AR; 318 (b), V&A Images, London/AR; 319 (tl), The Trustees of The British Museum/AR; 319 (tr), Private Collection/Peter Newark American Pictures/BAL; 319 (b), Robert W. Nicholson/NGS Image Collection.

CHAPTER 8: 320-321, Erich Lessing/AR; 322, Bildarchiv Preussischer Kulturbesitz/AR; 324, Private Collection/Christie's Images/BAL; 325 (t), Adoc-photos/AR; 325 (b), Erich Lessing/AR; 326, Réunion des Musées Nationaux/AR; 327 (t), HIP/AR; 327 (b), National Army Museum, London/BAL; 328 (t), Musee de la Ville de Paris, Musee Carnavalet, Paris, France Archives Charmet/BAL; 328 (b), Alinari/AR; 329, Scala/AR; 330 (l), National Army Museum, London/BAL; 330 (r), Bildarchiv Preussischer Kulturbesitz AR; 331 (t), Library of Congress; 331 (c), National Army Museum, London/BAL; 331 (b), SSPL/National Media Museum/AR; 332, Bildarchiv Preussischer Kulturbesitz/AR; 333 (t), Hulton Archive/Getty Images; 333 (b), Private Collection/ Roger-Viollet, Paris/BAL; 334 (l), Réunion des Musées Nationaux/AR; 334 (r), restyler/Shutterstock; 335 (t), Musee d'Orsay, Paris, France/Lauros/Giraudon/BAL; 335 (b), The Pierpont Morgan Library/AR; 336 (t), NG Books; 336 (b), Stephen Morrison/epa/Corbis; 337 (t), Private Collection/BAL; 337 (b), Bildarchiv Preussischer Kulturbesitz/AR; 338, James L. Stanfield/NGS Image Collection; 338-339, Library of Congress; 339, Robert Clark/NGS Image Collection; 340, Luis Marden/NGS Image Collection; 342 (l), AR; 342 (r), Brooklyn Museum of Art, New York, USA/Gift of F. Ethel Wickham in memory of W. Hull Wickham/BAL; 343 (t), The Academy of Natural Sciences, Ewell Sale Stewart Library , and the Albert M. Greenfield Digital Imaging Center for Collections; 343 (b), Butler Institute of American Art, Youngstown, OH, USA/Gift of Joseph G. Butler III 1946/BAL; 344 (t), Private Collection/BAL; 344 (b), Woolaroc Museum, Oklahoma, USA/Peter Newark Western Americana/BAL; 345 (t), Edward S. Curtis/NGS Image Collection; 345 (b), Private Collection/Peter Newark American Pictures/BAL; 346 (t), Bildarchiv Preussischer Kulturbesitz/AR; 346 (b), Library of Congress; 347 (t), SSPL/National Media Museum/AR; 347 (b), Austin History Center, Austin Public Library, Lawrence T. Jones III, Austin, Texas; 348 (t), Private Collection/Peter Newark American Pictures/BAL; 348 (b), The New York Public Library/AR; 349 (t), Private Collection/Peter Newark Western Americana/BAL; 349 (b), David J. & Janice L. Frent Collection/Corbis; 350 (t), R. Gino Santa Maria/Shutterstock; 350 (c), NG Books; 350 (b), Bridgeman-Giraudon/AR; 351, Museo Nacional de Historia, Castillo de Chapultepec, Mexico/Giraudon/BAL; 352 (t), Private Collection/Archives Charmet/BAL; 352 (b), Réunion des Musées Nationaux/AR; 353 (l), Wikipedia (JaMAC.jpg); 353 (r), Private Collection/Peter Newark American Pictures/BAL; 354, Katherine Carl/Wikipedia; 356 (t), HIP/AR; 356 (b), Wikipedia (Lin_Zexu_1.jpg); 357 (l), The Granger Collection, New York; 357 (r), Bibliotheque des Arts Decoratifs, Paris, France/Archives Charmet/BAL; 358 (t), Private Collection/BAL; 358 (b), Erich Lessing/AR; 359 (t), Library of Congress; 359 (b), AR; 360 (l), George Baxter/Getty Images; 360 (r), Private Collection/BAL; 361 (t), Alexander Turnbull Library, Wellington, New Zealand/BAL; 361 (b), Royal Geographical Society, London, UK/BAL; 362 (tl), Private Collection/Peter Newark American Pictures/BAL; 362 (tr), SEF/AR; 362 (b), Erich Lessing/AR; 363 (tl), Tom Lovell/NGS Image Collection; 363 (tr), HIP/AR; 363 (b), Royal Geographical Society, London, UK/BAL.

CHAPTER 9: 364-365, Hulton Archive/Getty Images; 366, Private Collection/Archives Charmet/BAL; 368 (t), HIP/AR; 368 (b), Library of Congress; 369 (t), Victor R. Boswell, Jr./NGS Image Collection; 369 (b), Hulton Archive/Getty Images; 370 (l), Bettmann/CORBIS; 370 (r), Private Collection/BAL; 371 (t), Library of Congress; 371 (b), Bildarchiv Preussischer Kulturbesitz/AR; 372 (l), Réunion des Musées Nationaux/AR; 372 (r), Private Collection/Peter Newark American Pictures/BAL; 373 (t), Library of Congress; 373 (b), Private Collection/DACS/Archives Charmet/BAL; 374, FDR Library; 376, AR; 377 (tr), Brown Brothers/FDR Library; 377 (c), Library of Congress; 377 (b), Snark/AR; 378 (tr), Corbis; 378 (c), Snark/AR; 378 (b), Library of Congress; 379 (t), Bettmann/Corbis; 379 (b), Wikipedia (Francisco_Villa.gif); 380, Bildarchiv Preussischer Kulturbesitz/AR; 382, Archives Larousse, Paris, France/Giraudon/BAL; 383 (t), NG Books; 383 (b), Private Collection/Peter Newark American Pictures/BAL; 384 (l), Library of Congress; 384 (r), Library of Congress; 385 (l), Library of Congress; 385 (r), Private Collection/Archives Charmet/BAL; 386 (t), Scala/White Images/AR; 386 (b), Library of Congress; 387 (l), Library of Congress; 387 (r), Deutsches Plakat Museum, Essen, Germany/Archives Charmet/BAL; 388 (l),Bettmann/Corbis; 388 (br), AR; 389 (t), Hulton-Deutsch Collection/Corbis; 389 (b), Tereshchenko Dmitry/Shutterstock; 390 (t), Central Press/Getty Images; 390 (b), Private Collection/BAL; 391 (t), Library of Congress; 391 (b), SZ Photo/BAL; 392 (t), Library of Congress; 392 (b), Private Collection/Peter Newark American Pictures/BAL; 393 (t), NG Books; 393 (b), Library of Congress; 394 (t), Bildarchiv Preussischer Kulturbesitz/AR; 394 (b), H. Hoffmann/Wikipedia; 395 (tr), Bettmann/Corbis; 395 (c), Private Collection/Peter Newark Military Pictures/BAL; 395 (b), NG Books; 396, AFP/Getty Images; 398 (l), FDR Library; 398 (r), City of Edinburgh Museums and Art Galleries, Scotland/BAL; 399 (t), Private Collection/The Stapleton Collection/BAL; 399 (b), Private Collection/Archives Charmet/BAL; 400 (t), Private Collection/BAL; 400 (b), James P. Blair/NGS Image Collection; 401 (t), AFP/Getty Images; 401 (b), Private Collection/Archives Charmet/BAL; 402, LAPI/Roger Viollet/Getty Images; 403 (t), Fox Photos/Getty Images; 403 (b), Private Collection/Dinodia/BAL; 404 (tl), SSPL/Science Museum/AR; 404 (tr), Snark/AR; 404 (b), DeA Picture Library/AR; 405 (tl), The New York Public Library/AR; 405 (tr), Wikipedia (Nagasakibomb.jpg); 405 (bl), Private Collection/DACS/BAL; 405 (br), SZ Photo/BAL.

CHAPTER 10: 406-407, Michael Melford/NGS Image Collection; 408, Sergei Guneyev/Time & Life Pictures/Getty Images; 410 (t), Zettler/dpa/Corbis; 410 (b), Erwin Lux/Wikipedia; 411 (t), Private Collection/Roger-Viollet, Paris/BAL; 411 (b), SZ Photo/BAL; 412 (t), epa/Corbis; 412 (b), Serge Ligtenberg/POOL/epa/Corbis; 413 (t), Horacio Villalobos/Corbis; 413 (b), Homer Sykes/Getty Images; 414, James Leynse/Corbis; 416 (l), NASA; 416 (r), NASA; 417 (t), Ed Kashi/AuroraPhotos; 417 (cr), Graeme Dawes/Shutterstock; 417 (l), Matthew Yohe/Wikipedia; 418 (t), james steidl/iStockphoto; 418 (b), Bettmann/Corbis; 419 (t), Hung Chung Chih/Shutterstock; 419 (b), Joe Scherschel/NGS Image Collection; 420, Adoc-photos / AR; 422 (t), CBS Photo Archive/Getty Images; 422 (b), Library of Congress; 423 (t), Library of Congress; 423 (b), James P Blair/NGS Image Collection; 424 (t), Justin Sullivan/Getty Images; 424 (b), Kevin Lamarque/Reuters/Corbis; 425 (r), Lucas Dolega/epa/Corbis; 425 (l), Diego Goldberg/Sygma/Corbis; 426, Peter Turnley/Corbis; 428 (tl), Mohammed Salem/Reuters/Corbis; 428 (cr), B. Anthony Stewart/NGS Image Collection; 428 (b), Bettmann/Corbis; 429 (t), Mirrorpix/Getty Images; 429 (b), Bettmann/Corbis; 430, James Marshall/Corbis; 431, Mike Hutchings/Reuters/Corbis; 432, Jack Birns//Time Life Pictures/Getty Images; 434 (t), Wang Xiaochuan/Xinhua Press/Corbis; 434 (b), Jacques Langevin/Sygma/Corbis; 435 (t), Private Collection/Peter Newark Military Pictures/BAL; 435 (b), W.E. Garrett/NGS Image Collection; 436 (t), Kapoor Baldev/Sygma/Corbis; 436 (b), Library of Congress; 437 (t), Thomas J. Abercrombie/NGS Image Collection; 437 (br), David McLain/NGS Image Collection; 437 (bl), Andrejs Jegorovs/Shutterstock; 438, Susan Seubert/NGS Image Collection; 440 (t), Pascal Maitre/NGS Image Collection; 440 (b), Jay Dickman/NGS Image Collection; 441, Library of Congress; 442, Reuters/Corbis; 442 (r), From The 9/11 Commission Report; 443 (l), From The 9/11 Commission Report; 443 (tr), Library of Congress; 443 (br), Reuters/Corbis; 444 (t), Yoan Valat/epa/Corbis; 444 (b), Paul Nicklen/NGS Image Collection; 445 (t), Frank May/epa/Corbis; 445 (b), Einstein/Shutterstock; 446 (tl), Stan Rohrer/iStockphoto; 446 (tr), JP Laffont/Sygma/Corbis; 446 (b), Bettmann/Corbis; 447 (tl), Bettmann/Corbis; 447 (tr), NASA; 447 (b), Aero Graphics, Inc./Corbis.

CREDITS AND BIBLIOGRAPHY

SELECTED BIBLIOGRAPHY

Bentley, Jerry H., and Herbert F. Ziegler. *Traditions and Encounters: A Global Perspective on the Past.* Boston: McGraw Hill, 2000.

Daniels, Patricia, and Steven Hyslop. *Almanac of World History.* Washington, DC: National Geographic, 2003.

Davies, Norman. *Europe: A History*. Oxford: Oxford University Press, 1996.

Duiker, William J. and Jackson J. Spielvogel. *World History, Vols. 1 & 2.* Minneapolis: West Publishing Co., 1994.

Farrington, Karen. *Historical Atlas of Empires.* New York: Checkmark Books, 2002.

Goldsworthy, Adrian. *How Rome Fell.* New Haven: Yale University Press, 2009.

Hanawalt, Barbara. *The Middle Ages: An Illustrated History.* Oxford Univ. Press, 1998.

Hunt, Lynn. *The Making of the West: Peoples and Cultures.* Boston: Bedford/St. Martin's, 2001.

Kagan, Donald, Steven Ozment, and Frank M. Turner. *The Western Heritage.* Upper Saddle River, N.J.: Pearson Prentice Hall, 2007

Kishlansky, Mark A., ed. *Sources of World History, Vols 1 & 2.* Belmont, CA: Thomson Wadsworth, 2007.

National Geographic. *1000 Events That Shaped the World.* Washington, DC: National Geographic, 2007.

National Geographic. *Concise History of the World.* Washington, DC: National Geographic, 2006.

National Geographic. *Visual History of the World.* Washington, DC: National Geographic, 2005.

Roberts, J. M. *Ancient History.* London: Duncan Baird Publishers, 2002.

Rosenwein, Barbara H. *A Short History of the Middle Ages.* Peterborough, ON: Broadview, 2004.

WEBSITES

The Internet History Sourcebooks Project *http://www.fordham.edu/halsall/*

The Avalon Project *http://avalon.law.yale.edu/*

The National Archives *http://www.archives.gov/exhibits/*

AUTHORS AND CONTRIBUTORS

STEPHEN G. HYSLOP (Chapters 7, 8, 9, & 10) is the author of several books on American and world history, including *Eyewitness to the Civil War* and *National Geographic Almanac of World History* (with Patricia S. Daniels). His articles have appeared in *American History* and the *History Channel Magazine.*

BOB SOMERVILLE (Chapters 1 & 3) worked for 20 years at Time-Life Books, writing and editing books on a wide variety of subjects. He now works as a freelance writer and editor based in Forest Heights, Maryland. His book *Dogtown: A Sanctuary for Rescued Dogs* was named Best Book of the Year in 2009 by the Independent Book Publishers Association.

JOHN MILLIKEN THOMPSON (Chapters 2, 4, 5 & 6) has authored 10 books and contributed to more than 30. His most recent books, both published by National Geographic, are *The Medieval World: An Illustrated Atlas* and *Dakotas: Where the West Begins.* His historical novel, *The Reservoir,* is forthcoming from the Other Press in 2011.

DR. JOSEPH KETT (Consultant) is the James Madison Professor History at the University of Virginia, specializing in American intellectual and cultural history.

JAMES RESTON, JR. (Foreword) is the author of 15 books, three plays, and numerous articles in national magazines. His last five historical works, *Galileo: A Life, The Last Apocalypse, Warriors of God, Dogs of God,* and *Defenders of the Faith,* have been translated into 12 foreign languages. He has been a fellow at the American Academy in Rome, a scholar in residence at the Library of Congress, and is currently a senior scholar at the Woodrow Wilson International Center for Scholars in Washington.

ACKNOWLEDGMENTS

The editors would like to thank the following for their permission to reprint excerpts from their texts: p. 33 Lichtheim, *Ancient Egyptian Literature: Volume III,* by permission of the University of California Press; p. 173 Goetz, *Popul Vuh: The Sacred Book of the Ancient Quiche Maya,* by permission of the University of Oklahoma Press; p. 183 *The Letters of John of Salisbury,* by permission of Oxford University Press; p. 298 *Popular Culture in Late Imperial China,* by permission of the University of California Press; p. 418 by permission of Scribner, a division of Simon & Schuster, Inc. from *The Double Helix* by James D. Watson.

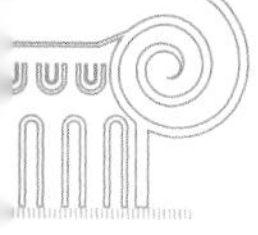

INDEX

Boldface indicates illustrations.

B

C

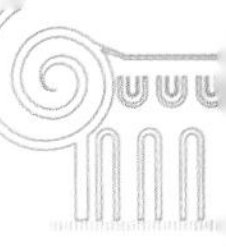

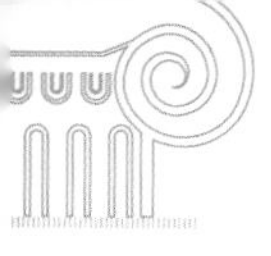

H

I

K

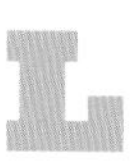

M

N

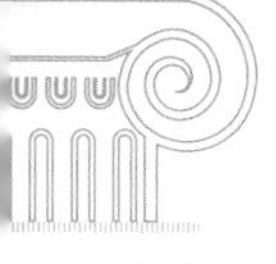

S

Published by the National Geographic Society

John M. Fahey, Jr., *President and Chief Executive Officer*
Gilbert M. Grosvenor, *Chairman of the Board*
Tim T. Kelly, *President, Global Media Group*
John Q. Griffin, *Executive Vice President; President, Publishing*
Nina D. Hoffman, *Executive Vice President; President, Book Publishing Group*

Prepared by the Book Division

Barbara Brownell Grogan, *Vice President and Editor in Chief*
Marianne R. Koszorus, *Director of Design*
Lisa Thomas, *Senior Editor*
Carl Mehler, *Director of Maps*
R. Gary Colbert, *Production Director*
Jennifer A. Thornton, *Managing Editor*
Meredith Wilcox, *Administrative Director, Illustrations*

Staff for This Book

Patricia Daniels, *Project Editor*
Melissa Farris, *Art Director*
Kay Kobor Hankins, *Designer*
Linda B. Meyerriecks, *Illustrations Editor*
Dan O'Toole, *Contributing Writer*
Elizabeth Levine, *Researcher*
Mary Beth Oelkers-Keegan, *Copy Editor*
Sarajane Herman, *Proofreader*
Connie D. Binder, *Indexer*
Al Morrow, *Design Assistant*
Rob Waymouth, *Illustrations Specialist*
Matt Propert, *Illustrations Assistant*
Scott Pospiech, *Editorial Intern*
Rebecca Quarella, *Editorial Intern*

Manufacturing and Quality Management

Christopher A. Liedel, *Chief Financial Officer*
Phillip L. Schlosser, *Vice President*
Chris Brown, *Technical Director*
Nicole Elliott, *Manager*
Rachel Faulise, *Manager*

Founded in 1888, the National Geographic Society is one of the largest nonprofit scientific and educational organizations in the world. It reaches more than 285 million people worldwide each month through its official journal, *National Geographic,* and its four other magazines; the National Geographic Channel; television documentaries; radio programs; films; books; videos and DVDs; maps; and interactive media. National Geographic has funded more than 9,000 scientific research projects and supports an education program combating geographic illiteracy.

For more information, please call 1-800-NGS LINE (647-5463) or write to the following address:

National Geographic Society
1145 17th Street N.W.
Washington, D.C. 20036-4688 U.S.A.

Visit us online at www.nationalgeographic.com

For information about special discounts for bulk purchases, please contact National Geographic Books Special Sales: ngspecsales@ngs.org

For rights or permissions inquiries, please contact National Geographic Books Subsidiary Rights: ngbookrights@ngs.org

This 2013 edition printed for Barnes & Noble, Inc. by the National Geographic Society.

ISBN: 978-1-4351-4807-9 (B&N ed.)

Library of Congress Cataloging-in-Publication Data

Eyewitness to history / edited by Patricia Daniels.
p. cm.
Includes bibliographical references and index.
ISBN 978-1-4262-0652-8 (alk. paper)
1. World history--Sources. 2. Civilization--History--Sources.
D21.3.E96 2010
909--dc22
2010012991

Printed in Hong Kong

13/THK/1